Input–Output Analysis
Volume I

The International Library of Critical Writings in Economics

Series Editor: Mark Blaug

Professor Emeritus, University of London
Professor Emeritus, University of Buckingham
Visiting Professor, University of Exeter

This series is an essential reference source for students, researchers and lecturers in economics. It presents by theme a selection of the most important articles across the entire spectrum of economics. Each volume has been prepared by a leading specialist who has written an authoritative introduction to the literature included.

A full list of published and future titles in this series is printed at the end of this volume.

Wherever possible, the articles in these volumes have been reproduced as originally published using facsimile reproduction, inclusive of footnotes and pagination to facilitate ease of reference.

For a list of all Edward Elgar published titles visit our site on the World Wide Web at
http://www.e-elgar.co.uk

Input–Output Analysis
Volume I

Edited by

Heinz D. Kurz

Professor of Economics
University of Graz, Austria

Erik Dietzenbacher

Associate Professor of Mathematical Economics
University of Groningen, Netherlands

and

Christian Lager

Assistant Professor of Economics
University of Graz, Austria

THE INTERNATIONAL LIBRARY OF CRITICAL WRITINGS IN ECONOMICS

An Elgar Reference Collection
Cheltenham, UK • Northampton, MA, USA

Published by
Edward Elgar Publishing Limited
8 Lansdown Place
Cheltenham
Glos GL5O 2HU
UK

Edward Elgar Publishing, Inc.
6 Market Street
Northampton
MA 01060
USA

A catalogue record for this book
is available from the British Library

Library of Congress Cataloguing in Publication Data
Input-output analysis / edited by Heinz D. Kurz, Erik Dietzenbacher
    and Christian Lager.
        (The international library of critical writings in economics ; 92)
    (Elgar reference collection)
        Includes bibliographical references and index.
        1. Input-output analysis. I. Kurz, Heinz D. II. Dietzenbacher,
    Erik, 1958-   . III. Lager, Christian, 1951   . IV. Series.
    V. Series : Elgar reference collection.
    HB142.I523   1998
    339.2'3--dc21   98-17059
                                                         CIP

ISBN 1 85898 357 6 (3 volume set)

Printed and bound in Great Britain by
MPG Books Ltd, Bodmin, Cornwall

Contents

Acknowledgements

The editor and publishers wish to thank the authors and the following publishers who have kindly given permission for the use of copyright material.

Academic Press, Inc. for article: Leif Johansen (1978), 'On the Theory of Dynamic Input–Output Models with Different Time Profiles of Capital Construction and Finite Life-Time of Capital Equipment', *Journal of Economic Theory*, **19** (2), December, 513–33.

Blackwell Publishers Ltd for articles: R.M. Goodwin (1949), 'The Multiplier as Matrix', *Economic Journal*, **LIX** (236), December, 537–55; A. Ghosh (1958), 'Input–Output Approach in an Allocation System', *Economica*, **XXV** (97), February, 58–64; Kenichi Miyazawa and Shingo Masegi (1963), 'Interindustry Analysis and the Structure of Income-Distribution', *Metroeconomica*, **XV** (2–3), 89–103; Graham Pyatt and Jeffery I. Round (1979), 'Accounting and Fixed Price Multipliers in a Social Accounting Matrix Framework', *Economic Journal*, **89** (356), December, 850–73; F. Duchin and D.B. Szyld (1985), 'A Dynamic Input–Output Model with Assured Positive Output', *Metroeconomica*, **XXXVII** (3), October, 269–82; Heinz D. Kurz (1985), 'Effective Demand in a "Classical" Model of Value and Distribution: The Multiplier in a Sraffian Framework', *Manchester School of Economic and Social Studies*, **LIII** (2), June, 121–37.

Anne P. Carter for her own excerpt: (1970), 'A Linear Programming System Analyzing Embodied Technological Change', in A.P. Carter and A. Bródy (eds), *Contributions to Input–Output Analysis*, Chapter 4, 77–98.

Chapman & Hall for excerpt: Christian Lager (1988), 'The Use of a Social Accounting Matrix for Comparative Static Equilibrium Modelling', in Maurizio Ciaschini (ed.), *Input–Output Analysis. Current Developments*, Chapter 5, 75–89.

The Econometric Society for article: David Hawkins and Herbert A. Simon (1949), 'Note: Some Conditions of Macroeconomic Stability', *Econometrica*, **17**, 245–8; Clopper Almon (1963), 'Numerical Solution of a Modified Leontief Dynamic System for Consistent Forecasting or Indicative Planning', *Econometrica*, **31** (4), October, 665–78.

Elsevier Science B.V. for article: Wassily Leontief (1936), 'Quantitative Input and Output Relations in the Economic System of the United States', *Review of Economic Statistics*, **XVIII** (3), August, 105–25; Thijs ten Raa (1986), 'Dynamic Input–Output Analysis with Distributed Activities', *Review of Economics and Statistics*, **LXVIII** (2), May, 300–310; Sherman Robinson and David W. Roland-Holst (1988), 'Macroeconomic Structure and Computable General Equilibrium Models', *Journal of Policy Modeling*, **10** (3), Fall,

353–75; Peter Kalmbach and Heinz D. Kurz (1990), 'Micro-Electronics and Employment: A Dynamic Input–Output Study of the West German Economy', *Structural Change and Economic Dynamics*, **1** (2), December, 371–86; Wassily Leontief (1928/1991), 'The Economy as a Circular Flow', *Structural Change and Economic Dynamics*, **2** (1), 181–212; Paul A. Samuelson (1991), 'Leontief's "The Economy as a Circular Flow": An Introduction', *Structural Change and Economic Dynamics*, **2** (1), 177–9; Wassily Leontief (1991), 'An Introductory Note by Professor Leontief', *Structural Change and Economic Dynamics*, **2** (1), 179.

International Economic Review for article: K. Tokoyama and Y. Murakami (1972), 'Relative Stability in Two Types of Leontief Models', *International Economic Review*, **13** (2), June, 408–15.

International Regional Science Review for article: Peter W.J. Batey and Adam Z. Rose (1990), 'Extended Input–Output Models: Progress and Potential', *International Regional Science Review*, **13** (1–2), 27–49.

International Input–Output Association for article: A. Bródy (1995), 'Truncation and Spectrum of the Dynamic Inverse', *Economic Systems Research*, **7** (3), 235–47.

Augustus M. Kelley, Publishers for excerpt: Ladislaus von Bortkiewicz (1907), 'On the Correction of Marx's Fundamental Theoretical Construction in the Third Volume of *Capital*', in P. M. Sweezy (ed.) (1949), *Karl Marx and the Close of His System & Böhm-Bawerk's Criticism of Marx*, 199–221.

Kluwer Academic Publishers for article: Richard Stone (1966), 'Input–Output and Demographic Accounting: A Tool for Educational Planning', *Minerva*, **IV** (3), Spring, 365–80.

Wassily Leontief for his own excerpt: (1970), 'The Dynamic Inverse', in A.P. Carter and A. Bródy (eds), *Contributions to Input–Output Analysis*, Chapter 1, 17–46.

Ulrich Meyer for his own article: (1982), 'Why Singularity of Dynamic Leontief Systems Doesn't Matter', in *Input–Output Techniques, Proceedings of the Third Hungarian Conference on Input–Output Techniques 3–5 November, 1981*, 181–9.

Domenico M. Nuti for excerpts: V.K. Dmitriev (1898), 'The Theory of Value of David Ricardo: An Attempt at a Rigorous Analysis, Part 1. Introduction: The Theory of "Production Costs" Before Ricardo' and 'Part 2. Ricardo's Theory of Value', translated by D. Fry in D.M. Nuti (ed.) (1974), *V.K. Dmitriev: Economic Essays on Value, Competition and Utility*, 39–80.

Oxford University Press, Inc. for excerpt: Wassily Leontief (1953), 'Dynamic Analysis', *Studies in the Structure of the American Economy*, Chapter 3, 53–90 and 486–93.

Review of Economic Studies, Ltd. for articles: J.v. Neumann (1937), 'A Model of General Economic Equilibrium', translated in *Review of Economic Studies*, **XIII**, 1945–6, 1–9; Dale W. Jorgenson (1961), 'Stability of a Dynamic Input–Output System', *Review of Economic Studies*, **XVIII**, 105–16; V. Mukerji (1964), 'Output and Investment for Exponential Growth in Consumption – The General Solution and Some Comments', *Review of Economic Studies*, **XXXI** (1) No. 85, January, 77–82.

Every effort has been made to trace all the copyright holders but if any have been inadvertently overlooked the publishers will be pleased to make the necessary arrangement at the first opportunity.

In addition the publishers wish to thank the Library of the London School of Economics and Political Science and the Marshall Library of Economics, Cambridge University for their assistance in obtaining these articles.

General Introduction

Heinz D. Kurz, Erik Dietzenbacher and Christian Lager

According to the authors of an article titled 'Input–Output analysis: the first fifty years', published in 1989, 'not only is input–output a rare *original idea*, but also one that has stood the *test of time*' (Rose and Miernyk, 1989, p. 259; emphases in the original). In their view Wassily Leontief's paper on 'Quantitative input–output relations in the economic system of the United States' (Leontief, 1936) 'was the beginning of what has become a major branch of quantitative economics' (Rose and Miernyk, 1989, p. 229).

There can be no doubt that input–output economics is 'a genuinely new and original idea' (Dorfman, 1973, p. 430), which can be traced back far into the history of economics. And it is also true that input–output analysis has stood the test of time: over the years its theoretical structure has been refined and its practical applications have been widened. Today it is a multifaceted area of economics. Contemporary applied economics is unthinkable without input–output and many economic and social policy issues rely heavily on its findings. It is used in a large number of fields, including national accounting, regional economics, environmental economics, trade and transport economics, the study of technological change and employment, growth economics and development economics. Further fields to which it can be applied are in sight. It had an important impact on fact finding activities in many countries and has contributed to the harmonization of their accounting systems. The huge amount and the quality of economic data routinely collected nowadays reflect at least partly the rise of quantitative economics in general and input–output analysis in particular. As Leontief succinctly put it: 'The general nature of the approach has made the development of input–output analysis a cumulative process. Each refinement in theoretical structure and each addition to or improvement in the accuracy of factual information incorporated in its data base potentially improved the performance of the general model in application to all special problems' (Leontief, 1987, p. 864).

The fact that input–output analysis is alive and well is also documented by the activities of the International Input–Output Association (IIOA) and several national associations. The IIOA was founded in 1986; its main activities include the organization of conferences and the publication of *Economic Systems Research: Journal of the International Input–Output Association*. Another journal that is devoted entirely to input–output related issues is the *Journal of Applied Input–Output Analysis*, published by the Pan Pacific Association of Input–Output Studies (PAPAIOS). However, these two journals are by no means the only ones that publish work in the field of input–output analysis. For example, also *Metroeconomica, Structural Change and Economic Dynamics* and the *Journal of Regional Science* include many articles in the field of input–output. In general, papers using input–output analysis and tools find their way into virtually all major journals in economics; important contributions have been published, for example, in *Econometrica*, the *Review of Economics and Statistics* and the *Economic Journal*. In addition there are series of books devoted to input–output and a broad stream of monographs dealing with its different areas of application. The field of input–output analysis has indeed expanded over time so much and has been subdivided into so many specialized branches that it would be difficult, not to say impossible, for a single person to overlook it in its entirety.

With a quickly growing field of economics such as the one under consideration, characterized by an ever more sophisticated division of labour, from time to time it is useful to take stock, look at the development the subject has taken and assess the present state of the art. This can be done in several ways, including survey articles, special issues of journals, collections of commissioned papers dealing with the different sub-fields and so on. These three volumes of readings are designed to contribute to, or rather facilitate, such an assessment. They contain a selection of altogether 85 essays and two notes, organized in ten parts. All essays and notes have been previously published. In contrast to most collections in this series of books, we felt it was appropriate to have each of the ten parts preceded by a separate introduction to the specific subject at hand. These introductions attempt to give the reader an overview of the relevant literature within that subject, the main research topics and the links between them. The introductions are meant to provide some guidance to the reader and to sketch the background against which the essays in that part should be viewed. These introductions have not been published before; they were specially written for these volumes.

It goes without saying that the present volumes may be considered a complement to the available survey articles and textbooks on input-output analysis. With regard to surveys, see in particular Stone (1984), Leontief (1987) and Rose and Miernyk (1989); with regard to textbooks, see in particular Schumann (1968), Bulmer-Thomas (1982), Miller and Blair (1985), Holub and Schnabl (1994) and ten Raa (1995). For appraisals of Leontief's contribution, see Dorfman (1973) and Carter and Petri (1989).

The structure of the volumes is outlined below.

Volume I

Volume I contains three parts. Part I deals with the 'Foundations of Input–Output Analysis' and has six papers plus two notes related to the (abridged) English translation of Leontief's 1928 paper (Leontief, 1928), one by Paul A. Samuelson, the other one by Wassily Leontief. The papers deal with the theory of linear economic systems in which commodities are produced by means of commodities. Both the reproduction or *quantity and growth* aspect and the *price and distribution* aspect are dealt with, and it is made clear that input–output analysis is firmly rooted in the 'classical' tradition of economic thought, incepted in the seventeenth and eighteenth century. The most advanced version of classical analysis is, of course, Piero Sraffa's *Production of Commodities by Means of Commodities* (Sraffa, 1960). The reader is asked to consider that book as firmly belonging to Part I.

Part II is devoted to 'Dynamic Input–Output Analysis' and comprises thirteen papers. The starting point of the development of this branch was the publication of a dynamic version of Leontief's basic model (Leontief, 1953). This has triggered a rich literature on theoretical and applied problems of dynamic analysis. One of the main fields of dynamic input–output analysis so far has been the problem of the displacement and reabsorption of workers due to technological progress. See in particular Leontief and Duchin (1986); see also Kalmbach and Kurz (1992).

Part III deals with 'Multiplier Analysis, Extended Input–Output Models and Social and Demographic Accounting' and comprises nine papers. 'Extended' input–output models combine the Leontief propagation process arising from demand for circulating capital inputs with additional income multiplier effects by incorporating socioeconomic variables such as income shares and propensities to consume. The original approach is to treat the household sector as an industry whose output is labour and whose inputs are consumer goods. Disaggregated versions of the extended input–output model presuppose a dis-aggregated and consistent database usually referred to as Social Accounting Matrix (SAM) which is an input–output table augmented by disaggregated income formation and consumption expenditure accounts. Quesnay's *Tableau Economique* might be considered as the earliest example of a SAM. Two types of multipliers have been developed. 'Accounting multipliers' which are based on average coefficients directly derived from a base year SAM are of limited analytical use – hence the concept of 'fixed price multipliers' which are based on marginal coefficients. In contrast to that multisectoral extension of the 'Keynesian' multiplier there is the neoclassical concept of 'flexible price multipliers' given by the Jacobian of a computable general equilibrium model. Multiplier analysis is not confined to economic analysis but has been applied to demographic problems by making use of Systems of Demographic Accounts (SDA).

Volume II

Volume II contains four parts. Part I is concerned with input–output studies of 'Energy and Environment' and contains six papers. The basis of these types of models are IO-tables (or SAMs) augmented by additional accounts showing the physical flows from the environmental system to the economic system (inputs of resources) and vice versa (outputs of pollutants). Leontief (1970) proposed a model which calculates the amounts of pollutants generated for given amounts of final demand as well as prices for given levels of abatement. Leontief's pollution abatement model has been widely discussed, refined and used. Energy demand studies emphasize the importance of product mix and substitution effects. The latter effects are usually taken into account by introducing well behaved neoclassical production or cost functions.

The five papers of Part II are devoted to an analysis of 'Foreign Trade and International Models'. Most studies in that field are concerned with the so-called 'Leontief paradox', that is, the US exports are less capital intensive than its imports. On the premise that the US capital endowment is relatively abundant, this contradicts the Heckscher–Ohlin–Samuelson trade theory. Several attempts have been made to explain the paradox. Some of them contradict or reinterpret, whilst others replicate Leontief's findings. Two types of world models are considered: The UN World Model proposed by Leontief and the interlinked national input–output models of the INFORUM group.

Part III deals with 'Regional and Interregional Models' and comprises eight papers. Multipliers derived from regional IO-tables account for propagation effects within that particular region but fail to recognize interconnections between regions. To include these latter effects, an interregional approach has to be considered. Being a spatial disaggregation of a national table, an interregional input–output table requires a tremendous amount of data which are not always available. Therefore, methods to derive such tables from national data as well as interregional models which require less detailed information have been developed. Other studies are concerned with the empirical importance of interregional feedbacks.

The statistical information provided by industry surveys can be arranged within the framework of make (output) and use (input) matrices drawing a clear distinction between commodities and industries. The four papers of Part IV, 'Systems with Input and Output Matrices', are concerned with methods which recast make and use matrices into the usual form of square sector by sector matrices used in input–output analysis. The industry and the commodity technology-assumption as well as some hybrid models and methods which require additional information are discussed.

Volume III

Volume III contains three parts. Part I deals with 'Structural Analysis' and comprises eleven papers. In the early days, the focus was on comparing the production structures of different countries. Due attention was paid to measuring sectoral interdependencies or linkages. A multitude of different concepts have been developed for this purpose, ranging from simple summary measures to advanced mathematics-oriented approaches. These measures have been widely used for the identification of so-called key sectors. Most of the methodologies discussed are readily applicable to a comparison of economic structures over time. The recent interest in aspects of economic growth, however, has also revived the interest in a methodology that was proposed especially for studying structural changes over time. This 'structural decomposition analysis' has nowadays become a major tool for disentangling the sources of growth.

The seven papers of Part II are devoted to input–output 'Price Models', A considerable number of early theoretical contributions were concerned with the *Nonsubstitution theorem* which demonstrates that Leontief's model has a somewhat greater generality than its assumptions concerning fixed coefficients might suggest at first. On the assumptions that (i) there is only a single primary factor (labour) with a positive price (all other primary factors, for example land, being 'free goods'); (ii) there are constant returns to scale throughout the economy; and (iii) there is no joint production, then generally only one technique can be used in the long run, being cost-minimizing. Hence the (optimal) coefficients of production are determined and constant and, therefore, prices of production are independent of demand. Other versions of multisectoral price models such as two- or three-channel prices discussed in centrally planned societies, Seton's concept of 'eigenprices' and price models for small open economies are also considered.

The compilation of input–output tables is a tedious process that requires a lot of time and energy. The sixteen papers of Part III deal with 'Data-Related Topics'. Given the large amount of data to be handled, it is inevitable that the data have to be aggregated and that they contain measurement errors. The research on aggregation has focused on two issues: (i) to specify conditions for an aggregation that is free of errors; and (ii) to develop aggregation schemes that minimize aggregation errors. The literature devoted to analysing the effects of measurement errors can be distinguished into deterministic and stochastic approaches. The third topic in this part is related to the fact that compiling input–output tables is rather time-consuming. As a result, tables are published with a significant time-lag and usually they are not issued for each year. Consequently, input–output analysts often have to rely on updates of older tables. For this purpose, several updating procedures have been developed.

Selecting the material for these volumes inescapably forced us to make hard, indeed very hard choices. The received literature on input–output analysis is voluminous and it was clear from the beginning that we could reprint only a minor fraction of it in this series. Which papers to include and which not? We felt that we should not rely exclusively on our own judgements, given the dimension of the problem. We thought it would be a good idea to make use of the expert knowledge of several major practitioners of input–output analysis. We therefore sent a first proposal of the structure of the project and a provisional selection of essays to a number of colleagues, asking for their advice.

The reaction was reassuring in important respects and saved us a lot of headache. First, almost all colleagues we approached responded and gave us comments. While a few restricted themselves to suggesting some of their own contributions that could or should be included in the volumes, others gave detailed and careful advice on papers we might want to drop or add. However, the number of additional essays suggested for inclusion in the volumes greatly exceeded the number suggested for dropping. Given the overall size of the project, expressed in the maximum number of pages available to us, which had already largely been exhausted by our initial proposal, this fact caused us considerable difficulties. The way we dealt with them is closely related to another fact: we were surprised how little the opinion of many of those invited to comment deviated from our first proposal. While a few commentators pleaded for substantial changes, the vast majority approved of the overall structure and content of the project and advocated only small changes, generally asking for a few additions. We scrutinized carefully the suggestions made and incorporated them as best we could. We decided not to follow recommendations to drop a given paper or (more frequently) include a new one, if it was advocated by a single commentator only. However, if it turned out that several people argued independently of one another (as we assumed) the same point of view, we were prepared to follow them.

We benefited a great deal from the exchange of ideas with the scholars we were able to involve in this sort of refereeing process. We are especially grateful to Clopper Almon, Pirkko Aulin-Ahmavaara, András Bródy, Anne P. Carter, Klaus Conrad, Faye Duchin, Emilio Fontela, Ambica Ghosh, Hans-Werner Holub, Peter Kalmbach, Wassily Leontief, Jan Oosterhaven, Graham Pyatt, Adam Z. Rose, Paul A. Samuelson, Hermann Schnabl, Jochen Schumann, Jiří V. Skolka, Reiner Stäglin, Bert Steenge, Thijs ten Raa and Lucja Tomaszewicz for their often detailed and most helpful comments and suggestions. Without their expert knowledge, which they kindly put at our disposal, the present volumes would be even more imperfect than they are now. Apologies are due to those whose suggestions we did not follow. Space constraints prevented us from doing so.

References

Bulmer-Thomas, V. (1982), *Input–Output Analysis in Developing Countries*, New York. John Wiley.

Carter, A. and Petri, P.A. (1989), 'Leontief's contributions to economics', *Journal of Policy Modeling*, **11**, 7–30.

Dorfman, R. (1973), 'Wassily Leontief's contribution to economics', *Swedish Journal of Economics*, **28**, 430–49.

Holub, H.-W. and Schnabl, H. (1994), *Input–Output-Rechnung – Input–Output-Analyse*, München:: Oldenbourg.

Kalmbach, P. and Kurz, H.D. (1992), *Chips und Jobs. Zu den Beschäftigungswirkungen des Einsatzes programmgesteuerter Arbeitsmittel in der Bundesrepublik Deutschland*, Marburg: Metropolis.

Leontief, W. (1928), 'Die Wirtschaft als Kreislauf', *Archiv für Sozialwissenschaft und Sozialpolitik*, **60**, 577–623.

Leontief, W. (1936), 'Quantitative input and output relations in the economic system of the United States', *Review of Economic[s and] Statistics*, **XVIII** (3), 105–25. [Reprinted as Chapter 4 in Volume I.]

Leontief, W. (1953), 'Dynamic analysis', in *Studies in the Structure of the American Economy*, Chapter 3, New York: Oxford University Press, 53-90. [Reprinted as Chapter 7 in Volume I.]

Leontief, W. (1970), 'Environmental repercussions and the economic structure: an input–output approach', *Review of Economics and Statistics*, **LII** (3), 262–71. [Reprinted as Chapter 2 in Volume II.]

Leontief, W. (1987), 'Input–output analysis'. in J. Eatwell, M. Milgate and P. Newman (eds), *The New Palgrave. A Dictionary of Economics*, vol. 2, London: Macmillan, 860–64.

Leontief, W. and Duchin, F. (1986), *The Future Impact of Automation on Workers*, New York: Oxford University Press.

Miller, R.E. and Blair, P.D. (1985), *Input–Output Analysis*, Englewood Cliffs, New Jersey: Prentice-Hall.

Raa, T. ten (1995), *Linear Analysis of Competitive Economies*, London: Harvester Wheatsheaf.

Rose, A. and Miernyk, W. (1989), 'Input–output analysis: the first fifty years'. *Economic Systems Research*, **1**, 229–71.

Schumann, J. (1968), *Input–Output Analyse*, Berlin: Springer.

Sraffa, P. (1960), *Production of Commodities by Means of Commodities*, Cambridge: Cambridge University Press.

Stone, R. (1984), 'Where are we now? A short account of the development of input–output studies and their present trends', in *Proceedings of the Seventh International Conference on Input–Output Techniques*. New York: UN, 439–59.

Introduction to Part I:
Foundations of Input–Output Analysis

'Everything important has already been said by someone who did not discover it' (A.N. Whitehead). *Cum grano salis*, this applies also to input–output analysis. Many of the ideas and concepts that became prominent in the aftermath of Wassily Leontief's 'The economy as a circular flow' (Leontief, [1928] 1991; Chapter 3a, this volume) and his *Tableau Economique* of the US economy (Leontief, 1936; Chapter 4, this volume) have been anticipated in the writings of earlier authors. Leontief himself has frequently drawn the attention to some of his precursors. Part I contains Leontief's two classic essays and a few papers which either prepared the ground for modern input–output analysis or represent the culmination of earlier theoretical developments that are closely related to it.

According to Leontief, 'Input–output analysis is a practical extension of the classical theory of general interdependence which views the whole economy of a region, a country and even of the entire world as a single system and sets out to describe and to interpret its operation in terms of directly observable basic structural relationships' (Leontief, 1987, p. 860). The key terms in this characterization are 'classical theory', 'general interdependence' and 'directly observable basic structural relationships'. The purpose of this introduction is to provide a short account of the classical approach and to relate Leontief's work to this tradition.

We shall adopt the following distinction between a *classical* and an alternative *neoclassical* approach to the theory of production, distribution and value. The classical tradition focuses attention on goods that are reproducible. Production is conceived as a circular flow: commodities are produced by means of commodities. The means of production are divided into scarce and reproducible: scarce means of production such as land yield their owners a (differential) rent, whereas reproducible means of production, that is capital goods, yield their owners profits which in conditions of free competition tend to be proportional to the value of the capital invested. The elaborated versions of the classical approach typically start from the following data, or independent variables:

1. The set of technical alternatives from which cost-minimizing producers can choose. (In an extreme case, only one technique is taken to be available, that is, the problem of the choice of technique is set aside.)
2. The size and composition of the social product, reflecting the needs and wants of the members of the different classes of society and the requirements of reproduction and capital accumulation. (In an extreme case, the economy is assumed to be stationary, that is, net saving and net investment are zero.)

3. The ruling real wage rate(s) (or, alternatively, the general rate of profit).
4. The quantities of different qualities of land available and the known stocks of depletable resources, such as mineral deposits. (In an extreme case, natural resources are for simplicity set aside, that is, taken to be 'free goods'.)

The treatment of wages as an independent variable and of the other distributive variables, the rate of profit and the rents of land, as dependent residuals exhibits a fundamental *asymmetry* in the classical approach. Prices are considered the means of distributing the social surplus.

It deserves to be emphasized that the above data, or independent variables, bear a close resemblance to the premises of Leontief's approach, especially circular production, an exclusive concern with magnitudes that are observable, and an exogenously given final demand. Moreover, these data are sufficient to determine the unknowns, or dependent variables: the rate of profit, the rent rates, and the set of relative prices supporting the cost-minimizing system of producing the given levels of output. No other data, such as, for example, demand functions for commodities and factors of production are needed. The classical approach allows the consistent determination of the variables under consideration. It does so by separating the determination of income distribution and prices from that of quantities, which are taken as given or independently variable in (2) above. Quantities were considered as determined in another part of the theory, that is, the analysis of capital accumulation, structural change and socioeconomic development.

In contradistinction, the data in terms of which the neoclassical approach attempts to determine normal income distribution and relative prices exhibits some striking differences with respect to the classical approach. First, it introduces independent variables, or explanatory factors, that are not directly observable, such as preferences or utility functions. Second, it takes as given not only the amounts of natural resources available but also the economy's 'initial endowments' of labour and capital. The data from which neoclassical theory typically begins its reasoning are:

(a) The set of technical alternatives from which cost-minimizing producers can choose.
(b) The preferences of consumers.
(c) The initial endowments of the economy with all 'factors of production', including capital, and the distribution of property rights among individual agents.

The basic novelty of marginalist theory consists of the following. While the received classical approach conceives the real wage as determined prior to profits and rents, in the neoclassical approach all kinds of income are explained *symmetrically* in terms of supply and demand with regard to the services of the respective factors of production: labour, capital and land. Supply and demand are conceptualized as functional relationships (or correspondences) between the price of a factor service (or good) and the quantity supplied or demanded. Here there is no need to enter into a discussion of the marginalist long-period theory and its shortcomings, because these have been dealt with in some detail elsewhere (see, for example, Kurz and Salvadori, 1995, ch. 14). Suffice it to say that while Leontief's above characterization of input–output analysis appears to be fully compatible with the classical approach, it is not obvious whether and how it could be reconciled with the neoclassical one.

'General interdependence' involves two intimately intertwined problems, which, in a first step of the analysis, may, however, be treated separately. First, there is the problem of *quantity* for which a structure of the levels of operation of processes of production is needed in order to guarantee the reproduction of the means of production used up and the satisfaction of some final demand, that is, the needs and wants of the different groups (or 'classes') of society, perhaps making allowance for the growth of the system. Secondly, there is the problem of *price* for which a structure of exchange values of the different products is needed in order to guarantee a distribution of income between the different classes of income recipients consistent with the repetition of the productive process on a given (or an increasing) level.

The practical importance of the requirement that all magnitudes referred to should be 'observable' is obvious. But there is also a theoretical motivation for it: as Leontief (1928, pp. 619–20) stressed, the starting point of the marginalist theory, the *homo oeconomicus*, gives too much room to imagination and too little to facts. Economic analysis should rather focus on the concept of circular flow which expresses one of the fundamental 'objective' features of economic life. A careful investigation of its 'technological' aspects is said to be an indispensable prerequisite to any economic reasoning.

It is hardly an exaggeration to say that input–output analysis is an offspring of systematic economic analysis incepted in the seventeenth and eighteenth centuries. The importance of early contributions to the development of classical Political Economy lies first and foremost in the concepts and method put forward. Thus, the notions of production as a circular flow, of productive interdependences between different sectors of the economy and of social surplus are clearly discernible in authors such as William Petty (1623–87) and Richard Cantillon (1697–1734). Scrutinizing their works, the attentive reader will come across some primitive conceptualizations of input–output systems designed to portray the relationships of production in the economy. These generally form the basis of an inquiry into the laws governing the distribution and growth of the wealth of a nation. In the works of these authors we also encounter early formulations of the distinction between market and 'normal' price and the idea that in competitive conditions the former tends to gravitate around the latter. The norrnal price is envisaged to be governed by systematic, permanent, nonaccidental forces, whereas the market price is subject to a myriad of additional influences of a more or less short-lived and accidental character about which nothing general can be said. Therefore, only natural prices can be the object of scientific investigation.

François Quesnay and the Physiocrats

An important step forward in analysing the interrelated problems of the production, distribution and use of the wealth of a nation was made by François Quesnay (1694–1774) and his followers. The physiocratic view that only agriculture can generate a surplus, a *produit net*, was most clearly expressed in the *Tableau économique*, a first version of which was published in 1758 (INED, 1958). The *Tableau* contains a sophisticated two-sector expression of the production of commodities by means of commodities. It portrays the whole process of production, distribution and expenditure as a reproduction process, with circulation of commodities and money as an integral part of it. Phillips (1955) regarded it as an early input–output table and interpreted it as a closed model. An important goal of the *Tableau* was to lay bare the origin of revenue and thus the factors affecting its size – factors which could be manipulated by economic policy aimed at fostering national wealth and power.

According to their economic role in the reproduction process, Quesnay distinguished between the 'productive class', the 'sterile class' and the class of proprietors of land and natural resources. The productive class comprises those working in primary production, in particular agriculture; they are called productive because the value of the commodities produced by them exceeds the incurred costs of production. The difference between total proceeds and total costs, where the latter include the upkeep of those employed in the primary sector, is distributed as rent to the propertied class. In contradistinction to the productive class, the sterile class which comprises those employed in manufacturing (and commerce) do not generate a revenue, or surplus: the prices of manufactures cover just costs of production, including, of course, the subsistence of artisans, tradesmen and so on. In the two-sector scheme put forward neither sector can exist on its own. In addition to *intra*sectoral flows of commodities there are *inter*sectoral flows: agriculture receives produced means of production from industry, and industry receives raw materials and means of subsistence from agriculture. Indeed, both (composite) commodities enter directly or indirectly into the production of both commodities. Hence the system of production underlying the *Tableau* could be represented by a matrix of material inputs (means of production-cum-means of subsistence) that is indecomposable.

The characteristic features of the *Tableau* can be summarized as follows. First, the *Tableau* starts from the following set of data or independent variables: the system of production in use, defined in terms of (i) the (average) methods of production employed to produce (ii) given levels of (aggregate) output; and (iii) given real rates of remuneration of those employed in the two sectors of the economy, that is, essentially wages. The reference is to some 'normal' levels of output, defined in terms of some average of the conditions of production over a sequence of years (balancing good and bad harvests). Second, the *Tableau* distinguishes between capital of different durability, where all kinds of capital relate to productive capital only. The *avances annuelles* refer to yearly advances or circulating capital (raw materials, sustenance of workers and so on); the *avances primitives* to fixed capital (tools, buildings, machines, horses and so on); and the *avances foncières* to capital incorporated in the land (land melioration of all kinds and so on). Exclusively those parts of capital which are used up during the process of production and have to be replaced periodically are taken into account in the table. This presupposes that the stocks of durable means of production employed in different branches of the economy, their modes of utilization and thus their patterns of wear and tear (and therefore depreciation) are known. Third, all shares of income other than wages are explained in terms of the surplus product (representing a certain surplus value), or residual, left after the means of subsistence in the support of workers (and masters) and what is necessary for the replacement of the used-up means of production have been deducted from the annual output. Hence, the distributive variables are treated *asymmetrically*: the wage rate is taken to be an *exogenous* variable, whereas the (rate of) rent is an *endogenous* variable. Fourth, and closely related to what has just been said, the physiocrats conceived of any surplus product that may exist as *generated* in the sphere of production and only *realized* in the sphere of circulation. Fifth, the process of circulation is assumed to work out smoothly. This involves, *inter alia*, the existence of a system of *relative* prices which support the process of reproduction, and a system of *absolute* prices compatible with the stock of money available in the economy and the going habits of payment. While in the *Tableau* the problem of accumulation of capital is set aside, it is well known that Quesnay was concerned with the sources of economic growth and stressed the role of accumulation.

Achille-Nicolas Isnard

Before we turn to the English classical economists the work of a man must be mentioned, not least because it is hardly known and yet can be said to have anticipated important findings of the subsequent literature: Achille-Nicolas Isnard (1749–1803), a French engineer, was a critic of the physiocratic doctrine that only agriculture is productive (see also Gilibert, 1981). In his *Traité des richesses* (Isnard, 1781) he argued that this doctrine was contradicted already by the fact that the *produit net* in the *Tableau* consisted both of agricultural and manufactured products. More important, Isnard argued that whether a sector of the economy generates an income in excess of its costs of production cannot be decided independently of the exchange ratios between commodities, or *relative* prices. The latter do not only reflect the real physical costs of production of the various commodities, but in addition the rule according to which the surplus product is distributed between the propertied classes.

Isnard's analysis revolved around the concepts of production as a circular flow and of surplus, or 'disposable wealth'. He wrote: 'In the whole of the riches, and setting aside values, there are in reality two parts, one required in production, the other destined to enjoyments ... The latter is the noble part of goods and the part which is nobly enjoyed by the proprietors' (ibid., pp. 36–7; our translation). Isnard added that a part of the surplus may also be accumulated in order 'to increase the mass of productive wealth' (ibid., p. 37). He emphasized that the magnitude of the surplus depends on the technical conditions of production and the 'exigence of nature' (ibid.). The impression generated by the physiocrats that only agriculture is productive is closely related to the system of prices underlying their schema. These prices are such that the entire *produit net* is indeed appropriated by the landowners in the form of rent. Other rules of distribution would immediately reveal the peculiarity of the physiocratic doctrine. Isnard stressed: 'The values of the different products determine the portions of total wealth allotted to the various producers; these portions change with the values of the objects which each producer has to acquire for production' (ibid., p. *xv*; similarly p. 37). The first book of the *Traité* was designed to clarify, by way ay of a mathematical argument, the role of relative prices as the media to realize a given distribution distribution of income.

Isnard started with a system of the division of labour with only two commodities. Each producer produces a certain amount of one commodity, a part of which he uses as a means of production and as a means of subsistence. He swaps the sectoral surplus for the other commodity he is in need of, but does not produce himself. Isnard put forward the following system of simultaneous equations:

$$(1 - a)p_1 + bp_2 = p_1 \tag{1a}$$
$$ap_1 + (1 - b)p_2 = p_2, \tag{1b}$$

where a represents the surplus of the first commodity, b that of the second, and p_1 and p_2 are the unit prices of commodities 1 and 2, respectively . He showed that the exchange ratio which guarantees the repetition of the process of production and consumption is given by: $p1/p2 = b/a$.

He then turned to a system with three commodities and argued that the exchange ratios between the commodities can again be determined, provided we are given (i) the commodity surplus in each line of production and (ii) the way it is distributed between the two remaining sectors. The system investigated is a closed system in the sense that the given coefficients reflect both the amounts of the means of production plus the means of subsistence needed in the three sectors (per unit of output), that is, what the classical economists were to call 'productive consumption', and the consumption of the propertied classes, that is, 'unproductive consumption'. Obviously, the sum of the quantities of any column is equal to the sum of the corresponding row. This means that only two of the three equations are independent. Taking one of the commodities as standard of value, or numeraire, the system of equations allows one to determine the remaining two prices. In this view prices reflect the dominant conditions of production and distribution. The prices of the *Tableau* represent but a special system of prices which gives rise to the mis-conception that only agriculture is productive. If the producers in agriculture would have to pay more of their own (composite) product per unit of the manufactured (composite) product, the situation would be different: the surplus of agriculture would be smaller or, in the extreme, nil, whereas the surplus of industry would be positive or, in the extreme, equal to the surplus of the system as a whole. He concluded: 'Quesnay and *les économistes* were therefore wrong in asserting that industry is generally not productive' (ibid., pp. 38–9).

Adam Smith, David Ricardo and Robert Torrens

The concepts of production as a circular flow and of the surplus product surfaced again in the writings of Adam Smith (1723–90), who also provided a careful analysis of the inter-dependence of the different sectors of the economy (Smith [1776] 1976, Book V, ch. V). The concept was put into sharp relief in David Ricardo's (1772–1823) *Essay on the Influence of a Low Price of Corn on the Profits of Stock* published in 1815 (cf. Ricardo, *Works* VI), in Ricardo's *Principles* (cf. Ricardo, *Works* I), and in the second edition of Robert Torrens's (1780–1864) *Essay on the External Corn Trade* (cf. Torrens, 1820). The surplus product was now generally considered to be shared out between the owners of land and the owners of capital. The emphasis was on the factors determining the general rate of profit. In these formulations the two problems identified above – that of relative quantities and the rate of growth and that of relative prices and the rate of profit – emerged ever more clearly.

Torrens emphasized that the concept of surplus provides the key to an explanation of the general rate of profit. In the *Essay* he determined the agricultural rate of profit in physical terms as the ratio between the net output of corn and corn input (corn as seed and food for the workers) and took the exchange value of manufactured goods relative to corn to be so adjusted that the same rate of profit obtains in manufacturing. This he called a 'general principle' (ibid., p. 361) and acknowledged his indebtedness to Ricardo's 'original and profound inquiry into the laws by which the rate of profits is determined' (ibid., p. *xix*).

It was, of course, clear to the older authors that the capital advanced in a sector is never homogeneous with the sector's product. We encounter a relaxation of this bold assumption in Torrens's *Essay on the Production of Wealth*, published in 1821. There he put forward an example with two sectors, both of which use both products in the same proportions as inputs (see Torrens, 1821, pp. 372–3). He concluded that the rate of profit is given in terms of the surplus left after the amounts of the used up means of production and the means of subsistence in the support of labourers have been deducted from gross output. With the surplus and the social capital consisting of the same commodities in the same proportions, the general rate of profit can be determined without having recourse to the system of relative prices.

However, the physical schema is not only important for the determination of the rate of profit (and relative prices), it also provides the basis for assessing the potential for expansion of the economy. As Torrens stressed, 'this surplus, or profit of ten per cent, they [that is the cultivators and manufacturers] might employ either in setting additional labourers to work, or in purchasing luxuries for immediate enjoyment' (ibid., p. 373). If in each sector the entire surplus were to be used for accumulation purposes, then the rates of expansion of the two sectors would be equal to one another and equal to the rate of profit. Champernowne in his commentary on von Neumann's growth model was later to call a constellation of equi-proportionate growth a 'quasi-stationary state' (Champernowne, 1945, p. 10).

Karl Marx

Karl Marx (1818–83) was an attentive student both of the writings of the physiocrats and the classical economists. He praised Quesnay and his followers as 'the true fathers of modern political economy' (Marx [1956] 1963, p. 44) and called the *Tableau* 'an extremely brilliant conception, incontestably the most brilliant for which political economy has up to then been responsible' (ibid., p. 344). The *Tableau* was the foil against which he developed his own *schemes of reproduction* in Volume II of *Capital* ([1885] 1956, part III). The schemes are concerned with the allocation of labour amongst the different sectors of the economy. That allocation was envisaged by Marx to depend on the socially dominant techniques of production, the distribution of income between wages and profits, and the expenditures out of these incomes, especially whether or not parts of profits are accumulated. In principle the quantity system could be studied without any recourse to the problem of valuation. Marx nevertheless chose to provide both a description of the requirements of reproduction in physical terms (use-values) and in value terms (labour values). (In addition he dealt with the problem of money circulation.) Thus he intended to show that the physical reproduction of capital and its value reproduction are two sides of a single coin.

Marx started from a description of the economic system divided into two main sectors or spheres of production: sector I produces means of production and sector II means of subsistence. Each sphere i (i = I, II) is represented by an equation giving the (labour) value of the sectoral output (z_i) as the sum of the sectoral constant capital (c_i), its variable capital (v_i) and the surplus value (s_i) generated in the sector. In contrast to Quesnay's *Tableau*, here the labour performed in both sectors is taken to be productive, that is, generating a surplus value. This description involves given methods of production and a given real wage rate. Otherwise it would be impossible to derive the labour-value magnitudes. With a given and uniform real wage rate and a given and uniform length of the working day (reflecting free competition in the labour market), the rate of surplus value (s_i/v_i) is uniform across sectors. The larger the real wage rate, the larger is the variable capital and the smaller is the sectoral surplus value. Setting aside the problem of fixed capital, we have

$$z_I = c_I + v_I + s_I \tag{2a}$$
$$z_{II} = c_{II} + v_{II} + s_{II}, \tag{2b}$$

Simple reproduction, that is, stationary conditions, imply

$$c_{II} = v_I + s_I. \tag{3}$$

If a part of the surplus value is saved and invested, the system reproduces itself on an upward spiralling level. This is dealt with in Marx's schemes of *extended* reproduction (cf. ibid., ch. XXI) which provide a theory of the relationship between quantities, or sectoral proportions, and the rate of growth of the economic system as a whole.

    However, Marx saw that the importance of the *Tableau* was not restricted to the problem of quantities and growth: it also provided a much needed *general* framework to consistently determine the general rate of profit. His theory of the rate of profit and prices of production in part II of Volume III of *Capital* (Marx [1894] 1959) can indeed be interpreted as an amalgamation and elaboration of insights Marx owed first and foremost to the physiocrats and Ricardo. There the problem of the rent of land is set aside altogether. The entire surplus is assumed to accrue in the form of profits at a uniform rate. Marx proposed a two-step procedure which was aptly dubbed 'successivist', as opposed to 'simultaneous' (see von Bortkiewicz, 1906–7, essay I, p. 38). In a first step he specified the general rate of profit as the ratio between the (labour) value of the economy's surplus product, or surplus value, and the (labour) value of total social capital. In a second step this (value) rate of profit was then used to calculate prices by discounting forward sectoral costs of production, or 'cost prices', measured in terms of labour values. This is the (in)famous problem of the 'Transformation of Values of Commodities into Prices of Production'.

   Marx's successivist procedure cannot be sustained. A first and obvious error concerns the fact that the capitals ought to be expressed in price rather than in value terms. Marx was aware of this slip in his argument (Marx [1894] 1959, pp. 164–5 and 206–7), but apparently thought that it could easily be remedied without further consequences. He was wrong. Once the necessary corrections suggested by Marx himself are carried out, it becomes clear that it cannot generally be presumed that the 'transformation' of values into prices of production is relevant with regard to single commodities only, while it is irrelevant with regard to commodity aggregates, such as the surplus product or the social capital, the ratio of which gives the rate of profit. Since the rate of profit cannot be determined before knowing the prices of commodities, and since the prices cannot be determined before knowing the rate of profit, the rate of profit and prices have to be determined *simultaneously* rather than successively.

Does Marx's blunder also falsify his intuition that starting from the set of data (i)–(iii) (and thus setting aside the problem of rent), which he had discerned in the *Tableau* and Ricardo, relative prices and the rate of profit can be determined in a logically coherent way? An answer to this question was provided by Vladimir K. Dmitriev (1868–1913) and Ladislaus von Bortkiewicz (1868–1931).

Vladimir K. Dmitriev and Ladislaus von Bortkiewicz

In 1898 the Russian mathematical economist Dmitriev published, in Russian, 'An attempt at a rigorous analysis' of Ricardo's theory of value and distribution (Dmitriev [1898] 1974; Chapter 1, this volume). Dmitriev investigated first how the total amount of labour expended in the production of a commodity is to be ascertained. He disposed of the mis-conception that this involved an infinite 'historical regress' by showing that it is from a knowledge of the current conditions of production of the different commodities alone that one can determine the quantities of labour embodied (see ibid., p. 44). Assuming single production and using matrix notation, the problem amounts to solving the following system of simultaneous equations

$$\mathbf{z}^T = \mathbf{z}^T \mathbf{A} + \mathbf{l}^T \tag{4}$$

where $\mathbf{A}$ is the $n \times n$ matrix of material inputs, $\mathbf{l}$ is the n-vector of direct (homogeneous) labour inputs and $\mathbf{z}$ is the n-vector of quantities of labour embodied in the different commodities, or labour values. (T is the sign for transpose). Replacing repeatedly the $\mathbf{z}$ on the right-hand side of the equation by the right-hand side gives

$$\mathbf{z}^T = \mathbf{l}^T + \mathbf{l}^T \mathbf{A} + \mathbf{l}^T \mathbf{A}^2 + \mathbf{l}^T \mathbf{A}^3 + ... \tag{5}$$

where equation (5) is known as the 'reduction to dated quantities of labour'. In the single-products case contemplated by Dmitriev there are as many series of dated quantities of labour as there are products, and thus there are as many equations as unknowns.

Next Dmitriev turned to an analysis of the rate of profit and 'natural' prices. He praised Ricardo who had clearly specified the factors determining the general rate of profit, that is, (i) the real wage rate and (ii) the technical conditions of production in the wage goods industries: 'Ricardo's immortal contribution was his brilliant solution of this seemingly insoluble problem' (ibid., p. 58). Prices are explained in terms of a reduction to (a finite stream of) dated wage payments, properly discounted forward. With $\mathbf{p}$ as the n-vector of prices, w as the nominal wage rate and r as the competitive rate of profit, and taking wages as paid *ante factum*, from equation (5) we get

$$\mathbf{p}^T = (1 + r)w[\mathbf{l}^T + (1 + r)\mathbf{l}^T \mathbf{A} + (1 + r)^2 \mathbf{l}^T \mathbf{A}^2 + (1 + r)^3 \mathbf{l}^T \mathbf{A}^3 + ...] \tag{6}$$

Dmitriev also confirmed Ricardo's finding that relative prices are proportional to relative quantities of labour embodied in two special cases only: (i) when the reduction series are linearly dependent pairwise; and (ii) when the rate of profit is zero.

Finally, Dmitriev demonstrated that Ricardo was right in stating that there is an inverse relationship between the rate of profit and the real wage rate, given the technical conditions of production; and that the rate of profit does not depend (as Marx contended) on the conditions of production in the industries that produce 'luxuries'.

Von Bortkiewicz who taught economics and statistics at the University of Berlin, the same university which in the late 1920s also had Wassily Leontief, John von Neumann and Robert Remak among its members, elaborated on Dmitriev's approach in his criticism of Marx's labour value-based reasoning (von Bortkiewicz, 1906–7, 1907; the second article is reprinted as Chapter 2, this volume). He accused Marx of variously retrogressing to opinions which had already been shown to be defective by Ricardo.

Von Bortkiewicz, like Dmitriev before him, pointed out that the *data* from which the classical approach to the theory of value and distribution starts are sufficient to determine the rate of profit and relative prices; no additional data are needed to determine these variables. He developed his argument both in terms of an approach in which it is assumed that commodities are obtained by a finite stream of labour inputs, that is, production is 'linear', which is also known as the 'Austrian' view of production, and one in which production is 'circular'. He cast his argument in algebraic form. Considering the set of price equations associated with a given system of production with n commodities, it is recognized that the number of unknowns exceeds the number of equations by two: there are $n + 2$ unknowns (n prices, the nominal wage rate, and the rate of profit) and n equations. With the real wage bundle given from outside the system of production, and fixing a standard of value or numeraire, two additional equations (and no extra unknown) are obtained and the system can be solved for the rate of profit and prices in terms of the numeraire. Von Bortkiewicz generalized the approach to cover fixed capital.

Georg von Charasoff

While von Bortkiewicz was predominantly concerned with the price and distribution aspect and gave only slight attention to the quantity and growth aspect, Georg von Charasoff (1877–?) pointed out a fundamental *duality* between the two. Charasoff, who was born in Tiflis, wrote his Ph.D. thesis in mathematics at the University of Heidelberg. In 1910 he published a book entitled *Das System des Marxismus. Darstellung und Kritik* (The System of Marxism. Presentation and Critique) in which he anticipated several results of later reformulations of the classical approach and of input–output analysis. Because of his highly condensed and abstract argument, which is mathematical without making use of formal language, his contribution was largely ignored at the time of its publication and has only recently been rediscovered (see Egidi and Gilibert, 1984).

Von Charasoff (1910) developed his argument within the framework of an interdependent model of (single) production, which exhibits all the properties of the later input–output model. The central concept of his analysis is that of a 'series of production': it consists of a sequence, starting with any (semipositive) net output vector (where net output is defined exclusive of wage goods), followed by the vector of the means of production and means of subsistence in the support of workers needed to produce this net output vector, then the vector of the means of production and means of subsistence needed to produce the previous vector of inputs, and so on. He called the first input vector 'capital of the first degree', the second input vector 'capital of the second degree', and so on. This series 'has the remarkable property that each element of it is both the product of the following and the capital of the preceding element; its investigation is indispensable to the study of all the theoretical questions in political economy' (ibid., p. 120).

The series under consideration is closely related to the expanded Leontief inverse. Let $\mathbf{y}$ denote the n-dimensional vector of net outputs and $\mathbf{C}$ the $n \times n$ matrix of 'augmented' input coefficients; each coefficient represents the sum of the respective material and wage good input per unit of output, since von Charasoff, like the classical economists and Marx, reckoned wage payments among capital advances. Then the series is given by

$$\mathbf{y}, \mathbf{Cy}, \mathbf{C}^2\mathbf{y}, ..., \mathbf{C}^k\mathbf{y}, ...$$

With circular production this series is infinite. Tracing it backward: first, all commodities that are 'luxury goods' disappear from the picture; next, all commodities that are specific means of production needed to produce the luxury goods disappear; then the specific means of production needed in the production of these means of production disappear, and so on. On the assumption that none of the commodities mentioned so far enters in its own production, 'it is clear that from a certain finite point onwards no further exclusions have to be made, and all the remaining elements of the series of production will always be made up of the selfsame means of production, which in the final instance are indispensable in the production of all the different products and which therefore will be called *basic products*'. He stressed: 'The whole problem of price boils down ... to the determination of the prices of these basic products' (ibid., pp. 120–21).

A further property of the series of production deserves to be stressed: the capital of the second degree ($\mathbf{C}^2\mathbf{y}$) is obtained by multiplying the capital of the first degree ($\mathbf{Cy}$) by $\mathbf{C}$. 'Yet since the physical composition of a sum of capitals is obviously always a medium between the physical compositions of the summands, it follows that capitals of the second degree deviate from one another to a smaller extent than is the case with capitals of the first degree' (ibid., p. 123). The farther one goes back, the more equal the compositions of the capitals become, that is, capitals of a sufficiently high degree 'may practically be seen as different quantities of one and the same capital: the *original* or *prime capital*'. This finding is of the utmost importance for determining the rate of profit and the maximum rate of growth of the system. For it turns out that 'this original type, to which all capitals of lower degree converge, possesses the property of growing in the course of the process of production without any qualitative change, and that the rate of its growth gives the general rate of profit' (ibid., p. 124).

The rate of profit, r, can thus be ascertained in terms of a comparison of two quantities of the same composite commodity: the 'original capital'. Let $\mathbf{u}$ designate the n-dimensional vector of an elementary unit of the original capital, $\mathbf{u} \geq \mathbf{0}$, then $\mathbf{Cu}$ is the (original) capital corresponding to $\mathbf{u}$, and we have

$$\mathbf{u} = (1 + g)\mathbf{Cu} \tag{7}$$

with g as the uniform rate of growth, where $r = g$. Von Charasoff emphasized: 'The original capital expresses the idea of a surplus-value yielding, growing capital in its purest form, and the rate of its growth appears in fact as the general capitalist profit rate' (ibid., p. 112); and: 'The original capital is nothing else than the basic production, whose branches are taken in particular dimensions. As regards these dimensions the requirement is decisive that gross profits of the basic production ... are of the same type as its total capital' (ibid., p. 126). This finding can be said to generalize Torrens's 'general principle' referred to above: it relies neither on the existence of a single sector whose capital is physically homogeneous with its product and whose product is used by all sectors as an input nor on the special case in which all sectors exhibit the same input proportions.[1]

These considerations provide the key to a solution of the problem of price. For, if the various capitals can be conceived of 'as different amounts of the selfsame capital ..., then prices must be proportional to the dimensions of these, and the problem of price thus finds its solution in this relationship based on law' (ibid., p. 123). Let $\mathbf{p}$ designate the n-dimensional vector of prices, $\mathbf{p} \geq 0$ then we have the following price system

$$\mathbf{p}^T = (1 + r)\mathbf{p}^T\mathbf{C}. \tag{8}$$

Thus, while $\mathbf{u}$ equals the right-hand eigenvector of $\mathbf{C}$, $\mathbf{p}$ equals the left-hand eigenvector; $1/(1 + r)$ equals the dominant eigenvalue of matrix $\mathbf{C}$. The solution to the price problem can therefore be cast in a form, in which 'the notion of labour is almost entirely by-passed' (ibid., p. 112). Implicit in this reasoning is the abandonment of the labour theory of value as a basis for the theory of relative prices and the rate of profit.

Von Charasoff shared with von Neumann ([1937] 1945) a concern with the potential for equi-proportionate growth. In the hypothetical case in which all profits are accumulated, the proportions of the different sectors equal the proportions of the original capital. In this case the actual rate of growth equals the rate of profit: the system expands along a von Neumann ray. Von Charasoff was perhaps the first author to note clearly what von Neumann more than two decades later was to call 'the remarkable duality (symmetry) of the monetary variables (prices p_j, interest factor β) and the technical variables (intensities of production q_i, coefficient of expansion of the economy α)' (von Neumann [1937] 1945, p. 1).

Wassily Leontief

Wassily Leontief was born in 1905 in St Petersburg. After his studies at the university of his home town, then Leningrad, he went to Berlin to work on his doctorate under the supervision of von Bortkiewicz. In 1928 he published a part of his thesis entitled 'Die Wirtschaft als Kreislauf' (Leontief, 1928; an abridged English translation of this paper (Chapter 3a, this volume) was published in 1991). In it Leontief put forward a two-sector input–output system which was designed to describe the production, distribution and consumption aspects of an economy as a single process. In 1932 he joined the faculty at Harvard University and began with the construction of the first input–output tables of the American economy. These tables together with the corresponding mathematical model were published in 1936 and 1937 (see Leontief, 1941). He related his 1936 paper (Chapter

4) explicitly to the work of Quesnay: 'The statistical study presented ... may be best defined as an attempt to construct, on the basis of available statistical materials, a *Tableau Economique* of the United States for 1919 and 1929' (Leontief, 1936, p. 105).

In his thesis Leontief advocated the view that economics should start from 'the ground of what is objectively given' (Leontief, 1928, p. 583). He distinguished between 'cost goods' and 'revenue goods', that is, inputs and goods satisfying final demand. The argument is developed within the confines of what was to become known as the *Nonsubstitution Theorem* (see Samuelson, 1951, and Kurz and Salvadori, 1994). A nonsubstitution theorem is a uniqueness theorem which asserts that under certain specified conditions an economy has one particular price structure for each admissible value of the rate of profit, that is, relative prices are independent of the pattern of final demand. The conditions are (i) constant returns to scale, (ii) a single primary factor of production only (generally homogeneous labour), and (iii) no joint production, that is, circulating capital only. In much of Leontief's analysis it is also assumed that the system of production (and consumption) is indecomposable. Leontief suggested (1928, p. 585) that the process of production should be described in terms of three sets of 'technical coefficients': (i) 'cost coefficients', that is, the proportion in which two cost goods h and k participate in the production of good j (in familiar notation: a_{hj}/a_{kj}); (ii) 'productivity coefficients', that is, the total quantity produced of good j in relation to the total quantity used up of the ith input (in familiar notation: $1/a_{ij}$); (iii) 'distribution coefficients', that is, the proportion of the total output of a certain good allotted to a particular point (or pole) in the scheme of circular flow; as is explained later in the paper, such a point may represent a particular group of property income receivers. A major concern of Leontief's was with a stationary system characterized by constant technical coefficients; in addition he discussed cases in which one or several coefficients change, thereby necessitating adjustments of the system as a whole.

Starting from a physically specified system of production-cum-distribution, Leontief is to be credited with having provided a clear idea of the concept of *vertical integration* (Leontief, 1928, p. 589). With regard to the reduction to dated quantities of labour (ibid., pp. 596 and 621–2), he pointed out that because of the circular character of production 'a complete elimination of a factor of production from the given system is in principle impossible. Of course, the size of the "capital factor" can be reduced to any chosen level by referring back to even earlier periods of production' (ibid., p.622 [p. 211]; page numbers in square brackets refer to the 1991 English translation of Leontief, 1928). This reduction has nothing to do with an historical regress (ibid., p. 596, fn. 6 [p.192 fn]).

Next Leontief addressed the problem of the exchange relationships. Emphasis is on 'the general conditions which must be fulfilled within the framework of a circular flow' (ibid., p. 598 [p. 193]). The concept of 'value' adopted is explicitly qualified as one which has nothing to do with any intrinsic property of goods, such as utility; it rather refers to the 'exchange relation deduced from all the relationships ... analysed so far' (ibid.). In the case of a model with two goods, the 'relations of reproduction' are tabulated as follows:

$$aA + bB \to A$$
$$(1 - a)A + (1 - b)B \to B$$

where A and B give the total quantities produced of two, possibly composite, commodities, and a and b [$(1 - a)$ and $(1 - b)$] give the shares of those commodities used up as means of production and means of subsistence in the first (second) sector. The reader will notice a striking similarity between Leontief's considerations and those of Isnard.

It should be stressed that the system contemplated, albeit stationary, generates a surplus, just as that of Isnard. Moreover, Leontief assumed that a part of the product of each sector is appropriated by a so-called ownership group: 'In the general circular flow scheme, income from ownership is of course considered alongside other cost items without the slightest direct reference to how it originates (the phenomenon of ownership). It is the task of interest theory to investigate these fundamental relationships' (ibid., p. 600 [p. 196]). His argument resulted in setting up price equations which reflect the going rule that fixes the distribution of income. Counting unknowns and equations, Leontief found that the number of variables exceeds the number of equations by one. He concluded: 'No clear resolution of this problem is possible. One may vary at will the exchange proportions and consequently the distribution relationships of the goods without affecting the circular flow of the economy in any way' (ibid., pp. 598–9 [p. 194]). In other words, the same quantity system is assumed to be compatible with different price systems reflecting different distributions of income. He added: 'The sense of the surplus theory is represented by the classical school (for example, even by Ricardo) and ... is best understood if one enquires into the use of this "free" income. The answer is: it either accumulates or is used up unproductively' (ibid., p. 619 [p. 209]). Hence the exchange ratios of goods reflect not only 'natural', that is, essentially technological, factors, but also 'social causes'. Given the rate of interest together with the system of production, relative prices can be determined. 'But this is the "law of value" of the so-called objective value theory' (ibid., p. 601 [p. 196], Leontief concluded.

Before we turn briefly to Leontief's contributions to input–output analysis, more narrowly defined, it should be recalled that in the late 1920s he was a member of a research group at the University of Kiel, Germany. The group was led by Adolf Löwe, later Adolph Lowe, and included Fritz (later Fred) Burchardt (1902–58) and Alfred Kähler (1900–1981), among others. One of the main questions tackled by this group was the problem of the displacement of workers due to technical progress and their absorption, or lack thereof, as a consequence of capital accumulation. In order to be able to take into account both the direct and indirect effects of technical progress, they developed multisectoral analyses. In 1931 and 1932 Burchardt published an essay in which he attempted to cross-breed Marx's scheme of reproduction and Eugen von Böhm-Bawerk's temporal view of production (Burchardt, 1931–2). Alfred Kähler in his Ph.D. thesis of 1933 put forward a sophisticated argument which revolved around a static input–output model and the way different forms of technical progress affect the coefficients of production of the different sectors and how these effects have secondary effects and so on (Kähler, 1933). He also tried to calculate the change in the price system made necessary by technical change, assuming that any improvement is eventually passed on to workers in the form of a higher wage rate.

While Leontief conceived of his early contribution as firmly rooted in the classical tradition, he called his input–output method developed in the 1930s and 1940s 'an adaptation of the neo-classical theory of general equilibrium to the empirical study of the quantitative interdependence between interrelated economic activities' (Leontief, 1966, p. 134). Scrutiny shows, however, that in his input–output analysis he preserved the concept of circular flow and did not, as is maintained by some interpreters, adopt the Walras–Cassel view of production (on this see Gilibert, 1981, and Kurz, 1997). In the second edition of *The Structure of American Economy*, published in 1951, a decade after the first edition (Leontief, 1941), he even explicitly rejected the view of production as a one-way avenue that leads from the services of the 'original' factors of production: land, labour and capital – the 'venerable trinity' – to final goods (Leontief, 1951, p. 112). Unlike the theories of Walras and Cassel, in Leontief there are no given initial endowments of these factors.

When all sales and purchases are taken to be endogenous, the input–output system is called *closed*. In this case final demand is treated as if it were an ordinary industry: the column associated with it represents the 'inputs' it receives from the various industries, and the corresponding row giving the value added in the various industries is assumed to represent its 'output' allocated to these industries. The price system which is dual to the quantity system associated with the closed input–output model is

$$\mathbf{p}^T = \mathbf{p}^T\mathbf{A} \tag{9a}$$

that is,

$$\mathbf{p}^T(\mathbf{I} - \mathbf{A}) = \mathbf{0}^T \tag{9b}$$

In the second edition of *The Structure of the American Economy* (1951), Leontief elaborated the *open* input–output model which treats the technological and the final demand aspects separately. Now the input matrix represents exclusively the matrix of interindustry coefficients; the vector of final demand is taken to be given from outside the system. The matrix of input coefficients is then used to determine the sectoral gross outputs as well as the necessary intersectoral transactions that enable the system to meet final demand and reproduce all used up means of production. As to the determination of prices in the open input–output model, Leontief proposed a set of 'value-added price equations'. The price each productive sector is assumed to receive per unit of output equals the total outlays incurred in the course of its production. These outlays comprise the payments for material inputs purchased from the same or other productive sectors plus the *given* 'value added'. Assuming a closed economy without a government, the latter represents payments to the owners of productive factors: wages, rents, interest and profits. The price system which is dual to the quantity system associated with the open input–output model is given by

$$\mathbf{p}^T(\mathbf{I} - \mathbf{A}) = \mathbf{v}^T \tag{10a}$$

where **p** is the *n*-vector of prices and **v** is the *n*-vector of values added per unit of output. Solving for **p** gives

$$\mathbf{p}^T = \mathbf{v}^T(\mathbf{I} - \mathbf{A})^{-1}. \tag{10b}$$

The Leontief inverse matrix $(\mathbf{I} - \mathbf{A})^{-1}$ is semipositive if the largest real eigenvalue of matrix **A** is smaller than unity (cf. Hawkins and Simon, 1949; Chapter 6, this volume). The main problem with this approach is that the magnitudes of value added per unit of output in the different sectors cannot generally be determined prior to, and independently of, the system of prices. Another way of putting it is that in this formulation two things are lost sight of: the constraint binding changes in the distributive variables, and the dependence of relative prices on income distribution – facts rightly stressed by Leontief in his 1928 paper.

Robert Remak

The problem of the existence of a (non-negative) solution of system (9) was first investigated by Robert Remak (1888–1942) in a paper published in 1929 (Remak, 1929). Its author had studied mathematics and in 1929 acquired the *venia legendi* at the University of Berlin and was a *Privatdozent* there until 1933. According to the information gathered by Wittmann, Remak was in all probability stimulated by a group of economists around Bortkiewicz to study the problem of the conditions under which positive solutions of systems of linear equations obtain (Wittmann, 1967, p. 401).

Remak's paper begins with a definition of what is meant by an exact science which bears a striking resemblance to Leontief's point of view: an exact science regards as 'exactly correct' only what can be ascertained by physical observation, counting or calculation (Remak, 1929, p. 703). Conventional economics, which Remak tended to equate with Marshallian demand and supply analysis, is said not to allow 'quantitative calculations that can also be carried out practically' (ibid., p. 712). The alternative are 'superposed' or 'reasonable' prices: 'A superposed price system has nothing to do with values. It only satisfies the condition that each price covers the prices of the things required in production, and the consumption of the producer on the assumption that it is both just and feasible' (ibid., p. 712). Its calculation requires a detailed knowledge of the socio-technical relations of production, that is, the methods of production in use and the needs and wants of producers (ibid., pp. 712–13).

Remak then constructs 'superposed prices' for an economic system in stationary conditions in which there are as many single-product processes of production as there are products, and each process or product is represented by a different 'person' or rather activity or industry.[2] The amounts of the different commodities acquired by a person over a certain period of time in exchange for its own product are of course the amounts needed as means of production to produce this product and the amounts of consumption goods in support of the person (and its family), given the levels of sustenance. With an appropriate choice of units, the resulting system of 'superposed prices' can be written as

$$\mathbf{p}^T = \mathbf{p}^T\mathbf{C} \tag{11}$$

where $\mathbf{C}$ is the augmented matrix of inputs per unit of output, and $\mathbf{p}$ is the vector of exchange ratios. Discussing system (11) Remak arrived at the conclusion that there is a solution to it which is semipositive and unique except for a scale factor.

John von Neumann

Von Neumann (1903–1957) was born in Budapest. He studied mathematics, among other things, and in 1927 assumed the position of a *Privatdozent* at the University of Berlin. In 1929 be transferred to the University of Hamburg and in 1930 he went to Princeton University where in 1933 he joined the Institute for Advanced Study as a professor. Von Neumann read his paper on the growth model for the first time in the winter of 1932 at the Mathematical Seminar of Princeton University. In 1936 he gave the paper in Karl Menger's Mathematical Colloquium at the University of Vienna (von Neumann, 1937); in 1945 an English translation of the paper appeared (von Neumann, 1945; Chapter 5, this volume). The paper is interesting for several reasons, not least because it may be interpreted as containing an implicit comment on Remak (for this interpretation, see Kurz and Salvadori, 1993).

Von Neumann assumed that there are n goods which can be produced by m constant returns to scale production processes. The problem is to establish which processes will actually be chosen and which not, being 'unprofitable'. He took the real wage rate, consisting of the 'necessities of life', as given and paid at the beginning of the (uniform) production period. In addition he assumed 'that all income in excess of necessities of life will be reinvested' (von Neumann, 1945, p. 2). The characteristic features of the model include: (i) 'Goods are produced not only from "natural factors of production", but in the first place from each other. These processes of production may be circular'; (ii) the processes 'can describe the special case where good G_j can be produced only jointly with certain others, viz. its permanent joint products'; (iii) both circulating and fixed capital can be dealt with: 'wear and tear of capital goods are to be described by introducing different stages of wear as different goods, using a separate P [rocess] $_i$ for each of these' (ibid., pp. 1–2). These assumptions are coupled with the Rule of Free Goods: 'if there is excess production of G_j, G_j becomes a free good and its price $[p_j] = 0$' (ibid., p. 3).

Von Neumann's approach can be summarized as follows. Let $\mathbf{A}$ and $\mathbf{B}$ be the $n \times m$ input and output matrices, respectively, where $\mathbf{A}$ includes the means of subsistence in the support of workers; and let $\mathbf{q}$ be the m-dimensional vector of activity levels and $\mathbf{p}$ the n-dimensional price vector. $\alpha = 1 + g$ is the expansion factor, where g is the growth rate; $\beta = 1 + r$ is the interest factor, where g is the rate of interest (or profit). The model is subject to the following axioms.

$$\mathbf{Bq} \geq \alpha \mathbf{Aq}, \tag{12a}$$
$$\mathbf{p}^T \mathbf{B} \leq \beta \mathbf{p}^T \mathbf{A}, \tag{12b}$$
$$(\mathbf{B} - \alpha \mathbf{A})\mathbf{q} = 0, \tag{12c}$$
$$\mathbf{p}^T(\mathbf{B} - \beta \mathbf{A})\mathbf{q} = 0, \tag{12d}$$
$$\mathbf{q} \geq 0 \text{ and } \mathbf{p} \geq 0. \tag{12e}$$

Axiom (12a) implies that α times the inputs for a given period are not larger than the outputs of the previous period. Axiom (12b) is the no extra profits condition. Axiom (12c) states the free disposal assumption. Axiom (12d) implies that processes which incur extra cost will not be operated. Finally, (12e) requires that both the intensity and the price vector are semipositive. In order to demonstrate that for any pair of non-negative matrices $\mathbf{A}$ and $\mathbf{B}$ there exist solutions for $\mathbf{q}$ and $\mathbf{p}$ and for α, $\alpha \geq 0$, and β, $\beta \geq 0$, von Neumann assumed in addition:

$$\mathbf{A} + \mathbf{B} > 0, \tag{12f}$$

which implies that every process requires as an input or produces as an output some positive amount of every good. On the basis of these givens he demonstrated the existence of a solution. He determined (i) which processes will be operated; (ii) at what rate the economic system will grow; (iii) what prices will obtain; (iv) what the rate of interest will be; and (v) that, of necessity, the growth and the interest factor are equal.

There are striking similarities between the contributions of the classical economists and von Neumann. These concern: (i) the concept of production as a circular flow; (ii) the concept of the surplus product which forms the basis of an explanation of all shares of income other than wages; (iii) the notion of a uniformly expanding economy in which the rate of expansion is determined endogenously; (iv) the concept of duality of the relationship between relative quantities and the rate of growth on the one hand and that between relative prices and the rate of interest on the other; (v) the way in which the problem of the choice of technique is approached and the use of inequalities in it; and (vi) the way the Rule of Free Goods is applied to primary factors of production and to products, respectively. Von Neumann in fact applied that rule in the same way as the classical economists did. While he assumed 'that the natural factors of production, including labour, can be expanded in unlimited quantities' (1945, p. 2), this did not make him treat all these factors alike. Rather, he singled out labour as the only factor that is exempt from that rule; all other primary factors, although needed in production, 'disappear' from the scene because they are taken to be non-scarce. Labour is assumed to receive a given wage bundle which is independent of the degree of employment.

Piero Sraffa

Piero Sraffa (1898–1983) graduated from Turin University and then went to the London School of Economics (1921–2). After appointments in Perugia and Cagliari, Italy, he was offered a lectureship in Cambridge, UK. In 1930 he assumed the position of the librarian of the Marshall Library which he held until his retirement.

Shortly after his arrival in Cambridge Sraffa showed John Maynard Keynes the set of propositions which were to grow into *Production of Commodities by Means of Commodities* (Sraffa, 1960). The slim volume contains the hitherto most sophisticated treatment of circular flow systems, tackling the issues of scarce natural resources, fixed capital and pure joint production – issues which in spite of their great empirical importance are often avoided in input–output analyses. Scrutiny shows that in his investigation Sraffa proceeds through a number of stages towards ever more general constellations concerning the data (1)–(4) mentioned at the beginning of this introduction (see above, pp. xix–xx). He was concerned with reviving the 'standpoint ... of the old classical economists from Adam Smith to Ricardo' (ibid., p. v). He developed his argument essentially in a two-part structure. In one part he investigated *given* 'systems of production'. The emphasis is on the relationship between relative prices, the general rate of profit and the wage rate implicit in a given system, or 'technique'. In another part he turned to the problem of which system of production will be adopted from a set of alternative systems, that is, the problem of the choice of technique. Hence, what was initially taken as given is now an *unknown*. Sraffa assumed that the choice between alternative techniques 'will be exclusively grounded on cheapness' (ibid., p. 83). In other words, he was concerned with determining the *cost-minimizing* system(s) of (see also Kurz and Salvadori, 1995).

It can be shown that as regards its technical core many input–output models are but special cases of Sraffa's more general analysis (see Lager, 1997). In addition Sraffa provided a meticulous account of how the technical conditions of production shape the relationship between the distributive variables and relative prices – issues commonly avoided in input–output models or dealt with in a cavalier way. These are some of the reasons why input–output theorists might want to study carefully Sraffa's contribution which, after all, belongs to the same intellectual tradition: classical economic analysis.

Notes

1. Von Charasoff's construction also bears a close resemblance to Sraffa's device of the standard system in which the rate of profit 'appears as a ratio between quantities of commodities irrespective of their prices' (Sraffa, 1960, p. 22).
2. The somewhat unfortunate phrasing of the problem by Remak may have been the source of the misconception that his concern was with a pure exchange economy; for this interpretation, see Gale (1960, p. 290).

References

Bortkiewicz, L. von (1906–7), 'Wertrechnung und Preisrechnung im Marxschen System', *Archiv für Sozialwissenschaft und Sozialpolitik*, **23** (1906), 1–50, **25** (1907), 10–51 and 445–88; in the text referred to as essays I, II and III. Essays II and III were translated into English; see von Bortkiewicz (1952), 'Value and price in the Marxian system', *International Economic Papers*, **2**, 5–60.

Bortkiewicz, L. von (1907), 'Zur Berichtigung der grundlegenden theoretischen Konstruktion von Marx im 3. Band des "Kapital"', *Jahrbücher für Nationalökonomie und Statistik*, **34**, 319–35.

Burchardt, F. (1931–2), 'Die Schemata des stationären Kreislaufs bei Böhm-Bawerk und Marx', *Weltwirtschaftliches Archiv*, **34** (1931), 525–64, **35** (1932), 116–76.

Champernowne, D.G. (1945), 'A note on J. v. Neumann's article on "A model of economic equilibrium"', *Review of Economic Studies*, **13**, 10–18.

Charasoff, G. von (1910), *Das System des Marxismus: Darstellung und Kritik*, Berlin: H. Bondy.

Dmitriev, V.K. (1898), 'The theory of value of David Ricardo: An attempt at a rigorous analysis', translated by D. Fry in D.M. Nuti (ed.) (1974), *V.K. Dmitriev: Economic Essays on Value, Competition and Utility*, with an introduction by D.M. Nuti, Cambridge: Cambridge University Press. [Reprinted as Chapter 1 in Volume I.]

Egidi, M. and Gilibert, G. (1984), 'La teoria oggettiva dei prezzi', *Economia Politica*, **1**, 43–61. An English translation of the paper titled 'The objective theory of prices' was published in *Political Economy. Studies in the Surplus Approach*, **5** (1989), 59–74.

Gale, D. (1960), *The Theory of Linear Economic Models*, New York: McGraw-Hill.

Gilibert, G. (1981), 'Isnard, Cournot, Walras, Leontief. Evoluzione di un modello', *Annali della Fondazione Luigi Einaudi*, Turin, **XV**, 129–53.

Hawkins, D. and Simon, H.A. (1949), 'Note: Some conditions of macroeconomic stability', *Econometrica*, **17**, 245–8. [Reprinted as Chapter 6 in Volume I.]

INED (1958), *François Quesnay et la physiocratie*, 2 vols, Paris: Institut Nationale d'Etudes Démographiques.

Isnard, A.-N. (1781), *Traité des richesses*, 2 vols, London and Lausanne: F. Grasset.

Kähler, A. (1933), *Die Theorie der Arbeiterfreisetzung durch die Maschine*, Greifswald: Julius Abel.

Kurz, H.D. (1997), '"Classical" roots of input–output analysis: a short account of its long prehistory', manuscript, to be published.

Kurz, H.D. and Salvadori, N. (1993), 'Von Neumann's growth model and the "classical" tradition', *European Journal of the History of Economic Thought*, **1**, 129–60.

Kurz, H.D. and Salvadori, N. (1994), 'The non-substitution theorem: making good a lacuna', *Journal of Economics*, **59**, 97–103.

Kurz, H.D. and Salvadori, N. (1995), *Theory of Production. A Long-Period Analysis*, Cambridge, Melbourne and New York: Cambridge University Press.

Lager, C. (1997), 'On the treatment of fixed capital in a Sraffian framework and in the theory of dynamic input–output analysis', *Economic Systems Research*, **9**, 357–73.

Leontief, W. (1928), 'Die Wirtschaft als Kreislauf', *Archiv für Sozialwissenschaft und Sozialpolitik*, **60**, 577–623.

Leontief, W. (1936), 'Quantitative input and output relations in the economic system of the United States', *Review of Economic[s and] Statistics*, **18** (3), 105–25. [Reprinted as Chapter 4 in Volume I.]

Leontief, W. (1941), *The Structure of American Economy, 1919–1939: An Empirical Application of Equilibrium Analysis*, White Plains, New York: International Arts and Sciences Press. Second enlarged edition published 1951.

Leontief, W. (1966), *Input–Output Economics*, New York: Oxford University Press.

Leontief, W. (1987), 'Input–output analysis', in J. Eatwell, M. Milgate and P. Newman (eds), *The New Palgrave. A Dictionary of Economics*, vol. 2, 860–64.

Leontief, W. (1991), 'The economy as a circular flow', *Structural Change and Economic Dynamics*, **2** (1), 177–212, English translation of parts of Leontief (1928) with an introduction by P.A. Samuelson. [Reprinted as Chapter 3 in Volume I.]

Leontief, W. *et al.* (1951), *Studies in the Structure of the American Economy: Theoretical and Empirical Explorations in Input–Output Analysis*, White Plains, New York: International Arts and Sciences Press.

Marx, K. (1956), *Capital*, vol. II, Moscow: Progress Publishers. English translation of *Das Kapital*, vol. II, edited by F. Engels (1885), Hamburg: Meissner.

Marx, K. (1959), *Capital*, vol. III, Moscow: Progress Publishers. English translation of *Das Kapital*, vol. III, edited by F. Engels (1894), Hamburg: Meissner.

Marx, K. (1963), *Theories of Surplus Value*, part I. Moscow: Progress Publishers. English translation of *Theorien über den Mehrwert*, part 1, Berlin 1956: Dietz.

Neumann, J.v. (1937), 'Über ein ökonomisches Gleichungssystem und eine Verallgemeinerung des Brouwerschen Fixpunktsatzes', *Ergebnisse eines mathematischen Kolloquiums*, **8**, 73–83.

Neumann, J.v. (1945), 'A model of general economic equilibrium', *Review of Economic Studies*, **13**, 1–9; English translation of von Neumann (1937). [Reprinted as Chapter 5 in Volume I.]

Phillips, A. (1955), 'The Tableau économique as a simple Leontief model', *Quarterly Journal of Economics*, **69**, 137–44.

Remak, R. (1929), 'Kann die Volkswirtschaftslehre eine exakte Wissenschaft werden?', *Jahrbücher für Nationalökonomie und Statistik*, **131**, 703–35.

Ricardo, D. (1951–73), *The Works and Correspondence of David Ricardo*, edited by Piero Sraffa with the collaboration of Maurice H. Dobb, Cambridge: Cambridge University Press, 11 vols. In the text referred to as *Works*, volume number.

Samuelson, P.A. (1951), 'Abstract of a theorem concerning substitutability in open Leontief models', in T.C. Koopmans (ed.), *Activity Analysis of Production and Allocation*, New Haven, London: Yale University Press, 142–6. [Reprinted as Chapter 12 in Volume III.]

Smith, A. (1776), *An Inquiry into the Nature and Causes of the Wealth of Nations. The Glasgow Edition of the Works and Correspondence of Adam Smith*, vol. I, 1976, Oxford: Oxford University Press.

Sraffa, P. (1960), *Production of Commodities by Means of Commodities*, Cambridge: Cambridge University Press.

Torrens, R. (1820), *An Essay on the Influence of the External Corn Trade upon the Production and Distribution of National Wealth*, 2nd edition, London: Hatchard.

Torrens, R. (1821), *An Essay on the Production of Wealth*, London: Longman, Hurst, Rees, Orme, and Brown. Reprint edited by J. Dorfman, New York 1965: Augustus M. Kelley.

Wittmann, W. (1967), 'Die extremale Wirtschaft. Robert Remak – ein Vorläufer der Aktivitätsanalyse', *Jahrbücher für Nationalökonomie und Statistik*, **180**, 397–409.

Introduction to Part II : Dynamic Input–Output Analysis

Hawkins (1948), Holley (1952, 1953) and Leontief (1953, 1970; Chapters 7 and 8 this volume, respectively)[1] were first to come up with a multi-sector generalization of the Harrod–Domar growth model. In contrast to the static input–output model, this type of model, which was later labelled the dynamic input–output model, takes into account interindustry transactions not only for intermediate products but also for fixed capital items.

Leontief (1970) presented a time discrete version of the dynamic input–output model developed in Leontief (1953). Neglecting technical progress, that model is given by

$$\mathbf{q}_t = \mathbf{f}_t + \mathbf{A}\mathbf{q}_t + \mathbf{B}(\mathbf{q}_{t+1} - \mathbf{q}_t) \tag{1}$$

where $\mathbf{A}$ is a square matrix of flow–flow coefficients that specifies flows of inputs of circulating capital per unit of output flow, and $\mathbf{B}$ is a stock flow matrix of stocks of fixed capital goods required at the beginning of the period per unit of output produced during that period. Consumption of commodities during period t, denoted by vector $\mathbf{f}_t$, plus consumption of circulating capital ($\mathbf{A}\mathbf{q}_t$) plus additions to stocks of fixed capital, that is, $\mathbf{B}(\mathbf{q}_{t+1} - \mathbf{q}_t)$, equals gross outputs produced during period t, denoted by vector $\mathbf{q}_t$.

The model is based on three restrictive assumptions:

1. there is no choice of technique,
2. there is full capacity production, and
3. fixed capital products are transferable between different lines of production at zero cost (reversibility of capital in place).

These restrictive assumptions give rise to the following conceptual problems:

1. *Instability.* A large number of studies provide conditions for stability of the quantity model in relation to the eigenvalues of the matrices describing the technology.[2] Since the magnitude of capital coefficients is inversely related to the length of the period of production, Wurtele (1959), Leontief (1970) and Petri (1972) demonstrated that the size of this time interval is critical. Stability can be obtained by changing the unit of time which changes the length of time required for adjustment of capital to the rate of output. Szyld (1985) provided necessary and sufficient conditions for the existence of a balanced growth solution for the case of a reducible matrix of input coefficients. Tokoyama and Murakami (1972; Chapter 10) identified stability zones for forward-lag

models with gestation lags of one and two production periods as well as for backward-lag models where the anticipated increase in outputs is a weighted average of the actual increase of the past two periods.

Solow (1959) observed *dual instability*. The larger the potential rate of balanced growth the more likely it is that the quantity model is unstable and the price model is stable. But if the rate of interest is close to the maximum potential rate of balanced growth, then it is likely that the price model will be unstable. A *dual (in)stability theorem* has been proved by Jorgenson (1960): if – for any initial rates of output – the output levels determined over time by a dynamic Leontief model can be assured to remain non-negative, then prices must become negative for some initial price vector and vice versa.

The instability of Leontief's model led to a debate between Sargan (1958, 1961) and Leontief (1961a, b). Sargan pointed out that Leontief's model is a multisectoral version of Harrod's dynamic model of growth. Hence the dynamic input–output model exhibits the same difficulties. Sargan's critique is closely related to the problem of:

2. *Causal Indeterminacy* detected by Dorfinan, Samuelson and Solow (1958). Stocks of fixed capital goods available at the end of a period are given by the stocks available at the beginning of that period plus net investment, that is, those products which are available after current consumption has been deducted from gross outputs;

$$\mathbf{k}_{t+1} = \underbrace{\mathbf{Bq}_{t+1}}_{\substack{terminal \\ stocks}} = \underbrace{\mathbf{q}_t - \mathbf{Aq}_t - \mathbf{f}_t}_{net\ investment} + \underbrace{\mathbf{Bq}_t.}_{\substack{initial \\ stocks}} \tag{2}$$

Leontief's dynamic model has no explicit investment hypothesis. There is no active planned investment or capacity with regard to (expected) demand. Investment is taken to be what is left at the end of the period after final and intermediate consumption has been deducted. This leads to the related problems of:

3. *Singularity and the Possibility of Negative Solutions*. Since choice of technique is ruled out and capital items in place are assumed to be transferable, stocks available at the beginning of period t are allocated to production processes in such a way that full capacity production is guaranteed, that is, $\mathbf{k}_{t+1} = \mathbf{Bq}_{t+1}$. Consequently gross outputs in period $t + 1$ are not determined by (expected) demand but are determined by full utilization of what is left over from the previous period. Hence gross production during period t is calculated according to:

$$\mathbf{q}_t = \mathbf{B}^{-1}\mathbf{k}_t \tag{3}$$

The solution of Leontief' s forward-lag model requires the inversion of the matrix of fixed capital coefficients. Since not all products are fixed capital goods, it is most likely that some of the rows of this matrix have only zero elements and hence the matrix is singular. This problem is analysed and solved in Kendrick (1972), Livesey (1973, 1976) and Luenberger and Arbel (1977). A comprehensive discussion and solutions to the so called *problem of singularity* is provided by Meyer (1982; Chapter II) and ten Raa (1986a; Chapter 12).

But there is another problem. The structure of given endowments (initial stocks) need not fit full capacity requirements specified by matrix **B**. Therefore it is possible that negative outputs appear. The full capacity assumption together with the absence of choice of technique makes the model rigid. The consequence is that the system may end up with negative outputs and/or stocks. The following suggestions are proposed to overcome these problems.

One suggestion is to circumnavigate the problem of stability and to reinterpret the Leontief model either as a multisectoral version of a Domar type equilibrium model of steady growth (Meyer and Schumann, 1977) or as a planning system (Sargan, 1958) rather than as a model describing the actual behaviour of a decentralized economy. In *Proportions. Prices and Planning*, Bródy (1970) provided sufficient conditions for the existence of a positive and unambiguous steady state solution of a closed (homogeneous) version of Leontief's dynamic model and emphasized the classical roots of input–output analysis. He presented a rigorous formulation of the Marxian schemata of simple and extended reproduction and provided a comparison of that model with Leontief's dynamic model as well as with von Neumann's model of steady growth. Lager (1997) showed that Leontief's dynamic model as well as most of its recent generalizations are special cases of the model of balanced growth developed by von Neumann (1937, 1945; Chapter 5).

The second route is to relax the full-capacity assumption and to allow for disequilibria in the sense that capacity is not fully adjusted to output at any moment of time. Without the full capacity assumption the system is indeterminate and requires (or allows for) additional technological constraints or behavioural assumptions. Leontief (1953, p. 68) was aware that his approach – a multisectoral version of the acceleration principle – '*has one particular serious defect – it neglects the irreversibility of the accumulation process*' by transferring fixed capital from sectors with idle capacity to rapidly growing sectors with a scarcity of capital. Hence Leontief (1953) and Uzawa (1956) assured *irreversibility* of capital already in place by introducing a flexible accelerator such that demand for capital is proportional to the rate of change of outputs when the latter is rising but zero in the case of declining outputs and thus admitting excess capacity in declining sectors.

Dorfman, Samuelson and Solow (1958) and Solow (1959) argued that there is no technological reason for assuming that at any moment of time capacity is fully adjusted to outputs. All the technological constraints allow one to assert is that output must be smaller than or equal to full capacity. In this case the dynamic model is not fully determinate and thus allows for an analysis of intertemporal choice of efficient capacity plans, that is, factor substitution in production. An optimal capital accumulation is obtained by solving a linear programme. In contrast to the activity analysis approach Johansen (1960), Almon (1963a, b; Chapter 15) and Schumann (1968) used production functions which allow for the substitution of capital and labour.

Another way to give up the full capacity assumption is to avoid indeterminacy by the introduction of planned investment. Substituting in equation (1) actual outputs of period $t + 1$ by anticipated outputs, $\hat{\mathbf{q}}_{t+1}$, and assuming that changes in outputs are expected to remain as they were in the previous period, that is, $\tilde{\mathbf{q}}_{t+1} - \mathbf{q}_t = \mathbf{q}_t - \mathbf{q}_{t-1}$ gives the backward lag model,

$$\mathbf{q}_t = \mathbf{f}_t + \mathbf{A}\mathbf{q}3_t + \mathbf{B}(\mathbf{q}_t - \mathbf{q}_{t-1}) \tag{4}$$

proposed by Wurtele (1959) or Carter (1963).

Jorgenson (1961; Chapter 14). Almon (1963a, b) and Duchin and Szyld (1985; Chapter 16) also introduced explicit investment hypotheses which are based on planned or desired capacities. Almon presumed that investment and employment decisions are made by firms which form their expectations by using the forecasts of the model (rational expectations) and allowed for substitution of capital and labour. Hence investment does not only result from the growth of output, but also from the substitution of capital for labour as the wage goes up and the productivity of new capital increases. Duchin and Szyld introduced different gestation periods. Hence the expansion of future capacities must be planned several periods in advance. These plans are based on expected rates of growth of outputs which are a weighted average of the rates observed in the recent past. The model proposed by Duchin and Szyld has been used for empirical investigations by Leontief and Duchin (1986). It has been further developed and used by Kalmbach and Kurz (1990 (Chapter 17), 1992) and Edler and Ribakova (1993). While the latter types of models are pure quantity models, Jorgenson (1961) proposed a fully integrated quantity and price model. On the one hand, apart from technical requirements there is speculative holding of stocks which is assumed to be proportional to the difference between current price and expected – that is, long-run normal – price of the respective commodity. On the other hand, changes in the gap between current and long-run prices are related to the level of stocks held in excess of requirements for transaction and productive purposes. The complete model can be decomposed in two parts, an equilibrium part of proportional growth and its dual, and a disequilibrium part based on the theory of speculative stocks. Steadily growing outputs and stationary equilibrium prices are both stable provided that the money rate of interest is at least equal to the equilibrium rate of growth.

Leontief's dynamic model has been further refined and developed in many directions. Carter (1963, 1970; Chapter 18) suggested that structural change may be introduced into dynamic input–output models by consideration of capital embodied technical progress. Technology is represented by (i) average technical coefficients reflecting existing capacity observable from past periods and (ii) 'best practice' coefficients characterizing new technologies. An optimal mix of input structures, in the sense that demand for labour is minimized, subject to an overall investment ceiling given by the total amount of gross new investment available to the system, is calculated by means of a linear programming model. Applications of dynamic input–output models for the analysis of technical change and the diffusion of new technologies can be found in Edler (1990), Edler *et al.* (1990) and Kalmbach and Kurz (1990, 1992).

Stone and Brown (1962), Mathur (1964) and Mukerji (1964; Chapter 13) investigated the dynamic Leontief system for the case of differentiated rates of growth of final demands. While Stone and Brown (1962) considered only a particular (long-run) solution, Mukerji (1964) generalized this approach to interconnected growth in consumption of commodities and provided a general solution.

Various contributions were devoted to a further elaboration of the dynamic structure of Leontief's model. Transit and production lags (Bródy, 1965), gestation lags and a finite life of fixed capital (Johansen, 1978; Åberg and Persson, 1981) were considered. Ten Raa (1986a, b) recast vectors of inputs into temporal distributions. Aulin-Ahmavaara (1990) proposed a generalized dynamic model which includes all properties of some earlier models. While most of these studies are concerned with the particular case of balanced growth, ten Raa (1986a, b) offered a general solution which also applies to unbalanced growth.

Leontief (1970) introduced the notion of the *dynamic inverse*, which allows for a (backward) solution if technical coefficients change arbitrarily over time, and thus provided a comprehensive tool for empirical investigations of technological change. Bródy (1995; Chapter 9) argued that the dynamic inverse should be, in principle, based on an infinite series of interlinked processes. Therefore calculating the dynamic inverse requires either the inversion of a doubly infinite matrix or the inversion of a square truncated system. Simple truncation will give a doomsday result, that is, at the end of the period the whole product will be consumed and the economy will vanish. Another scenario provides funds for simple reproduction after the end of the period but neglects flows for further growth.

While most of the studies in the field of dynamic input–output analysis are primarily concerned with fixed capital investment, Lovell (1962) and Meyer (1990) analysed the dynamic behaviour of a multisector buffer-stock inventory model.

Notes

1. Georgescu-Roegen (1951, p. 117) mentioned that Leontief presented his dynamic model in a paper read in February 1949 before the staff of the Harvard Fconomic Research Project.
2. See, for instance, Steenge (1978, 1990)

References

Åberg, M. and Persson, H. (1981), 'A note on a closed input–output model with finite life-times and gestation lags', *Jou rnal of Economic Theory*, **24**, 446–52.

Almon, C. (1963a), 'Consistent forecasting in a dynamic multi-sector model' , *Review of Economics and Statistics*, **45**, 148–61.

Almon, C. (1963b), 'Numerical solution of a modified Leontief dynamic system for consistent forecasting or indicative planning', *Econometrica*, **31** (4), 665–78. [Reprinted as Chapter 15 in Volume I.]

Aulin-Ahmavaara, P. (1990), 'Dynamic input–output and time', *Economic Systems Research*, **2**, 329–44.

Bródy, A. (1965), *The Model of Expanding Reproduction*, Application of Mathematics to Economics, Budapest: Akadémiai Kiadó, 61–3.

Bródy, A (1970), *Proportions, Prices and Planning: A Mathematical Restatement of the Labour Theory of Value*, Amsterdam and Budapest: Akadémiai Kiadó and North-Holland Publishing Company.

Bródy, A (1995), 'Truncation and spectrum of the dynamic inverse', *Economic Systems Research*, **7**, 235–47. [Reprinted as Chapter 9 in Volume I.]

Carter, A.P. (1963), 'Incremental flow coefficients for a dynamic input output model with changing technology', in T. Barna *et al.* (eds), *Structural interdependence and Economic Development: Proceedings of an International Conference on Input–Output Techniques, Geneva, September 1961*, New York: Macmillan and Co. Ltd, 277–302.

Carter, A.P. (1970), 'A linear programming system analyzing embodied technological change', in A.P. Carter and A. Bródy (eds), *Contributions to Input–Output Analysis*, Amsterdam and London: North-Holland Publishing Company, 77–98. [Reprinted as Chapter 18 in Volume I.]

Dorfman, R., Samuelson, P.A. and Solow, R.M. (1958), *Linear Programming and Economic*

Analysis, New York: McGraw-Hill.

Duchin, F. and Szyld, D. (1985), 'A dynamic input–output model with assured positive output', *Metroeconomica*, **XXXVII** (3), 269–82. [Reprinted as Chapter 16 in Volume I.]

Edler, D. (1990), 'Ein dynamisches Input–Output-Modell zur Abschätzung der Auswirkungen ausgewählter neuer Technologien auf die Beschäftigung in der Bundesrepublik Deutschland', Deutsches Institut für Wirtschaftsforschung, Beiträge zur Strukturforschung, Heft 116, Berlin: Duncker & Humblot.

Edler, D. *et al.* (1990), 'Intersectoral effects of the use of industrial robots and CNC machine tools – an empirical input–output analysis', in R. Schettkat and M. Wagner (eds), *Technological Change and Employment*, Berlin: Walter de Gruyter. 293–314.

Edler, D. and Ribakova, T. (1993), 'The Leontief–Duchin–Szyld dynamic input–output model with reduction of idle capacity and modified decision function', *Structural Change and Economic Dynamics*, **4**, 279–97.

Georgescu-Roegen, N. (1951), 'Some properties of a generalized Leontief model', in T.C. Koopmans (ed.), *Activity Analysis of Production and Allocation*, New Haven and London: Yale University Press, 165–76.

Hawkins, D. (1948). 'Some conditions of macro-economic stability', *Econometrica*, **16**, 309–22.

Holley, J.L. (1952), 'A dynamic model', *Econometrica*, **20**, 616–42.

Holley, J.L. (1953), 'A dynamic model', *Econometrica*, **21**, 298–324.

Johansen, L. (1960), *A Multisectoral Study of Economic Growth*, Amsterdam: North-Holland Publishing Company.

Johansen, L. (1978), 'On the theory of dynamic input–output models with different time profiles of capital construction and finite life-time of capital equipment', *Journal of Economic Theory*, **19** (2), 513–33. [Reprinted as Chapter 19 in Volume I.]

Jorgenson, D.W. (1960), 'A dual stability theorem', *Econometrica*, **28**, 892–9.

Jorgenson, D.W. (1961), 'Stability of a dynamic input–output system', *Review of Economic Studies*, **28**, 105–16. [Reprinted as Chapter 14 in Volume I.]

Kalmbach, P. and Kurz, H.D. (1990), 'Micro-electronics and employment: a dynamic input–output study of the West German economy', *Structural Change and Economic Dynamics*, **1** (2), 371–86. [Reprinted as Chapter 17 in Volume I.]

Kalmbach, P. and Kurz, H.D. (1992), *Chips and Jobs: Zu den Beschäftigungswirkungen programmgesteuerter Arbeitsmittel*, Marburg: Metropolis.

Kendrick, D. (1972), 'On the Leontief dynamic inverse', *Quarterly Journal of Economics*, **86**, 693–6.

Lager, C. (1997), 'On the treatment of fixed capital in the Sraffian framework and in the theory of dynamic input–output analysis', *Economic Systems Research*, **9**, 357–73.

Leontief, W. (1953), 'Dynamic analysis', in *Studies in the Structure of the American Economy*, Chapter 3, New York: Oxford University Press, 53–90.[Reprinted as Chapter 7 in Volume I.]

Leontief, W. (1961a), 'Lags and the stability of dynamic systems', *Econometrica*, **29**, 659–69.

Leontief, W. (1961b), 'Lags and the stability of dynamic systems: a rejoinder', *Econometrica*, **29**, 674–5.

Leontief, W. (1970), 'The dynamic inverse', in A.P. Carter and A. Bródy (eds), *Contributions to Input–Output Analysis*, Amsterdam: North-Holland Publishing Company, 17–46. [Reprinted as Chapter 8 in Volume I.] Reprinted in Leontief, W. (1986), *Input–Output Economics*, New York: Oxford University Press, 2nd edition, 294–320.

Leontief, W. and Duchin, F. (1986), *The Future Impact of Automation on Workers*, New York and Oxford: Oxford University Press.

Livesey, D.A. (1973), 'A minimal realization of the Leontief dynamic input–output model', in K.R. Polenske and J.V. Skolka (eds), *Advances in Input–Output Analysis*, Cambridge: Ballinger, 527–41.

Livesey, D.A. (1976), 'The singularity problem in the dynamic input–output model', *International Journal of Systems Science*, **4**, 437–40.

Lovell, M.C. (1962), 'Buffer stocks, sales expectations, and stability: a multi-sector analysis of the inventory cycle', *Econometrica*, **30**, 267–96.

Luenberger, D.G. and Arbel, A. (1977), 'Singular dynamic Leontief systems', *Econometrica*, **45**, 991–5.

Mathur, P.N. (1964), 'Output and investment for exponential growth in consumption', *Review of Economic Studies*, **31**, 73–6.

Meyer, U. (1982), 'Why singularity of dynamic Leontief systems doesn't matter', in *Input–Output Techniques, Proceedings of the Third Hungarian Conference on Input–Output Techniques*, Budapest: Statistical Publishing House, 181–9. [Reprinted as Chapter 11 in Volume I.]

Meyer, U. (1990), 'Time profiles of adjustment processes in input output analysis', Paper presented at The Input–Output Workshop; Stuttgart, 1990.

Meyer, U. and Schumann, J. (1977), 'Das dynamische Input–Output-Modell als Modell gleich-gewichtigen Wachstums', *Zeitschrift für die gesamte Staatswissenschaft*, **133**, 1–37.

Mukerji, V. (1964), 'Output and investment for exponential growth in consumption – the general solution and some comments', *Review of Economic Studies*, **XXXI** (1), 77–82. [Reprinted as Chapter 13 in Volume I.]

Neumann, J.v. (1937), 'Über ein ökonomisches Gleichungssystem und eine Verallgemeinerung des Brouwerschen Fixpunktsatzes', *Ergebnisse eines mathematischen Kolloquiums*, **8**, 1935–36, Leipzig und Wien: Franz Deuticke.

Neumann, J.v. (1945), 'A model of general economic equilibrium', *Review of Economic Studies*, **13**, 1–9.

Petri, P.A. (1972), 'Convergence and temporal structure in the Leontief dynamic model', in A. Carter and A. Bródy (eds), *Input Output Techniques*, Amsterdam: North-Holland Publishing Company.

Raa, T. ten (1986a), 'Dynamic input–output analysis with distributed activities', *Review of Economics and Statistics*, **LXVIII** (2), 300–310. [Reprinted as Chapter 12 in Volume I.]

Raa, T. ten (1986b), 'Applied dynamic input–output analysis with distributed activities', *European Economic Review*, **30**, 805–31.

Sargan, J.D. (1958), 'The instability of the Leontief dynamic model', *Econometrica*, **26**, 381–92.

Sargan, J.D. (1961), 'Lags and the stability of dynamic systems: a reply', *Econometrica*, **29**, 670–73.

Schumann, J. (1968), *Input–Output-Analyse*, Berlin: Springer.

Solow, R. (1959), 'Competitive valuation in a dynamic input–output system', *Econometrica*, **27** (1). 30–53. [Reprinted as Chapter 14 in Volume III.]

Steenge, A.E. (1978), 'On two types of stability in the dynamic Leontief model', *Economics Letters*, **1**, 105–9.

Steenge, A .E. (1990), 'On the complete instability of empirically implemented dynamic Leontief models', *Economic Systems Research*, **2**, 3–16.

Stone, R. and Brown, J.A. (1962), 'Output and investment for exponential growth in consumption', *Review of Economic Studies*, **XXIX**, June, 241–5.

Szyld, D. (1985), 'Conditions for the existence of a balanced growth solution for the Leontief dynamic input–output model', *Econometrica*, **53**, 1411–19.

Tokoyama, K. and Murakami, Y. (1972), 'Relative stability in two types of dynamic Leontief models', *International Economic Review*, **13** (2), 408–15. [Reprinted as Chapter 10 in Volume I.]

Uzawa, M. (1956), 'Note on Leontief's dynamic input–output system', *Proceedings of the Japan Academy*, **32**, 79–82.

Wurtele, Z. (1959), 'A note on some stability properties in Leontief's dynamic models', *Econometrica*, **27**, 672–5.

Introduction to Part III: Multiplier Analysis, Extended IO-Models and Demographic Accounting

In the standard open Leontief model consumption is treated as exogenous so that the usual Leontief matrix multiplier lacks the effects generated by income on consumption expenditure. *Extended IO-models* combine the Leontief propagation process and functional relationships between production, income and consumption. There are three historical roots to be considered: following the classical theory of 'subsistence consumption' and the concept of 'natural price of labour', the first attempt of such extensions is to treat the household sector as an industry whose output is labour and whose inputs are consumer goods. This approach is implicit in von Neumann (1937, 1945; Chapter 5, this volume), and explicit in Leontief (1937) and Goodwin (1949; Chapter 20). Using the neoclassical conceptions of preference and utility, Duesenbery and Kistin (1953) discussed the relation between consumers' demand and relative prices, real income and other explanatory variables within a multisectoral framework. The introduction of Keynes/Kalecki type of consumption functions disaggregated by commodities as well as by types of households is due to Miyazawa and Masegi (1963; Chapter 21), Miyazawa (1976), Schumann (1968) and Stäglin (1976).

Extended IO-models and disaggregated multiplier analysis call for a disaggregated and consistent database usually referred to as *social accounting matrix* (SAM). The earliest example of a SAM is provided by Quesnay's *Tableau Economique*. The modern conception of social accounting goes back to conceptual and methodological work on national accounting by Richard Stone (1961, 1978) which finally leads to the guidelines provided by the United Nations Statistical Office (1968). While IO places emphasis on interindustry transactions by disaggregating the national production account into accounts for different industries and commodities, a SAM also aims at the description of interactions among those institutional sectors which collect, spend and save income. Thus a SAM is an extension of an IO-table. Pyatt (1991) provides a detailed account of the principles and notions of social accounting. The concepts of 'institutions', 'assets' and 'transactions' are discussed. Starting with fundamental transaction identities Pyatt develops a comprehensive accounting framework which covers institutions, production activities, real and financial assets and their appreciation.

Given a SAM it is straightforward to generalize the multisectoral multiplier provided by the Leontief inverse and to establish an extended version of the static IO-model which endogenizes income generation and consumption expenditure of groups of households. These *Miyazawa multipliers* do not only take into account the transfers of goods between activities of the standard Leontief model but also consider the interactions within and between industries and households. Thus the effects of changes in the volume or the structure of final demands as well as the effect on output and employment due to an exogenous change in the distribution of income can be estimated. Depending on the scope of analysis households may he grouped according to various characteristics. SAMs constructed for less developed countries[1] usually distinguish groups of rural and urban households. Studies evaluating alternative strategies of distribution of income disaggregate the household sector by income classes. Rose and Beaumont (1988) calculated Miyazawa multipliers for the West Virginia economy using an income disaggregated consumption matrix. Lager (1988; Chapter 24) and Cloutier and Thomassin (1994) used a matrix of income share coefficients to relate income by source to household income. In a pioneering exercise Miernyk *et al.* (1967) and Tiebout (1969) distinguished households by previous residence. Extensive income and (proportional) consumption is associated with an increase of the labour force due to immigration. Intensive income and (marginal) consumption arise from an increase in per capita income of existing workers. Trigg and Madden (1994) distinguished between income and consumption of employed and unemployed workers. A first step towards the extension of input–output analysis to the area of public choice was made by Rose, Stevens and Davis (1989). Results obtained from a multisectoral model of income formation and distribution are transformed into operational measure of distributional impacts. The methodology is illustrated in the context of a policy to increase coal surface mining on public lands.

As a major methodological innovation in relation to SAMs and extended IO-models, *multiplier decomposition analysis* is used to achieve a better insight into the complex interdependencies between and within industries and households. One type of decomposition, proposed by Miyazawa (1976), is based on block inversion and gives multipliers which relate changes in the volume and the structure of exogenous demand or income to changes in sectoral production and distribution of income. Studies by Henry and Martin (1984) and Lager (1988) found that a redistribution of income towards lower income groups results in an overall higher level of production and income (due to a decline of aggregate savings and imports). Another type of decomposition, proposed by Pyatt, Roe *et al.* (1977) and used by Pyatt and Round (1979; Chapter 22) and Stone (1978, 1984), separated intra-, inter- and extra-group effects. While the first of these effects captures interindustry relations or transfers within groups of households, the latter effects refer to the interrelations between producers and households. Further developments in decomposition analysis are discussed in greater detail in Part I (Structural Analysis) of Volume III.

Multipliers which are derived directly from a SAM of a certain period are based on average expenditure propensities of the respective year. Since effects of additional injections are of interest, these *accounting multipliers* are of limited analytical value. Thus Pyatt and Round (1979) advocated multipliers based on marginal rather than average expenditure propensities. By complementing the initial SAM with estimates of income elasticities, *fixed price multipliers* can be derived which are, of course, in general lower than the corresponding accounting multipliers. Fixed price multipliers measure demand driven effects of exogenous injections in the absence of any capacity constraints and thus represent a multisectoral and multi-institutional disaggregation of the aggregate Keynesian multiplier.

A different perspective on the effects of exogenous shocks is provided by *flexible price multipliers* given by the Jacobian matrix of a computable general equilibrium model (CGE).

Comparing the input–output approach with CGE models Rose (1995) identifies conceptual differences as well as similarities. Robinson and Roland-Hoist (1988; Chapter 23) compared multipliers calculated directly from a SAM with 'marginal' multipliers derived from a CGE model using the Jacobian matrix of partial derivatives at a given equilibrium. CGE based multipliers are significantly smaller than accounting multipliers. In contrast to SAM based multipliers, the diagonal elements of the Jacobian multiplier matrix are less than unity and most of the off diagonal elements are negative. The Keynesian model behind the SAM multipliers assumes that supply immediately adapts to demand. Consequently, the beneficial process of propagation of initial injections results in more or less incremental gains for all sectors. The neoclassical CGE model starts from given initial capacities. Exogenous injections lead to bottlenecks reflected by rising prices. Therefore a rise in exogenous demand is accompanied by a decline in price elastic endogenous demands. Taking final demands as exogenous and applying CES production functions with a given capital stock, Tokutsu (1994) obtained similar results. Sancho (1992) was concerned with price effects due to an exogenous change in sectoral wages. Calculations carried out with fixed coefficients, Cobb Douglas and CES value added functions demonstrated that price effects vary inversely with the elasticity of substitution between labour and capital. An intermediate step towards general equilibrium models (not necessarily in the neoclassical sense) is taken by making demand for consumer goods depend on prices. Lager (1988) applied a stepwise Linear Expenditure System (LES). Marginal propensities to consume depend on purchaser prices whereas the latter depend on producer prices, tax rates and transport margins. An Almost Ideal Demand System (AIDS) was estimated by Trigg and Madden (1994) and the corresponding Jacobian multipliers were compared to SAM based fixed price multipliers. Assuming different consumption patterns and saving propensities for workers and capitalists, Kurz (1985; Chapter 26) argued that there is no such thing as 'the multiplier'. He showed that the multiplier effects depend on technical conditions of production, consumption and saving patterns but also on prices which themselves depend on the distribution of income between workers and capitalists.

The application of accounting matrices is not confined to economics. Stone (1966; Chapter 27) developed a System of Demographic Accounts (SDA) which assigns individuals to stages as age or education, occupation and retirement. Given a SDA, a matrix of transition probabilities indicating the probability of annual transition from one state to another can be calculated. Stone (1984) showed some IO applications for demographic analyses. The lower triangular Leontief inverse of this transition matrix measures the probability of reaching a state (for example, university degree) indicated by the row starting from a state (for example, primary school) indicated by the column. Given the educational cost of each state, a dual 'price' model can be used to calculate total costs of completing the education of an individual in a certain state.

A comprehensive survey of research on extended input–output models, emphasizing recent developments in demographic-economic and socio-economic analysis is presented in Batey and Rose (1990; Chapter 25). With reference to a representative selection of extended models the basic principles of model design and construction are reviewed. As examples for the direction of current work two topics – labour market analysis and income distribution – are discussed in greater detail.

A completely different type of extension on the traditional input–output analysis is based on the 'supply-driven input–output model proposed by Ghosh (1958; Chapter 28). Its major distinguishing features are (i) constant allocation of outputs over sectors based on fixed output (or allocation) coefficients, (ii) the calculation of impacts of the sectoral outputs generated by exogenous changes in primary factors and (iii) perfectly elastic final demand (see Rose and Miernyk, 1989, p. 240). Ghosh suggested that his model would be appropriate in cases where different sectors are under monopoly control and all except one factor is scarce. A centrally planned economy or an economy operating by decree, as in national emergency, might fit that picture.

The Ghosh model has been criticized on several occasions by Giarratani (1980) and Chen and Rose (1991). Oosterhaven (1988) even termed the 'supply-driven' model implausible. His critique can be summarized as follows. An increase of, for example, labour in only one sector, induces all sectoral outputs to increase. Hence, in all but one sector the output rises without using extra labour. Recently, Dietzenbacher (1997) addressed this implausibility and interpreted the 'supply-driven' input–output model as a price model which could be used to describe the effects of an exogenously specified cost-push. Its results will be the same as those obtained from the Leontief price model. The differences between these two models are the endogenous results. Given sectoral value added, the Ghosh model computes output values whereas the Leontief model calculates price indices.

Empirical investigations (see for example Augustinovics, 1970 or Giarratani, 1980) found that input and output coefficients have a comparable degree of stability over time.

Note

1. For an overview and comparison of SAMs for some LDCs see Pyatt and Round (1985).

References

Augustinovics, M. (1970), 'Methods of international and intertemporal comparison of structure', in A.P. Carter and A. Bródy (eds), *Contributions to Input Output Analysis*, Amsterdam: North-Holland Publishing Company, 249–69.

Batey W.J. and Rose, A.Z. (1990), 'Extended input–output models: progress and potential', *International Regional Science Review*, **13** (1–2), 274–9. [Reprinted as Chapter 25 in Volume I.]

Chen, C.Y. and Rose, A.Z. (1991), 'The absolute and relative joint stability of input–output production and allocation coefficients', in W. Peterson (ed.), *Advances in Input–Output Analysis*, New York: Oxford University Press, 25–36.

Cloutier, L.M. and Thomassin, P.J. (1994), 'Closing the Canadian input–output model: homogeneous vs. non-homogenous household sector specifications', *Economic Systems Research*, **6**, 397–414.

Cronin, F.J. (1984), 'Analytical assumptions and causal ordering in interindustry modeling', *Southern Economic Journal*, **50**, 521–9.

Dietzenbacher, E. (1997), 'In vindication of the Ghosh model: a reinterpretation as a price model', *Journal of Regional Science*, **37**, 629–51.

Duesenberry, J.S. and Kistin, H. (1953), 'The role of demand in the economic structure', in W. Leontief *et al.* (eds), *Studies in the Structure of the American Economy*, Chapter 12, New York: Oxford University Press, 451–85.

Ghosh, A. (1958), 'Input–output approach in an allocation system', *Economica*, **XXV** (97) 58–64. [Reprinted as Chapter 28 in Volume I.]

Giarratani, F. (1980), 'The scientific basis for explanation in regional analysis', *Papers, Regional Science Association*, **45**, 185–96.

Goodwin, R.M. (1949), 'The multiplier as matrix', *Economic Journal*, **LIX** (236) 537–55. [Reprinted as Chapter 20 in Volume I.] Reprinted in: Goodwin, R.M. (1983), *Essays in Linear Economic Structures*, London: Macmillan, 1–21.

Henry, M. and Martin, T. (1984), 'Estimating income distribution effects on regional input–output multipliers', *Regional Science Perspectives*, **12**, 334–5.

Kurz, H.D. (1985), 'Effective demand in a "classical" model of value and distribution: the multiplier in a Sraffian framework', *Manchester School of Economics and Social Studies*, June, **LIII** (2), 121–37. [Reprinted as Chapter 26 in Volume I.]

Lager, C. (1988), 'The use of a social accounting matrix for comparative static equilibrium modelling', in M. Chiascini (ed.), *Input–Output Analysis: Current Developments*, London and New York: Chapman and Hall, 75–89. [Reprinted as Chapter 24 in Volume I.]

Leontief, W. (1937), 'Interrelations of prices, output, savings, and investment', *Review of Economic[s and] Statistics*, **19**, 109–32.

Miernyk, W.H. *et al.* (1967), *Impact of the Space Program on a Local Economy: An Input–Output Analysis*, Morgantown, WV: West Virginia University Library.

Miyazawa, K. (1976), *Input–Output Analysis and the Structure of Income Distribution*, Lecture Notes in Economics and Mathematical Systems, Mathematical Economics, 116, Berlin: Springer.

Miyazawa, K. and Masegi, S. (1963), 'Interindustry analysis and the structure of income-distribution', *Metroeconomica*, **XV** (2–3), 89–103. [Reprinted as Chapter 21 in Volume I.]

Neumann, J.v. (1937), 'Über ein ökonomisches Gleichungssystem und eine Verallgemeinerung des Brouwerschen Fixpunktsatzes', *Ergebnisse eines mathematischen Kolloquiums*, **8**, 73–83.

Neumann, J.v. (1945), 'A model of general economic equilibrium', *Review of Economic Studies*, **13**, 1–9.

Oosterhaven, J. (1988), 'On the plausibility of the supply-driven input–output model', *Journal of Regional Science*, **28**, 203–17.

Pyatt, G. (1991), 'Fundamentals of social accounting', *Economic Systems Research*, **3**, 315–41.

Pyatt, G. and Roe, A.R. *et al.* (1977), *Social Accounting for Development Planning: With Special Reference to Sri Lanka*, Cambridge: Cambridge University Press.

Pyatt, G. and Round, J. (1979), 'Accounting and fixed price multipliers in a social accounting matrix framework', *The Economic Journal*, **89** (356), 850–73. [Reprinted as Chapter 22 in Volume I.]

Pyatt, G. and Round, J. (1985), 'Social accounting matrices for development planning', in G. Pyatt and J. Round (eds), *Social Accounting Matrices: A Basis for Planning*, Washington, D.C.: The World Bank, 186–206.

Robinson, S. and Roland-Holst, D.W. (1988), 'Macroeconomic structure and computable equilibrium models', *Journal of Policy Modeling*, **10** (3), 353–75. [Reprinted as Chapter 23 in Volume III.]

Rose, A. (1995), 'Input–output economics and computable general equilibrium models', *Structural Change and Economic Dynamics*, **6**, 295–304.

Rose, A. and Beaumont, P. (1988), 'Interrelational income-distribution multipliers for the West Virginia economy', *Journal of Regional Science*, **28**, 461–75.

Rose, A. and Miernyk, W. (1989), 'Input–output analysis: the first fifty years', *Economic Systems Research*, **1**, 229–71.

Rose, A., Stevens, B. and Davis, G. (1989), 'Assessing who gains and who loses from natural resource policy: distributional information and the public participation process', *Resources Policy*, **6**, 282–91.

Sancho, F. (1992), 'Multiplier Analysis with flexible Cost Functions', *Economic Systems Research*, **4**, 311–23.

Schumann, J. (1968), *Input–Output-Analyse*, Berlin: Springer.

Stäglin, R. (1976), Multiplikatorwirkungen des Konjunkturprogramms von 1975: Anwendung des um den Keynes'schen Multiplikator erweiterten Input–Output-Modells. Beiträge zur Strukturforschung, **45**, Berlin: Duncker & Humblot.

Stone, R. (1961), *Input–Output and National Accounts*, OECD.

Stone, R. (1966), 'Input–output and demographic accounting', *Minerva*, **IV** (3), 365–80. [Reprinted as Chapter 7 in Volume I.]

Stone, R. (1978), 'The Disaggregation of the Household Sector in the National Accounts', Paper presented at the World Bank SAM Conference, Cambridge, England, 16–21 April, 1978.

Stone, R. (1984), 'Accounting Matrices in Economics and Demography', in F. van der Ploeg, *Mathematical Models in Economics*, Chichester: John Wiley and Sons, Ltd. 10–36.

Tiebout, C.M. (1969), 'An Empirical Regional Input–Output Projection Model: The State of Washington 1980', *Review of Economics and Statistics*, **51**, 334–40.

Tokutsu, I. (1994), 'Price-endogenized Input–Output Model: A General Equilibrium Analysis of the Production Sector of the Japanese Economy', *Economic Systems Research*, **6**, 323 46.

Trigg, A.B. and Madden, M. (1994), 'Using a Demand System to Estimate Extended Input–Output Multipliers', *Economic Systems Research*, **6**, 385–96.

United Nations Statistical Office (1968), *A System of National Accounts*, United Nations, New York.

Part I
Foundations of Input–Output Analysis

[1]

THE THEORY OF VALUE OF DAVID RICARDO

An attempt at a rigorous analysis

I. INTRODUCTION: THE THEORY OF 'PRODUCTION COSTS' BEFORE RICARDO

The simplest formula expressing the relationship between price and production cost is

$$\text{Price} \geqslant \text{production costs.} \qquad (1)$$

This formula is not a result of a scientific analysis of the phenomena of economic life, but a simple statement of the self-evident fact that production cannot continue (at least for any appreciable length of time) if the price of the product does not cover the costs incurred.

It is strange, therefore, to ascribe the discovery of this truth to any given economist.[1] What had to be done to pass from this *fact* to a complete *theory of production costs* in economics was, first, to state the laws defining the magnitude of that surplus which is incorporated in a price over and above the costs incurred; second, to analyse actual costs incurred in production by the entrepreneur. The first problem was not satisfactorily solved even by Smith: he, of course, defines profit in terms of the relationship between demand and supply of capital, i.e. by a feature dependent on market conditions. Very little had been done before Smith also for the analysis of real production costs in the narrow sense, *not including profit*.

Note that we completely disregard, as having nothing in common with science, all the *unsubstantiated* assertions concerning laws of value proclaimed by various 'thinkers' without any more foundation than the 'authority' of their propounders. They include, for example, the 'theory' which states that value is determined by the amount of labour expended on the production of the product (Franklin and Petty)[2] or by the amount of labour and land (Cantillon, Locke and others).[3]

---

[1] See for instance P. Bois-Guillebert, *Les détails de la France*, Paris, 1843; K. Marx, *Zur Kritik der politischen Oekonomie*, Berlin, 1859, p. 32, and N. Sieber, *D. Ricardo i K. Marx v' ikh ekonomicheskikh issledovaniakh* [D. Ricardo and K. Marx in their economic research], Moscow, 1885.

[2] See *The Works of Benjamin Franklin*, edited by J. Sparks, 1856 ['Trade in general being nothing else but the exchange of labor for labor, the value of all things is . . most justly measured by labor'], Vol. 2, p. 267. Petty, however, attempts to make his assertion less arbitrary by stipulating *caeteris paribus*: 'If a man can bring to *London* an ounce of Silver out of the Earth in *Peru* in the same time that he can produce a bushel of Corn, then one is the natural price of the other; now if by reason of new and more easie Mines a man can get two ounces of Silver as easily as formerly he did one, then Corn will be as cheap at ten shillings the bushel, as it was before at five shillings *caeteris paribus*'; W. Petty, *A treatise of taxes and contributions*, London, 1662, Ch. 5, pp. 50–1 of the 1899 edition. The approach is undoubtedly scientific, but even so it limits the very meaning and sphere of application of the law as stated.

[3] R. Cantillon, *Essai sur la nature du commerce en général*, London, 1755; edited with an English translation by H. Higgs, London, 1931; Locke, *Works*, London, 1823, Vol. 5, *Of civil government*, para. 40.

The theory of value of David Ricardo

We find the most detailed analysis of production costs in the works of Smith's immediate forerunner, Steuart. According to Steuart's theory (*Principles of Political Economy*, 1767, Book 2) the actual value of a thing is made up of the following elements: 'The value of the workman's subsistence and necessary expense both for supplying his personal wants and providing the instruments belonging to his profession' and 'the value of the materials, that is the first matter employed by the workman'.

According to Steuart, these three elements combined define the lower limit, below which the market price of the product cannot fall. What we see here is essentially a simple, detailed list of the expenditure which the capitalist producer incurs (as before, profit is related to market conditions, i.e. to the supply and demand of the given commodity); no traces of *scientific* analysis are, as yet, to be noted in this 'theory' of production costs. The only exception is the subsistence wage theory. Even before Adam Smith's work appeared, the theory had become established in economic science that wages tended toward the means of subsistence. It is even possible to find a fairly detailed development of the concept of the 'means of subsistence' (Cantillon, Petty and Turgot).[1]

However, it was only in Adam Smith's work that an explanation was given of the mechanism of the process by which wages are constantly maintained at the level of the means of subsistence. To sum up what has been said, we may express the state of the theory concerning the relationship between value and production costs at a time immediately preceding the appearance of Adam Smith's work by the following formula:

Price = outlay on wages (= the number of working days × the daily subsistence of the worker *in terms of the product* × *the price of the produce consumed by the workers*)

    + outlay in the replacement of tools and materials (= the quantity of tools and materials consumed in production × *the price of the tools and materials*)

    + *the total of profit*

    + *rent* (= the sum paid for 'the assistance of natural forces').   (2)

The quantities set in italics are the unknowns.

Naturally, at this stage of development the theory of production costs

---

[1] See Cantillon, 1755, who is quoted by Smith himself.

W. Petty defines the value of the average daily pay by what the worker needs to live, work and reproduce himself (*The Political Anatomy of Ireland*, London, 1691, p. 64, p. 181 of 1899 edition). Turgot states 'Workers are continuously obliged to lower the price one against the other. For all kinds of labour it must happen and does in fact happen that the worker's wage is limited to what is necessary for his subsistence' (A. R. J. Turgot, *Réflexions sur la formation et la distribution des richesses*, 1770, § vi, p. 10 of the 1844 edition).

1. The theory of 'production costs' before Ricardo

fully merits the reproach so often levelled at the theory of production costs *in general* (consequently also in its fully developed form), that it defines price from prices, that it defines one unknown from other unknowns.[1] The problem facing Adam Smith was not an easy one, and it is therefore not surprising that his solution of it was far from complete. It was only in the writings of his successor, Ricardo, that the theory of production costs was completed. Nevertheless, Smith did contribute a very great deal to the correct solution of the problem. Above all, we find in Adam Smith a correct formulation of the problem to be solved which is undoubtedly very important for its correct solution.

Smith states that 'the relative or exchangeable value of goods' is determined by 'rules which men naturally observe in exchanging them either for money or for one another'.[2] This first eliminated any question of the *intrinsic* value of commodities: the object of research should be merely the *relative* value of commodities, their ratio of exchange (the term is borrowed from Jevons[3]) to avoid confusion arising from the use of the word value in two senses: exchange value and use value; use of the term 'ratio of exchange' eliminates the need for any qualification concerning the different meanings of the word 'value', such as is made by Smith[4] and Ricardo.

Smith then proceeds to an analysis of the concept of production costs or, to be more precise, to an analysis of those elements from which they are made up for the capitalist entrepreneur. In his theory of wages Adam Smith merely develops and provides greater basis for the hypothesis

---

[1] E.g. Sieber, 1885, p. 109. Sieber quotes the words of Kamorzhinsky: 'It may be objected against theories of production costs that they explain the price of a good not from such elements as would be independent of price, but from other prices, because production costs are calculated from the price of all the goods needed for production'. Sieber adds to this: 'The formulation of the question of production costs given by us is a clear expression of the discontent which arises in the minds of some, unfortunately very few of the newest economists when discussing terms which *only seemingly* contain a known and definite meaning. . . .'

[2] A. Smith, *An enquiry into the nature and causes of the wealth of nations* (1776), Book I, Ch. 4, p. 42, of the 1814 edition.

[3] Jevons uses the term 'the ratio of exchange'; Zalessky translates this in his thesis, quite unsuccessfully in our opinion, by the words *otnoshenie obmena* [exchange relation]. See Zalessky *Uchenie o tsennosti* [Theory of value], Kazan, 1893, Book II, p. 122.

[4] 'The word *value*', states Smith, 'has two different meanings and sometimes expresses the utility of some particular object, and sometimes the power of purchasing other goods which the possession of that object conveys. The one may be called "value in use"; the other, "value in exchange"' (Book I, Ch. 4, p. 42 of the 1814 edition). Although Adam Smith explained the concept of exchange value excellently he did not venture to give an equally precise definition of 'use value' or 'usefulness'. The first completely correct definition of the concept of 'usefulness' is found in F. Galiani, an Italian economist of the last century: 'I call utility the attitude of an object to procure us happiness', *Della moneta* (1750), Ch. 2, p. 59.

The theory of value of David Ricardo

already stated by preceding economists that real wages have a tendency to coincide with the essential means of subsistence of the worker.[1]

The main changes made by Smith to the formula of production costs relate to the second and third terms of the second part of equation (2). Smith was the first to point out that the second term, the value of the tools and materials used in production, could invariably be broken down, in its turn, into *wages, profit* and *rent* (by 'profit' and 'rent' we shall invariably understand *the sum of profit* and the *sum of rent* in money) so that all production costs may be reduced to the three elements: wages, profit and rent. These three parts, states Smith,

> 'seem either immediately or ultimately to make up the whole price of corn. A fourth part, it may perhaps be thought, is necessary for replacing the stock of the farmer, or for compensating the wear and tear of his labouring cattle, and other instruments of husbandry. But it must be considered that the price of any instrument of husbandry, such as a labouring horse, is itself made up of the same three parts; the rent of the land upon which he is reared, the labour of tending and rearing him, and the profits of the farmer who advances both the rent of this land, and the wages of this labour. Though the price of the corn, therefore, may pay the price as well as the maintenance of the horse, the whole price still resolves itself either immediately or ultimately into the same three parts of rent, labour and profit.'

This hypothesis is subsequently extended by Smith to all other products (Smith, Book I, Ch. 6, p. 81 of 1814 Edition).

Smith himself notes instances when one (and sometimes even two) of these three basic elements of price are absent, so that the price of the product is reduced in the last analysis to only two elements, *wages and profits* (*Ibid.*).

In view of the inconsistency of Smith's views on rent, we shall subsequently consider only the latter case. Since, as is explained by Ricardo, the cause for the appearance of rent is that different portions of the same commodity sold in the same market (and consequently commanding the same price) are produced with different costs, in order to exclude rent from price, we have to make the *conventional* assumption that all units of a given commodity are produced with equal costs (and as a corollary of this, that all portions of the capital employed in the given production are *equally productive*). Formula (2) then becomes:

$$X_A = (n_A a X_a + n_1 a X_a + n_2 a X_a + \cdots + n_m a X_a) + (y_A + y_1 + y_2 + \cdots + y_m) \quad (3)$$

[1] Smith himself cites Cantillon on this question (Smith, Book I, Ch. 8, p. 110 of 1814 edition); the theory of the 'iron' law of wages reached its final development, of course, in the writings of David Ricardo, and we shall therefore defer closer examination of this question until we analyse Ricardo's theory of value.

1. The theory of 'production costs' before Ricardo

where X_A is the price of product A; n_A, n_1, n_2, ..., n_m are the number of working days expended in production; a is the amount of a product, e.g. corn, consumed by a worker in a day (in order to simplify the formula we assume that a worker consumes one product, e.g. corn, which is of course a simplification that Ricardo also makes in his analysis; we shall see subsequently that nothing is altered in our analysis if we accept that the workers consume several products); X_a is the price of product a; y_A, y_1, y_2, ..., y_m are the profits incorporated in the price of product A; these include both the profit obtained by the producer of product A himself, and the profit of the producers of the tools and materials consumed in the production of product A. Or if

$$\begin{cases} n_A + n_1 + n_2 + \cdots + n_m = N_A \\ y_A + y_1 + y_2 + \cdots + y_m = Y_A \end{cases} \tag{4}$$

then we obtain

$$X_A = N_A a x_a + Y_A, \tag{5}$$

where N_A is the total sum of the labour directly or *indirectly* expended in the production of product A, and Y_A is the total sum of the profit received by all the producers involved directly or *indirectly* (i.e. by the production of materials and tools) in the production of commodity A.

Therefore, the total price of product A is, in the absence of rent, made up of only two elements: wages and profit. Smith repeatedly objected to this hypothesis;[1] these objections have once again been advanced comparatively recently, as an argument against the labour theory of value, by economists of the 'Austrian school', supporters of the theory of marginal utility.

What these objections amount to is that because capital is essential in all branches of production in the *modern* economy, it is impossible to eliminate the element of capital when calculating production costs. For the production of capital it is once again capital which is invariably needed. It is asked how it is possible to calculate the amount of labour expended for the production of a given economic good from the very beginning of history, when man managed without capital, down to the present time. There is no doubt that at present capital is invariably produced by capital; it is also correct that it is an impossible task to calculate the amount of labour expended in a given product from the time of the creation of the first capital by labour alone. However, there is no need for such a calculation: the sum of the labour expended on the production of a given product may be determined without such historical digressions.

[1] See K. Marx, *Capital*, Vol. i (1867), Part 3.

The theory of value of David Ricardo

Let us denote by N the total amount of labour directly and indirectly expended on the production of a unit of commodity A; let the amount of labour directly consumed in production be n_A; let several kinds of 'technical capital' $K_1, K_2, \ldots, K_m$ be involved in production; let there be consumed in production $1/m_1$ of the capital K_1, $1/m_2$ of the capital $K_2, \ldots, 1/m_M$ of the capital K_M; further, let the amount of labour directly and indirectly expended on the production of the capital K_1 be N_1, that expended on production of the capital K_2 be $N_2, \ldots$, that expended on production of the capital K_M be N_M, in which case the total sum of the labour expended on the production of a unit of commodity A will be:

$$N_A = n_A + \frac{1}{m_1} N_1 + \frac{1}{m_2} N_2 + \cdots + \frac{1}{m_M} N_M. \tag{6}$$

Since n_A and $m_1, m_2, \ldots, m_M$ are here quantities given by the technical conditions of production of the product A, $N_A, N_1, N_2, \ldots, N_M$ are unknowns.

Other capital goods, some of which are included in this series and others not, are involved in their turn in the production of capital goods $K_1, K_2, \ldots, K_M$, to which the quantities of labour $N_1, N_2, \ldots, N_M$ of this equation correspond. Let the number of all the *different* capital goods involved both directly and indirectly in the production of the product A be M (the number is always finite).[1]

For the amount of labour needed for the production of any capital K_1 out of the M capital goods it is obviously possible to compile an equation completely similar to equation (6); quantities N corresponding to the capital goods involved in the production of the capital K_I will be incorporated in the second part of such an equation, and since M is a finite number, we shall obtain M equations with M unknowns ($N_1, N_2, N_3, \ldots, N_M$); adding in equation (6), we obtain a system of $(M+1)$ equations with $(M+1)$ unknowns (N_A, N_1, N_2, N_M) which is always adequate for the determination of N, giving the required sum of labour expended on the production of the product A. Therefore, without any digressions into the prehistoric times of the first inception of technical capital, we can always find the total sum of the labour directly and indirectly expended on the production of any product *under present-day production conditions*, both of this product itself and of those capital goods involved in its production. As we have seen, the fact that all capital under *present-day* conditions is itself produced with the assistance of other capital in no way hinders a precise solution of the problem.

It should not, however, be thought that the whole system of our $(M+1)$ equations is indispensable for the determination of the total

---

[1] This is because, despite the diversity and complexity of present-day technology, even the number of *all possible* qualitatively different capital goods is always a finite quantity.

1. The theory of 'production costs' before Ricardo

labour expended on the production of any product I; all the unknowns incorporated in the expression of this sum may frequently be excluded from the smallest number of equations. For example, let the capital good K_1 be involved in production of the product; the capital goods K_2 and K_3 in production of capital good K_1; K_1 and K_3 in production of K_2; K_1 and K_2 in production of K_3 and so on; in that case, using the same notations as before, we shall have a system of four equations with four unknowns, from which N_I is determined by successive substitution:*

$$\left.\begin{aligned}
N_I &= n_I + \frac{1}{m_1} \cdot N_1 \\[2mm]
N_1 &= n_1 + \frac{1}{m_2} \cdot N_2 + \frac{1}{m_3} N_3. \\[2mm]
N_2 &= n_2 + \frac{1}{m_4} \cdot N_1 + \frac{1}{m_5} N_3 \\[2mm]
N_3 &= n_3 + \frac{1}{m_6} \cdot N_1 + \frac{1}{m_7} N_2
\end{aligned}\right\} \tag{7}$$

It is, of course, possible to imagine even simpler cases.[1]

Thus the production costs formula may always be reduced to the expression:

$$X_A = N_A a X_a + Y_A. \tag{8}$$

---

* *Ed. note.* The system of equations given by Dmitriev does not lend itself to solution by substitution: commodities 1 and 3 require commodity 2 and vice versa; commodity 1 requires commodity 3 and vice versa, i.e. there are feedbacks in the determination of the price system by substitution. However, Dmitriev is right in thinking that the solution of the system is simplified by the existence of a number of zero-technical coefficients (for instance, when the input–output matrix is triangular, or quasi-triangular) and that it can sometimes be solved by substitution, although in the following footnote he rejects the idea of progressive 'layers' of production.

[1] We are absolutely unable to agree with the opinion of Tugan-Baranovsky who, while quite correctly opposing von Wieser's objection to the labour theory of value, states that 'In passing from one branch of industry to another manufacturing goods of increasingly higher orders relative to our product . . . we ultimately arrive at branches of industry which manufacture their own constant capital (in the terminology of Marx)' (*Yuridicheskii Vestnik*, October 1890, p. 223). Such a completely arbitrary assumption deprives the solution of the problem of the generality which is required. Nor can we accept, either in form or in content, the 'mathematical' solution of the problem which he proposes at the end of the paper; the conclusion at which he arrives may be obtained only thanks to the completely arbitrary and unreal assumption that the denominator of an infinite descending progression remains continuously the same. Furthermore, it is impossible to equate incommensurate quantities.

The theory of value of David Ricardo

If we take the appropriate formula for any product, $B, C, \ldots$

$$\left.\begin{aligned} X_B &= N_B a X_a + Y_B \\ X_C &= N_C a X_a + Y_C \end{aligned}\right\} \tag{9}$$
$$\ldots$$

and if we bear in mind that the task of the theory of value is to determine the proportion in which products are exchanged, we shall have

$$\left.\begin{aligned} X_{AB} &= \frac{X_A}{X_B} = \frac{N_A a X_A + Y_A}{N_B a X_A + Y_B} \\[2mm] X_{AC} &= \frac{X_A}{X_C} = \frac{N_A a X_A + Y_A}{N_C a X_A + Y_C} \end{aligned}\right\} \tag{10}$$
$$\ldots$$

and so on, where X_{AB} will denote the value of product A in terms of B, i.e. the number of units of the product B given in the market for a unit of the product A.[1] For X_{AB} to be known, the quantities Y_A and Y_B must be given; Adam Smith's second important contribution to development of the theory of value was the analysis of these quantities. Smith first notes that the quantity Y is always related to the sum of the capital expended in production and to the time during which it is in circulation (in the production concerned). If, therefore, we denote the capital by Z and the time by T and assume that all the other quantities on which the amount of profit may depend are constant, we shall have:

$$Y = F(Z, T). \tag{11}$$

If we denote the sum of the profit attained in the given production A by a unit of capital (expressed in the same unit of value as the sum of the profit) in a time unit[2] by r_A (which we shall refer to as 'the rate of profit in the production of A'), the sum of the profits attained in the same production by Z units of capital in unit time will be Zr_A, if we take into consideration our assumption made above (with the methodological aim of excluding the phenomenon of rent from our analysis) that *all capital goods* expended in production *are equally productive*. Adding this profit in unit time to the initial capital Z, we obtain $Z + Zr_A = Z(1 + r_A)$; if this

---

[1] We adopt the condition $X_{AB} = X_A/X_B$ without special proof as being sufficiently evident; for a detailed proof see L. Walras, *Eléments d'économie politique pure*, Lausanne, 1874, Lesson 11, pp. 153–63 of the English translation of the 1926 edition, by W. Jaffé, *Elements of pure economics*, London, 1954. Walras shows by mathematical analysis that '*We do not have* perfect, *or general* market equilibrium unless the price of any two commodities in terms of the other is equal to the ratio of the prices of these two commodities in terms of any third commodity' (p. 157 of the English edition). See also Smith, *Wealth of nations*, Book I, Chs. 6 and 10.

[2] The 'period of the production concerned' may be taken as the unit in the interests of simplicity.

1. The theory of 'production costs' before Ricardo

sum is left in production, after a further unit of time (assuming that the conditions of production remain unaltered) we have: $Z(1+r_A)(1+r_A) = Z(1+r_A)^2$, and repeating T times, we shall have $Z(1+r_A)^T$, from which the sum of the profit from Z units of capital in T units of time will be:

$$Y_A = Z(1+r_A)^T - Z = Z[(1+r_A)^T - 1]. \tag{12}$$

(See Smith, Book I, Ch. 9, p. 160–1 of the 1814 edition.)

In setting this expression of profit as a function of the sum of capital and of time in our formulas of production costs, we obtain for the simplest case in which N_A working days are expended on the production of a unit of the product without the participation of technical capital:

$$Y_A = N_A a X_a [(1+r_A)^{T_A} - 1] \tag{13}$$

where T_A will denote the time having elapsed between expenditure of the capital $N_A a x_a$ (it is assumed in the interests of simplicity that the whole sum is expended simultaneously) and sale of the product.

In addition to the labour directly expended in the production of A, let there also be expended some capital K_1, and let this capital itself be produced by n_1 days of labour with the assistance of the capital K_2, and let us assume in the interest of simplicity that this capital K_2 is itself produced without the participation of new technical capital by n_2 days of labour (this methodological approach is, of course, regularly used by Ricardo in his researches on value with the object of simplifying formulas and thus making them more suitable for analysis). Let the capitals K_1 and K_2 involved in the productions A and K_1 be completely used up in production without residue (such an assumption will undoubtedly simplify the formulas more than the equally arbitrary assumption made by Ricardo that capital goods are perpetual).

Suppose the time expended in production of the capital K_2 be T_{K2}, in which case, assuming in the interests of simplicity that the whole sum expended on production of the capital K_2, which equals $n_2 a X_a$, is expended simultaneously, we shall have as an expression of the price of the capital K_2:

$$X_{K2} = n_2 a X_a (1+r_{K2})^{T_{K2}} \tag{14}$$

where r_{K2} is the 'rate of profit' in the production of K_2. Further, let the time expended on production of the capital K_1 be T_{K1}, in which case, deliberating in the same way as before (and making the same arbitrary assumptions), we shall have for X_{K1}:

$$X_{K1} = n_1 a X_a (1+r_{K1})^{T_{K1}} + n_2 a X_a (1+r_{K2})^{T_{K2}} (1+r_{K1})^{T_{K1}}. \tag{15}$$

47

The theory of value of David Ricardo

If, finally, the time expended on manufacture of the product A is equal to T_A, we shall have for X_A

$$X_A = n_A a X_a (1+r_A)^{T_A} + n_1 a X_a (1+r_{K1})^{T_{K1}} (1+r_A)^{T_A} +$$
$$+ n_2 a X_a (1+r_{K2})^{T_{K2}} (1+r_{K1})^{T_{K1}} (1+r_A)^{T_A}. \quad (16)$$

If we compare this expression of price with the former expression

$$X_A = N_A a X_a + (y_A + y_1 + y_2 + \cdots + y_m) \quad (17)$$

we see that instead of the unknowns $y_{A1}, y_1, \ldots$, which denoted the *sums* of the profits of the different entrepreneurs directly or indirectly involved in production of product A, we now have another series of unknowns r_A, $r_{K1}, r_{K2}, \ldots$ denoting the *rate of profit* in the different branches of industry involved in the production of A. Therefore, the number of unknowns still remains the same ($T_A, T_{K1}, T_{K2}, \ldots$ incorporated in the new expression of price are known quantities dependent on the technical conditions of production of $A, K_1, K_2 \ldots$ and so on). The importance of the transformations made by us to the production costs formula is revealed only in connection with another hypothesis of prime importance established by Adam Smith, namely the hypothesis that the 'rate of profit' tends to be equalised in all branches of industry. By virtue of this hypothesis we shall have $r_A = r_{K1} = r_{K2} \ldots = r$, where r is taken to mean the *general* level towards which the rate of profit of individual branches of industry tends.[1]

Adam Smith arrives at this hypothesis deductively from the basic premise that every man aspires to the greatest advantage (Smith, Book I, Ch. 10, p. 162 of 1814 edition). Smith reasons as follows: if profit in some branch of industry A is higher than in others, this will compel industrialists from other branches to convert to production of the product A; *as a consequence of this production will expand, the supply of the product A will increase* and the price of the product which is, *caeteris paribus*, inversely proportional to the supply, will fall. But since *production costs will remain the same*, the profit on capital, which is the difference between the price and the production costs, will fall; if, nevertheless, it were still to be above the general level, this would cause a new conversion of producers from other branches and a new reduction of the price until, finally, profit reached the general level; there could be no further reduction of profit, since this would destroy the motive (exceptional profit) for the conversion of producers from other branches.

At this point we shall not make a critical analysis of this theory, which is completely accepted by Ricardo: we shall demonstrate its incorrectness and arbitrary nature in the Second Essay when analysing the 'theory

---

[1] We naturally assume that $r, r_{K1}, r_{K2}, \ldots$ are all adjusted to a common unit of time and unit of value expended.

1. The theory of 'production costs' before Ricardo

of competition' (all that we have done here has been to indicate the arbitrary assumptions by setting them in italics). The whole of Smith's reasoning in this case is based on the arbitrary assumption that the amount of a given good may be increased without limit by the application of labour and capital and that its production is under the influence of free competition, and that therefore the law of the equality of the 'profit rate' in different branches of production applies only to goods which satisfy this *arbitrary* assumption.

If we make the corresponding transformations to the expressions X_A, X_B, ... we shall have

$$X_A = n_A a X_a (1+r)^{t_A} + n_1 a X_a (1+r)^{t_A + t_{A1}} + n_2 a X_a (1+r)^{t_A + t_{A1} + t_{A2}} + \cdots$$
(18)

for any product A, where the terms t_{A1}, t_{A2}, ... denote the periods of time expended on the production of capital goods of the first, second and higher orders involved in manufacture of product A, and

$$X_B = m_B a X_a (1+r)^{t_B} + m_1 a X_a (1+r)^{t_B + t_{B1}} + m_2 a X_a (1+r)^{t_B + t_{B1} + t_{B2}} + \cdots$$
(19)

for any product B [where m_B, m_1 and m_2 are labour outlays occurred respectively t_B, t_{B1}, t_{B2} time periods earlier].

We take the ratio of X_A to X_B and obtain:

$$X_{AB} = \frac{n_A a X_a (1+r)^{t_A} + n_1 a X_a (1+r)^{t_A + t_{A1}} + n_2 a X_a (1+r)^{t_A + t_{A1} + t_{A2}} + \cdots}{m_B a X_a (1+r)^{t_B} + m_1 a X_a (1+r)^{t_B + t_{B1}} + m_2 a X_a (1+r)^{t_B + t_{B1} + t_{B2}} + \cdots}.$$
(20)

If r is given, X_{AB} will also be a quite definite quantity and, consequently, the problem of the exchange proportion will be solved (since all the other exchange proportions may be similarly determined for a given product A: X_{AC}, X_{AD}, X_{AE} etc.).

However, Adam Smith did not proceed any further in his analysis of production costs. The honour for a complete solution of the problem belongs to his great successor Ricardo. Smith himself related the magnitude of r to the abundance of the supply of capital. He says: 'The increase of stock, which raises wages, tends to lower profit. When the stocks of many rich merchants are turned into the same trade, their mutual competition naturally tends to lower its profits; and when there is a like increase of stock in all the different trades carried on in the same society, the same competition must produce the same effect in them all' (Smith, Book I, Ch. 9, p. 143 of the 1814 edition).

If we denote the supply of capital by D, then $r = \phi(D)$ and $d\phi(D)/dD < 0$, i.e. as the supply of capital increases the profit rate declines. The actual form of the function ϕ is taken by Smith to be empirically given,

The theory of value of David Ricardo

despite the fact that the relationship between r and D undoubtedly already belongs to the sphere of *economic analysis* (as is shown by the writings of Ricardo); Smith does not give us any such analysis, although we find a completely accurate statement of the cause of the reduction in profit when capital goods increase *independent of competition* (see Smith, Book I, Ch. 9, p. 151 of the 1814 edition).

2. RICARDO'S THEORY OF VALUE

The most important point in Ricardo's theory is undoubtedly his theory of the conditions defining the 'average' profit rate to which, according to Smith's theory, profit tends in the individual branches of industry. As we have seen, this question was left unanswered in the writings of Smith, if we disregard his references to the relationship between the demand and supply of capital. We have to ask ourselves whether it was actually solved by Ricardo. Strange as it may seem, in view of the remarkable clarity of Ricardo's writings, negative answers to this question are still to be found in economic literature. It will suffice to mention the critical writings on the question of profit of E. Böhm-Bawerk (*Kapital und Kapitalzins*, Vol. 1, *Geschichte und Kritik der Kapitalzins Theorien*, pp. 101–11) and Zalessky (*Uchenie o proiskhozhdenii pribyli na kapital* [The theory of the origin of profit on capital], Kazan, 1898, Vol. II, p. 52); such views are particularly surprising when they are expressed by economists who have used the precise mathematical method for their analysis.[1]

Thus, in his most interesting analysis of Ricardo's theory of value[2] (which contains a model analysis of the theory of rent), Yu. Zhukovsky states, after having expounded Ricardo's theory of profit,

> 'But all this defines only the relative magnitude of the profit on capital or the order of its reduction. Ricardo however does not provide any answer to the question of how to determine the initial magnitude of the profit from which wages are subsequently deducted, the initial magnitude of the percentage on capital, and we would note that from this aspect the question still remains unanswered' (p. 345).
> '. . . Ricardo gave no answer at all on how to determine this absolute initial magnitude of the percentage *and whether this initial magnitude of the percentage,* from which wages have to be subtracted, *remains constant* when the product becomes dearer;. from this aspect this quantity remains completely undefined' (pp. 356–7).

[1] We should also include here in part the general criticisms which Thünen makes of the theory of production costs; see p. 58, footnote 2.

[2] Yu. Zhukovsky 'Istoriya politicheskikh uchenii XIX veka' [A history of nineteenth century political theories], Vol. I.

2. *Ricardo's theory of value*

'The only theory to which we may point as defining the initial level of the profit which may be taken by the capitalist *consists in the level or excess of capital goods*, and this level should be dependent *on the ratio between the supply and demand for capital* or *r/s*' (p. 357).

'Ricardo assumes that capital goods may flow freely like a fluid under the influence of gravity from one place and point to another and may tend toward equalisation of profits and to a general level of them, *the height of which is determined by nothing other than their greater or lesser excess*'. . . .

'If we denote the volume of the capital goods by (*a*), the space over which they are poured by (*b*), and the height by (*h*), we shall have the condition: $hb = a$; from which $h = a/b$' (p. 342).

We would be in complete agreement with all these remarks by Zhukovsky had they been made in relation to Smith's theory, but to assert that we find no other definition for the general level of profit in Ricardo's work than the formula $x = r/s$ is to fail to understand the very basis of Ricardo's theory.

Walras states the same criticism even more clearly.

'Let *P* be the aggregate price received for the products of an enterprise; let *S*, *I* and *F* be respectively the wages, interest charges and rent laid out by the entrepreneurs, in the course of production, to pay for the services of personal faculties, capital and land. Let us recall now that, according to the English School, the selling price of products is determined by their costs of production, that is to say, it is equal to the cost of the productive services employed. Thus we have the equation

$$P = S + I + F$$

and *P* is determined for us. It remains only to determine *S*, *I* and *F*. Surely, if it is not the price of the products that determines the price of productive services, but the price of productive services that determines the price of the products, [we must be told what determines the price of the services]. This is precisely what the English economists try to do. To this end, they construct a theory of rent according to which rent is not included in the expenses of production,

$$P = S + I.$$

Having done this, they determine *S* directly by the theory of wages. Then, finally, they tell us that "the amount of interest or profit is the excess of the aggregate price received for the products over the wages expended on their production", in other words, that it is determined by the equation

$$I = P - S.$$

It is clear now that the English economists are completely baffled by the problem of price determination; for it is impossible for *I* to deter-

51

The theory of value of David Ricardo

mine P at the same time that P determines I. In the language of mathematics one equation cannot be used to determine two unknowns. This objection is raised without any reference to our position on the manner in which the English School eliminates rent before setting out to determine wages' (Walras, *Elements*, 1874, Lesson 40, § 368, pp. 424–5 of the English edition).

The subsequent analysis will show us how justified these reproaches are.

The last formulas derived by us on p. 49, expressing the farthest point reached by Adam Smith in his analysis of the connection between the price of a product and its production costs relate, as we have noted, only to commodities: (1) whose quantity may be increased without limit by the application of labour and capital, (2) separate portions of which are produced with identical production costs (in order to exclude rent), (3) whose production and sale take place under the influence of 'unlimited competition'. These are precisely the forms that are also the starting point for Ricardo's analysis;

> 'In speaking, then, of commodities, of their exchangeable value, and of the laws which regulate their relative prices, we mean always such commodities only as can be increased in quantity by the exertion of human industry, and on the production of which competition operates without restraint.'[1]

Before turning to an examination of the conditions determining 'the general rate of profit' r, Ricardo pauses to analyse instances in which the sought-after quantities X_{AB}, X_{AC}, X_{AD} and so on (i.e. the value of any product A in terms of the value of the product B, C etc.) may be determined *independently* of the magnitude of r. Let the products A, B and so on be produced solely by 'current labour', without the use of capital goods (i.e. of tools and materials which are themselves a result of the expenditure of labour). Let N_A days of labour have been expended on the production of a unit of product A, N_B days of labour on the production of product B and so on; further, let the time needed for manufacture and delivery to the market be t_A for product A, t_B for the product B and so on (Ricardo invariably assumes that a product is sold immediately on delivery to the market). If in each period a worker consumes a units of corn (which Ricardo assumes is the only consumption of workers) and the price of corn is X_a, the price of N_A days of labour is $N_A a X_a$ and the price of N_B days of labour is $N_B a X_a$. If we now assume that the 'profit rate' in industries

[1] D. Ricardo: *On the principles of political economy and taxation*, London, 1817, Ch. I, 'On Value'; throughout this chapter Ricardo assumes that individual units of the same product are obtained at the same cost, *but he does not specifically state* this assumption; the conditions under which rent may arise are not introduced until the second chapter.

2. *Ricardo's theory of value*

A, B and so on is r, and assume for simplicity that the capital used to hire workers is all expended simultaneously at the beginning of production, we shall have the following expression for X_{AB}:

$$X_{AB} = \frac{N_A a X_a (1+r)^{t_A}}{N_B a X_a (1+r)^{t_B}} \qquad (21)$$

If $t_A = t_B$ in this expression, we shall have for X_{AB}, after the appropriate simplifications:

$$X_{AB} = \frac{X_A}{X_B} = \frac{N_A}{N_B} \qquad (22)$$

i.e. the relative value of products A and B equals the ratio of the amount of labour expended on the production of a unit of product A to the amount of labour expended on the production of a unit of product B; the cost of a unit of product A is related to the cost of a unit of product B as the amount of labour expended on the production of a unit of product A is related to the amount of labour expended on the production of a unit of product B.

Suppose the same number of workers are occupied from the beginning to the end in the production of A and in the production of B; this number will be N_A/t_A for A and N_B/t_B for B; let the payment to these workers be advanced not for the whole time until production of the product is completed, but only for a unit of time (e.g. for one day); in this case the expenditure at the beginning of each unit of time will be expressed by $N_A a X_a/t_A$ for product A and $N_B a X_a/t_B$ for product B; if the profit from a unit of capital over a unit of time remains equal to r, we shall have for X_{AB}:

$$X_{AB} = \frac{N_A a X_a (1+r)^{t_A}/t_A + N_A a X_a (1+r)^{t_A-1}/t_A + \cdots + N_A a X_a (1+r)/t_A}{N_B a X_a (1+r)^{t_B}/t_B + N_B a X_a (1+r)^{t_B-1}/t_B + \cdots + N_B a X_a (1+r)/t_B} =$$

$$= \frac{N_A t_B [(1+r)^{t_A} + (1+r)^{t_A-1} + \cdots + (1+r)]}{N_B t_A [(1+r)^{t_B} + (1+r)^{t_B-1} + \cdots + (1+r)]}; \qquad (23)$$

and if we set $t_A = t_B$ in this expression, we once again have $X_{AB} = N_A/N_B$.

In addition to the directly expended or 'current' labour, let there now be additionally expended in the production of A a certain amount of capital; this capital good is itself the product of a certain amount of current labour assisted by a certain amount of new capital good; ascending ever higher and higher to 'production goods of higher orders' (the *Productivgüter höherer Ordnung* of the theoreticians of marginal utility), let us finally arrive at a capital good (or capital goods) produced solely

The theory of value of David Ricardo

by current labour. In that case, as we have shown when describing Smith's theory, the total sum of the production costs of a unit of product A (in the Ricardian sense, i.e. including profit) will be given by

$$X_A = n_A a X_a (1+r)^{t_A} + n_1 a X_A (1+r)^{t_A + t_1} + n_2 a X_A (1+r)^{t_A + t_1 + t_2}$$

$$+ \cdots + n_m a X_a (1+r)^{t_A + t_1 + t_2 + \cdots + t_m}, \quad (24)$$

where n_A, n_1, n_2 and so on are the amounts of current labour expended on the production of product A and of the capital goods $(K_1, K_2, K_3, \ldots)$ used in the production of product A; t_A, t_1, t_2 and so on denote the 'production period' of the product A and of capital goods $K_1, K_2, K_3, \ldots$ If, in the interests of brevity, we employ the notations $t_A + t_1 = t_{A1}$, $t_A + t_1 + t_2 = t_{A2}$ and so on, we have:

$$X_A = n_A a X_a (1+r)^{t_A} + n_1 a X_a (1+r)^{t_{A1}} + n_2 a X_a (1+r)^{t_{A2}}$$

$$+ \cdots + n_m a X_a (1+r)^{t_{Am}} \quad (25)$$

where

$$t_{Am} > t_{A(m-1)} > t_{A(m-2)} > \cdots > t_{A2} > t_{A1} > t_A,$$

correspondingly for increasingly long periods of time separating the times at which the amounts of labour n_m, $n_{m-1}, \ldots n_1$, n_A are expended from the time at which the finished product A is delivered to the market.

If we assume that in our formula terms having the same powers have already been summed (so that, for example, $n_1 a X_a (1+r)^{t_1} = m_1 a X_a \times (1+r)^{t_1} + m_2 a X_a (1+r)^{t_1} + \cdots + m_m a X_a (1+r)^{t_1}$), we may also employ it for cases in which any number of different forms of capital goods are *directly* involved in the production of the product A.

This formula serves equally to express the case in which the labour n_1, n_2 and so on preliminarily expended is involved in production of A in the form of machines, tools and 'auxiliary materials' created by it, and to express the case in which the product A itself passes successively through different stages of processing (in this case t_A, t_1, t_2, $\ldots$ will denote the periods of the separate stages of processing; n_A, n_1, n_2 $\ldots$ will denote the amounts of labour used in each stage).

The *structure* of the formula will not be altered if, instead of assuming that the amounts $n_A a X_a$, $n_1 a X_a$ and so on are advanced simultaneously at the beginning of the corresponding production processes A, $K_1, \ldots$ and so on, we assume that they are advanced in parts during the production period; the only difference from equation (25) will be that the term $n_A a X_a (1+r)^{t_A}$ will be replaced by a sum:

$$m_A (1+r)^{t_A} + m_{A1} (1+r)^{t_{A1}} + m_{A2} (1+r)^{t_{A2}} + \cdots + m_{AV} (1+r)^{t_{AV}}, \quad (26)$$

where $m_A + m_{A1} + m_{A2} + \cdots + m_{AV} = n_A$ and $t_A > t_{A1} > t_{A2} > \cdots > t_{AV} > 0$; the term $n_1 a X_a (1+r)^{t_{A1}}$ will be replaced by a sum:

$$m_1 a X_a (1+r)^{t_{A1}} + m_2 a X_a (1+r)^{t_{A11}} + m_3 a X_a (1+r)^{t_{A12}} + \cdots + m_W a X_a (1+r)^{t_{A1W}}$$

$$(27)$$

2. *Ricardo's theory of value*

where $m_1 + m_2 + \cdots + m_W = n_1$, and $t_{A1} > t_{A11} > t_{A12} > \cdots > t_A$, and so on. (Compare with the case considered earlier [p. 54].) Consequently a formula of the type

$$X_A = n_A a X_a (1+r)^{t_A} + n_1 a X_a (1+r)^{t_{A1}} + \cdots + n_m a X_a (1+r)^{t_{Am}} \quad (25)$$

in which $n_A, n_1, n_2, \ldots, t_A, t_{A1}, t_{A2}, \ldots$ can be taken to stand for any magnitudes, will also serve us in this case to express the connection between the price of the product and its production costs.

Accordingly, having selected a formula for the production costs of any product B, we obtain

$$X_{AB} = \frac{n_A(1+r)^{t_A} + n_1(1+r)^{t_{A1}} + \cdots + n_m(1+r)^{t_{Am}}}{m_B(1+r)^{t_B} + m_1(1+r)^{t_{B1}} + \cdots + n_p(1+r)^{t_{Bp}}} \quad (28)$$

as an expression of the exchange ratio X_{AB}, i.e. as an expression of the value of product A in terms of B.

Let the number of terms having different indices be equal both in the numerator and in the denominator, so that $m = p$ and let:

$$t_A = t_B; \quad t_{A1} = t_{B1}; \quad \ldots; \quad t_{Am} = t_{Bp}. \quad (29)$$

In that case

$$X_{AB} = \frac{n_A(1+r)^{t_A} + n_1(1+r)^{t_{A1}} + \cdots + n_m(1+r)^{t_{Am}}}{m_B(1+r)^{t_A} + m_1(1+r)^{t_{A1}} + \cdots + m_m(1+r)^{t_{Am}}}. \quad (30)$$

Let us further have:

$$\frac{n_A}{m_B} = \frac{n_1}{m_1} = \frac{n_2}{m_2} = \cdots = \frac{n_m}{m_m} = R. \quad (31)$$

We shall then have $n_A = m_B R, \ldots, n_k = m_k R$ and

$$X_{AB} = \frac{R[m_B(1+r)^{t_A} + m_1(1+r)^{t_{A1}} + \cdots + m_m(1+r)^{t_{Am}}]}{m_B(1+r)^{t_A} + m_1(1+r)^{t_{A1}} + \cdots + m_m(1+r)^{t_{Am}}} =$$

$$= R = \frac{n_A + n_1 + n_2 + \cdots + n_m}{m_B + m_1 + m_2 + \cdots + m_m}, \quad (32)$$

i.e. in this case the value of product A in terms of B once again will not depend on the level of r, but only on the amount of labour expended on the production of products A and B.

The expression usually given to assumptions (29) and (31) made to obtain this result is that 'the capital goods used up in the branches A and B are of *identical organic composition*'. We should take this vague expression to mean (1) that the turnover periods of the different portions of the

The theory of value of David Ricardo

capital expended in the production of B and of that expended in the production of A are the same, i.e. that it is impossible to find in the production of A a turnover period which could not be found in the production of B *and vice versa*; (2) that the ratios of the portions of capital with correspondingly equal turnover periods in both branches of production are equal. Any attempt to give a briefer definition of the conditions under which value is equal simply to the ratio of the amount of labour expended on the production of a unit of both products renders the definition less *general* than is required and makes it necessary to supplement it by a number of qualifications and special rules, which is the approach followed by Ricardo.[1] Now let t_A not be equal to t_B in the simplest formula (equation (21) on p. 53) expressing the exchange value of the commodities A and B produced by the same current labour as a function of their production costs. Let, for example, $t_A > t_B$, in which case we have $(1+r)^{t_A} > (1+r)^{t_B}$ and in consequence of this:

$$\frac{N_A a X_a (1+r)^{t_A}}{N_B a X_a (1+r)^{t_B}} > \frac{N_A}{N_B} \quad \text{and} \quad X_{AB} > \frac{N_A}{N_B}, \tag{33}$$

i.e. the value of A in terms of B will be greater than the ratio of their 'labour values' (the amounts of labour used in their production).

It may readily be appreciated from the formula that when t_A and t_B are invariable this difference will be greater, the greater is the magnitude of r. Thus, in this case, the magnitude of X_{AB} is a function not only of N_A and N_B, but also of the level of r and, consequently, cannot be determined independently of it. The same will hold for any X_{MN}:

$$X_{MN} = \frac{n_M(1+r)^{t_M} + n_1(1+r)^{t_{M1}} + \cdots + n_k(1+r)^{t_{Mk}}}{m_N(1+r)^{t_N} + m_1(1+r)^{t_{N1}} + \cdots + m_p(1+r)^{t_{Np}}} \tag{34}$$

since (as has been shown above) the second part of the equality cannot be expanded into

$$R \cdot \frac{m_M(1+r)^{t_M} + m_1(1+r)^{t_{M1}} + \cdots + m_k(1+r)^{t_{Mk}}}{m_M(1+r)^{t_M} + m_1(1+r)^{t_{M1}} + \cdots + m_k(1+r)^{t_{Mk}}} \tag{35}$$

[1] In referring to the conditions by virtue of which products are exchanged in the market *other than in proportion* to the amounts of labour expended on their production, Ricardo first considers the division of capital in *different* proportions into fixed and 'circulating' capital, and then adds those cases in which both commodities are produced by 'current' labour, but more time is needed for the production of one than for the production of the other. 'This case', states Ricardo, 'appears to differ from the last, but is, in fact, the same': finally, all this is qualified by the statement: 'It is hardly necessary to say, that commodities which have the same quantity of labour bestowed on their production, will differ in exchangeable value, if they cannot be brought to market in the same time' (Ricardo, *Principles*, Ch. 1, Section IV, p. 37 of the Sraffa edition).

2. Ricardo's theory of value

where R is a quantity that is independent of r. Ricardo examines various special cases that are relevant here (see *Principles*, Ch. 1). Note that to convert from our formulas to the Ricardian examples we first have to introduce the condition of the 'durability' of the capital goods $K_1, K_2, \ldots$, in which case we obtain equation (25) (a simplification of (24))

$$X_A = n_A a X_a (1+r)^{t_A} + n_1 a X_a (1+r)^{t_{A1}} + \cdots + n_m a X_a (1+r)^{t_{Am}}. \quad (25)$$

Thus, in all cases when the organic composition of the capital goods used in the production of A and B is not the same, the exchange ratio X_{AB} of the products A and B cannot be determined independently of the level of r; in this case

$$X_{AB} = f(n_A, n_1, n_2, \ldots; m_B, m_1, m_2, \ldots; t_A, t_{A1}, t_{A2}, \ldots; t_B, t_{B1}, t_{B2}, \ldots; r)$$
$$(37)$$

from which, if $n_A, n_1, \ldots, m_B, m_1, \ldots, t_A, t_{A1}, \ldots, t_B$ and $t_{B1}, \ldots$ have been adopted as quantities dependent on the technical conditions of production of the products A and B, we obtain $X_{AB} = f(r)$, where X_{AB} will be a determined quantity when r is given.

How may the required magnitude of r be determined? Is it possible to use our 'production cost equations' (see p. 55) for its determination? Let us write them in the form:

$$\left.\begin{array}{l} X_A = a X_a [n_A (1+r)^{t_A} + n_1 (1+r)^{t_{A1}} + \cdots + n_m (1+r)^{t_{Am}}] \\[2mm] X_B = a X_a [m_B (1+r)^{t_B} + m_1 (1+r)^{t_{B1}} + \cdots + m_p (1+r)^{t_{Bp}}]. \end{array}\right\} \quad (38)$$

If we assume, as previously, that the quantities $n_A, n_1, \ldots, m_B, m_1, \ldots,$ $t_A, t_{A1}, \ldots, t_B, t_{B1}, \ldots$ are constants, it is possible to write the expression in square brackets in the form $f_A(r), f_B(r) \ldots$ where $f'_A(r) > 0, f'_B(r) > 0,$ $\ldots$ (i.e. when r increases, $f_A(r), f_B(r), \ldots$ is also increased, and *vice versa*). We then have from the equations for A and B

$$\frac{X_A}{a X_a} = f_A(r); \qquad \frac{X_B}{a X_a} = f_B(r), \text{ and so on.} \quad (39)$$

It is evident from these equations that when $X_A/aX_a,\ X_B/aX_a, \ldots$ increase, r also increases by virtue of $\mathrm{d}f_A(r)/\mathrm{d}r > 0;\ \mathrm{d}f_B(r)/\mathrm{d}r > 0$. Consequently, when $X_A, X_B, \ldots$ remain unchanged, r will be greater the less is aX_a and *vice versa*; i.e. *a reciprocal relationship will exist between the profit rate and the level of wages*.[1]

---

[1] Too much importance is often attached to this Ricardian hypothesis. Ricardo's main contribution to the theory of profit does not lie here, but in his establishment of the laws governing the *absolute* level of profit.

The theory of value of David Ricardo

Nevertheless, this analysis does not give us the magnitude of r; in the equations

$$\left.\begin{array}{l} X_A = aX_a \cdot f_A(r) \\ X_B = aX_a \cdot f_B(r) \end{array}\right\} \tag{40}$$
$$\cdots$$

and in the equations derived from them:

$$X_{AB} = \frac{f_A(r)}{f_B(r)}; \qquad X_{AC} = \frac{f_A(r)}{f_B(r)}; \cdots \tag{41}$$

r will be a determined quantity if the magnitude $X_{AB}, X_{AC}, \ldots$ are given. *However, without proceeding from production conditions, we have no other* equations for the determination of X_{AB} and X_{AC} apart from the same equations (41), and the same equation cannot serve for the determination of two unknowns. Thus, we are apparently trapped in a logical circle: profit must be known in order to determine value, but profit itself is dependent on value. There would appear to be no way out of this circle other than to relate value or profit to conditions lying *outside the sphere of production*. As we have seen, Adam Smith took this way out, when he related the profit rate to the demand and supply of capital. To proceed in this manner is, however, to acknowledge the untenability of the theory of production costs itself.[1]

Ricardo's immortal contribution was his brilliant solution of this seemingly insoluble problem. Let us take a series of 'production cost equations' expressing the connection between price and production cost for the commodities A, B, C, ...

$$\left.\begin{array}{l} X_A = aX_a[n_A(1+r)^{t_A} + n_1(1+r)^{t_{A1}} + n_2(1+r)^{t_{A2}} + \cdots + n_m(1+r)^{t_{Am}}] \\ X_B = aX_a[m_B(1+r)^{t_B} + m_1(1+r)^{t_{B1}} + m_2(1+r)^{t_{B2}} + \cdots + m_p(1+r)^{t_{Bp}}] \end{array}\right\}$$
$$\cdots \tag{42}$$

Each new equation incorporates the unknowns X_a and r as in the preceding equations, and additionally a further new unknown X with the appropriate index. Therefore, if the number of equations is n, then the number of unknowns is $(n+2)$. However, no more than n unknowns may be eliminated with n equations. When we arrive at the product N taken by us as the unit of value (e.g. silver), we shall have:

$$1 = aX_a[P_N(1+r)^{t_N} + P_1(1+r)^{t_{N1}} + P_2(1+r)^{t_{N2}} + \cdots + P_S(1+r)^{t_{NS}}]. \tag{43}$$

---

[1] Compare Thünen's criticisms of Smith (J. H. von Thünen *Le salaire naturel et son rapport au taux l'intérêt*, Paris, 1857).

2. *Ricardo's theory of value*

This equation does not contain a new unknown. If we add to it the n former equations, we shall have $(n+1)$ equations with $(n+2)$ unknowns. The number of equations will still be inadequate, and the question of the level of the profit rate will apparently remain unsolved.

It is to Ricardo's credit that he was the first to note that there is one production equation by means of which we may determine the magnitude of r *directly* (i.e. without having recourse for assistance to the other equations). This equation gives us the production conditions of the product a to which in the final analysis the expenditure in all the products A, B, C, ... is reduced. Let us take the 'production costs' equation for this product a compiled in the same way as we compiled the equations for the other products:

$$X_a = aX_a[N_a(1+r)^{t_a} + N_1(1+r)^{t_{a1}} + \cdots + N_q(1+r)^{t_{aq}}] \tag{44}$$

from which:

$$a[N_a(1+r)^{t_a} + N_1(1+r)^{t_{a1}} + \cdots + N_q(1+r)^{t_{aq}}] - 1 = 0 \tag{45}$$

and if we determine r from this equation, we have:

$$r = F(N_a, N_1, N_2, \ldots, N_q; t_a, t_{a1}, t_{a2}, \ldots, t_{aq}; a). \tag{46}$$

But since N_a, N_1, ...; t_a, t_{a1}, ... and a are given quantities dependent on the technical conditions of production of the product a (i.e. the product forming the essential means of existence of the worker), r is also a given magnitude, i.e. is independent of the economic circumstances.

If we now insert the magnitude of r found by us in the production cost equations (42) and so on (on the basis of the law of the equality of profit rates in different branches of industry), we shall obtain X_A, X_B, ... and correspondingly X_{AB}, X_{AC}, ... as functions of the same *given* quantities N, n, m, ... (with the appropriate indices), t's ... (with the appropriate indices) and of the quantity a. Before proceeding to a general analysis of the expression found by us for the magnitude of r, let us consider whether the solution of the problem remains the same if, instead of taking one product (a) consumed by the workers (e.g. corn, as is done by Ricardo) we take several such products in accordance with reality.[1]

Let α, β, γ, ... be products consumed by the workers. Let the daily consumption of a single worker be a for the product α, b for the product β

---

[1] Ricardo himself makes a stipulation along these lines (after he has established his law of profit). He states 'The effects produced on profits would have been the same, or nearly the same, if there had been any rise in the price of those other necessaries, besides food, on which the wages of labour are expended' (Ricardo, *Principles*, Ch. 6, p. 118 of the Sraffa edition).

The theory of value of David Ricardo

and c for the product γ; if we now take the production costs equation for (α), we obtain:

$$X_\alpha = N_\alpha(aX_\alpha + bX_\beta + cX_\gamma \ldots)$$

$$(1+r)^{t_\alpha} + N_{\alpha 1}(aX_\alpha + bX_\beta + cX_\gamma \ldots)(1+r)^{t_{\alpha 1}} + \cdots \quad (47)$$

Clearly this equation does not make it possible to determine r directly as in the preceding case, but if we add to this equation the production costs equation for $\beta, \gamma, \ldots$, we obtain the equation system:

$$\left.\begin{array}{l} X_\beta = N_\beta(aX_\alpha + bX_\beta + cX_\gamma \ldots) \\ \qquad (1+r)^{t_\beta} + N_{\beta 1}(aX_\beta + bX_\beta + cX_\gamma \ldots)(1+r)^{t_{\beta 1}} + \cdots \\ X_\gamma = N_\gamma(aX_\alpha + bX_\beta + cX_\gamma \ldots) \\ \qquad (1+r)^{t_\gamma} + N_{\gamma 1}(aX_\beta + bX_\beta + cX_\gamma \ldots)(1+r)^{t_{\gamma 1}} + \cdots \end{array}\right\} \quad (48)$$

$\ldots$

Let us multiply both parts of equation (47) by a, both parts of the following by b, of the next by c and so on and then add all our equations term by term. We shall obtain:

$$\begin{aligned} (aX_\alpha + bX_\beta + cX_\gamma \ldots) = {} & aN_\alpha(aX_\alpha + bX_\beta + cX_\gamma \ldots)\ (1+r)^{t_\alpha} \\ & + aN_{\alpha 1}(aX_\alpha + bX_\beta + cX_\gamma \ldots)\ (1+r)^{t_{\alpha 1}} + \cdots + \\ & + bN_\beta(aX_\alpha + bX_\beta + cX_\gamma \ldots)(1+r)^{t_\beta} \\ & + bN_{\beta 1}(aX_\alpha + bX_\beta + cX_\gamma \ldots)\ (1+r)^{t_{\beta 1}} + \cdots + \\ & + cN_\gamma(aX_\alpha + bX_\beta + cX_\gamma \ldots)\ (1+r)^{t_\gamma} \\ & + cN_{\gamma 1}(aX_\alpha + bX_\beta + cX_\gamma \ldots)\ (1+r)^{t_{\gamma 1}} + \cdots \quad (49) \end{aligned}$$

Having divided both sides of the equation by $(aX_\alpha + bX_\beta + cX_\gamma, \ldots)$ we shall obtain:

$$1 = aN_\alpha(1+r)^{t_\alpha} + aN_{\alpha 1}(1+r)^{t_{\alpha 1}} + \cdots + bN_\beta(1+r)^{t_\beta} +$$

$$bN_{\beta 1}(1+r)^{t_{\beta 1}} + \cdots + cN\gamma(1+r)^{t_\gamma} + cN_{\gamma 1}(1+r)^{t_{\gamma 1}} + \cdots \quad (50)$$

Consequently:

$$r = F(N_\alpha, N_{\alpha 1}, \ldots; N_\beta, N_{\beta 1}, \ldots; N_\gamma, N_{\gamma 1}, \ldots;$$

$$a, b, c, \ldots; t_\alpha, t_{\alpha 1}, \ldots; t_\beta, t_{\beta 1}, \ldots; \quad (51)$$

$$t_\gamma, t_{\gamma 1}, \ldots; \ldots).$$

Therefore, our system of equations (47), (48) of the 'production costs' of products consumed by the workers still yields r as a function of the same given quantities.[1] Consequently we may establish that the *level of*

----

[1] If the number of products consumed by the workers is n, we shall have n equations in which we have $(n+1)$ unknowns; $(X_\alpha, X_\beta, X_\gamma, \ldots)$ yielding n unknowns, to which the unknown r is added.

2. Ricardo's theory of value

the profit rate r is determined by the production costs of products consumed by the workers. (There is no need for us to repeat the qualification made by Ricardo 'on that land or with that capital which yields no rent',[1] since it has already earlier been proposed to exclude rent from our investigation.) Production costs in this case should be understood as '*only costs in the "objective sense"*' (similar to what was denoted by Rodbertus by the term *Kosten des Gutes* [cost of the good] in contrast with *Auslagen des Unternehmers* [expenditure of the entrepreneurs] or *Kosten des Betriebs* [cost of running the enterprise],[2] namely *the quantity of goods used in production, and the period of reproduction* (i.e. the time between the moment or moments of expenditure of 'production goods' and the time at which the ready product appears on the market).

If we assume $a, b, c, \ldots$ to be constants (which, if the 'iron law of wages' prevails, amounts to the assumption that the minimum of means of subsistence of the worker is invariable), we obtain r exclusively as a function of the *quantities of labour and time* $N_\alpha, N_{\alpha 1}, \ldots;\; N_\beta, N_{\beta 1}, \ldots;$ $N_\gamma, N_{\gamma 1}, \ldots;\; t_\alpha, t_{\alpha 1}, \ldots;\; t_\beta, t_{\beta 1}, \ldots;\; t_\gamma, t_{\gamma 1}, \ldots;\; \ldots;$ corresponding to industries, $\alpha, \beta, \gamma, \ldots$ making products consumed by the workers. Once these quanties are given, the magnitude of r, i.e. the profit rate, is a fully defined quantity.

Consequently, Ricardo succeeded in finding a solution to the problem. Our formulas of 'production costs' have now taken the general form:

$$\left.\begin{aligned}
X_A &= F(n_A, n_1, n_2, \ldots, t_A, t_{A1}, \ldots;\; N_\alpha, N_{\alpha 1}, \ldots, \\
&\quad t_\alpha, t_{\alpha 1}, \ldots;\; N_\beta, N_{\beta 1}, \ldots, t_\beta, t_{\beta 1}, \ldots;\; \ldots) \\
X_B &= F(m_B, m_1, m_2 \ldots, t_B, t_{B1}, \ldots;\; N_\alpha, N_{\alpha 1}, \ldots, \\
&\quad t_\alpha, t_{\alpha 1}, \ldots;\; N_\beta, N_{\beta 1}, \ldots, t_\beta, t_{\beta 1}, \ldots;\; \ldots)
\end{aligned}\right\} \tag{52}$$

where the element of 'price' does not appear at all in the second part of the equation. To level at Ricardo's theory the hackneyed reproach that it 'defines price in terms of price' is to manifest a complete lack of understanding of the writings of this very great theoretical economist.

The *starting point* for Ricardo's analysis was provided by the present-day *capitalist system* based on the use of *hired human labour*; it would, however, be extremely erroneous to imagine that the *conclusions* at which he arrived have a bearing only on the present time. Zhukovsky has quite correctly understood and explained in his book the importance of Ricardo's theoretical conclusions.[3] Ricardo's theory of rent may serve as an

---

[1] Ricardo, *Principles*, Ch. 6, p. 126 of the Sraffa edition.
[2] See C. Rodbertus, *Zur Erkenntniss unserer staatswirthschaftlichen Zustände*, 1842, pp. 25–6.
[3] *History of 19th Century Political Theories* (Vol. 1, pp. 388–9). Zhukovsky states that 'Ricardo deals with the question of distribution only in the sense of the division of separate

The theory of value of David Ricardo

example: the movement of individuals from more fertile to less fertile areas of land is taken as the starting point, but the theory retains its significance even if the opposite assumptions are made. Ricardo subsequently clarifies the laws of rent only in land rent and rent from mines, but this does not prevent the laws established by him from being of general significance for all cases to which the conditions of the origin of rent stated by him apply. (See, in this respect, Zhukovsky, *History* . . . , p. 318.) In our equations for 'production costs' (see equation (25), p. 54), let us set the magnitudes an_A, an_1, an_2, . . . , am_B, am_1, am_2, . . . to be respectively A_A, A_{A1}, A_{A2}, . . . , A_B, A_{B1}, A_{B2}, . . . : in this case A_A, A_{A1}, . . . , A_B, A_{B1}, . . . will denote the quantity of some good α to the expenditure of which we may, in the final analysis, reduce the production costs of the products A, B, . . . Having effected such a transformation in the 'production costs' equation of the product α, we have:

$$X_\alpha = A_\alpha X_\alpha (1+r)^{t_\alpha} + A_{\alpha 1} X_\alpha (1+r)^{t_{\alpha 1}} + \cdots \tag{53}$$

Shortening as necessary and solving the equation with respect to r, we shall have:

$$r = F(A_\alpha, A_{\alpha 1}, \ldots, t_\alpha, t_{\alpha 1}, \ldots). \tag{54}$$

Since the periods of production t_α, $t_{\alpha 1}$, . . . are always finite, it follows that when

$$A_\alpha + A_{\alpha 1} + A_{\alpha 2} + \cdots < 1, \tag{55}$$

we have $r > 0$.

Equation (54) does not contain the quantities n_α, $n_{\alpha 1}$, . . . , i.e. the quantity of labour used in the production of the product α, and it yields r as a function of the *production period* and the *quantity of the good* α expended in production.

Equation (54) shows that whenever a known quantity of some product α has been used up in the production of α and we can obtain a *larger* quantity *of the same* product within some finite period of time as a result of the production process, the profit rate in the given branch of industry will be a fully-determined quantity *greater than zero, irrespective of the price of the product* α. If the production costs of the other goods, A, B, C, . . . are

---

parts of a product between the three elements of price–rent, past labour and current labour *in the sense of elements of price* (p. 388).

It is a matter of indifference for Ricardo's theory whether these elements correspond in a given society to individual classes and persons or not, since 'by worker, rentier and capitalist he always understands more or less abstract fictitious persons'. However, 'Not merely does this not do any harm to the formulation of the problem of distribution given by Ricardo but, on the contrary, it is an indication of the theoretical, philosophical nature of this formulation, which ensures that Ricardo's deductions, should they be correct, have the nature of general laws' (p. 389).

2. *Ricardo's theory of value*

reduced *in the final analysis* to the same product α, the same profit rate should also be established in these branches under conditions of free mobility from one branch of production to another (irrespective of what the ratios $X_{A\alpha}$, $X_{B\alpha}$, ... will be). The essence of the production process by means of which a 'production good' α yields as a result the products A, B, C, ... and new quantities of the same good α is a matter of complete indifference for determination of the rate of profit. Whether the potential energy incorporated in the production good α is released and used in production in the form of *human labour*, as happens at present, or by means of some other process (*not involving the participation of human labour*) is a matter of indifference; whenever we have:

$$1 = A_\alpha(1+r)^{t_\alpha} + A_{\alpha 1}(1+r)^{t_{\alpha 1}} + \cdots \qquad (56)$$

on condition that

$$A_\alpha + A_{\alpha 1} + \cdots < 1, \qquad (55)$$

the profit r will be a fully-defined quantity and greater than zero. For example, suppose some production good β, to which the production costs of all the economic goods A, B, C, ... may be ultimately reduced, be utilised in production by means of the conversion of its potential energy into the work of some living creatures *other than man*. On the basis of the conditions of production we can have and we shall have all the conditions needed for the occurrence of a profit. In this case the profit rate will be a fully-defined magnitude greater than zero, despite the fact that no unit of *human* labour was used in production.[1]

Finally, it is theoretically possible to imagine a case in which all products are produced exclusively by the work of machines, so that no unit of *living labour* (whether human or of any other kind) participates in production, and nevertheless an industrial profit may occur in this case under certain conditions; this is a profit which will not differ essentially in any way from the profit obtained by present-day capitalists using hired workers in production.

Suppose that a machine M is able, without the participation of human labour, and using natural forces as a motor, to produce machines of the following orders: M_1, M_2, M_3, ...; let these machines in their turn singly or in combination automatically produce machines of an even higher order M_1', M_2', M_3', ... until we ultimately arrive at machines M_A, M_B, M_C, ... which directly produce the consumer products A, B, C, ...

---

[1] The quantities A_β, $A_{\beta 1}$, ... are determined in a completely similar manner to the determination of production costs when human labour is used: $A_\beta = N_\beta b$, $A_{\beta 1} = N_1 b$, $A_{\beta 2} = N_2 b$, ..., where N_β, N_1, N_2, ... are the quantities of living labour (in any unit), and b is the quantity of product β which must be expended for the production of one unit of labour.

The theory of value of David Ricardo

In this case the production costs of these products $A, B, C, \ldots$ may always be reduced in the final analysis to the number (or parts) of machines M consumed in the production of the products $A, B, C, \ldots$

Suppose also that among the machines directly or indirectly produced by the machine M, there is the machine M itself, i.e., in other words, let the machine M be *capable of reproduction*. In this case we shall have

$$\left. \begin{aligned} X_A &= n'_M X_M (1+r)^{t_A} + n''_M X_M (1+r)^{t_{A1}} \ldots \\ & \vdots \\ X_M &= N'_M X_M (1+r)^{t_M} + N''_M X_M (1+r)^{t_{M1}} \ldots \end{aligned} \right\} \tag{57}$$

where $n'_M, n''_M, \ldots, N'_M, N''_M, \ldots$ will denote the number of machines M (or parts of the machine M, if $n'_M, n''_M, \ldots$ are less than unity) used up in the production of units of the products $A, B, C, \ldots, M, \ldots$ If $N'_M + N''_M + \ldots < 1$ in the equation for M, *then r will be greater than zero and a fully-defined quantity, provided that the quantities* $N'_M, N''_M, \ldots, t_M, t_{M1}, \ldots$ *are given*.

We have therefore seen, proceeding from Ricardo's analysis, that the origin of industrial profit does not stand in any 'special' relationship to the human labour used in production. Profit may equally well occur in other production processes provided that they satisfy the quite definite conditions stated above. Whether or not such modes of production are capable of existing in the present state of technical knowledge is not a subject for political economy.

Let us assume that the production costs of the economic goods, $A, B, C, \ldots$ may be reduced in the final analysis to the expenditure of the production good α, whose production costs are themselves determined by the formula:

$$X_\alpha = A_\alpha X_\alpha (1+r)^{t_\alpha} + A_{\alpha 1} X_\alpha (1+r)^{t_{\alpha 1}} \ldots \tag{58}$$

Let us assume that by using a different production process (e.g. by using the work of *animals* in place of *human* labour) we can reduce the production costs of the goods $A, B, C, \ldots$ to the expenditure of a production good β, whose production costs are themselves determined by the formula:

$$X_\beta = A_\beta X_\beta (1+r)^{t_\beta} + A_{\beta 1} X_\beta (1+r)^{t_{\beta 1}} \ldots \tag{59}$$

Let us assume that by using a further production process (e.g. exclusively the work of machines employing natural forces as a motor) we shall have correspondingly:

$$X_M = A_M X_M (1+r)^{t_M} + A_{M1} X_M (1+r)^{t_{M1}} + \cdots \tag{60}$$

Let r, determined from equation (58), be r_α and let r from equation (59)

2. *Ricardo's theory of value*

be denoted by r_β and so on. Which of the possible production processes will in reality be used? Obviously, the one which yields the greatest value for r (this follows directly from the hypothesis that an economic subject tends to pursue the greatest advantage). Consequently, for any given production process *actually* to determine the profit rate, it is still insufficient that it *could in general* serve as a source of profit, and it is further necessary that it should yield a *higher profit* rate than all other possible processes. Consequently, for example, if the present state of technology could realise the hypothesis made above of production of all commodities exclusively by machines capable of reproducing themselves, the condition $A_M + A_{M1} + \cdots < 1$ would still be inadequate for the rate of profit in fact to be defined by the equation

$$1 = A_M(1+r)^{t_M} + A_{M1}(1+r)^{t_{M1}} \ldots \tag{61}$$

from which

$$r_M = f(A_M, A_{M1}, \ldots, t_M, t_{M1}, \ldots); \tag{62}$$

it would further be necessary for r_M to be greater than the profit rate r_α established when human labour is used in production. We have previously assumed for simplicity that there is only one series of production costs equations corresponding to each production good $\alpha, \beta, \gamma, \ldots$, to the expenditure of which the production costs of each product $A, B, C, \ldots$ (including the products $\alpha, \beta, \gamma, \ldots$ themselves) may be reduced:

$$
\left.
\begin{aligned}
X_A &= A_A X_\alpha (1+r)^{t_A} + A_{A1} X_\alpha (1+r)^{t_{A1}} + \cdots \\
X_B &= A_B X_\alpha (1+r)^{t_B} + A_{B1} X_\alpha (1+r)^{t_{B1}} + \cdots \\
&\;\;\vdots \\
X_\alpha &= A_\alpha X_\alpha (1+r)^{t_\alpha} + A_{\alpha 1} X_\alpha (1+r)^{t_{\alpha 1}} + \cdots
\end{aligned}
\right\} \tag{63}
$$

In reality, however, there may undoubtedly be several equations systems corresponding to each of them; thus, in addition to the system (63), it is also possible to have any system (64) for the same production good α.

$$
\left.
\begin{aligned}
X_A &= A'_A X_\alpha (1+r)^{t'_A} + A'_{A'} X_\alpha (1+r)^{t'_{A'}} + \cdots \\
X_B &= A'_B X_\alpha (1+r)^{t'_B} + A'_{B'} X_\alpha (1+r)^{t'_{A'}} + \cdots \\
&\;\;\vdots \\
X_\alpha &= A'_\alpha X_\alpha (1+r)^{t'_\alpha} + A'_{\alpha'} X_\alpha (1+r)^{t'_{\alpha'}} + \cdots
\end{aligned}
\right\} \tag{64}
$$

Thus, for example, let the product α be a product consumed by the workers and at the same time a product consumed by some other living creatures to whose work it is also possible to reduce the production

The theory of value of David Ricardo

costs of each of the products A, B, C, $\ldots$, so that $A_A = n_1 a$, $A_{A1} = n_2 a$, $\ldots$, $A_B = m_1 a$, $A_{B1} = m_2 a$, $\ldots$, $A'_A = n'_1 a'$, $A'_{A1} = n'_2 a'$, $\ldots$, $A'_B = m'_1 a'$, $A'_{B1} = m'_2 a'$, where n_1, n_2, $\ldots$, m_1, m_2, $\ldots$ are the *quantities of human work* used in production; n'_1, n'_2, $\ldots$, m'_1, m'_2, $\ldots$ are the *quantities of the work of animals* capable of being used instead of people in the productions A, B, $\ldots$; a is the amount of the product α per unit of work consumed by a *man*; a' is the amount of the product consumed per unit of work completed by an *animal*.

The systems (63), (64), and so on will correspond to *different production processes* by means of which the potential energy of a production good α is used in the production A, B, C, $\ldots$ There can be assumed to be any number of such processes corresponding to each of the production goods α, β, $\ldots$

But in reality one out of all these equation systems will be in force, namely the one which will yield the greatest value for r (determined from the equation for α). This is because no one will begin to use modes of production which yield a low-profit rate if it is possible to use a mode determining a higher rate.

Now let us assume that the production costs of the products A, B, C, D, $\ldots$, L may be reduced to the expenditure of the product D; let the production good D be the *only* good to which the production costs of all the products A, $\ldots$, L (including D itself) may be reduced. The 'production costs' equation for D from the foregoing gives us a fully determined magnitude of r. From the equation

$$X_D = A_D X_D (1+r)^{t_D} + A_{D1} X_D (1+r)^{t_{D1}} + \cdots \tag{65}$$

we have

$$r_D = f_D(A_D, A_{D1}, \ldots; t_D, t_{D1}, \ldots); \tag{66}$$

the same profit rate is also established in the productions A, B, $\ldots$, L. Now let us assume that the production costs of the remainder of the products M, N, $\ldots$, P, cannot be reduced to the product D.[1] Let the only product to which they may be reduced be N,[2] in which case the production costs equation of the product N:

$$X_N = A_N X_N (1+r)^{t_N} + A_{N1} X_N (1+r)^{t_{N1}} + \cdots \tag{67}$$

still yields a fully-determined quantity for r:

$$r_N = f_N(A_N, A_{N1}, \ldots, t_N, t_{N1}, \ldots). \tag{68}$$

---

[1] For example, let D be a product consumed by animals; in that case only the production costs of commodities producible by the labour of animals may be reduced to the product D, since if the products M, N, $\ldots$, P may be produced only by human labour, their production costs can no longer be expressed in terms of D.

[2] If products M, N, $\ldots$, P are products of human labour, N should be understood as the product consumed by the workers.

2. Ricardo's theory of value

This profit level is also established in the branches of production M, $N, \ldots, P$.

Therefore, we shall have one rate of profit r_D for one part of the production $A, B, \ldots, L$, and another rate r_N for the other part $M, N, \ldots, P$.

Let $r_D > r_N$; in that case producers will begin to forsake the branches $M, N, \ldots, B$ and transfer to the branches $A, B, C, \ldots, L$. The price of the products $A, B, C \ldots, L$ will begin to fall (owing to the excess of supply over demand), but since the profit rate determined from the equations

$$\left. \begin{aligned} r_D &= f_D(A_D, A_{D1}, \ldots, t_D, t_{D1}, \ldots) \\ r_N &= f_N(A_N, A_{N1}, \ldots, t_N, t_{N1}, \ldots) \end{aligned} \right\} \tag{69}$$

is not dependent on X_D and X_N, and consequently is not dependent on $X_{DN} = X_D/X_N$, the profit level r_D will continue to remain above r_N however much capital may be 'poured' from the branches $M, N, \ldots, P$ into the branches $A, B, \ldots, L$. However much value the product D may lose owing to the excess of supply, it will nevertheless be more advantageous to entrepreneurs to lay out capital in the production of D than in production of the product N (or any other product from among $M, N, \ldots, P$), which is very costly, since the entrepreneur will receive a larger sum *per unit of value expended in unit time in* the production of D than *per unit of value* in the production of N. The reason for this is that a drop in the price of the finished product D will invariably be matched by a proportionate drop in its production costs, since these costs are reduced to the product D itself.

Whatever quantities we insert for X_D in equation D we obtain the same magnitude for the rate of profit r_D (the amount of profit per unit of value expended in unit time). Consequently, there is apparently no natural limit to the movement of capitalists from the branches $M, \ldots, P$ into the branches $A, \ldots, L$ apart from complete cessation of the production of $M, \ldots, P$. Such a conclusion would be correct if, when $r_D > r_N$, economic expectation always led producers to transfer from the branch N to D. In fact, the hypothesis that producers tend to transfer from branches with a low *rate* of profit to branches with a high rate holds only for cases in which all the quantities entering into the economic calculation of the entrepreneurs have a *finite* value. Since this latter condition does in fact hold in most instances, the foregoing hypothesis is in general found to be correct in practice, but if adopted as the basis of abstract analysis it may lead to false conclusions. Let us assume that an entrepreneur previously expended N units of value (in an arbitrary unit) in production of A, so that in a unit of time we have $N(1+r_A) - N$ units

The theory of value of David Ricardo

of profit, and in T units of time we have $N(1+r_A)^T - N$ units of profit; were he to place this amount of value in production B, he would have $N(1+r_B)^T - N$. If $r_B > r_A$, we have in general

$$N(1+r_B)^T - N > N(1+r_A)^T - N \qquad (70)$$

from which

$$N[(1+r_B)^T - (1+r_A)^T] > 0. \qquad (71)$$

The situation will, however, be different if one of the factors in the first part of the inequality disappears. For example, let the price of product B fall to nothing owing to excess of supply (assuming as the unit of value the value of any of the products produced by expenditure of the product A), in which case, however much of product B is produced, N will also be zero, and consequently so will the entire expression

$$N[(1+r_B)^T - (1+r_A)^T] = 0, \qquad (72)$$

i.e. all motive for the movement of producers from A to B is destroyed. Therefore, when the value of product B (and of others produced by its means), expressed in terms of product A (or by some other commodity produced by its means), falls to zero, the incentive for conversion from A to B will cease, despite the fact that the *rate* of profit continues to remain higher in B than in A (since the rate is not dependent on price). Consequently, when different constant profit rates exist in different branches of production, a balance will be established either when products yielding a high profit rate pass into the realm of *free goods* or when the production of products with a low rate of profit is discontinued. What is actually produced in such a specific case is a question of fact and is dependent on the form of $f_A(D_A), f_B(D_B), \ldots, f_M(D_M), f_N(D_N), \ldots$ expressing the price of products $A, B, \ldots$ as a function of their sale: $D_A, D_B, \ldots$ The smaller is the group represented by the goods $A, \ldots, L$ (by comparison with the group $M, \ldots, P$) and the smaller is the demand for these goods (i.e. the smaller is the quantity of these goods which *completely* satisfies the demand for them), the greater is the probability that they will become 'free' goods before all capital leaves the branches $M, \ldots, P$ (and *vice versa*). Therefore, even were there actually to exist at present some exceptional production processes which were able *without the participation of human labour* to reproduce their real production costs *in natura* (and not in the form of equivalent value) and consequently to determine an *independent* level of profit unrelated to the production costs of the means of subsistence of the workers, the only result of such a situation, in view of the limited nature of the demands which these processes could satisfy, would be to render these products completely valueless and to transfer them to

2. *Ricardo's theory of value*

the realm of free (non-economic) goods. There is, therefore, no foundation for any of the references to various 'natural' processes (such as the breeding of animals and yields which do not necessitate human tending of the plants etc.) as independent sources of 'profit on capital'.[1]

Let us now present our 'production costs' formulas in a more general form (more general than the formula $X_A = A_A X_a (1+r)^{t_A} + A_{A1} X_a \times (1+r)^{t_{A1}} + \cdots$), namely let us set:

$$A_A X_\alpha = P_A; \qquad A_{A1} X_\alpha = P_{A1}; \qquad \ldots \tag{73}$$

in which case we obtain:

$$X_A = P_A (1+r)^{t_A} + P_{A1}(1+r)^{t_{A1}} + \cdots \tag{74}$$

where P_A, P_{A1}, ... will directly denote the number of units of value expended in production or, in other words, will denote the real production costs expressed in a common unit of value with the finished product.[2] Equation (74) is the most general expression of the connection between the price of a product and production costs, and therefore it enables us to extend our analysis beyond *present-day* forms of production.

Let us imagine* a situation in which manpower is withdrawn from market circulation (for whatever reason: without or by means of legislation) so that it is impossible to buy or sell human labour on the *market*. In that case, obviously, it will no longer be possible to reduce the real *production costs* of products to the *expenditure of products* (the means of subsistence of the workers): human labour will be the last level to which they can all be reduced. Let the value of a unit of labour expressed in the same common measurement unit in which the values of the finished

---

[1] See pp. 77–78 for the characteristics distinguishing 'profit on capital', as a special form of income, from other forms of 'income from ownership'.

[2] This formula may be derived directly from the definition of the concept of 'profit' as the difference between the value expended in production and the value obtained as a result of production:

$$A_A = P_A + Z + P_{A1} + Z_1 + \cdots$$

where the sums of the profits are replaced by expressions corresponding to them in terms of the rate of profit r.

* *Ed. note.* In this passage Dmitriev argues that if labour ceased to be a commodity (i.e. if it were 'withdrawn from market circulation') all other commodities would exchange at prices equal to their direct and indirect labour contents (*labour values*). Obviously Dmitriev needs an additional assumption, that labourers as free (i.e. non-hired) producers should not be able to rent capital goods from capitalists (or from each other) and sell capital goods to capitalists (or to each other); for otherwise there would be no reason why relative prices should be different, whether workers are hired by capitalists or machines are hired by workers. If we add this assumption then we must be either in a world without capital goods or in a world without capitalists (including the State among capitalists). In either case there would be no profit, hence relative prices could conceivably be equal to relative values. However, under this necessary additional assumption Dmitriev's proposition seems somewhat trivial.

The theory of value of David Ricardo

products X_A, X_B, ... are expressed be K. In that case, if the quantity of labour used (directly and indirectly) in the production of a unit of the products A, B, ... is expressed by M_A, M_{A1}, ..., M_B, M_{B1}, ..., we shall have a series of equations:

$$
\left.
\begin{aligned}
X_A &= M_A K(1+r)^{t_A} + M_{A1}K(1+r)^{t_{A1}} + \cdots \\
X_B &= M_B K(1+r)^{t_B} + M_{B1}K(1+r)^{t_{B1}} + \cdots
\end{aligned}
\right\}
\tag{75}
$$
$$ \cdots $$

The unknowns in the equations for X_A, X_B, ... will be K and r. Having regard to the fact that we shall have one equation in the equation system (75) (for the commodity used as a measure of value, i.e. a commodity whose value is taken to be unity):

$$ 1 = M_p K(1+r)^{t_p} + M_{p1}K(1+r)^{t_{p1}} + \cdots \tag{76} $$

which does not add a new unknown, we shall therefore have a total of n equations with $(n+1)$ unknowns. In our previous analysis we excluded the superfluous $(n+1)$ unknown by means of the equation:

$$ X_\alpha = A_\alpha X_\alpha(1+r)^{t_\alpha} + A_{\alpha1}X_\alpha(1+r)^{t_{\alpha1}} + \cdots \tag{53} $$

which directly yielded us r as a function of the known quantities. It is natural to consider whether it is also possible to find a similar equation in the system (75). Clearly this is not possible; for this to be possible one would have to obtain, as a result of production, the same 'production good' to which all real production costs could be reduced. But this is impossible, because *production costs will always consist of labour* (since labour cannot be bought by the price of its means of subsistence), *and the result of production will always be a product*, and not labour. Therefore the production cost equation for product α will be *included in labour* (since labour cannot be bought by the price of the means of its subsistence), *and the result of production will always be a product*, and not labour. Consequently, the production costs equation for the product α will be:

$$ X_\alpha = M_\alpha K(1+r)^{t_\alpha} + M_{\alpha1}K(1+r)^{t_{\alpha1}} + \cdots \tag{77} $$

where X_α, K and r are unknowns. If we take the value of the product α to be the unit of value (i.e. if we take the commodity α to be the commodity used as a measuring unit), the equation becomes:

$$ 1 = M_\alpha K(1+r)^{t_\alpha} + M_{\alpha1}K(1+r)^{t_{\alpha1}} + \cdots \tag{78} $$

In order to determine r from this, K would have to be a known quantity. However, for K to be known, r would have to be known. Therefore, the question *apparently* remains unresolved, at least within the limits of the

2. *Ricardo's theory of value*

data of *production* conditions (expressed by the production costs equation). This is, however, only apparent. In reality, the quantity K, expressing the equivalent ratio of product α and labour, *cannot be determined on the market,* by virtue of the assumption made at the beginning of the present analysis (since labour has been removed from market exchange). It follows therefore that the *only process* by means of which the two different goods (the product α and labour) may replace each other in equivalent quantities will be the *process of production* of product α.

Every man who has in his possession some quantity of units of labour *has no means of replacing them by the product α other than by expending his labour in the production of the product* (he cannot sell his labour on the market). The coefficient K cannot therefore remain *undetermined,* but will have a quite precise (and *unique*) value determined by the conditions of production of product α. If N units of labour are capable of producing S units of the product α, it follows that $K = S/N$.[1] Consequently, we shall have $M_\alpha K + M_{\alpha 1} K \ldots = 1$ in our equation (78), from which the only value for r satisfying this equation will be $r = 0$. Therefore despite the apparent inadequacy of equation system (75), we obtain a *fully determined magnitude for r* which, by the law of the equality of the profit level in all industries, is also established in the industries $A, B, \ldots$

Setting $r = 0$ in the system (75), we obtain:

$$\left.\begin{array}{l} X_A = M_A K + M_{A1} K + \cdots \\ X_B = M_B K + M_{B1} K + \cdots \end{array}\right\} \tag{79}$$

$$\cdots$$

From this

$$X_{AB} = \frac{X_A}{X_B} = \frac{M_A + M_{A1} + \cdots}{M_B + M_{B1} + \cdots}, \quad \text{and so on,} \tag{80}$$

i.e. *the exchange ratio of commodities will be determined exclusively by the quantity of labour used in their production, irrespective of the time that will have elapsed between the time labour was expended and the time when the finished product was obtained.*[2] Therefore, the law of 'labour value' would *always* hold were human labour to be withdrawn from circulation in the market (whereas in the present state of affairs it holds only for products produced by capital goods of the same organic composition, as is noted and *emphasised* by Ricardo).

---

[1] $N \cdot K = S \cdot X_\alpha$, from which $K/X_\alpha = S/N$ and, since $X_\alpha = 1$ (because we have taken the product α as the commodity used as a unit of measure), we have: $K = S/N$.

[2] In the absence of hired labour, the introduction of capital goods (*capitale tecnico*) will not therefore serve to infringe the 'labour theory of value' (see, in this respect, the remarks by A. Loria, *Analisi della proprietà capitalista,* 1889. Loria does not directly assume the absence of hired labour, but this stems indirectly from the other conventional assumptions which he makes, such as free land (*terra libera*)).

The theory of value of David Ricardo

The same conclusion may be arrived at by a different route. For there to be equilibrium in the sphere of production it is essential that entrepreneurs should be identically rewarded in all branches of industry. This condition is satisfied if equal amounts *of value expended in equal periods of time* yield *equal amounts of value* in all branches of production. Let us assume that we have two industries A and B; let the process of production of product A require t units of time for its completion and let the process for B require nt units of time. Let us assume that when N units of labour have been expended we obtain M_A units of the product A or M_B units of the product B.

Let K_N, X_A and X_B respectively denote the value of a unit of labour and of units of the products A and B expressed in some arbitrary but *common* unit. In that case the amount of value *expended* in the productions A and B will equal $K_N N$; the amount of value *obtained* in the production of B on completion of the production process, i.e. after nt units of time (from the expenditure of labour) will equal $X_B M_B$. For equilibrium to exist between sectors A and B it is essential that the value of the total quantity of the product obtained in sector A *over the same period of time* should also equal $X_B M_B$ (since otherwise there would be infringement of the condition that equal quantities of value yield equal quantities of value in all branches in equal periods of time).[1] In order now to determine the value of one unit of the product A, it is necessary to divide $X_B M_B$ by y, the number of units of the product A obtained in sector A for N units of labour expended in nt units of time. The question which arises is how large y will be in the absence of hired labour? It is not difficult to see that in this case (in contrast to what is observed under present-day conditions) $X_A M_A$ units of value obtained in the production of A at the end of t units of time cannot be exchanged in the market for an equivalent quantity of labour (which, when $r > 0$, is always greater than N, i.e. is greater than the quantity of labour expended in the production of M_A units of product A). Therefore, N units of labour will yield as many units of the product in the production of A in nt units of time as will be yielded in t units of time, i.e. M_A since the production process for A cannot be repeated without the expenditure in production of N *further new* units of labour.

Hence, for sectors A and B to be in equilibrium, the value of a unit of product A should equal:

$$\frac{X_B M_B}{M_A} = X_A \quad \text{from which} \quad \frac{X_A}{X_B} = \frac{M_B}{M_A} \qquad (81)$$

---

[1] By virtue of the law of the 'equality of profit rates' already established by Adam Smith.

2. *Ricardo's theory of value*

and since the quantities of labour needed for a unit of product A and of product B are respectively

$$N_A = \frac{N}{M_A} \quad \text{and} \quad N_B = \frac{N}{M_B}, \tag{82}$$

we have:

$$\frac{N_A}{N_B} = \frac{N \cdot M_B}{M_A \cdot N} = \frac{M_B}{M_A}, \quad \text{from which} \quad \frac{X_A}{X_B} = \frac{N_A}{N_B}, \tag{83}$$

i.e. the relation between the values of units of products A and B, expressed in any common unit, should be equal to the relation between the quantities of labour used in their production, irrespective of the length of the production processes of A and B.

Let us now proceed from this general analysis of the conditions affecting the appearance and rate of profit to the present state of affairs. Hardly anyone will dispute[1] that the *only* process determining the level of profit at the *present time* is the process of production of the means of subsistence of the workers (*capitale alimento*[2]). Let us consider this special case of the existence of profit on capital in greater detail. Take the production costs equation of the means of subsistence a of the workers:

$$X_a = n_a a X_a (1+r)^{t_a} + n_{a1} a X_a (1+r)^{t_{a1}} + \cdots \tag{84}$$

which, when shortened, yields

$$1 = n_a a (1+r)^{t_a} + n_{a1} a (1+r)^{t_{a1}} + \cdots \tag{85}$$

from which

$$r = F_a(t_a, t_{a1}, \ldots; n_a, n_{a1}, \ldots; a). \tag{86}$$

It is evident from equation (85) that the derivatives of F_a with respect to the variables $t_{a1}, t_a, \ldots, n_a, n_{a1}, \ldots, a$ will all be negative. This means that the quantity r will be smaller: (1) the greater is the labour expended on production of a unit of a subsistence product of the workers, (2) the greater is the time elapsing between the moment that the labour is expended and the time when the finished product is obtained, (3) the greater is the amount of the consumer product of the workers consumed per unit of work.

In Ricardo's opinion, the most important factor affecting an increase

---

[1] Although discussion of this question is not within the competence of political economy.
[2] The terminology of Loria; see his *Analisi della proprietà capitalista*, 1889.

The theory of value of David Ricardo

in the quantity of labour expended on the production of a unit of a product consumed by the workers is the need to go over to the cultivation of less fertile land as the population increases. This point can be largely nullified by improvement in the techniques of land cultivation and, in particular, by the acceleration of production processes.

The quantity denoting the amount of the product consumed per unit of work, when the iron law of wages prevails,[1] will be dependent on the level of needs of the worker and will increase together with them. If we imagine a situation in which the iron law of wages does not hold, the quantity a will in general be determined by the actual struggle of the mutually opposed interests of the capitalists striving to establish the greatest possible value for r and therefore striving to reduce the quantity a to the minimum possible, and of the workers striving conversely to raise a to the greatest possible value. The level of a at which equilibrium is established is a question of fact and is dependent on the strength of the contending parties. In this state of affairs investigation of the conditions affecting the level of a falls outside the scope of political economy and within that of other disciplines; in this case also, as when the iron law of wages prevails and a is determined by the physiological needs of the worker's body, political economy should take the quantity a to be given in its analysis. To proceed in any other way would be to offend against the requirements of correct methodology, by virtue of which every science should have its own special subject and corresponding strictly defined limits.

At all events we invariably have two limits for a: a lower limit, which will be the quantity a established when the iron law of wages (determined

---

[1] The action of this law is manifested only over long periods of time; for short periods, for which the *number of workers is a constant*, the relationship between the level of wages and the supply of *labour* will sometimes be completely the opposite; when wages rise the supply of labour may not only not increase, but may even decrease. In fact, if we take the number of *workers* to be invariable, we obtain the following curve for variation of the supply of labour as a function of the wage rate:

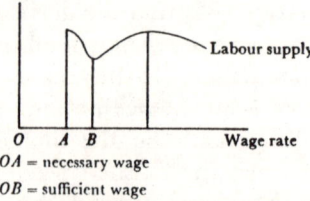

OA = necessary wage
OB = sufficient wage

Figure 1.1

Clearly when the wages rate rises from OA to OB not only will the supply of labour not increase, but on the contrary it will fall. A detailed and thorough analysis of the 'labour supply curve' (and also of the prototype curves from which it is derived) is to be found in W. Launhardt: *Mathematische Begründung der Volkswirthschaftslehre*, Leipzig, 1885, pp. 94–5 and also p. 90 [the figure is from Launhardt, p. 95].

74

2. *Ricardo's theory of value*

by the physiological needs of the worker's body) prevails, and an upper limit, which will be the total quantity of the product produced per unit of work.

A question which arises is whether it is possible to find a value for *a* between these limits which, even if only in some hypothetical ideal system, would be *simultaneously the most advantageous both for the capitalist employers and for the workers* and consequently would be determined by an *economic* factor.

We know that this is a problem which the celebrated economist J. H. von Thünen, one of the first economists to decide to apply higher mathematical analysis to economic problems, set himself. Thünen refers to the wages which satisfy such conditions as 'natural wages' (in contrast to the wages established by the struggle of the mutually opposed interests of capitalists and workers). Thünen concludes as a result of his study that it is possible to achieve complete harmony of the interests of capitalists and workers under certain ideal conditions; Thünen defined the level of wages most advantageous both to the capitalists and to the workers by the formula $\sqrt{(ap)}$, where *a* are the means of subsistence necessary to the worker in a unit of time and *p* is the entire production of the worker in the same unit of time.

Unfortunately, despite its apparent rigour, Thünen's research suffers from many omissions, each of which is sufficient in itself (owing to the very nature of the study) to make his conclusion unconvincing. We shall not here make a detailed analysis of Thünen's work (see the criticism of Thünen's theory in Launhardt)[1] but shall confine ourselves to an indication of his principal error (thanks to which alone he was able to obtain a *definite* answer to the problem which he had set himself), which is of general fundamental (methodological) importance. We refer to Thünen's incorrect use of *maximum formulas.* There is no doubt that the techniques made available by higher mathematics for determination of the value of a variable which maximises a

---

[1] See Launhardt, 1885, p. 150. 'This doctrine is erroneous. By contenting themselves with the necessary wages, the workers employed in the factory incur a privation which cannot be measured by the number of days during which they are subject to this privation but by the magnitude of this privation which is equal to *y* for each day. The magnitude of the privation is therefore equal to $na(a+y)$; if this is divided by the profit of the firm one obtains $[1/(a+y) - 1]/q$; this expression is greatest for $y=0$. And this cannot be otherwise if one considers the question of the wage rate from the viewpoint of the entrepreneur, since the entrepreneurial profit will be greater the smaller the wage.'

Launhardt's correction would be right if people did strive under the influence of economic calculation to the *highest level of income on their capital*; in fact this occurs *only* when capital is a constant or a *variable independent of the rate of interest.* We are not justified in assuming either case on the basis of the main assumptions made by Thünen. And that is why the aspiration of people toward the greatest well being may be regarded as satisfied (and consequently a balance of interests as established) *only when the total sum of income on capital is greatest.* The maximum formula given by Launhardt does not satisfy this requirement.

The theory of value of David Ricardo

function ought to find extremely important application in political economy, which studies the actions of individuals under the influence of their striving for the *greatest advantage*. Nevertheless, great care ought to be taken to ensure that the differential formulas which serve to determine the value of a variable corresponding to the maximum of a function should not be applied purely mechanically to economic problems. Under the influence of the pursuit of the greatest benefit every economic subject in fact strives (in as far as this is dependent on his will) to impart to all variables on which his net income depends, values such that the *total sum* of this net income should be *greatest*, but from this it does not at all follow that the same may be accepted in relation to any partial income (*revenue partiel*) of the subject. A value of the variable which yields the maximum value for some one partial income of the subject may completely fail to correspond to the maximum value of his *total* income and, consequently, may contradict the basic striving of every economic subject toward the greatest benefit. The sole exception is the case in which a given *partial* income does not stand in any functional relationship to the other parts of the total income.

The differential equation $\mathrm{d}\{[(p-a-y)y]/[q(y+a)]\} = 0$ from which Thünen determines the most advantageous level of wages $(a+y)$ for a hired worker obviously contradicts this basic methodological rule: in fact, given the conventional assumptions which Thünen makes in order to present the worker as completely free of the effect of the 'iron law of wages', the formula $[(p-a-y)y]/[q(y+a)]$ expresses only a part of the worker's *total income*[1] and moreover a part which cannot be accepted as an independent variable relative to the remaining income (since the income from previously accumulated capital is also a function of the variable y).

It was only thanks to the methodological error that Thünen was able to obtain a *definite* answer to the task which he has set himself. Had he based his analysis on an expression of the worker's *total income*, and not on an arbitrarily selected part of it, he would have found that the question which he had formulated did not have and could not have any *definite* solution since, given the assumptions made by him, the sum of total income is a quantity independent of y and consequently also of $(a+y)$ (despite the fact that *taken separately* each of the parts of the total income is a function of the variable y), so that in such a hypothetical state of affairs the amount of wages would be a matter of complete indifference both for the workers and for their employers.

---

[1] This formula would express the *total sum* of the worker's income only if the worker *had no previously accumulated savings at all*, but under such conditions it would obviously also not be possible to refer to any 'natural' wages.

2. Ricardo's theory of value

Now let us turn to our equation (85), which defines the quantity r under present conditions:

$$1 = n_a a (1+r)^{t_a} + n_{a1} a (1+r)^{t_{a1}} + \cdots \qquad (85)$$

Setting in it $n_a a + n_{a1} + \cdots = 1$, we have $r = 0$. With this state of affairs any extraction of profit from capital becomes impossible and, in consequence of this, any capitalist production (i.e. with hired workers) should cease (in fact it would cease even before r became zero). This at least is how it would be if the conventional assumptions made by us at the beginning of our analysis of the phenomenon of profit on capital were in fact to hold. But since in fact these conventional assumptions are realised only in exceptional cases, the incentive to continue production and exchange would still remain in force for some of the entrepreneurs even when $r = 0$. The point is that *profit on capital* is not the only form of income yielded by capital. Following Ricardo, we take *profit on capital* to mean only one quite definite form of income regulated by its own precisely defined laws. The characteristic distinguishing this form of income from the group of remaining (rent-like) incomes governed by their own laws is that the 'profit on capital' is obtained by virtue of the mere possession of capital, whereas all other forms of income connected with capital are obtained by virtue of the various *advantages* of some capitalists over others. These advantages may relate both to the sphere of production and to the sphere of sale (exchange) and even to the sphere of consumption; they may be either temporary or permanent (the former correspond to what are known as incomes depending on the general conditions of markets [*kon"yunktural'nyye dokhody*], and the latter to rent-like incomes in the strict sense). However they may be expressed, the incomes produced by them are subject to their own definite laws *which have nothing in common with the laws governing the origin and level of the 'profit on capital'*. It would be not merely unscientific but impossible to study these two groups of incomes together,[1] since the difference existing between them is not merely superficial but *fundamental*. The actual classification of incomes (into profit on capital and rent-like incomes) cannot present the slightest difficulty: all that needs to be done to decide to which group a given income belongs in each specific case is to consider whether this income would be possible if all the capitalist entrepreneurs were placed under *completely identical conditions* both in relation to production and in relation to sale and consumption. Such a conventional assumption excludes all possibility of the occurrence of rent-like profits and the only possible

---

[1] For this reason the extension of the concept of 'rent' (made by Rodbertus) to 'all income which any person obtains without personal labour, solely on the basis of some possessions' is highly irrational. (C. Rodbertus, *Zur Erkenntniss*, 1842, p. 64; *Zur Beleuchtung der socialen Frage*, Berlin, 1875, Vol. I, p. 32.)

The theory of value of David Ricardo

income from capital will be 'profits on capital' in the strictly scientific sense (i.e. understood as a quite definite form of income governed by its own unique laws). This is the approach which we have previously used in our analysis of the 'profit on capital'. Given such an assumption, all possibility of the extraction of income from capital is eliminated when $r = 0$ (since all the conditions for the development of rent-like income have thus been excluded beforehand and 'profit on capital' is the *only* possible income from capital).

We still have to consider whether or not our conclusion will be modified if, instead of calculating income in exchange units, we calculate it (as is in fact done by every economic subject) in its *use value*.* For this purpose we must calculate the sum of the use value (utility) represented to a given individual by the product expended by him in production and to subtract this sum from the sum of the use value represented to the same individual by the finished product of the production. If, in the interests of simplicity, the actual period of production is taken as the unit of time, the profit rate r may be arrived at by dividing the difference obtained by us by the sum of the use value expended.

Let the use value of a unit of the product α be K. In this case, under the production conditions we have assumed we shall have for the determination of r:

$$K = n_a a K (1+r)^{t_a} + n_{a1} a K (1+r)^{t_{a1}} + \cdots$$

$$\text{or} \quad 1 = n_a a (1+r)^{t_a} + n_{a1} a (1+r)^{t_{a1}} + \cdots \quad (87)$$

from which $r = 0$ when $n_a a + n_{a1} a + \cdots = 1$. But this will be so only while we assume that the *use of a unit of the given product is a constant for the given individual*, at least within the effective limits of economic calculation. In fact, however, this is not so: the use value of a unit of a given product for a given individual is a *function of time*. It was on this basis that Böhm-Bawerk attempted to construct an independent theory of profit on capital (i.e. independent of production conditions) in his work *Kapital*

---

* *Ed. note.* It is difficult to think what Dmitriev seeks in this passage (up to the end of Section 2 of the First Essay) by calculating income (and inputs) in terms of 'use value', unless he has in mind a situation of equal marginal and average (cardinal) utility of commodities, *and* admits the interpersonal additivity of utility levels. The weakest point of his analysis is his criticism of Böhm-Bawerk, on the ground that it is sufficient 'to postulate that all people "overvalue" present goods by comparison with future goods to *an equal degree* for this overvaluation to cease' to be a source of income'. In modern terminology 'overvaluation' of this kind does not require a rate of substitution between present and future consumption equal to $(1+r)$, where r is the interest rate, whatever the relation between present consumption c_0 and consumption at a future date c_1; 'overvaluation' would be interpreted as $(1+r) > 1$ for $c_0 = c_1$. Even if economic agents had the same rate of 'overvaluation', or more generally if they had identical time preference functions, as long as their relative endowments of dated consumption differ there would be a positive mutual gain from exchange.

2. *Ricardo's theory of value*

und Kapitalzins. He states: 'Present goods are generally of greater value than future goods of the same sort and number. This proposition is the kernel and centre of the theory of interest, which I have to propose' (*Positive Theorie*, 1889, p. 248).[1]

It is not difficult to demonstrate that although Böhm-Bawerk wished to indicate the source of 'profit on capital' he in fact indicated only a new source of *rent-like* (differential) *income*. In fact, we only have to postulate that all people 'overvalue' present goods by comparison with future goods *to an equal degree* for this overvaluation to cease to be a source of income.

In fact, let us assume that an individual A gives an individual B a sum of 100 roubles to be returned with interest a year later. Let the ratio of the usefulness of one rouble at the present time to the usefulness of one rouble after a year be 2:1, denoting these usefulnesses by K_p and K_f and we have $K_p : K_f = 2:1$, from which $K_f = \frac{1}{2}K_p$; if B agrees to give A 200 roubles at the end of a year, his income from this operation expressed in use value is:

$$100K_p - 200K_f = 100K_p - 200 \cdot \tfrac{1}{2}K_p = 100K_p - 100K_p = 0. \quad (88)$$

Were he to return more than 200 roubles at the end of a year, his income would be expressed by a negative quantity: therefore 200 will be the highest sum which B may in general return to the creditor A. Let us consider what will be A's income at this highest sum of 200 roubles which B may return to him. Since we assume that neither of the contracting parties A and B has an advantage over the other in the sphere of consumption, the coefficients K_p and K_f will be the same for both. Consequently, the benefit obtained from the operation by contracting party A will also be expressed by $100K_p - 200K_f = 100K_p - 100K_p = 0$.

A transaction between A and B under conditions which exclude the

---

[1] Böhm-Bawerk notes three main 'overvaluations' of goods in hand. It is only the second of these three bases (the difference in the use value of goods in hand and future goods) that is an essentially new factor capable of providing a basis for the construction of an independent theory 'of the origin of profit on capital'. Böhm-Bawerk gives the following formulation of the second basis (*Zweiter Grund*): 'We underestimate systematically our future needs and the means for their satisfaction' (p. 266). '. . . The existence of this fact is beyond doubt. It is more difficult to say why the fact exists' (p. 267). Böhm-Bawerk subsequently indicates three bases for this fact. 'It seems to me that a first reason stems from the fragmentary character of the idea we have about the future state of our needs' (p. 268). '. . . While this reason seems to amount to erroneous estimation, a second reason seems to stem from an erroneous decision. I believe that it occurs frequently that somebody who is faced with a choice between a present and a future pleasure or pain decides in favour of the lesser present pleasure although he knows exactly and is aware at the moment of his choice that the future disadvantage is greater and hence that his choice is disadvantageous for his wellbeing as a whole' (p. 268). '. . . Finally as a third reason, the consideration of the short duration and insecurity of our life seems also, to me, to be important' (p. 269).

The theory of value of David Ricardo

possibility of the development of rent does not therefore give any advantage to either of the contracting parties; it is further not difficult to prove that *under such conditions an advantage will be completely impossible* provided, of course, that the contracting parties are guided in their actions by correct economic calculus.

In fact, correct economic calculus is incompatible with any *economically purposeless* acts (i.e. acts as a result of which the benefits do not exceed the sacrifices), even when a given act does not entail any risk (since every act invariably entails some expenditure of energy, which could be otherwise used on something else with greater benefit or satisfaction). But every transfer of value to other hands *always* entails some risk. There is no point in incurring this risk if the transaction is *unprofitable*, and therefore the very transfer of value to other hands under such conditions is opposed to the economic calculation of a contracting party acting in good faith. Consequently, under conditions which exclude the possibility of the occurrence of rent, no overvaluation of goods in hand can provide an independent source of profit on capital. Therefore, if production conditions are such as we have assumed at the beginning of this section, profit on capital cannot arise whatever the units in which the balance of the economic operation is calculated (units of exchange or use).

All the foregoing is fully applied in the theory in which Launhardt attempted several years before the appearance of the second volume of *Kapital und Kapitalzins* (in which Böhm-Bawerk's own views are set out) to construct a theory of profit on capital on the same basis as Böhm-Bawerk.[1]

Although the 'overvaluation' of goods in hand by comparison with future goods, which is noted by Böhm-Bawerk, does not contribute anything new to the theory of the development of profit and the level of profit, it is a significant factor under the *given* conditions of production in the question of the accumulation of capital. (For a detailed analysis of this question see Launhardt, 1885, pp. 67–9).

3. THE THEORY OF MONOPOLY PRICES

Ricardo pays hardly any attention to the laws determining the price of scarce products. Nor is any clear distinction to be found in his writings between scarce products in the true sense and monopoly products (the

---

[1] Compare Launhardt, 1885. '... an enjoyment is the less appreciated the more distant the future when it can be had ...' (p. 5). 'The secure prospect of an enjoyment in the future is thought to be of lesser value than the same enjoyment in the present ...' (p. 6). This hypothesis is subsequently related to interest: 'Interest is the compensation for waiting for an enjoyment or for the temporary renunciation of an enjoyment ...' (p. 7).

[2]

"On the Correction of Marx's Fundamental Theoretical Construction in the Third Volume of *Capital*," by

Ladislaus von Bortkiewicz

CRITICS of Marx have hitherto shown little inclination to examine more closely the procedure which is used in the third volume of *Capital*[1] for the transformation of values into prices of production and for the determination of the average rate of profit, in order to see whether this procedure is free of contradictions.

Tugan-Baranowsky provides an exception in this respect.[2] He has shown specifically that the way Marx calculates the average rate of profit is not valid. Moreover, Tugan-Baranowsky has pointed out how with given prices of production and a given average rate of profit it is possible to calculate correctly the corresponding values and the rate of surplus value. In this case there is posed a problem which is the opposite of that which Marx tried to solve.

It is nevertheless interesting to show that Marx erred, and in what way, without reversing his way of posing the problem. For this purpose, it will be convenient, in order not to complicate the presentation, to introduce the same limiting assumption which Tugan-Baranowsky made use of, namely, that the entire advanced capital (including the constant capital) turns

[1] Vol. III, pp. 182-203.
[2] *Theoretische Grundlagen des Marxismus* (Leipzig, 1905), pp. 170-188.

over once a year and reappears again in the value or the price of the annual product.[1] Insofar as it is a question of demonstrating Marx's errors it is quite unobjectionable to work with limiting assumptions of this kind, since what does not hold in the special case cannot claim general validity.

In still another respect the procedure followed here agrees with that of Tugan-Baranowsky. The different spheres of production from which Marx composes social production as a whole can be put together into three departments of production. In Department I means of production are produced, in Department II workers' consumption goods, and in Department III capitalists' consumption goods. At the same time we shall assume that in the production of all three groups of means of production, that is, those which are used respectively in Departments I, II, and III—the organic composition of capital is the same.

Finally, we shall assume "simple reproduction."

Let c_1, c_2, c_3 stand for the constant capital, v_1, v_2, v_3 for the variable capital, and s_1, s_2, s_3 for the surplus value in Departments I, II, and III respectively. The conditions of simple reproduction are expressed in the following system of equations:

(1) $$c_1 + v_1 + s_1 = c_1 + c_2 + c_3$$
(2) $$c_2 + v_2 + s_2 = v_1 + v_2 + v_3$$
(3) $$c_3 + v_3 + s_3 = s_1 + s_2 + s_3$$

If we now designate the rate of surplus value by r, then we have

$$r = \frac{s_1}{v_1} = \frac{s_2}{v_2} = \frac{s_3}{v_3}$$

and equations (1), (2), and (3) can be rewritten as follows:

(4) $$c_1 + (1 + r)v_1 = c_1 + c_2 + c_3$$
(5) $$c_2 + (1 + r)v_2 = v_1 + v_2 + v_3$$
(6) $$c_3 + (1 + r)v_3 = s_1 + s_2 + s_3$$

[1] This assumption is also found, for example, in Kautsky, *Karl Marx' Ökonomische Lehren* (Stuttgart, 1903), p. 98.

Appendix 201

The problem now is to convert these value expressions into price expressions which conform to the law of the equal rate of profit.

Marx's solution consists, first, in forming the sums

(7) $\qquad c_1 + c_2 + c_3 = C$
(8) $\qquad v_1 + v_2 + v_3 = V$
(9) $\qquad s_1 + s_2 + s_3 = S$

next, in determining the sought-for average rate of profit, which will be designated by ρ, from the formula

(10) $$\rho = \frac{S}{C+V}$$

and, finally, expressing the production prices of the commodities produced in the three departments by

$$c_1 + v_1 + \rho\,(c_1 + v_1)$$
$$c_2 + v_2 + \rho\,(c_2 + v_2)$$
$$c_3 + v_3 + \rho\,(c_3 + v_3)$$

from which it emerges that the sum of these three price expressions, or the total price, is identical with the sum of the corresponding value expressions, or the total value $(C + V + S)$.

This solution of the problem cannot be accepted because it excludes the constant and variable capitals from the transformation process, whereas the principle of the equal profit rate, when it takes the place of the law of value in Marx's sense, must involve these elements.[1]

The correct transition from value quantities to price quantities can be worked out as follows:

Suppose that the relation between the price and the value of the products of Department I is (on the average) as x to 1, in the case of Department II as y to 1, and in the case of Department III as z to 1. Furthermore let ρ be the profit rate which

[1] For a closer examination of this point, see the second article of my work "Wertrechnung und Preisrechnung im Marxschen System," *Archiv für Sozialwissenschaft und Sozialpolitik*, Vol. XXV, No. 1 (July, 1907).

is common to all departments (though now formula (10) can no longer be regarded as the correct expression for ρ).

The counterpart of equations (4), (5), and (6) is now the following system:

(11) $\qquad (1 + \rho)(c_1x + v_1y) = (c_1 + c_2 + c_3)x$

(12) $\qquad (1 + \rho)(c_2x + v_2y) = (v_1 + v_2 + v_3)y$

(13) $\qquad (1 + \rho)(c_3x + v_3y) = (s_1 + s_2 + s_3)z$

In this manner we obtain three equations with four unknowns (x, y, z, and ρ). In order to supply the missing fourth equation we must determine the relation between the price unit and the value unit.

If we were to choose the price unit in such a way that total price and total value are equal, we would have to set

(14) $\qquad\qquad Cx + Vy + Sz = C + V + S$

where

(15) $\qquad\qquad C = c_1 + c_2 + c_3$

(16) $\qquad\qquad V = v_1 + v_2 + v_3$

(17) $\qquad\qquad S = s_1 + s_2 + s_3$

If, on the other hand, the price unit and the value unit are to be regarded as identical, then we have to consider in which of the three departments the good which serves as the value and price unit is produced. If gold is the good in question, then Department III is involved and in place of (14) we get

(18) $\qquad\qquad\qquad z = 1$

Let us follow this last procedure. In this fashion the number of unknowns is reduced to three (x, y, and ρ).

To arrive at the simplest possible formulas, let us form the following expressions:

$$\frac{v_1}{c_1} = f_1 \quad , \quad \frac{v_1 + c_1 + s_1}{c_1} = g_1$$

$$\frac{v_2}{c_2} = f_2 \quad , \quad \frac{v_2 + c_2 + s_2}{c_2} = g_2$$

$$\frac{v_3}{c_3} = f_3 \quad , \quad \frac{v_3 + c_3 + s_3}{c_3} = g_3$$

and

$$1 + \rho = \sigma$$

Equations (11), (12), and (13) can be rewritten, taking account of (1), (2), and (3), as follows:

(19) $$\sigma\,(x + f_1 y) = g_1 x$$

(20) $$\sigma\,(x + f_2 y) = g_2 y$$

(21) $$\sigma\,(x + f_3 y) = g_3$$

From equation (19) we get:

(22) $$x = \frac{f_1 y\,\sigma}{g_1 - \sigma}$$

If we substitute this value for x in equation (20) the result is

(23) $$(f_1 - f_2)\,\sigma^2 + (f_2 g_1 + g_2)\,\sigma - g_1 g_2 = 0$$

from which it follows that

(24) $$\sigma = \frac{-(f_2 g_1 + g_2) + \sqrt{(f_2 g_1 + g_2)^2 + 4\,(f_1 - f_2)\,g_1 g_2}}{2\,(f_1 - f_2)}$$

or, otherwise written,

(25) $$\sigma = \frac{f_2 g_1 + g_2 - \sqrt{(g_2 - f_2 g_1)^2 + 4\,f_1 g_1 g_2}}{2\,(f_2 - f_1)}$$

It is easy to show that in this case the quadratic equation (23) yields only one solution which is relevant to the terms of the problem. If $f_1 - f_2 > 0$, we get $\sigma < 0$ by putting a minus sign in front of the square root in formula (24). If on the other hand $f_1 - f_2 < 0$, the result of putting a plus sign in front of the square root in formula (25) is

$$\sigma > \frac{g_2}{f_2 - f_1}$$

and *a fortiori*

$$\sigma > \frac{g_2}{f_2}$$

This contradicts equation (20) which yields

$$\sigma < \frac{g_2}{f_2}$$

From equations (20) and (21) we find:

(26) $$y = \frac{g_3}{g_2 + (f_3 - f_2)\,\sigma}$$

and when we have solved for σ and y, x can be calculated according to formula (22).

Let us now see by several numerical examples how these formulas can be used to transform values into prices. Suppose for example that the given value expressions are the following:

TABLE 1: VALUE CALCULATION

Dept. of Production	Constant Capital	Variable Capital	Surplus Value	Value of Product
I	225	90	60	375
II	100	120	80	300
III	50	90	60	200
Total	375	300	200	875

From this we derive the following numerical values:

$$c_1 = 225, c_2 = 100, c_3 = 50, v_1 = 90, v_2 = 120, v_3 = 90,$$

$$s_1 = 60, s_2 = 80, s_3 = 60, \text{ and further: } f_1 = \frac{2}{5}, f_2 = \frac{5}{6},$$

$$f_3 = \frac{9}{5}, g_1 = \frac{5}{3}, g_2 = 3, g_3 = 4.$$

Formulas (25), (26), and (22) yield:

$$\sigma = \frac{5}{4}, \text{ therefore } \rho = \frac{1}{4}, y = \frac{16}{15}, x = \frac{32}{25}, \text{ and we get:}$$

TABLE 2: PRICE CALCULATION

Dept. of Production	Constant Capital	Variable Capital	Profit	Price of Product
I	288	96	96	480
II	128	128	64	320
III	64	96	40	200
Total	480	320	200	1,000

In Department I the price expression for constant capital (288) comes from multiplying the corresponding value expression (225) by $\frac{32}{25}$, and the price expression for variable capital

(96) from multiplying the corresponding value expression (90) by $\frac{16}{15}$. The profit in this department consists of the sum of the two price expressions $(288 + 96)$ multiplied by the profit rate $(\frac{1}{4})$. The figures for the other departments are calculated in exactly the same way.[1]

That the total price exceeds the total value arises from the fact that Department III, from which the good serving as value and price measure is taken, has a relatively low organic composition of capital. But the fact that total profit is numerically identical with total surplus value is a consequence of the fact that the good used as value and price measure belongs to Department III.

It is not without interest to compare the price and profit relations of Table 2 with the price and profit relations which Marx would have obtained in this case. According to formula (10) Marx would have written $\rho = \frac{200}{675} = \frac{8}{27}$, since (according to Table 1) S = 200, C = 375, V = 300.

We get:

TABLE 3: PRICE CALCULATION ACCORDING TO MARX

Dept. of Production	Constant Capital	Variable Capital	Profit	Price of Product
I	225	90	$93\frac{9}{27}$	$408\frac{8}{27}$
II	100	120	$65\frac{5}{27}$	$285\frac{5}{27}$
III	50	90	$41\frac{13}{27}$	$181\frac{13}{27}$
Total	375	300	200	875

[1] Table 1 is taken from the above-mentioned work of Tugan-Baranowsky, and all figures in Table 2 are related to the corresponding figures of Tugan-Baranowsky (*ibid.*, p. 171) as 8 to 5. Tugan-Baranowsky sets up his value schema in terms of labor units instead of money units. This is legitimate enough, but it turns attention away from the real difference between value calculation and price calculation.

Appendix

There thus emerges a discrepancy between the prices of the quantities produced in the various departments ($408\frac{9}{27}$, $285\frac{5}{27}$, $181\frac{13}{27}$) and the numerical expressions for constant capital, variable capital, and profit. As already indicated, Marx would have had to determine the average rate of profit in this case to be $\frac{8}{27}$, or 29.6 percent, while according to the correct procedure it amounts to $\frac{1}{4}$, or 25 percent.[1]

But Marx not only failed to indicate a valid way of determining the rate of profit on the basis of given value and surplus value relations; more, he was misled by his wrong construction of prices into an incorrect understanding of the factors on which the height of the rate of profit in general depends.[2] He took the position that with a given rate of surplus value the rate of profit is greater or smaller according as the total social capital, including all spheres of production, has a lower or higher organic composition. This view follows from the fact that Marx expressed the rate of profit by formula (10). If we designate, as before, the rate of surplus value by r and the relation of the value of constant capital to total capital by q_0, according to which

$$r = \frac{S}{V} \text{ and } q_0 = \frac{C}{C + V}$$

we should then have:

(27) $$\rho = (1 - q_0)\, r$$

According to this, with a given rate of surplus value the only circumstance which affects the height of the rate of profit is whether the share of constant capital in total capital, the quotient q_0 is larger or smaller; and it would make no difference at all what differences existed between the organic composition of the capitals in the different spheres of production.

---

[1] See the first article of my work "Wertrechnung und Preisrechnung," in *Archiv für Sozialwissenschaft und Sozialpolitik*, Vol. XXIII, No. 1, p. 46.
[2] By rate of profit we understand here and in what follows, unless the contrary is expressly stated, the average rate of profit.

It is true that in *Capital* we read that the general rate of profit is determined by two factors: (1) the organic composition of the capitals in the different spheres of production, hence the different profit rates of the individual spheres, and (2) the distribution of the total social capital among these different spheres.[1] But the way Marx works these two factors into his calculation schema is such as to allow us to reduce them to one single factor, namely the organic composition of the total social capital.

Let q_1 represent the relation of constant capital in our Department I to the total capital of that department, γ_1 the share of the latter in the total social capital. Similarly let q_2, γ_2 and q_3, γ_3 represent the analogous quantities in Departments II and III. These designations can be expressed in the following formulas:

$$\frac{c_1}{c_1 + v_1} = q_1, \quad \frac{c_2}{c_2 + v_2} = q_2, \quad \frac{c_3}{c_3 + v_3} = q_3;$$

$$\frac{c_1 + v_1}{C + V} = \gamma_1, \quad \frac{c_2 + v_2}{C + V} = \gamma_2, \quad \frac{c_3 + v_3}{C + V} = \gamma_3$$

From these formulas it appears that:

$$\frac{c_1 + c_2 + c_3}{C + V} = \gamma_1 q_1 + \gamma_2 q_2 + \gamma_3 q_3$$

or also, since $c_1 + c_2 + c_3 = C$ and $\dfrac{C}{C + V} = q_0$,

(28) $$q_0 = \gamma_1 q_1 + \gamma_2 q_2 + \gamma_3 q_3$$

If one now substitutes this formula for q_0 in (27) and takes account of the fact that $\gamma^1 + \gamma^2 + \gamma_3 = 1$, one gets:

(29) $$\rho = \frac{\gamma_1 (1 - q_1) r + \gamma_2 (1 - q_2) r + \gamma_3 (1 - q_3) r}{\gamma_1 + \gamma_2 + \gamma_3}$$

This formula expresses the Marxian standpoint very clearly: the general rate of profit (ρ) appears as the arithmetic average

[1] Vol. III, pp. 191-192.

of the particular rates of profit $(1 - q_1)r$, $(1 - q_2)r$, and $(1 - q_3)r$, which contribute to the formation of the average with the respective "weights" $\gamma_1, \gamma_2, \gamma_3$. And of the two factors which in Marx's view determine the general rate of profit, one, according to formula (29), is represented by q_1, q_2, q_3 and the other by $\gamma_1, \gamma_2, \gamma_3$. It is, however, obvious from formula (28) that these two factors can be reduced to one single factor, that is to say, to the organic composition of the total social capital which is represented by q_0.

In opposition to this view we shall now show by means of a suitably constructed numerical example that, because formulas (27) and (29) are false, cases are possible in which, with a given rate of surplus value, one and the same rate of profit is compatible with different organic compositions of the total social capital. Take the following value schema as a starting point:

TABLE 4: VALUE CALCULATION

Dept. of Production	Constant Capital	Variable Capital	Surplus Value	Value of Product
I	300	120	80	500
II	80	96	64	240
III	120	24	16	160
Total	500	240	160	900

If we compare this table with Table 1 we find that the rate of surplus value is the same (66⅔ percent), while the organic composition of capital is higher. According to Table 1, $q_0 = \dfrac{375}{675} = .556$; while according to Table 4, $q_0 = \dfrac{500}{740} = .676$. Marx would say that the rate of profit must fall from 29.6 percent to 21.6 percent.

If we now apply to this table the correct method of transformation, as we did in going from Table 1 to Table 2, we find $x = \frac{32}{35}$, $y = \frac{16}{21}$, $\rho = \frac{1}{4}$, and as a complete result:

TABLE 5: PRICE CALCULATION

Dept. of Production	Constant Capital	Variable Capital	Profit	Price of Product
I	$274\tfrac{2}{7}$	$91\tfrac{3}{7}$	$91\tfrac{3}{7}$	$457\tfrac{1}{7}$
II	$73\tfrac{1}{7}$	$73\tfrac{1}{7}$	$36\tfrac{5}{7}$	$182\tfrac{6}{7}$
III	$109\tfrac{5}{7}$	$18\tfrac{2}{7}$	32	160
Total	$457\tfrac{1}{7}$	$182\tfrac{6}{7}$	160	800

The reason why Table 4 gives the same rate of profit as Table 1 (25 percent) is that according to formula (25) the rate of profit ($\rho = \sigma - 1$), given a certain rate of surplus value, depends exclusively on the organic composition of the capitals in Departments I and II (in this connection it is necessary to keep in mind the meaning of the quantities f_1, f_2, g_1, and g_2), and that in this respect Tables 1 and 4 are identical. But the circumstance that the ratio of constant capital to total capital in Department III has grown from about 36 percent to about 83 percent has no bearing on the height of the rate of profit. For the rest, however, this result is hardly surprising from the point of view of the theory of profit which sees the origin of profit in "surplus labor." Ricardo had already taught that a change in the relations of production which touches only such goods as do not enter into the consumption of the working class cannot affect the height of the rate of profit.[1]

Let us now consider a case where the rate of profit changes in spite of the fact that the organic composition of the total social capital remains the same. This happens if one contrasts with Tables 1 and 2 the following tables:

[1] For a closer examination of this point, see the third article of my work "Wertrechnung und Preisrechnung."

Appendix

TABLE 6: VALUE CALCULATION

Dept. of Production	Constant Capital	Variable Capital	Surplus Value	Value of Product
I	205	102	68	375
II	20	168	112	300
III	150	30	20	200
Total	375	300	200	875

Following formulas (25), (26), and (22) we get

$$\sigma = \frac{415 - 5\sqrt{409}}{216} = 1.453,\ y = .432,\ x = .831$$

and as a complete result:

TABLE 7: PRICE CALCULATION

Dept. of Production	Constant Capital	Variable Capital	Profit	Price of Product
I	170.3	44.1	97.1	311.5
II	16.6	72.6	40.5	129.7
III	124.6	13.0	62.4	200
Total	311.5	129.7	200	641.2

Marx's method of transformation would have produced the same rate of profit again, 29.6 percent (instead of 45.3 percent), and the distribution of the total profit among the three departments would have been as follows: Department I, $90\frac{26}{27}$ (instead of 97.1), Department II, $55\frac{19}{27}$ (instead of 40.5), and Department III, $53\frac{9}{27}$ (instead of 62.4).

The erroneous character of Marx's transformation method comes out even more clearly in the special case where there is no constant capital in Department II. We have this case in the following table:

Appendix

TABLE 8: VALUE CALCULATION

Dept. of Production	Constant Capital	Variable Capital	Surplus Value	Value of Product
I	180	90	60	330
II	0	180	120	300
III	150	30	20	200
Total	330	300	200	830

In this case we can no longer use formula (25) for the purpose of calculating ρ or σ, because $f_2 = \infty$ and $g_2 = \infty$. We have instead to go back to equations (11), (12), and (13). We find from (12), since $c_2 = 0$, that

$$1 + \rho = \frac{v_1 + v_2 + v_3}{v_2}$$

By reason of formula (2) we can also write (again because $c_2 = 0$):

$$1 + \rho = \frac{v_2 + s_2}{v_2}$$

and finally

$$\rho = \frac{s_2}{v_2}$$

or

$$\rho = r$$

The rate of profit is equal to the rate of surplus value, thus according to Table 8 equal to $\frac{2}{3}$ or $66\frac{2}{3}$ percent. If we put this value of ρ into formulas (11) and (13) we get two equations of the first degree with two unknowns (x and y), since here too $z = 1$, and we find: $x = 1\frac{0}{13}$, $y = \frac{2}{13}$. The conversion of values into prices and of surplus value into profit gives:

TABLE 9: PRICE CALCULATION

Dept. of Production	Constant Capital	Variable Capital	Profit	Price of Product
I	$138\frac{6}{13}$	$13\frac{11}{13}$	$101\frac{7}{13}$	$253\frac{11}{13}$
II	0	$27\frac{9}{13}$	$18\frac{6}{13}$	$46\frac{2}{13}$
III	$115\frac{5}{13}$	$4\frac{8}{13}$	80	200
Total	$253\frac{11}{13}$	$46\frac{2}{13}$	200	500

212   *Appendix*

According to Marx, however, the relevant quantity relations would be as follows:

TABLE 10: PRICE CALCULATION ACCORDING TO MARX

Dept. of Production	Constant Capital	Variable Capital	Profit	Price of Product
I	180	90	$85\frac{5}{7}$	$355\frac{5}{7}$
II	0	180	$57\frac{1}{7}$	$237\frac{1}{7}$
III	150	30	$57\frac{1}{7}$	$237\frac{1}{7}$
Total	330	300	200	830

The rate of profit would be $\dfrac{200}{630}$ or 31.8 percent (instead of $66\frac{2}{3}$ percent!).

In this case, characterized by the absence of constant capital in Department II, the incorrectness of Marx's derivation of prices and profit is particularly obvious. For it is clear that here in Department II, where the outlay of capitalists consists solely of variable capital and indeed of the very commodities which are produced in that department, the gain of the capitalists must always remain in the same relation to their outlay whether the prices of the relevant commodities are higher or lower. There is no way, either through exchange of commodities or through "price regulation," by which this relation could be reduced from $66\frac{2}{3}$ percent to 31.8 percent.

Following Table 9 we can represent commodity exchanges as follows:[1]

The capitalists of Department

I   II   III

(1) hold commodities priced at:

$138\frac{6}{13}$ $27\frac{9}{13}$ 80

---

[1] For the sake of simplicity it is assumed that the capitalists advance consumption goods to their workers *in natura* so that the workers take no direct part in commodity exchanges.

(2) buy commodities priced at:

	I	II	III
	—	—	$115\frac{5}{13}$
from $\{$ II	$13\frac{11}{13}$	—	$4\frac{8}{13}$
III	$101\frac{7}{13}$	$18\frac{6}{13}$	—

(3) sell commodities priced at:

	I	II	III
	—	$13\frac{11}{13}$	$101\frac{7}{13}$
to $\{$ II	—	—	$18\frac{6}{13}$
III	$115\frac{5}{13}$	$4\frac{8}{13}$	—

As can be seen, in the case of each group of capitalists the sum of the prices at which commodities are bought is the same as the sum of the prices at which commodities are sold. Table 10 would show a different picture:

The capitalists of Department

I	II	III

(1) hold commodities priced at:

I	II	III
180	180	$57\frac{1}{7}$

(2) buy commodities priced at:

	I	II	III
	—	—	150
from $\{$ II	90	—	30
III	$85\frac{5}{7}$	$57\frac{1}{7}$	—

(3) sell commodities priced at:

	I	II	III
	—	90	$85\frac{5}{7}$
to $\{$ II	—	—	$57\frac{1}{7}$
III	150	30	—

Here the capitalists of Departments I and III would take in less than they pay out, while contrariwise the capitalists of Department II would take in more than twice what they pay out.

The case where $c_2 = 0$ is, however, useful not only for showing up very clearly to what paradoxes Marx's method of converting values into prices leads, it is also very well suited to serve as a starting point for an essential supplement to our previous exposition.

One would be inclined to conclude from the fact that in this particular special case the rate of profit is simply equal to the rate of surplus value, and also from the fact that it is entirely independent of the organic composition of capital in Departments I and III, that the organic composition in these two departments could be of any height without there ensuing a decline in the rate of profit. If this were true, and regardless of its being a special case, one could hardly suppress a strong doubt about the correctness of explaining profit by the principle of "surplus labor."

The truth of the matter, however, is that the share of constant capital in the total investment of Departments I and III cannot exceed a certain limit if the rate of profit in these two departments is also to equal r. If we substitute r for p in equation (11) and take account of equation (4), we get:

$$(1 + r)(c_1 x + v_1 y) = [c_1 + (1 + r)v_1]x$$

from which follow

$$c_1 x r < (1 + r)v_1 x$$

and also

$$c_1 < \frac{1 + r}{r} v_1$$

On the other hand, by reason of equation (1), with $c_2 = 0$, we have

$$c_3 = (1 + r)v_1$$

Let us introduce the new expressions

$$\frac{(1 + r)^2}{r} = \beta \qquad \text{and} \qquad \frac{c_1 + c_3}{c_1 + v_1 + c_3 + v_3} = q'$$

We now have the inequality

(30) $$c_1 + c_3 < \beta v_1$$

Therefore

$$1 + \frac{v_1 + v_3}{c_1 + c_3} > 1 + \frac{v_1 + v_3}{\beta v_1}$$

or

$$\frac{1}{q'} > \frac{(1 + \beta) v_1 + v_3}{\beta v_1}$$

and as a consequence

(31)
$$q' < \frac{\beta v_1}{(1 + \beta) v_1 + v_3}$$

We then have *a fortiori*:

$$q' < \frac{\beta}{1 + \beta}$$

or

(32)
$$q' < \frac{1 + 2r + r^2}{1 + 3r + r^2}$$

The quantity q' is, however, the expression for the organic composition of the combined capitals of Departments I and III. The independence of the rate of profit from the organic composition of the capitals in I and III, in the case where there is no constant capital in II, therefore, does not at all mean that the organic composition of capital in the other two departments can be indefinitely high. The truth of the matter is rather that if the share of constant capital in these departments, the quantity q', exceeds a certain limit, the equalization of the rate of profit becomes impossible.

In order to determine the upper limit for q_0, in other words for the share of constant capital in the total social capital, it is most convenient to start from the inequality (30) which can also be written as follows (with $c_2 = 0$):

$$C < \beta v_1$$

We have

$$q_0 = \frac{C}{C + V}$$

and therefore:

$$(33) \qquad q_0 < \frac{\beta v_1}{\beta v_1 + V}$$

From the relation

$$(34) \qquad \frac{V}{v_2} = 1 + r$$

we get, however,

$$V = v_2 + rv_2$$

and since on the other hand

$$V = v_1 + v_2 + v_3$$

it emerges that:

$$v_1 + v_3 = rv_2$$

and as a consequence

$$v_1 < rv_2$$

If we now substitute rv_2 for v_1 in (33), we get *a fortiori*

$$q_0 < \frac{\beta rv_2}{\beta rv_2 + V}$$

or also, taking account of (34),

$$(35) \qquad q_0 < \frac{1 + r}{2 + r}$$

Hence if the rate of surplus value is 66⅔ percent, as we have assumed in the foregoing examples, then the constant capital invested in Departments I and III can in no case exceed ⅝ of the total social capital.

So much for the case in which $c_2 = 0$, that is to say in which constant capital is absent from Department II.

Likewise if $c_1 = 0$ it is impossible to determine the rate of profit by means of formulas (24) or (25), because here $f_1 = \infty$ and $g_1 = \infty$. If we take equations (11) and (12) as a basis for the determination of ρ or σ, we easily find:

$$(36) \qquad \frac{1}{1 + r} \sigma^2 + f_2 \sigma - g_2 = 0$$

where r, as formerly, signifies the rate of surplus value $\left(\dfrac{s_1}{v_1}\right)$. This last equation can also be derived from equation (23) if one divides its coefficients by g_1. With $c_1 = 0$,

$$\frac{f_1}{g_1} = \frac{v_1}{v_1 + s_1} = \frac{1}{1 + r}$$

It would be entirely wrong to assume from the fact that r appears in (36) and not in (23) that in the case where c_1 is not zero the rate of profit is independent of the rate of surplus value. This is because the quantities g_1 and g_2 depend on r. We have:

$$g_1 = 1 + (1 + r)f_1$$

and

$$g_2 = 1 + (1 + r)f_2$$

If we eliminate the quantities f_1, f_2, g_1, g_2 from equations (23) and (36) by introducing the quantities q_1, q_2, and r, then the following relations emerge:

$$f_1 = \frac{1 - q_1}{q_1}, f_2 = \frac{1 - q_2}{q_2}$$

$$g_1 = \frac{1 + r(1 - q_1)}{q_1}, g_2 = \frac{1 + r(1 - q_2)}{q_2}$$

From this it is at once apparent that the rate of profit depends only on the rate of surplus value (r) and the organic composition of the capitals invested in Departments I and II.

The rate of profit is always smaller than the rate of surplus value, if we abstract from the special case where $c_2 = 0$. This can be proved as follows:

From equation (11) we find

$$c_1x + v_1y < (c_1 + c_2 + c_3)x$$

and, taking account of (4),

$$v_1y < (1 + r)v_1x,$$

from which it follows that

$$x > \frac{y}{1 + r}$$

218   *Appendix*

From equation (12) there thus emerges the inequality:

$$(1+\rho)\left(\frac{c_2 y}{1+r}+v_2 y\right) < (v_1+v_2+v_3)y$$

or, taking account of (9),

$$(1+\rho)\left(\frac{c_2}{1+r}+v_2\right) < c_2+(1+r)v_2$$

and finally

$$1+\rho < 1+r$$

and

(37) $$\rho < r$$

Another upper limit for ρ can be derived from (11) in the following way. We have:

$$(1+\rho)c_1 x < (c_1+c_2+c_3)x$$

and hence

(38) $$\rho < \frac{c_2+c_3}{c_1}$$

This inequality allows us to conclude that with a given rate of surplus value (r) and a given quantity of variable capital (V), an unlimited growth of constant capital cannot take place without bringing about a decline in the rate of profit.

It follows from (4) that:

$$c_2+c_3 = (1+r)v_1$$

and this means that the growth of constant capital in Departments II and III finds a limit in the height of the rate of surplus value and in the size of the total disposable variable capital. It is to be remembered, too, that v_1 forms a part of V.

We could say with equal justification that the growth of constant capital in Departments II and III finds a limit in the quantity of labor which society has at its disposal in a given economic period. Let this quantity be H. Of this h_1 belongs to Department I, h_2 to II, and h_3 to III, so that $H = h_1 + h_2 + h_3$.

Appendix 219

If we designate the quantity of labor contained in one unit of value as η then we have:

$$h_1 = (v_1 + s_1)\eta, \; h_2 = (v_2 + s_2)\eta, \; h_3 = (v_3 + c_3)\eta, \text{ and}$$

$$H = (V + S)\eta$$

We can now write

$$(c_2 + c_3)\eta = h_1$$

and since h_1 is a part of H, it appears that the constant capital invested in Departments II and III, measured in terms of the quantity of (stored-up) labor which it contains, is limited by the quantity of (living) labor which is available for use in production during the relevant economic period.

Nevertheless, so far as the constant capital invested in Department I (c_1) is concerned, one can imagine it as growing indefinitely without disturbing the conditions of economic equilibrium as they find expression in equations (4), (5), and (6). But, as formula (38) shows, sooner or later the consequence of the growth of constant capital in Department I must be a decline in the rate of profit. For the rest, the inequality (38) is valid even in the case where $c_2 = 0$.

It follows from what has been said that it would be entirely incorrect to state in opposition to Marx that the rate of profit does not depend in general on the organic composition of the total social capital. The simple relation between ρ and q_0 with which Marx operates—see equation (27)—does not exist, and cases can be constructed in which, with a given rate of surplus value (r), the rate of profit (ρ) remains unchanged although q_0 takes on different values, just as cases are possible in which ρ assumes different values although q_0 remains unchanged. But— and this should not be overlooked—such cases are based on the supposition that the organic composition of capital is different in the three departments. If, on the other hand, the condition $q_1 = q_2 = q_3$ is fulfilled, then values and prices are identical and formula (27) comes into force.

This last remark cannot serve to excuse Marx. For if the con-

Appendix

dition which would validate formula (27) is fulfilled, then the entire operation of converting values into prices is pointless, while Marx makes use of this formula precisely in connection with this operation.

The above remark is directed only against the criticism which holds that, regardless of whether the quantities q_1, q_2, and q_3 are equal or not, the Marxian thesis of the influence of the organic composition of the total social capital on the height of the rate of profit, as this thesis finds expression in formula (27), is false.

Tugan-Baranowsky in particular makes this mistake. The two numerical examples with which he tries to refute the Marxian thesis are precisely characterized by the assumption that the organic composition of capital is equal in all three departments, in other words that $q_1 = q_2 = q_3 = q_0$.

In one example,[1] r (the rate of surplus value) falls from 1 to $\frac{7}{9}$, while at the same time q_0 increases from $\frac{2}{3}$ to $\frac{20}{29}$, from which it emerges, entirely in keeping with formula (27), that ρ (the rate of profit) declines from $\frac{1}{3}$ to $\frac{7}{29}$.[2]

In the other example,[3] r rises from 1 to $\frac{81}{44}$, while at the same time q_0 increases from $\frac{2}{3}$ to $\frac{25}{36}$, from which, once again in keeping with formula (27), ρ increases from $\frac{1}{3}$ to $\frac{9}{16}$.

Tugan-Baranowsky concludes from the fact that in the one case a growth in the share of constant capital accompanies a fall and in the other case a rise in the rate of profit, that the general

[1] *Op. cit.*, p. 177.
[2] By q_0 I always understand the relation of the *value* of variable capital to the *value* of the total capital, while in Tugan-Baranowsky's examples it is a question of *price* expressions. In the place of q_0, which equals $\frac{C}{C+V}$, there thus appears $\frac{Cx}{Cx+Vy}$. But the latter expression is identical with q_0 if one assumes, as Tugan-Baranowsky does, that the organic composition of capital is identical in all three departments. For in this case we have $x = y$ or alternatively $x = y = 1$.
[3] *Ibid.*, pp. 180-181.

Appendix   221

rate of profit is entirely independent of the organic composition of the social capital, and that therefore the Marxian theory of profit is false.[1]

As though such numerical examples could in any way touch the Marxian theory of the influence of the organic composition of the total social capital on the rate of profit! According to Marx, this influence makes itself felt in the indicated way only if the rate of surplus value remains unchanged.[2]

[1] See the first article in my work "Wertrechnung und Preisrechnung," pp. 48-49.
[2] *Capital*, Vol. III, for example p. 75 and p. 248. The extent to which this limiting condition figures in the Marxian law of the falling rate of profit I have discussed thoroughly in the third article of my work "Wertrechnung und Preisrechnung im Marxschen System."

[3]

[a]

THE ECONOMY AS A CIRCULAR FLOW[1]

WASSILY LEONTIEF

1. A GENERAL SCHEME OF THE CIRCULAR FLOW OF AN ECONOMY

1.1. *Technology and the Economy*

It is astonishing that in spite of all other disagreements, theorists of different persuasions seem to agree on one issue: that the separation between technology and the economy is an essential precondition for economic theorizing. [. . .] For us, on the contrary, both 'technical' and 'economic' facts are established data which are used as a point of departure for further analysis.

[. . .] If one were to investigate the characteristics of the various individual elements in the circular flow of an economy, one would be forced to enlist the aid of a large number of the social and natural sciences. The interconnections which shape all these elements into a unified whole—an economy—are not specifically economic in nature; indeed, they are as varied as the elements themselves, drawn from the realms of physics, biology, psychology, sociology and so on. And if the economic theorist, as opposed to the practitioner, needs no particular knowledge of physics or biology or any other specialist field, this is because he takes the existence of the above mentioned interconnections for granted, seeking no further elucidation. It is also quite possible that within the domain occupied by these other disciplines the necessary specialist research has not yet been carried out: for example, psychology has only in a very limited fashion explained its idea of the laws governing the satisfaction of needs. The economist can set about filling this gap, and in doing so he is acting as a psychologist. [. . .] In methodological terms, all these areas of research [. . .] go well beyond the boundaries of the actual problem under investigation.

1.2. *The Economy as a Circular Flow*

The form of the relationship which exists between the individual elements in any economic process is always [. . .] a causal relationship. In production certain elements are generated by certain other elements and are then themselves used and consumed in further production. The two basic concepts here are costs and returns. *Cost items* (inputs) are those elements whose consumption in production causes the generation of corresponding *return items* (output).[2]

---

[1] Translated by Robert Aylett (Goldsmith's College. London, UK) from the original German article which appeared in *Archiv für Sozialwissenschaft und Sozialpolitik*, Volume 60, 1928, pp. 577–623. This translation omits certain passages; these are indicated by [. . .].

[2] This paragraph has been taken over from a previous section (the Editors).

182 W. LEONTIEF

Economic phenomena are characterized by a multiplicity of causal relationships. For example, there is a variety of inputs which may be used in the production of a particular good, and each good in turn may be used in a variety of ways. [...] This leads to a system of economic interrelationships between economic processes. However, it does not mean that the economic sphere is isolated from other spheres; precisely because of the many-sidedness of economic relationships the interaction with the non-economic sphere will be particularly close.

[...] At this point the concept of a circular flow comes into play as a tool which enables us to identify those causal relationships that are specific to the economic sphere. Circular flow analysis only takes into account those relationships which allow us to return to the initial starting point. [...] For example, in the case of cost items such as used-up coal or worn-out machinery, the principle of the circular flow allows us to follow step by step the entire process of their 'reproduction'.

In visual terms, the system of economic interrelationships may be represented as a long path describing a wide circle and ending up again at its starting point. All along the way, it branches off into numerous smaller paths, some of which interweave in all manner of combinations, whilst others lead off into the non-economic sphere. The researcher, however, will only be interested in those paths which contribute towards a complete circuit.

In this manner we are offered the chance of avoiding the gulf between 'technological' and 'economic' approaches. The two approaches are indeed not mutually exclusive: they share an intimate relationship, since we must understand the objective technological framework before we can begin to construct a theory of the economic system.

1.3. *Technical Coefficients*

Every production process is determined in two ways: qualitatively in terms of the nature of its inputs and outputs, and quantitatively in terms of the numerical proportions between these items. An unambiguous *qualitative* description of the various input and output items can be obtained easily by using a careful terminology. Once a particular production process is qualitatively described in terms of its input and output items, the quantitative proportions between these items may be described in a wide variety of ways. To us it seems that a combination of the following ratios—technical coefficients—would provide the best solution:

(i) *Cost coefficients.* For each individual input, we form the ratio between the number of units of that input used in the given production process, on the one hand, and the number of units of some specified other input (or cost group), on the other hand. Normally, it is not an individual cost group which is used as the denominator, but the output. However, this ratio is useless for our purposes, since it is dependent on the level of productivity, for which we have to introduce an independent indicator.

(ii) *Productivity coefficients*. This coefficient identifies the quantitative relation between costs and returns. We form the ratio between the number of units of total output and the number of units of some specified kind of input (or cost group).

(iii) *Coefficients of distribution*. This coefficient indicates the distribution of total output between the various uses in the circular flow. For each kind of output and each individual production process, we form the ratio between the number of units of that output used in the given process, on the one hand, and the total number of units of that output on the other.

We are not concerned with the *absolute* size of our technical coefficients, and hence it does not matter what kind of cost item is selected as the denominator in calculating the first two of the coefficients. Suppose for example that 4 units of item 2 and 10 units of item 3 are used in producing 6 units of item 1. Select group 2 as our denominator. Then the cost coefficient of item 2 is 1 and that of item 3 is 2.5. The productivity coefficient is 1.5. Suppose further that item 1 is used by two production processes, and that the total output of that item is distributed in such a way that 2 units are used in the first process and 6 units in the second; then the corresponding coefficients of distribution will be 1/3 and 2/3.

1.4. *New Combinations*

Thus far, we have considered the circular flow as a process of rotation which is eternally repeated. Let us now examine the possibilities for change which are contained in the circular flow. Here we are not concerned with any sort of driving force or prime mover, but merely with the formal conditions for economic change.

If the circular flow were to represent a 'technically' closed system, then of course no change of any sort would be possible. It would represent a sort of *perpetuum mobile* which, having been set in motion, would endlessly repeat its regular movement. But in reality the economic process is only a fragment of a much larger system of events, and as such, its nature may well be changed by the addition of new elements or the elimination of old elements.

It is customary to pigeon-hole technical change under the label 'new combinations'. In itself, this term is not wrong, but it is so vague that it would be better to say nothing at all. Suppose, for example, that the combination of three looms, one worker, and a certain quantity of cotton produces a certain amount of yarn. If one uses better machines which produce less waste but otherwise use the same combination of inputs, a greater quantity of yarn can be manufactured. A technical change has taken place, but the combination remains the same: three looms, one worker, and the given quantity of raw material. One could be tempted to think that this counter-example is merely due to a misunderstanding of the terminology, and that in fact a new combination has taken place, namely concerning the production factor 'machinery'. And, indeed, if we 'break down' the new machines into their cost elements we will probably find that they have been produced with a different set of inputs than the old machines.

We can see from this example that a given 'new combination' may only be identified at a particular level of conceptual refinement. But we have shown above that the very existence of the subject 'economics' relies on the fact that the elements of the analysis are still broad enough to enable us to capture a multiplicity of causal relationships between such elements. Once we overstep this mark, the various causal chains fall apart and with them the object of economic theory. The lower the level at which the new combination appears, the finer the net of technical coefficients must be cast in order to capture and identify it. But, as we have seen, economic dissection can follow the 'technological' dissection only up to certain limits. If the change we are seeking to identify lies beyond those limits, then any new combination which may be present can no longer be identified as an economic phenomenon. [. . .]

2. THE ELEMENTARY SCHEME OF THE CIRCULAR FLOW OF AN ECONOMY

In order to conduct a rigorous analysis, we must first establish more precisely what we mean by the notion of a 'circular flow'. Let us imagine the economic process as a closed causal chain. Between any two neighbouring elements in the chain—where one may be seen as a cause, the other as its immediate effect—there lies a distinct, if infinitely small time interval. Let us call this the *elementary period of production*. During this short interval a certain quantity of specific economic items is produced and consumed at every *stage of the production process*: these quantities are also infinitely small. Let us call them the *elementary incomes* or *elementary costs*. If a relationship is established between these infinitely small flows, then finite ratios may be derived with which calculations may easily be performed.

Out of all the elementary concepts—periods of production, elementary costs, elementary incomes—only the period of production is the same across all production processes. Therefore it would seem the most practical approach to define it as the *unit period* and to relate all the various elementary costs and incomes to this unit period. (If as our discourse continues we operate with absolute numbers, we only do so for the sake of simplicity.)

Two other concepts must be taken into consideration. First there is the shortest path, measured in periods of production, which any item would have to follow in order to describe a full cycle in our circular flow—starting from any one point and proceeding along one of the many potential production paths before returning to the starting point. This we shall call the '*shortest reproduction period*'.

However, the item might follow numerous other paths, since the production system has numerous branches. The longest of these paths we shall call the '*longest reproduction period*'. Naturally, at no point may the same path be

THE ECONOMY AS A CIRCULAR FLOW   185

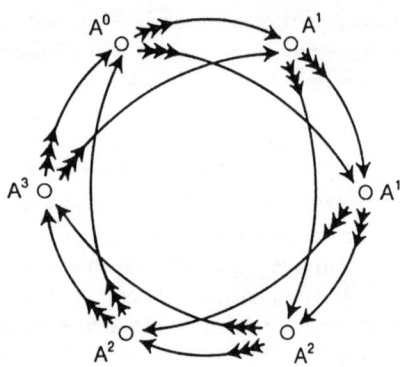

Fig. 1.

followed twice, even for the shortest period of time. There is, of course, no need to assume that all goods have reproduction periods of the same length.

This scheme will help us examine the entire network of the circular flow with particular reference to any element 'A' within the system. We may then sub-divide other elements into groups—depending on their distance from point 'A' of production; that distance is measured by the number of unit periods following the direction of production. Each of these elements may then be defined by that measure of distance. For example: all items whose distance in the production flow from point 'A' is equal to one unit period, i.e. all those where element 'A' is consumed as a cost element, may be labelled as group 'A^1'. Points in the next group are then called 'A^2', and so on (see Fig. 1).

Similar systems may be set up for all individual items in the circular flow. If one were to express in one single formula all the relative positions, considered from all possible vantage points, which any individual item obtains, this formula would describe, uniquely and exhaustively, the position of that element within the circular flow.

The formula cannot simply be reversed, as the distances may only be defined for a certain direction: however, it is permissible to introduce the notion of negative distances, whereby 'A^{-1}', for example, would describe all the cost elements of 'A^0'.

2.1. *Stages of Production*

The production network within the circular flow system may be structured either in an integrated fashion, so that in the final analysis the reproduction of each individual element is directly or indirectly dependent on the simultaneous independent existence of all the other elements, or it may be seen as a composite structure, in which the whole consists of several independently reproduceable groups, of which each (directly or indirectly) satisfies the conditions for producing the others, and thus satisfies the conditions for its own reproduction. In this latter

186   W. LEONTIEF

case we are really talking about several wholly identical reproduction systems, which exist alongside each other but are separated by a phase difference.

Let us take, by way of example, the following four-stage system:

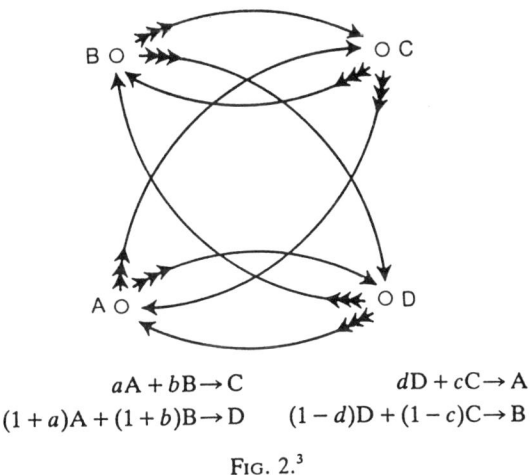

$$aA + bB \rightarrow C \qquad\qquad dD + cC \rightarrow A$$
$$(1 + a)A + (1 + b)B \rightarrow D \qquad (1 - d)D + (1 - c)C \rightarrow B$$

FIG. 2.[3]

Here, the elements A and B, on the one hand, and C and D on the other hand form the independently reproducible groups. Thus we are really talking about the duplication of the cycle $(A + B) \rightarrow (C + D) \rightarrow (A + B) \rightarrow (C + D)$, etc., together with a phasing element which means that $(A + B)$ and $(C + D)$ exist simultaneously.

The independent elementary groups A, B and C, D may be designated as different production stages.[4] Of course, each production stage of this kind may represent a highly complex system in itself.

2.2. *Three Phases of a Local Decline in Productivity*

Using our basic circular flow scheme we can now analyse the effects of a local decline in productivity. The whole process may be divided into individual periods of production:

Period 0—where simple reproduction still takes place without variations occurring.

---

[3] a and $(1 - a)$, b and $(1 - b)$, c and $(1 - c)$, d and $(1 - d)$ are the coefficients of distribution of A, B, C and D. Individual economic elements appear in the form of specific units which cannot be subjected to division and thus represent the lowest limit of all technical coefficients. On this subject see our essay 'Ueber die Theorie und Statistik der Konzentration' in *Jahrbücher für Nationalökonomie und Statistik*, Volume 126, p. 301).

[4] We are using the term production stage deliberately. In principle, our use of the term corresponds wholly to what is normally understood by the term. Of course, one always thinks when using it of a one-sided state of affairs. However, this is only because one is not looking at the entire circle, but just at a segment of it.

Period 1—at stage 'A^0' productivity falls by $1/n$ of its previous level. The following state of affairs is produced: at all stages in the first group which obtain their intermediate inputs from 'A^0', the consumption of 'A' is $1/n$ less than in Period 0. Everything else remains as in period 0.

Period 2—at stage A^0 output remains at the level of period 1, as the supply of intermediate inputs remains the same as in period 0. At the various stages of production in the first zone output will fall by $1/n$ as a result of the decreased supply of intermediate inputs. At the same time, $1/n$ of the complementary elements, which are consumed here alongside the output of A^0, remain unconsumed.

Period 3—at stage A^0 and in group A^1 everything remains unchanged. The changes which occur in the previous period in the first group are repeated in group A^2.

The changes proceed in this manner until a second phase of change develops. We have already seen that apart from a gradual effect on groups A^1, A^2 and A^3 of the original decline in productivity at stage A^0, the consumption of all other complementary elements declines in proportion to the consumption of element A. But insofar as the points of production of these elements have not been reached by the reverberation of declining production elsewhere in the system, there arises an unusable excess production of these elements. However, these production stages will in turn receive a shortened ration of intermediate inputs. Output will fall. The excess production disappears.

In schematic terms, the process may be represented as follows: A^0 is the starting point for the change, A^p and $(A^{p-1})A^q$ two other stages of production. The indices p, q and $p - 1$ describe the relationships between these three elements. If $p > q$, then, since the position of the third group vis-a-vis the second is indicated by the index (-1), $p - 1$ must equal q. In this case they are two successive groups of A^0. However, if $p < q$, we are presented with the case described above. The decline in consumption of $(A^{p-1})A^q$ will occur in Period P, and the resulting excess production will last $(q - p)$ periods, until it is balanced out in the Period Q by a corresponding shortfall in output.

Period 4—Now comes the fourth phase. It is characterized by the fact that the reverberations of a fall in output return to the same points in the productive system via the shortest route. The individual parts of the system are affected by this phenomenon at quite different times. Whilst some stages of production have hardly begun to be touched by the first consequences of the primary decline in productivity, others may already have experienced a second decline in output.

As time goes on, this phase difference becomes greater. If the distances between two stages of production and the starting point of the entire movement are equal to K^1 and K^2, and their shortest reproduction periods are equal to M^1 and M^2, respectively, then in V periods following the primary decline in productivity the following phase difference D will be produced between them:

$$\left(1 + \frac{V - K^1}{M^1}\right) - \left(1 + \frac{V - K^2}{M^2}\right) = \mathrm{D}$$

188 W. LEONTIEF

or

$$\frac{V(M^2 - M^1) + (I - M^2)K^2M^1 - (I - M^1)K^1M^2}{M^1M^2} = D.$$

It is evident that the greater V is, the greater D is.

However, after a sufficient number of periods, the relative differences in output caused by a phase difference of this sort begin to decline steadily. Where the primary shortfall in productivity equals $1/n$, this latter decline may be expressed by the formula:

$$\left(1 - \frac{1}{n}\right)\frac{V + 1 - M^1 + K^1}{M^1} - \left(1 - \frac{1}{n}\right)\frac{V + 1 - M^2 + K^2}{M^2}$$

2.3. *Local Increase in Productivity*

Where cost coefficients remain unchanged in the first group, a local increase in productivity effects no change in the circular flow system—by contrast to the case where there is a decline in productivity. The additional output produced by the increase in productivity finds no practical application if the supply of complementary elements remains constant. It remains outside the circular flow system.

2.4. *Changes in Cost Coefficients*

We can now turn our attention to the second kind of quantitative change—the altering of the cost coefficients.

If the cost coefficient of an element in group A^{-1} at production stage A^0 increases by $1/n$, the output at A^0 will be restricted by $1/n$, since, given the new distribution of costs, supplies from stage A^{-1} geared to the previous scale of production will no longer be adequate. At the same time, on the other hand, $1/n$ of all other elements in group A^{-1} will find no practical use. Of course, the fall in output at stage A^0 will necessarily have the same effects as in the case of a simple decline in productivity.

In the opposite case—if the cost coefficient of an element decreases—output will remain unchanged, but $1/n$ of the relevant intermediate inputs will be rendered surplus. This phenomenon may be attributed to the now familiar effects of local overproduction.

2.5. *Changes in the Distribution Coefficients*

A local change in distribution coefficients must, in the final analysis, make itself felt in the form of underproduction at those production stages suffering from reduced supplies, and in the form of overproduction in those stages favourably affected by its repercussions.

2.6. *Combined Changes*

We now need to investigate the effects of combined elementary quantitative changes. The effects of changes in the same direction (i.e. only positive or only negative) may simply be added together. Changes in opposite directions, on the other hand, must be offset against each other. In this context it is easily established that a full compensation is only possible between opposing changes of differing types; changes of the same type, even with opposite signs, can never wholly offset one another.

Any change in productivity at stage A^0 may be compensated for in group A^1 by a counterbalancing change in cost coefficients. Opposing changes of the same type, however, can only offset one another in the context of a corresponding change in distribution coefficients.

In the wake of a local increase in productivity the balance of the circular flow system can never be fully restored by redistribution; however, it is possible by using relatively small changes temporarily to delay acute overproduction.

A simple example may serve to explain this state of affairs. Let us imagine an economic system consisting of three elements, which are initially produced in the quantities A, B and C. Production follows the formula:

$$\tfrac{1}{2}B + \tfrac{1}{2}C \rightarrow A$$
$$\tfrac{1}{2}A + \tfrac{1}{2}C \rightarrow B$$
$$\tfrac{1}{2}A + \tfrac{1}{2}B \rightarrow C$$

Now let us assume that at juncture 0 the output of A rises by 1/10; we will proceed to draw up a scheme to represent the corresponding changes in distribution. It should be pointed out that the circular image we have used up to now will hardly suffice to give a picture of the situation, so we will use the following tabulation:

Period	Output A	Consumption of A relative to production of		Output of B	Consumption of B relative to production of		Output of C	Consumption of C relative to production of	
		B	C		A	C		A	B
−1	1	0.5	0.5	1	0.5	0.5	1	0.5	0.5
0	1.1	0.55	0.55	1	0.45	0.55	1	0.45	0.55
+1	0.99	0.495	0.495	1.1	0.605	0.495	1.1	0.605	0.495
+2	1.331	0.6655	0.6655	0.99	0.3245	0.6655	0.99	0.3245	0.6655
+3	0.7139	0.30645	0.30645	1.331	1.02455	0.30645	1.331	1.02455	0.30645
+4	2.25301			0.7139			0.7139		

One can see that in the wake of the assumed increase in production the circular flow system does not undergo a regular change, but behaves in a pendulum fashion. The swing from one period of production to the next increases in a constant manner, with the result that it becomes impossible fully to utilize the goods resulting from the increase in production. The speed with which this 'absolute disproportionality' manifests itself depends on the magnitude of the original change in productivity. In our example it occurs in the fourth period of production. Given an increase in productivity of 50%, overproduction becomes impossible to avoid after two periods. However, where there is a 1% increase in productivity, overproduction will not manifest itself until the 10th period.

190 W. LEONTIEF

In the case of a decline in productivity, the whole process follows an analogous course.

2.7. *Qualitative Changes*

Qualitative changes, like quantitative changes, may also be divided into positive and negative: the appearance of new kinds of economic elements and the disappearance of old kinds.

Let us once again take an elementary example. At a certain stage in the circular flow system, and without any change in cost, a new product 2 has been produced to replace an old product 1. If the new elements constituting 2 fail to match the requirements at the various stages in the next group, then this amounts to a decrease in productivity at the starting point, to zero. The circle is completely destroyed, just as if instead of 1 nothing at all had been produced.

If the composition of intermediate inputs at any one stage of production changes in such a way that one element disappears, or indeed several elements disappear, a corresponding overproduction arises of the now unusable goods. One may see, then, that the effects of any local qualitative change manifest themselves in a corresponding quantitative shift.

2.8. *The Total Picture of Economic Change*

Now that we have familiarized ourselves with the individual elements of economic change, let us attempt to gain an overall view of a changing circular flow system. The opportunites for technical change, as we have mentioned, are assumed to remain limitless.

The precise question we must ask is the following: which sort of changes in the technical data of an economic process preserve the characteristics of a circular flow system? What we have to do is create, *ex definitione,* a complete scheme for defining economic change.

2.9. *Steady Changes*

Firstly, in accordance with our basic assumptions, we must eliminate all those sequences of change which do not correspond to our principle of reproduction. But we do have a type of circular flow system which wholly satisfies our basic assumptions, and yet can manifest steady changes.

We came across a system of this sort when we were analysing a local decline in productivity. Given unchanging cost components and the presence of unchanging elements, total output is in a process of steady decline from one period of production to the next. The counterbalance to this regressive change is formed by an analogous progressive development. Of course the latter, as we have seen, cannot be brought about by a local increase in productivity, but only by a simultaneous proportional productivity increase in all stages of the cycle.

This image of a steady and uniform kind of development may easily be conceived of as forming a special case of the steadily uniform circular flow system, thus:

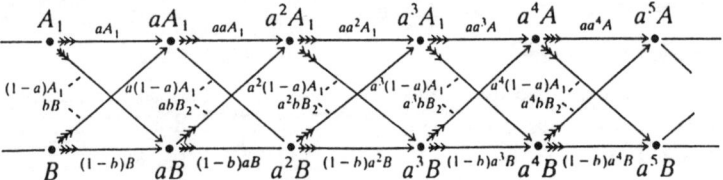

Where $a = 1$ development is steady and unchanging. Where $a < 1$ and $a > 1$ we see regressive and progressive change respectively.

2.10. *Irregular Change*

Absolutely irregular change may be conceived of as a situation where one varies particular elements in a process of reproduction and leaves others unchanged, then leaves the new elements unchanged while subjecting the old ones to change. Where step-by-step changes of this sort occur, the repetition of the same elements in all neighbouring periods of production preserves the circular flow principle; yet in the long run limitless possibilities for change are presented.

However, this apparently so arbitrary scheme also corresponds to the 'practical', unprejudiced way of seeing things. If one wishes to see the economy as a rational, planned activity, then any change must of necessity be linked to a partial repetition. It is precisely from this 'practical' point of view that continuous and constant change in the economic process becomes quite inconceivable—since an endless and continuous process like the economic process can, rationally and consciously, only be structured and managed as a process of constant repetition. Any new element appears as a new means to reach an old goal. A new machine produces 'old' goods. And even if the latter prove to be new, they are in their turn used for the old established purpose. No matter how long a detour may be, it must ultimately lead back to the old path. Subsequently, the new can in turn become a fixed point. But precisely because of this state of affairs it must of necessity repeat itself.

2.11. *Cost Substitution*

Up to now we have examined the circular flow of an economy as represented in our elementary scheme. But a closer examination of its elements shows that it only represents a certain marginal case. The cost–output relationship, as indeed any other notion of a causal relationship, exhibits a certain degree of latitude.

What are the costs involved in producing 100 lbs of bread? Exhaustive knowledge of the circumstances might produce many quite differing answers to this question, all of which are right. One analysis might refer to so much dough plus so much coal and so much work on the part of the baker; another to so much flour, yeast, water and coal; a third, equally impeccable analysis, might even refer to so much seed, fertilizer, agricultural machinery, so much coal-bearing land and so on.

192 W. LEONTIEF

Any preceding link in a causal chain may be seen as the cause of the subsequent link. Accordingly, we may modify our scheme in any direction we choose. The circular flow system originally consisting of four elements might, for example, be reduced to three elements:[5]

$$4_3^{n-1} + 1_4^{n-1} \rightarrow 15_1^n \qquad 4_1^{n-1} + 2_2^{n-1} \rightarrow 10_3^n$$

$$8_1^{n-1} + 12_4^{n-1} \rightarrow 4_2^n \qquad 3_1^{n-1} + 2_2^{n-1} + 6_3 \rightarrow 13_4^n.$$

Let us replace 1_2 by its cost $(2_1 + 3_4)$

$$4_3^{n-1} + 1_4^{n-1} \rightarrow 15_1^n$$
$$4_1^{n-1} + (4_1 + 6_4)^{n-2} \rightarrow 10_3^n$$
$$3_1^{n-1} + (4_1 + 6_4)^{n-2} + 6_3 \rightarrow 13_4^n.$$

In a similar fashion one might be able to eliminate a second element.[6]

This gives rise to a new form of cost composition, where the individual elements not only differ qualitatively and quantitatively, but also in terms of their respective positions in the sequence of successive periods of production. Our new, reduced scheme contains, for example, not only single production periods but also double periods. This must also be taken into account in drawing up group distributions.

A change in the point which has been eliminated can only express itself indirectly in this new scheme. The process which allowed itself to be portrayed quickly and simply in our first scheme could only be reflected here in a highly complex fashion.

2.12. *'Capital Goods'*

It one takes into consideration the economic elements present at the end of period $(n-1)$, we have first of all the output from this period, equal to 15_1, 10_4 and 13_3. In addition, we have 8_1 and 12_4, which were indeed produced in the period $(n-2)$ but did not become usable until the point 'n' in time; in the meantime, according to our abbreviated mode of representation, they stand outside the flow. Let us call these elements 'capital goods'.

The notion of capital in this sense, then, is neither a specific nor a general characteristic nor indeed any kind of feature pertaining to individual economic elements: it is merely an expression of a particular method of conception—or rather calculation. The size of the 'capital reserve' increases in proportion to the number of points of production substituted by their corresponding cost elements.

---

[5] Superscripts refer to time differentials, subscripts to various forms of economic elements.

[6] The limits for possible substitution are set by the qualitative cost make-up of the last of the substituted elements. In our example, no single cost group comprises less than two complementary kinds of goods. Since the example contains a total of four points of production, no more than two may be eliminated.

No especial proof is necessary of the fact that the entire process must be carried out on the basis of the production scheme in force at any one moment. In this, we are not concerned with the real genesis of individual elements, which has perhaps been effected by technical changes.

2.13. *Buffer Stocks*

We are by now familiar with changes in technical coefficients and with the formal conditions for combining these basic elements. We now know, however, that the last elements in the economic system are not absolutely simple elements; correspondingly, their mutual interrelationships cannot possess the absolute constancy of truly 'final' relationships. Thus the constant technical coefficients which we have investigated are, strictly speaking, only average values around which real individual cases oscillate. If that is so, the smooth running of the economic process can only be conceived in the way that at every point of production there is a certain amount of buffer stocks capable of balancing out any deviations in the cost coefficients or productivity coefficients. The volume of these 'buffer stocks' depends on the magnitude of the chance fluctuations and the time they take to balance each other out. Since, however, it is impossible to distinguish absolutely between chance and non-chance changes, one can only view these buffer stocks as economic elements with a limited degree of probability.

There is no need to go through the entire argument that the periodically returning but non-chance technical changes (changes whose causes are known, in other words), also need buffer stocks of this sort, in the same way as chance changes do. (For more details about 'buffer stocks' see pp. 205–208).

2.14. *Excursus: The Proportions of Exchange*

The circular flow of an economy is determined down to the finest detail by inherent laws of cost. But these are insufficient where the economy is organized on an exchange basis: for now a second phenomenon is lined up alongside the by now familiar relations of production: those of exchange.

2.15. *General and Specific Exchange*

In both cases the goods in question are really the same: items of output on the one hand and the corresponding cost items on the other. If the exchange process were organized in such a way that all producers stockpiled their products to be exchanged and then proceeded to select the input items they needed—and this image is frequently used to portray the course of social exchange—no particular problem would arise. The exchange would simply embody the by now familiar cost–return relationship. In reality, the offsetting of costs against returns is not general in nature, but quite specific: the items are not set off against each other in large groups, as in the production process, but in pairs. The final outcome of the exchange is the same in the case of both general and specific exchange: it is achieved, though, by differing means.

2.16. *Underdetermined Exchange Equations*

Without analysing the foundations of and the innermost reasoning behind any particular formulation of the exchange relationship, let us examine the general conditions which must be fulfilled within the framework of a circular flow. The precise problem is as follows:

194   W. LEONTIEF

The total output, i.e. the sum of the individual intermediate outputs from all stages of production within a single production period, is distributed over individual spheres of ownership in such a manner that further production cannot take place within individual stages of production. A redistribution must take place by means of specific acts of exchange: this will assemble into cost groups complying with the existing cost structure all those goods needed to continue the circular flow. The question arises of which exchange proportion will enable this grouping to take place.

To simplify things, let us assume that the original distribution of ownership corresponds to the qualitative classification of the output, i.e. that the output of each individual product forms an independently owned group of goods. We need at this juncture to introduce the concept of value in order to provide a comprehensive algebraic view of this argument. This does not imply the introduction of any new characteristic inherent in these goods—but rather the introduction of an exchange relation deduced from all the relationships we have analysed thus far.

We have assumed a system containing two elements which stand in the following production relationship to each other:

$$aA + bB \rightarrow A,$$
$$(1 - a)A + (1 - b)B \rightarrow B.$$

The two original groups of goods under different ownership are assumed to correspond to the output items, which are qualitatively different from each other.

Groups of input items may be expressed by the following general formula:

$$k(aA + bB) \quad \text{and} \quad m[(1 - a)A + (1 - bB)],$$

where the coefficients of ownership, k and m, may assume any value between 0 and 1.

The two general exchange formulae are thus as follows:

$$Ap_1 = k(aAp_1 + bBp_2) + m[(1 - a)Ap_1 + (1 - b)Bp_2],$$
$$Bp_2 = l(aAp_1 + bBp_2) + r[(1 - a)Ap_1 + (1 - b)Bp_2]. \tag{I}$$

Of the two prices p_1 and p_2, the one may immediately be set at 1, as we are only dealing with a ratio.

On the other hand

$$k + l = 1$$
$$m + r = 1. \tag{II}$$

We are presented with four equations and five unknowns. No clear resolution of this problem is possible. One may vary at will the exchange proportions and consequently the distribution relationships of the goods without affecting the circular flow of the economy in any way. Seen from this point of view, any particular system of price relationships is a merely accidental phenomenon.

2.17. *Income from Ownership*

From the above one may see that an unambiguous solution to the problem of exchange lies outside the scope of our previous conceptual parameters. All the factors which find immediate expression in the form of technical coefficients have already been used in our calculations. The problem will have to be viewed from another angle.

Among the various factors which determine this or that cost structure, there are, as we have said, social agents which coexist alongside all the possible natural data. Up to now, it has been possible to see these, like all the other factors, as exogenously given facts, without any need for further investigation.

But now, in the realm of income exchange analysis, one of these initial conditions—namely the distribution of ownership—comes under direct scrutiny. Of course, its indirect effect on the cost structure still remains. Thus a thorough analysis of the relationship between distribution of income and its effect on the existing technical coefficients becomes necessary if one is to gain a complete understanding of exchange relationships. This effect consists in the fact that the income phenomenon corresponds to a particular kind of cost element, the so-called income from ownership. (On income as cost element see p. 208–209)

2.18. *A Simple Exchange Economy without Profits*

The close relationship between the value problem and the problem of income from ownership becomes particularly clear when one takes into account that a hypothetical system of exchange without income from ownership is wholly lacking in any 'necessary' price system.

Let us imagine the production of two types of commodities, e.g. 'consumption goods' and 'production goods' (so-called 'capital goods'). In a given exchange relationship—established according to quite arbitrary price relationships—each of the two production branches belongs to a particular 'owner'.

If, however, prices are altered, one of the two (owners) will be able to exchange fewer cost items than previously, and thus fewer of his personally owned goods, which he requires to produce his own capacity to work. Simply as an owner, he would receive no income in a simple 'profitless' economy.

The other owner, however, who has benefited from the change in prices, will now be in a position to widen his customary purchases of cost goods. If the capital goods producer is thus affected, he will not only acquire capital goods as cost elements, but also that proportion of the elements necessary for the production of consumed goods which the other owner has not been able to purchase because of his loss of purchasing power. Accordingly, a proportion of consumer goods production will come under the ownership and control of the capital goods producer. At the same time, the partially under-utilized work capacity of the consumer goods producer, who has been adversely affected by the price change, will be used in the same 'branch', but under different ownership. His personal income will remain the same as before the price change. In this case, there would be absolutely no vested interest in any particular pricing system, and thus absolutely no equilibrium position in the price system.

196 W. LEONTIEF

2.19. *The Second Value Equation*

In the general circular flow scheme, income from ownership is of course considered alongside other cost items without the slightest direct reference to how it originates (the phenomenon of ownership). It is the task of interest theory to investigate these fundamental relationships.

We cannot involve ourselves here in this specialist area; we simply wish to anticipate the result relevant to the theory of exchange—which is the tendency to attribute the same value to cost items in a given ownership group and the output items produced from them.

This phenomenon may lead us to extend our system of comparisons. In order to avoid unnecessarily complicated calculations, let us examine the familiar elementary case of a two-branch circular flow system.

In this pattern, the first group of exchange equations is as follows:

$$Ap_1 = k(aAp_1 + bBp_2) + m[(1-a)Ap_1 + (1-b)Bp_2],$$
$$Bp_2 = (1-k)(aAp_1 + bBp_2) + (1-m)[(1-a)Ap_1 + (1-b)Bp_2)]. \qquad \text{(III)}$$

Two new equations now come into consideration, both drawn up on the basis of the above-mentioned principle;

$$Ap_1 = kAp_1 + mBp_2$$
$$Bp_2 = (1-k)Ap_1 + (1-m)Bp_2 \qquad p_2 = 1. \qquad \text{(IV)}$$

In order to ascertain the exchange proportion, the entire equation must be solved for p_1. In this process, in each pair of equations one equation must remain the same, since to proceed otherwise would ultimately produce an identity. Let us then take the two following formulae:

$$Ap_1 = k(aAp_1 + bB) + m[(1-a)Ap_1 + (1-b)B]. \qquad \text{(III}_1, \text{I)}$$
$$Ap_1 = kAp_1 + mB. \qquad \text{(IV}_1, \text{I)}$$

Hence it follows that:

$$k(aAp_1 + bB) + m[(1-a)Ap_1 + (1-b)B] = kAp_1 + mB \qquad \text{(V)}$$

or:

$$(k-m)(aAp_1 + bB - Ap_1) = 0$$

It follows from this that either $(k-m) = 0$ or $aAp + bB - Ap = 0$. The first solution $(k = m)$ means that the individual branches of production are distributed proportionally across the two ownership groups. In this case there is no stimulus towards exchange. The corresponding value of p_1 does not come into question as an exchange proportion.

There remains the equation $aAp + bB - Ap = 0$. This formula implies that the value of an item and that of its costs are the same. But this is the 'law of value' of the so-called objective value theory. This law of costs plays almost the same role in value theory as quantity theory plays in monetary theory. The functional relationship expressed in the formula is recognized by all theories. The disagreements are all the more animated, then, as to which element should be ascribed the determining function.

At this point, where we are discussing the circular flow problem, it would seem relevant to break down this proposition into its two components—the first and second kinds of exchange equations—and to separate the circular flow element from the other, which one might perhaps designate the 'value principle'.

2.20. *The Exchange Proportion in a Changing Circular Flow*

The same equations can be used in a changing system of circular flow as in the case of steady reproduction. Let us assume, for example, that in the period following the period of production just examined there is produced at stage 2 a new item, which then goes on to fit in and link up with other items in the production chain.

Let the new production formula be:

$$aA + bB \rightarrow A \qquad \text{and later:} \qquad aA + cC \rightarrow A$$
$$(1-a)A + (1-b)B \rightarrow C \qquad\qquad (1-a)A + (1-c)C \rightarrow C.$$

In the third period of production, the new element will be used to reproduce iteslf and to produce item 1. In this process, two new and unknown prices come to light—that of the new product and that of the old item 1, now produced with new cost coefficients.

For the sake of brevity, let us assume that the price of item 1 is unknown as early as in period 2: this will make any separate proofs for the following periods redundant.

The first pair of equations, deriving from formula (IV), is as follows:

$$kAp_1 + mB = l(aAp_1 + bB) + r[(1-a)Ap_1 + (1-b)B]$$
$$(1-k)Ap_1 + (1-m)B = (1-l)(aAp_1 + bB) + (1-r)[(1-a)Ap_1 + (1-l)B],$$

(VI)

the second:

$$kAp_1 + mB = lAp_3 + rCp_4$$
$$(1-k)Ap_1 + (1-m)B = (1-l)Ap_3 + (1-r)Cp_4.$$

(VII)

The two unknown prices are p_3 and p_4, the new equally unknown ownership coefficients l and r. The prices p_1 and p_2 are known from the preceding period.

As previously, one equation from the first pair must be eliminated. On the other hand, the other two may be used together, since their sum does not produce an identity, by contrast to the situation where there is steady production. We now have three equations with four unknowns—and yet there is a clear solution for p_3 and p_4.

$(kAp + mB)$ and $[(1-k)Ap_1 + (1-m)B]$ can, for the sake of simplicity, and in line with equation (II), be replaced by Ap_1 and B.

Let us call $(aAp + bB)$ 'x' and $[(1-a)Ap_1 + (1-b)B]$ 'y'.

From (VII) it follows that:

$$(1-l)rCp_4 - (1-l)Ap_1 = l(1-r)Cp_4 - lB,$$

or

$$rCp_4 - Ap_1 + lAp_1 = 1Cp_4 - lB.$$

$$P_4 = \frac{Ap_1 - lAp_1 - lB}{rC - lC}.$$

(VIII)

198   W. LEONTIEF

From (VI) we get: $Ap_1 = lx + ry$ or

$$l = \frac{Ap_1 - ry}{x}. \tag{IX}$$

From (VIII) and (IX) it follows:

$$P_4 \frac{Ap_1 \dfrac{Ap_1(Ap_1 - ry)}{x} - \dfrac{B(Ap - ry)}{x}}{C\left[r - \dfrac{(Ap_1 - ry)}{x}\right]} = \frac{Ap_1 x - (Ap + B)(Ap - ry)}{C(rx - Ap_1 + ry)}$$

but since $Ap + B = x + y$, then

$$P_4 = \frac{y(rx - Ap_1 + ry)}{C(rx - Ap_1 + ry)} = \frac{y}{C}$$

or

$$P_4 = (1 - a)Ap_1 + (1 - b)B.$$

P_3 may be worked out by the same method.

One sees, then, that the 'cost law' also applies to changing circular flow.

3. AN EMPIRICAL ANALYSIS OF THE CIRCULAR FLOW

Thus far we have familiarized ourselves with economic flow in the form of a cycle built up of elementary cost and income relationships. The object of our analysis has not been the economic process itself, but rather a model of a system of economic flows. Our next task is to undertake the transition from this general scheme to empirical facts. In doing so, we are in no way leaving our high level of abstraction. The new problem is of the same theoretical nature as all the others we have handled up to this juncture.

3.1. *The Empirical Notion of Capital*

The difficulty in making the transition from the realm of schematic constructions to the realm of the circular flow of a real economy lies in the fact that in the former our calculations involved infinitely small time spans and we assumed an exhaustive knowledge of the chain of causes, whereas in the latter neither of these is possible. In the real economic process one may establish any number of points of production with all their relevant technical coefficients—but never all of them, since they are endlessly large in number.

This is where the notion of 'capital' comes to our aid. In our schematic analysis, cost substitution amounted to an unnecessary complication of our elementary portrayal of matters; here, it offers the only means of mastering an endless diversity of concepts by reducing them to as few as one wishes.

As has been indicated, the substitution process consists in directly relating back the output from a chain of production of any length to the initial costs. All intermediate links in the chain are replaced by a capital sum which is equal to the product of the starting costs and the number of substituted intermediate periods.

But since the initial costs ('elementary costs' in our scheme) are equal to the return in one period (in our scheme an 'elementary production period'), the capital sum can be defined as being equal to the sum of the initial costs consumed in the course of the substituted segment of time.

This quantity can be established for each real economic item with practically no further ado. Thus using the concept of capital, one may reduce any economic cycle to as small a number of items as one might wish.

3.2. *Length of the Production Path*

As a consequence of this, the working out of an empirical circular flow scheme must of necessity begin with the establishing of temporal distributions, i.e. of the distances between arbitrarily selected stages.

But here we encounter a significant problem. Individual stages of production may be interconnected by various production paths of differing lengths. The shortest of these is easily established, of course; for as we have seen, the decline in output at any one point spreads via the shortest path, and in principle the measurement of distances is only possible with the aid of an 'experiment' of this nature.[7] But to establish all the other connecting paths one must trace them step by step. If all the endless number of production stages were connected to one another via paths leading in numerous directions, one would be confronted with the same sort of diversity we were able to overcome earlier by using the substitution procedure.

The doctrine of the circular flow only deals with possible forms of the economic process, and thus the question of whether the number of branches on any individual production path really is infinite, or does indeed have a limit, cannot be answered on the basis of any deductive considerations.

However, the structure of the circular flow can never finally be established by empirical means—because of its endless multiplicity, which furthermore is in a constant process of change. Thus one is forced either to adduce other theoretical considerations, which analyse not only the form but also the context of the system, or to content oneself with imperfect empirical knowledge. For a complete evaluation of these 'fragmentary' data the methodology of theory is all the more indispensable.

3.3. *'Structural Research'*

Empirical investigation also obtains its formal structure from theory.

In our analysis of the general scheme of the circular flow we have become familiar with a kind of staged structure in the relationships of reproduction. We have labelled as production stages each of those elementary groups within a scheme of the circular flow which contributes towards the production of all the others. It follows, then, that the distance between the links in one chain of this kind of production stage and those of another similar chain remains constant.

---

[7] Despite external similarities, this 'experiment' is fundamentally different from that which forms the basis of the so-called 'principle of attributing costs', where the 'specific productivity' of a cost factor is established by changing its cost coefficient—a process afflicted by an internal malaise, since 'specific productivity' actually presupposes a certain technical coefficient. In our case, technical coefficients remain unchanged: the consumption of intermediate inputs sinks proportionally.

200 W. LEONTIEF

But since each point of production within a complex system forms part of a production stage, it means that all elements forming part of a single production stage lie within the same group—when compared to any other point in the system—with the result that other, longer production paths simply cannot exist.

Inasmuch as empirical economics is concerned with leaning on theory in order to get to the heart of the way the economic process proceeds, its task must lie in researching the stages structure of the economic cycle.

It seems to us that the now modern 'structural research' really ought to see its task in this light. Two sets of questions may be distinguished: on the one hand, the delineating of various stages of production from each other—one might speak in terms of zonal research—on the other, the establishing of the interrelationships between the elements within one and the same production stage—strictly speaking, knowledge of one single stage of production would suffice. The relation of 'circular flow theory' to 'structural research' would be a typical case of the cooperation between a purely 'nomological' view and an equally pronounced 'idiographic' research method.

For the sake of simplicity, the abovementioned stages forming one and the same stage of production may, of course, be further amalgamated; but for this further substitution properly to reflect the basic relationships, all these stages must be established in advance.

3.4. *'Capitalization'*

The temporal distribution of individual stages of production, no matter how they are established, may be clearly represented by the following formula. By way of example, let us take a circular flow scheme reduced to two points:

$$a\mathrm{A}^{n-K} + b\mathrm{B}^{n-l} \to \mathrm{A}^n$$
$$(1-a)\mathrm{A}^{n-d} + (1-b)\mathrm{B}^{n-r} \to \mathrm{B}^n.$$

Of course, any unit of time may be taken as a measure. A and B represent the output which may be produced in the course of this unit of time.

This interim scheme may now be 'capitalized' thus:

$$[a\mathrm{A}(n-k)]^{n-1} + [b\mathrm{B}(n-l)]^{n-1} \to \mathrm{A}^n$$
$$[(1-a)\mathrm{A} \cdot (n-d)]^{n-1} + [(1-b)\mathrm{B}(n-r)]^{n-1} \to \mathrm{B}^n.$$

In this new system, the relationship between cost and return is quite different from that in an elementary scheme. The capitalization coefficients—the units of time between 'initial costs' and 'end products'—are constant values.

3.5. *Capital Accumulation and/or Consumption*

If the cost elements at the point of consumption increase, the 'technically required' capital sum grows by the product of the increase and the capitalization coefficients. Consequently, the increase in output corresponding to the increase in consumption will only appear if the increased capital is 'accumulated'. A space of time equal to the capitalization period is necessary before this can happen.

Decreased costs, on the other hand, mean a proportional decrease in the capital required. The difference between this and the real capital sum may then be 'consumed'—as a result, output will be able to maintain its original level for a while.

We will dispense with further analysis, since in methodological terms the matter would seem to be clear on the basis of the example we have offered.

Among modern theoreticians, Fisher, E. v. Böhm-Bawerk and Clark have thoroughly treated the capital problem from a morphological—if one may use that term—standpoint of the circular flow of an economy.

3.5.1. *Fisher's definition of capital*

Fisher's brief definition goes as follows:

> "A stock of wealth at an instant in time is called capital (*I.F.*) A flow of service through a period of time is called income".[8]

Of the two pairs of concepts—stock and flow on the one hand, wealth and service on the other—on which this differentiation between capital and income is based, only the first lies within the scope of our analysis. According to Fisher's own conception of things, the juxtaposing of stock and flow may only be applied to material goods (wealth), since services can only be imagined in a state of flow. We can thus set the latter aside for the time being.

Flow is "the quantity of any specified thing undergoing any specified change during any specified period of time".

Stock is "the quantity of any specified thing at any instant".[9]

3.5.2. *Continuity in the economic process*

If one imagines the circular flow of an economy as fundamentally a continuous process, then this concept of capital corresponds to the elementary return and/or costs in our elementary scheme.[10] In strict terms, Fisher's 'stock' amounts to the sum of all elementary returns. 'Flow', then, is nothing other than a multiple of this sum.

Missing from Fisher, though, is any indication of how one might determine this infinitely large number of infinitely small units. We have already seen that in principle it is impossible to establish this number by direct methods. The way Fisher simply ignores the problem of calculating capital would only be

---

[8] *I.F. The nature of capital and income*, 2nd edn. New York, 1923, p. 52.

[9] *Ibid.* p. 332, p. 336.

[10] A brief example by way of explanation: a certain volume of a certain item is produced annually. One may represent the whole process as taking place once a year, for example on the 31st December. In this case, a 'stock' would always be present which is equal to the annual output. If the conversion process took place twice a year, for example on the 30th June and the 31st December, only half as much stock would need to be stored; monthly production would require stock amounting to only 1/12 of the annual output. In a continuous process, only an infinitely small fraction of the total output would need to be present.

202 W. LEONTIEF

comprehensible if, counter to our notions, he conceived of the flow of an economy as a fundamentally discontinuous process. But we find no direct reference to this state of affairs in his work. Let us then discuss this question separately.

Strictly, there is nothing which can be proved: it all depends on what one means by 'an economy'. However, we are in a position to demonstrate that, based on traditional notions, an economy can scarcely be viewed as a discontinuous process.

First, it hardly seems contentious that an absolute discontinuity, measured by mere 'astronomical' time, is wholly irrelevant to the circular flow of an economy. Imagine, for example, the totality of economic life with all its requirements being brought to a complete standstill as if by a magic wand—and then resuming its course again. It is absolutely clear that this general moratorium, whether it lasts a second or a century, may not be designated an economic fact.

If one speaks of a discontinuity in the economic process, then one can only mean a relative inconstancy. To put it another way: the change within a circular flow which—measured in absolute time and compared with other changes—takes place most uniformly, i.e. with the smallest pauses, can in economic terms be considered as absolutely continuous change. Only those parts of the entire process which during their course exceed this minimal measure of absolute discontinuity may be counted as 'economic', that is relatively discontinuous.

There is no lack of practical examples: 50 years are required to produce a good wine; the production of finished cloth starting from raw wool takes, let us say, around a year; some chemical process or other is completed within a few minutes. The same is true for consumption, which in this case is only production seen from the cost side.

But now there comes the following objection: the period required to produce wool cloth appears so long only if you calculate it from the day when the sheep are shorn in Australia. If, by contrast, you take as the starting point the moment when the yarn is stretched onto the loom, the process takes hardly any longer than our chemical process, above. But if you want to stretch out the producing of the chemical product back to the stage of raw materials, one comes up with a production period lasting several months. The same is true for the wine: a 50 year old Tokay can easily be produced within a year—if you take a 49 year old as your raw material. The same is true for consumption.

It all simply depends on where one starts counting, or ceases to count. The theoretician seeking to introduce his system of the concept of capital, as a fundamental concept alongside that of the flow of goods, must of necessity construct a clear 'classification of industries',[11] otherwise his concept of capital will have absolutely no determinable sense.

This is where Irving Fisher's otherwise so sharp analysis comes to grief. He speaks of a momentary stock of goods as if it were the most natural thing in the world; but instead of systematically analysing the concept, he consults some 72 dictionaries for a definition.

---

[11] See for example Jevons, *The Principles of Economics*, 1905, pp. 107, 114 ff.

In dealing with the notion of income he comes across the idea of a flow of goods and he is confronted—inevitably—with the problem of differentiating between individual phases of production; he simply states that by using one's own discretion one can draw a line along any sequence of production; and he adds, quite rightly, that the position of this boundary is irrelevant when calculating income—where for him income means the same as flow. He fails to notice that in the process his notion of capital loses its foundations.

3.5.3. *E. v. Böhm-Bawerk's notion of capital*

In his critique of Fisher's theory, Böhm-Bawerk also failed to take into account the abovementioned flaw. Indeed he goes as far as to ask: "In what sense then does the invoked antithesis (between capital and income *W.L.*) really and incontestably exist?". He goes on to provide the following answer: "Certainly in this sense, to which Fisher refers frequently and explicitly, that capital is a 'stock' and income a 'flow' ".[12]

In his own formulation, Böhm-Bawerk has avoided these dangerous waters with rare theoretical skill:

'Capital' he says "is none other than the sum total of all the intermediate *products* (*W.L.*) which arise on the individual stages of the roundabout production paths".[13]

But when it comes to giving an example, these 'intermediate products' suddenly disappear, to be replaced by preserved labour.

If Böhm-Bawerk had attempted to enumerate all these intermediate products, following his own 'realistic' definition, as he calls it, his position would scarcely have been any more felicitous than that of Fisher.

3.5.4. *Clark's notion of capital*

Among modern theoreticians it would seem that Clark has best recognized the logical difficulties inherent in capital theory. But even Clark's work lacks an unimpeachable definition of capital.

"Capital is this permanent fund of productive goods the identity of whose component elements is forever changing. Capital goods are the shifting component parts of this permanent aggregate".[14]

Elsewhere he says:

"We describe these real things by the use of an abstract term (capital *W.L.*) just as we describe a thousand other realities".[15]

But Clark does not himself seem to be fully clear about the nature of this, his own generic concept. In the large number of analogies he uses to further his

---

[12] *Kapital und Kapitalzins*, 4th edn. Jena, 1921. Volume III. p. 4.
[13] *Ibid.* p. 16.
[14] *Essentials of Economic Theory*, New York. 1922. p. 29.
[15] *Ibid*, p. 22.

case—without giving a single example—he demonstrates a typical vacillation between stating what is self-evident and being extremely unclear. There is a very illuminating analysis of how 'capital goods' find themselves in constant flow, and of how one must imagine these capital goods 'in some way constituting a stock' in order to come to a true definition of capital. What 'some way' constitutes is never said. Even his indication that businessmen mainly see capital as a sum of money does not make the whole matter any clearer—before one introduces one's measuring equipment, one should first establish the nature of the thing to be measured.

3.5.5. *The flow of goods*

For Clark, as for other theoreticians, the image of a flow of water seems to be particularly illuminating. The comparison is worked out more or less along the lines of the following parallel statements:

1. The length of a defined section of river.

2. The movement of individual water particles along the flow of the river

3. The reserves of water in a defined length of river remains constant although individual water particles are constantly being replaced

The 'total stock' within a defined segment of the circular flow.

The transition of economic goods from one phase of production to the next.

The 'stock of goods' within a defined segment of the circular flow remains unchanged, although the individual units of goods change and supersede each other.

But there is a fundamental difference between these two flows: the 'supply of water', if one ignores the position of its individual elements, represents a homogeneous mass, whereas the flow of goods consists of a varied series of endlessly differing elements. Might it perhaps be possible, though, to abstract the 'use value' and find in the 'exchange value' a generally valid instrument of measurement?

"Instrument of production composes the fund but the dollars serve to describe it", says Clark.[16]

Another erroneous conclusion is drawn from a false analogy. As we have indicated, no evaluation may be undertaken if it is impossible precisely to enumerate the elements to be evaluated.

One can either establish the volume of water in a stretch of river by direct methods—taking a cross-section at any one point and then measuring the length of the stretch—or indirectly—by establishing the amount of water which passes a sectional area in the course of the time it takes each individual particle to traverse the entire stretch. However, the volume of a flow of goods may only be established by the second, indirect method, with the aid of the capitalization process. This should always be borne in mind when drawing analogies and conclusions using 'flow theory'.

[16] *Ibid*, p. 31.

3.6. *Buffer Stocks*

If one finally asks oneself why it is that 'realistic' definitions of capital seem so plausible, then it is undoubtedly because within the economic process there are momentarily present stocks of finite size. These are buffer stocks.

Strictly speaking, there must be a stock of this type at hand for every element in the circular flow (see pp. 192–193). Only at certain stages, however, does this stock reach a finite level—otherwise the total stock would have to be infinite, given the infinite number of stages of production. One can already see that the sum of all these stocks in no way corresponds to the notion of a momentary total stock, which, for example, formed the basis of Fishers's definition of capital.

Much more difficult is the question of whether the existence of buffer stocks will not also wreck our 'nominalist' definition of capital. The problem can best be examined by using our by now thoroughly familiar elementary scheme. Let us take a section from the circular flow model lasting two production periods. For the sake of simplicity, we will only take into consideration one production path. Product 2 is produced from product 1, and then goes towards producing product 3. The elementary consumption of product 1 is equal to A. The output from 3 is C. The output and consumption of 2, on the other hand, are subject to certain

TABLE 1.

206 W. LEONTIEF

fluctuations as a result of certain technical changes. If the output and consumption changes ran in parallel, the harmonious running of the production cycle would be guaranteed, without the need for any stock. But if the production coefficients move independently of one other, a buffer stock must be on hand.

Let us take the following sequence by way of example: (see Table 1).

The output of element 2 in the first period equals B, but in the course of the next three periods it climbs to twice that figure, before going on to assume its original level. The consumption of 2, on the other hand, remains equal to B in the course of the first 4 periods and to 2B in the final three (of course with a corresponding displacement by one period).

In periods 1 to 4 there is consequently an accumulation of 2, which is then used up in the subsequent 3 periods.

This oscillating pattern then starts again.

Production conditions take on a somewhat different shape if one production process periodically comes to a complete standstill (as is the case, for example, in seasonal industries). In this case, two buffer stocks must alternately be accumulated and consumed. On the one hand they constitute the output generated by the production process, on the other, they represent intermediate inputs.

In schematic terms these interrelationships may be portrayed as follows (see Table 2):

TABLE 2.

	No. 1	No. 2	No. 3	No. 4	Capitalization period between Nos 1 and 3	Capitalization period between Nos 1 and 5
Period 0	0 → A	1 B	2 C C C	3 D →	4	5
Period 1	1 → A	2 B B	3 C C	4 D →	$3\frac{1}{2}$	5
Period 2	2 → A	3 B B B	4 C	5 D →	3	5
Period 3	3 → A	4 B B B B →	5 C C →	6 D →	$2\frac{1}{2}$	5
Period 4	4 → A	5 B B B →	6 C C C →	7 D →	2	5
Period 5	5 → A	6 B B →	7 C C C C →	8 D →	1,5	5

In order to be able to 'capitalize' these supplies one must first establish the capitalization period—using the now familiar hypothetical 'experiment'.

We induce at stage 1 (Table 1) a change, and establish the span of time which must elapse before a corresponding change becomes noticeable at stage 3. But what do we mean by a corresponding change? We mean that the output—presupposing complete constancy of all technical coefficients in the intermediate stage—undergoes a change proportional to the original change, and remains at this new level as long as the original costs do.

Both the constancy of the technical coefficients as well as the mutability of output are held to be relative in nature. In the present cases, e.g. where the two values undergo certain fluctuations without there being any particular 'disturbing' factor, they must be drawn into the realm of the 'constant'.

Imagine, for example, that as a result of increased productivity at a preceding stage there has been twofold consumption at stage 1 since time period 0, and thus twofold output. After one period has elapsed the consumption of this latter product may undergo a corresponding increase. If one carries the calculation through the entire 'period of oscillation', there will be a complete balance at the end.

$$
\begin{array}{cccc}
\text{Period} & 6 & 7 & 8 \\
 & N_1 & N_2 & N_3 \\
 & A \longrightarrow & B \longrightarrow & C \\
 & & B & \nearrow \\
 & & B \longrightarrow & C \\
 & & B & \nearrow
\end{array}
$$

This applies to all changes in output of product 1 in period 0. Thus the capitalization period here is equal to 1. It remains the same even when the changes in the first period are taken into account.

If, however, the primary changes in output of 1 has only been manifested in period 2, there would have to be a deficit produced at the end of the period of oscillation if the consumption of product 2 had increased in the next period of production. The reason for this is clear. Quantity B, produced in period 2 under the old production conditions in order to be absorbed into the inventory and to serve to produce a balance at the end of the period of oscillation, no longer suffices to meet the now increased consumption. Where there is a twofold output of product 1 in the second period and an immediate corresponding proportional increase in consumption, the deficit in the seventh and last period would be equal to 1B. If, on the other hand, the increase in consumption does not appear in the fourth, but rather in the fifth period, there would be complete balance achieved at the end.

Where primary costs are doubled in the second period, the capitalization period equals 2. Just as in the case of a simple production sequence, the size and the direction of the change plays no role in determining the capitalization period. In the third period the capitalization coefficient of 1 equals 2.5, in the fourth also 2.5, in the fifth it falls to 2, and in the sixth it finally amounts to only 1.5 periods.

208 W. LEONTIEF

In this manner we may also calculate the capitalization periods in the second case—that is between stages 1 and 3, on the one hand, and 2 and 4, on the other (see Table 2). In the latter case the capitalization period forms, as expected, a constant value—for the opposing changes of both stocks cancel each other out.[17]

[There follows a section (pp. 614–618) on the flow of commodities and the flow of money (the Editors)].

3.7. *Man in the Circular Flow*

Let us now consider the position of man within the circular flow of an economy. This question might seem a little odd, as if man were somehow not the 'natural' focus of the economic process.

In most theories, the notion of economic man really does form the starting point for all deductions; other matters are adduced as it were where required and in a quite undifferentiated form. We have attempted to put a more systematic construction on these 'other matters' by using the idea of circular flow. But if the latter, in defiance of custom, is chosen to be the starting point for our entire analysis, this is for two reasons (the methodological right to do this need not be doubted).

On the one hand, there is our duty as critical thinkers. Any discrepancies in a theoretical construct may be far easier indicated from a new point of view than when they are seen from a traditional viewpoint. In the former case, there are no prior associations present, and one does not run the risk of unconsciously ironing out flaws by using one's imagination.[18]

On the other hand, the circular flow principle seems to deserve a higher logical rating than the extremely complex notion of economic man—for purely systematic reasons, and because of its very simplicity.

3.8. *Income and 'Costs'*

The above-mentioned problems may be formulated very simply in schematic terms. If economic man is seen as a 'point of transformation' within the entire cycle, one may relate all the various elements within the system to this starting point in two different ways: either along the direction of production, as income, or against the flow of production, as costs in the narrow sense of the word. Every element can thus be seen both as income and as 'cost'. The income from the last (equals the first negative) zone may be seen as direct income, the costs in the first zone as direct costs.

[17] It would be absolutely wrong to speak of a 'constant inventory'. The concept contains a contradiction. Inventory is always a reserve, a balancing fund. As such it not only has of necessity to fluctuate, but it must also at certain times be reduced to nil. The 'minimal stock' is not part of the economic circular flow.

[18] Although F. Wieser might see association as 'one of the most effective tools of research' and condemns all 'new' terminology which distances the reader from associations (see *Grundriß der Sozialökonomik,* 1, Volume 2, p. 11), we see a wholly unambiguous terminology, free of all associations, as the prime prerequisite for scientific analysis. If terminology is over-descriptive and slips out of the researcher's control, then, like all blunt tools, it belongs on the scrapheap.

3.9. *Pure Income*

But now we come up against the customary distinction between net and gross income, 'necessary' maintenance costs and 'free' profit.

The tendency in some way to extract income from the rest of the flow is as old as the subject of economics itself. The example of the Aristotelian calves has always cropped up in some way or other. The arguments designed to justify this notion, however, are of quite differing sorts. In the case of Adam Smith, for example, they consisted of quite sober considerations of the productivity of labour—and the cow came out of it scarcely any worse than the man. In the case of Schmoller, the considerations were of a more ethical nature, which forbid man's being reduced to the level of a mere machine.

As far as the latter line of reasoning is concerned, it has to do on the one hand with a question of conviction, and on the other with a purely terminological matter: neither of which is worth discussing. The sense of the surplus theory is represented by the classical school (e.g. even by Ricardo) and, as accepted for the most part nowadays, is best understood if one enquires into the use of this 'free' income. The answer is: it either accumulates or is used up unproductively.

3.10. *Accumulation*

Accumulation means here a measurable economic change. That economic changes are at all possible cannot be doubted. But one must ask how and to what extent they may be measured.

Where steady change takes place, where each individual return experiences the same steady increase or decrease, it suffices to establish the coefficients of change at any one stage of production in order to be able to draw conclusions about all the changes. But if the technical coefficients change in an uneven fashion, one is faced with a problem which is in principle insoluble: reducing these non-steady changes in individual returns to a common denominator.

The value measure which is unnecessary where regular change takes place fails in the face of irregular change, as does measurement in kind. The size, indeed even the direction of the change, will appear different, according to which element is taken to be the standard measure.

3.11. *Productive and Unproductive Consumption*

The question of productive and unproductive consumption is very closely bound up with the general problem of productivity, which we discussed thoroughly when establishing the basis for the circular flow principle (see pp. 181–182). Is the consumption of goods brought about by a fire, or the 10–20% of infertile seed which even the best batch contains, productive or unproductive consumption? Well, one can call it what one likes. In the given state of the economy these cost elements are just as unavoidable as, for example, the undoubtedly 'productive' consumption of raw materials. Any attempt to distinguish an unproductive and a productive side to personal consumption is just as arbitrary as it is when dealing with 'objective' cost goods.

210 W. LEONTIEF

3.12. *'Unproductive' Services*

Many theorists juxtapose unproductive consumption and unproductive services. In this sense they are talking of 'derived income'. In its purest form this construction reminds one of a benevolent lady in an old English novel: "Mylady was very charitable in her own way. She had a charity school for poor children where they were taught to read and write gratis, and where they were kept well to spinning gratis for mylady in return".

Of course, 'unproductive' services are usually characterized as such without reference to the 'derived income' one may obtain for oneself from it. Frequently, it is only material efforts producing accumulable products which are seen as productive—where accumulation equates with hoarding. Thus Malthus, for example, drew up an entire scale of more or less productive labour, differentiated by the 'perishability' of their products. Fisher actually means the same thing when he applies his notion of stock only to the flow of goods and not to the flow of services.

In the wake of what has been said about the definition of capital and accumulation, it would be idle to contest the validity of this argumentation. However, the possibility of being able to relate all 'derived' income and all 'unproductive' labour back to 'primary' income and/or 'productive' labour may be seen as powerful methodological argument. The primacy of labour over 'capital' is sometimes proved in the same way.

3.13. *'Primary Production Factors'*

Since in both cases we are talking about one and the same line of reasoning, let us examine the second problem somewhat more closely. It is here that as a means of proof the reduction method seems to have been particularly misused.

Since Adam Smith there has been a major dispute as to whether both production factors should be seen as primary factors, or whether it is merely labour which is primary, whereas capital is a derived factor which can be referred back to this one original factor.

Putting the problem in this fashion can quickly lead to a confusion of two quite different questions, of which one is purely historical in nature, the other purely analytical. In the one instance we are dealing with investigating the genesis of capital goods in their relationship to labour, in the other, the position of both in a given production system.

Let us turn our attention to this latter problem. The basic relationship between the two elements may be investigated using a twofold scheme:

$$a A^{n-1} + k K^{n-1} \to A^n$$

$$(1 - a) \cdot A^{n-1} + (1 - k) K^{n-1} \to K^n.$$

The substitution of K (Capital) could be carried out as follows:

Period:

$n - 1 \quad aA + \underbrace{kK}$

$n - 2 \quad \overbrace{k[(1 - a)A + \underbrace{(1 - k)K]}}$

$n - 3 \quad \overbrace{k(1 - k)[(1 - a)A + \underbrace{(1 - k)K]}}$

$n - 4 \quad \overbrace{k(1 - k)^2[(1 - a)A + (1 - k)K]}$

etc.

As might be expected from our earlier discussion, a complete elimination of a factor of production from the given system is in principle impossible. Of course, the size of the 'capital factor' can be reduced to any chosen level by referring back to even earlier periods of production.

But what purpose can this reduction serve? The 'priority' of labour over capital is just as impossible to prove in this way as it would be impossible to disprove by relating the labour factor to the capital factor using the same method.

Substitution has the perfectly clear methodological task of enabling us to comprehend the nature of the real circular flow of an economy—at first with the aid of the notion of capital—and secondly of helping, in certain special cases, to eliminate elements which are not vital for our analysis. For example, in a two-factor system of reproduction one may juxtapose capital as a homogeneous element with labour, and investigate the developing interrelationships of the two within a given production period. A twofold, threefold or even further reduction of these elements is out of the question as far as our first-named purpose (above) is concerned. Moreover, it does not represent a simplification; the elements examined are not referred to each other in a direct relationship, that is within a single production period, but are at a certain mutual distance: where the reduction becomes infinite, so does this distance.

At the start of our investigation we indicated that its fundamental task was of a critical nature; it has assumed an analytical character simply out of methodological considerations.

4. CONCLUSION

Let us finally provide a brief summary of our critical conclusions.

In his time, J. S. Mill objected to the notion of 'catallactics'.[19] Since then, this tendency to view the economy as a price system and to conduct economic theory as if it were purely a price theory has increased. Quite rightly, voices have been raised against this fundamental neglect of the 'material' point of view. It seems

---

[19] The concept of 'catallactics'—the science of exchange—was first used by R. Whateley in 1834. See also discussion in Hicks (1975) (the Editors).

212   W. LEONTIEF

wrong to us to try to rehabilitate the latter by setting measurement in kind alongside the value measure, as if the entire problem of economics lay in finding the 'right' measure.

One need only look somewhat more closely at the basis of 'pure price theory' to be in a position to establish how strongly it is pervaded by the material point of view. In order to re-establish the correct relationship between the material and value points of view, one need only arrange the two views somewhat more systematically and locate them within the broader theoretical structure.

The question is not one of whether this or that point of view is correct. To each its due—although when the matter is judged impartially, the 'value' point of view ought to recognize a proper field of analysis in which the material approach will be of considerable importance.

[b]

LEONTIEF'S 'THE ECONOMY AS A CIRCULAR FLOW': AN INTRODUCTION

PAUL A. SAMUELSON

It was Wassily Leontief who said that a scientist's first work, like a person's first love, is of key importance. However, in his own case, Leontief has never grown old; and having been incredibly precocious, Leontief's beginnings must be traced back to adolescence and childhood in Petersburg, Petrograd and Leningrad. Still the scientist is his major work, and this translation of Leontief's 1928 *The Economy as a Circular Flow* sounds the first note of the overture to his *Ring* of Input–Output.

A 22-year-old, working in Kiel but out of the Berlin stable of Bortkiewicz, Wassily labored on his own. Except for perfunctory references to Irving Fisher, Jevons and Böhm-Bawerk, he seems not even to have mentioned such obvious works as Quesnay's *Tableau Economique,* Marx's Tableaux of Steady and Expanded Reproduction (appearing in *Capital's* little-studied Volume 2 of 1885), or the virtually unknown 1898 Russian essay of Dmitriev with its vindication of Adam Smith's resolution of all income into the values-added of wages, land rents and profit–interest. Of course he did not refer—nor could he have before 1960—to the tentative researches, then being done in Cambridge by 30-year-old Piero Sraffa, on the intricacies of production of commodities by means of commodities.

A historian of science like Robert K. Merton, knowing about Newton and Leibniz and about Darwin and Wallace, would expect that somewhere a Leontief and a Sraffa would be *independently* discovering at about the same time the theory of input–output.[1] If Wassily did not know Piero in 1928, Piero did not know Wassily. What is more interesting—and it tells us much about the two personalities—in the half century that followed neither one seems ever to have referred explicitly by name to the other. The tub of genius stands on its own bottom!

A new embryo contains the future organism, but not even the most discerning eye can see in the constellation of early cells the beautiful baby that is to come. Reviewing the present translation, one sees a considerable gap between it and the 1936 paper my Harvard teacher published in the *Review of Economics and*

Address: Massachussets Institute of Technology, Cambridge, MA, USA.

[1] Neither Leontief nor Sraffa knew that, in 1928, the 24-year-old John von Neumann was perfecting his model of a two-person zero-sum game—a model whose duality and saddlepoint properties pointed him toward his general equilibrium growth model (of 1932, 1937 and 1945) with its considerable overlap with input–output and linear programming analysis. As Merton knows, good things in science often come in threes.

178   P. A. SAMUELSON

Statistics. (Since Wassily, like Joseph Schumpeter, rarely lectured at Harvard on his own current researches, I had to learn about input–output on my own—much as I had to puzzle out for myself Schumpeter's curious 1911 theory about the necessity of a zero interest rate in circular-flow equilibrium *sans* developmental innovations.)

This 1928 maiden voyage includes nothing in its ballast of what has always been a hallmark of Leontief's research: nothing of manageable empirical measurement. No mother would be confused between her baby gorilla and yonder baby chimpanzee. In embryo, when all mammals begin superficially alike, the resemblance is much greater. Therefore, the Sraffian paradigms that remained forever innocent of empirical investigation started out more closely resembling the 1928 Leontief formulations than did the ultimate 1960 classic, *The Production of Commodities by Commodities*. Oddly, the 1928 non-mathematical Italian began more with algebra and formal mathematics than did the *wunderkind* of mathematical economics. The present article contains no matrix, much less a determinant. It is, so to speak, primarily taxonomic and topological. The pioneer is carving our a new language, prior to composing a scientific poem in that language. Directed arrows connect points A, B, C and D with each other, depicting flows of cash or more basically the temporal production of outputs from earlier-time application of inputs. The coal needed last period to make this period's coal was preceded by the smaller fractional total of day-before-yesterday's coal needed for yesterday's coal—and so on in what is implicitly a converging geometric progression of scalar or matrix type. What in 1958 Dorfman–Samuelson–Solow dubbed Leontief–Cornfield and Gaitskill infinite series are already glimpsed in 1928 by the bold pioneer. The formal cases of Perron–Frobenius non-negative matrices that are or are not *decomposable* and *cyclic* are sketched with a broad brush. The blackboard is prepared for the time-phased production functions, in which output of a good at time $t + 1$ depends on inputs at time t of labor, and of different raw materials and produced factors (including, possibly, input of the good itself). To make his model empirically identifiable, Leontief approximated reality by the special assumption of a single set of techniques (fixed technical coefficients of labor a_{0j} and of produced inputs a_{ij}) and by aggregation into at first a dozen sectors and ultimately into several hundred.

The rest is history. Indicative planning for peacetime reconversion. Planning for growth and development. Estimating the impacts of OPEC energy shocks. These and scores of similar policy applications and econometric measurements have been the harvests of Leontief's research groups at Harvard, the US Bureau of Labor Statistics and at NYU (well into his ninth decade of life!).

The public at large thank Wassily Leontief for his Nobel-class research findings. The guild of professional economists blesses him for his brilliant, deep and many scientific breakthroughs. His pupils, colleagues and friends appreciate Wassily Leontief for his creative productivity, serene integrity and generous kindnesses. By shear good luck I met my Master young and have coasted along ever since on the impulse of his wisdom and knowledge.

REFERENCES

DORFMAN, R. SAMUELSON, P. and SOLOW, R. (1958). *Linear Programming and Economic Analysis.* McGraw-Hill, New York.

DMITRIEV, V. K. (1898). 'The Theory of Value of David Ricardo', in D. M. Nuti (ed.), *Economic Essays on Value, Competition and Utility.* Cambridge University Press, London.

LEONTIEF, W. W. (1928). 'The Economy as a Circular Flow', *Archiv für Sozialwissenschaft und Sozialpolitik*, **60**, 577–623.

—— (1936). 'Quantitative Input and Output Relations in the Economic System of the United States', *Review of Economics and Statistics*, **18**, 105–25.

—— (1941). *The Structure of the American Economy, 1919–1929.* Harvard University Press, Cambridge, MA. The 1951 Oxford University Press second edition is an expanded version.

MARX, K. (1885). *Capital.* Volume 2.

QUESNAY, F. (1758). *Tableau Oeconomique* (so-called 'first edition' as reproduced and translated in Appendix A of Kuczynski and Meek, 1972, *Quesnay's Tableau Economique.* Macmillan, London).

SRAFFA, P. (1960). *Production of Commodities by Means of Commodities.* Cambridge University Press, Cambridge.

VON NEUMANN, J. (1928). 'Zur Theorie der Gesellschaftsspiele', *Math. Annalen*, **100**, 295–320.

—— and MORGENSTERN, O. (1964). *The Theory of Games and Economic Behavior.* John Wiley, New York.

[c]

AN INTRODUCTORY NOTE BY PROFESSOR LEONTIEF

The text of the following article was submitted in the Fall of 1927 to the Dean of the University of Berlin with my application for a PhD degree.

In a confidential appraisal of it, requested by the Dean, a copy of which was recently located in that University's archives, Professor Ladislaus Bortkiewicz, the author of the well known statistical 'law of small numbers', said:

'Although I find much that is objectionable in it, this dissertation is without any doubt acceptable. In developing his—in my opinion very doubtful—theoretical constructs the candidate received no guidance whatsoever from his academic teachers. He arrived at his present position quite independently, one might say, despite them. It is very likely that he will maintain this scientific point of view also in the future.'

Wassily Leontief

[4]

The Review *of* Economic Statistics

VOLUME XVIII AUGUST, 1936 NUMBER 3

QUANTITATIVE INPUT AND OUTPUT RELATIONS IN THE ECONOMIC SYSTEM OF THE UNITED STATES

INTRODUCTION

The statistical study presented in the following pages may be best defined as an attempt to construct, on the basis of available statistical materials, a *Tableau Economique* of the United States for the year 1919.[1]

One hundred and fifty years ago, when Quesnay first published his famous schema, his contemporaries and disciples acclaimed it as the greatest "invention" since Newton's laws. The idea of general interdependence existing among the various parts of the economic system has become by now the very foundation of economic analysis. And yet, when it comes to the practical application of this theoretical tool, modern economists must rely exactly as Quesnay did upon fictitious numerical examples. What would be the present state of the theory and policy of international trade if, instead of actual balances of foreign trade, the economist had to base his analysis upon assumed numerical set-ups, supplemented by scattered items of actual statistical information? This is the situation in which the student of economics finds himself at present when he faces a problem of national production, consumption, and distribution. Despite the remarkable increase in the volume of primary statistical data, the proverbial boxes of theoretical assumptions are in this respect as empty as ever. Considerable progress has been achieved in the field of national income statistics. The economic balance of some of the most important branches of the national economy, particularly that of agriculture, has been studied with much success. Thus the ground has been prepared, at least in part, for a more complete analysis of the interrelations of the whole economic system. Nevertheless, the difficulty of the task still remaining can hardly be exaggerated.

[1] The research project, a summary of the results of which are presented in this paper, has been financed by the Harvard University Committee on Research in the Social Sciences. Mr. Maynard C. Heins worked on it as a full-time assistant for four years. Without his able collaboration, the statistical task could hardly have been accomplished.

The publication of this preliminary survey is prompted by the conviction that the inevitable path of any empirical research is that of trial and error.

Governmental publications constitute the main source of primary statistical information used in this study. Additional data were gathered from trade publications, and in some instances the results of special investigations have been utilized. In many cases, use was made of the work of the National Bureau of Economic Research on national income.

At the time that this study was initiated (1932), the publication of the detailed results of the 1929 Census was still far from complete. As a result, the Census of 1919 had to be used. It is because of this fact that the entire investigation is based on 1919 data.

CHART I.—SERIES INDICATIVE OF BUSINESS CONDITIONS

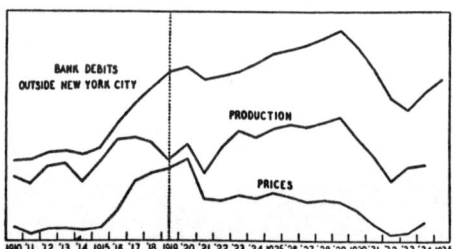

The general business conditions prevailing during that year are described in W. L. Thorp's *Business Annals* in the following terms:

> Revival; prosperity.
> Uncertainty gives way to extraordinary activity, late spring; building revival; enormous output of new securities; speculation; steel, coal, and railroad shopmen's strikes, autumn; commodity prices rise; active foreign trade.
> Money eases slightly but tightens late in year; stock exchange booms, railroads reaching peak, May, and industrials, November; falling bond prices; embargo on gold export removed, June.
> Large wheat, fair cotton and corn crops; prices very high.[2]

[2] *Business Annals* (National Bureau of Economic Research, New York, 1926), p. 143.

The position of the year 1919 within the framework of cyclical fluctuations of adjoining decades is fairly well indicated by the three basic economic series presented on Chart 1.

THE THEORETICAL SCHEME AND ITS STATISTICAL APPLICATION

FUNDAMENTAL CONCEPTS

I

The theoretical basis of the subsequent statistical analysis is rather simple. The economic activity of the whole country is visualized as if it were covered by one huge accounting system. Not only all branches of industry, agriculture, and transportation, but also the individual budgets of all private persons, are supposed to be included within this system. Each business enterprise as well as each individual household is treated as a separate accounting unit. A complete bookkeeping system consists of a large number of different types of accounts. For our particular purpose, however, only one of them is of importance: the expenditure and revenue account. It registers on its credit side the outflow of goods and services from the enterprise or household (which corresponds to total receipts or sales) and on the debit side the acquisition of goods or services by the particular enterprise or household (i.e., corresponding to total outlays). In other words, such an account gives a description of the flow of commodities and services as it enters the given enterprise (or household) through one end and leaves it by the other. In contrast to a balance sheet, this type of account is related not to a single "instant" but rather to a period of time, say a year, a month, or a week. It differs from the usual profit and loss account in so far as it includes *all* sales and *all* purchases. In the case of purchases, it includes not only those representing expenses in the accounting sense, but also "capital outlays," etc. Our expenditure and revenue account covers in other words the entire "balance of trade" of the individual enterprise (or household).

Profits paid out to the "owners," as well as expenditures connected with additional investment (in plant, etc.), are supposed to be debited, together with payments for all the current operating expenses, purchases, replacements of machinery, etc. Purchases made on credit or paid for with borrowed money are also entered, along with all other expenditures, on the debit side; while the sales, even if made on credit, are credited in the same way as are the cash sales.

An expenditure and revenue account of this kind may show over a period of time a negative balance (sales smaller than purchases) only to the extent that a given household or enterprise disburses its previously accumulated cash, bank balances, or other negotiable titles, or spends funds obtained by additional borrowings. A positive balance (sales greater than expenditures), on the other hand, can result from an accumulation of cash, repayment of debts, or an increase in bank deposits or security holdings. The structure of the expenditure and revenue account thus described is very similar to that of the "balance of trade" of a country; it covers explicitly all the commodity and service transactions, but not the so-called capital items.

II

It follows from the obvious nature of economic transactions that each revenue item (as defined above) of an enterprise or household must reappear as an outlay item in the account of some other enterprise or household. This consideration makes it possible to present the whole system of interconnected accounts in a single two-way table (Table 1).

TABLE 1

Distribution of Outlays (Input)	DISTRIBUTION OF OUTPUT (REVENUE)					
	A	B	C	D	E	Total
A		A_b	A_c	A_d	A_e	$\sum\limits_a^e A_i$
B	B_a		B_c	B_d	B_e	$\sum\limits_a^e B_i$
C	C_a	C_b		C_d	C_e	$\sum\limits_a^e C_i$
D	D_a	D_b	D_c		D_e	$\sum\limits_a^e D_i$
E	E_a	E_b	E_c	E_d		$\sum\limits_a^e E_i$
Total	$\sum\limits_A^E i_a$	$\sum\limits_A^E i_b$	$\sum\limits_A^E i_c$	$\sum\limits_A^E i_d$	$\sum\limits_A^E i_d$	S

The capital letters, A, B, C, D, and E, indicate business and household units.

Each row contains the revenue (output) items of one separate business (or household), subdivided according to the origin of revenue, or, what amounts to the same thing, the destination of its products. The figures in row A, for example, show that the product of firm A was distributed during some specified period of time in the following way: the amount b was taken by the firm B, the amount c by the firm C, and the amounts d and e were sold to the firms D and E, respectively. The last item ΣA_i represents the sum total of these separate entries and shows the total revenue or production of firm A. In a similar manner, the subsequent rows show the production-revenue distribution of firms B, C, D, and E.

If read vertically, column by column, the table shows the expenditure sides of the successive accounts. The last item $\sum_{A}^{E} i_a$ of the first column shows, for example, the total expenditures of firm A; the entries above it in the same column indicate the distribution of these expenditures among all the different sources of supply; B_a was obtained from B, C_a from C, etc. The succeeding columns reveal the cost distribution of the firms B, C, D, and E.

If it contained empirical data, the table would naturally have a number of empty squares. Those lying along the main diagonal are necessarily left open because our accounting principle does not allow for registration of any transaction within the same firm. Actually, no firm or household exists which sells its products or supplies its services to *all* the other households or firms, and which makes its purchases also from every one of them. This means that not only the diagonal but also many other boxes of our revenue-expenditure table will remain blank.

The grand total of all transactions S, placed in the lower right corner, may be obtained by adding up the revenues of all the different firms as shown in the last column or the expenditures as listed in the last row. Although, as was pointed out before, the credit and the debit side of the account for each particular enterprise or household will not necessarily balance, the total expenditures of all the firms and households must, for obvious reasons, equal the sum total of their revenues.

The simple system of letters and subscripts used in the present description leads to an abridged method of identifying each separate box of the combination table; box AB is situated on the intersection of row A and column B, CD defines the square belonging to row C and column D, etc.

III

Even if the construction of an exhaustive table describing all the transactions taking place between the independent economic units within a national economy were actually possible, the very size of such a table would constitute a serious impediment to any profitable use of the information contained in it. Obviously, considerable simplification of the original scheme is essential. The first step toward such simplification is the grouping of accounts. The majority of theoretical and practical economic problems for the solution of which the *tableau économique* may be used are not formulated in terms of individual business enterprises and households but relate rather to whole classes of such independent units.

The grouping can be based on many different principles. The business enterprises can be classified, for example, according to the type of their products and segregated into separate *industries*, or — if location differences are to be brought out — a regional grouping must be applied.

Whatever the principle of classification, the actual technique of consolidating the accounts is fundamentally always the same. If, for example, the firms B and C of Table 1 had to be combined into one "industry," a new accounting unit, B+C, must be formed (Table 2).

The new B+C row is obtained by adding (vertically) the corresponding items of the rows B and C of the original Table 1. An addition (horizontally) of the corresponding items of the columns B and C produces the new group column B+C.

One difference between the old table and the new is that the latter contains a smaller number of separate accounts. The grand total S remains the same as before. The consolidated account B+C differs, however, from the original "primary" account; the box which lies on the main diagonal is not necessarily an empty one. If the firms B and C buy commodities or services from each other, as well as from other concerns, the new consolidated account will show purchases or sales from B+C to B+C. This kind of registered internal turnover gives rise to a distinction between gross accounts and net accounts. The former registers *all* the value transfers between the original, simple accounting units, irrespective of any further grouping. The latter suppresses all the transactions between the members of the consolidated accounting group; in other words, it reveals only the external relations and treats the newly formed groups as if they were the original firms and households.

TABLE 2

Distribution of Outlays (Input)	DISTRIBUTION OF OUTPUT (REVENUE)				
	A	B+C	D	E	Total
A		A_b+A_c	A_d	A_e	$\sum_a^e A_i$
B+C	B_a+C_a	B_c+C_b	B_d+C_d	B_e+C_e	$\sum_a^e (B_i+C_i)$
D	D_a	D_b+D_c		D_e	$\sum_a^e D_i$
E	E_a	E_b+E_c	E_d		$\sum_a^e E_i$
Total	$\sum_\Lambda^E i_a$	$\sum_\Lambda^E (i_b+i_c)$	$\sum_\Lambda^E i_d$	$\sum_\Lambda^E i_e$	S

Table 2 is constructed on the principle of gross accounting. In order to convert it to a net transaction basis, the content (if any) of the box [(B+C)(B+C)], that is the entry B_e+C_b, has to be suppressed. The total revenue sum at the right end of row (B+C) and the total outlays sum at the bottom of column (B+C) must be diminished by the same amount.

The result is shown in Table 3. The notation of Table 2 is now somewhat modified. The consolidated items are defined not as sums of the originally independent accounting elements, but simply as homogeneous transactions between the new *composite* groups. For example, the content of the box (B+C)A, which was described in Table 2 as B_a+C_a, is now defined as $(B+C)_a$ ["the product of the firm (B+C) going to the firm A"]; similarly we write $D_{(b+c)}$ instead of D_b+D_c.

The grand total S of the consolidated Table 3

TABLE 3

Distribution of Outlays (Input)	DISTRIBUTION OF OUTPUT (REVENUE)				
	A	B+C	D	E	Total
A		$A_{(b+c)}$	A_d	A_e	$\sum_a^e A_i$
B+C	$(B+C)_a$		$(B+C)_d$	$(B+C)$	$\sum_a^e (B+C)_i$
D	D_a	$D_{(b+c)}$		D_e	$\sum_a^e D_i$
E	E_a	$E_{(b+c)}$	E_d		$\sum_a^e E_i$
Total	$\sum_\Lambda^E i_a$	$\sum_\Lambda^E i_{(b+c)}$	$\sum_\Lambda^E i_d$	$\sum_\Lambda^E i_e$	S

is smaller than that of Table 2. The difference is due to the exclusion of the internal transactions (B_c+C_b).

The process of consolidation, i.e., the reduction in the number of independent accounts, may proceed up to the point where the whole table is reduced to a single box [(A+B+C+D+E) (A+B+C+D+E)]. The *net* content of these completely unified accounts equals zero.

It hardly needs to be said that such integration of accounts reduces the volume of information conveyed. The statement that the total amount of transactions between firms B and C equals (B_c+C_b) (Table 2) is considerably less informative than a separate listing of sales from B to C and from C to B.

As has already been mentioned, even the most detailed economic study would hardly require an individual treatment of all the actually independent households and firms. On the other hand, many modern business enterprises combine such a conglomeration of heterogeneous economic activities that a distribution of all their transactions among a number of smaller, more homogeneous, quasi-independent accounting units appears to be highly desirable.

IV

Up to this point the discussion has been based on the assumption that the primary statistical material, consisting of the expenditure and revenue accounts of all the separate firms and households, is absolutely complete. In view of the practical difficulties which make such a thorough coverage of all economic transactions actually impossible, the question arises as to what effect the inevitable gaps in the primary accounts will have on the form and content of the final table.

The absence of a single individual account would not in any way impair the completeness of the picture. As every transaction is always credited to one firm or household and debited to another, the missing item can always be found in the corresponding "opposite" account. In case of a larger gap, only partial reconstruction is possible. All transactions taking place among the firms whose accounts are missing in our records are definitely irreplaceable. Only those revenue and outlay items which originate in sales to or purchases from the "reporting" firms can be picked out indirectly from the opposite entries. This means that the final result of the completed tabulation will be the same as that which we should get if the accounts of the "unreported" firms were consolidated into a single group and reduced to a net basis. For instance, taking our previous example, if the reports of firms B and C were missing, the revenue and outlay table would be identical with Table 3, which presents the "net" accounts.

V

The meaning and economic nature of a national revenue and outlay table may be further elucidated by relating it to some of the basic concepts of national income statistics such as "value added," "social product," etc.

This relation would be particularly simple in a static economy. By dividing all the accounts into two large groups, one containing the Household accounts, the other, all the rest, which might be called Business, and consolidating each of the two groups into a single item (H and B, respectively, of Table 4), we can reduce the total number of boxes to four.

TABLE 4

Distribution of Outlays (Input)	DISTRIBUTION OF OUTPUT (REVENUE)		
	H (Households)	B (Business)	Total
H (Households)	H_h	H_b	$H_h + H_b$
B (Business)	B_h	B_b	$B_h + B_b$
Total	$H_h + B_h$	$H_b + B_b$	S

Since, under static conditions, the corresponding row and column sums are necessarily equal, we find that the sum of the values transferred from Business to Households is equal to the total value movement in the opposite direction. The sum total of the Household expenditures (column H) represents the "National Income"; it is equal to the total value of services credited to Households (row H). The "value added" in Business is equal in its magnitude to H_b (i.e., the services contributed to Business by Households), and this is equal, under static conditions, to the value of goods and services supplied from Business to Households (B_h). The total product of industry $B_h + B_b$ equals $H_b + B_b$.

B_b represents the payments from Business to Business. Its inclusion is often defined as "double counting" and it is very often struck from the final accounts. $B_h (= H_b)$ is defined as the "net product" of industry. The Household accounts can also be reduced to a net basis by disregarding the services furnished and paid for from Household to Household (H_h). On such a net basis the National Income is B_h, which equals the "value added" H_b.

Under dynamic conditions the relations are less symmetric. The value added H_b is not necessarily equal to the Household expenditures B_h. In an expanding economy, the second item will often be somewhat smaller than the first one. The difference, measuring the "active balance of trade" between Household and Business, would indicate the transfer of purchasing power from Household to Business (see p. 115). Such transfer will also be revealed in a corresponding surplus of total industrial expenditures (input), column B, over the aggregate industrial sales (output), row B.

The foregoing analysis is based on the assumption that the saving and investment accounts are strictly separable. In some instances — as in the case of farming — strict separation of Household and Business units is not only practically but also theoretically impossible. A combined unit of this kind can increase its capital assets by the full amount of its revenue, buying capital goods, for example, yet keeping its expenditure and revenue account as balanced as ever.

The same is true of an industrial enterprise which is incurring "capital losses," or accumulating "undistributed surplus." Its current expenditures may still be equal to its total revenue (see below, p. 113). In order to discover the deficit or surplus, it is necessary to examine the status of its fixed assets account. But "capital accounting" in this sense leads to an entirely new range of economic problems, such as depreciation, evaluation of assets, etc. The straightforward methods of registering the actual value of all commodities and services as they cross the border lines of separate accounting units cannot contribute anything to the solution of these problems.

VI

In the statistical literature dealing with methods of calculating the National Income, much attention has been given to the concept of "double counting."

It is hardly an exaggeration to say that the principle of double entry constitutes the very foundation of a rational accounting system. Double counting emerges from a process of consolidation of accounts. If two interrelated accounts are added together, the same item may appear simultaneously on the credit and on the debit side of the new account. If the purpose of such an addition happens to be the elimination of all traces of the mutual interrelation of the two accounts, this item can be suppressed on both sides.

Whether or not some particular transaction appears on both sides of the same (consolidated) account depends upon the method of grouping the accounting units for the purpose of consolidation. If, instead of segregating the household accounts in one, and all the others in a second, group, as has been done in Table 4, we should separate all agricultural from all nonagricultural items, an entirely different picture would emerge. A grouping of the latter kind reveals, for example, the "balance of trade" between industry and agriculture. Many value items which according to the first arrangement might have been excluded because of "double counting" would have to be retained in the second, while some of the original income items of the first table would have to be eliminated after the subsequent regrouping.

In its actual application, the elimination of the doubly counted items means the suppression from our record of all those statistical data which describe the mechanism of inter-industrial rela-

tions. But it is exactly this mechanism which to a large degree determines the size of the net income flow and its variations.

For the understanding of the economic structure of a business enterprise and evaluation of the prospects of its future development, even an approximate knowledge of the itemized expenditure and revenue account is more important than the most accurate information concerning the single figure given for its net revenue or deficit. The same is true regarding empirical analysis of the structure of the whole national economy. It is true that, from the point of view of welfare economics, the part of the annual flow of values which is more or less arbitrarily defined as the National Income deserves particular attention. To a more detached observer, however, it may appear to be a mere by-product of the whole highly complex process of production and distribution of economic values.[1]

STATISTICAL APPLICATION

I

The classification of accounts used in the following statistical study is a compromise between a theoretical ideal and practical necessity.

According to the abstract theoretical scheme, all production enterprises should be segregated into a number of homogeneous industrial groups, homogeneity being defined in terms of (a) identity of products and (b) qualitative and quantitative similarity of the cost structure of the firms within each group. Further, all the households should be subdivided into separate classes according to the kind of services they supply, i.e., the type of income received. Actually, neither of these desiderata can be achieved.

To begin with, a definite departure from the basic "functional" classification and grouping of industries has been made in dealing with international transactions. The consolidation of all foreign economic units into a single foreign-countries' (imports and exports) account is obviously based upon a geographic, i.e., locational principle.

Even more important is the fact that the very

---

[1] In this connection it may be interesting to note the extreme variability of the theoretical concept of National Income. Ricardo, for example, definitely treated all wages as a doubly counted item and identified the net income of society with the sum total of rents and profits.

QUANTITATIVE INPUT AND OUTPUT RELATIONS   III

nature of the actual process of production and consumption precludes a clean-cut differentiation of industries. In the case of agriculture, even the fundamental distinction between enterprise and household is impossible. On the other hand, the primary statistical information for industry as a whole is fragmentary and incomplete. Practically none of it could be used directly; a large part of the entries in our final table (Table 5, inserted between pages 124–25) represents more or less indirect estimates. Among the lines of economic activity completely ignored in the present analysis, the most important are the entire fields of (a) distribution, wholesale and retail, (b) banking and finance, and (c) all non-rail transportation. Not less serious is the omission of (d) the income-expenditure accounts of all public bodies, including the budgets of federal, state, and local governments.

It would be erroneous, however, to conclude that these omissions, significant as they are, destroy the fundamental coherence of the final table. The relation of all the "unaccounted" economic units to the rest of the system is implicitly reflected in the anonymous "Undistributed" account (Table 5).

A detailed presentation of methods of computation and a description of all statistical sources will be given in a later part of this paper. The purpose of the present analysis is to show what the meaning of the general table (Table 5) would be if the numerical data contained in it were accepted at their face value.

The major part of the 44 accounts of the main table consists of 41 production accounts: of these, one represents agriculture; 34 represent industrial groups; 4, mining; one, transportation (railroads); and one, electric utilities. Agriculture is represented by a combination of production and household items. The household expenditures and receipts are consolidated in the Total Services row and the Consumption column. Foreign commodity trade is entered in the Export column and the Import row.

A systematic examination of the table can be undertaken from three different angles. If distribution of products of different industries is to be selected as the starting point, the analysis must proceed row by row; on the other hand, if the cost aspect be put in the foreground, the table should be studied column by column. Finally, the question of industrial balance will lead to a comparison of each column with the corresponding row.

II

A typical industrial distribution is exemplified by row 32, Yarn and Cloth. The gross total of 5,578 million dollars represents the value of the output of this industrial group in 1919, appraised "at factory." Exports amounted to 318 million dollars; 41 millions were used in agricultural production; 8 millions, in automobile manufacturing; 31 millions, in other wood industries (furniture). 911 millions were traded among the different stages of the yarn and cloth manufacturing industry itself, while 1,208 millions were absorbed by the clothing industry, and 290 millions by other textile products. The leather-shoe industry took in 6 millions; the other leather industries, 1 million; and 189 millions went to the rubber industry. One million can be traced to the heterogeneous group of industries under the single heading Industries N.E.S. (not elsewhere specified), and 1,812 millions went to consumption.

Thus 4,816 millions of yarn and cloth products are allocated to definite accounts; subtracting this from the sum total of 5,578 millions, we obtain a residual of 762 millions. This balancing item is entered into the special "Undistributed" column. This column includes both those products the use of which is entirely unknown and those whose classification (as derived from available statistical data) is not determinate enough to assign them to one of the other accounts. This means that the undistributed column, on one hand, contains the net debits of the unreported accounts as defined above (page 109), and on the other hand, includes the aggregated errors in allocation of the respective products among the 43 reported accounts. It is quite likely that a certain portion of the undistributed product may actually have been absorbed by industries which, according to the present distribution, are not credited with any takings of yarn and cloth products. The underestimation of some of the distributed amounts represents another source of the undistributed surplus.

The 9,102 millions of its own product absorbed by agriculture include both feed and other intermediate products as well as those consumption goods which were, according to available statistical information, retained on the farm. There is little doubt, however, that a considerable amount of agricultural products consumed by the farmer is obtained through the medium of the usual distributary channels. This means that some part of the 2,209 millions of agricultural products assigned in our table to Consumption was, in fact, used on the farm.

The distribution of transportation (steam railroad) services raises a new problem: Into whose cost schedule should the transportation costs of commodities moved by rail be included? Even if it were practically possible to distinguish between the cases in which the producer sells at factory, and those in which he delivers his goods free at the purchaser's door, such a twofold system of entry would hardly be advisable. One of the principal aims of the present statistical analysis is to reveal the typical productive and distributive interrelations which determine the structure of the national economy. This requires such a classification and grouping of the different elements of the system as will reveal the most stable aspect of these interrelations. Differentiation between "f.o.b." and "c.i.f." transactions, as well as any other classification by mode of payment, scarcely meets this criterion. Thus a systematic presentation of all transactions on a uniform (f.o.b. or c.i.f.) basis appears to be theoretically preferable. In Table 5, the transportation costs of each class of goods are charged to the industry which produces them, i.e., the value of every product includes the sum total of revenue obtained by the railroads for transportation of this particular kind of commodity. In distributing the products of an industry, however, the available statistical information does not enable us to identify the value (quantity times price including transportation costs) of the finished commodity according to location of the buyers. The freight costs allocated to the product of an industry are, therefore, spread in our table in an equal ratio over all units, which would be correct only under the obviously unrealistic assumption that the actual freight charges constitute a fixed proportion of the total price paid by each and every buyer.

Application of our method to imports makes it necessary to augment the import values of foreign commodities by a proportional amount of domestic transportation costs. An equivalent of the sum total of these transportation costs is

charged — in the distribution row of railway services — to exports. This item must not be confused with that part of transportation services which is charged directly to the cost accounts of the particular industries and thereby increases the "at factory" value of American export goods.

It will be seen that 4,161 million dollars of the railroad "product" are allocated to definite accounts. The undistributed 1,464 millions contain less than 1,000 millions of transportation costs still unaccounted for; the rest represents the so-called non-operating revenues.

In allocating imports, we meet in part the same difficulty which was discussed in connection with the distribution of transportation services. One portion of the wares obtained from abroad consists of goods which, like rubber, silk, or diamonds, cannot possibly come from domestic sources. The data revealing the consumption of these particular kinds of commodities by different industries indicate at the same time the distribution of the imports of these goods. This simple solution cannot be applied, however, to imports which are directly competing with domestic products of the same kind. In this case, the consumption data still leave open the question as to what part of the total amount absorbed by any single industry was of foreign origin. In this, as in the instance of freight costs, proportional distribution has been used throughout as the only practicable solution of the problem. The ratio between total domestic production and foreign imports of each particular kind of goods was applied as a fixed distribution key to all the different categories of users of this commodity. Import duties are included in the value of commodities obtained from abroad.

III

The service row (43) is, for the sake of convenience, subdivided into two parts. Distribution of Labor Services (row 43a) is rather simple: each industry is debited with the total amount of wages and salaries disbursed. As the figures in this row include only payments to hired labor, agriculture is credited only with the money wages of hired farm workers.

The definition and evaluation of Capital and Entrepreneurial Services (row 43b) raise an extremely difficult theoretical and statistical problem. Capital services are clearly discernible only in so far as an enterprise is working with borrowed funds and makes contractual interest payments. But even in this case, ever-changing economic conditions regularly produce a situation in which the contractual rate differs considerably from the current one. The remuneration of that part of the capital investment which belongs to the owners of the enterprise is hardly distinguishable from entrepreneurial returns, monopolistic revenue, windfall profits resulting from appreciation of commodity stocks on hand, etc. So far as monopolistic and speculative profits are concerned, it is highly doubtful whether they could and should be considered as remuneration for some specific kind of service.

The theoretical difficulty and practical impossibility of distinguishing these different kinds of remuneration made it necessary to lump all of them into one single group, loosely defined as "Capital and Entrepreneurial Services." It corresponds rather closely to the bookkeeping concept of net revenue (minus taxes) augmented by the sum total of all interest payments on borrowed capital, and it includes the following three elements of a typical corporate revenue and expenditure account: (a) interest paid, (b) dividends paid, and (c) undistributed profits. According to this set-up, the undistributed surplus plays, so to speak, a double rôle in the cost account of an enterprise. On the one hand, it represents the value of materials, additional pay rolls, and other cost elements on which it usually is spent in the process of new investment; on the other hand, it measures (in addition to the two other items mentioned above) the productive services of capital and entrepreneurship. This twofold function would be more apparent if each enterprise were to pay out the total of its net revenue to the stockholders and other owners and subsequently would obtain from them, in form of a loan or in exchange for a new stock issue, an equal sum of money to be spent on new investment. The formal difference between this and the usual method of retaining undistributed surplus lies only in the fact that the former operation involves two additional monetary transactions; the immediate material consequences are in both cases identical. The identity of the material consequences in this case holds even to the extent that, should the valuation of services obtained be arbitrarily

changed, it would make no difference so long as it were offset by corresponding write-up (or reduction) of the loan value (if profits were distributed and then immediately borrowed). From a certain point of view, therefore, it may be said that the surplus values entered in the table are fictitious. Their meaning is entirely dependent upon the interpretation of the actual valuation and accounting practices of the industry.[1]

According to our definition, therefore, the value of capital services will be nil, if no interest or dividend payment is forthcoming during the period under consideration and no additional surplus has been accumulated during that time. Every payment on interest and dividend account is debited as a capital service, even if accompanied by a deficit.

The fundamental set-up of our table necessitates a radical departure from the conventional accounting practices so far as the treatment of deficits is concerned. The existence of a deficit either (a) indicates the fact that the given enterprise purchased more goods and services (including dividend and interest payments) than it sold, or (b) shows that it failed to maintain its fixed investment, inventories, etc.

In the first case, the enterprise must have spent some of its previously accumulated cash balances or, if this proves to be impossible or impracticable, the "loss" is "financed" out of "additional" investment. In either situation, we have a surplus of expenditures over sales which influences the "balance of trade" of this enterprise in exactly the same way as a new additional investment.

In the second case, the deficit is confined to so-called book losses. It is indeed accompanied by revaluation of some assets but does not affect in any direct way the equilibrium of external payments and receipts. The "balance of payments" as well as the "balance of trade" of an enterprise remains entirely unaffected by internal revaluations of this kind.

[1] Without embarking upon a fundamental discussion of the evaluation problem, it is important to indicate that the explanation of actual economic forces should be clearly distinguished from any attempt to improve existing financial practices. Thus it would be as inadmissible to contest the validity of corporate surplus data on the ground of inadequacy of existing accounting systems as it would be wrong, for example, to dismiss our wage statistics with the remark that the existing wage rate cannot provide an adequate standard of living for the working class.

This leads to the conclusion that, unless they are financed by reduction of cash holdings or additional investment, deficits in our set-up should be disregarded; negative surpluses (deficits) can be left entirely out of the picture (see below, page 125).

Official financial statistics for obvious reasons do not follow this line of reasoning. The revenue data computed for any industrial group on the basis of usual accounting practices show only the net difference between the aggregate positive net revenue of all enterprises showing net income and the net losses sustained by the remaining part of the industry. The income statistics published by the Bureau of Internal Revenue, however, give separately figures for incomes of "Corporations Reporting Net Income" as well as for the aggregate deficits of "Corporations Reporting No Net Income." The former figure can be used in the calculation of the services of capital as defined for our special purpose.

In using official net income data, we still introduce a systematic underestimation of the entrepreneurial and capital services. The sum total of dividend payments and other capital services actually exceeds by a certain amount the aggregate net income of industry because a number of business concerns pay dividends in excess of actual earnings. The exact extent of these overpayments for the year 1919 cannot be ascertained readily; for the manufacturing and mining industries alone, they appear not to have exceeded 100 million dollars.[1]

The situation of an industry which is suffering losses is, in certain respects, identical with that which arises in the case of additional investment (which might be financed by undistributed profits, security sales, or out of already available cash resources). From the point of view of the present analysis, it is of no import that in one case the surplus of expenses over receipts is accompanied by a decrease in the value of "capital assets," while in the other this value is increasing. The whole approach is based on registration of the current stream of goods and services; the appreciation and depreciation of

capital *assets* are explicitly not taken into account.

These considerations lead to a corresponding interpretation of the Total Expenditures row (see page 115).

The theoretical and statistical difficulties in dealing with agricultural labor and capital services are essentially the same as in the case of the corresponding industrial cost schedules. In addition, these difficulties are enhanced by the impossibility of falling back on objective accounting figures. Any attempt to split the gross expenditures of agricultural accounting units into the standard components of wages, entrepreneurial and capital income, and other production costs is bound to lead back to arbitrary principles of imputation.

The most radical method of solving the problem would be that of including the farm purchases of consumers' goods among all the other outlays and placing in the service row only the amounts of wages, interest, etc. actually paid out. This type of reasoning has been applied in the general table to the distribution of that part of agricultural production which was consumed directly on the farm (see page 116). Obvious statistical difficulties make the consistent use of this procedure impracticable. Furthermore, there exists a good theoretical reason for keeping, so far as possible, the distribution of marketable consumption goods separate from that of other kinds of commodities.

A simple non-controversial solution of our difficulty is to relegate all agricultural outlays other than those which are already allocated among other industries to the Undistributed row. This device is essentially that used in our table. The residual amount (with the exception of taxes) is shifted, however, from the undistributed to the service row. This allocation is justified by the fact that most of these monetary expenditures are analogous in their economic nature to the industrial incomes entered in the adjacent boxes of the service row. Strictly speaking, the value of agricultural service-expenses obtained in this indirect way represents an overestimate. They include a certain amount of trade services absorbed in connection with the purchase of agricultural cost-goods; if the exact figure for this item were known, it would go in the Undistributed row. On the other hand, in using this figure, one has to keep in mind that,

---

[1] The aggregate net income (minus income tax) of "Manufacturing and Mining Corporations Reporting Net Income" in 1919 amounted to 4,217 million dollars, according to *Statistics of Income* (Bureau of Internal Revenue), while total dividend payments and corporate savings as estimated by W. I. King (*National Income and Its Purchasing Power*, New York, 1930) amounted to 4,276 million dollars.

as indicated above, one part (approximately 1,900 or 2,000 million dollars) of the sum total of the commodities charged from Agriculture to Agriculture consists of consumption goods.

The 5,382 millions of capital and entrepreneurial services charged to consumption include rental payments for hired houses and apartments, as well as the contribution of these factors to the so-called service industries, liberal professions, etc.

IV

Each vertical column of Table 5 shows the structure of expenditures of the corresponding industrial (or household) accounts. It gives a list of commodities and services which were absorbed by each particular branch of economic activity during the period under consideration. In an entirely static system, this distribution could be defined as the cost structure. Under the actual dynamic conditions prevailing, however, a large part of the total outlay represents not only current production costs but also additional investment. No attempt is made in the present investigation to split the expenditures of an enterprise into two parts corresponding to these two types of outlay.

The primary statistical data do not contain direct information concerning the total expenditures of the different industries similar to that which the census data on the total "value of product" give for total receipts. The magnitude of the total outlays can be determined, however, in an indirect way, through augmenting the total value of product by the value of additional new capital investment and the reduction of cash holdings. The difficulties involved in the capital accounting problem in so far as they reflect the difficulty of distinguishing current costs from new capital expenditures do not impair the validity of the sum totals thus obtained — so long as we are interested in aggregate expenditures and not in their two separate parts (current and additional expenditures as defined above). The evaluation practices in current use affect, however, the magnitude of the total outlay in so far as they determine that part of the value of capital and entrepreneurial services which is reflected in the surplus accounts.

The general principle for treatment of corporate surpluses as service items has been laid down in the preceding discussion of capital and entrepreneurial services. The total outlays of an enterprise can be defined accordingly as value of sales (product) plus additional capital investment and borrowing plus increment of positive surplus minus net changes in the cash balance (which might be positive as well as negative). The available statistical information does not give any clue for an evaluation of the last item. There is good reason to believe, however, that the financing of new investment through disbursement of previously accumulated cash balances was in 1919 a relatively minor item. Much more serious is the omission of short-term bank credits obtained by the various industries between the beginning and the end of the year 1919. A very rough estimate shows that approximately one billion dollars was added in this way to total industrial expenditures.[1] The absolute lack of any statistical evidence concerning distribution of the sum total among the separate industries precludes any attempt to use this estimate in our study.

The total outlay items at the bottom of columns 1 to 45 represent the total values of product, including imputed transportation costs (see page 112), augmented by additional positive surpluses and long-term capital investments, of the respective individual industries.

The undistributed-outlays figure (row 44c) is a balancing item which fills the gap between the total outlay for each industry and the sum total of the individual outgo items distributed among the other rows. Taxes are segregated in a special subdivision of the Undistributed account in order to show to what extent the expenditure accounts of industries and households were linked to the revenue accounts of the government. The total of expenditures for consumption (column 43) is taken from the most recent and careful estimate made by Arthur R. Gainsborough.[2]

The elementary structural characteristics of the economic system represented in Table 5 can be seen more clearly in Table 6 (insert), where all

[1] According to the *Report of the Comptroller of the Currency* for the year 1920 (Vol. I, page 31), 23 per cent of the total loans and discounts made by national banks during this year were absorbed by industrial enterprises, including railroads and public utilities. Applying this percentage to the average annual increase in total loans and discounts by all reporting banks between June, 1918, and June, 1920, we find that the proportional share of industry for the year 1919 would be approximately one billion dollars.

[2] As given in W. H. Lough, *High Level Consumption* (New York, 1935).

entries are expressed as percentages of the *net* sum totals of the corresponding rows and columns. Each box contains two figures. The figure that is not in parentheses shows the value of the particular item in its relation to the total *net output* of the industry or service group from which it originates; the other, in parentheses, gives the magnitude of the same item in relation to the total *net outlay* of the industrial or household account by which it was absorbed.

It is interesting to note that the undistributed items in the agricultural and industrial rows and columns (numbered 1 to 41) are relatively much smaller than in the service row and in the consumption column. The explanation seems to lie in the fact that a large part of total household expenditures are directed toward undistributed non-material production branches, which in their turn absorb a great amount of services but a relatively small quantity of material costs.

V

The statistical research — the results of which are presented in this paper — has been undertaken with the definite aim of supplying an empirical background for the study of the interdependence between the different parts of our national economy on the basis of the theory of general economic equilibrium. These results are incomplete; in many respects they are open to criticism; and certainly, subsequent revisions will modify many important details of the picture. Work on a similar *Tableau Economique* for the year 1929 is already under way. But even the available material, however imperfect it may be, seems to justify a laboratory test of the pertinent theoretical formulations. Such an attempt will be presented in a later article.

The statistical data collected in our main table fill in the "empty boxes" of the theory of general equilibrium. Hypothetical production and consumption equations gain explicit meaning as soon as the symbolic algebraic signs are replaced by observed numerical values. Once an empirical foundation is thus established, the vague generalities of abstract theoretical statements will acquire concrete empirical significance.

STATISTICAL SOURCES AND METHODS OF CALCULATION

The fundamental theoretical framework of our analysis, as well as the main outlines of its statistical application, is developed in the first part of this article. The following pages contain a systematic explanation of the final numerical results which are embodied in the general table (Table 5).

Lack of space precludes the possibility of a complete reproduction of all the preliminary calculations. No attempt is made here to acquaint the reader with the details of individual computations or to present the series of alternative estimates which in many instances were used for checking purposes.

Preliminary Comments

a. The values of the total output of all the separate industries from "Flour and grist mills" (row 2) to "Industries not elsewhere specified" (row 39), with the exception of "Electric utilities" (row 25), are based on the Census of Manufactures and the Census of Mines and Quarries, both for the year 1919.

b. Whenever total production or total consumption data are used as a basis of distribution, adjustments for exports or imports are carried through. These adjustments are not commented upon separately in each particular instance.

c. References to "production" indicate that the particular items are based on production statistics; references to "cost" or "consumption data" show that cost statistics of the industry which uses the particular product have been utilized.

d. Whenever the output of an industry is distributed on the basis of production values, transportation costs (if any) are added separately on the basis of a fixed proportion of the total value of the output. In all of the cases where the distribution is based on cost data of the industries which use the particular product, no such adjustment is necessary.

e. Abbreviations: *Mfr.* and *Min.* indicate, respectively, the Census of Manufactures and the Census of Mines and Quarries, both for the year 1919 unless stated as being for some other year. The abbreviation "n. e. s." stands for "Not Elsewhere Specified." For brevity, the term Transportation (Steam Railroads) is written Transportation (Railroads).

f. All original calculations are made in thousands of dollars. The rounding off is carried out in such a way as to avoid any discrepancy between the sum totals and their respective parts.

g. The following comments are arranged by distribution rows and within each row according to the order of the items, reading from left to right, in the general table. The italicized main headings refer to the rows of the table, while reference to the items within each row is introduced by the word "*To*."

1. Agriculture

Agriculture is basically defined as farming, and, in accordance with the Census, includes the entire field of crop production, fruits and vegetables, livestock and livestock products, and forest products produced on farms. The value of the total output at farm is taken from the Census of Agriculture, and increased by the amounts of transportation costs of agricultural products. (See row 41 of the general table and the discussion on page 112 above.)

To Agriculture: determined on the basis of the average percentage of products sold from the farm in the years 1924–28 (*Farm Value, Gross Income and Cash Income from Farm Products 1924–1929*, Part V [Bureau of Agricultural Economics United States Department of Agriculture, Washington, Oct. 1930]). *To* Flour and Grist Mills: quantity milled (*Mfr.*, at farm prices). *To* Canning and Preserving: estimated on basis of *Mfr.*, 1929. *To* Bread and Bakery Products: milk, eggs, nuts, and fruits (estimated). *To* Sugar, Glucose and Starch: production and cost data, Census of Agriculture and *Mfr.* *To* Liquors and Beverages: data taken from Senate Hearings (S. 436 and S. 2473, 72d Congress, 1st session). *To* Tobacco Manufactures: U. S. production. *To* Slaughter and Meat Packing: data from Census of Agriculture, *Mfr.*, and Department of Agriculture.

To Butter, Cheese, etc.: data from *Mfr.* *To* Other Food Products: dairy products, fruits, and nuts (estimated on the basis of *Mfr.*, 1923–29). *To* Chemicals: cottonseed, flaxseed, etc. (production [Census of Agriculture], sold at farm [See Agriculture to Agriculture, above]). *To* Paper and Wood Pulp: straw (costs, *Mfr.*). *To* Yarn and Cloth: quantities consumed (*Mfr.*) at farm prices. *To* Leather, Tanning: estimated; difference between total consumption of hides and skins and supply from meat packing and imports. *To* Consumption: edible products not distributed to other industries plus part of nursery and greenhouse products. *To* Undistributed: includes increase in cotton, wheat, and corn stocks, undistributed part of forest products.

2. Flour and Grist Mill Products

Includes flour and grist mill products (including output of custom mills), rice cleaning and polishing, prepared feeds for animals.

To Agriculture: animal feeds (*Mfr.*). *To* Bread and Bakery Products: flour consumption (estimated on basis of biennial Censuses of Mfr., 1923–29). *To* Consumption: residual of all edible products. *To* Undistributed: residual inedible products.

3. Canning and Preserving

Includes canning and preserving fish, fruits and vegetables, oysters, and pickles, preserves and sauces.

To Consumption: total output of all specified products (*Mfr.*). *To* Undistributed: "all other products."

4. Bread and Bakery Products

Includes bread and bakery products, breadstuff preparations, and macaroni, vermicelli, etc.

To Consumption: total value of products.

5. Sugar, Glucose and Starch

Includes sugar (cane, beet), sugar refining, glucose and starch, and sweetening sirups.

To Agriculture: stock feed. *To* Canning and Preserving: estimated on basis of *Mfr.*, 1929. *To* Bread and Bakery Products: estimated on basis of biennial Censuses of Mfr., 1923–29. *To* Sugar: raw sugar and cornstarch (*Mfr.*). *To* Liquors and Beverages: quantity of sugar used (Senate Hearings, S. 436 and S. 2473, 72d Congress, 1st session). *To* Butter, Cheese, etc.: cost of materials (*Mfr.*). *To* Other Food Products: report of cost of materials (*Mfr.*). *To* Yarn and Cloth: consumption of starch in cotton manufacture (*Mfr.*). Consumption in other parts of yarn and cloth industry could not be determined. *To* Consumption: residual of edible products. *To* Undistributed: beet pulp, oil cake, and "other products."

6. Liquors and Beverages

Includes liquors (distilled, malt and vinous), malt, and mineral and soda waters.

To Liquors and Beverages: malt (estimate; total output of malt industry is 39 millions). *To* Consumption: remainder of products.

7. Tobacco Manufactures

Includes tobacco (chewing, smoking, and snuff), cigars, and cigarettes.

To Consumption: total production.

8. Slaughter and Meat Packing

Includes slaughtering and meat packing, poultry killing,

sausage, lard, lard compounds and other substitutes, meat products not elsewhere specified.

To Agriculture: all fertilizers. *To* Bread and Bakery Products: lard and lard substitutes (estimated on basis of biennial Censuses of Mfr., 1923–29). *To* Slaughter and Meat Packing: meat, sausage casings, etc., reported as products and materials (*Mfr.*). *To* Butter, Cheese, etc.: oleo oils and stock. *To* Yarn and Cloth: wool. *To* Chemicals: stearin, soap stock, other oils and greases, and fertilizer materials (last item estimated roughly at 45 millions). *To* Leather: hides and skins, oils and greases (last item estimated roughly at 10 millions). *To* Consumption: meats, oleomargarine, lard, and lard substitutes (consumption of lard is estimated on basis of family budget studies). *To* Undistributed: residual amount.

9. Butter, Cheese, etc.

Includes butter, butter reworking, cheese, condensed milk, oleomargarine.

To Bread and Bakery Products: butter and condensed and evaporated milk (estimated on basis of biennial Censuses of Mfr., 1923–29). *To* Other Food Products: condensed and powdered milk (estimated; one-half the cost of milk and milk products to confectionery and ice cream). *To* Consumption: remaining cream, cheese, butter and substitutes, condensed and evaporated milk, and buttermilk. *To* Undistributed: casein and other products.

10. Other Food Products

Includes baking powder and yeast, chocolate and cocoa products, coffee and spices (roasting and grinding), confectionery and ice cream, cordials and flavoring sirups, flavoring extracts, food preparations not elsewhere specified (peanut butter, all other preparations for human consumption), peanut roasting and grading, vinegar and cider.

To Bread and Bakery Products: baking powder and yeast, chocolate and malt extract (estimated on basis of biennial Censuses of Mfr., 1923–29). *To* Other Food Products: chocolate, cocoa and other materials (cost of materials; *Mfr.* and estimates). *To* Consumption: remaining products assignable to consumption. *To* Undistributed: undistributed chocolate, cocoa, peanut grading, etc.

11. Iron Mining

Includes mining of iron ore.

To Blast Furnaces: blast furnace consumption, cost data, (*Mfr.*). *To* Undistributed: remainder of products.

12. Blast Furnaces

Includes blast furnaces and ferroalloys.

To Steel Works and Rolling Mills: consumption of domestically produced pig iron, ferroalloys, and blast furnace gases, computed on basis of *Mfr.* *To* Automobile Industry: estimated. *To* Other Iron and Steel Industries: consumption by foundries, etc., less amount taken by the automobile industry, computed on basis of *Mfr.* *To* Construction: slag (sold). *To* Undistributed: residual.

13. Steel Works and Rolling Mills

Includes steel works and rolling mills.

To Agriculture: staples, barbed and woven wire, horseshoes (calculated on basis of *Mfr.*). *To* Iron Mining: This, as well as a number of subsequent items, is calculated on the basis of the statistics of distribution of rolled steel products compiled by the *Iron Age* for 1922 and later years. These distributions show certain relatively constant proportions, on the basis of which a corresponding table for 1919 has been constructed. In the *Iron Age* distribution, all mining industries are treated as a single industry. The final distribution to individual mining industries is made on the basis of the total cost of materials as given in the Census. *To* Blast Furnaces: mill cinder, scale, slag, etc. (cost data, *Mfr.*). *To* Steel Works and Rolling Mills: cost of materials (*Mfr.*). *To* Automobiles;

estimates based on the *Iron Age* distribution (see Steel Works and Rolling Mills to Iron Mining). *To* Other Iron and Steel: This item is the result of a detailed analysis of census data. It is the difference between the total outputs of products of the types and qualities used by "Other Iron and Steel" and the amount of these materials distributed to other industries. *To* Non-Ferrous Metal Mining: estimated (see Steel Works and Rolling Mills to Iron Mining). *To* Petroleum and Natural Gas: estimated (see Steel Works and Rolling Mills to Iron and Steel). *To* Coal: estimated (see Steel Works and Rolling Mills to Iron Mining). *To* Rubber: estimate of wire used in tire production. *To* Construction: estimated on basis of *Mfr*. *To* Transportation (Railroads): railway track materials and cars. *To* Undistributed: residual item consisting partly of rolled products and partly of advanced products such as nails, bolts, wire manufactures, etc., made in rolling mills.

14. Other Iron and Steel Industries

Includes aeroplanes, agricultural implements, ammunition, carriage and wagon materials, carriages and sleds, children's carriages and wagons and repairs, cars and general shop construction including railway repair shops, cash registers and calculating machines, copper, tin and sheet iron work, cutlery and edge tools, cream separators, electrical machinery, engines (steam, gas and water), files, firearms, foundry and machine shop products, furniture (metal), galvanizing and other coating processes, gas and electric fixtures, gas machines and gas and water meters, hardware, hardware (saddlery), horseshoes, iron and steel bolts and nuts, cast pipe, doors and shutters, forgings, nails and spikes, tempering and welding, wrought pipe, locomotives, machine tools, motorcycles, bicycles and parts, needles, pins, hooks and eyes, ordnance, steel pens, plumbers' supplies, n. e. s., pumps (not power), pumps (power), safes and vaults, saws, scales and balances, screws (machine), screws (wood), sewing machines and attachments, shipbuilding (steel), soda water apparatus, springs (steel), stamped and enameled ware, steam fittings, etc., steel barrels and drums, stoves and hot air furnaces, stoves (gas and oil), structural ironwork, textile machinery and parts, tin and terne plate, tinware, n. e. s., tools, n. e. s., typewriters and parts, vault lights and ventilators, windmills, window and door screens, wire, wirework, n. e. s.

The highly intricate structure of this important industrial group defies any attempt to introduce a finer distinction among its separate component parts. Even on the basis of the census classification accepted above, it overlaps in many instances the adjoining industries, particularly "Steel Works and Rolling Mills," "Non-Ferrous Metal Smelting and Refining," and "Brass, Bronze, and Copper Products." Such commodities as copper wire, for example, are produced in rolling mills and copper works as well as in special wire works. The distribution of these goods among the different consumers is made in this, as in all other similar cases, on a strictly proportional basis. For each particular kind of use, each source of supply is drawn upon in proportion to its total output.

To Agriculture: agricultural machinery, carriages, traction engines, and other products used by agriculture (production data, *Mfr*.). *To* Flour and Grist Mills: machinery (production data, *Mfr*.). *To* Cannings and Preserving: tin cans (estimated on basis of Census of Mfr., 1929. Comparing this amount with the total number of containers used by the canning industry in 1929 — 3,036 million cans — we obtain an average price of 2.96 cents per can, which might be somewhat high.) *To* Bread and Bakery Products: machinery (production data, *Mfr*.). *To* Sugar, Glucose, and Starch: sugar machinery (production data, *Mfr*.). *To* Liquors and Beverages: bottling machinery (production data, *Mfr*.). *To* Butter, Cheese, etc.: dairy machinery and tin cans (*Mfr*.). *To* Other Food Products: confectioners' machinery (*Mfr*.). *To* Iron Mining: estimate; mining machinery is distributed among the different branches

of mining in proportion to the horsepower used. *To* Steel Works and Rolling Mills: 30 per cent of metal working machinery (estimated on basis of *Mfr*., 1925–29). *To* Automobiles: electrical equipment, engines, vehicle hardware, machine tools, stamped ware, etc. (machine tools purchased estimated on basis of statement in *Iron Trade Review*, Jan. 5, 1920, p. 56. Stamped ware estimated on basis of *Mfr*., 1929. All other items, *Mfr*.). · *To* Other Iron and Steel: forgings, engines for shipbuilding, tin and terne plate and other products used in the same industry for further manufacture (*Mfr*.). *To* Non-Ferrous Metal Mining: ore crushers and mining machinery (for explanation of the latter item, see Other Iron and Steel to Iron Mining).

To Non-Metal Minerals: clay and glass working machinery (*Mfr*.). *To* Petroleum and Natural Gas: oil well machinery and wrought pipe. *To* Refined Petroleum: metal containers and wrought pipe (estimated on basis of *Mfr*. and *Iron Age* distribution; see Steel Works and Rolling Mills to Iron Mining). *To* Coal: machinery (estimate; see Other Iron and Steel to Iron Mining). *To* Chemicals: oil mill machinery (*Mfr*.). *To* Electric Utilities: machinery and apparatus (telephone and telegraph apparatus and supplies and line materials). *To* Lumber and Timber: estimated on basis of *Mfr*. *To* Paper and Wood Pulp: paper and pulp machinery (*Mfr*.). *To* Printing and Publishing: machinery (*Mfr*.). *To* Yarn and Cloth: textile machinery (*Mfr*.). *To* Other Textile Products: industrial sewing machines. *To* Leather: machinery (*Mfr*.). *To* Shoes: machinery (*Mfr*.). *To* Other Leather Products: hardware (*Mfr*.). *To* Rubber: machinery (*Mfr*.). *To* Construction: electric machinery and fixtures, etc., electric wire (estimated on basis of data of American Bureau of Metal Statistics on copper consumption), gas and water meters, etc., building hardware, cast pipe, iron and steel doors and shutters, nails and spikes (estimated), wrought pipe (estimated), plumbing supplies, hot air furnaces, stamped and enameled ware (tubs and sinks), dredging, excavating, and road making machinery, concrete mixers, safes and vaults, steam fittings, structural iron work, vault lights and ventilators. Unless otherwise stated, all data are obtained from *Mfr*. *To* Transportation (Railroads): products of railway repair shops (*Mfr*.), locomotives, cars and machinery purchased (*Statistics of Railways*, 1919). *To* Consumption: electric wire, machinery and appliances, stoves and ranges, cutlery and edge tools, hardware, enameled ware, sewing machines, etc. (*Mfr*.). *To* Undistributed: This item contains among other products the total output of the steel shipbuilding industry, which in 1919 amounted to 1,456 million dollars.

15. Automobiles

Includes automobile bodies and parts, automobiles, and automobile repairing.

To Automobile Industry: products of bodies and parts industry (*Mfr*.) and 50 per cent (estimated) of the "other products" of the automobile industry (*Mfr*.). *To* Consumption: passenger cars, product of repair shops, and 50 per cent of "other products" of automobile industry (*Mfr*.). *To* Undistributed: trucks and other special types of motor vehicles (*Mfr*.).

16. Non-Ferrous Metal Mining

Includes mining of copper, lead and zinc, gold and silver, and metals, n. e. s.

To Non-Ferrous Metal Mining: purchased ore, etc. (*Min*.). *To* Smelting and Refining: production of copper, lead, and zinc ore (*Min*.). *To* Undistributed: principally products of gold and silver mining.

17. Non-Ferrous Metals: Smelting and Refining

Includes smelting and refining of copper, lead, and zinc, metals n. e. s., and smelting not from ore.

QUANTITATIVE INPUT AND OUTPUT RELATIONS

To Steel Works and Rolling Mills: consumption by steel works and rolling mills of copper (*Mfr.*), zinc (quantity as given by the American Bureau of Metal Statistics, 1919); valued at point of production. *To* Automobiles: lead and zinc (American Bureau of Metal Statistics). *To* Other Iron and Steel: lead and zinc (American Bureau of Metal Statistics). *To* Smelting and Refining: rough estimate on basis of *Mfr.* *To* Brass, Bronze, etc.: estimated on basis of metal content of products of the industry. *To* Printing and Publishing: zinc (American Bureau of Metal Statistics). *To* Chemicals: lead and zinc, including pigments from ore. *To* Paint Industry: estimated on the basis of American Bureau of Metal Statistics and *Mineral Industry*. *To* Construction: lead (American Bureau of Metal Statistics). *To* Consumption: lead and zinc (American Bureau of Metal Statistics). *To* Undistributed: includes addition to copper stocks valued at 59 million dollars.

18. Brass, Bronze and Copper Products, etc.

Includes aluminum manufacture, Babbit metal and solder, bells, brass, bronze, and copper products, gold and silver leaf and foil, gold and silver not from ore, lead (pipe, bar and sheet), silver smithing and silverware, tin and other foils, plated ware.

To Tobacco Manufactures: tin and other foils (rough estimate on basis of production of tin and other foils). *To* Other Food Industries: rough estimate on basis of production of tin and other foils. *To* Automobiles: brass, bronze and copper, and aluminum (calculated on basis of American Bureau of Metal Statistics and *Automobile Facts and Figures*). *To* Other Iron and Steel Industries: calculated on basis of American Bureau of Metal Statistics and *Mfr.* *To* Electric Utilities: copper wire and cable. *To* Consumption: hardware, lamps, etc. (production data, *Mfr.*). *To* Undistributed: residual (includes gold and silver not from ore). *To* Construction: copper wire.

19. Non-Metal Minerals

Includes mining of stone, clay, gypsum, phosphate rock, sulphur, and miscellaneous mineral mining, artificial stone, asbestos (building material and other asbestos products), brick, tile, etc., cement, crucibles, emery and other abrasive wheels, glass, graphite (ground and refined), grindstones, hones and whetstones, marble and stone work, millstones, minerals and earths (ground and prepared), paving materials, pottery, sand, lime, brick, wall plaster and composition flooring.

To Agriculture: limestone, lime, etc. (*Min.*). *To* Canning and Preserving: glass containers (estimated on basis of *Mfr.*). *To* Sugar: lime and limestone (*Mineral Resources of the U. S.*). *To* Liquors and Beverages: glass containers (estimated on basis of *Mfr.*). *To* Blast Furnaces: limestone flux (*Mineral Resources of the U. S.*). *To* Steel Works and Rolling Mills: fluor spar (*Mineral Resources of the U. S.*). *To* Automobiles: plate glass (estimated consumption on basis of *Mfr.*, 1923). *To* Other Iron and Steel: glass and brick. *To* Smelting and Refining: brick, tile, etc.

20. Petroleum and Natural Gas

Includes petroleum and natural gas industry. The distribution of natural gas constitutes a part of the general industrial fuel and power distribution, for the detailed description of which see the distribution of products of the coal industry. The following explanation covers only the crude petroleum and natural gas not included in the general fuel and power distribution.

To Petroleum and Natural Gas: contains 29 million dollars of natural gas purchased for resale (*Min.*). *To* Refined Petroleum: contains 657 million dollars of petroleum and 60 millions of natural gas for refining (*Mfr.*). *To* Manufactured Gas: contains 2 million dollars of natural gas purchased for resale. *To* Consumption: includes 19 million dollars of natural-gas gaso-

line other than that going to refined petroleum. *To* Undistributed: contains 22 million dollars of petroleum.

21. Refined Petroleum

Includes lubricating greases and refined petroleum. The distribution of refined petroleum constitutes a part of the general industrial fuel and power distribution, for the detailed description of which see the distribution of products of the coal industry. The following explanation covers only the distribution of petroleum products not included in the general fuel and power distribution.

To Agriculture: axle grease (*Mfr.*). *To* Refined Petroleum: contains 152 million dollars of distillates purchased and rerun. *To* Electric Utilities: fuel oil (*Statistical Abstract of United States*). *To* Construction: road oils (*Mfr.*). *To* Transportation (Railroads): fuel oil and lubricants (*Statistics of Railways*, 1919). *To* Undistributed: includes fuel oil to shipping and additions to stocks.

22. Coal

Includes coal, anthracite and bituminous. The total value of coal distributed (including transportation costs) exceeds by 3.3. per cent (70 million dollars) the actual output of the coal mines in the year 1919. Due to a prolonged strike, a considerable part of the current consumption was drawn from stocks. According to the fundamental set-up of our general table, all stock accounts belong in the consolidated "Undistributed" account. For want of better knowledge, it is assumed that the distribution from stock is proportional to the distribution from mines. Accordingly, the distribution of the product of the coal industry as described below is subsequently stepped down by 3.3. per cent all along the line.

The main part of the coal distribution is derived from the general fuel and power distribution which is outlined below.

General Fuel and Power Distribution for Manufacture and Mining

The physical quantities of coal (bituminous and anthracite), coke, fuel oil, gasoline, and gas used for fuel by the different industries, as reported in *Mfr.* and *Min.*, were multiplied by the average unit price of the respective products as given at the point of production. The values thus obtained are increased in the case of coal, coke, and oil through addition of average rail transportation costs (see page 112 above). For obvious reasons, no transportation costs have been added to the value of coal used in coal mines and bituminous coal used by cokeries. Fuel oil and gasoline absorbed by the oil refining industry and coke used in cokeries are also valued at average producers' prices without addition of transportation costs.

The subtraction of these hypothetical fuel costs from the total fuel and power costs as given in the Census yields a residual for purchased power which is taken to consist entirely of purchased electric power.

The use of average prices and transportation charges necessarily impairs the reliability of these preliminary estimates. Particular bias is to be expected with respect to those industries in which the fuel costs constitute a large proportion of total expenses or in which the quantity of fuel used is determined by special technical requirements. On the basis of these qualifications, the preliminary estimates were revised for the following twelve industries: Iron Mining, Blast Furnaces, Steel Works and Rolling Mills, Non-Ferrous Metal Mining, Smelting and Refining, Non-Metal Minerals, Petroleum and Natural Gas, Refined Petroleum, Coal, Coke, Manufactured Gas, and Sugar. The revision consists in recalculation of the purchased power costs on the basis of an average outlay of $17.50 per horsepower of prime movers operated on purchased power in each particular industry. For all branches of the mining industry, the actual cost of purchased power is given in the Census of Mining. Subsequently the costs of other fuels were adjusted correspondingly. Thus, for example, the price of coal used in coal mining is reduced below the average, while its unit cost to gas manufacturers is considerably increased. Fuel oil costs to the sugar industry are reduced because of special locational advantages.

The final distribution of gas requires additional calculations because this product is supplied from three different sources; one part comes from the petroleum and natural gas industry, another originates in gas manufacture, and the rest is a by-product of the coke industry. The distribution among these three sources is proportional throughout.

The following comments cover only that part of the coal distribution which is not derived from the general fuel and power distribution.

To Electric Utilities: estimate based on quantities consumed (*Statistical Abstract of the United States*). *To* Transportation (Railroads): estimated on the basis of *Statistics of Railways*, 1919. *To* Consumption: estimate of National Coal Commission (*What the Coal Commission Found*). *To* Undistributed: contains 27 million dollars consumed by shipping (*Statistical Abstract of United States*).

23. Coke

Includes coke and manufactured fuel. The main part of the coke distribution is derived from the general fuel and power distribution (see coal distribution). The following remarks cover only that part of the coke and coke gas distribution which is not derived from the general fuel and power distribution.

To Electric Utilities: proportional distribution of gas on the basis of *Statistical Abstract of United States*. *To* Consumption: rough estimate. *To* Undistributed: residual.

24. Manufactured Gas

Includes manufactured gas industry. The main part of the manufactured gas distribution is derived from the general fuel and power distribution (see coal distribution). The following comments cover only that part of manufactured gas which is not included in the general fuel and power distribution.

To Electric Utilities: proportional distribution on the basis of consumption data (*Statistical Abstract of United States*). *To* Consumption: undistributed gas, coke, and appliances (*Mfr.*). *To* Undistributed: undistributed by-products.

25. Electric Utilities

Includes electric railroads, electric light and power, telephone and telegraph. The main part of the electric power distribution is derived from the general fuel and power distribution. (See coal distribution.) The following comments cover only those items which are not derived from the general fuel and power distribution.

To Electric Utilities: power sold by central electric stations to electric railways and to other central electric stations, power sold by electric railroads to central electric stations, etc. *To* Consumption: (*a*) passenger and baggage revenue of electric railroads (estimated on basis of the Census of Electric Railroads, 1917 and 1922); (*b*) domestic and farm consumption of electric power (estimated on basis of Census of Electric Industries: Central Electric Stations, 1917, 1922, 1927, and 1932). It is assumed that two-thirds of "small power and light" sales consisted of power and that one-third was used for commercial lighting; (*c*) thirty per cent of total telegraph and telephone revenue (rough estimate). *To* Undistributed: residual.

26. Chemicals

Includes blackings, stains, and dressings, bluing, candles, chemicals, cleaning and polishing preparations, coal tar products, drug grinding, druggists' preparations, natural dyestuffs and extracts, essential oils, explosives, fireworks, fertilizers, glue, n.e.s., adhesives, cottonseed oil and cake, oil, n.e.s., paints, patent medicines and compounds, perfumery and cosmetics, salt, soaps, sulphuric, nitric, and mixed acids, turpentine and rosin, varnishes, wood distillation.

To Agriculture: fertilizers (*Mfr.*), cottonseed oil and cake (*Mfr.*), sprays (estimate given in W. I. King, *The National Income and Its Purchasing Power* [National Bureau of Economic Research, New York, 1930]). *To* Slaughter and Meat Packing: cottonseed oil (seventy per cent of the total output as estimated by Philip G. Wright, *The Tariff on Animal and Vegetable Oils* [New York, 1928]). *To* Iron Mining: explosives (estimate based on *Production of Explosives in the United States* [Bureau of Mines, Technical Paper 259, May, 1920]). *To* Blast Furnaces: charcoal from wood distillation (production, *Mfr.*). *To* Automobiles: estimate based on *Automobile Facts and Figures*. *To* Non-Ferrous Metal Mining: explosives (see Chemicals to Iron Mining). *To* Non-Metal Minerals: explosives (see Chemicals to Iron Mining). *To* Petroleum Refining: sulphuric acid, etc. (cost data, *Mfr.*). *To* Coal: explosives (see Chemicals to Iron Mining). *To* Chemicals: chemicals, oils, and tallow (cost data, *Mfr.*). *To* Printing and Publishing: ink (production, *Mfr.*). *To* Yarn and Cloth: dyes and bleaches (estimated on basis of *Mfr.*). *To* Paper and Wood Pulp: bleaching powder (cost data, *Mfr.*). *To* Leather, Tanning: tanning materials (cost and production data, *Mfr.*). *To* Rubber: bone, carbon, and lampblack (estimated on basis of *Mineral Industry*, 1920). *To* Construction: paints (rough estimate on basis of Census of Construction, 1929). *To* Consumption: patent medicines, drugs, soap, cosmetics, paint, etc. (Soap and paint estimated on basis of Census, 1929; other items taken from *Mfr.*). *To* Undistributed: contains chemicals, paints, soap, etc. There is good reason to believe that a considerable part of undistributed chemical products consists of consumption goods.

27. Lumber and Timber Products

Includes lumber and timber products, lumber, planing mill products, boxes (wood), and custom saw mills. This distribution is not intended to include lumber and timber products produced on farms for farmers' own use. Available statistical information does not provide, however, a sufficient basis for a clear-cut distinction among the different sources of the lumber supply.

To Agriculture: fence posts (total output, *Statistical Abstract of United States*). *To* Iron Mining: estimated on basis of 1923 distribution as given by the Department of Agriculture (Statistical Bulletin 21). *To* Automobiles: estimated on basis of *Automobile Facts and Figures* for 1923. *To* Other Iron and Steel Industries: includes wood used in car construction, agricultural implements, and carriages and wagons, estimated on basis of *Wood Using Industries of New York* (Technical Publication No. 14 of New York State College of Forestry, 1921). *To* Non-Ferrous Metal Mining: estimated on basis of 1923 distribution as given by the Department of Agriculture (Stat. Bull. 21). *To* Refined Petroleum: containers (cost data, *Mfr.*). *To* Coal Mining: estimated on basis of 1923 distribution as given by Department of Agriculture (Stat. Bull. 21). *To* Lumber and Timber Products: saw logs consumed by lumber industry, lumber consumed by planing mills and box factories (estimated on basis of *Mfr.*). *To* Other Wood Products: used in wooden shipbuilding, furniture, cooperage, wood (turned and carved), etc. (estimated on basis of Census of Mfr. and *Wood Using Industries of New York*. For reference, see above). *To* Chemicals: material for production of tanning extracts and dyestuffs and wood distillation (*Mfr.*). *To* Shoe Industry: materials for wooden heels (*Mfr.*). *To* Construction: lumber and millwork (estimated on basis of Census of Construction, 1929). *To* Transportation (Railroads): ties (*Statistics of Railways*). *To* Industries not elsewhere specified: estimated on basis of *Wood Using Industries of New York* (for reference, see above).

QUANTITATIVE INPUT AND OUTPUT RELATIONS 121

28. Other Wood Products

Includes baskets, rattan and willow ware, billiard tables and bowling alleys, brooms, brushes, coffins and burial cases, charcoal, cooperage (slack and tight), cork cutting, furniture (wood, rattan, and willow), store and office fixtures, show cases, lasts, looking glass and picture frames, matches, musical instruments, pianos, organs and materials, refrigerators, sewing machine cases, shipbuilding (wooden), wood (turned and carved), woodenware products not elsewhere specified, wood preserving.

To Tobacco: cigar boxes (*Mfr.*). *To* Other Iron and Steel Industries: sewing machine cases (*Mfr.*). *To* Other Wood Products: musical instruments, parts (*Mfr.*). *To* Shoes: lasts (*Mfr.*). *To* Consumption: wooden furniture, musical instruments, coffins and burial cases, wooden goods n.e.s., etc. (*Mfr.*). To Undistributed: includes 165 million dollars of wooden shipbuilding products.

29. Paper and Wood Pulp

Includes paper and wood pulp, pulp from fiber, not wood, and pulp goods.

To Paper and Wood Pulp: pulp (*Mfr.*). *To* Other Paper Products: paper for boxes, bags, etc. (rough estimates on basis of cost of materials, *Mfr.*). *To* Printing and Publishing: printing paper and board (production, *Mfr.*). *To* Construction: building and roofing paper (production, *Mfr.*). *To* Consumption: wallpapers, writing paper, tissue paper, etc. (production, *Mfr.*). *To* Undistributed: wrapping paper, paper board, etc.

30. Other Paper Products

Includes bags (paper), boxes (paper and other n. e. s.), carbon paper, cardboard, cardcutting and designing, envelopes, paper goods, n. e. s., paper novelties, paper patterns, wall paper not made in paper mills.

To Consumption: wall paper not made in paper mills, playing cards, and paper novelties (production, *Mfr.*). *To* Undistributed: bags, boxes, etc.

31. Printing and Publishing

Includes printing and publishing (book and job), music, newspapers and periodicals, book binding and blank book making, engraving (steel and copperplate), lithographing, photo-engraving, engraving materials, printing materials, stereotyping and electrotyping, typefounding, and wood engraving.

To Printing and Publishing: printing for others, photoengraving, bookbinding, etc. (*Mfr.*). *To* Transportation (Railroads): job printing, blank books, etc. (estimated on basis of cost data, *Statistics of Railways*). *To* Consumption: newspaper and periodical sales and subscriptions, books and pamphlets, sheet music (*Mfr.*). *To* Undistributed: contains job printing, newspaper and periodical advertising, lithographing, etc.

32. Yarn and Cloth

Includes cotton goods, cotton small wares, cotton lace woolen goods, worsted goods, carpets and rugs, wool felt hats, felt goods, knit goods, silk manufactures, cordage and twine, jute, linen, wool shoddy, wool pulling, wool scouring, fur felt hats, dyeing and finishing textiles, flax and hemp (dressed), haircloth, oilcloth and linoleum, straw hats.

To Agriculture: twine (*Mfr.*). *To* Automobiles: upholstery material (estimated on basis of *Automobile Facts and Figures*). *To* Other Wood Products: upholstery goods (production, *Mfr.*). *To* Yarn and Cloth: yarn, etc. (cost data, *Mfr.*). *To* Clothing: distribution based on a special study made by the Bureau of Business Research, Harvard Graduate School of Business Administration (*Distribution of Textiles*, Bulletin No. 56). As this study covers only a part of the industry, the application of its findings to the total output required a series of additional calculations. The estimates were made for each type of fabric

and marketing channel separately. *To* Other Textile Products: bag materials, etc. (estimated on basis of cost of materials and output data, *Mfr.*). *To* Shoes: lining materials (production, *Mfr.*). *To* Other Leather Products: saddle felts (production, *Mfr.*). *To* Rubber Industry: tire duck (production, *Mfr.*) and cloth for rubberizing (estimate on basis of yardage). *To* Consumption: difference between the total product of the industry and the amounts distributed among all other uses, including undistributed (see below). *To* Undistributed: consists of products for further manufacture which could not be assigned to particular industries, products of unknown use, unspecified products and contract work (production, *Mfr.*).

33. Clothing

Includes men's clothing, buttonholes, men's collars and cuffs, men's furnishings, suspenders, garters, etc., shirts, women's clothing, corsets, gloves and mittens, cloth, hats and caps (other than felt, straw, or wool), millinery and lace goods.

To Clothing: sixty per cent (rough estimate) of products of contract clothing manufacture, buttonholes, fur trimmings from fur goods industry (estimated on basis of *Mfr.*, 1929). *To* Consumption: difference between total output of clothing industry and the amounts distributed to other uses. *To* Undistributed: "Other Products" estimated on basis of *Mfr.*, 1929.

34. Other Textile Products

Includes asbestos textile mill products, awnings, tents and sails, bags other than paper, belting and hose (not rubber), carpets (rag), cloth sponging and refinishing, clothing (horse), flags and banners, furs (dressed), hairwork, hammocks, hat and cap materials, house furnishings, n. e. s., mattresses and bedspreads, nets and seines, oakum, regalia, etc., upholstery materials, n. e. s., waste (cotton and other).

To Agriculture: clothing (horse, *Mfr.*). *To* Other Wood Products: imitation leather and coiled hair (*Mfr.*). *To* Yarn and Cloth: cloth sponging and finishing (production, *Mfr.*). *To* Clothing: hat and cap materials and dressed furs (*Mfr.*). *To* Consumption: house furnishings, mattresses, etc. (*Mfr.*). *To* Undistributed: bags, awnings, tents and sails, asbestos products, etc. (*Mfr.*).

35. Leather, Tanning

Includes leather tanning and finishing. The value of the total product of the industry includes 77 million dollars of hides and skins tanned on contract, which is not included in the value of the product of the industry as given in the Census.

To Automobiles: estimated on basis of *Automobile Facts and Figures*. *To* Other Wood Products: upholstery leather other than that assigned to automobile industry. *To* Chemicals: glue stock and fertilizer materials (*Mfr.*). *To* Printing and Publishing: bookbinders leather (*Mfr.*). *To* Yarn and Cloth: wool and hair (*Mfr.*). *To* Clothing: textile leather and hat sweats (*Mfr.*). *To* Leather, Tanning: rough leather (cost data, *Mfr.*). *To* Shoes: sole, upper, patent, and welting leather, less 55 million dollars assigned to consumption. *To* Other Leather Industries: estimated on basis of cost of materials as given in *Mfr.* *To* Consumption: rough estimate of leather used in shoe repairing. *To* Undistributed: residual.

36. Shoes

Includes boots and shoes, boot and shoe cut stock, boot and shoe findings.

To Boots and Shoes: cut stock and findings (*Mfr.*). *To* Consumption: boots and shoes (*Mfr.*).

37. Leather, Other Products

Includes belting leather, gloves and mittens (leather), saddlery and harness, pocketbook leather, trunks and valises, leather goods, n.e.s.

To Consumption: trunks and valises, gloves and mittens, etc. (production, *Mfr.*). *To* Undistributed: includes 40 million dollars of leather belting.

38. Rubber Manufactures

Includes belting and hose (rubber), boots and shoes (rubber), rubber tires and tubes, and rubber goods, n. e. s.

To Automobiles: tires (estimated; four tires and tubes per automobile produced in 1919) and rubberized cloth (estimated on basis of *Mfr.*). *To* Rubber Manufacture: reclaimed rubber (production, *Mfr.*). *To* Consumption: tires (total production of pneumatic tires less amount assigned to automobile industry), boots and shoes, druggists' and stationers' supplies, etc. (production, *Mfr.*). *To* Undistributed: includes solid tires (less amount assigned to automobile industry), hard rubber products, hose, etc.

39. Industries Not Elsewhere Specified.

Includes buttons, dairymen's and poultrymen's, etc. supplies, electroplating, enameling, engraving and die sinking, feathers and plumes, fire extinguishers (chemical), foundry supplies, glass cutting and staining, hand stamps, instruments (professional and scientific), japanning, jewelry and instrument cases, labels and tags, lamps and reflectors, models and patterns, musical instruments and materials, n. e. s., photographic apparatus, photographic materials, roofing materials, sand and emery paper and cloth, stencils and brands, surgical appliances, typewriter supplies, upholstery materials, n. e. s., wheelbarrows, artificial flowers, artificial limbs, artists' materials, china decorating, clocks, combs and hairpins not made of rubber, dental goods, fancy goods, n.e.s., ice manufactured, ivory, shell, and bone work, jewelry, lapidary work, mirrors, optical goods, pencils (lead), pens (fountain and stylographic), pens (gold), phonographs, pipes (tobacco), signs and advertising novelties, sporting and athletic goods, stationery, n.e.s., statuary and art goods, theater scenery, toys and games, umbrellas and canes, watch and clock materials, watch cases and watches, whips, window shades and fixtures, washing machines and wringers, all other industries.

To Agriculture: dairymen's, poultrymen's, etc. supplies (production, *Mfr.*). *To* Other Iron and Steel: foundry supplies (production, *Mfr.*). *To* Other Wood Products: upholstery materials, n. e. s. (production, *Mfr.*). *To* Yarn and Cloth: buttons for knit goods (cost data, *Mfr.*). *To* Clothing: buttons (rough estimate). *To* Construction: roofing materials (production, *Mfr.*). *To* Consumption: includes products of all industries from artificial limbs to all other industries as listed above. *To* Undistributed: residual.

40. Construction

Includes construction of multiple dwellings, public works and public utilities, business buildings, industrial buildings, residential projects by operators, individual-built homes, etc., educational buildings, social and recreational buildings, religious and memorial buildings, hospitals and institutions, public and government buildings, military and naval structures.

The total value of products, as given in the table, is an authoritative estimate made on the basis of contracts awarded in 25 states as reported by the F. W. Dodge Corporation ("Who Builds the Homes in Which You Live," *Literary Digest*, 1926, p. 6).

To Consumption: multiple dwellings, residential projects and individual-built homes, stables, etc. (estimate; Dodge data for 25 states are increased by 21.7 per cent, which is the ratio between the total construction in the United States as given above and the Dodge figures of construction in 25 states). *To* Undistributed: residual. No attempt has been made to dis-

tribute the 625 million dollars of industrial construction (estimate) among the various industries.

41. Transportation (Steam Railroads)

Includes Class I, II, and III railroads, switching and terminal companies.

The total value of product is equal to the total operating and non operating revenue of all railways, diminished by 899 million dollars, a sum which represents the total of financial transactions between separate railroads and consists of rent payments to other roads, interest and dividend payments to other roads, and the net income of "federal" roads.

The interpretation of railroad finances for the year 1919 is considerably complicated by the repercussions of governmental control. The non-operating revenue of "corporate" railroads includes approximately 900 million dollars paid by the Federal Treasury in compensation for "leased lines." On the other hand, in operating these "federal" roads, the government earned some net income. In the official accounting sheets, this amount appears twice, once in the income schedule of the "corporate" roads as a part of payment received for "leased lines," and again in the revenue account of the "federal" roads. In order to avoid this double counting, the latter item had to be subtracted from the aggregate railroad revenue.

The general scheme of distribution of transportation services is described in the first part of this article (see page 112).

To all branches of industry and agriculture: distribution of freight services is based on the "Revenue Freight Tonnage by Classes of Commodities" as published in *Statistics of Railways* for 1919. The freight revenue on each of the different types of commodities "per ton" is estimated on the basis of the "Estimate of the Freight Revenue of Class I Roads by Classes of Commodities on Basis of 1922 Tonnage and 1923 Rates," Interstate Commerce Commission, Bureau of Statistics, 1923. The average per ton revenue on each particular type of commodity as given in this study is corrected for the main freight rate changes which took place between 1919 and 1922.

To Consumption: total revenue earned in connection with passenger traffic, which includes, in addition to the revenue on passenger account, receipts from transportation of excess baggage, the revenue from hotel accommodations owned by the railroads, etc. *To* Exports: estimated costs of domestic transportation of imported commodities (see page 112). *To* Undistributed: this residual item includes the *net* governmental payment for lease of lines to the amount of approximately 400 million dollars.

42. Imports

Includes commodity imports into the United States entered for domestic consumption (as listed in *Foreign Commerce and Navigation of the United States*, 1919). Imports of gold and silver are excluded. The general principles of the import distribution are presented in the first part of this article (see page 112).

The declared values of each particular kind of imports are augmented by the amount of duty collected and by the proportional amount of domestic rail-transportation costs paid within the country (see Transportation to Exports). The statistical scheme used in distribution of imports is analogous to the set-up of the general table: it may best be represented by a two-way tabulation, in which the rows show the distribution of all the individual kinds of imports while the columns indicate the quantities of the different foreign goods absorbed by the respective industries. The detailed figures are given below in non-tabular form. Main headings refer to type of imports; subheadings indicate the industries in which the imports were absorbed.

QUANTITATIVE INPUT AND OUTPUT RELATIONS

IMPORTS
(Unit: thousand dollars)

Agricultural
To: Agriculture	38,700
Flour and grist mills	17,156
Bread and bakery products	8,865
Liquors and beverages	238
Tobacco	75,146
Slaughter and meat packing	56,772
Other food products	335,677
Yarn and cloth	714,502
Chemicals	64,868
Consumption	138,161
Undistributed	8,363
	1,458,448

Flour and grist mill products
To: Bread and bakery products	738
Consumption	9,905
	10,643

Canning and preserving
To: Consumption	27,509

Bread and bakery products
To: Consumption	6,842

Sugar, etc.
To: Sugar, etc. (refining)	393,171
Undistributed	4,420
	397,591

Liquors and beverages
To: Consumption	798

Tobacco mfrs.
To: Consumption	11,339

Slaughtering and meat packing
To: Slaughtering and meat packing	5,629
Chemicals	1,820
Leather, tanning	306,509
Consumption	16,020
Undistributed	8,050
	338,028

Butter, cheese, etc.
To: Consumption	11,013
Undistributed	2,010
	13,023

Other food products
To: Consumption	2,807

Iron mining
To: Blast furnaces	2,386

Blast furnaces
To: Steel works and rolling mills	5,443
Other iron and steel industries	1,652
	7,095

Steel works and rolling mills
To: Steel works and rolling mills	3,849
Other iron and steel industries	808
Transportation	652
	5,309

Automobiles
To: Consumption	123

Other iron and steel industries
To: Agriculture	4,083
Other iron and steel industries	589
Textiles, yarn and cloth	1,136
Construction	134
Consumption	773
Undistributed	9,314
	16,029

Non-ferrous metal mining
To: Blast furnaces	19,200
Smelting and refining	21,868
	41,068

Smelting and refining
To: Blast furnaces	144
Steel works and rolling mills	22,188
Other iron and steel industries	28,702
Smelting and refining	29,331
Brass, bronze, etc.	9,277
Undistributed	12
	139,654

Brass, bronze, etc.
To: Other iron and steel industries	3,923
Brass, bronze, etc.	5,811
Clothing	1,283
Other textile products	1,283
Chemicals	471
Other industries n. e. s.	3,770
Consumption	1,669
Undistributed	4,613
	22,823

Non-metal minerals
To: Brass, bronze, etc.	37
Non-metal minerals	9,674
Chemicals	983
Construction	1,800
Consumption	83,218
Other industries n. e. s.	28,526
Undistributed	13,881
	138,119

Petroleum and natural gas
To: Petroleum refining	26,443

Petroleum refining
To: Consumption	4,997
Undistributed	974
	5,971

Coal
To: Consumption	5,473

Coke
To: Consumption	141

Lumber and timber
To: Agriculture	137
Lumber and timber	32,768
Other wood products	5,772
Paper and pulp	10,459
Construction	11,883
Transportation	355
Electric utilities	182
Consumption	536
Undistributed	13,222
	75,314

Other wood products
To: Other wood products	236
Consumption	5,819
Undistributed	4,401
	10,456

Paper and wood pulp
To: Tobacco mfr.	6,124
Paper and wood pulp	37,049
Printing and publishing	43,732
Consumption	143
Undistributed	2,677
	89,725

Other paper products
To: Consumption	104
Undistributed	1,814
	1,918

Printing and publishing
To: Consumption	4,894
Undistributed	237
	5,131

Yarn and cloth
To: Agriculture	2,696
Flour and grist mills	590
Other wood products	427
Yarn and cloth	28,130
Clothing	32,457

Other textile products.....................	50,000
Consumption............................	25,102
Undistributed...........................	53,393
	192,795

Clothing

To: Consumption.........................	21,020

Other textile products

To: Yarn and cloth	497
Clothing..............................	12,452
Consumption...........................	2,843
Undistributed..........................	26,680
	42,472

Chemicals

To: Agriculture...........................	33,345
Textiles...............................	5,466
Chemicals.............................	41,700
Construction..........................	1,236
Consumption..........................	9,330
Undistributed.........................	14,254
	105,331

Vegetable oils

To: Canning and preserving..................	8,000
Slaughtering and meat packing.............	41,181
Other food products......................	1
Steel works and rolling mills...............	98
Other iron and steel......................	127
Yarn and cloth..........................	10,606
Chemicals..............................	42,107
Consumption...........................	10,014
Undistributed..........................	15,700
	127,834

Chemicals including vegetable oils................	233,165

Leather, tanning

To: Other wood products....................	1
Tanning................................	5,751
Shoes..................................	3,966
Other leather products....................	11,376
Undistributed..........................	123
	21,217

Shoes

To: Consumption.........................	226

Other leather products

To: Agriculture..........................	230
Consumption..........................	6,261
Undistributed..........................	287
	6,778

Rubber

To: Consumption.........................	368
Undistributed..........................	636
	1,004

Rubber, crude

To: Rubber industries......................	221,626

Industries n. e. s.

To: Industries n. e. s.......................	70
Consumption...........................	40,368
Undistributed..........................	8,411
	48,849

Miscellaneous

To: Tobacco mfrs..........................	3,865
Other food products......................	6,217
Steel works and rolling mills...............	3,341
Brass, bronze, etc........................	3,267
Other wood products.....................	6,036
Paper and pulp..........................	7,185
Other textiles...........................	74,235
Chemicals..............................	22,688
Leather, tanning.........................	10,225
Industries. n. e. s.	3,337

Consumption...........................	12,919
Undistributed	
Special imports........................	32,377
Other.................................	16,092
Household effects......................	8,449
U. S. mfrs. returned...................	44,777
	255,010
Total Imports..............................	3,904,368

43a. Wages and Salaries

To Agriculture: total of money wages paid to farm laborers (Census of Agriculture). To Manufacturing and Mining Industries (all industries from Flour and Grist Mills to Industries Not Elsewhere Specified, with the exception of Electric Utilities): calculated on the basis of *Mfr.* and *Min.* To Electric Utilities: calculated on the basis of the Census of Electric Utilities. To Construction: rough estimate. The percentage relation of wages and salaries and cost of materials to the value of product of the industry in the year 1929 was calculated on the basis of the Census of Construction. These ratios were corrected for the change in wage level and variation in the cost of materials between 1919 and 1929 and then applied to the total value of output in 1919. To Transportation (Railroads): total wages and salaries (*Statistics of Railways*, 1919) diminished by the amount of wages and salaries paid out by steam railroad repair shops. (The latter are included in the Other Iron and Steel Industries.) To Consumption: estimate; the total of direct services (intangibles) absorbed by households amounted, according to W. H. Lough (*High Level Consumption* [New York, 1935]), to 6,546 million dollars. It is assumed that the material costs connected with the direct services are negligible and that consequently the total amount is distributed among wages, salaries, and capital and entrepreneurial services. The ratio between the two shares is obtained on basis of the income distribution within the "Unclassified Industries" as given by W. I. King (*The National Income and Its Purchasing Power*, 1930). To Undistributed: includes wages and salaries paid out in banking, mercantile industry, Pullman and express industry, shipping, undistributed unclassified (W. I. King: *The National Income . . .*). The last amount represents the difference between the total wages and salaries paid out in unclassified industries and the amount of wages and salaries assigned to Consumption (see Wages and Salaries to Consumption).

43b. Capital and Entrepreneurial Services (for definition and general discussion, see page 113.)

To Agriculture: see page 114. To Manufacturing Industries and Mining: calculated on the basis of the corporate income tax data in *Statistics of Income*, 1919 (published by the Bureau of Internal Revenue). For each industry, the amount of the net corporate income, earned by "corporations reporting net income" less tax, is augmented by the estimated amount of interest paid. In the official income statistics for 1919 the industrial classification used in the distribution of interest charges is somewhat less detailed than that which is given in our table. The necessary subdivision is obtained through a very rough estimate: the interest charges within each industrial group are distributed in proportion to the value of product. The results obtained thus for corporate enterprises only are stepped up so as to cover each industry as a whole (see "Gross Total Outlays" for manufacturing, below).

To Electric Utilities: comprises net income earned by "corporations reporting net income" less tax (*Statistics of Income*, Bureau of Internal Revenue), plus interest paid (W. I. King, *The National Income . . .*). To Construction: see "*To* Electric Utilities." To Railroads: see "*To* Electric Utilities." To Consumption: comprises rents for hired dwellings (estimated by W. H. Lough in *High Level Consumption*) and capital and

Table 5
QUANTITATIVE INPUT AND OUTPUT RELATIONS
IN THE ECONOMIC SYSTEM OF THE UNITED STATES, 1919

(Unit: million dollars)

DISTRIBUTION OF OUTPUT OF CLASSES LISTED AT LEFT OF TABLE

DISTRIBUTION OF OUTLAYS (INPUT) OF CLASSES LISTED AT TOP OF TABLE	Agriculture	Flour and grist mill products	Canning and preserving	Bread and bakery products	Sugar, glucose, and starch	Liquors and beverages	Tobacco manufactures	Slaughtering and meat packing	Butter, cheese, etc.	Other food industries	Iron mining	Blast furnaces	Steel works and rolling mills	Other iron and steel and electric mfrs.	Automobiles	Non-ferrous metal mining	Smelting and refining	Brass, bronze, copper, etc., mfrs.	Non-metal minerals	Petroleum and natural gas
	1	2	3	4	5	6	7	8	9	10	11	12	13	14	15	16	17	18	19	20
1 Agriculture	9102	1771	208	21	163	57	202	3033	797	53										
2 Flour and grist mill products	686			354																
3 Canning and preserving																				
4 Bread and bakery products																				
5 Sugar, glucose, and starch	27		24	50	11	6			30	116										
6 Liquors and beverages						35														
7 Tobacco manufactures																				
8 Slaughtering and meat packing	19			92					354	17										
9 Butter, cheese, etc.				27						36										
10 Other food industries				22						67										
11 Iron mining												269	5							
12 Blast furnaces													669	161	5					
13 Steel works and rolling mills	46										12	6	482	1154	86	31			13	76
14 Other iron and steel and electric mfrs.	522	18	91	10	1	11			51	10	4		17	503	381	11			7	46
15 Automobiles																997				
16 Non-ferrous metal mining																	7	267		
17 Smelting and refining													24	36	1		406	216		
18 Brass, bronze, copper, etc., mfrs.							5			13				251	46					
19 Non-metal minerals	7			19	1	21						22	4	22	14		3		20	
20 Petroleum and natural gas													10		4		3		7	41

Refined petroleum	Coal	Coke	Manufactured gas	Electric utilities	Chemicals	Lumber and timber products	Other wood products	Paper and wood pulp	Other paper products	Printing and publishing	Yarn and cloth	Clothing	Other textile products	Leather tanning	Leather shoes	Other leather products	Rubber manufactures	Industries n.e.s.	Construction	Transportation (steam railroads)	Exports	Consumption	Undistributed	Gross total output	Net total output	
21	22	23	24	25	26	27	28	29	30	31	32	33	34	35	36	37	38	39	40	41	42	43	44	45	46	
					308			4			1117			30							2100	2209	972	22147	13045	1
																					318	968	136	2462	2462	2
																					151	462	15	628	628	3
																					23	1325		1348	1348	4
											6										159	749	23	1201	1190	5
																					28	552		615	580	6
																					47	966		1013	1013	7
					79						20			247							1035	2626	87	4576	4222	8
																					146	874	65	1148	1148	9
																					56	1189	66	1400	1333	10
																					4		21	299	299	11
																				1		13	8	857	857	12
	89																		2	130	98	327	374	2926	2444	13
30	30			341	11	48	2	24		47	108	7	2	5	14	14	17		810	1431	896	634	5456	11610	11107	14
																					152	1773	383	3305	2308	15
																					1	74		349	342	16
					41														7		130	5	173	1039	633	17
			2																		52	113	300	783	783	18
3			13	54				9						1					622	15	66	189	336	1441	1421	19
722		2			6														1	2	15	90	29	932	891	20

Continued Overleaf

Table 5 Continued

No	Item	1	2	3	4	5	6	7	8	9	10	11	12	13	14	15	16	17	18	19	20
21	Refined petroleum	2	3	2	2	6	2		5	1	1			22	32	5	5	7	3	17	10
22	Coal		6	2	6	14	10	1	15	5	7	9	10	95	85	7	10	16	5	76	
23	Coke				2	1							230	7	20	1		7	1	4	
24	Manufactured gas					1			1					18	8	1		5		12	3
25	Electric utilities		7	2	10		3	1	5	5	5	2	1	12	44	11	10	2	7	14	1
26	Chemicals	356							159		4	3		10		9				1	
27	Lumber and timber products	258									3				96	44	12				
28	Other wood products						13							14							
29	Paper and wood pulp																				
30	Other paper products																				
31	Printing and publishing																				
32	Yarn and cloth	41														8					
33	Clothing																				
34	Other textile products	6																			
35	Leather tanning															19					
36	Leather shoes																				
37	Other leather products	75																			
38	Rubber manufactures													1	153						
39	Industries n.e.s.	21												10							
40	Construction																				
41	Transportation (steam railroads)	744	82			26	11		77			80	24	97	165		19	17		187	
42	Imports	85	21	8	8	468		91	106		353		23	35	36			115	18	11	
43a	Wages and salaries	1099	97	91	227	73	101	153	286	60	190	83	92	738	4096	677	148	72	171	488	169
43b	Capital and entrepreneurial services	9818	78	37	61	127	55	88	61	40	141	8	36	383	866	207	67	42	34	158	179
43c	Total services	10917	175	128	288	200	156	241	347	100	331	94	128	1121	4962	884	215	114	205	646	348
44a	Undistributed: Taxes	133	20	15	20	24	112	249	19	10	49	31	21	88	427	148	19	7	20	32	39
44b	Other		403	176	458	326	200	267	530	150	419	136	173	402	4445	673	156	126	351	546	903
44c	Total	133	423	191	478	350	312	516	549	160	468	167	194	490	4872	821	175	133	371	578	942
45	Gross total outlays	23047	2506	656	1390	1241	624	1070	4650	1166	1461	372	910	3108	12482	3488	504	1095	826	1593	1467
46	Net total outlays	13945	2506	656	1390	1230	589	1070	4296	1166	1394	372	910	2626	11979	2491	497	689	826	1573	1426
		1	2	3	4	5	6	7	8	9	10	11	12	13	14	15	16	17	18	19	20

21	22	23	24	25	26	27	28	29	30	31	32	33	34	35	36	37	38	39	40	41	42	43	44	45	46	
177		1	50	21	6	3	1	5		1	5					1	5	5		73	363	649	281	1772	1595	21
20	36	189	49	121	45	8	7	34	2	3	39	2	1	6	2		8	20		441	120	595	96	2223	2187	22
2		3	13		4			1			1						1				5	5	61	369	366	23
7			17	4	11				1							2						227	12	330	313	24
1	13	1	1	101	8	2	5	15	2	10	38	6	2	4	5	1	5	14				979	778	2133	2032	25
13	23			194			6		25	58			47			2		30			388	725	1249	3302	3108	26
35	36		9	48	485	453							13			14	252	95	86			469	2408	1923		27
				37								12									61	757	391	1285	1248	28
			77	210	233									18							58	99	117	812	735	29
																					15	38	397	450	450	30
										184										30	19	404	1118	1755	1571	31
							31			911	1208	290		6	1	189	1				318	1812	762	5578	4667	32
												145									42	3109	75	3371	3226	33
												30		4	47						44	172	282	585	538	34
						8	17			3	6	4	14	482	106						219	55	73	1006	992	35
															233						82	1064		1379	1146	36
																					10	130	88	303	303	37
																	19				53	651	261	1138	1119	38
												14		3	20				86		97	1134	391	1776	1776	39
																						1034	2108	3142	3142	40
131	713	50		9	337														5		141	1246	1464	5625	5620	41
26			181	33	12	56		44	792	129	55	371	4	11	222	43	18	1				572	257	4205	4205	42
118	975	50	78	782	497	713	402	171	106	589	1095	731	86	108	292	68	279	514	762	2228	3464	10137	33356			43 (a)
140	126	22	18	281	243	184	103	74	45	133	585	271	47	85	100	37	107	407	95	815	5382	9151	30937			43 (b)
258	1101	72	96	1063	740	897	505	245	151	722	1680	1002	133	193	392	105	386	921	857	3043	8846	19288	64293	55447		43 (c)
78	49	9	19	143	104	50	32	35	15	32	249	34	15	26	25	6	38	55	78	244		1355		4174		44 (a)
405	268	63	102	716	1547	663	220	341	93	545	792	1027	68	101	235	73	396	856	252	450	50	11980	32083			44 (b)
483	317	72	121	859	1651	713	252	376	108	577	1041	1061	83	127	260	79	434	911	330	694	50	13335	36257	36257		44 (c)
1908	2358	388	349	2534	3404	2540	1352	852	473	1850	5825	3588	613	1045	1423	317	1285	1933	3167	5928	7890	52362	38536	205576		45
1731	2322	385	332	2433	3210	2055	1315	775	473	1666	4914	3443	566	1031	1190	317	1266	1933	3167	5923	7890	43516	38536		182020	46

Table 6
QUANTITATIVE INPUT AND OUTPUT RELATIONS IN THE ECONOMIC SYSTEM OF THE UNITED STATES, 1919 : PERCENTAGE DISTRIBUTION +

(Unit: one per cent)

DISTRIBUTION OF OUTPUT OF CLASSES LISTED AT LEFT OF TABLE

DISTRIBUTION OF OUTLAYS (INPUT) OF CLASSES LISTED AT TOP OF TABLE	1 Agriculture	2 Flour and grist mill products	3 Canning and preserving	4 Bread and bakery products	5 Sugar, glucose, and starch	6 Liquors and beverages	7 Tobacco manufactures	8 Slaughtering and meat packing	9 Butter, cheese, etc.	10 Other food industries	11 Iron mining	12 Blast furnaces	13 Steel works and rolling mills	14 Other iron and steel and electric mfrs	15 Automobiles	16 Non-ferrous metal mining	17 Smelting and refining	18 Brass, bronze, copper, etc., mfrs.	19 Non-metal minerals	20 Petroleum and natural gas
1 Agriculture		13.6 (70.7)	1.6 (31.7)	.2 (1.5)	1.2 (3.3)	.4 (9.7)	1.5 (8.8)	23.3 (70.6)	6.1 (68.4)	.4 (3.8)										
2 Flour and grist mill products	27.9 (4.9)			14.4 (25.5)																
3 Canning and preserving																				
4 Bread and bakery products																				
5 Sugar, glucose, and starch	2.3 (.2)		2.0 (3.7)	4.2 (3.6)		.5 (1.0)			2.5 (2.6)	9.7 (8.3)										
6 Liquors and beverages																				
7 Tobacco manufactures																				
8 Slaughtering and meat packing	.5 (.1)			2.2 (6.6)					.4 (1.5)											
9 Butter, cheese, etc.				2.4 (1.9)						3.1 (2.6)										
10 Other food industries				1.7 (1.6)																
11 Iron mining												90.0 (29.6)	1.7 (.2)							
12 Blast furnaces													78.1 (25.5)	18.8 (1.3)	.6 (.2)					
13 Steel works and rolling mills	1.9 (.3)										.5 (3.2)	.2 (.7)	47.2 (9.6)	3.5 (3.5)	1.3 (6.2)				.5 (.8)	3.1 (5.3)
14 Other iron and steel and electric mfrs.	4.7 (3.7)	.2 (.7)	.8 (3.9)	.1 (.7)	* (.1)	.1 (.9)			.5 (4.4)	.1 (.7)	* (1.1)		.2 (.6)	3.4 (15.3)	.1 (2.2)				.1 (.4)	.4 (3.2)
15 Automobiles																				
16 Non-ferrous metal mining																	78.1 (38.8)			
17 Smelting and refining													3.8 (.9)	5.7 (.3)	.2 (*)			34.1 (26.2)		
18 Brass, bronze, copper, etc., mfrs.							.6 (.5)			1.7 (.9)			32.1 (2.1)	5.9 (1.8)						
19 Non-metal minerals	.5 (.1)			1.3 (1.3)	.1 (.1)	1.5 (3.6)						1.5 (2.4)	.3 (.2)	1.5 (.6)	1.0 (.6)		.2 (.4)			
20 Petroleum and natural gas													1.1 (.4)		.4 (.2)		.3 (.4)		.8 (.4)	
21 Refined petroleum	.1 *	.2 (.1)	.1 (.3)	.1 (.1)	.4 (.5)	.1 (.3)		.3 (.1)	.1 (.1)	.1 (.1)			1.4 (.8)	2.0 (.3)	.3 (.2)	.3 (1.0)	.4 (1.0)	.2 (.4)	1.1 (1.1)	.6 (.7)

+ The figures in this table are based upon the data in Table 5. Figures not in parentheses are percentages of the net totals of the rows (net total output) of Table 5; figures in parentheses are percentages of the net totals of the columns (net total outlays) of Table 5. Asterisks indicate percentages of less than 5/100 of one per cent.

Column legend (column numbers 21–46):

21 Refined petroleum · 22 Coal · 23 Coke · 24 Manufactured gas · 25 Electric utilities · 26 Chemicals · 27 Lumber and timber products · 28 Other wood products · 29 Paper and wood pulp · 30 Other paper products · 31 Printing and publishing · 32 Yarn and cloth · 33 Clothing · 34 Other textile products · 35 Leather tanning · 36 Leather shoes · 37 Other leather products · 38 Rubber manufactures · 39 Industries n.e.s. · 40 Construction · 41 Transportation (steam railroads) · 42 Exports · 43 Consumption · 44 Undistributed · 45 Gross total output · 46 Net total output

21	22	23	24	25	26	27	28	29	30	31	32	33	34	35	36	37	38	39	40	41	42	43	44	45	46	
					2.4 (9.6)			* (.5)			8.6 (22.7)			.2 (2.9)							16.1 (26.6)	16.9 (5.1)	7.5 (2.9)	169.8	100.0	1
																					12.9 (4.0)	39.3 (2.2)	5.5 (.4)	100.0	100.0	2
																					24.0 (1.9)	73.6 (1.1)	2.4 *	100.0	100.0	3
																					1.7 (.3)	98.3 (3.0)		100.0	100.0	4
											.5 (.1)										13.4 (2.0)	62.9 (1.7)	1.9 (.1)	100.9	100.0	5
																					4.8 (.4)	95.2 (1.3)		106.0	100.0	6
																					4.6 (.6)	95.4 (2.2)		100.0	100.0	7
					1.9 (2.5)						.5 (.4)			5.9 (24.0)							24.5 (13.1)	62.2 (6.0)	2.1 (.2)	108.4	100.0	8
																					12.7 (1.9)	76.1 (2.0)	5.7 (.2)	100.0	100.0	9
																					4.2 (.7)	89.2 (2.7)	5.0 (.2)	105.0	100.0	10
																					1.3 (.1)	7.0 (.1)		100.0	100.0	11
																			.1 *		1.5 (.2)		.9 *	100.0	100.0	12
	3.6 (3.8)																		.1 (.2)	5.3 (4.1)	4.0 (1.7)	13.4 (4.1)	15.3 (1.0)	119.7	100.0	13
.3 (1.7)	.3 (1.3)		3.1 (14.0)	.1 (.3)	.4 (2.3)	* (.2)		.2 (3.1)		.4 (2.8)	1.0 (2.2)	.1 (.2)	* (.4)	* (.5)	.1 (1.2)	.1 (4.4)	.2 (1.3)		7.3 (11.4)	12.9 (24.2)	8.1 (1.4)	5.7 (1.5)	49.1 (4.2)	104.5	100.0	14
																					6.6 (1.9)	76.8 (4.1)	16.6 (1.0)	143.2	100.0	15
																					.3 *		21.6 (.2)	102.0	100.0	16
					6.5 (1.3)															1.1 (.2)	20.5 (1.6)	.8 *	27.3 (.4)	164.1	100.0	17
			.3 (.1)																.1 *	*	6.6 (.7)	14.4 (.3)	38.3 (.8)	100.0	100.0	18
.2 (.2)			.9 (.5)	3.8 (1.7)				.6 (1.2)						.1 (.1)						43.8 (19.6)	4.6 (.8)	13.3 (.4)	23.6 (.9)	101.4	100.0	19
81.0 (41.7)			.2 (.6)	.7 (.2)														.1 (.1)	.2 *		1.7 (.2)	10.1 (.2)	3.3 (.1)	104.6	100.0	20
	.1 (.3)	3.1 (15.1)	1.3 (.9)	.4 (.2)	.2 (.1)	.1 (.1)		.3 (.6)			.1 (.1)	.3 (.1)					.1 (.1)	.3 (.3)	.2 (.2)	4.6 (.2)	22.8 (4.6)	40.7 (1.5)	17.6 (.7)	111.1	100.0	21

Continued Overleaf

Table 6 Continued

Item	1	2	3	4	5	6	7	8	9	10	11	12	13	14	15	16	17	18	19	20
22 Coal		.3 (.2)	.1 (.3)	.3 (.4)	.6 (1.1)	.5 (1.7)	* (.1)	.7 (.3)	.2 (.4)	.3 (.5)	.4 (2.4)	.5 (1.1)	4.3 (3.6)	3.9 (.7)	.3 (.3)	.5 (2.0)	.7 (2.3)	.2 (.6)	3.5 (4.8)	
23 Coke													62.8 (25.3)	1.9 (.3)	5.5 (.2)	.3 *	1.9 (1.0)	.3 (.1)	1.1 (.3)	
24 Manufactured gas				.5 (.1)	.3 (.1)					.3 (.1)			5.8 (.7)	2.6 (.1)	.3 *		1.6 (.7)		3.8 (.8)	1.0 (.2)
25 Electric utilities		.3 (.3)	.1 (.3)	.5 (.7)		.1 (.5)	* (.1)	.2 (.1)	.2 (.4)	.2 (.4)	.1 (.5)	* (.1)	.6 (.4)	2.2 (.1)	.5 (.4)	.5 (2.1)	.1 (.3)	.3 (.8)	.7 (.9)	* (.1)
26 Chemicals	11.5 (2.6)						5.1 (3.7)				.1 (1.1)	.1 (.3)		.3		.3			* (.1)	
27 Lumber and timber products	13.4 (1.9)										.2 (.8)		5.0 (.8)	2.3 (1.8)	.6 (2.4)					
28 Other wood products					1.0 (1.2)								1.2 (.1)							
29 Paper and wood pulp																				
30 Other paper products																				
31 Printing and publishing																				
32 Yarn and cloth	.9 (.3)													.2 (.3)						
33 Clothing																				
34 Other textile products	1.1 *																			
35 Leather tanning														1.9 (.8)						
36 Leather shoes																				
37 Other leather products	24.8 (.5)																			
38 Rubber manufactures													.1 *	13.7 (6.1)						
39 Industries n.e.s.	1.2 (.2)												.6 (.1)							
40 Construction																				
41 Transportation (steam railroads)	13.2 (5.3)	1.5 (3.3)		.5 (2.1)	.2 (1.9)		1.4 (1.8)				1.4 (21.5)	.4 (2.6)	1.7 (3.7)	2.9 (1.4)		.3 (3.8)	.3 (2.5)		3.3 (11.9)	
42 Imports	2.0 (.6)	.5 (.8)	.2 (1.2)	.2 (.6)	11.1 (38.0)		2.2 (8.5)	2.5 (2.5)		8.4 (25.3)		.5 (2.5)	.8 (1.3)	.9 (.3)			2.7 (16.7)	.4 (2.1)	.3 (.7)	
43 a Wages and salaries																				
43 b Capital and entrepreneurial services																				
43 c Total services	19.7 (78.2)	.3 (7.0)	.2 (19.5)	.5 (20.7)	.4 (16.3)	.3 (26.5)	.4 (22.5)	.6 (8.1)	.2 (8.6)	.6 (23.7)	.2 (24.5)	.2 (14.1)	2.0 (12.7)	8.9 (41.4)	1.6 (35.5)	.4 (43.3)	.2 (16.5)	.4 (24.8)	1.2 (41.1)	.6 (24.4)
44 Undistributed: a Taxes																				
44 b Other																				
44 c Total	.4 (0.0)	1.2 (6.9)	.5 (29.0)	1.3 (34.4)	1.0 (28.5)	.9 (53.0)	1.4 (48.2)	1.5 (12.8)	.4 (13.7)	1.3 (33.5)	.5 (44.9)	.5 (21.3)	1.4 (8.7)	13.4 (40.7)	2.3 (32.9)	.5 (35.2)	.4 (19.3)	1.0 (44.9)	1.6 (36.7)	2.6 (66.0)
45 Gross total outlays	(65.3)	(100.0)	(100.0)	(100.0)	(100.9)	(105.9)	(100.0)	(108.2)	(100.0)	(104.8)	(100.0)	(100.0)	(118.4)	(104.2)	(140.0)	(101.4)	(58.9)	(100.0)	(101.3)	(102.9)
46 Net total outlays	(100.0)	(100.0)	(100.0)	(100.0)	(100.0)	(100.0)	(100.0)	(100.0)	(100.0)	(100.0)	(100.0)	(100.0)	(100.0)	(100.0)	(100.0)	(100.0)	(100.0)	(100.0)	(100.0)	(100.0)

21	22	23	24	25	26	27	28	29	30	31	32	33	34	35	36	37	38	39	40	41	42	43	44	45	46	#
.9 (1.2)	8.6 (49.1)	2.2 (14.8)	5.5 (5.0)	2.1 (1.4)	.4 (.4)	.3 (.5)	1.6 (4.4)	.1 (.4)	.1 (.2)	1.8 (.8)	.1 (.1)	.1 (.2)	.3 (.6)	.1 (.2)		.4 (.6)	.9 (1.0)		20.2 (7.4)	5.5 (1.5)	27.2 (1.4)	4.4 (.2)		101.6	100.0	22
.5 (.1)		3.6 (3.9)	1.1 (.1)				.3 (.1)			.3 *							.3 (.1)			1.4 (.1)	1.4 *	16.7 (.2)		100.8	100.0	23
2.2 (.4)			1.3 (.2)	3.5 (.3)						.3 (.1)							.6 (.1)				72.5 (.5)	3.8 *		105.4	100.0	24
* (.1)	.6 (.6)	* (.3)	* (.4)		.4 (.2)	.1 (.1)	.2 (.4)	.7 (.9)	.1 (.4)	.5 (.6)	1.9 (.8)	.3 (.2)	.2 (.4)	.2 (.4)	.2 (.4)	* (.3)	.2 (.4)	.7 (.7)			48.2 (2.2)	38.3 (2.0)		105.0	100.0	25
.4 (.8)	.7 (1.0)						.2 (.8)			.8 (1.5)	1.9 (1.2)			1.5 (4.6)		* (.2)		1.0 (.9)		12.5 (4.9)	23.3 (1.7)	40.2 (3.2)		106.2	100.0	26
1.8 (2.0)	1.9 (1.6)		.5 (.4)	2.5 (1.5)			23.6 (34.4)							.7 (1.1)			.7 (.7)	13.1 (8.0)	4.9 (1.6)	4.5 (1.1)		24.4 (1.2)		125.2	100.0	27
														1.0 (1.0)						4.9 (.8)	60.6 (1.7)	31.3 (1.0)		103.0	100.0	28
							28.6 (44.4)	31.7 (14.0)										2.4 (.6)		7.9 (.7)	13.5 (.2)	15.9 (.3)		110.5	100.0	29
																				3.3 (.2)	8.4 (.1)	88.2 (1.0)		100.0	100.0	30
																		1.9 (.5)		1.2 (.2)	25.7 (.9)	71.2 (2.9)		111.7	100.0	31
						.7 (2.8)					25.9 (35.0)	6.2 (51.2)		.1 (.5)	* (.3)	4.0 (14.9)	* (.1)			6.8 (4.3)	38.8 (4.2)	16.3 (2.0)		119.5	100.0	32
																				1.3 (.5)	96.3 (7.1)	2.3 (.2)		104.5	100.0	33
						5.6 (2.4)							.7 (.1)							8.2 (.6)	31.8 (.4)	52.4 (.7)		108.7	100.0	34
						1.7 (2.2)			.3 (.2)	.6 (.1)	.4 (.1)			48.6 (40.5)	10.7 (33.4)					22.1 (2.8)	5.5 (.1)	7.4 (.2)		101.4	100.0	35
																				7.2 (1.0)	92.8 (2.4)			120.3	100.0	36
																				3.3 (.1)	42.9 (.3)	29.0 (.2)		100.0	100.0	37
																				4.7 (.7)	58.2 (1.5)	23.3 (.7)		101.7	100.0	38
					.8 (.7)					.2 (.1)	1.1 (.6)								4.8 (2.7)	5.5 (1.2)	63.9 (2.6)	22.0 (1.0)		100.0	100.0	39
																				32.9 (2.4)	22.2 (2.9)	67.1 (5.5)		100.0	100.0	40
2.3 (7.6)	12.7 (30.7)	.9 (3.0)		.2 (.3)	6.0 (6.4)															2.5 (1.8)	22.2 (2.9)	26.0 (3.8)		100.1	100.0	41
.6 (1.5)				4.3 (5.6)	.8 (1.6)	.3 (1.3)	1.3 (7.2)		1.0 (2.6)	18.8 (16.1)	3.1 (3.7)	1.3 (9.7)	8.8 (36.0)	.1 (.3)	.3 (3.5)	5.3 (17.5)	1.0 (2.2)	.4 (.6)	* (*)		13.6 (1.3)	6.1 (.7)		100.0	100.0	42
																										43 ⟨a,b
.5 (04.9)	2.0 (47.4)	.1 (18.7)	.2 (28.9)	1.9 (43.7)	1.3 (23.1)	1.6 (43.6)	.9 (38.4)	.4 (31.6)	.3 (31.9)	1.3 (43.3)	3.0 (34.2)	1.8 (29.1)	.2 (23.5)	.3 (18.7)	.7 (32.5)	.2 (33.1)	.7 (30.5)	1.7 (47.6)	1.5 (27.1)	5.5 (51.4)		34.8 (50.1)		116.0	100.0	c
																										44 ⟨a,b
1.3 (27.9)	.9 (03.7)	.2 (18.7)	.3 (06.4)	2.4 (05.3)	4.6 (51.4)	2.0 (34.7)	.7 (19.2)	1.0 (48.5)	.3 (22.8)	1.6 (34.6)	2.9 (21.2)	2.9 (30.8)	.2 (04.7)	.4 (12.3)	.7 (21.8)	.2 (24.9)	1.2 (34.3)	2.5 (47.1)	.9 (10.4)	1.9 (11.7)	.1 (.6)	36.8 (30.6)		100.0	100.0	c
(10.2)	(001.6)	(00.8)	(005.0)	(04.2)	(006.0)	(23.6)	(02.8)	(009.9)	(100.0)	(111.0)	(18.5)	(04.2)	(108.3)	(001.4)	(19.6)	(100.0)	(001.5)	(100.0)	(100.0)	(100.0)	(100.0)	(20.3)	(100.0)			45
(100.0)	(100.0)	(100.0)	(100.0)	(100.0)	(100.0)	(100.0)	(100.0)	(100.0)	(100.0)	(100.0)	(100.0)	(100.0)	(100.0)	(100.0)	(100.0)	(100.0)	(100.0)	(100.0)	(100.0)	(100.0)	(100.0)	(100.0)	(100.0)			46
21	22	23	24	25	26	27	28	29	30	31	32	33	34	35	36	37	38	39	40	41	42	43	44	45	46	

QUANTITATIVE INPUT AND OUTPUT RELATIONS   125

entrepreneurial income derived from personal services (see Wages and Salaries to Consumption). *To* Undistributed: calculated on basis of the estimates given in W. I. King's *The National Income* . . . . Includes (*a*) profit, dividends, and interest derived from banking, mercantile industry, Pullman and express services, transportation by water, and income derived from governmental properties; (*b*) total annual addition to the undistributed surplus in all industries, less that part of it which is attributed by W. I. King to factories, mines, quarries and oil wells, railroads, and electric utilities; (*c*) profit, dividends, and interest derived from "Unclassified Industries," as defined by W. I. King in *The National Income* . . . , less capital and entrepreneurial services (excluding rents) charged to consumption (see above); (*d*) aggregate corporate deficit in all industries, minus deficits of industries covered in the distribution columns 1 to 41.

44a. Taxes

Taxes Paid by Agriculture: estimate made by W. I. King (*The National Income* . . .). Taxes paid by manufacturing industries and mining (from Flour and Grist Mills to Industries Not Elsewhere Specified, excluding Electric Utilities); federal, state, county, and local, including excises, as reported in *Mfr.* and *Min.* Taxes paid by the Electric Utilities: comprise corporate income, war profit, excess profit, and other domestic taxes as listed in *Statistics of Income* (Bureau of Internal Revenue). Taxes paid by Construction: include the same items as taxes paid by Electric Utilities. Taxes paid by consumers: comprise income taxes, direct personal property taxes, poll taxes, licenses, and fees for personal activities. Estimate taken from W. H. Lough, *High Level Consumption.*

44b. Other Undistributed

Each item represents the difference between the Total Expenditures and the total of all other items included in each column.

45. Gross Total Outlays

The definition of the concept of Gross Total Outlays, as well as the general outlines of its statistical derivation, is given on page 115 above. The following comments are limited to description of actual statistical calculations.

To Agriculture: this item is obtained by adding the value of the total product (22,147 million dollars) as given in row 1 to the estimated net increase in agricultural indebtedness between the beginning and the end of the year 1919.

According to data presented in the *Federal Reserve Bulletin* (April, 1936) the increase in agricultural mortgage indebtedness amounted in 1919 to four or five hundred million dollars. Agricultural loans by commercial banks expanded between July 31, 1918, and December 31, 1920, from 3,517 million dollars to 5,317 million dollars, which gives an average annual increase of 720 million dollars. Augmenting this sum by the 400 million dollars of new mortgage credits we have 1,120 million dollars as the total of additional agricultural credits. To obtain a net figure, it will be necessary to subtract from this amount that part of the mortgage credit which originated in financing sales of agricultural land by non-farmers. Furthermore, the increase in bank savings and other non-agricultural financial investments by the farm population has also to be taken into consideration. Neither of these items can be determined with any degree of accuracy. Thus the gross total of 1,120 million dollars is simply reduced to 900 million dollars, 220 million dollars being allowed for the two items mentioned above.

To Manufacturing Industries and Mining (from Flour and Grist Mills to Industries Not Elsewhere Specified with exception of Electric Utilities): the aggregate additional corporate investment is obtained by combining the data on corporate savings as estimated by W. I. King (*The National Income* . . .) with the statistics of new capital issues (stock and bond, excluding refunding) compiled by the *Commercial and Financial Chronicle.* The distribution of this total among the separate industries is based upon the analysis of the financial statistics of approximately 2,000 corporations covered in the *Source Book for the Study of Industrial Profits,* compiled by Ralph C. Epstein and published by the Department of Commerce.

The increment in the total capital investment between 1919 and 1920 has been calculated for each particular industrial group as represented among these 2,000 corporations. In order to make the industrial groups of the sample representative, the relative size of each of them was brought into accord with the relative size of the respective total industries. This was accomplished in two steps: first, the capital increase within each sample industrial group was related to the value of product (sales) as given for the identical sample; *i.e.,* the capital increase per dollar of output (sales) was calculated. Next, the ratios thus obtained were weighted by the total corporate product of each particular industry as given in the Census, and each of these weighted ratios was expressed as a proportion of the sum of such weighted ratios. Finally, after these two steps were taken, the estimate of the *relative* corporate capital increase within the different industrial groups was applied to the sum total of new investment.

The capital increase as calculated for each industry must be further augmented by the total of the deficits for the corresponding industry (as given in *Statistics of Income,* published by the Bureau of Internal Revenue). According to conventional accounting principles, these are charged against the net income of profitable corporations but in our set-up (see page 114) the offsetting influence of deficits has to be eliminated, which means that they have to be "added back."

The last stage in these calculations consists in stepping up the results which apply only to the corporate part of the industry so as to include all producers covered in the Census. The ratio between the total output of each separate industry and that part of it which was produced by corporations is used as a multiplier in each case.

The "Gross Total Outlays" were obtained by adding the new capital investment in each industry as derived above to the value of its total product.

To Electric Utilities: the total is obtained by adding to the total value of product new stock and bond issues (estimate taken from W. I. King, *The National Income* . . .) and additional corporate surplus, roughly estimated at 15 million dollars. *To* Construction: no attempt is made to estimate additional stock and bond issues or additions to undistributed surplus. Thus this item represents the total output of the industry increased by the total deficits of corporate construction enterprises (*Statistics of Income,* Bureau of Internal Revenue). *To* Railroads: total of new issues, additions to undistributed surplus (W. I. King, *The National Income* . . .), augmented by total corporate deficit (*Statistics of Income,* Bureau of Internal Revenue), added to the total value of product. *To* Exports: total exports of domestic products augmented by domestic transportation costs charged to imported goods (see Transportation to Exports). *To* Consumption: total consumption expenditures, *i.e.,* total consumers' spendings and withholdings (received income), less savings as estimated in *High Level Consumption* by Lough. *To* Undistributed: total of undistributed products and services listed in column 44.

WASSILY W. LEONTIEF

HARVARD UNIVERSITY

[5]

A Model of General Economic Equilibrium[1]

The subject of this paper is the solution of a typical economic equation system. The system has the following properties:

(1) Goods are produced not only from "natural factors of production," but in the first place from each other. These processes of production may be circular, i.e. good G_1 is produced with the aid of good G_2, and G_2 with the aid of G_1.

(2) There may be more technically possible processes of production than goods and for this reason "counting of equations" is of no avail. The problem is rather to establish which processes will actually be used and which not (being "unprofitable").

In order to be able to discuss (1), (2) quite freely we shall idealise other elements of the situation (see paragraphs 1 and 2). Most of these idealisations are irrelevant, but this question will not be discussed here.

The way in which our questions are put leads of necessity to a system of inequalities (3)—(8') in paragraph 3 the possibility of a solution of which is not evident, i.e. *it cannot be proved by any qualitative argument*. The mathematical proof is possible only by means of a generalisation of Brouwer's Fix-Point Theorem, i.e. by the use of very fundamental *topological* facts. This generalised fix-point theorem (the "lemma" of paragraph 7) is also interesting in itself.

The connection with topology may be very surprising at first, but the author thinks that it is natural in problems of this kind. The immediate reason for this is the occurrence of a certain "minimum-maximum" problem, familiar from the calculus of variations. In our present question, the minimum-maximum problem has been formulated in paragraph 5. It is closely related to another problem occurring in the theory of games (see footnote 1 in paragraph 6).

A direct interpretation of the function $\phi(X, Y)$ would be highly desirable. Its rôle appears to be similar to that of thermodynamic potentials in phenomenological thermodynamics; it can be surmised that the similarity will persist in its full phenomenological generality (independently of our restrictive idealisations).

Another feature of our theory, so far without interpretation, is the remarkable duality (symmetry) of the monetary variables (prices y_j, interest factor β) and the technical variables (intensities of production x_i, coefficient of expansion of the economy a). This is brought out very clearly in paragraph 3 (3)—(8') as well as in the minimum-maximum formulation of paragraph 5 (7**)—(8**).

Lastly, attention is drawn to the results of paragraph 11 from which follows, among other things, that the normal price mechanism brings about—if our assumptions are valid—the technically most efficient intensities of production. This seems not unreasonable since we have eliminated all monetary complications.

The present paper was read for the first time in the winter of 1932 at the mathematical seminar of Princeton University. The reason for its publication was an invitation from Mr. K. Menger, to whom the author wishes to express his thanks.

1. Consider the following problem: there are n goods $G_1, \ldots, G_n$ which can be produced by m processes $P_1, \ldots, P_m$. Which processes will be used (as "profitable") and what prices of the goods will obtain? The problem is evidently

[1] This paper was first published in German, under the title *Über ein Ökonomisches Gleichungssystem und eine Verallgemeinerung des Brouwerschen Fixpunktsatzes* in the volume entitled *Ergebuisse eines Mathematischen Seminars*, edited by K. Menger (Vienna, 1938). It was translated into English by G. Morgenstern. A commentary note on this article, by D. G. Champernowne, is printed below.

non-trivial since either of its parts can be answered only after the other one has been answered, i.e. its solution is implicit. We observe in particular :

(*a*) Since it is possible that $m > n$ it cannot be solved through the usual counting of equations.

In order to avoid further complications we assume :

(*b*) That there are constant returns (to scale) ;

(*c*) That the natural factors of production, including labour, can be expanded in unlimited quantities.

The essential phenomenon that we wish to grasp is this : goods are produced from each other (see equation (7) below) and we want to determine (*i*) which processes will be used ; (*ii*) what the relative velocity will be with which the total quantity of goods increases ; (*iii*) what prices will obtain ; (*iv*) what the rate of interest will be. In order to isolate this phenomenon completely we assume furthermore :

(*d*) Consumption of goods takes place only through the processes of production which include necessities of life consumed by workers and employees.

In other words we assume that all income in excess of necessities of life will be reinvested.

It is obvious to what kind of theoretical models the above assumptions correspond.

2. In each process P_i ($i = 1, \ldots, m$) quantities a_{ij} (expressed in some units) are used up, and quantities b_{ij} are produced, of the respective goods G_j ($j = 1, \ldots, n$). The process can be symbolised in the following way :

$$P_i : \sum_{j=1}^{n} a_{ij} \, G_j \rightarrow \sum_{j=1}^{n} b_{ij} \, G_j \dots\dots\dots\dots\dots\dots\dots\dots (1)$$

It is to be noted :

(*e*) Capital goods are to be inserted on both sides of (1) ; wear and tear of capital goods are to be described by introducing different stages of wear as different goods, using a separate P_i for each of these.

(*f*) Each process to be of unit time duration. Processes of longer duration to be broken down into single processes of unit duration introducing if necessary intermediate products as additional goods.

(*g*) (1) can describe the special case where good G_j can be produced only jointly with certain others, viz. its permanent joint products.

In the actual economy, these processes P_i, $i = 1, \ldots, m$, will be used with certain *intensities* x_i, $i = 1, \ldots, m$. That means that for the total production the quantities of equations (1) must be multiplied by x_i. We write symbolically :

$$E = \sum_{i=1}^{m} x_i \, P_i \dots\dots\dots\dots\dots\dots\dots\dots\dots(2)$$

$x_i = 0$ means that process P_i is not used.

We are interested in those states where the whole economy expands without change of structure, i.e. where the ratios of the intensities $x_1 : \ldots : x_m$ remain unchanged, although $x_1, \ldots x_m$ themselves may change. In such a case they are multiplied by a common factor a per unit of time. This factor is the *coefficient of expansion of the whole economy.*

3. The numerical unknowns of our problem are : (*i*) the *intensities* $x_1, \ldots, x_m$ of the processes $P_1, \ldots, P_m$; (*ii*) the *coefficient of expansion* of the whole economy a ; (*iii*) the *prices* $y_1, \ldots, y_n$ of goods $G_1, \ldots, G_n$; (*iv*) the interest factor β ($= 1 + \dfrac{z}{100}$, z being the rate of interest in % per unit of time. Obviously :

$$x_i \geqq 0, \dots\dots\dots\dots(3) \qquad\qquad y_j \geqq 0, \dots\dots\dots\dots(4)$$

A MODEL OF GENERAL ECONOMIC EQUILIBRIUM 3

and since a solution with $x_1 = \ldots = x_m = 0$, or $y_1 = \ldots = y_n = 0$ would be meaningless:

$$\sum_{i=1}^{m} x_i > 0, \ldots \ldots \ldots \ldots (5) \qquad \sum_{j=1}^{n} y_j > 0, \ldots \ldots \ldots \ldots (6)$$

The economic equations are now:

$$a \sum_{i=1}^{m} a_{ij} x_i \leqq \sum_{i=1}^{m} b_{ij} x_i, \ldots \ldots \ldots \ldots \ldots \ldots \ldots \ldots \ldots \ldots (7)$$

and if in (7) $<$ applies, $y_j = 0$ $\ldots \ldots \ldots \ldots \ldots \ldots \ldots \ldots \ldots (7')$

$$\beta \sum_{j=1}^{n} a_{ij} y_j \geqq \sum_{j=1}^{n} b_{ij} y_j, \ldots \ldots \ldots \ldots \ldots \ldots \ldots \ldots \ldots \ldots (8)$$

and if in (8) $>$ applies, $x_i = 0 \ldots \ldots \ldots \ldots \ldots \ldots \ldots \ldots \ldots \ldots (8')$

The meaning of (7), (7′) is: it is impossible to consume more of a good G_j in the total process (2) than is being produced. If, however, less is consumed, i.e. if there is excess production of G_j, G_j becomes a free good and its price $y_j = 0$.

The meaning of (8), (8′) is: in equilibrium no profit can be made on any process P_i (or else prices or the rate of interest would rise—it is clear how this abstraction is to be understood). If there is a loss, however, i.e. if P_i is unprofitable, then P_i will not be used and its intensity $x_i = 0$.

The quantities a_{ij}, b_{ij} are to be taken as given, whereas the x_i, y_j, a, β are unknown. There are, then, $m + n + 2$ unknowns, but since in the case of x_i, y_j only the ratios $x_1 : \ldots : x_m, y_1 : \ldots : y_n$ are essential, they are reduced to $m + n$. Against this, there are $m + n$ conditions (7) + (7′) and (8) + (8′). As these, however, are not equations, but rather complicated inequalities, the fact that the number of conditions is equal to the number of unknowns does not constitute a guarantee that the system can be solved.

The dual symmetry of equations (3), (5), (7), (7′) of the variables x_i, a and of the concept " unused process " on the one hand, and of equations (4), (6), (8),)8′) of the variables y_j, β and of the concept " free good " on the other hand seems remarkable.

4. Our task is to solve (3)—(8′). We shall proceed to show:

Solutions of (3)—(8′) *always exist*, although there may be several solutions with different $x_1 : \ldots : x_m$ or with different $y_1 : \ldots : y_n$. The first is possible since we have not even excluded the case where several P_i describe the same process or where several P_i combine to form another. The second is possible since some goods G_j may enter into each process P_i only in a fixed ratio with some others. But even apart from these trivial possibilities there may exist—for less obvious reasons—several solutions $x_1 : \ldots : x_m, y_1 : \ldots : y_m$. Against this it is of importance that a, β should have the same value for all solutions; i.e. a, β *are uniquely determined*.

We shall even find that a and β can be directly characterised in a simple manner (see paragraphs 10 and 11).

To simplify our considerations we shall assume that always:

$$a_{ij} + b_{ij} > 0 \ldots \ldots \ldots \ldots \ldots \ldots \ldots \ldots \ldots \ldots \ldots \ldots \ldots \ldots (9)$$

(a_{ij}, b_{ij} are clearly always $\geqq 0$). Since the a_{ij}, b_{ij} may be arbitrarily small this restriction is not very far-reaching, although it must be imposed in order to assure uniqueness of a, β as otherwise W might break up into disconnected parts.

Consider now a hypothetical solution x_i, a, y_j, β of (3)—(8′). If we had in (7) always $<$, then we should have always $y_j = 0$ (because of (7′)) in contradiction to (6).

4   THE REVIEW OF ECONOMIC STUDIES

If we had in (8) always $>$ we should have always $x_i = 0$ (because of (8')) in contradiction to (5). Therefore, in (7) $\leqq$ always applies, but $=$ at least once ; in (8) $\geqq$ always applies, but $=$ at least once.

In consequence :

$$a = \frac{\text{Min.}}{j = 1, \ldots, n} \left[\frac{\sum\limits_{i=1}^{m} b_{ij}\, x_i}{\sum\limits_{i=1}^{m} a_{ij}\, x_i} \right] \quad\ldots\ldots\ldots\ldots\ldots\ldots (10),$$

$$\beta = \frac{\text{Max.}}{i = 1, \ldots, m} \frac{\sum\limits_{j=1}^{n} b_{ij}\, y_j}{\sum\limits_{j=1}^{n} a_{ij}\, y_j} \quad\ldots\ldots\ldots\ldots\ldots\ldots (11).$$

Therefore the x_i, y_j determine uniquely a, β. (The right-hand side of (10), (11) can never assume the meaningless form $\frac{0}{0}$ because of (3)—(6) and (9)). We can therefore state (7) + (7') and (8) + (8') as conditions for x_i, y_j only :

$y_j = 0$ for each $j = 1, \ldots, n$, for which :

$$\frac{\sum\limits_{i=1}^{m} b_{ij}\, x_i}{\sum\limits_{i=1}^{m} a_{ij}\, x_i}$$

does not assume its minimum value (for all $j = 1, \ldots, n$) $\ldots$ (7*).

$x_i = 0$ for each $i = 1, \ldots, m$, for which :

$$\frac{\sum\limits_{j=1}^{n} b_{ij}\, y_i}{\sum\limits_{j=1}^{n} a_{ij}\, y_i}$$

does not assume its maximum value (for all $i = 1, \ldots, m$) $\ldots$ (8*).

The $x_1, \ldots, x_m$ in (7*) and the $y_1, \ldots, y_n$ in (8*) are to be considered as given. We have, therefore, to solve (3)—(6), (7) and (8) for x_i, y_j.

5. Let X' be a set of variables $(x'_1, \ldots, x'_m)$ fulfilling the analoga of (3), (5) :

$$x'_i \geqq 0, \ldots\ldots\ldots\ldots\ldots (3') \qquad \sum\limits_{i=1}^{m} x'_i > 0, \ldots\ldots\ldots\ldots\ldots (5')$$

and let Y' be a series of variables $(y'_1, \ldots, y'_n)$ fulfilling the analoga of (4), (6) :

$$y'_j \geqq 0, \ldots\ldots\ldots\ldots\ldots (4') \qquad \sum\limits_{j=1}^{n} y'_j > 0, \ldots\ldots\ldots\ldots\ldots (6')$$

Let, furthermore,

$$\phi(X'_i, Y'_i) = \frac{\sum\limits_{i=1}^{m} \sum\limits_{j=1}^{n} b_{ij}\, x'_i\, y'_j}{\sum\limits_{i=1}^{m} \sum\limits_{j=1}^{n} a_{ij}\, x'_i\, y'_j} \quad\ldots\ldots\ldots\ldots\ldots (12)$$

A MODEL OF GENERAL ECONOMIC EQUILIBRIUM 5

Let $X = (x_1, \ldots, x_m)$, $Y = (y_1, \ldots, y_n)$ the (hypothetical) solution, $X' = (x'_i, \ldots, x'_m)$, $Y' = (y'_1, \ldots, y'_n)$ to be freely variable, but in such a way that (3)—(6) and (3')—(6') respectively are fulfilled ; then it is easy to verify that (7*) and (8*) can be formulated as follows :

$\phi(X, Y')$ assumes its minimum value for Y' if $Y' = Y \ldots \ldots (7^{**})$.

$\phi(X', Y)$ assumes its maximum value for X' if $X' = X \ldots \ldots (8^{**})$.

The question of a solution of (3)—(8') becomes a question of a solution of (7^{**}), (8^{**}) and can be formulated as follows :

(*) *Consider (X', Y') in the domain bounded by (3')—(6'). To find a saddle point $X' = X$, $Y' = Y$, i.e. where (X, Y') assumes its minimum value for Y', and at the same time (X', Y) its maximum value for Y'.*

From (7), (7*), (10) and (8), (8*), (11) respectively, follows :

$$a = \frac{\sum\limits_{j=1}^{n} \left[\sum\limits_{i=1}^{m} b_{ij}\, x_i \right] y_j}{\sum\limits_{j=1}^{n} \left[\sum\limits_{i=1}^{m} a_{ij}\, x_i \right] y_j} = \phi(x, y) \quad \text{and} \quad \beta = \frac{\sum\limits_{i=1}^{m} \left[\sum\limits_{j=1}^{n} b_{ij}\, y_j \right] x_i}{\sum\limits_{i=1}^{m} \left[\sum\limits_{j=1}^{n} a_{ij}\, y_j \right] x_i} = \phi(x, y)$$

respectively.

Therefore :

(**) *If our problem can be solved, i.e. if $\phi(X', Y')$ has a saddle point $X' = X$, $Y' = Y$ (see above), then :*

$$a = \beta = \phi(X, Y) = \text{the value at the saddle point} \ldots \ldots \ldots \ldots (13)$$

6. Because of the homogeneity of $\phi\,(X', Y')$ (in X', Y', i.e. in $x', \ldots, x_m'$ and $y_1', \ldots y_m'$) our problem remains unaffected if we substitute the normalisations

$$\sum_{i=1}^{m} x_i = 1, \ldots \ldots \ldots \ldots (5^*) \qquad \sum_{j=1}^{n} y_j = 1, \ldots \ldots \ldots \ldots (6^*)$$

for (5'), (6') and correspondingly for (5), (6). Let S be the X' set described by :

$$x_i' \geqq 0, \ldots \ldots \ldots \ldots (3') \qquad \sum_{i=1}^{m} x_i' = 1, \ldots \ldots \ldots \ldots (5^*)$$

and let T be the Y' set described by :

$$y_j' \geqq 0, \ldots \ldots \ldots \ldots (4') \qquad \sum_{j=1}^{n} y_j' = 1, \ldots \ldots \ldots \ldots (6^*)$$

(S, T are simplices of, respectively, $m-1$ and $n-1$ dimensions).

In order to solve[1] we make use of the simpler formulation (7*), (8*) and combine these with (3), (4), (5*), (6*) expressing the fact that $X = (x_1, \ldots, x_m)$ is in S and $Y = (y_1, \ldots, y_n)$ in T.

7. We shall prove a slightly more general lemma : Let R_m be the m-dimensional

---

[1] The question whether our problem has a solution is oddly connected with that of a problem occurring in the Theory of Games dealt with elsewhere. (Math. Annalen, 100, 1928, pp. 295–320, particularly pp. 305 and 307–311). The problem there is a special case of (*) and is solved here in a new way through our solution of (*) (see below). In fact, if $a_{ij} \equiv 1$, then $\sum\limits_{i=1}^{m} \sum\limits_{j=1}^{n} a_{ij}\, x'_i\, y'_j = 1$ because of (5*), (6*). Therefore $\phi\,(X', Y') = \sum\limits_{i=1}^{m} \sum\limits_{j=1}^{n} b_{ij}\, x'_i\, y'_j$, and thus our (*) coincides with loc. cit., p. 307. (Our $\phi\,(X', Y')$, b_{ij}, x'_i, y'_j, m, n here correspond to $h\,(\xi, \eta)$, $a_{pq,\xi p}$, ηq, $M+1$, $N+1$ there).

It is, incidentally, remarkable that (*) does not lead—as usual—to a simple maximum or minimum problem, the possibility of a solution of which would be evident, but to a problem of the saddle point or minimum-maximum type, where the question of a possible solution is far more profound.

6 THE REVIEW OF ECONOMIC STUDIES

space of all points $X = (x_1, \ldots, x_m)$, R_n the n-dimensional space of all points $Y = (y_1, \ldots, y_n)$, R_{m+n} the $m + n$ dimensional space of all points $(X, Y) = (x_1, \ldots x_m, y_1, \ldots, y_n)$.

A set (in R_m or R_n or R_{m+n}) which is *not empty, convex closed and bounded* we call a set C.

Let $S°$, $T°$ be sets C in R_m and R_n respectively and let $S° \times T°$ be the set of all (X, Y) (in R_{m+n}) where the range of X is $S°$ and the range of Y is $T°$. Let V, W be two closed subsets of $S° \times T°$. For every X in $S°$ let the set $Q(X)$ of all Y with (X, Y) in V be a set C; for each Y in $T°$ let the set $P(Y)$ of all X with (X, Y) in W be a set C. Then the following lemma applies.

Under the above assumptions, V, W have (at least) one point in common.

Our problem follows by putting $S° = S$, $T° = T$ and $V =$ the set of all $(X, Y) = (x_1, \ldots, x_m, y_1, \ldots, y_n)$ fulfilling (7*), $W =$ the set of all $(X, Y) = (x_1, \ldots, x_m, y_1, \ldots, y_n)$ fulfilling (8*). It can be easily seen that $V . W$ are closed and that the sets $S° = S$, $T° = T$, $Q(X)$, $P(Y)$ are all simplices, i.e. sets C. The common points of these V, W are, of course, our required solutions $(X, Y) = (x_1, \ldots, x_m, y_1, \ldots, y_m)$.

8. To prove the above lemma let $S°$, $T°$, V, W be as described before the lemma.

First, consider V. For each X of $S°$ we choose a point $Y°(X)$ out of $Q(X)$ (e.g. the centre of gravity of this set). It will not be possible, generally, to choose $Y°(X)$ as a continuous function of X. Let $\epsilon > 0$; we define:

$$w^\epsilon(X, X') = \text{Max.} \left(0, 1 - \frac{1}{\epsilon} \text{ distance } (X, X')\right) \quad \ldots\ldots\ldots\ldots (14)$$

Now let $Y^\epsilon(X)$ be the centre of gravity of the $Y°(X')$ with (relative) weight function $w^\epsilon(X, X')$ where the range of X' is $S°$. I.e. if $Y°(X) = (y_1°(x), \ldots, y_n°(x))$, $Y^\epsilon(X) = (y_1^\epsilon(x), \ldots, y_n^\epsilon(x))$, then:

$$y_j^\epsilon(X) = \int_{S°} w^\epsilon(X, X') \, y_j°(X') \, dX' \Big/ \int_{S°} w^\epsilon(X, X') \, dX', \ldots\ldots (15)$$

We derive now a number of properties of $Y^\epsilon(X)$ (valid for all $\epsilon > 0$):

(*i*) $Y^\epsilon(X)$ is in $T°$. Proof: $Y°(X')$ is in $Q(X')$ and therefore in $T°$, and since $Y^\epsilon(X)$ is a centre of gravity of points $Y°(X')$ and $T°$ is convex, $Y^\epsilon(X)$ also is in $T^\bullet$.

(*ii*) $Y^\epsilon(X)$ is a continuous function of X (for the whole range of $S°$). Proof: it is sufficient to prove this for each $y_j^\epsilon(X)$. Now $w^\epsilon(X, X')$ is a continuous function of X, X' throughout; $\int_{S°} w^\epsilon(X, X') \, dX'$ is always > 0, and all $y_j°(X)$ are bounded (being co-ordinates of the bounded set $S°$). The continuity of the $y_j^\epsilon(X)$ follows, therefore, from (15).

(*iii*) For each $\delta > 0$ there exists an $\epsilon_0 = \epsilon_0(\delta) > 0$ such that the distance of each point $(X, Y^{\epsilon_0}(X))$ from V is $< \delta$. Proof: assume the contrary. Then there must exist a $\delta > 0$ and a sequence of $\epsilon_\nu > 0$ with $\lim_{\nu \to \infty} \epsilon_\nu = 0$ such that for every $\nu = 1, 2, \ldots$ there exists a X_ν in $S°$ for which the distance $(X_\nu, Y^{\epsilon_\nu}(X_\nu))$ would be $\geq \delta$. A fortiori $Y^{\epsilon_\nu}(X_\nu)$ is at a distance $\geq \frac{\delta}{2}$ from every $Q(X')$, with a distance $(X_\nu, X') \leq \frac{\delta}{2}$.

All X_ν, $\nu = 1, 2, \ldots$, are in $S°$ and have therefore a point of accumulation X^* in $S°$; from which follows that there exists a subsequence of X_ν, $\nu = 1, 2, \ldots$, converging towards X^* for which distance $(X_\nu, X^*) \leq \frac{\delta}{2}$ always applies. Substituting this subsequence for the ϵ_ν, X_ν, we see that we are justified in assuming: $\lim X_\nu = X^*$,

A MODEL OF GENERAL ECONOMIC EQUILIBRIUM 7

distance $(X_\nu, X^*) \leqq \dfrac{\delta}{2}$. Therefore we may put $X' = X^*$ for every $\nu = 1, 2, \ldots,$

and in consequence we have always $Y^{\epsilon\nu}(X_\nu)$ at a distance $\geqq \dfrac{\delta}{2}$ from $Q(X^*)$.

$Q(X^*)$ being convex, the set of all points with a distance $< \dfrac{\delta}{2}$ from $(Q(X^*)$ is also convex. Since $Y^{\epsilon\nu}(X_\nu)$ does not belong to this set, and since it is a centre of gravity of points $Y^\circ(X')$ with distance $(X_\nu, X') \leqq \epsilon_\nu$ (because for distance $(X_\nu, X') > \epsilon_\nu$, $w^{\epsilon\nu}(X_\nu, X') = 0$ according to (14)), not all of these points belong to the set under discussion. Therefore: there exists a $X' = X_\nu$ for which the distance $(X_\nu, X'_\nu) \leqq \epsilon_\nu$ and where the distance between $Y^\circ(X'_\nu)$ and $Q(X^*)$ is $\geqq \dfrac{\delta}{2}.$

Lim $X_\nu = X^*$, lim distance $(X_\nu, X'_\nu) = 0$, and therefore lim $X'_\nu = X^*$. All $Y^\circ(Y_\nu)$ belong to T° and have therefore a point of accumulation Y^*. In consequence, (X^*, Y^*) is a point of accumulation of the $(X_\nu, Y^\circ(X_\nu))$ and since they all belong to V, (X^*, Y^*) belongs to V too. Y^* is therefore in $Q(X^*)$. Now the distance of every $Y^\nu(Y_\nu)$ including from $Q(X^*)$ is $\geqq \dfrac{\delta}{2}$. This is a contradiction, and the proof is complete.

(*i*)—(*iii*) together assert: for every $\delta > 0$ there exists a continuous mapping $Y_\delta(X)$ of S° on to a subset of T° where the distance of every point $(X, Y_\delta(X))$ from V is $< \delta$. (Put $Y_\delta(X) = Y^\epsilon(X)$ with $\epsilon = \epsilon_0 = \epsilon_0(\delta)$).

9. Interchanging S° and T°, and V and W we obtain now: for every $\delta > 0$ there exists a continuous mapping $X_\delta(Y)$ of T° on to a subset of S° where the distance of every point $(X_\delta(Y), Y)$ from W is $< \delta$.

On putting $f_\delta(X) = X_\delta(Y_\delta(X))$, $f_\delta(X)$ is a continuous mapping of S° on to a subset of S°. Since S° is a set C, and therefore topologically a simplex[1] we can use L. E. J. Brouwer's Fix-point Theorem[2]; $f_\delta(X)$ has a fix-point. I.e., there exists a X^δ in S° for which $X^\delta = f_\delta(X^\delta) = X_\delta(Y_\delta(X^\delta))$. Let $Y^\delta = Y_\delta(X^\delta)$, then we have $X^\delta = X_\delta(Y^\delta)$. Consequently, the distances of the point (X^δ, Y^δ) in R_{m+n} both from V and from W are $< \delta$. The distance of V from W is therefore $< 2\delta$. Since this is valid for every $\delta > 0$, the distance between V and W is $= 0$. Since V, W are closed and bounded, they must have at least one common point. This proves our lemma completely.

10. We have solved (7^*), (8^*) of paragraph 4 as well as the equivalent problem $(*)$ of paragraph 5 and the original task of paragraph 3: the solution of (3)—$(8')$. If the x_i, y_j (which were called X, Y in paragraphs 7—9) are determined, a, β follow from (13) in $(**)$ of paragraph 5. In particular, $a = \beta$.

We have emphasised in paragraph 4 already that there may be several solutions x_i, y_j (i.e. X, Y); we shall proceed to show that there exists only one value of a (i.e. of β). In fact, let X_1, Y_1, a_1, β_1 and X_2, Y_2, a_2, β_2 be two solutions. From (7^{**}), (8^{**}) and (13) follows:

$$a_1 = \beta_1 = \phi(X_1, Y_1) \leqq \phi(X_1, Y_2),$$
$$a_2 = \beta_2 = \phi(X_2, Y_2) \geqq \phi(X_1, Y_2),$$

therefore $a_1 = \beta_1 \leqq a_2 = \beta_2$. For reasons of symmetry $a_2 = \beta_2 \leqq a_1 = \beta_1$, therefore $a_1 = \beta_1 = a_2 = \beta_2$.

---

[1] Regarding these as well as other properties of convex sets used in this paper, c.f., e.g. Alexandroff and H. Hopf, *Topologie*, vol. I, J. Springer, Berlin, 1935, pp. 598–609.
[2] Cf., e.g. 1 c, footnote 1, p. 480.

We have shown :

At least one solution X, Y, α, β exists. For all solutions :

$$\alpha = \beta = \phi \ (X, Y) \ \dots\dots\dots\dots\dots\dots\dots\dots\dots \ (13)$$

and these have the same numerical value for all solutions, in other words : The interest factor and the coefficient of expansion of the economy are equal and uniquely determined by the technically possible processes $P_1, \dots, P_m$.

Because of (13), $\alpha > 0$, but may be $\lessgtr 1$. One would expect $\alpha > 1$, but $\alpha \leq 1$ cannot be excluded in view of the generality of our formulation : processes $P_1, \dots, P_m$ may really be *unproductive*.

11. In addition, we shall characterise α in two independent ways.

Firstly, let us consider a state of the economy possible on purely technical considerations, expanding with factor α' per unit of time. I.e., for the intensities $x_1, \dots, x_m$ applies :

$$x_i \geq 0 \dots\dots\dots\dots (3') \qquad \sum_{i=1}^{m} x_i' > 0 \dots\dots\dots\dots (5') \text{ and}$$

$$\alpha' \sum_{i=1}^{m} a_{ij} \, x_i' \leq \sum_{i=1}^{m} b_{ij} \, x_i' \dots\dots\dots\dots\dots\dots\dots\dots\dots \ (7'')$$

We are neglecting prices here altogether. Let $x_i, y_j, \alpha = \beta$ be a solution of our original problem (3)—(8') in paragraph 3. Multiplying (7'') by y_j and adding $\sum_{j=1}^{n}$ we obtain :

$$\alpha' \sum_{i=1}^{m} \sum_{j=1}^{n} a_{ij} \, x_i' \, y_j \leq \sum_{i=1}^{m} \sum_{j=1}^{n} b_{ij} \, x_i' \, y_j,$$

and therefore $\alpha' \leq \phi \ (X', Y)$. Because of (8**) and (13) in paragraph 5, we have :

$$\alpha' \leq \phi \ (X', Y) \leq \phi \ (X, Y) = \alpha = \beta \ \dots\dots\dots\dots\dots \ (15).$$

Secondly, let us consider a system of prices where the interest factor β' allows of no more profits. I.e. for prices $y_1', \dots y'_n$ applies :

$$y'_j \geq 0, \dots\dots\dots\dots (4') \qquad \sum_{j=1}^{n} y'_j > 0, \dots\dots\dots\dots (6') \text{ and}$$

$$\beta' \sum_{j=1}^{n} a_{ij} \, y'_j \geq \sum_{j=1}^{n} b_{ij} \, y'_j \dots\dots\dots\dots\dots\dots\dots\dots\dots \ (8'')$$

Hereby we are neglecting intensities of production altogether. Let $x_i, y_j, \alpha = \beta$ as above. Multiplying (8'') by x_i and adding $\sum_{i=1}^{m}$ we obtain :

$$\beta' \sum_{i=1}^{m} \sum_{j=1}^{n} a_{ij} \, x_i \, y'_j \leq \sum_{i=1}^{m} \sum_{j=1}^{n} b_{ij} \, x_i \, y'_j$$

and therefore $\beta' \geq \phi \ (X, Y')$. Because of (7**) and (13) in paragraph 5, we have :

$$\beta' \geq \phi \ (X, Y') \geq \phi \ (X, Y) = \alpha = \beta \dots\dots\dots\dots\dots\dots \ (16)$$

These two results can be expressed as follows :

The greatest (purely technically possible) factor of expansion α' *of the whole economy is* $\alpha' = \alpha = \beta$, *neglecting prices.*

The lowest interest factor β' *at which a profitless system of prices is possible is* $\beta' = \alpha = \beta$, *neglecting intensities of production.*

A MODEL OF GENERAL ECONOMIC EQUILIBRIUM 9

Note that these characterisations are possible only on the basis of our knowledge that solutions of our original problem exist—without themselves directly referring to this problem. Furthermore, the equality of the maximum in the first form and the minimum in the second can be proved only on the basis of the existence of this solution.

Princeton, N.J. J. v. NEUMANN.

[6]

NOTE: SOME CONDITIONS OF MACROECONOMIC STABILITY

By David Hawkins and Herbert A. Simon

In a recent paper by one of us[1] there is an error in the statement of a supposed sufficient condition that a system of linear homogeneous equations should have solutions all of the same sign. The present note is intended to correct that error, to state and prove an apparently new, necessary and sufficient condition that the stated consequence should hold, and finally to interpret the significance of this condition in economic terms.

Two preliminary remarks are in order. First, the error in the theorem originally stated does not affect the substance of the paper to which reference is being made. That paper sets forth theorems on the stability of systems which *do* have stationary solutions with all variables positive. The lemma under consideration here gives necessary and sufficient conditions that a system *will* have stationary solutions with all variables positive. That is, it gives a criterion to test whether the theorems in the body of the paper are applicable to any particular system of equation.

Second, the conditions under which the variables satisfying a system of linear equations will be all positive are of economic interest in their own right. They are, in fact, the conditions determining whether a system of linear production functions is capable, given a sufficient supply of the "fixed" factors of production, of producing any desired schedule of consumption goods.

The system of equations[2] is the following:[3]

$$(1) \qquad \sum_{j=1}^{n} b_{ij} x_j = 0, \qquad (i = 1, \cdots, n)$$

with $\Delta = 0$ and of rank $n - 1$; $b_{ij} > 0$ for all $i \neq j$; $b_{ii} < 0$ for all i.

Instead of dealing directly with the system (1), it will be more convenient to consider the associated nonhomogeneous system:

$$(2) \qquad \sum_{j=1}^{m} a_{ij} x_j - k_i = 0, \qquad (i = 1, \cdots, m)$$

---

[1] David Hawkins, "Some Conditions of Macroeconomic Stability," Econometrica, Vol. 16, October, 1948, pp. 309–322. The theorem under discussion is on page 312.

[2] The system (1) is essentially that introduced by W. W. Leontief in *The Structure of American Economy*, 1919–1929, Cambridge: Harvard University Press, 1941. p. 48.

[3] In Hawkin's original system we require only that $b_{ij} \geqslant 0$ for $i \neq j$. The stronger condition $b_{ij} > 0$ employed here simplifies the statement of the theorem and its proof and, because of the continuity of solutions of these equations with respect to variations of these coefficients, does not involve any essential loss of generality.

with

$$m = n - 1; k_i = b_{in}; a_{ij} = -b_{ij}, \quad (i,j = 1, \cdots, m); |A| = |a_{ij}| \neq 0.$$

It is clear that, for $x_n = 1$, the solution of (1) is identical with that of (2), and the $[x_i]$ satisfying (1) will all be of the same sign if and only if the $[x_i]$ satisfying (2) are all positive. Further, without loss of generality, we can take $a_{ii} = -b_{ii} = 1$.

In equations (2), x_i is the total quantity of the ith commodity produced; k_i is the quantity of the ith commodity consumed; $-a_{ij}x_j$ is the quantity of the ith commodity used in producing the jth commodity. The nth equation in system (1), which is linearly dependent upon the first m equations, may be interpreted as a consumption function. Alternatively, the vector $[k_i]$ in (2), which gives the relative quantities of the various commodities consumed, may be considered the schedule of consumption goods.

The production system (2) is economically meaningful only if the $[x_i]$ satisfying it are all positive. Conceivably, the signs of the $[x_i]$ may depend upon the magnitude of the $[k_i]$—that is, upon the schedule of consumption goods. Hence we will be interested in knowing under what conditions the $[x_i]$ will be positive for some given set $[k_i]$, and under what conditions the $[x_i]$ will be positive for *any* set $[k_i \geqslant 0]$.

The defective theorem is the following: LEMMA: *The system of equations* (1) *is satisfied only for x_i all of the same sign.*

This theorem is true only for $n \leqslant 3$, as shown by the following counter-example:

$$-2x_1 + 4x_2 + x_3 + x_4 = 0$$

$$4x_1 - 2x_2 + x_3 + x_4 = 0$$

$$x_1 + x_2 - 2x_3 + 4x_4 = 0$$

$$x_1 + x_2 + 4x_3 - 2x_4 = 0$$

We verify immediately that $\Delta = 0$, and is of rank $n - 1$, and that $b_{ij} > 0$ for all $i \neq j$, while $b_{ii} < 0$ for all i. But the general solution of this system is: $x_1 = K; x_2 = K; x_3 = -K; x_4 = -K$; where K is an arbitrary constant.

The fallacy in the proof offered for the lemma lies in paragraph III of Hawkins' paper. Specifically, it is not correct that: if all members of a set of hyperplanes intersect in a common line through the origin, and if each member of the set has points lying in the first quadrant, then the common line of intersection must lie in the first quadrant.

We now proceed to a valid, necessary and sufficient condition that the equations (2) be satisfied only for $[x_i]$ all positive. THEOREM: *A necessary and sufficient condition that the x_i satisfying* (2) *be all positive is that all principal minors of the matrix* $||a_{ij}||$ *be positive.*

To prove this theorem we first consider the augmented $m \cdot n$ matrix $||a_{ij} - k_i||$ and proceed to reduce this matrix, row by row, to triangular form. That is, by adding to each row an appropriate linear combination of the preceding rows, we obtain a matrix in which all elements to the left of the main diagonal are zero. This procedure can always be carried out step by step until a row (say the jth) is reached with a nonpositive diagonal term. It does not alter the solution of the system and does not alter the values of the principal minors consisting of the first i rows and columns ($i = 1, \cdots, m$).

Because of the arrangement of signs in our particular matrix, all elements in the first column except the first can be made zero by adding to each row an appropriate *positive* multiple of the first row. The signs of all other elements off the main diagonal will remain negative. The sign of a_{22} may remain positive or become negative. In the former case, the third and all following elements in the second column can be made zero by adding to the corresponding rows an appropriate *positive* multiple of the second row. In general, if the first i elements on the main diagonal remain positive after the first $i-1$ steps in the triangularization, then the ith step in triangularization can be carried out by adding to the remaining rows a *positive* multiple of the ith row; otherwise by adding a *negative* multiple of the ith row. We carry out the triangularization until we reach a row with a nonpositive diagonal term.

For the matrix finally obtained, we distinguish two cases: (A) all the diagonal terms in the triangular matrix are positive, (B) at least one term on the main diagonal is nonpositive (and the jth term, say, is the first nonpositive one). We now prove that in case (A) all the principal minors are positive and all the x_i are positive; while in case (B) at least one principal minor is nonpositive and at least one of the x_i is negative—a statement equivalent to our theorem.

A. In case (A) we solve the corresponding system of equations successively for x_m, x_{m-1}, $\cdots$, x_1 in terms of the k_i. Since $k_m > 0$, we must have $x_m > 0$. Since $k_{m-j} > 0$, it follows that if all $x_{m-i} > 0$ ($i < j$), then $x_{m-j} > 0$. Hence by induction, all the x_i must be positive. But, since a triangular determinant equals the product of the elements on its main diagonal, all principal minors consisting of the first k rows and columns of the triangular matrix are positive ($k = 1, \cdots, m$). But these minors are equal to the corresponding minors of the original matrix $||a_{ij}||$.

B. In case (B), all elements to the right of the main diagonal in the jth row of the diagonalized matrix are negative, and the diagonal term is nonpositive. Suppose now that all x_i for $i > j$ are positive.

248   DAVID HAWKINS AND HERBERT A. SIMON

Then, since k_j is positive, x_j must be negative.[4] But the principal minor of the first j rows and columns of the triangularized matrix will be negative or zero, since the jth element in the principal diagonal is nonpositive, the others positive. Hence the corresponding minor in $||a_{ij}||$ will be nonpositive.

Since the signs of the x_i obviously do not depend on the order in which the equations are arranged before triangularization, in case (A) *all* the principal minors of $||a_{ij}||$ must be positive.

This completes the proof of the theorem. Moreover, our proof gives a direct method of testing whether the x_i satisfying a given matrix are all positive.

COROLLARY: *A necessary and sufficient condition that the x_i satisfying* (2) *be all positive for any set* $[k_i > 0]$ *is that all principal minors of the matrix* $||a_{ij}||$ *are positive.* This corollary follows immediately from the theorem, and from the consideration that the elements of the matrix $||a_{ij}||$ are independent of the $[k_i]$.

Economic Interpretations. From the corollary, we see that if the production equations are internally consistent in permitting the production of some fixed schedule of consumption goods, then these consumption goods can be obtained in any desired proportion from this production system. Hence the system will be consistent with *any* schedule of consumption goods.

The condition that all principal minors must be positive means, in economic terms, that the group of industries corresponding to each minor must be capable of supplying more than its own needs for the group of products produced by this group of industries. If this is true, and if the condition $\Delta = 0$ for equations (1) is satisfied, then we can say that each group of industries must be just capable of supplying its own demands upon itself *and* the demands of the other industries in the economy. For example, if the principal minor involving the ith and jth commodities is negative, this means that the quantity of the ith commodity required to produce one unit of the jth commodity is greater than the quantity of the ith commodity that can be produced with an input of one unit of the jth commodity. Under these circumstances, the production of these two commodities could not be continued, for they would exhaust each other in their joint production.

University of Colorado and
Illinois Institute of Technology

---

[4] Or, if the diagonal term is zero, we have a contradiction—i.e., all x for $i > j$ cannot be positive.

Part II
Dynamic Input–Output Analysis

[7]

DYNAMIC ANALYSIS

Wassily Leontief

I. STATIC AND DYNAMIC THEORY

A STATIC theory derives the changes in the variables of a given system from the observed changes in the underlying structural relationships: dynamic theory goes further and shows how certain changes in the variables can be explained on the basis of fixed, i.e. invariant, structural characteristics of the system.

Dynamic theory thus enables us to derive the empirical law of change of a particular economy from information obtained through the observation of its structural characteristics at one single point of time. This possibility, methodologically rather obvious, and practically very important, has unfortunately been obscured by the fact that most of the recent attempts to determine the structural characteristics of actual economic systems have been based on some kind of statistical time-series analysis, thus giving rise to the erroneous impression that the empirical laws of change necessarily must be derived from direct observations of past development.

This would not be true even if one had reason to believe that extended, say forty- or fifty-year, stretches of economic development were explainable in purely dynamic terms, that is, without explicit reference to significant structural change. Our knowledge of Western economic history of the last two hundred years proves such an assumption to be untenable.

The empirical approach designed to derive the operational properties of a national economy through direct and detailed observation of its structural characteristics at one particular point, or at least a relatively short interval, of time seems to commend itself for the purposes of dynamic as well as of static analysis.

Developed with this particular use in mind, the theory described below represents a dynamic extension of the static input-output scene. It is not a general theory if by general one means a formulation which, for the sake of conceptual completeness, incorporates all the hypothetically relevant determinants of the process to be explained, including those which—like the more subtle aspects of entrepreneurial decision-making, for example—will remain beyond the reach of the empirical investigator for a long

54   STATIC AND DYNAMIC THEORY

time to come. This implies, of course, the assumption that in its specialized form the proposed theory, implemented by accessible factual information, can advance the understanding of the actually observed dynamic
processes; it also implies the belief that as additional data become available the theory itself could be refined to take them into account.

Static input-output analysis describes the economic system in terms of
mutually interrelated and structurally conditioned, simultaneous flows of
commodities and services. The dynamic element—the dependence of the
future on the past states of the system—can and usually has been accounted for in the theoretical explanation through the introduction of
structural time lags, of structural stock-flow relationships, or of a combination of both.

The methodological emphasis on 'structural' is relevant for the following reason. The accumulation and decumulation of stocks can, in some
instances, be shown to result directly from the operation of primary structural lags. The fluctuation in the amount of 'work in progress' (which is
a stock of intermediate products) observed in the shipbuilding industry,
for example, can be successfully explained on the basis of the structural
lag measured by the time which elapses between the laying of the keel
of a vessel and its final completion. Conversely an observed lag between
the variation in the stream of inputs absorbed by an industry and the corresponding changes in the level of its output can often be traced back to
its changing capital requirements based on the technologically determined
stock-flow ratio between the amounts, i.e. the stock of equipment, building, and inventory of materials, on the one hand, and the corresponding
capacity to turn out the actually observed stream of finished products, on
the other.

As is often the case in this type of analysis, the selection of the theoretical scheme depends to a considerable extent on the level of detail at
which the empirical inquiry is to be conducted. The stock-flow relationship which, at one such level, would best be considered as a structural
datum, might turn out to be reducible on another, deeper level to fixed
structural lags and vice versa.

In general stock-flow ratios are more readily observable than lags between flows. It is interesting to note in this connection that the conventional standards of behavior, the rules-of-thumb actually, or at least apparently, adhered to by the practical decision-makers in economic enterprises—be they industrial managers, directors of commercial or financial
institutions, or even public budget-making authorities—most often are formulated in terms of some normal period of turnover, desirable inventory
ratios and other, similar stock-flow relationships; these conventional rules

DYNAMIC ANALYSIS   55

hardly ever contain explicit references to desirable or normal time lags.

This is the reason why stock-flow relationships, rather than structural time lags or a combination of both, are relied upon in this initial attempt at a dynamic approach to empirical input-output analysis.[1] A separate note appended to this chapter contains the description of a mathematical procedure which could be used in quantitative analysis of more general dynamic input-output systems involving both structural lags and stock-flow relationships.

II. Statement of Dynamic Theory

The static input-output scheme described in Chapter 2 (p. 18 ff.) explains the mutual interdependence of the distinct sectors of the national economy in terms of a given set of structural coefficients, a_{ik}. Each such coefficient represents the amount of a particular input, i, which is absorbed by industry k per unit of its output. A complete set of such coefficients pertaining to any one particular industry determines the flows of labor, all kinds of materials, fuels, replacement parts, etc., which this industry would have to absorb per unit of time, say per month or per year, in order to be able to produce a given flow of output, i.e. in order to be able to maintain a rate of output defined in terms of so many units of finished product per month or per year.

These input coefficients do not reflect, however, the stock requirements of the economy; they do not and cannot explain the magnitude of those input flows which serve directly to satisfy the capital needs of all its various sectors, either as additions to fixed investment in the form of permanent improvements, building and different kinds of equipment, or as an increase in the necessary inventories of raw material, goods in process, etc. In the open static system, such as is described in the last chapter, these inputs, instead of being assigned to the industries which actually absorb them, are simply considered to be a part of final demand. In equations (2, 1), (2, 2), and (2, 3) all investment demand for the product of any industry i is included in y_i; that means that the effects of investment demand on outputs of all commodities and services are explained, while the observed magnitude of this demand itself, though 'taken in account,' is not explained.

Such an explanation becomes possible as soon as the stock requirements of all the individual sectors of the economy are included in the structural

---

[1] Other discussions of the same dynamic system based on stock-flow relationships will be found in Hawkins, David, 'Some Conditions of Macroeconomic Stability,' *Econometrica*, October 1948; Georgescu-Roegen, N., 'Relaxation Phenomena,' in *Activity Analysis of Production and Allocation*, ed. by T. C. Koopmans, New York, 1951; Leontief, W., 'Dynamic Analysis of Economic Equilibrium,' *Proceedings of Second Symposium on Large-Scale Digital Calculating Machinery*, Harvard University Press, 1951, pp. 333-7.

56   STATIC AND DYNAMIC THEORY

map of the system along with its previously described flow requirements.

If $S_{ik}(t)$ represents the stock of a commodity produced by industry i and used by industry k at the time t, the rate of change, i.e. the rate of increase or decrease in that stock at this particular point of time, can be written as $\dfrac{dS_{ik}(t)}{dt}$ or, for short, as $\dot{S}_{ik}$.

The basic balance equation—equation (2, 2) on p. 18—can now be rewritten as follows:

$$X_i - \sum_{k=1}^{m} x_{ik} - \sum_{k=1}^{m} \dot{S}_{ik} = Y_i \qquad\qquad \begin{aligned} i &= 1, 2, \cdots, m \quad (3, 1) \\ k &= 1, 2, \cdots, m \end{aligned}$$

The second left-hand term represents here, as before, the sum total of those input flows of commodity i which serve the current production requirements of all the various sectors of the economy; the new, third term describes, on the other hand, the inputs absorbed on 'capital account,' i.e. that part of the total demand for commodity i which is being added to or subtracted (if $\sum_{k=1}^{m} \dot{S}_{ik}$ happens to be negative) from the stocks of that particular good used throughout the economy. All allocations of commodity i to current replacement and maintenance requirements of the capital goods and other stocks are to be thought of as being accounted for by the second term, $\sum_{k=1}^{m} X_{ik}$, unless of course they are included in the final demand, Y_i.

The set of structural equations (2, 2) describing the current input requirements of each sector of the economy on its rate of output, X_k, must now be supplemented by a corresponding set of structural stock-flow relationships:

$$S_{ik} = b_{ik}X_k \qquad\qquad \begin{aligned} i &= 1, 2, \cdots, m \quad (3, 2a) \\[4pt] k &= 1, 2, \cdots, m \end{aligned}$$

The b_{ik}'s will from now on be referred to as the stock or capital coefficients of the system. If i stands, say, for power tools and k for automobiles, the coefficient, b_{ik}, indicates the amount, i.e. the stock, of power tools used per unit of the annual automobile output. With b_{ik} known, the corresponding equation in (3, 2a) determines the total stock of machine tools which the automobile industry would use if it were to produce at a rate of X_k units of automobiles per year. The over-all balance between the input and the output flows expressed in (3, 1) comprises, however, only additions to and subtractions from stocks rather than the entire stocks themselves. Differentiation of both sides of (3, 2a) in respect to time transforms these structural equations into relations between

DYNAMIC ANALYSIS 57

changes in specific stocks held by various industries, S_{ik}, and changes in the rates of output of these industries, $\dot{X}_{ik}$:

$$S_{ik} = b_{ik}\dot{X}_k \qquad\qquad i = 1, 2, \cdots, m \quad (3, 2b)$$

$$k = 1, 2, \cdots, m$$

Substitution of the two sets of structural relationships (2, 2) and (3, 2b) in (3, 1) leads to the final system of dynamic input-output equations:

$$X_i - \sum_{k=1}^{m} a_{ik}X_k - \sum_{k=1}^{m} b_{ik}\dot{X}_k = Y_i \qquad\qquad i = 1, 2, \cdots, m \quad (3, 3)$$

$$k = 1, 2, \cdots, m$$

It is a system of m linear differential equations with constant coefficients. Its m 'unknowns' are the same as those of the corresponding static system (2, 3): the output flows of all the various commodities and services, X_1, X_2, $\cdots$, X_k, $\cdots$, X_m. Their mutual interdependence now involves also, however, the rates of change of all these flows, $\dot{X}_1$, $\dot{X}_2$, $\cdots$, $\dot{X}_k$, $\cdots$, $\dot{X}_m$. Because of that the solution of this dynamic system leads to the determination, or perhaps prediction, of the behavior of each one of these variables over time. Once the time shape of a particular output function, $X_k(t)$, has been determined, the corresponding variations in the input flows, $x_{ik}(t)$, absorbed and capital stocks, $S_{ik}(t)$, held in this k^{th} sector of the economy can be found by substituting $X_k(t)$ in the appropriate equations in (2, 2) and (3, 2a).

The complete set of capital coefficients of the m industries described above forms a square matrix,

$$b \equiv \begin{bmatrix} b_{11} & b_{12} & \cdots & b_{1m} \\ b_{21} & b_{22} & \cdots & b_{2m} \\ \cdot & \cdot & & \cdot \\ \cdot & \cdot & & \cdot \\ \cdot & \cdot & & \cdot \\ b_{m1} & b_{m2} & \cdots & b_{mm} \end{bmatrix} \qquad\qquad (3, 4)$$

each column of which lists the stock requirements of one particular sector of the economy. It can be referred to as the capital matrix or the capital structure of the economy. Together with the corresponding previously defined (see p. 19) matrix of the flow coefficients, a, it summarizes the primary structural information required for the derivation of the general dynamic properties of a given economic system.

As explained before, the 'bill of goods' entered on the right-hand side of system (3, 3) is considered to be some known function of time; the history of each individual component, Y_i, of this final demand is assumed to be given, i.e. determined by relationships other than those described in these equations themselves. System (3, 3), in other words, is an open system. To close it one would have to add to it the missing links.

58   STATIC AND DYNAMIC THEORY

If the Y_i's represented, for example, direct consumers' demand, the missing relations would be those pertaining to the description of the position of the households in their connection with the other parts of the economy. System (3, 3) could then be closed through the introduction of an additional equation (or equations, if households were broken down into several separate categories) with coefficients reflecting the structural properties of this particular sector. The treatment of households as an industry supplying its output, mainly labor services, to other industries and receiving its inputs, consumers' goods, from them has already been considered in connection with static input-output analysis.[2]

The components of final demand, $Y_1, Y_2, \cdots, Y_m$, will appear in the new enlarged system as input flows of the nth, the household, sector. Its structural properties like those of any other industry can, for purposes of dynamic analysis, be described in terms of two sets of parameters—the flow coefficients, $a_{1n}, a_{2n}, \cdots$, and the stock coefficients, $b_{1n}, b_{2n}, \cdots$; the latter determine consumers' investments in housing, automobiles, household appliances, and all other kinds of durables and 'storables.'

Closed through explicit inclusion of this n^{th} sector, the original open system (3, 3) will thus be replaced by the following $n \ (= m + 1)$ equations:

$$X_i - \sum_{i=1}^{n} a_{ik}X_k - \sum_{i=1}^{n} b_{ik}\dot{X}_k = 0 \qquad \begin{aligned} i &= 1, 2, \cdots, m, n \\ k &= 1, 2, \cdots, m, n \end{aligned} \qquad (3, 5)$$

X_n represents here the output of the households. The final bill of goods, $Y_1, Y_2, \cdots$, of the open system—which one must remember is, for argument's sake, assumed to have comprised household demand only—can now be written as $x_{1n}, x_{2n}, \cdots$ and derived from the following set of relationships:

$$Y_i \equiv x_{in} = a_{in}X_n + b_{in}\dot{X}_n \qquad i = 1, 2, \cdots, n \qquad (3, 6)$$

$a_{in}X_n$ represents the flow of commodities and services absorbed by households on the current consumption accounts while $b_{in}\dot{X}_n$ shows the additions to or—if $\dot{X}_n$ is negative—the subtractions from the consumers' stocks of durables and semi-durables. This investment demand by households obviously must be clearly distinguished from the investment demand of the other sectors of the economy.

III. The Economic Interpretation

A concise technical presentation of the solution of systems of linear differential equations with constant coefficients can be found in any standard

[2] See Leontief, W. W., *The Structure of American Economy*, 1919-1939, New York, 1951, pp. 41, 169-71.

mathematical text on advanced calculus. The following discussion concerns itself primarily with the interpretation of such solutions in specific economic terms.[8]

Closed (the mathematician calls them homogeneous) systems such as (3, 5) are easier to handle than the corresponding open, non-homogeneous systems like (3, 3). Because of that the former will be taken up first. Its solution can be written in the following form:

$$X_i(t) = c_1 k_{i1} e^{\lambda_1 t} + c_2 k_{i2} e^{\lambda_2 t} + \cdots + c_k k_{ik} e^{\lambda_k t} + \cdots + c_n k_{in} e^{\lambda_n t}$$

$$i = 1, 2, \cdots, n \quad (3, 7)$$

Each of these n equations describes the path through time of one of the n different outputs, $X_1(t)$, $X_2(t)$, $\cdots$. The numerical solution of a dynamic input-output system (3, 5) consists in determination of the values of the n 'roots,' $\lambda_1, \lambda_2, \cdots, \lambda_n$, the n^2 coefficients of the type k_{ik} and the n coefficients $c_1, c_2, \cdots, c_n$. Once the numerical values of these $n^2 + n$ coefficients are entered in (3, 7), the level of any output, $X_i(t)$, at any point of time, t_1, can be found by putting $t = t_1$ in the exponentials on the right-hand side of the appropriate equation.

The magnitude of each one of the n roots $\lambda_1, \lambda_2, \cdots$ and of each of the n^2 coefficients, k_{ik}, depends upon the structure of the economy as described by the two sets of the structural coefficients, a and b.[4]

The actual level of all the outputs at any particular point of time, $t = t_1$ (say $t = 1953$), depends, however, not only on these structural properties alone but also on the state of the system, i.e. the level of outputs at some

---

[8] A simple, step-by-step description and explanation of computations described here in general verbal terms is given in a separate note on p. 76 ff. A reader familiar with the elements of calculus might turn to it for additional clarification.

[4] Given the two square matrices, $\bar{a}$ and b, $\lambda_1, \lambda_2, \cdots, \lambda_n$ are the roots of the 'characteristic equation,' determinant $| \bar{a} - \lambda b | = 0$, where determinant $| \bar{a} - \lambda b |$ is the determinant of the matrix $[\bar{a} - \lambda b]$. In the usual case in which no two of these roots are identical, in the kth column, the coefficients k_{ik}, can be set to be equal (or more generally, proportional) to *any* one column of matrix $[F(\lambda_k)]$, adjoint of matrix $[\bar{a} - \lambda_k b]$, i.e. a matrix in which each element, $F_{ij}(\lambda_k)$, is the co-factor of the element $a_{ji} - \lambda_k b_{ji}$ in $| \bar{a} - \lambda b |$.
The matrix $\bar{a}$ written out in full reads as follows:

$$\begin{bmatrix} 1 - a_{11} & -a_{12} & \cdots & -a_{1n} \\ -a_{21} & 1 - a_{22} & \cdots & -a_{2n} \\ \vdots & \vdots & & \vdots \\ -a_{n1} & -a_{n2} & \cdots & 1 - a_{nn} \end{bmatrix}$$

and is thus related to the matrix a defined in (2, 5) by the following relationship:

$$\bar{a} = [I - a]$$

where I is a unit matrix. Since the basic set a of all structural flow coefficients enters practically all theoretical equations as a component of $\bar{a}$, the new notation offers the advantage of greater brevity.

60   STATIC AND DYNAMIC THEORY

original point of time, $t = t_o$ (say $t = 1950$). To predict the development of a dynamic system over a given interval of time, it is not sufficient to know its general law of change; one must have also specific information concerning its position at the start. These, as the mathematician calls them, initial conditions can be described, for example, in terms of the particular levels of output, $X_1(t_o)$, $X_2(t_o)$, $\cdots$, observed at the original point of time, t_o. Which particular point of time is chosen to serve as such a base of reference, in principle at least, does not matter; once some actual state of the system has been observed, the supposedly known dynamic law of change should make it possible to compute its position at any other, either earlier or later, point of time as well. Practically, taking into account the fact that the structural characteristics of an economy and also its law of change does vary with time, so that the actual course of its development is bound to veer away from the theoretically computed course, the initial point of observation should not be too far removed from those for which the indirect prediction is actually being made.

The quantitative information contained in the description of the 'initial conditions' of the given economic system is incorporated in solution (3, 7) through the numerical values of the constants, c_1, c_2, $\cdots$, c_n. Given the levels of all outputs for some initial point of time, t_o, this t_o (say $t = 0$) can be inserted in all the exponents on the right- and the corresponding $X_i(t_o)$'s on the left-hand side of the equations (3, 7). With the roots, λ, and the constants, k, already known, the system is thus transformed into a set of n linear equations which can be easily solved for the n unknown coefficients, c_1, c_2, $\cdots$, c_n.[5] With these inserted in (3, 7) and the time, t, as well as the outputs, $X_i(t)$, considered again as variables, the solution of the closed dynamic system (3, 5) is complete.

---

[5] There are many other ways to anchor the general structural law of change of a given economic system to the historically emergent circumstances of its existence. Instead of registering the magnitude of all the n variables, i.e. the levels of output of all the separate industries at any single point of time, one could observe the magnitude of one of them, say $X_1(t)$, representing, for example, the output of steel, at n different points of time, t_1, t_2, $\cdots$, t_n. Inserting alternatively the pairs of corresponding values t_1 and $X_1(t_1)$, t_2 and $X_1(t_2)$, and so on up to t_n and $X_1(t_n)$ in the appropriate—in this case it would be the first—equation of system (3, 7), one obtains a system of n linear equations with c_1, c_2, $\cdots$, c_n as the unknowns to be determined by it.

Empirically observed rates of change, $\dot{X}_1(t)$, of outputs even if the $X_1(t)$'s, that is the outputs themselves, are unknown, can also define the initial conditions of the system, sufficient for determination of the constants, c_i. The published Soviet Russian statistics indicate for example the percentage-wise growth of the individual industries in the interval between two years without making any mention of the absolute level of output at either year. Were the basic structural characteristics of the Soviet economy known, given ratios such as $\dfrac{X_1(t_1)}{X_2(t_2)}$, $\dfrac{X_2(t_1)}{X_2(t_2)}$, $\cdots$ combined with information on the actual, absolute level of output, $X_i(t_o)$ reached at any time in any one industry (or on its absolute increment, say $X_i(t_3) - X_i(t_4)$, between two points of time) would suffice for determination of the numerical values of the constants, c_1, c_2, $\cdots$. With these inserted in the dynamic solution (3, 7), the absolute levels of outputs of all industries could be determined for any point of time, t.

DYNAMIC ANALYSIS 61

The n roots, $\lambda_1, \lambda_2, \cdots, \lambda_n$, depending on the magnitude of the structural coefficients combined in the matrices, $\bar{a}$ and b, will be real or complex. The complex roots occur in conjugate pairs such as $\lambda_k = \alpha_k + i\beta_k$ and $\bar{\lambda}_k = \alpha_k - i\beta_k$, the constants, α and β being structurally determined. The terms on the right-hand side of equations (3, 7) containing such conjugate roots can be combined pairwise and, with imaginary terms cancelled out, they will appear in the following form:

$$c_i k_{ik} e^{\alpha_k t} \cos (\beta_k t + c'_{ik} + k'_i) \qquad (3, 8)$$

As t increases, i.e. as time goes on, $\cos (\beta_k t + c'_{ik} + k'_i)$ will fluctuate between -1 and $+1$.

All exponential terms, $e^{\lambda_k t}$ and $e^{\alpha_k t}$, if λ_k or α_k are positive, will grow in their absolute magnitude as t increases, while the terms with negative λ's and α's will become smaller and smaller tending toward 0. A term with $\lambda = 0$ would, of course, remain constant and a periodic term with $\alpha = 0$ would show a periodic wave-like motion of constant unchanging amplitude.[6]

Considering the solution as a whole, one can see that if all its roots are negative the system, with the passage of time, would shrink to nothing; all exponentials and consequently all the terms on the right-hand side of (3, 7) will tend toward 0. This will not happen if at least one root is positive (or rather, not negative). The largest of the roots, if time went on and all the constants in the system remained unchanged, would finally dominate the direction and the rate of change of all the individual variables: in each one of the equations describing the development of the various parts of the economy, the particular term containing this largest positive root will, sooner or later, begin to grow faster—or fall slower—in its absolute magnitude than all the other terms taken together. If, for example, λ_1 were the largest positive root in (3, 7) in the long run, i.e. after t had become large enough, the outputs of the separate industries could with an ever smaller percentage error be computed from the following truncated set of equations:

$$X_i(t) = c_1 k_{ik} e^{\lambda_1 t} \qquad i = 1, 2, \cdots, n \quad (3, 10)$$

The relative magnitude of the outputs of any two industries would become invariant with time, i.e. constant. From (3, 10), it follows that

$$\frac{X_i(t)}{X_j(t)} = \frac{k_{i1}}{k_{j1}} \qquad (3, 11)$$

---

[6] In case a root, λ_k, repeats itself s times, the terms containing it will appear on the right-hand side of the ith equation in (3, 7) in the following form:

$$[{}_1 c_k\, {}_{11} k_{ik} + {}_2 c_k ({}_{21} k_{ik} + {}_{22} k_{ik} t) + \cdots + {}_s c_k ({}_{s1} k_{ik} + {}_{s2} k_{ik} t + \cdots + {}_{ss} k_{ik} t^s)] e^{\lambda_k t} \qquad (3, 9)$$

The k coefficients are structurally determined while the constants, $c - s$ in number, depend upon the initial conditions.

62   STATIC AND DYNAMIC THEORY

The relative rate growth of all industries would accordingly become the
same and equal to the dominant root, λ_1:

$$\frac{\dot{X}_i(t)}{X_1(t)} = \frac{c_1 k_{ik} \lambda_1 e^{\lambda_1 t}}{c_1 k_{ik} e^{\lambda t}} = \lambda_1 \qquad (3, 12)$$

It is interesting to note that both the long-run rate of growth and the
equilibrium proportions between the outputs of the individual industries
are dependent upon the structural properties of the economy only; because of that, they can be determined without the knowledge of any
initial conditions. To determine the absolute level of outputs even for
the state of 'long-run equilibrium' the knowledge of some initial state of
the system is, however, indispensable.

Having mentioned these peculiar properties of the theoretical long-run
dynamic equilibrium—a concept which plays a considerable role in some
of the 'purer' theories of economic growth—one must at once say that,
for purposes of empirical analysis of the actual economic development,
they most probably will be of very little use.

The more the actual proportion of the outputs of the various industries
deviates at any given point of time from the long-run equilibrium ratios
corresponding to the existing structural properties of the system, the
greater role will the terms in (3, 7) containing the secondary, i.e. non-
dominant, roots play in the determination of the actual course of its
dynamic development in the immediate future. One can easily visualize
situations in which a term containing a relatively small and even the
smallest root, λ_k, but carrying the relatively large (positive or negative)
coefficient, $c_k k_{ik}$, will—as t increases—contribute more to the change in
the output of sector X_i than a term with a large root, λ_j, but a smaller
coefficient, $c_j k_{ij}$. In the long run, i.e. with a large enough t, the 'greatest'
root would actually come into its own, but by then the empirical significance of the original dynamic equations based on the structural properties
of the economy observed at the same time with its initial conditions
might long be dead.

In a homogeneous, dynamic system with constant coefficients containing no other than n real roots, and thus showing no periodic fluctuations
in its solution, each of the n variables representing the separate outputs
could—depending on the initial conditions—reverse the direction of its
movement up to $n - 1$ times before settling into a monotonic rise or
fall gradually approaching the long-run equilibrium rate of change of
the system as a whole.

DYNAMIC ANALYSIS 63

IV. THE OPEN SYSTEM

The solution of the original open, i.e. non-homogeneous, system (3, 3) will be of the following general form:

$$X_i(t) = c_1 k_{i1} e^{\lambda_1 t} + c_2 k_{i2} e^{\lambda_2 t} + \cdots + c_k k_{ik} e^{\lambda_k t} + \cdots + c_m k_{im} e^{\lambda_m t} + L_i(t)$$

$$i = 1, 2, \cdots, m \quad (3, 13)$$

All terms, but the last, on the right-hand side are obtained by solving (3, 3) as if it were a closed, homogeneous system, i.e. by assuming that all components of final demand, $Y_1, Y_2, \cdots, Y_m$, are equal to 0. The roots, $\lambda_1, \lambda_2, \cdots, \lambda_m$, and all the k coefficients can thus be determined by the method described above in connection with the solution of system (3, 7).

The functions $L_1(t), L_2(t), \cdots, L_m(t)$, on the other hand, represent what is called the particular part of the general solution of the non-homogeneous system (3, 3), the part which incorporates the specific effect of the final demand. The shape of these functions depends not only on the structural coefficients appearing on the left-hand side of (3, 3), but also on the specific shape of the functions, $Y_1(t), Y_2(t), \cdots, Y_m(t)$, i.e. the given changes over time of each of the separate components of final demand.

For a comprehensive discussion of the 'particular' solution of non-homogeneous systems of differential equations, the reader must again be referred to standard mathematical texts. The empirically observed or—if the analysis is to be used in connection with some kind of policy choices—hypothetically prescribed shapes of the $Y(t)$ functions will often be expressible in some standard functional form. The shapes of the corresponding $L(t)$ functions would then also be of a rather simple form. The numerical computation of the relevant parameters can, in such cases, easily be standardized.

If, for example, the course of final demand for the products of each industry is represented by an exponential polynomial

$$Y_i(t) = g_{i1} e^{\mu_1 t} + g_{i2} e^{\mu_2 t} + \cdots + g_{ik} e^{\mu_k t} + \cdots + g_{iv} e^{\mu_v t}$$

$$i = 1, 2, \cdots, m \quad (3, 14)$$

the particular solution of (3, 3) will be:

$$L_i(t) = w_{i1} e^{\mu_1 t} + w_{i2} e^{\mu_2 t} + \cdots + w_{ik} e^{\mu_k t} + \cdots + w_{iv} e^{\mu_v t}$$

$$i = 1, 2, \cdots, m \quad (3, 15)$$

The numerical values of each of the constants, $w_{i1}, w_{i2}, \cdots$, depend on the magnitude of the coefficients, g_{ik}, occurring in all the given-demand

64   STATIC AND DYNAMIC THEORY

functions, $L_i(t)$, as well as on the two sets of the structural flow and stock coefficients, a and b.[7]

In case the given bill of goods is described by a set of ordinary polynomials in t:

$$Y_i(t) = g_{i0} + g_{i1}t + g_{i2}t^2 + \cdots + g_{ik}t^k + \cdots + g_{iv}t^v$$

$$i = 1, 2, \cdots, m \quad (3, 17)$$

the corresponding particular solution of (3, 3) will consist also of polynomials of the order v in t:

$$L_i(t) = w_{i0} + w_{i1}t + w_{i2}t^2 + \cdots + w_{ik}t^k + \cdots + w_{iv}t^v$$

$$i = 1, 2, \cdots, m \quad (3, 18)$$

Each of the constants, w_{i0}, w_{i1}, $\cdots$, again depends on the structural matrices $\bar{a}$, b, and the set of constants characterizing the given-demand polynomials (3, 17).[8]

After the particular solution of the open system (3, 3)—that is, the shape of the functions, $L_i(t)$, and the values of all the coefficients occurring in them—has been found, the only elements in the solution (3, 13) still to be determined are, $c_1, c_2, \cdots, c_m$. As in the previously discussed solution of a homogeneous system, these constants reflect the specific state which the given system has reached in the course of its development up to some particular point or points of time.

---

[7] If $\bar{a}$ and b are the previously defined square matrices and g_k the *column* matrix g_{1k}, g_{2k}, $\cdots$, g_{mk} of constants which are associated in each of the equations of (3, 14) with the exponential term, $e^{\mu_k t}$, then the *column*, w_k, of the coefficients, w_{1k}, w_{2k}, $\cdots$, w_{mk}, associated with the same term $e^{\mu_k t}$ in the 'particular' solution (3, 15) can be computed by the formula,

$$w_k = [\bar{a} - \mu_k b]^{-1} g_k \quad (3, 16)$$

[8] If $\bar{a}$ and b are the previously defined square, structural matrices while g_k represents a *column* matrix of the constants, g_{1k}, g_{2k}, $\cdots$, g_{mk}, which are associated with t^k in each of the equations (3, 17) and if, furthermore, w_k is the *column* matrix of the similarly placed constants, w_{1k}, w_{2k}, $\cdots$, w_{mk}, in solution (3, 18), then all the $(v + 1)$ such columns, w_0, w_1, $\cdots$, w_v, can be computed on the basis of the following recursive formulae:

$$
\begin{aligned}
w_v &= \bar{a}^{-1} g_v \\
w_{v-1} &= \bar{a}^{-1}(g_{v-1} + vbw_v) \\
&\quad \vdots \\
w_k &= \bar{a}^{-1}(g_k + (k+1)bw_{k+1}) \\
&\quad \vdots \\
w_0 &= \bar{a}^{-1}(g_0 + bw_1)
\end{aligned}
\qquad (3, 19)
$$

Beginning at the top, one can first compute w_v, insert the magnitude thus found on the right-hand side of the next matrix equation, then compute w_{v-1} and thus work step-by-step down to w_0.

DYNAMIC ANALYSIS 65

If, for example, at $t = t_o$, $X_1 = X^o{}_1$, $X_2 = X^o{}_2$, $\cdots$, $X_m = X^o{}_m$, these particular values of time and of the output variables can be entered on the right- and left-hand side of the equations (3, 13); the $L_i(t)$ terms on the right having then been written out in their explicit form such as (3, 15) or (3, 18). Thus a system of m linear equations is obtained which can be solved for the m unknown coefficients, c_1, c_2, $\cdots$, c_m.

V. POLICY DECISIONS AND THE OPEN SYSTEM

In dynamic as in the static input-output analysis,[9] consideration of the national economy as an open system offers an analytical tool particularly well suited to the making of appraisals of the material implications of alternative policy decisions.

Questions of policy can have an operational meaning only if one assumes that the structure of certain sectors of the economy can be changed. To examine the possible effects of such changes on the rest of the economy, one can remove the balance equations of the sectors subject to such change from the original, closed set. As soon as the original system is thus opened, the number of equations becomes smaller than the number of the original unknowns. The additional degrees of freedom thus acquired by the explanatory scheme finds its expression in the transfer of certain input items from the left- to the right-hand side of the remaining balance equations. In this position they constitute the given bill of goods of the new open system. If the policies in question were supposed, for example, to modify directly the structure of consumers' demand, the household equations would be those to go from the closed system and the household purchases of the products of all the other sectors of the economy would make up the final bill of goods in the newly constituted open system. If the possible effects of alternative schedules of governmental purchases of military equipment were in question, these schedules would have to appear on the right-hand side of the non-homogeneous, dynamic input-output system (3, 3) to be solved.

In interpreting the operational significance of the final demand in an open system, it is important to emphasize the exclusion of certain sets of structural constants from the left-hand side of the basic dynamic equations rather than the inclusion of some particular kind of demand on their right-hand side. The final bill of goods described by functions Y_1, Y_2, $\cdots$, Y_m in (3, 3) can, strictly speaking, comprise any demand not derivable, i.e. not explainable, on the basis of the structural input-output relationships explicitly accounted for by the flow and stock coefficients appearing on the left-hand side of the particular open system used.

[9] See Leontief, op. cit. pp. 142, 168, 205.

66   STATIC AND DYNAMIC THEORY

With some basic structural characteristics of the economy considered as given and described by the appropriate sets of the flow and capital coefficients, the problem of possible choice must, first of all, be defined in terms of the particular interval of time within which the direct effects of the policy in question on the course of the dynamic development of the given economy are to be examined. With the beginning, say t_o, and the end— let it be t_g—of this period given, our attention for the purposes of policy decisions can be centered, first of all, on the interdependence between (1) the state of the economy, i.e. the levels of all the outputs, X^o_1, X^o_2, $\cdots$, X^o_m, at the time t_o; (2) the state of the economy, similarly described, at the time t_g; and (3) the development of the final demand in the interval of time between t_o and t_g as depicted by the m functions, $Y_1(t)$, $Y_2(t)$, $\cdots$, $Y_m(t)$.

With the general form of these bill-of-goods functions chosen in advance,[10] their particular time profiles can be described in terms of an appropriate set of constants, such as g and μ in (3, 14) or g in (3, 17).

The desired interrelationship can be obtained from the general solution (3, 13) of the open system (3, 3). Let the final demand, for example, be described in terms of the m exponential polynomials (3, 14). The levels of the m outputs, X^g_1, X^g_2, $\cdots$, X^g_m, characterizing the state of the economy at the final point of time, t_g, are, according to (3, 13), determined by the following set of equations:

$$X^g_i = c_1(X^o, g, \mu)k_{i1}e^{\lambda_1 t_g} + c_2(X^o, g, \mu)k_{i2}e^{\lambda_2 t_g} + \cdots$$
$$+ c_m(X^o, g, \mu)k_{im}e^{\lambda_m t_g} + w_{i1}(g, \mu)e^{\mu_1 t_g} + w_{i2}(g, \mu)e^{\mu_2 t_g} + \cdots$$
$$+ w_{iv}(g, \mu)e^{\mu_v t_g} \quad i = 1, 2, \cdots, m \quad (3, 20)$$

The parameters, c, are shown here to be functions of the initial levels of the individual outputs, X^o_1, X^o_2, $\cdots$, X^o_m—represented, in short, by X^o—and of all the bill-of-goods constants symbolized by g and μ; the constants, w, are shown to be dependent on g and μ. Both the c's and w's as well as the roots, λ, depend also, of course, on the magnitude of the basic sets of the structural flow and stock coefficients, a and b. This dependence will necessarily be taken into account when in the course of actual computations the c's and the w's are explicitly replaced on the right-hand side of (3, 20) by numerical functions of the X^o_1's, the g's, and the μ's.[11]

With these substitutions completed, system (3, 20) can be considered to represent a set of m equations in $2m + u$ variables: the m initial out-

---

[10] As already pointed out (p. 63), many alternative types of single-valued functions, $Y_i(t)$, can be used to describe, with any desired degree of approximation, the actually observed or hypothetically assumed time shape of final demand over any given interval of time.

[11] For purposes of actual computation, the right-hand terms of (3, 20) can be simplified by putting $t_g = 0$, i.e. by conventionally putting the origin of the time count at the end of the time interval in question.

DYNAMIC ANALYSIS 67

puts, X^o_1, X^o_2, $\cdots$, X^o_m; the m final outputs, X^g_1, X^g_2, $\cdots$, X^g_m; and the u constants which determine the particular shape of the m final-demand functions, $Y_1(t)$, $Y_2(t)$, $\cdots$, $Y_m(t)$, between $t = t_o$ and $t = t_g$. Providing only one constant for each such function, the number u cannot be smaller than m. Usually to provide a sufficient range of choice between alternative time paths of final demand, one would use for their description functions in which the total number of constants will be much larger than m. In the particular case discussed above, $u = m \cdot v + v$, where $m \cdot v$ is the total number of the g coefficients and v the number of the μ coefficients in $(3, 14)$.

With $2m + u$ variables, and m relations connecting them, one can generally fix arbitrarily the values of $m + u$ of these variables, and then determine the corresponding values of the remaining m from the m equations.

For purposes of many kinds of policy decisions, the initial state of the system, i.e. its position in the point of time t_o, when the first effects of alternative policies can be expected to set in, must be considered as given; that is, determined by direct observation or possibly by unconditional prediction based on a solution of an appropriate closed dynamic system. With the set X^o of the initial output given, the range of possible alternatives is thus reduced to free determination of the values of any u of the remaining $u + m$ variables, the corresponding magnitudes of the other m being obtained through the solution of system $(3, 20)$.

For certain purposes one would want to prescribe, for example, the final state of the economy, i.e. the levels of all outputs at the time t_g, insert them in $(3, 20)$, and then obtain a quantitative description of all the paths which the final demand could take while leading the economy from its given original to the prescribed final state. This presupposes, of course, that u is larger than m, i.e. that the number of parameters available for the description of the changing levels of final demand between t_o and t_g exceeds the number of equations limiting their admissible courses to those which would actually connect the two fixed positions of the system.

The variety of materially significant alternatives might be very great. A low level of final demand in the first part of the time period under consideration might, for example, be substituted by choice for a high level in its later stretch, or vice versa. Demand for one type of goods can be substituted for that of another kind. Each particular path of final demand would, of course, be associated with a specific solution of the entire dynamic system; the corresponding time paths of all the individual outputs can be found by inserting the alternative bill-of-goods functions in the general solution $(3, 13)$. The associated changes in stocks of all commodities in all the sectors of the economy can finally be computed

68 STATIC AND DYNAMIC THEORY

by simply multiplying every output function, $X_k(t)$, by all the capital coefficients, $b_{1k}, b_{2k}, \cdots, b_{mk}$.

Conjunctural discussion of special situations which might arise under difficult hypothetical assumptions lies beyond the scope of this chapter and indeed of this entire volume. The empirical description of the capital structure of the American economy in the year 1939, combined with the previously derived matrix of current input-output ratios, provides sufficient basis for the application of the analytical tool described in this chapter to the study of the dynamic properties of an actual economy.

VI. IRREVERSIBILITY

The straightforward elaboration of the so-called 'acceleration principle' developed above has one particularly serious defect—it neglects the irreversibilities of the accumulation process.

The dynamic balance equations (3, 3), as they have been set up above, provide for a strict and continued maintenance within each and every sector of the economy of the stock-flow ratios determined by the appropriate sets of capital coefficients. In most instances of expanding output under conditions of fully utilized capacity, this seems to be a pretty good description—at least in a first approximation—of the observed reality. Increasing output requires, in such cases, additional 'stocks' of building equipment, of raw material, and of goods in process, all of which constitute input requirements on the investment account which, in the description of the input-output balance of the economy, must be added to the amounts of the same commodities absorbed simultaneously on current production account.

But when the rate of output of an industry declines and stock requirements are reduced accordingly, the structurally determined stock-flow ratios can be maintained only through a corresponding reduction in stocks: a reduction which, if it actually is achieved, must be entered in the input-output balance of the economy as part of the positive flow available for coverage of the effective input requirements for the commodity in question. In the dynamic system (3, 3), whenever the rate of output, X_k, of some industry, k, declines, i.e. whenever $\dot{X}_k$ becomes negative, all the terms describing the investment input in that industry, $-b_{ik}\dot{X}_k, -b_{2k}\dot{X}_k, \cdots$, turn positive; therefore, in striking the input-output balance, they are added to—instead of being charged against—the 'new' production, $X_1, X_2, \cdots$.

At the time of a rapidly declining rate of production, an industry might even discontinue entirely all purchases of raw materials and satisfy its whole current input demand by living off inventories. In other instances, however, the previously accumulated stocks cannot be reduced. So-called permanent improvement to land obviously cannot be used up at all; the same applies to a large extent to buildings. Other kinds of fixed capital, such as machinery and equipment, can be consumed on current account through discontinued or re-

DYNAMIC ANALYSIS 69

duced maintenance, but even this can happen only to a strictly limited extent, i.e. at a relatively slow rate. The typical irreversibility of the accumulation process finds its expression in idle capacity and surplus inventories, i.e. in unused stocks of fixed and working capital.

Non-transferability of stocks in addition to technical irreducibility constitutes another cause of the irreversibility of the accumulation process. In each equation of the dynamic system (3, 3) the entire output of one particular industry is being balanced against the consumption of its products throughout the entire economy. This implies that the surplus stocks resulting from diminished capacity utilization in any one industry can be transferred to and put to use—either as part of the required stock or as input on current account—in any other expanding, or at least not too rapidly contracting, industry. Sales of surplus machinery, leasing of vacated floor space, and liquidation of surplus inventories of raw and semi-manufactured materials through sale to other more fortunate users are obvious alternatives to the downward adjustment of stockholdings of an industry through under-maintenance and internal consumption on current account. Frequently such transfers from one sector of the economy to another prove, however, to be impracticable. More often than not the balance, or better to say the imbalance, between the available and the required stocks has to be struck for each industry or even each individual establishment separately.[12]

To fix our ideas, let us consider a case in which one and only one kind of stock, say the stock of commodity i used in industry k, i.e. S_{ik}, is irreducible. At any time in which $S_{ik} = b_{ik}X_k$ and $\dot{X}_k \geq 0$, i.e. in which the available stock, S_{ik}, is being fully utilized and the output of X_k increases, or at least remains unchanged, the input-output balance will be adequately described by the kth equation in system (3, 3). In a situation with $\dot{X}_k < 0$, that is, under conditions of falling output, this equation ceases to apply: the reduction of the stock implied by the positive magnitude of the term, $-b_{ik}\dot{X}_k$, cannot actually occur. At the time of declining production, this term necessarily must be equal to 0. In other words, $b_{ik} = 0$ whenever $\dot{X}_k < 0$; that means that whenever $\dot{X}_k < 0$ the dynamic input-output balance of the whole economy has to be described not by the system (3, 3) but by another set of equations which can be obtained from the first by simply putting $b_{ik} = 0$.[13] The original solution (3, 13) must. for the time during which $\dot{X}_k < 0$, accordingly be replaced by an analogous but numerically different solution for which all the constants are computed on the assumption that $b_{ik} = 0$, while the rest of the structural b (stock) coefficients and all the a (flow) coefficients remain the same as before.

In some cases the investment process is not entirely irreversible but the previously accumulated stocks can be consumed only at a limited rate.

---

[12] The unequal degree of transferability of various commodities between different localities constitutes the basis of interregional input-output analysis described in Chapters 4 and 5.

[13] In this particular instance only the ith equation will be affected by this change.

70   STATIC AND DYNAMIC THEORY

Such a downward limit to negative accumulation could, for example, be set by the rate of normal replacement omitted in order to allow the stocks to run down. If $a_{ik}X_k$ represents such replacement requirements,[14] then, with $\dot{X}_k < 0$, the rate of negative accumulation, $b_{ik}\dot{X}_k$, cannot be smaller in its absolute value than $a_{ik}X_k$. As soon as $-a_{ik}X_k - b_{ik}\dot{X}_k$ becomes positive, i.e. as soon as the absolute magnitude of the second term becomes greater than that of the first, idle capital, that is surplus capacity, is bound to appear. The ith balance equation in system (3, 3) has to be replaced by a new one in which not only the coefficient, b_{ik}, but also a_{ik} is set to equal 0: the rate of stock reduction, $-b_{ik}\dot{X}_k$, will be just large enough to equal the replacement requirements.

In this second phase of dynamic change characterized by the existence of a surplus stock, the capital-output relationship described in (3, 2a) cannot be used any more to determine the magnitude of the total stock, $S_{ik}(t)$. The partly idle stock leads, in these conditions, a quasi-independent existence. In the case of complete irreversibility, it would remain constant through the entire duration of that regime. In the second case it would decline at a rate equal to the current maintenance requirement, $a_{ik}X_k$. The size of total stock at any one point of time, t, can, during that second phase, be computed from the following formula:

$$S_{ik}(t) = S_{ik}(t_1) - a_{ik}\int_{t_1}^{t} \dot{X}_k(t)dt \qquad (3, 21)$$

t_1 marks the point of transition from the first to the second regime, and $S_{ik}(t_1)$ represents the magnitude of stock at the time t_1. The rate of change of the output, $\dot{X}_k(t)$, is determined by the solution (3, 13) of the modified system (3, 3) with $a_{ik} = 0$ and $b_{ik} = 0$.

The difference between the total available and the required stock of commodity i in industry k—let it be called the surplus or idle stock and designated by $\bar{S}_{ik}(t)$—can be computed as follows:

$$\bar{S}_{ik}(t) = S_{ik}(t) - b_{ik}X_{ik}(t) \qquad (3, 22)$$

$\bar{S}_{ik}(t)$ cannot be negative. With $\bar{S}_{ik}(t) = 0$, the economy finds itself in the first phase; with $\bar{S}_{ik}(t) > 0$, in the second.

The transition from the first to the second phase must take place at that point of time in which—if the system had continued to move along the first-phase path—a positive surplus stock, $\bar{S}_{ik}$, would have appeared. In the case of absolute irreversibility discussed above, this would occur whenever the output, $X_k(t)$—with the stock, $S_{ik}(t)$, still fully utilized—turns from expansion to contraction, i.e. at the point of time, t_1, in which the state of industry k is characterized by the following three conditions:

$$\bar{S}_{ik}(t_1) = 0 \quad {}_1\dot{X}_k(t_1) < 0 \quad {}_1\dot{X}_k(t_1) = 0 \qquad (3, 23)$$

---

[14] In the case of most fixed capital goods, the entire consumption on current account consists of replacement inputs.

DYNAMIC ANALYSIS   71

The left-hand subscript '1' indicates that both the first and the second derivatives, $_1\dot{X}_k(t)$ and $_1\ddot{X}_k(t)$, refer to the 'rate of change' and the 'rate of the rate of change' of output $X_k(k)$ as determined by the dynamic equation governing the behavior of the economy in the first phase, i.e. under conditions of $\tilde{S}_1(t) = 0$. And the combined conditions indicate a situation in which the output, X_k, after rising up to the time, t_1, would have begun to fall if allowed to move further along the first-phase path. It is the last equation which in the form $_1\dot{X}_k(t) = 0$ must be used to determine the terminal point of time, t_1.

The levels of outputs, $X_1(t_1)$, $X_2(t_1)$, $\cdots$, reached at the end of the just-concluded first phase represent also the initial condition which must be used in the determination of the path to be followed by the economy in the course of the second phase.

That second phase lasts as long as $\tilde{S}_{ik}(t) > 0$ and it terminates if and when, at some point of time, t_2,

$$\tilde{S}_{ik}(t_2) = 0 \quad _2\dot{X}_k(t_2) > 0 \tag{3, 24}$$

Note the left-hand subscript '2' which means that $_2\dot{X}_k(t_2)$ is computed from the equations governing the behavior of the economy in the second phase, i.e. under the assumption of $b_{ik} = 0$. These conditions describe a situation in which the output, $X_k(t)$, rises and reaches, at the time t_2, the level at which the entire previously idle stock, $\tilde{S}_{ik}$, becomes absorbed into active use.

Since in the course of this second phase, and just up to the time t_2, $\tilde{S}_{ik}(t) > 0$, it is the equation $\tilde{S}_{ik}(t) = 0$ which can be used to determine the point of time, t_2, marking its end. Here again the outputs, $X_1(t_2)$, $X_2(t_2)$, $\cdots$, supply the initial conditions which must be inserted in the dynamic solution charting the further movement of the economy now again under the original first-phase regime.

To derive the general dynamic law of change for an economy with limited reversibility, one must thus have:

1. A set of general solutions of the alternative dynamic systems appropriate to all the various phases through which it will pass in the course of its development.

2. A set of rules specifying the conditions under which the process is switched from one phase to the next.

With one irreversible stock, the number of possible alternative phases is two; with two irreversible stocks, it is four.[15] In general, with n irreversible stocks, the total number of all possible phases is 2^n.

Actually, starting with a given initial state, an economy will hardly ever pass, in the course of its subsequent change, through all the theoretically possible phases. As an example of a development which would never abandon the original tracks, one can think of a homogeneous system which from the outset finds itself in the position of the 'long-run equilibrium' described on pages 59

---

[15] (1) Both stocks fully utilized, (2) the first partly, the second fully utilized, (3) both partly utilized, (4) the first fully, the second partly utilized.

to 62. With a positive dominant root, the course of its development will be marked by practically uniform growth of all the outputs. The proportional expansion of fully utilized stocks could, in this case, be interrupted only by fundamental structural variation. Otherwise the original full-utilization phase would continue *ad infinitum*.

VII. Defects of the Multi-phase Theory

The theory of the multi-phase process as presented above promises to become a useful tool in the empirical analysis of economic change. However it has certain defects which, even if they were negligible from the point of view of practical application, deserve special consideration since their examination will throw light on the internal logic of the theory of economic change in general and of the dynamic input-output analysis in particular.

These defects show up in the difficulties which may arise in the application of the rules under which the system is switched from one phase of its development to the next.

Consider an economy with a strictly irreversible stock, S_{ik}, at time t_1, i.e. at the point of transition from the first—the full-utilization—phase to the second phase characterized by the presence of a positive surplus stock, $\bar{S}_{ik}$.

The last two conditions in (3, 23) describe the movement of the output X_k at the time t_1 in terms of the dynamic law governing the first, full-utilization phase which is supposed to end exactly at that point of time, t_1. In its very next step, the economy will already have to follow the alternative, second path derived on the assumption of the presence of a positive surplus stock, $\bar{S}_{ik}$.

If in following this second path the output, X_k, proceeded to fall, idle stock would actually appear and the system would remain under the jurisdiction of the second-phase law up to the time when the idle stocks would again be absorbed in the course of some further developments.

But what would happen if, starting from the initial position of the economy at t_1, the second-phase law were to indicate a rise rather than a fall in the output X_k?

Increasing output at the time of full utilization of stock cannot lead to idle capacity; on the contrary, it implies additional investment. But additional investment can take place only under the rule of the first, not of the second, phase regime. This latter, however, cannot be established since, under conditions existing at time t_1, it would result in a declining output of X_k and a simultaneous appearance of idle stock.

In short, we are facing here a basic contradiction. A rule which—if applied in the existing situation—in effect requires that an industry,

DYNAMIC ANALYSIS 73

already operating at full capacity, should contract so long as it uses all its capital, but should expand if surplus capacity were to appear, obviously cannot be followed consistently.[16]

[16] Let $_1X_k(t_1)$ be the output of commodity k achieved under the law of the first phase at the point of transition, t_1 and let $_2X_k(t_1 + \Delta)$ represent the level which that output would reach at a slightly later point of time, $t_1 + \Delta$, if it had followed the second-phase law of change from t_1 onward.

Since the positive increment of time, Δ, is very small, one can use, for the purpose of comparing $_1X_k(t_1)$ and $_2X_k(t_1 + \Delta)$, the following three-term expansion:

$$_2X_k(t + \Delta) = {}_2X_k(t_1) + {}_2\dot{X}_k(t_1)\Delta + {}_2\ddot{X}_k(t_1)\Delta^2 \cdots \qquad (3, 25)$$

$_2X_k(t_1)$ by definition equals $_1X_k(t_1)$. To determine the value of $_2\dot{X}_k(t_1)$, let us first solve system (3, 3) for any one $\dot{X}_k$ in terms of the outputs, $X_1, X_2, \cdots, X_m$:

$$_1\dot{X}_k = \frac{\begin{vmatrix} b_{11} & b_{12} & \cdots & f_1(X) & \cdots & b_{1m} \\ b_{21} & b_{22} & \cdots & f_2(X) & \cdots & b_{2m} \\ \cdot & \cdot & & \cdot & & \cdot \\ \cdot & \cdot & & \cdot & & \cdot \\ \cdot & \cdot & & \cdot & & \cdot \\ b_{i1} & b_{i2} & \cdots & f_i(X) & \cdots & b_{im} \\ \cdot & \cdot & & \cdot & & \cdot \\ \cdot & \cdot & & \cdot & & \cdot \\ \cdot & \cdot & & \cdot & & \cdot \\ b_{m1} & b_{m2} & \cdots & f_m(X) & \cdots & b_{mm} \end{vmatrix}}{\begin{vmatrix} b_{11} & b_{12} & \cdots & b_{1k} & \cdots & b_{1m} \\ b_{21} & b_{22} & \cdots & b_{2k} & \cdots & b_{2m} \\ \cdot & \cdot & & \cdot & & \cdot \\ \cdot & \cdot & & \cdot & & \cdot \\ \cdot & \cdot & & \cdot & & \cdot \\ b_{i1} & b_{i2} & \cdots & b_{ik} & \cdots & b_{im} \\ \cdot & \cdot & & \cdot & & \cdot \\ \cdot & \cdot & & \cdot & & \cdot \\ \cdot & \cdot & & \cdot & & \cdot \\ b_{m1} & b_{m2} & \cdots & b_{mk} & \cdots & b_{mm} \end{vmatrix}} \qquad (3, 26)$$

The expressions, $f_1(X), f_2(X), \cdots$, which make up the kth column of the determinant on the top are linear functions of $X_1, X_2, \cdots, X_m$:

$$f_i(X) \equiv Y_i - X_i + \sum_{l=1}^{m} a_{il}X_l \qquad i = 1, 2, \cdots, m \quad (3, 27)$$

The outputs, $X_1, X_2, \cdots, X_m$, refer, of course, to the same point of time, say t_1, as the derivative $_1\dot{X}_k$. The left-hand subscript '1' indicates that the relation (3, 26) describes the condition prevailing in the first, full utilization phase. To determine the value which $_2\dot{X}_k(t)$ would have had at the same point of time, t_1, under the rules of the second phase, it is only necessary to change the right-hand side of (3, 26) to the extent of putting $b_{ik} = 0$ in the kth column of the determinant on the bottom, the top determinant remaining the same as before.

But, according to (3, 23), $_1\dot{X}_k(t_1) = 0$; this means that at $t = t_1$, the top determinant in (3, 26) equals 0. Barring the special case in which the bottom determinant vanishes when 0 is substituted for the original value of b_{ik} on the bottom, $_2\dot{X}_k(t_1) = 0$ if $_1\dot{X}_k(t_1) = 0$.

Returning to (3, 25), we see that with $_2X_k(t_1) = {}_1X_k(t_1)$ and $_2\dot{X}_k(t_1) = 0$,

$$_2X_k(t_1 + \Delta) < {}_1X_k(t_1) \quad \text{if} \quad _2\ddot{X}_k(t_1) < 0$$

and

$$_2X_k(t_1 + \Delta) > {}_1X_k(t_1) \quad \text{if} \quad _2\ddot{X}_k(t_2) > 0 \qquad (3, 28)$$

The transition from the first to the second phase can take place without difficulties if $_2\ddot{X}_k(t_1) < 0$ but a contradictory situation arises if $_2\ddot{X}_k(t_1) > 0$. If $_2\ddot{X}_k(t) = 0$ the same inequalities will hold for the third derivative, $_2\dddot{X}_k(t_1)$.

74   STATIC AND DYNAMIC THEORY

A similar contradiction might arise at a point of transition from the second back to the first phase. Having expanded its production up to the point where all the previously unused capacity has been absorbed, an industry conceivably can find itself in a situation in which the new regime, setting in as soon as idle stocks have disappeared, requires not a further increase but rather an immediate reduction of its output.

Before we turn to the consideration of the significance of this theoretical impasse, it is well to observe that in a large system containing many separate sectors the contradictory situations described above are not very likely to occur: the solution of the corresponding large systems of differential equations will depend on the numerical magnitudes of a great many structural coefficients. In the simple example considered above, the difference between the solution of the first- and the second-phase system hinges on the change in the value of one single coefficient, b_{ik}, which turns into 0 in the second phase. In other, more complicated cases in which a given industry uses more than one irreversible stock at the same time, two, three, or more coefficients might change their values simultaneously. However, so long as their number remains much smaller than the total number of all the structural constants in the entire system, such change will most likely result only in a relatively small difference between the two solutions corresponding to the two adjoining phases. This means that in the immediate vicinity of the point of transition the movement of the economy in general and of the critical output in particular will experience only a slight change of direction. If, under the first-phase law, the output, X_k, were about to begin to fall immediately after the point of transition, t_1, in a large system it will go down in the initial period of the second-phase rule too. Similar near-continuity can be expected to prevail also at the point of a changeover in the opposite direction.

The methodological significance of the inconsistent switching rules can be better understood if one realizes that the impasse caused by contradiction as described above finds its counterpart in possible indeterminacy resulting from too much choice. Consider, for example, an economic system smoothly moving along the path prescribed by the solution of a set of dynamic balance equations which neither assumes the existence nor provides for a necessary appearance of surplus stocks. So long as all the outputs involving the use of potentially irreducible stocks actually expand, the explanation of the observed dynamic process, given in terms of the corresponding mathematical system of the appropriate differential equations, seems to be entirely satisfactory.

A closer examination of this theoretical system might show, however, that if—at some arbitrarily chosen point of time, t_1—the equations were modified so as to correspond to the assumption that industry k suddenly begins to operate under conditions of surplus capacity, the new path,

DYNAMIC ANALYSIS   75

followed by the economy from t_1 onward, would actually indicate a reduction in the output of that industry and simultaneous appearance of
idle capacity.

Once the existence of this second alternative has been admitted, the
original set of equations and its solution can be accepted as an explanation of the actually observed process only in a qualified sense.

One, it could be called the preliminary, justification of such an accept-
ance might be based on the fact that 'it works,' i.e. on the fact that the
observed economic system actually follows the original path without ever
deviating into the second. The final vindication of the original theory
would have to wait, however, for an explicit statement of the specific reasons why such deviation does not actually happen. This means that it
would require the formulation of a more general theory, a theory which
would probe into the background of some of the relationships taken for
granted by the present theory and explain, that is derive, them in terms
of some more fundamental factors.

If, for example, the theory described above referred not to a free or a
quasi-free exchange economy but to a centrally guided system, the choice
between the two alternative dynamic systems would have to be made on
the deeper level of analysis involving consideration of the final objec-
tives of the planning authority and possibly an application of certain
maximizing rules. In terms of these principles, the deviation into the
second, alternative path would—as one actually has reason to believe—be
explicitly rejected.

In the case of the apparent contradiction described before, only an
appeal to the same, more basic consideration would obviously lead to a
correct solution, a solution which incidentally will necessarily involve
an actual increase in some stocks which already exceed the capacity
requirements computed on the basis of current production rates.

Returning to the unplanned economy that operates in a quasi-automatic
manner, the preliminary rejection of the alternative path in the latent
indeterminacy case will also have to be ultimately justified in terms of
a more general theory, i.e. a theory entering deeper layers of structural
relationships. It is very possible that in the explanation of the ordinary
course of dynamic change the role of more general analysis could still be
limited to that of an arbiter between alternative solutions reached on the
lower level of refinement. In certain special circumstances, the coarser
approach might fail altogether and the more detailed analysis has to take
over entirely. Such is the case of the contradictory switching rule.

A more detailed analysis of the internal operating conditions of the
individual sectors of the economy might, for example, show that so long
as it is subject to apparently contradictory impulses, the output of the
particular industry in question will simply remain constant while the

76   STATIC AND DYNAMIC THEORY

rest of the system will move on. Such, for example, would be the case if, under conditions of considerable stress, an industry could, for a short time, operate beyond the limits of its normal capacity, i.e. with stocks inferior to those computed on the basis of the standard capital coefficients, but then nearly at once would contract again, over-shoot in the downward direction only to turn back again.

Essentially this means the introduction, in our dynamic system, of a third, intermediary phase, a regime which would last up to the point at which—as a result of changes in the outputs of all the other industries and incidental variations in stocks—the second, the idle capacity, phase could take over without internal contradiction.[17]

Even without entering into a detailed discussion of such a compromise regime, it can be shown that it necessarily will involve accumulation somewhere in the economy of surplus stocks.

The constancy of the critical output, X_k, would have to be described in terms of a separate equation, $X_k = X^1{}_k$, where $X^1{}_k$ represents its level at the beginning of the phase, i.e. at the time t_1. But with the introduction of such an additional equation into the fundamental set (3, 3) of the dynamic balance equations, some other equation would have to be dropped. Otherwise the system as a whole could not be satisfied. Since each equation reflects the balance between the total available outputs and the required inputs of one particular commodity, the omission of any one of them means the admission of the possible and practically the necessary accumulation of a surplus stock of at least one of the commodities in question.

From here on, the theoretical analysis, if pursued any further, is bound to be highly speculative. Only a large amount of additional empirical information—very different in kind from that for the use of which the theory developed in the main part of this chapter has been designed— will be able to give it the necessary direction.

MATHEMATICAL NOTE 1

GENERAL AND SPECIAL SOLUTION OF A SIMPLE DYNAMIC INPUT-OUTPUT SYSTEM CONTAINING STOCKS AND FLOWS BUT NO LAGS

This note contains a systematic step-by-step description of the solution of a simple two-part dynamic input-output system. A reader acquainted with elementary algebra and familiar with the rudiments of

---

[17] The introduction of an additional phase can, under certain assumptions, be described as a recourse to higher-order systems of differential equations. The higher terms of such equations would influence the course of events (i.e. the solution of the system), however, at the critical turning points only.

DYNAMIC ANALYSIS 77

calculus will find in this example a concrete illustration of the analytical and computational procedures discussed verbally in Chapter 3.

I

To illustrate the analysis of a dynamic system presented in Chapter 3 one can consider the following set of two homogeneous linear differential equations of the first order with constant coefficients representing a dynamic input-output equilibrium of a closed two-sector economy.

$$X_1 - a_{11}X_1 - a_{12}X_2 - b_{11}\dot{X}_1 - b_{12}\dot{X}_2 = 0$$
$$-a_{21}X_1 - a_{22}X_2 + X_2 - b_{21}\dot{X}_1 - b_{22}\dot{X}_2 = 0$$
(3n, 1)

To determine the magnitude of the two roots, λ_1 and λ_2, and the various other constants involved in its general solution,

$$X_1 = c_1 k_{11}e^{\lambda_1 t} + c_2 k_{12}e^{\lambda_2 t}$$
$$X_2 = c_1 k_{21}e^{\lambda_1 t} + c_2 k_{22}e^{\lambda_2 t}$$
(3n, 2)

let us make an anticipatory assumption that,

$$X_1 = k_1 e^{\lambda t}$$
$$X_2 = k_2 e^{\lambda t}$$
(3n, 3a)

and consequently that,

$$\dot{X}_1 = \lambda k_1 e^{\lambda t}$$
$$\dot{X}_2 = \lambda k_2 e^{\lambda t}$$
(3n, 3b)

Substituting from (3n, 3a) and (3n, 3b) in (3n, 1), we have

$$e^{\lambda t}\{k_1(1 - a_{11} - b_{11}\lambda) + k_2(-a_{12} - b_{12}\lambda)\} = 0$$
$$e^{\lambda t}\{k_1(-a_{21} - b_{21}\lambda) + k_2(1 - a_{22} - b_{22}\lambda)\} = 0$$
(3n, 4a)

Considered as a system of two homogeneous equations with two unknowns, k_1 and k_2, (3n, 4a) can be rewritten in the following form:

$$\frac{k_1}{k_2} = \frac{a_{12} + b_{12}\lambda}{1 - a_{11} - b_{11}\lambda}$$
$$\frac{k_1}{k_2} = \frac{1 - a_{22} - b_{22}\lambda}{a_{21} + b_{21}\lambda}$$
(3n, 4b)

Comparing these two equations, we see that they can be consistent only if

$$\frac{a_{12} + b_{12}\lambda}{1 - a_{11} - b_{11}\lambda} = \frac{1 - a_{22} - b_{22}\lambda}{a_{21} + b_{21}\lambda}$$
(3n, 5)

Multiplying out and shifting all terms over to the left side, we have

$$[b_{22}b_{11} - b_{12}b_{21}]\lambda^2 - [(1 - a_{11})b_{22} + (1 - a_{22})b_{11} + a_{12}b_{21} + a_{21}b_{12}]\lambda$$

$$+ [(1 - a_{11})(1 - a_{22}) - a_{21}a_{12}] = 0 \quad \text{(3n, 6a)}$$

or, in short,

$$A\lambda^2 - B\lambda + C = 0 \quad \text{(3n, 6b)}$$

where A, B, and C represent the similarly placed expression in structural constants.

According to the well-known formula, this quadratic equation is satisfied by the following two values of λ:

$$\lambda_1 = \frac{1}{2A}(B + \sqrt{B^2 - 4AC})$$

$$\lambda_2 = \frac{1}{2A}(B - \sqrt{B^2 - 4AC}) \quad \text{(3n, 7)}$$

The special case of $\lambda_1 = \lambda_2$ can be disregarded since, as shown below, in a two-part economic system $\sqrt{B^2 - 4AC} > 0$ and thus $\lambda_1 \neq \lambda_2$.

Since both λ_1 and λ_2 will satisfy (3n, 4b), two different ratios of the coefficients, k_1 and k_2, can be computed from that formula. Using a second subscript to distinguish the two pairs and introducing two arbitrary constants, c_1 and c_2, to indicate that a proportional change in both coefficients belonging to the same pair is admissible, since it would not affect their ratios, one can write,

$$k_{11} = c_1(a_{12} + b_{12}\lambda_1) \qquad k_{12} = c_2(a_{12} + b_{12}\lambda_2)$$

$$k_{21} = c_1(1 - a_{11} - b_{11}\lambda_1) \quad k_{22} = c_2(1 - a_{11} - b_{11}\lambda_2) \quad \text{(3n, 8)}$$

These are based on the first of the two equations in (3n, 4b); the second, because of (3n, 5), would obviously give the same ratio, $\dfrac{k_1}{k_2}$.

Substitution from (3n, 8) in (3n, 3a) gives two 'constituent' solutions of the original system (3n, 1), one for each of the two roots λ_1 and λ_2.

$$X_1 = c_1 k_{11} e^{\lambda_1 t} \qquad X_1 = c_2 k_{12} e^{\lambda_2 t}$$

$$\text{and} \quad \text{(3n, 9)}$$

$$X_2 = c_1 k_{21} e^{\lambda_1 t} \qquad X_2 = c_2 k_{22} e^{\lambda_2 t}$$

Since each pair of these expressions for X_1 and X_2 taken separately satisfies (3n, 1), an additive combination of both will satisfy it too. Thus we arrive at the general solution (3n, 2) with all coefficients—but c_1 and c_2—explicitly described in terms of the two sets of the structural

DYNAMIC ANALYSIS 79

constants which make up the empirical background of the original dynamic system (3n, 1).

The numerical magnitudes of c_1 and c_2 can be determined only through the introduction of additional empirical data consisting of information on the values of the variables or on the magnitude of their changes at some specific points of time.

For example, let $X_1(t_o)$ and $X_2(t_o)$ represent the values of $X_1(t)$ and $X_2(t)$ observed at the point of time, $t = t_o$. Substituted in (3n, 2) they give,

$$X_1(t_o) = c_1 k_{11} e^{\lambda_1 t_o} + c_2 k_{12} e^{\lambda_2 t_o}$$

$$X_2(t_o) = c_1 k_{21} e^{\lambda_1 t_o} + c_2 k_{22} e^{\lambda_2 t_o}$$

(3n, 10)

The equations can be solved for c_1 and c_2:

$$c_1 = \frac{k_{22} X_1(t_o) - k_{12} X_2(t_o)}{(k_{22} k_{11} - k_{12} k_{21}) e^{\lambda_1 t_o}}$$

$$c_2 = \frac{k_{11} X_2(t_o) - k_{21} X_1(t_o)}{(k_{22} k_{11} - k_{12} k_{21}) e^{\lambda_2 t_o}}$$

(3n, 11)

These formulae can be simplified if one conventionally decides to count the time from the point, t_o, from which the initial state of the system happens to be given: If $t_o = o$, each of the exponential expressions on the right-hand side is reduced to 1.

Substituting for A, B, and C, their explicit definitions in terms of the a's and b's as shown in (3n, 6a), one can verify the following identity:

$$B^2 - 4AC = [(1 - a_{11})b_{22} - (1 - a_{22})b_{11} - a_{21}b_{12} + a_{12}b_{21}]^2$$

$$+ 4[(1 - a_{11})b_{22}a_{21}b_{12} + (1 - a_{22})b_{11}a_{12}b_{21} + b_{22}b_{11}a_{21}a_{12}$$

$$+ b_{12}b_{21}(1 - a_{11})(1 - a_{22})] \quad \text{(3n, 12)}$$

The first term on the right-hand side is positive because it is a square; the second, since $(1 - a_{11})$ and $(1 - a_{22})$, representing the fraction of the outputs of each of the two industries not absorbed on current account, are by themselves also essentially positive.

Systems consisting of three or more separate sectors can, however, have complex roots and thus contain periodic components in their solutions.

II

The general solution of an open, i.e. non-homogeneous, system with 'final demand' functions of an exponential type on the right-hand side:

80   STATIC AND DYNAMIC THEORY

$$X_1 - a_{11}X_1 - a_{12}X_2 - b_{11}\dot{X}_1 - b_{12}\dot{X}_2 = y_1 \equiv g_{11}e^{\mu_1 t} + g_{12}e^{\mu_2 t}$$
$$X_2 - a_{21}X_1 - a_{22}X_2 - b_{21}\dot{X}_1 - b_{22}\dot{X}_2 = y_2 \equiv g_{21}e^{\mu_1 t} + g_{22}e^{\mu_2 t}$$

$$(3n, 13)$$

can be written as follows:

$$X_1 = c_1 k_{11}e^{\lambda_1 t} + c_2 k_{12}e^{\lambda_2 t} + w_{11}e^{\mu_1 t} + w_{12}e^{\mu_2 t}$$
$$X_2 = c_1 k_{21}e^{\lambda_1 t} + c_2 k_{22}e^{\lambda_2 t} + w_{21}e^{\mu_1 t} + w_{22}e^{\mu_2 t}$$

$$(3n, 14)$$

The first two right-hand terms in each of these equations are obtained from solution (3n, 2) of the corresponding homogeneous system (3n, 1); the roots λ_1 and λ_2 and the coefficients, k_{11}, k_{12}, k_{21}, and k_{22}, are computed by equations (3n, 7) and (3n, 8).

The last two terms represent the particular solution of (3n, 13). The constants μ_1 and μ_2 are known; to determine w_{11}, w_{12}, w_{21}, and w_{22} assume that,

$$X_1 = w_{11}e^{\mu_1 t} + w_{12}e^{\mu_2 t}$$
$$X_2 = w_{21}e^{\mu_1 t} + w_{22}e^{\mu_2 t}$$

$$(3n, 15)$$

Substitute these values of X_1 and X_2 and the corresponding values of the derivatives $\dot{X}_1$ and $\dot{X}_2$ in (3n, 13), and group the terms containing $e^{\mu_1 t}$ separately from those containing $e^{\mu_2 t}$. If the two resulting equations,

$$[(1 - a_{11} - b_{11}\mu_1)w_{11} - (a_{12} + b_{12}\mu_1)w_{21} - g_{11}]e^{\mu_1 t}$$
$$+ [(1 - a_{11} - b_{11}\mu_2)w_{12} - (a_{12} + b_{12}\mu_2)w_{22} - g_{12}]e^{\mu_2 t} = 0$$
$$[-(a_{21} + b_{21}\mu_1)w_{11} + (1 - a_{22} - b_{22}\mu_1)w_{21} - g_{21}]e^{\mu_1 t}$$
$$+ [-(a_{21} + b_{21}\mu_2)w_{12} + (1 - a_{22} - b_{22}\mu_2)w_{22} - g_{22}]e^{\mu_2 t} = 0$$

$$(3n, 16)$$

are to hold for all possible values of t, each one of the four expressions enclosed in square brackets taken separately must equal 0. Thus we have four equations of which the first and the third can be solved for w_{11} and w_{21} while the second and the fourth can be solved for w_{12} and w_{22}:

$$w_{11} = \frac{g_{11}(1 - a_{22} - b_{22}\mu_1) + g_{21}(a_{12} + b_{12}\mu_1)}{(1 - a_{11} - b_{11}\mu_1)(1 - a_{22} - b_{22}\mu_1) - (a_{12} + b_{12}\mu_1)(a_{21} + b_{21}\mu_1)}$$

$$w_{21} = \frac{g_{21}(1 - a_{11} - b_{11}\mu_1) + g_{11}(a_{21} + b_{21}\mu_1)}{(1 - a_{11} - b_{11}\mu_1)(1 - a_{22} - b_{22}\mu_1) - (a_{12} + b_{12}\mu_1)(a_{21} + b_{21}\mu_1)}$$

$$(3n, 17)$$

$$w_{12} = \frac{g_{12}(1 - a_{22} - b_{22}\mu_2) + g_{22}(a_{12} + b_{12}\mu_2)}{(1 - a_{11} - b_{11}\mu_2)(1 - a_{22} - b_{22}\mu_2) - (a_{12} + b_{12}\mu_2)(a_{21} + b_{21}\mu_2)}$$

$$w_{22} = \frac{g_{22}(1 - a_{11} - b_{11}\mu_2) + g_{12}(a_{21} + b_{21}\mu_2)}{(1 - a_{11} - b_{11}\mu_2)(1 - a_{22} - b_{22}\mu_2) - (a_{12} + b_{12}\mu_2)(a_{21} + b_{21}\mu_2)}$$

DYNAMIC ANALYSIS 81

The constants c_1 and c_2 are finally determined on the basis of the given initial conditions. If, for example, at $t = 0$, $X_1 = X^o_1$, and $X_2 = X^o_2$, the insertion of these particular values of the three variables in (3n, 14) gives:

$$X^o_1 = c_1 k_{11} e^{\lambda_1 t_o} + c_2 k_{12} e^{\lambda_2 t_o} + w_{11} e^{\mu_1 t_o} + w_{12} e^{\mu_2 t_o}$$
$$X^o_2 = c_1 k_{21} e^{\lambda_1 t_o} + c_2 k_{22} e^{\lambda_2 t_o} + w_{21} e^{\mu_1 t_o} + w_{22} e^{\mu_2 t_o}$$

(3n, 18)

Solved for c_1 and c_2 these two equations yield,

$$c_1 = \frac{(X^o_1 - w_{11} e^{\mu_1 t_o} - w_{12} e^{\mu_2 t_o}) k_{22} - (X^o_2 - w_{21} e^{\mu_1 t_o} - w_{22} e^{\mu_2 t_o}) k_{12}}{(k_{11} k_{22} - k_{12} k_{21}) e^{\lambda_1 t_o}}$$

(3n, 19)

$$c_2 = \frac{(X^o_2 - w_{21} e^{\mu_1 t_o} - w_{22} e^{\mu_2 t_o}) k_{11} - (X^o_1 - w_{11} e^{\mu_1 t_o} - w_{12} e^{\mu_2 t_o}) k_{21}}{(k_{11} k_{22} - k_{12} k_{21}) e^{\lambda_2 t_o}}$$

III

An analogous procedure can be used in solving a non-homogeneous system in which the bill of goods is represented by ordinary polynomials. The solution of

$$X_1 - a_{11} X_1 - a_{12} X_2 - b_{11} \dot{X}_1 - b_{12} \dot{X}_2 = y_1 \equiv g_{10} + g_{11} t + g_{12} t^2$$
$$X_2 - a_{21} X_1 - a_{22} X_2 - b_{21} \dot{X}_1 - b_{22} \dot{X}_2 = y_2 \equiv g_{20} + g_{21} t + g_{22} t^2$$

(3n, 20)

is of the following form:

$$X_1 = c_1 k_{11} e^{\lambda_1 t} + c_2 k_{12} e^{\lambda_2 t} + w_{10} + w_{11} t + w_{12} t^2$$
$$X_2 = c_1 k_{21} e^{\lambda_1 t} + c_2 k_{22} e^{\lambda_2 t} + w_{20} + w_{21} t + w_{22} t^2$$

(3n, 21)

Again λ_1, λ_2, k_{11}, k_{12}, k_{21}, and k_{22} are defined by (3n, 7) and (3n, 8).

To determine the constants occurring in the last three terms of the two equations, let

$$X_1 = w_{10} + w_{11} t + w_{12} t^2$$
$$X_2 = w_{20} + w_{21} t + w_{22} t^2$$

(3n, 22)

and substitute those values of X_1, X_2 and of the corresponding derivatives in (3n, 20). In each of the two resulting equations (which are not being written out here because of their great length), the terms associated with t^2, t, and those not containing the variable, t, can be segregated in separate brackets. Each one of these bracketed expressions (three in each equation) must equal 0, if the two equations are to hold for all values of t. Thus a system of six equations is obtained, which can be solved for w_{10}, w_{11}, w_{12}, w_{20}, w_{21}, and w_{22}.

To determine the magnitudes of the two 'constants of integration,' c_1 and c_2, corresponding to the initial condition of the system described, for example, in terms of the particular levels of output $X^o{}_1$ and $X^o{}_2$ reached by the two industries at the time $t = t_o$ it is only necessary to insert $t = t_o$ on the right- and $X_1 = X^o{}_1$ and $X_2 = X^o{}_2$ on the left-hand side of the equation (3n, 21).

MATHEMATICAL NOTE 2

Formulation and Solution of Dynamic Input-Output Systems Containing Flows, Stocks, and Structural Lags

I

The similarity which exists between some of the more obvious properties of dynamic systems described in terms of difference—and those defined with the help of differential—equations has led to a nearly interchangeable use of these two types of mathematical formulation in modern business-cycle theory and the recently much debated theory of long-run economic growth. So far as conventional model building is concerned, that is, so long as the theoretical argument is aimed primarily at deriving general implications of certain simple theoretical assumptions, one of these two alternative methods of introducing dynamics into the system can serve as well as the other. Both can lead to periodic solutions, i.e. generate cyclical fluctuations or—with a properly chosen structural assumption—produce progressively expanding or evenly contracting long-run 'trends.'

Whenever the theoretical framework is designed with the specific purpose of incorporating in its mathematical formulation directly observed empirical parameters, the distinction between the difference and the differential equations acquires crucial importance.

In the particular instance of dynamic input-output analysis, the empirically observed structural stock-flow ratios, which are so fundamental to the explanation of the investment process, lead directly to relationships between the *levels* of output of the various industries and the *rates of change* of these outputs, i.e. to differential equations. On the other hand, other observations establish the existence throughout the system of structural lags. Specifically in each particular production process the determination of the levels of required inputs by the level of finished output involves, more often than not, structurally necessary time gaps between the two—a relationship to which one can give direct analytical expression only by setting up corresponding sets of difference equations.

To preclude a possibly over-simplified interpretation of these remarks, it is necessary to admit that the notion of immediate observation like that of direct measurement is conditioned by the general level of concreteness on which the particular analysis is being carried out. A rela-

DYNAMIC ANALYSIS 83

tionship looked upon as a basic structural characteristic of the system in the light of one given kind of empirical information will, in the context of a closer, more differentiated description, be treated as a derived property, explainable in terms of more detailed primary data. Some of the structural lags used in current descriptions of empirical input-output relationships imply, for example, the existence of causation operating over a gap of time—a somewhat mysterious relationship which in terms of a more detailed fine-grained observation will prove to be reducible to intuitively more satisfying and mathematically more manageable differential formulation.

Whatever the future may bring, in the present state of factual information, a simple method of solving simultaneously mixed difference-differential equations can most decidedly increase the empirical validity of dynamic input-output theory.

II

In order to present the proposed solution of this specific mathematical problem without unnecessary complication, it is best to consider a very simple example of a dynamic input-output system incorporating both lags and stock-flow relationships.

Let it be an open economy consisting of only two industries. The output of each one of them is used first to provide for the investment requirements of the other, and second to satisfy the final, i.e. outside, demand. In accordance with the well-known implication of the acceleration principle, the investment requirements of each industry are determined by the rate of change of its output. Structural lags enter the system through fixed 'lead times,' which—for technological and organizational reasons—have to elapse between the delivery of the capital goods to the investing industry and the increase in its output ensuing from actual utilization of the newly created productive facilities.

The dynamic input-output balance of this simple system is described by the following two mixed difference and differential equations:

$$X_1(t) - b_{12}X'_2(t + \tau_{12}) = Y_1(t) \qquad (3n, 23)$$

$$X_2(t) - b_{21}X'_1(t + \tau_{21}) = Y_2(t) \qquad (3n, 24)$$

$X_1(t)$, $X_2(t)$ represent the production rates of the two industries; while $Y_1(t)$ and $Y_2(t)$ describe the development of the final, i.e. independently determined, demand for their respective outputs; b_{12} is the technical capital coefficient of the second industry; it shows the stock of the product of the second industry used by the first industry per unit of its output, $X_1(t)$. Similarly, b_{21} is the capital coefficient of the first industry; τ_{12} and τ_{21} are the two investment lead periods as defined above.

84   STATIC AND DYNAMIC THEORY

In order to eliminate one of the two variables—say, $X_2(t)$—differentiate (3n, 24), substitute in the resulting equation, $t + \tau_{12}$ for t and insert the corresponding expression for $X'_2(t + \tau_{12})$ in (3n, 23):

$$X_1(t) - b_{12}b_{21}X''_1(t + \tau_{12} + \tau_{21}) = Y_1(t) + b_{12}Y'_2(t + \tau_{12}) \quad (3n, 25)$$

This equation can be finally rewritten as:

$$X''(t) - bX(t - \tau) = Y(t) \quad\quad\quad\quad (3n, 26)$$

where the time count is shifted by the substitution of $t - \tau$ for t and

$$b \equiv \frac{1}{b_{12}b_{21}},$$

$$Y(t) \equiv \frac{Y'_2}{b_{12}}(t - \tau_{21}) + Y_1(t - \tau)\frac{1}{b_{12}b_{21}}, \text{ and} \quad\quad (3n, 27)$$

$$\tau \equiv \tau_{12} + \tau_{21}.$$

All subscripts can obviously be conveniently omitted.

III

The method of solving this kind of mixed difference-differential equation shown below is based on application of the Laplace transform.[18] It consists of three consecutive steps. First the original variable $X(t)$ is replaced in the given equation by a new variable $x(s)$. This transformation is based on the definitional relationship,

$$x(s) \equiv L[X(t)] = \int_0^\infty e^{-st}X(t)dt \quad\quad (3n, 28)$$

In the second step the transformed—and, incidentally, greatly simplified—equation is solved for $x(s)$ and finally this solution is changed back into the terms of the original variable $X(t)$ with the help of the inverse transformation symbolically described by

$$X(t) \equiv L^{-1}[x(s)] \quad\quad\quad\quad (3n, 29)$$

IV

The solution of a dynamic system must generally provide for the introduction of independent, i.e. exogenously determined, 'initial conditions.' In our particular case these would comprise, for example,

---

[18] A systematic exposition of the application of the Laplace transform to solution of difference and differential equations can be found in such standard texts as Churchill, Ruel V., *Modern Operational Mathematics in Engineering*, McGraw-Hill, New York, 1944; or Van der Pol, B., and Bremmer, H., *Operational Calculus*, Cambridge University Press, Cambridge, England, 1950.

DYNAMIC ANALYSIS 85

a. the magnitude $X(0)$ of the level of output $X(t)$ at some initial point of time, $t = 0$,

b. the rate of change $X'(0)$ of that output at $t = 0$,

c. the shape of the output function $X(t)$ over the period of time extending from $t = -\tau$ up to $t = 0$.

The introduction of this third condition is made necessary by the presence of the structural lag, τ: The level of output, $X(t)$, from $t = 0$ and up to $t = \tau$ would, for example, be undetermined so long as the 'past history' of the system from $t = -\tau$ up to $t = 0$ remained unknown.[19]

Applying to the mixed difference-differential equation (3n, 26) the Laplace transform as defined in (3n, 28) we have:

$$\int_0^\infty e^{-st} X''(t) dt - b \int_0^\infty e^{-st} X(t - \lambda) dt = \int_0^\infty e^{-st} Y(t) dt \qquad (3n, 30)$$

In the middle term the first or lower part of the integral—which depends on the given 'initial history' of $X(t)$, i.e. on the interval of time stretching from $t = -\lambda$ to $t = 0$ can be conveniently separated from its upper part extending over the later period of time, $0 \le t \le \infty$:

$$\int_0^\infty e^{-st} X(t - \lambda) dt = \int_{-\lambda}^\infty e^{-s(\tau + \lambda)} X(\tau) d\tau =$$

$$e^{-\lambda s} \left\{ \int_{-\lambda}^0 e^{-s} X(\tau) d\tau + \int_0^\infty e^{-s} X(\tau) d\tau \right\} \qquad (3n, 31)$$

The new time variable τ is defined by $\tau = t - \lambda$; in the last two integrals it obviously can be simply replaced by t.

It follows that (3n, 30) can be written as,

$$L[X''(t)] - be^{-\lambda s} L[X(t)] = L[Y(t)] + be^{-\lambda s} \int_{-\lambda}^0 e^{-st} X(t) dt \qquad (3n, 32)$$

Applying to the first term the standard transformation formula,[20]

$$L[X^{(n)}(t)] = s^n L[X(t)] - s^{n-1} X(0) - s^{n-2} X^{(1)}(0) - \cdots - X^{(n-1)}(0) \qquad (3n, 33)$$

and using the simplified notation introduced in (3n, 28), the equation above can be rewritten as,

---

[19] The removal of structural lags from the original system, i.e. the reduction of the mixed difference-differential equation to a simple differential equation, would lead to elimination of the last but not the first two of these three initial conditions as formulated above. For this reason the otherwise possible combination of a and b with c is inadvisable.

[20] See Churchill, op. cit. p. 8.

86   STATIC AND DYNAMIC THEORY

$$s^2 x(s) - sX(0) - X'(0) - be^{-\lambda s}x(s) = y(s) + be^{-\lambda s}\int_{-\lambda}^{0} e^{-st}X(t)dt$$

or, if solved for $x(s)$, as,

$$x(s) = \{y(s) + sX(0) + X'(0) + be^{-\lambda s}\int_{-\lambda}^{0} e^{-st}X(t)dt\} \frac{1}{s^2 - be^{-\lambda s}} \quad (3n, 34)$$

The final step consists in the application of the inverse transform, L^{-1}, to both sides of the last equation.

The actual operation of inversion is facilitated if the fraction, $\dfrac{1}{s^2 - be^{-\lambda s}}$, is put in the form of the convergent infinite series,

$$\frac{1}{s^2}\left(1 + \frac{be^{-\lambda s}}{s^2} + \frac{b^{-2\lambda s}}{s^4} + \cdots\right),$$

of which it represents the sum,[21] i.e. if (3n, 34) is rewritten as,

$$x(s) = \{y(s) + sX(0) + X'(0) + be^{-\lambda s}\int_{-\lambda}^{0} e^{-st}X(t)dt\} \frac{1}{s^2}\sum_{n=0}^{\infty}\frac{b^n e^{-n\lambda s}}{s^{2n}} \quad (3n, 35)$$

V

Now this method of solving a mixed difference and differential equation will be applied to the particular case in which the final demand functions $Y_1(t)$ and $Y_2(t)$ occurring in the original system (3n, 23) and (3n, 24) are represented by two constants, C_1 and C_2, and the initial history of the economy, as reflected in the output level of the first industry between $t = -\lambda$ and $t = 0$, is described by a straight line.

Equation (3n, 26) must be solved for $X(t)$ under the conditions that:

$$Y(t) = C \quad\quad\quad\quad\quad\quad\quad\quad (3n, 36)$$

$$X(t) = A + Bt \quad \text{for} \quad -\lambda \leq t \leq 0 \quad\quad (3n, 37)$$

First the integral occurring in (3n, 35) can be explicitly computed on the basis of (3n, 37).

Integrating by parts and omitting the constant of integration, we have,

$$\int e^{-st}X(t)dt = \int e^{-st}(A + Bt)dt = -A\frac{e^{-st}}{s} - B\frac{e^{-st}}{s^2}(st + 1)$$

Consequently,

$$\int_{-\lambda}^{0} e^{-st}X(1)dt = \frac{1}{s}\{A(e^{st} - 1) - B\lambda e^{s\lambda}\} + \frac{1}{s^2}B(e^{s\lambda} - 1) \quad (3n, 38)$$

---

[21] The convergence of the series is secured since the arbitrary parameter, s, can always be assumed to be large enough to make of $\dfrac{be^{-\lambda s}}{s^{2n}}$ a true positive fraction.

DYNAMIC ANALYSIS 87

The L-transformation of the constant, C, is obtained on the basis of the following general formula, which incidentally will also be resorted to at the last stage of the argument,

$$L\left[C\frac{(t-k)^{\mu-1}}{(\mu-1)!}U(t-k)\right] = C\frac{e^{-ks}}{s^{\mu}} \qquad (3n, 39)$$

where

C and K are arbitrary constants,

μ is a positive integer, and

$U(t-k)$ is the so-called unit function, defined by

$$U(t-k)\begin{cases} = 1 & \text{when } t > k \\ = 0 & \text{when } t \leq k \end{cases} \qquad (3n, 40)$$

Putting $k = 0$ and $\mu = 2$ in (3n, 39), gives,

$$y(s) \equiv L[CU(t)] = \frac{C}{s} \qquad (3n, 41)$$

It must be noted that this transformation is only valid for $t > 0$. Since the history of the system between $t = -\lambda$ and $t = 0$ is described in the form of the given initial conditions, (3n, 39), and because we are interested only in the determination of its subsequent path, for $t > 0$, this constitutes no objectionable limitation on the final solution.

Substitution from (3n, 38) and (3n, 41) in (3n, 35) gives,

$$x(s) = \left\{\frac{1}{s}C + sX(0) + X'(0) + \frac{1}{s}b\{A(e^{s\lambda} - 1) - Bb\lambda e^{s\lambda}\} + \frac{1}{s^2}bB(e^{\lambda s} - 1)\right\}$$

$$\frac{1}{s^2}\sum_{n=0}^{\infty}\frac{b^n e^{-n\lambda s}}{s^{2n}}$$

$$= X(0)\sum_{n=0}^{\infty}\frac{b^n e^{-n\lambda s}}{s^{2n+1}} + X'(0)\sum_{n=0}^{\infty}\frac{b^n e^{-n\lambda s}}{s^{2n+2}} + (C - Ab)\sum_{n=0}^{\infty}\frac{b^n e^{-n\lambda s}}{s^{2n+3}}$$

$$- Bb\sum_{n=0}^{\infty}\frac{b^n e^{-n\lambda s}}{s^{2n+4}} + (A - \lambda B)\sum_{n=0}^{\infty}\frac{b^{n+1}e^{-\lambda s(n+1)}}{s^{2n+3}}$$

$$+ B\sum_{n=0}^{\infty}\frac{b^{n+1}e^{-\lambda s(n+1)}}{s^{2n+4}} \qquad (3n, 42)$$

Now it only remains to perform the inverse transformation, L^{-1}, i.e. to determine the equation in t of which equation (3n, 42) in s represents a Laplace transform. The previously used special transformation formula, (3n, 39), applied to every term under each summation sign leads thus to

88   STATIC AND DYNAMIC THEORY

the following solutions of the original mixed difference-differential equation (3n, 26) : [22]

$$L^{-1}[x(s)] = X(t) = X(0) \sum_{n=0}^{\infty} \frac{b^n(t - n\lambda)^{2n}}{(2n)!} U(t - n\lambda)$$

$$+ X'(0) \sum_{n=0}^{\infty} \frac{b^n(t - n\lambda)^{2n+1}}{(2n+1)!} U(t - n\lambda)$$

$$+ (C - bA) \sum_{n=0}^{\infty} \frac{b^n(t - n\lambda)^{2n+2}}{(2n+2)!} U(t - n\lambda) - bB \sum_{n=0}^{\infty} \frac{b^n(t - n\lambda)^{2n+3}}{(2n+3)} U(t - n\lambda)$$

$$+ (A - \lambda B) \sum_{n=0}^{\infty} \frac{b^{n+1}(t - n\lambda - \lambda)^{2n+2}}{(2n+2)!} U(t - n\lambda - \lambda)$$

$$+ B \sum_{n=0}^{\infty} \frac{b^{n+1}(t - n\lambda - \lambda)^{2n+3}}{(2n+3)!} U(t - n\lambda - \lambda) \quad (3n, 43)$$

For any given positive finite t and λ the number of terms under each summation sign will necessarily be also finite.[23] The cut-off point is determined in each instance by the argument of the corresponding unit function, $U(\ )$. Under the first four summation signs, for example, for any given t, the largest n, let it be called m, is determined by the combination of the following two inequalities:

$$t - m\lambda > 0 \quad \text{and} \quad t - (m + 1)\lambda < 0$$

which can be rewritten as

$$\frac{1}{\lambda} - 1 < m < \frac{t}{\lambda} \quad (3n, 44)$$

For the last three terms the corresponding formula is

$$\frac{t}{\lambda} < m < \frac{t}{\lambda} + 1 \quad (3n, 45)$$

[22] Let it be noted that for $n = 0$, $(2n)! = 1$.

[23] A positive λ is, because of obvious formal reasons, essential for the following argument. Should λ as it appears in the original dynamic equation (3n, 26) be negative, i.e. represent a 'lead' rather than a 'lag,' the foregoing formal requirement will still be satisfied if the same relationship is rewritten as:

$$X''(t - \alpha) - bX(t) = Y(t - \alpha)$$

where α stands for $-\lambda$ and thus is positive. The solution of this equation can be obtained by a procedure quite analogous to that described above and based on the same special transformation formulae (3n, 33), (3n, 39), and (3n, 40).

DYNAMIC ANALYSIS 89

VI

Substitutions of $X(t)$, as explicitly described on the right-hand side of (3n, 31), in (3n, 26) show that this indeed is the solution of the original mixed difference-differential equation.

The function $X(t)$ as defined by (3n, 43) represents the right-hand portion of the $X(t)$ curve shown in the schematic Figure 1. Its left-hand part covering the stretch from P_1 to P_2 depicts the past history of $X(t)$. The jump from P_2 to P_3 reflects the fact that the 'initial conditions' of our problem define the shape of $X(t)$ as described by (3n, 37) between

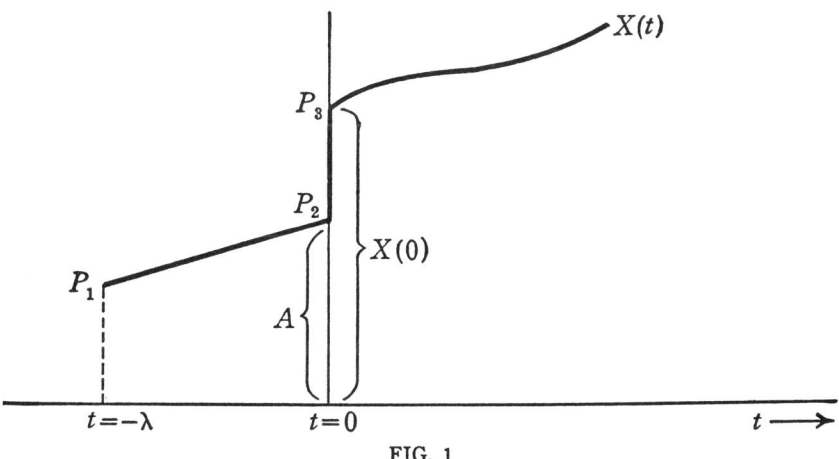

FIG. 1

$t = -\lambda$ and $t = 0$—including its level and its 'left-hand slope,' at P_2—separately from the values of $X(0)$ and $X'(0)$ as they appear in (3n, 43) describing the level and the 'right-hand slope' of the curve in point P_3, i.e. its slope at the origin of its right-hand part.

These additional degrees of freedom of the initial conditions will prove to be useful in special applications, such, for example, as comparison of various policy alternatives: Past history is unalterable and must be considered as given; action as a change in initial conditions can be taken in the future which begins with the present, that is at $t = 0$. It is at that point that an alteration and the consequent discontinuity in the initial condition are likely to occur.

The discontinuity in the initial condition at $t = 0$ will, of course, be eliminated if the constants $X(0)$ and $X'(0)$, as they appear in (3n, 43), are identified with the level and, respectively, the rate of change reached by the output, $X(t)$ at the end of its initial history at P_2. In the special case discussed above in which the history of the system is described by

90   STATIC AND DYNAMIC THEORY

(3n, 37), the jump between P_2 and P_3 as shown in Figure 1 would vanish if the magnitude of $X(0)$ as entered in (3n, 43) be defined by

$$X(0) = A \qquad\qquad (3\text{n, }46)$$

The difference between the right-hand and the left-hand slope of the curve at $t = 0$ would disappear if its derivative as entered in (3n, 43) were determined by

$$X'(0) = B \qquad\qquad (3\text{n, }47)$$

The use of the Laplace transform also allows introduction of any number of discontinuities in the final bill of goods. The last term in (3n, 26) can, for example, be of the following form:

$$Y(t) = Y_1(t)U(t) + Y_2(t)U(t - k) \qquad\qquad (3\text{n, }48)$$

where

$Y_2(t)$, according to (3n, 40), enters or rather jumps into the picture only at the time, $t = k$,

and where

k represents an empirically given shift constant, i.e. an observed or prescribed lag.

486 APPENDICES

SUMMARY OF 1939 CAPITAL STRUCTURE OF AMERICAN INDUSTRIES
(In Millions of 1939 Dollars)

INDUSTRIES	OUTPUT (1)	CAPACITY (2)	FIXED CAPITAL STOCK Undepreciated (3)	Replacement cost (4)	Depreciated (5)
1-8 Agriculture	9815.4	12250.0	16585.3		9959.3
9 Fishing	113.8	130.9	98.0		64.2
10 Flour and grist mill products	1250.3	1987.8	386.0		197.4
11 Canning and preserving	838.1	1178.8	352.6		176.3
12 Bread and bakery products	1458.0	2582.6	782.0		478.3
13 Sugar refining	557.8	934.4	312.9		177.1
14 Starch and glucose products	119.4	171.1	140.3		74.8
15 Alcoholic beverages	722.6	795.9	355.8		241.6
16 Nonalcoholic beverages	367.8	367.8	126.9		95.6
17 Tobacco manufactures	1322.2	1342.8	158.2		80.0
18 Slaughtering and meat packing	3003.0	3273.3	752.4		384.3
19 Manufactured dairy products	2093.8	2773.2	761.0		406.0
20 Edible fats and oils, n.e.c.	220.4	255.6		72.9	
21 Other food products	1218.1	2114.0		470.8	
22 Iron mining	150.9	309.5	489.6		300.4
23 Blast furnaces	550.8	898.5		1376.0	
24 Steel works and rolling mills	2790.4	4326.2		7782.0	
25 Iron and steel foundry products	463.7	995.1		863.8	
26 Shipbuilding	437.6	834.0	192.2		112.6
27 Firearms	17.7	21.6		21.4	
28 Munitions	100.1	174.5		348.9	
29 Agricultural machinery	422.6	626.9	292.2		144.9
30 Engines and turbines	135.1	135.1	66.7		30.9
31 Automobiles	4047.9	5419.6	1924.5		967.9

/Continued overleaf

APPENDIX 1

SUMMARY OF 1939 CAPITAL STRUCTURE OF AMERICAN INDUSTRIES
(Continued)

DOLLARS OF FIXED CAPITAL PER DOLLAR OF CAPACITY			REPLACEMENT REQUIREMENTS	TOTAL INVENTORIES HELD BY AND FOR THE INDUSTRY	DOLLARS OF INVENTORIES REQUIRED PER DOLLAR OF ANNUAL OUTPUT
Undepreciated (6)	Replacement cost (7)	Depreciated (8)	(9)	(10)	(11)
1.354		.813	1731.5	674.2	.069
.754		.491	10.9	17.0	.150
.194		.099	13.0	871.8	.697
.299		.150	16.2	118.7	.141
.303		.185	31.0	104.9	.072
.334		.190	9.5	165.1	.294
.820		.437	6.9	72.2	.605
.447		.303	13.1	158.6	.220
.345		.260	5.4	41.6	.113
.119		.060	6.9	502.0	.308
.200		.117	23.0	117.4	.039
.275		.147	49.6	54.4	.026
	.286		3.2	40.5	.184
	.222		22.1	126.7	.104
1.582		.970	23.7	0.3	.002
	1.531		47.6	161.5	.293
	1.798		272.5	535.9	.192
	.867		30.2	54.5	.118
.231		.135	6.6	58.7	.134
	.991		1.0	8.3	.470
	2.000		14.9	16.5	.164
.466		.231	11.0	95.5	.226
.493		.228	2.8	33.3	.247
.355		.179	86.8	563.4	.139

488   APPENDICES

SUMMARY OF 1939 CAPITAL STRUCTURE OF AMERICAN INDUSTRIES
(Continued)

		(1)	(2)	(3)	(4)
32	Aircraft	279.5	614.8	103.4	
33	Transportation equipment, n.e.c.	265.1	1732.9	486.8	
34	Industrial and household equipment, n.e.c.	2243.4	3560.0	1416.2	
35	Machine tools and metal-working equipment	451.7	645.3	323.6	
36	Merchandising and service machines	327.5	519.2	206.9	
37	Electrical equipment, n.e.c.	2130.6	2843.3	630.6	
38	Iron and steel, n.e.c.	2228.4	3909.5	1574.8	
39	Nonferrous metal mining	372.2	435.2		465.1
40	Smelting and refining of nonferrous metals	1127.4	1651.3		989.0
41	Aluminum products	206.9	206.9		123.6
42	Nonferrous metal manufactures and alloys	810.5	1526.3	478.6	
43	Nonmetallic mineral mining	394.4	604.0	660.9	
44	Nonmetallic mineral manufactures	1580.7	2100.6	2031.7	
45	Petroleum and natural gas	1679.0	1679.0	7233.3	
46	Petroleum refining	2461.1	3001.4	1978.8	
47	Anthracite coal	189.6	310.4	439.5	
48	Bituminous coal	733.5	1146.4	1570.9	
49	Coke and manufactured solid fuel	309.1	441.6		552.0
50	Manufactured gas	391.9	583.3	1468.1	
51	Communications	1523.7	1546.9	5513.6	
52	Electric public utilities	2445.5	3801.6	10154.1	
53	Chemicals	3745.0	5067.7	1879.6	
54	Lumber and timber	1435.9	2279.1	1226.0	
55	Furniture and other manufactures of wood	1173.4	1599.5	542.2	
56	Wood pulp, paper and paper products	2019.6	2531.9	1532.6	
57	Printing and publishing	2646.0	3400.5	1451.7	
58	Cotton yarn and cloth	1396.9	1942.0		1601.0
59	Silk and rayon products	619.0	827.9		579.8
60	Woolen and worsted manufactures	896.2	1956.3	805.0	

/Continued overleaf

APPENDIX 1   489

SUMMARY OF 1939 CAPITAL STRUCTURE OF AMERICAN INDUSTRIES
(Continued)

(5)	(6)	(7)	(8)	(9)	(10)	(11)
80.2	.168		.130	3.7	99.3	.356
285.6	.281		.165	17.7	75.4	.284
688.9	.398		.194	51.0	415.1	.185
158.5	.501		.246	12.0	75.3	.167
100.6	.398		.194	8.2	70.4	.215
332.7	.222		.117	23.4	386.6	.181
744.4	.403		.190	73.1	385.7	.173
		1.069		20.9	1.4	.004
		.599		35.7	188.5	.167
		.597		5.5	40.5	.196
282.7	.314		.185	17.0	135.1	.167
435.7	1.093		.721	26.4	1.2	.003
1001.1	.967		.477	81.3	172.1	.109
3458.8	4.308		2.060	362.2	18.3	.011
962.2	.659		.321	56.5	286.0	.079
236.6	1.416		.762	18.3	1.0	.005
878.8	1.370		.767	71.4	2.5	.004
		1.250		21.9	46.2	.099
1087.6	2.517		1.865	39.9	31.2	.080
3913.5	3.564		2.530	209.0	0.5	.003
8852.0	2.671		2.329	319.8	180.6	.070
1256.3	.371		.248	85.9	733.5	.196
764.0	.538		.335	39.4	193.5	.135
268.7	.339		.168	17.6	210.4	.179
832.5	.605		.329	55.7	278.7	.138
684.5	.427		.201	58.5	223.8	.085
		.825		50.7	541.6	.388
		.700		19.9	80.1	.129
392.4	.412		.201	27.9	195.8	.219

490   APPENDICES

SUMMARY OF 1939 CAPITAL STRUCTURE OF AMERICAN INDUSTRIES
(Continued)

		(1)	(2)	(3)	(4)
61	Clothing	3824.5	4153.1	291.1	
62	Other textile products	707.2	810.0	400.9	
63	Leather	346.4	475.9		96.6
64	Leather shoes	864.1	1120.7	199.0	
65	Leather products, n.e.c.	177.0	227.4	24.9	
66	Rubber products	903.3	1273.5	472.6	
67	Industries, n.e.c.	1749.1	1912.4	2873.1	
68 , 69	Construction	10091.1	19002.3		1437.7
70	Transportation, n.e.c.	1105.0	1615.1	4851.3	
71	Coastwise and inland water transportation	254.0	274.0	428.0	
72	Transoceanic water transportation	205.7	248.9		641.5
73	Steam railroad transportation	4449.0	7981.3	25750.0	
74	Trade	17121.0	19877.0	10602.4	
76	Banking	3747.6	7495.0	2630.7	
77	Insurance	3370.7	3910.0	391.0	
78	Other business services	328.1	397.1	77.5	
79	Advertising	1871.8	2264.8	441.9	
80	Services allied to transportation	172.1	243.4	73.0	
81	Automobile repair	432.3	432.3	204.6	
82	Other repair	301.8	301.8	142.7	
83	Rental agencies	64.4	#	#	#
85	Home renting	9914.0	9914.0		70577.8†
86	Hotels, etc.	527.6	850.0	1253.8	
87	Laundry, etc.	837.6	879.5	632.1	
88	Personal services	847.3	953.2	613.9	
89, 90 91	Professional entertainment, motion picture theaters, amusement places	992.8	1157.6	760.5	

#No data available. †Market value   /Continued overleaf

APPENDIX 1

SUMMARY OF 1939 CAPITAL STRUCTURE OF AMERICAN INDUSTRIES
(Continued)

(5)	(6)	(7)	(8)	(9)	(10)	(11)
137.9	.070		.033	13.9	469.2	.123
192.1	.497		.237	13.0	138.3	.195
		.203		2.2	83.2	.240
90.0	.179		.081	8.0	115.2	.133
11.9	.110		.052	1.0	24.1	.136
227.1	.371		.179	21.2	101.4	.112
1453.3	1.502		.760	114.7	230.1	.131
		.076		164.9	869.9	.086
3410.5	3.004		2.112	181.6	51.9	.047
218.7	1.562		.798	10.7	7.0	.028
		2.577		19.5	2.0	.010
	3.226			762.4	378.1	.084
5764.3	.534		.290	464.8	118.9	.007
2345.9	.351		.313	62.4	0.5	*
369.1	.100		.094	9.3	0.6	*
40.9	.195		.103	0.1	1.2	.004
233.3	.195		.103	9.0	127.6	.068
38.9	.300		.160	1.6	0.2	.001
130.9	.473		.303	8.9	2.8	.006
91.4	.473		.303	6.0	6.6	.022
#	#	#	#		0.1	.001
		7.119†		1764.4	0.8	*
834.9	1.475		.982	37.0	20.1	.038
302.4	.719		.344	37.8	47.5	.057
308.7	.644		.324	54.0	40.2	.047
417.9	.657		.361	56.4	85.4	.086

*Less than .0005   #No data available

492   APPENDICES

SUMMARY OF 1939 CAPITAL STRUCTURE OF AMERICAN INDUSTRIES
(Continued)

MAJOR CATEGORIES

	(1)	(2)	(3)	(4)
Agriculture and fishing (1-9)	9929.2	12380.9	16683.3	
Manufacturing (10-21, 23-38, 40-42, 44, 46, 49, 53-67)	59062.9	83539.8	27533.8	14877.8
Mining (22, 39, 43, 47, 48, 45)	3519.6	4484.5	10394.2	465.1
Construction (68, 69)	10091.1	19002.3		1434.7
Public utilities (50-52, 70-73)	10374.8	16051.1	48165.1	641.5
Total Services	40529.1	48675.7	17824.1	70577.8†
Trade (74)	17121.0	19877.0	10602.4	
Home Renting (85)	9914.0	9914.0		70577.8†
Other Services (76-83, 86-91)	13494.1	18884.7	7221.7	
TOTAL	133506.7	184134.3	120600.5	87996.9

† Market value

APPENDIX 1   493

SUMMARY OF 1939 CAPITAL STRUCTURE OF AMERICAN INDUSTRIES
(Continued)

(5)	(6)	(7)	(8)	(9)	(10)	(11)
10023.5	1.348		.810	1742.4	691.2	.070
14515.3	.330	.178	.174	1639.9	9896.6	.168
5310.3	2.318	.104	1.184	522.9	24.7	.007
		.076		164.9	869.9	.086
17482.3	3.001	.040	1.089	1542.9	660.3	.064
10788.6	.366	1.450	.222	2511.7	452.4	.011
5764.3	.533		.290	464.8	118.9	.007
		7.119†		1764.4	0.8	*
5114.3	.382		.271	282.5	332.7	.025
58120.0	.655	.478	.316	8124.7	12595.1	.094

†Market value *Less than .0005

[8]

*The dynamic inverse** *

Wassily LEONTIEF

Harvard University

1. The purpose of this paper is to introduce the notion of the Dynamic Inverse that could play a role in the empirical study of economic change analogous to the role played in static input-output analysis by the inverse of the flow coefficient matrix.

First I shall describe the open dynamic input-output system in terms of a simple set of linear equations. Next, I shall present a general solution of that system, that is, the inverse of its structural matrix. Each element of this inverse represents the combined direct and indirect inputs required from the row industry to permit an additional output of $1 million by the column industry. While in a static inverse such effects can be described by a single number, within the framework of dynamic analysis they have to be presented in a time series: as soon as capacity expansion and the corresponding investment processes are introduced explicitly into the system, the inputs contributing directly or indirectly to the delivery of a certain final output in a given year must be dated too. These come out of the computer as a sequence of numbers stretched back in time. The last sections of this paper are devoted to a brief discussion of the corresponding dynamic price system.**

2. Let the column vector x represent the n sectoral outputs, $_tx_1$, $_tx_2, ..., _tx_n$, produced in year t, and c the corresponding column vec-

---

* In preparation of this paper the author was assisted by Brookes Byrd, Richard Berner and Peter Petri.

** Basic concepts, the industry classification system, and the sources of data used in the study are presented in appendices II, III and IV.

18   W. LEONTIEF

tor, $_tc_1, _tc_2, \ldots, _tc_n$, of deliveries to final demand. This final demand does *not* include the annual additions to the stocks of fixed and working capital (inventories) used by the n productive sectors mentioned above. The structural characteristics of the economy are described by A_t, the square ($n \times n$) matrix of technical flow coefficients that specifies the direct current input requirements of all industries, and B_t, the corresponding square matrix of capital coefficients. Capital goods produced in year t are assumed to be installed and put into operation in the next year, $t + 1$.

The direct interpendence between the outputs of all the sectors of a given national economy in two successive years can be described by the following familiar balance equation:

$$x_t - A_t x_t - B_{t+1}(x_{t+1} - x_t) = c_t. \tag{1}$$

The second term on the left-hand side represents the current input requirements of all n industries in year t; the third, the investment requirements, i.e. additions to productive stock that would permit all industries to expand their capacity outputs from the year t to the next year, $t + 1$, from x_t to x_{t+1}. The time subscripts attached to both structural matrices provide the possibility of using different sets of flow and capital coefficients for different years, thus incorporating technological change into the dynamic system. It should be noted that the time subscript attached to matrix B_{t+1} identifies not the year in which the particular capital goods are produced, but rather the year in which they are first put to use. Equation (1) can be rewritten as:

$$G_t x_t - B_{t+1} x_{t+1} = c_t \tag{2}$$

where $G_t = (I - A_t + B_{t+1})$. A set of interlocked balance equations of this type describing the development of the given economy over a period of $m + 1$ years can be combined to form a system of $m + 1$ linear equations:

$$\begin{bmatrix} G_{-m} - B_{-m+1} & & & & \\ & G_{-m+1} - B_{-m+2} & & & \\ & & \ddots & \ddots & \\ & & & G_{-2} - B_{-1} & \\ & & & & G_{-1} - B_0 \\ & & & & & G_0 \end{bmatrix} \begin{bmatrix} x_{-m} \\ x_{-m+1} \\ \vdots \\ x_{-2} \\ x_{-1} \\ x_0 \end{bmatrix} = \begin{bmatrix} c_{-m} \\ c_{-m+1} \\ \vdots \\ c_{-2} \\ c_{-1} \\ c_0 \end{bmatrix} \tag{3}$$

THE DYNAMIC INVERSE   19

3.   The solution of this system determines the sequence of annual total sectoral outputs that would enable the economy to yield the sequence of final annual deliveries described by the array of column
vectors entered on the right-hand side. Starting with the last equation,
substituting its solution into the equation next to the last and thus
proceeding stepwise to the first, we arrive at the following solution of
system (3) for the unknown x's in terms of a given set of the c's.

$$
\begin{bmatrix} x_{-m} \\ \vdots \\ x_{-2} \\ x_{-1} \\ x_0 \end{bmatrix} = \begin{bmatrix} G_{-m}^{-1} \cdots R_{-m} \cdots R_{-3}R_{-2}G_{-1}^{-1} & R_{-m} \cdots R_{-3}R_{-2}R_{-1}G_0^{-1} \\ \vdots & \vdots \\ & R_{-2}G_{-1}^{-1} & R_{-2}R_{-1}G_0^{-1} \\ & G_{-1}^{-1} & R_{-1}G_0^{-1} \\ & & G_0^{-1} \end{bmatrix} \begin{bmatrix} c_{-m} \\ \vdots \\ c_{-2} \\ c_{-1} \\ c_0 \end{bmatrix}
$$

(4)

where $R_t = G_t^{-1}B_{t+1} = (I - A_t + B_{t+1})^{-1} B_{t+1}$.

The square matrix on the right-hand side of eq. (4) is the inverse of
the structural matrix that appears on the left-hand side of eq. (3). Every
element of this inverse is itself a square matrix.

The wedge-shaped column on the right describes the direct and indirect input requirements generated by the delivery to final demand
of one unit (or one million dollars' worth) of the products of any one
of the n industries in the year 0. These requirements are distributed
backward over time. Matrix G_0^{-1} shows the input requirements that
must be filled in year 0, i.e. the same year in which the final deliveries
are made; as in a static inverse each column of G_0^{-1} identifies the industry making the delivery to final demand, each row, the industry
supplying the specific input. The preceding term, $R_{-1}G_0^{-1}$, specifies
the requirements that have to be filled in the preceding year -1,
$R_{-2}R_{-1}G_0^{-1}$ specifies those to be filled in year -2, and so on. The
longest term, $R_{-m} \cdots R_{-2}R_{-1}G_0^{-1}$, describes the increments in the
outputs of all industries in the year $-m$, i.e., the inputs that have
to be provided m years before an additional batch of goods can be
delivered to final users. Each term of eq. (4) located above the diagonal
can be computed by multiplying the term located below it by an appropriate transformation matrix, R_{-t}.

4. In the absence of any technical change the time subscript can be eliminated from all the structural constants. The elements of each column can in this case be described in receding order by the same simple geometric series,

$$G^{-1}, RG^{-1}, R^2G^{-1}, \ldots, R^tG^{-1}, \ldots, R^mG^{-1}. \tag{5}$$

It is well known that as the exponent, t, becomes sufficiently large, the ratio between the magnitudes of all the similarly located elements of R^t and R^{t+1} asymptotically approaches the same constant, equal to the real part of the dominant characteristic root of R. If μ is the dominant root, then $R^{t+1} \to R(\mu) R^t$ as $t \to \infty$, where $R(\mu)$ denotes the real part of the root μ. If μ *is* real, positive, and less than 1, the increments to outputs required to deliver any given combination of additional goods to final demand in the final year 0 – traced back a sufficiently large number of years – will become smaller and smaller, and will finally become infinitely small.*

Thus, for all practical purposes, the chains of inputs stretching backwards from the year in which the delivery to final users is actually made, can, in case of such convergence, be treated as if they were of finite length. The same will be true even if the technical structure of the economy changes from year to year, i.e., when the R matrices retain their time subscripts. The series of required inputs converges backward in this case too, although not necessarily as smoothly as it does without technological change.

The distribution of such required inputs over time, however, varies greatly among industries. Some of the input series even dip below the zero line at their forward ends. This is the well-known effect of the so-called acceleration principle. As soon as the additional goods demanded directly or indirectly by the final users have been produced, the stocks of capital goods employed in making them will be released. The balance eq. (1) is set up in such a way as to indicate negative investment, that is disinvestment, in case $x_{t+1} < x_t$. In fact such potentially idle capacity will usually be absorbed by the direct or indirect input requirements generated by increases in final deliveries scheduled for the

---

* A mathematical analysis of the convergence properties of the Dynamic Inverse is presented in appendix I.

next and subsequent years. As will be shown below these must be entered into dynamic input-output accounting in the form of separate but overlapping chains. So long as, in a given year, the sum total of positive incremental output requirements exceeds the sum total of the negative, the output of that sector will increase.

One of the analytically and operationally most useful properties of open input-output systems is the linear additivity of their solutions with respect to any changes in final demand. Each element of the final bill of goods generates a separate chain of direct and indirect input requirements. The total requirements generated by any given vector of final demand are thus represented by the sum of such chains, each corresponding to one particular component of that vector.

This remains true even if some of the separable sets have negative elements, provided the others contain corresponding positive elements large enough to yield a positive or, at least, a nonnegative sum total. In static input-output computations, competitive imports are treated, for example, as generating negative (direct and indirect) input requirements which are subtracted from the corresponding input requirements generated by the positive vector of domestic final demand, thus yielding a smaller, but still positive (or at least non-negative) sum total. Strictly speaking, this already constitutes a departure from true separability: If that total turns out, for some particular output, to be negative, the entire result is invalidated. A new computation has to be untertaken with the imports previously treated as competitive now shifted over into the non-competitive category. The treatment of the direct and indirect effects of one part of the final bill of goods turns out, in this case, to be dependent on the magnitude of the – admittedly separately computed – requirements generated by all the other components of that vector. This introduces into the analytical picture cross-dependencies typical of non-linear systems.

The use of the Dynamic Inverse brings the obvious advantages of separability and additivity into the empirical analysis of economic change. The presence of negative elements in many of the separate input chains (describing the time sequence of the direct – but mostly indirect – input requirements generated by each individual element of a given time-phased final bill of goods) imposes obvious limits on the

22   W. LEONTIEF

strict use of the additivity assumption. Consistent, i. e., feasible sequences of total input requirements can be determined on the basis of a given Dynamic Inverse only for those time-phased bills of goods that generate larger positive than negative output requirements for the products of each industry in each period of time.

A time-phased vector of final demand – premultiplied by a given dynamic inverse – may arithmetically yield negative total direct and indirect output requirements for some goods in some periods of time. If so, at least some of the balance equations in system (3) do not represent the real world. As everyone who has dealt with this kind of system knows, the problem arises because eq. (3) assumes full capacity utilization in all the sectors all the time. By applying, for example, the simplex method routine of linear programming we could find a number of feasible production programs capable of delivering such a time-phased bill of goods. Each one of them would involve a precisely phased switching in and switching out of productive capacities and possibly the planned stock-piling of current outputs.

The operation of an economic process of such a discontinuous kind would be much more difficult to understand and to explain than that of a system whose change can be described in terms of continuous and additive components. In other words, a system with a diverging Dynamic Inverse that contains negative elements, whose magnitude grows as one goes back in time, could be programmed; however, the actual existence of such an economy would be very difficult to imagine. The explanation of the convergence of the actually observed Dynamic Inverse of the American economy which I will now describe should possibly be sought in the gradual substitution of new for the old columns of *A* and *B* coefficients, characterizing long-run technological change.

5.   An open dynamic input-output system was constructed and its inverse computed on the basis of two sets of *A* and *B* matrices, one describing the structural properties of the American economy in the year 1947, the other in the year 1958. A third system was formed and inverted on the assumption that the shift from the 1947 to the 1958 technology occurred gradually over the intervening years. In all three instances the Dynamic Inverse turned out to be well behaved: All time series of which it consists converged backward toward zero.

The same sectoral breakdown is used for both years. It contains 52 endogenous industries and a final bill of goods subdivided into household consumption (durables and non-durables) and government consumption. An alternative treatment of private consumption separates final deliveries to households into deliveries of non-durables and of the estimated replacement requirements for consumers' durables. The rest of the latter is charged to a special household investment account, controlled by an appropriate vector of capital coefficients.

Labor requirements were computed on the basis of sectoral labor input coefficients, and total capital requirements for each sector were determined through summation of all elements of the appropriate column of the *B* matrix.

All inputs and outputs were measured both for 1947 and 1958 in 1958 prices. In other words, the units in terms of which the numerical computations were performed and their results presented should be

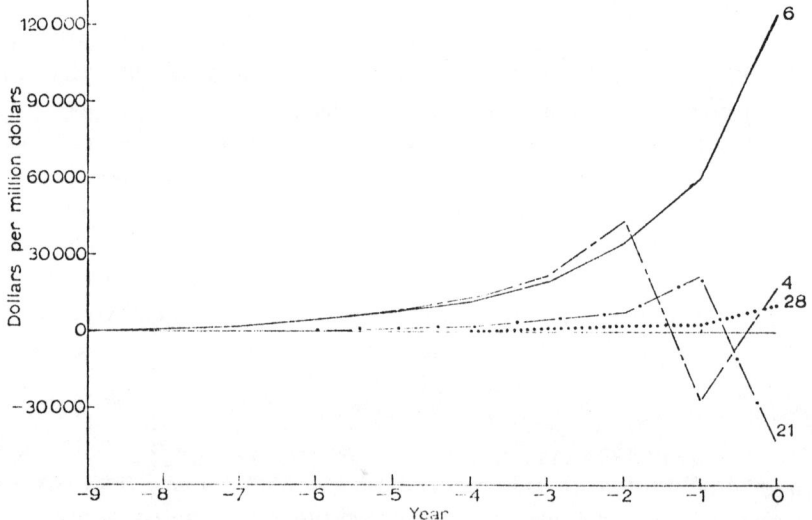

Fig. 1. Elements of the Dynamic Inverse showing the direct and indirect effects of a million dollars' increase in the final demand for the products of industry 3, machinery products, in year 0 on the outputs of industries 4, 6, 21, 28 in this and the preceding years. — – — – —: transportation equipment and consumer appliances (4); ————: metals (6); · — · — · —: lumber and products, excluding containers (21); ·······: rubber and plastic products (28).

24   W. LEONTIEF

interpreted as amounts of the respective commodities and services purchasable for one dollar at 1958 prices.

The entire computation absorbed about an hour's time on the I. B. M. 7094 computer. The program included automatic plotting of the resulting time series by the machine. A selection of such plots is presented in the eight figures that I will now discuss.

Fig. 1 illustrates the typical variety of shapes encountered among the time series each of which constitutes a single element of the Dynamic Inverse. Each of the four curves represents the time-phased amount of the product of one of the four different industries that were contributing directly or indirectly to supplying (in year 0) final users with one additional unit of the output of the machinery industry. Two of the inputs – 'metals', and 'rubber and plastic products' – are primarily materials; their input curves ascend gradually but steadily from the beginning to the end. The demand for primary metals is much larger and anticipates the final delivery in significant amounts by some eight

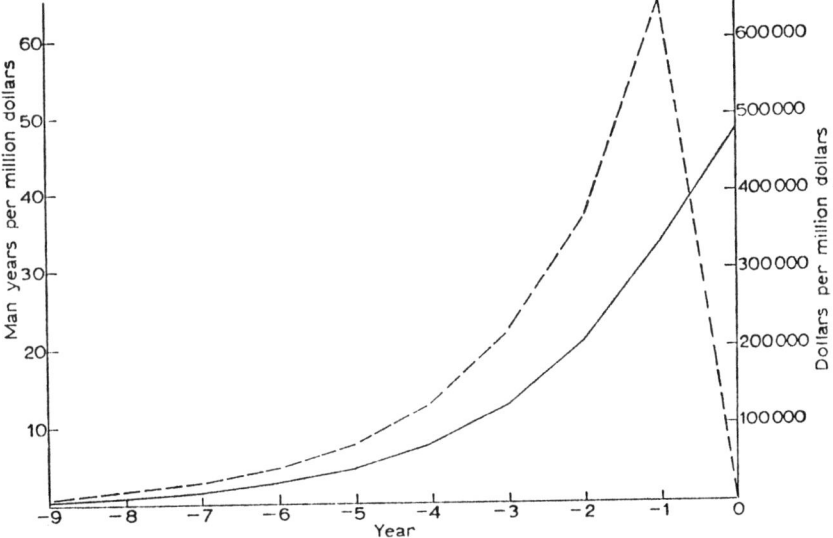

Fig. 2. Time series of total direct and indirect labor and capital inputs required to deliver one million dollars' worth of the products of industry 3, machinery products, to final demand in year 0 (the left scale refers to labor, the right scale to capital). ———: labor; -----: capital.

years. The first significant demand for rubber and plastic products is registered in the year -3.

The corresponding input requirements for transportation equipment and lumber, on the other hand, show a dip below the zero line in the years preceding the delivery of the final product. As explained above, this is typical of goods playing an important part in the process of capital accumulation.

Fig. 2 supplements fig. 1 by showing the amounts of labor and of capital, i.e., of investment goods, absorbed by *all industries* in the process of filling the direct and indirect input requirements for the delivery to final users (in year 0) of one million dollars' worth of the product of the machinery industry. The smoothness of the gradual rise is, of course, in both instances due to the mutual cancellation of irregularities in the employment and investment requirements of the many

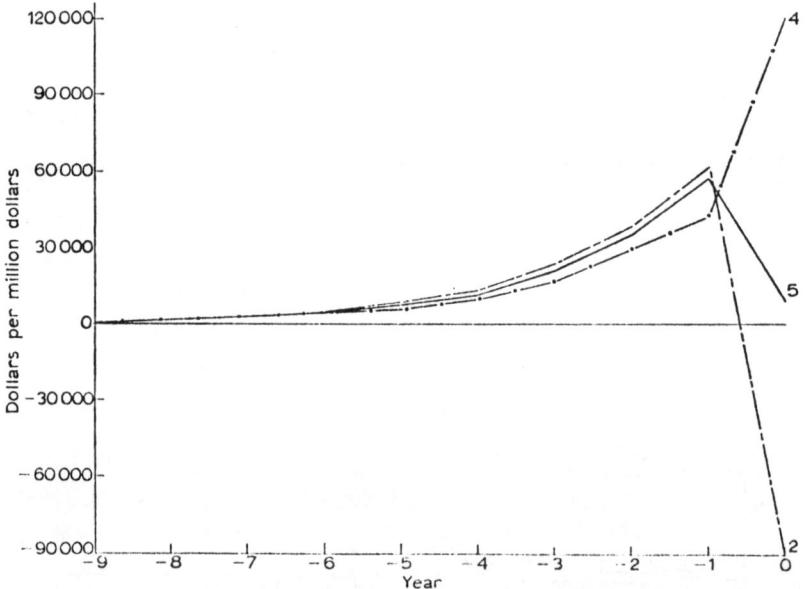

Fig. 3. Elements of the Dynamic Inverse showing the alternative direct and indirect effects on the output of industry 6, metals, of a million dollars' worth of deliveries to final demand for the products of industries 2, 4, 5 in year 0. $\cdot-\cdot-\cdot-$: transportation equipment and consumer appliances (4); $---$: textiles, clothing furnishings (2); $\underline{\qquad}$: construction (5).

26 W. LEONTIEF

different individual industries combined in each of these two totals. The one year time-lag between the installation of new capacities and the delivery of additional outputs explains the last year's drop in the investment curve.

The differences among the reactions of the same industry to various kinds of final deliveries are shown in fig. 3. Metals behave as a typical raw material in their contribution to the production of transportation equipment – that is mainly automobiles – delivered to final users; they react, however, as a typical investment good, in response to an increase in the final demand for textiles. An intermediate pattern of behavior marks the contribution of the metals sector to the satisfaction of the final demand for the output of the construction industry.

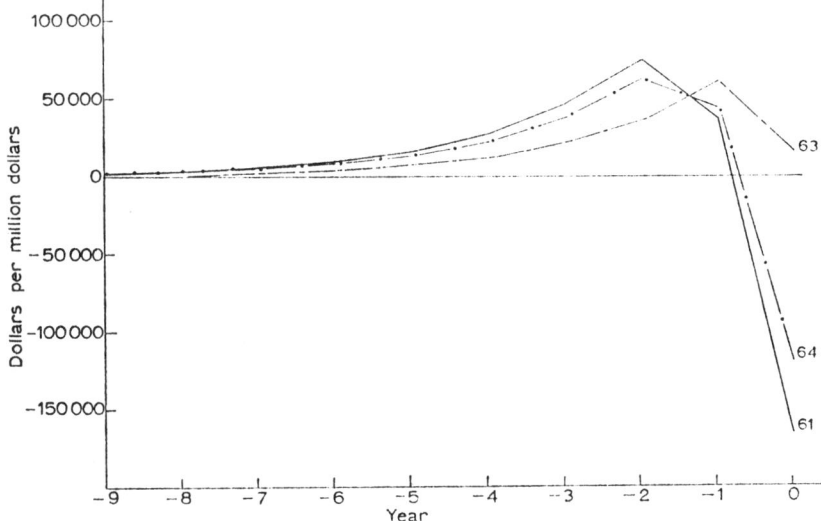

Fig. 4. Elements of the Dynamic Inverse showing the alternative direct and indirect effects on the output of industry 6, metals, of a million dollars' worth of increases in the household, government and total final demand in year 0. ——: household final demand (61); – – – – : government final demand (63); · — · — · — : total final demand (64).

A similar difference can be seen in fig. 4 between the shapes of two time series, both tracing the requirements for products of the metal sector, one reflecting an additional million dollars' worth of govern-

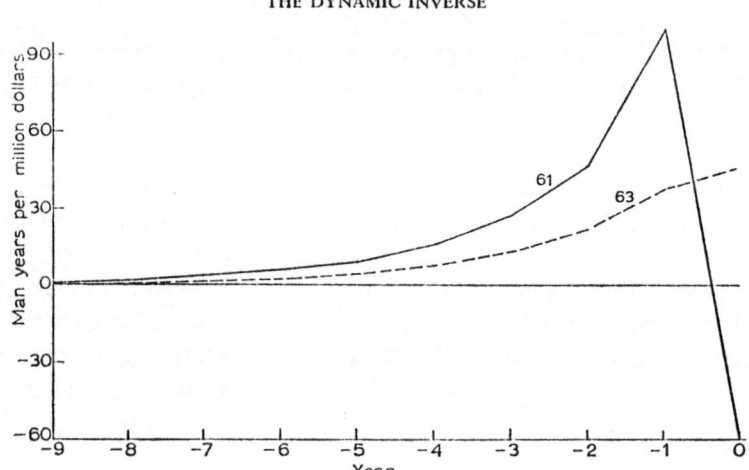

Fig. 5. Time series of alternative direct and indirect labor inputs required to deliver a million dollars' worth of increases in the government and household final demand vectors in year 0. ————: household final demand (61); ————: government final demand (63).

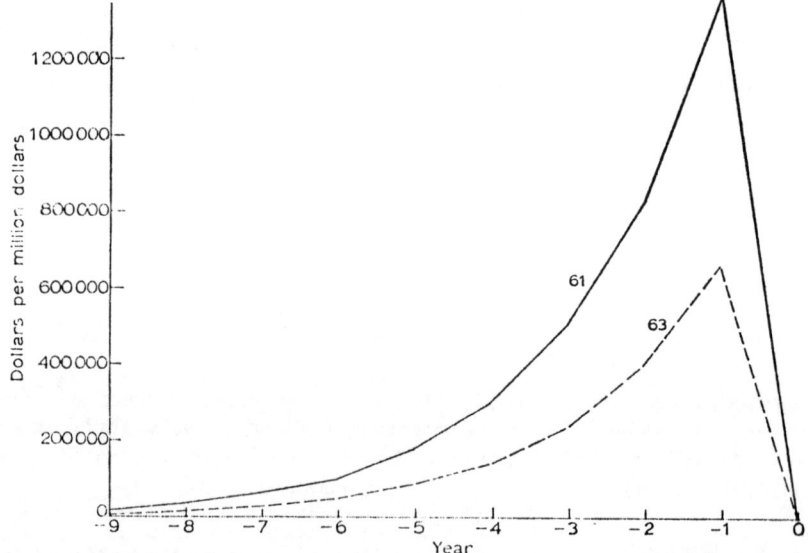

Fig. 6. Time series of alternative direct and indirect capital inputs required to deliver a million dollars' worth of increases in the government and household final demand vectors in year 0. ————: household final demand (61); ————: government final demand (63).

ment demand, the other anticipating a delivery of one million dollars' worth of goods and services demanded by households. The first curve reaches its crest one year before the final delivery can actually be made and stays above the zero line in the last; the second starts to fall off a year earlier and plunges below the zero line at the end. As should have been expected, the intermediate product mixture of the combined total demand yields an intermediate time-profile weighed in favor of households.

The time series of total labor inputs contributing to the two principal components of final demand, as shown in fig. 5, are similar in shape to those shown in fig. 4. The same is true of the corresponding total capital requirements shown in fig. 6.

The three sets of curves in fig. 7 demonstrate how the Dynamic Inverse can reveal the effects of specified technical change on the dynamic properties of a given economic system. Each part of the chart presents the same element of the Dynamic Inverse in three alternative versions.

All three curves at the top represent the time-phased increase in the output of chemicals contributing directly and indirectly to the delivery of one additional million dollars' worth of food and drug products to final demand in the year 0. The first is computed on the basis of A_{1947} and B_{1947}, i.e., of the flow and capital coefficients characterizing the input structures of the 52 producing sectors of the American economy of the year 1947, the second on the basis of A_{1958} and B_{1958}, i.e., of 1958 technology. The third inverse was computed – in accordance with eq. (4) – from a sequence of eleven different pairs of dated A and B matrices tracing the gradual shift from the 1947 to the 1958 technology. On the left this curve coincides with the first, but in the terminal year it catches up with the second.

The three sets of curves demonstrate how differently the same overall change can affect various elements of the same Dynamic Inverse. The combined effects of the many technical shifts reflected in the difference between the magnitude of the flow and the capital coefficients describing the input structures of the 52 sectors of the American economy in 1947 and 1958 led to an upward shift in the time series of chemical inputs required for delivery to final users of one million dollars' worth of food and drugs. The three curves in the middle part of the chart indicate that the same combination of structural changes reduced the

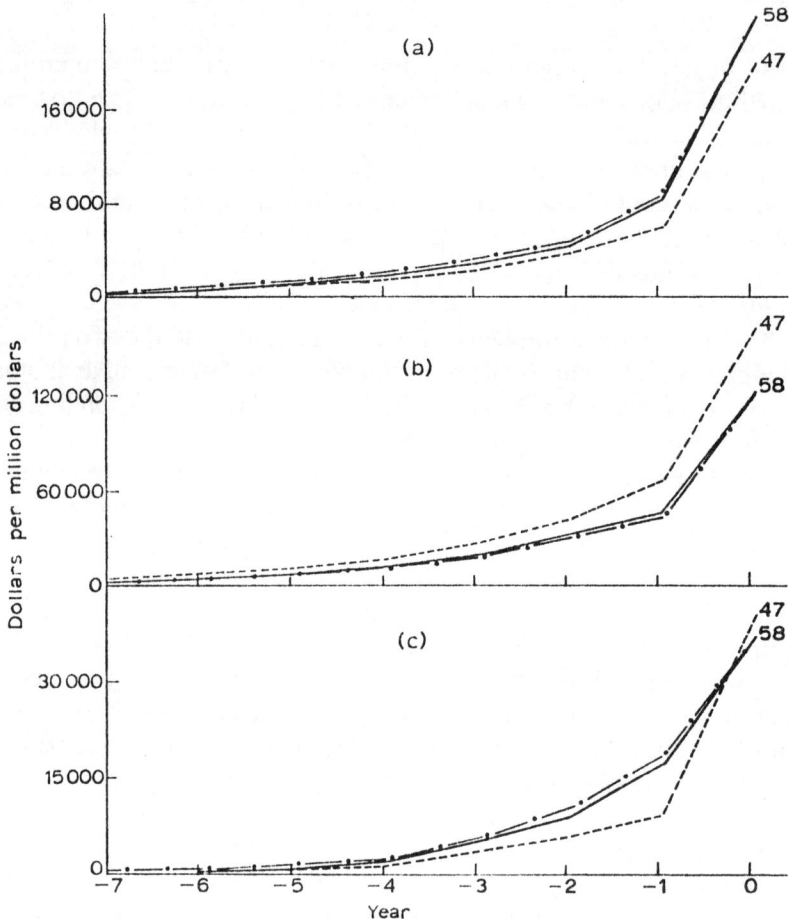

Fig. 7. Effects of technological change on the elements of the Dynamic Inverse. (a) Time series of direct and indirect requirements for chemicals (8) to deliver a million dollars' worth of food and drugs (1) in year 0, computed on the basis of flow and capital coefficients representing the technologies of: ---: 1947; ·—·—: 1958; ———: shifting, year by year, from 1947 to 1958. (b) Time series of direct and indirect requirements for metals (6) to deliver a million dollars' worth of transportation equipment (4) in year 0, computed on the basis of flow and capital coefficients representing the technologies of: ---: 1947; ·—·—: 1958; ———: shifting, year by year, from 1947 to 1958. (c) Time series of direct and indirect requirements for chemicals (8) to deliver a million dollars' worth of nonferrous mining products (16) in year 0, computed on the basis of flow and capital coefficients representing the technologies of: ---: 1947; ·—·—: 1958; ———: shifting, year by year, from 1947 to 1958.

inputs of metals contributing to the final delivery of consumers' appliances.

The contribution of chemicals to non-ferrous metals mining shown on the bottom was affected by the same structural shifts in a more complicated way: The input requirements dropped in the last year of the series, i.e., the year of the final delivery, but they rose in all the previous years.

6. The dynamic input-output system described above – not unlike the static input-output system – can be of little help in derivation of the Golden Rules of economic growth or in formulation of any other purely theoretical generalizations. It is too loosely jointed, too flexible for serving such an ambitious purpose. The Dynamic Inverse is primarily a storehouse of systematically organized factual information. This information is presented in a form particularly suitable for analytical description of intertemporal relations. The individual elements of the inverse can be spun into longer strands, each attached to a given time sequence of final deliveries. These strands can be woven into a broad fabric of intersectoral and intertemporal relationships which make up the analytical picture of economic growth.

Fig. 8 illustrates graphically the structure of one such simple strand describing – or explaining, if you will – the increase in the level of output of primary metals called for by a delivery to final users of one million dollars' worth of non-durable consumers' goods (and of proportionally increased services of durable consumers' goods) per year over a period of 17 years. The first delivery to final users is made in year 0, the last in the year +16.

Each of the partly superimposed curves represents the sequence of inputs required for delivery of an additional million dollars' worth of consumers' goods to households. The year of final delivery is indicated by the position of the forward end of the curve. While the first delivery is due in the year 0, the first incremental input of non-negligible size must be made in year −8. From then on, a new input sequence has to be started every year over a period of 17 years; the entire series of required total annual inputs – traced by the heavy black line on the chart – spans an interval of 25 years. The typical hump at the beginning reflects the buildup of the required additional capital stocks; the falling off at the end indicates, on the other hand, a reduction of these stocks, a gradual liquidation that sets in many years before the last delivery to households of an additional million dollars' worth of consumers' goods.

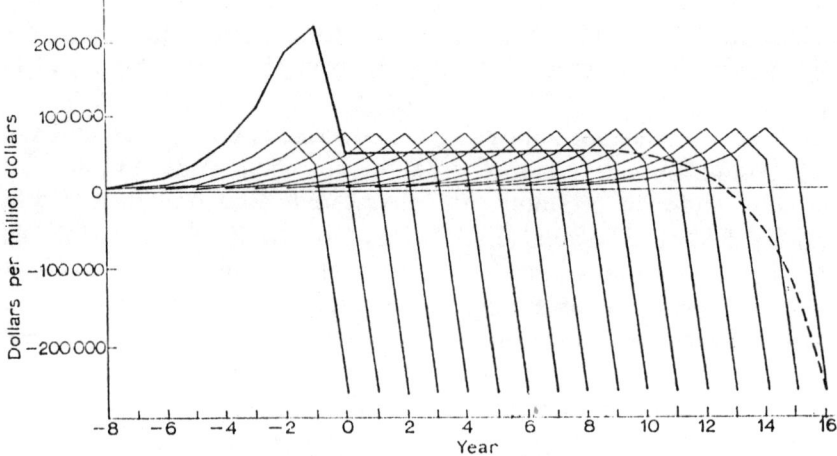

Fig. 8. Direct and indirect effects on the output of industry 6, metals, of annual increases of a million dollars, continued over a seventeen year period (years 0 through +16), in the household final demand vector (61). ———: effects of an increase in demand for a single year; ———: combined effects of all increases in annual demands.

The flat portion of the curve marks what might be called the period of stationary reproduction, during which only current annual input requirements, including capital replacements, have to be covered. With the A and B matrices invariant and the vector of final deliveries, c, constant over a sufficiently long period of time, the corresponding time-phased output vector, x, can – according to (5) – be determined as follows:

$$x = (I + R + R^2 + \cdots + R^m)\, G^{-1}c \tag{6}$$

If the series on the right-hand side converges,

$$x \to (I - R)^{-1}\, G^{-1}c = [G\,(I - G^{-1}B)]^{-1}\, c = (G - B)^{-1}\, c = (I - A)^{-1}\, c$$

as $m \to \infty$.

Under stationary conditions governing the flat portion of the cumulative curve in fig. 8, the dependence of sectoral outputs on final demand is controlled by the static inverse, $(I - A)^{-1}$.

Information anticipating the level of final demand eight years hence would, in this particular case, suffice for a reasonably accurate assessment of direct and indirect input needs. The degree of foresight required depends, of course, on the profile of the elements of the inverse from which the total input curve has to be built up. So long as the total final demand continues to rise from year to year, no liquidation of productive stock is likely to be called for. In the summation of the overlapping series of direct and indirect effects of successive changes in final deliveries, the positive elements of the Dynamic Inverse will tend to dominate its few negative components.

In recent contributions to the pure theory of economic growth the problem of so-called 'terminal conditions' has attracted much attention. According to the evidence presented above, the time horizon on which we could base our plans or make our projections should vary from sector to sector. The time-shape of the elements of the Dynamic Inverse that governs direct and indirect requirements for the products of one particular industry might be such that its output in a given year depends primarily on the composition and the level of the final demand vector of the same year. For another industry that shape might be such that the level of its output in a given year reflects final deliveries, say, four or five years later.

7. The balance equation (1), and consequently also the formulae describing the Dynamic Inverse derived from it, are based on the assumption of a uniform one-period ('one year') time lag between the installation of additional stocks of capital goods and the increase in the flow of output resulting from their first use. The same time unit enters into the definition of all the elements of the capital coefficient matrix B ('stocks per unit of *annual* output'). In fact, the time lags between the installation and initial full utilization of incremental capacities in various productive sectors of the U. S. economy – defined in terms of the degree of aggregation used in this study – seem to be around one year or somewhat shorter.

A change in the absolute magnitude of the time unit used in describing an actual economic system in terms of equations (1) would signify a corresponding real change in the length of all the lags. If, despite that change, the real capital requirements of all the sectors remain the same, the capital coefficients described by matrix B have to be 'translated' into the new time unit. Thus, if the time lag is reduced from one year to half a year, all elements of B have to be multiplied by 2.

The effects of such a shift on the dominant characteristic root of the system and, consequently, on its convergence are analyzed in appendix I; changes in the time lags and in the magnitudes of the B coefficients tend to offset each other. The three curves entered in fig. 9 show

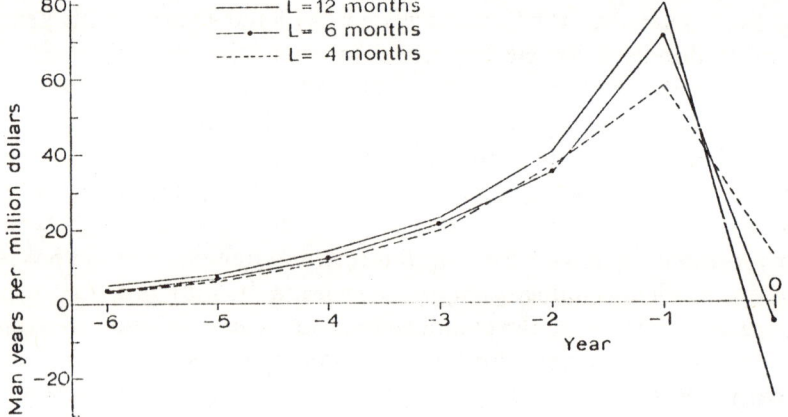

Fig. 9. Direct and indirect labor inputs required to deliver an additional one million dollars' worth of goods to total final demand in year 0, assuming investment lags of 12 months, 6 months and 4 months.

how the time sequence of labor inputs required to increase total deliveries to final demand by $ 1 million is affected if the basic structural investment lag is cut from one year to six or to four months. The horizontal axis of the graph is in natural years.

8.   In static input-output analysis, the inverse of the structural matrix of a particular economy post-multiplied by a given column vector of final demand yields the vector of corresponding total sectoral outputs. The transpose of the same inverse when post-multiplied by a given vector of values added (wage, profit, tax and other final payments disbursed by each industry per unit of its total physical output) yields

34   W. LEONTIEF

the corresponding vector of equilibrium prices, i.e., of prices at which the total outlay (including the values added) of each sector would equal its aggregate receipts. In dynamic input-output analysis the transpose of the Dynamic Inverse determines the relationship between the time-phased vectors of values added in each of the producing sectors and the set of equilibrium prices that would balance the total outlays and the total receipts of each producing sector over time.

Let p_t represent a column vector, $_tp_1, _tp_2, ..., _tp_n$, of the prices of goods and services sold and purchased by various sectors in year t and v_t a column vector, $_tv_1, _tv_2, ..., _tv_n$, of the values added in each sector per unit of its output in year t. Value added can be best defined residually as all current outlays of a producing sector other than payments for inputs purchased from the same or from other industries.

Equation (7) below states that in any year t the prices of all goods represented by the vector on the left-hand side must equal their unit costs as represented by the terms appearing on the right-hand side. The product of the transpose of the flow coefficient matrix A' and the price vector p_t represents the costs of current inputs purchased by each productive sector from itself and from other industries. The elements of the value-added (column) vector v_t comprise wages, rents, taxes, and profits paid out or charged per unit of its output by the respective industries in year t.

The two terms enclosed in the square brackets describe the unit cost or gains conventionally booked through the capital account. For purposes of proper cost accounting, the stocks of capital goods are assumed to be acquired by each sector, in accordance with technological requirements, one year before the delivery of the output they produce and then sold off together with that output; in fact the sale will, in most cases, be purely nominal since the sector disposing of the capital goods will repurchase them again and again. Both transactions, of course, are supposed to be made at prices prevailing in the time period during which they take place. The value of capital stock purchased in the year $t - 1$ is multiplied by $1 + r_{t-1}$; r_{t-1} represents the annual money rate of interest prevailing in that year. As has been observed before, the stocks of capital released from production of outputs delivered in year t are employed at once to produce goods that will be delivered in the following year $t + 1$. The A and B matrices on the right-hand side are dated to reflect the process of technical change.

$$p_t = A'_t p_t + [(1 + r_{t-1}) B'_t p_{t-1} - B'_{t+1} p_t] + v_t. \tag{7}$$

Equation (7) can be rewritten as

$$G'_t p_t - \alpha_{t-1} B'_t p_{t-1} = v_t \tag{8}$$

where

$$G'_t = (I - A'_t + B'_{t+1}) \quad \text{and} \quad \alpha_t = 1 + r_t$$

Assigning the values $-m$, $-m + 1$, $-m + 2$, ..., -2, -1, 0, to the time subscript t, we can construct a system of interlocked equations analogous to (3). The structural matrix on the left-hand side of that new system would resemble the transpose of the structural matrix appearing in (3) with the difference that each of the B_t's is multiplied by a corresponding scalar, α_{t-1}.

The solution of that system for the unknown price vector p_0 in terms of the value-added vectors of the same and all the previous years v_0, v_{-1}, v_{-2}, ... and of the corresponding 'force of interest' factors α_0, α_{-1}, α_{-2}, ... has the form:

$$p_0 = (G_0^{-1})' v_0 + (R_{-1} G_0^{-1})' \alpha_{-1} v_{-1} + (R_{-2} R_{-1} G_0^{-1})' \alpha_{-2} \alpha_{-1} v_{-2}$$

$$+, \cdots, + (R_{-m} \cdots R_{-2} R_{-1} G_0^{-1})' \alpha_{-m} \cdots \alpha_{-2} \alpha_{-1} v_{-m}$$

$$+ (R_{-m} \cdots R_{-2} R_{-1} G_0^{-1})' \alpha_{-m} \cdots \alpha_{-2} \alpha_{-1} B'_{-m} p_{-(m+1)} \tag{9}$$

The bracketed matrix products on the right-hand side of the first line are identical with the elements of the last column of the Dynamic Inverse appearing on the right-hand side of (4). These coefficients, however, enter into (9) in their transposed form. Since the series R_{-1}, $R_{-2} R_{-1}$, $R_{-3} R_{-2} R_{-1}$, ... converges toward 0, the last term on the right-hand side – containing the price vector $p_{-(m+1)}$ – can be disregarded provided that the sequence is extended back over a sufficient number of years.

The price vector of any given year has thus been shown to depend on the value-added vectors of that and of all preceding years. This dependence is governed by the transpose of the same Dynamic Inverse that determines the dated sequence of input requirements generated in the corresponding physical system by a given time phased bill of goods. For example, in the absence of technical change and on the assumption

36   W. LEONTIEF

that both the rate of interest and the value-added vectors remain constant over time, equation (9) is reduced to

$$p_o \rightarrow [G^{-1}]' [I + R' \wedge + (R')^2 \wedge^2 + (R')^3 \wedge^3 \cdots (R')^t \wedge^t] v \qquad (10)$$

as $t \rightarrow \infty$.

After t becomes sufficiently large, the ratio between two successive terms of the exponential series on the right-hand side tends to equal $\mu_1 \alpha$, where μ_1 is the dominant characteristic root of R'. The series will converge and thus yield a finite price vector p only if $\mu_1 \alpha < 1$ or, since $\alpha = 1 + r$, if

$$r < \frac{1 - \mu_1}{\mu_1}.$$

The conclusion that, under certain conditions, the characteristic root of the matrix of an open dynamic input-output system imposes an upper limit on the rate of interest has been presented many years ago by Michio Morishima.*

Fig. 10 shows how the price of the bundle** of consumers' goods delivered to final users in 1958 depends on the annual values added per unit of the metal industry's output. The solid curve, based on the unrealistic assumption that the rate of interest through the entire eleven-year period was equal to 0 (i.e., $\alpha = 1$), is identical with the corresponding solid curve in fig. 4. The dip below the zero line in the last year reflects negative costs, i.e., the revenue that would have been secured from the liquidation of capital stock purchased in the previous year. The positive expenditure on capital goods reflected in the other points of the same curve will, in most cases, offset this negative amount.

The other two curves were drawn on the assumption that interest rates of 10% and 25% respectively prevailed over the entire interval. They show how a rise in the interest rate increases the dependence of present prices on past values added (and, consequently, also on past prices).

Much of what I have said should have a familiar ring. The 'produc-

---

* Michio Morishima, 'Equilibrium, Stability, and Growth' Oxford University Press, London, 1964.

** A 'final demand bundle' consists of goods, weighted according to 1958 consumption patterns, costing $ 1 in 1958 prices.

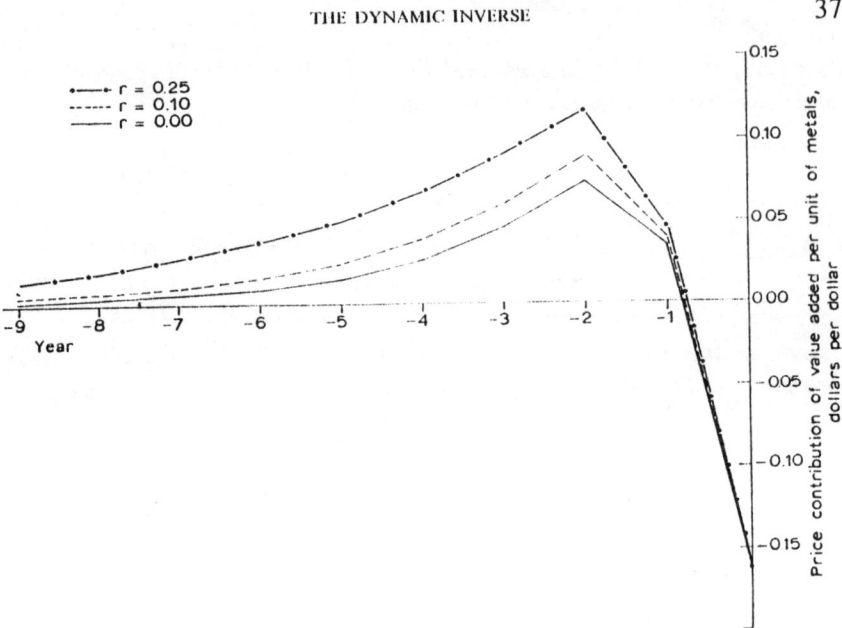

Fig. 10. Portion of the price of a 1958 final demand bundle, directly and indirectly attributable to value added paid by the metal industry in year *t*.

tive advances' of Francois Quesnay, the process of expanded reproduction of Karl Marx and the 'roundabout production' of Böhm-Bawerk all contain the basic theoretical notions incorporated in the derivation of the Dynamic Inverse. But while these great economists had to content themselves with verbal description and deductive reasoning, we can measure and we can compute. Therein lies the real difference between the past and the present state of economics.

38 W. LEONTIEF

Appendix I

To analyze the convergence properties of the series

$$R_{-1}, R_{-2}R_{-1}, R_{-3}R_{-2}R_{-1}, \ldots, R_{-t} \ldots R_{-3}R_{-2}R_{-1} \qquad (A1)$$

$$R_t = (I - A_t + B_{t+1})^{-1} B_{t+1}$$

we can first consider the case in which,

$A_t = A$ and $B_t = B$, for all t's and consequently,
$R_t = R$ for all t's.

In this case, series (1) is transformed into the geometric series,

$$R, R^2, R^3, \ldots, R^t \qquad (A2)$$

$$R = (I - A + B)^{-1} B \qquad (A3)$$

$$(I - A + B) = (I - A) [I + (I - A)^{-1} B] \qquad (A4)$$

$$(I - A + B)^{-1} B = [I + (I - A)^{-1} B]^{-1} (I - A)^{-1} B = (I + U)^{-1} U \qquad (A5)$$

where $U = (I - A)^{-1} B$.

Since $(I - A)^{-1} > 0$, and $B \geq 0$ and is irreducible, therefore $U > 0$.

$$[(I + U)^{-1} U]^{-1} = U^{-1} (I + U) = (I + U^{-1}); \qquad (A6)$$

consequently $\qquad R = (I + U^{-1})^{-1}. \qquad (A7)$

Let λ_i ($i = 1, 2, 3, \ldots, n$) represent the n roots of the square, non-singular and indecomposable matrix U. Since $U > 0$, it has – according to the well known theorem of Frobenius – a positive dominant simple root. Moreover, this root, and only this root, has associated with it a positive eigenvector. Let λ_1 be this root.

For real λ_i the corresponding roots of U^{-1} and of $I + U^{-1}$ are, $1/\lambda_i$ and $1 + (1/\lambda_i)$, respectively. Thus according to eq. (A7), the roots of R are

$$\mu_i = \frac{\lambda_i}{1 + \lambda_i} \quad \text{and in particular,} \quad \mu_1 = \frac{\lambda_1}{1 + \lambda_1}. \qquad (A8)$$

From $\lambda_1 > 0$, it follows that $0 < \mu_1 < 1$, which means that R always has a simple positive root μ_1 smaller than 1, associated with a positive eigenvector.

Fig. A1 depicts the relationship between μ_i and λ_i for all real λ_i. If some of these subdominant roots are smaller than -0.5, the correspond-

ing μ_i will be greater than 1 in absolute value. The eigenvectors associated with therm will have elements of different signs.†

This implies that series R^1, R^2, R^3 ... could be divergent. Depending
on whether the dominant root is real or complex and whether its
real part is positive or negative, the elements of the corresponding
dynamic inverse would, in this case, diverge – as one moves back in
time – expanding without limit either monotonically in the positive or
negative direction, or fluctuating with increasing amplitude between
the positive and negative domain.

If R_t changes with t, but does so within finite lower and upper
limits, say, $\underline{R}$ and $\overline{R}$, its higher terms will lie between the corresponding higher terms of the series $\underline{R}^1$, $\underline{R}^2$ ... and $\overline{R}^1$, $\overline{R}^2$.

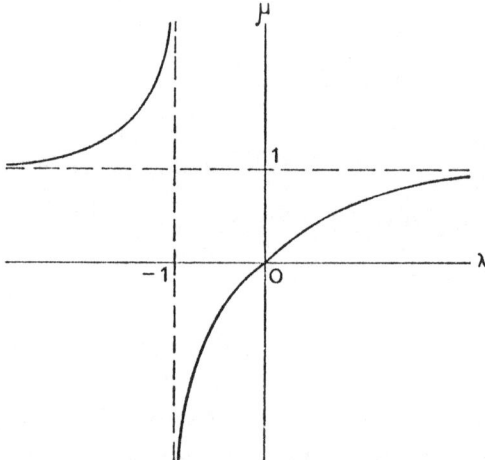

Fig. A 1. Schematic graph of relationship between μ and λ.

The convergence properties of the Dynamic Inverse depend on the
time unit in terms of which the capital coefficients that enter into matrix B are defined. In the basic balance equation (1) that unit also

---

† The analysis holds for complex roots with the following modification: Let $\lambda_i = a + b_i$. Then, the real part of the corresponding μ_i becomes $R(\mu_i) = \dfrac{a(a+1)+b^2}{(a+1)^2+b^2}$.
To guarantee convergence, we must have $(a^2 + 1.5a) > -(b^2 + 0.5)$. If $b = 0$,
these formulae reduce to the simpler form stated in the text.

40   W. LEONTIEF

represents the lag, i.e., the difference between the time when additional stocks of capital goods, or inventories of current inputs, are accumulated and the time when they can be put to use.

Let t be a given time interval described in original units and t^* the same time interval measured in different units. If α is the ratio of the length of the first to that of the second unit,

$$t^* = \alpha t \qquad (A9)$$

If, for example, t describes a given stretch of time in years and t^* measures it in months, then, $\alpha = 12$.

The technical flow coefficients have no time dimensions; hence the elements of matrix A will remain the same after the time unit – and consequently the lag built in into equation (A1) – has been changed from a year to, say, a month. But all the capital coefficients, that is the elements of matrix B, will become 12 times larger. Continuing to use an asterisk to mark the values of matrices and their roots after the change of the time unit, we have

$$B^* = B\alpha$$

$$U^* = U\alpha \quad \text{and} \quad I + U^{*-1} = I + U^{-1}/\alpha \qquad (A10)$$

It follows that,

$$\lambda_i^* = \lambda_i\alpha \quad \text{and, in accordance with (A8)}$$

$$\mu_i^* = \frac{\lambda_i/\alpha}{1 + \lambda_i/\alpha} \qquad (A11)$$

The relationship between μ_i^* and λ_i/α is thus the same as that between μ_i and λ_i explained above. Inspecting it we find that, if root μ_1 happens to be dominant, its dominance will not be affected by any change in the time unit and the lag. If, on the other hand, some other root μ_i were dominant and, consequently, the system were divergent, an increase in α, i.e., a shortening of the lag, if sufficiently large, could shift any negative magnitude λ_i/α into the interval between -0.5 and 0 and thus make μ_1^* dominant. A lengthening of the lag could, of course, have the opposite effect.

Appendix II

Concepts

I. A Matrix
    The A matrix includes current flow coefficients and replacement coefficients. It is on a domestic output base.

II. B Matrix
    The B matrix is made up of the capital stock coefficients for all industries. Residential construction is included in the real estate and rental industry. The capital coefficients are capacity based.

III. Labor row
    The labor row consists of 'man years' per thousand dollars of output.

IV. Total capital row
    This row is simply the column sums of the B matrix.

V. Alternative bills of goods
    A. Household non-durable goods including replacement of durable
       This vector of final demand includes current purchases of non-durable goods and replacement of durable goods by households. It also contains a capital coefficient column, consisting of the stock of consumer durables (the stock of residential construction is in the real estate and rental column). The labor entry into this vector is domestic help.
    B. Household goods, durable and non-durable
       This vector of final demand contains current purchases of durable and non-durable goods by households.
    C. Government
       The government vector of final demand consists of purchases by the federal, state and local governments.
    D. Total final demand
       Final demand includes expenditures by households (durable and non-durable goods), federal, state and local governments, exports, and competitive imports. It excludes the gross private capital formation and net inventory change vectors.

All items are in 1958 prices.

42   W. LEONTIEF

1947 through 1958 Data

Information regarding capital and technical coefficients is usually un-
available on a year-by-year basis. Since the dynamic model with technological change requires such data for, say, a dozen consecutive years,
and since data may exist for no more than three years in this interval,
most of the information has to be derived through interpolation. For
most coefficients exponential interpolation is used to approximate a
constant rate of growth. When one of the terminal year coefficients is
zero, the exponential method becomes impractical, and the program
approximates with a linear technique.

Suppose $a(47)$ and $a(58)$ represent corresponding elements of two
terminal year matrices. Then,

if $a(47) > 0$ and $a(58) > 0$ exponential interpolation is used,
if $a(47) = 0$ and $a(58) > 0$ linear interpolation is used,
if $a(47) > 0$ and $a(58) = 0$ linear interpolation is used, and
if $a(47) = 0$ and $a(58) = 0$ linear interpolation is used.

Appendix III

'59-order' classification

Number	Name	Corresponding 83-order sectors
1	Food and drugs	14, 15, 29
2	Textiles, clothing, furnishings	16, 17, 18, 19, 34 22, 23
3	Machinery (just final)	51, 44, 45, 46, 47, 48, 49, 50, 63
4	Transportation equipment and consumer appliances	52, 54, 56, 59, 60, 61, 62
5	Construction	11, 12
6	Metals	37, 38
7	Energy	7, 31, 68
8	Chemicals	27
9	--	—
10	—	—
11	Livestock	1
12	Crops	2
13	Forestry	3
14	Agricultural services	4
15	Iron ore mining	5
16	Nonferrous ore mining	6
17	Petroleum mining	8
18	Stone and clay mining	9
19	Chemical mining	10
20	—	—
21	Lumber and products, excluding containers	20
22	Wooden containers	21
23	Paper products and containers	24, 25
24	—	—
25	Printing and publishing	26
26	Plastics and synthetics	28
27	Paint and allied products	30
28	Rubber and plastic products	32
29	Leather tanning	33
30	Glass and glass products	35
31	Stone and clay products	36

44   W. LEONTIEF

'59-order' Classification

Number	Name	Corresponding 83-order sectors
32	Metal containers	39
33	Heating, plumbing, structural metals	40
34	Stampings, screw machine products	41
35	Hardware, plating, valves, wire products	42
36	Engines and turbines	43
37	Electric apparatus and motors	53
38	Electric lighting and wiring equipment	55
39	Electronic components	57
40	Batteries, X-ray and engine elect. eqp't.	58
41	Miscellaneous manufacturing	64
42	Transportation and warehousing	65
43	Communications, excl. radio and TV	66
44	Radio and TV broadcasting	67
45	Trade	69
46	Finance and insurance	70
47	Real estate and rental	71
48	Hotels, personal and repair services	72
49	Business services	73
50	Research and development	74
51	Automobile repair services	75
52	Amusements and recreation	76
53	Medical and educational institutions	77
54	—	—
55	—	—
56	Non-competitive imports	80
57	Entertainment and business travel	81
58	—	—
59	Scrap and by-products	83
60	Total labor row	
61	Household non-durables including replacement of durables column	
62	Household durables and non-durables column	
63	Government final demand column	
64	Total final demand, excluding gross private capital formation and net inventory change, column	
65	Total capital row	

Alternative bills of goods {61, 62, 63, 64}

Appendix IV

Sources of data

1958 A matrix, current flow coefficients
This matrix is based on the 1958 input-output table published by
the Office of Business Economics, Department of Commerce.
See A. P. Carter, 'Changes in the Structure of the American
Economy, 1947 to 1958 and 1962', *Review of Economics and
Statistics*, XLIX (May 1967).

1958 A matrix, replacement coefficients
This matrix was developed at the Harvard Economic Research
Project based on 1958 capital coefficients and U.S. Treasury
Department, Internal Revenue Service, *Depreciation Guidelines
and Rules*, Publication No. 456, U. S. Government Printing Office,
Washington, D. C. (1964).

1958 B matrix, capital coefficients
The capital coefficients for manufacturing sectors were obtained
from Waddell, Ritz, Norton, DeWitt, and Wood, *Capital Expansion Planning Factors, Manufacturing Industries*, National Planning Association, Washington, D. C. (April 1966). For non-manufacturing sectors, the capital coefficients were compiled at the
Harvard Economic Research Project by Samuel A. Rea, Jr. and
others in 1966–1967.

1958 Labor coefficients
The labor coefficients are based on Jack Alterman, 'Interindustry Employment Requirements', *Monthly Labor Review*,
88, No. 7 (July 1965).

1958 Final demand vectors
The final demand vectors are based on the 1958 input-output
table published by the Office of Business Economics, Department
of Commerce and on Raymond W. Goldsmith, *The National
Wealth of the United States in the Postwar Period*, National
Bureau of Economic Research, Princeton (1962).

1947 A matrix, current flow coefficients
This matrix is based on the Bureau of Labor Statistics 450-order
input-output table for 1947, which was obtained by the Harvard

46 W. LEONTIEF

Economic Research Project some years ago on cards (Deck A) from the Bureau of Labor Statistics along with mimeographed documentation for individual sectors. It is published at a 50-order level and is described in W. D. Evans and M. Hoffenberg, 'The Interindustry Relations Study for 1947', *The Review of Economics and Statistics*, XXXIV (May 1952). Adjustments have been made to the 1947 matrix in order to make it comparable with the 1958 matrix. See A. P. Carter, *op. cit.* Further work in this area is currently being done by Beatrice Vaccara and others at the Office of Business Economics and by the Harvard Economic Research Project.

1947 A matrix, replacement coefficients

This matrix was developed at the Harvard Economic Research Project, based on the 1947 capital coefficients and U.S. Treasury Department, *op. cit.*

1947 B matrix, capital coefficients

The 1947 capital coefficients are based on James M. Henderson and others, 'Estimates of the Capital Structure of American Industries, 1947', mimeographed, Harvard Economic Research Project (June 1953), and Robert N. Grosse, *Capital Requirements for the Expansion of Industrial Capacity*, Vol. 1, Part 1, Executive Office of the President, Bureau of the Budget, Office of Statistical Standards (November 1953). Further revisions were made to the coefficients by Alan Strout and others in 1958–1962. Additional adjustments to make the 1947 capital coefficients comparable with the 1947 were made by Samuel A. Rea, Jr. and others (1966–1967) at the Harvard Economic Research Project.

1947 Labor coefficients

Same source as 1958 labor coefficients

1947 Final demand vectors

The final demand vectors are based on the Bureau of Labor Statistics 450-order input-output table and on Raymond W. Goldsmith, *op. cit.*

[9]

Economic Systems Research, Vol. 7, No. 3, 1995

Truncation and Spectrum of the Dynamic Inverse

A. BRÓDY

(Received January 1995; revised April 1995)

ABSTRACT *The possibility of negative elements and perplexing computational problems hinder the widespread and universal use of this powerful instrument. A different solution for the truncation is proposed here that remedies some of the ills. It is also shown that— exploiting the skew-symmetric form, first suggested by Goodwin—we may obtain an interesting and important spectral decomposition of the system matrix. This decomposition, existing already for the simplest, one sector, totally aggregated model, describes those cycles that may disturb the path of a growing economy.*

KEYWORDS: *Equilibrium, cycles, aggregation, spectrum*

1. Introduction

When Leontief (1970) presented economics with the powerful tool of the dynamic inverse, he thoroughly explained its basic economic idea and logical set-up, its fundamental structure and mathematical equations. Furthermore, he displayed a comprehensive computation for the US.

The set-up of the model is based on an endless, that is infinite, process, whereby the economic system, in any given year, besides catering for a final bill of goods, $\mathbf{y}$, produces all the required flow inputs and also expands its productive capacities, to render high production possible in the next year.

The basic equation therefore has been the well-known dynamic model of the economy, already introduced earlier by Leontief (1953, pp. 82–88), as

$$\mathbf{x}_k = \mathbf{y}_k + \mathbf{A}\mathbf{x}_k + \mathbf{B}(\mathbf{x}_{k+1} - \mathbf{x}_k) \tag{1}$$

It is well known that if the economy is productive, the maximal eigenvalue of $\mathbf{A}$ is less than 1, then the inverse $\mathbf{Q} = (\mathbf{I} - \mathbf{A})^{-1}$ exists. Applying it to equation (1), it

A. Bródy, Institute of Economics, PO Box 262, H-1502 Budapest, Hungary. Research sponsored by Academic Grant T013795. I am grateful for the painstaking editorial work and suggestions of E. Dietzenbacher. Items (1) and (2) in the appendix particularly benefited from his ideas.

0953-5314/95/030235-13

236   *A. Bródy*

may be transcribed into

$$\mathbf{x}_k = \mathbf{Q}\mathbf{y}_k + \mathbf{Q}\mathbf{B}(\mathbf{x}_{k+1} - \mathbf{x}_k) \tag{2}$$

Thus the theoretical equilibrium of a closed model (with $\mathbf{y} = 0$) or the requirements for a prescribed investment portfolio can be easily computed.

Nevertheless, it remained obscure, how a forecasted path of final bills, say $\mathbf{y}_t$, (with $t = k$, $k+1$, ...) may influence the required yearly outputs. Each new year brings a new equation of the form (1), but all of them are interlinked, because the same successive $\mathbf{x}$ vectors must appear in the neighbouring years. This question has been solved by forming the (theoretically doubly infinite) set-up for the consecutive years

$$\begin{pmatrix} \cdots & & & \\ & \mathbf{I} - \mathbf{A} + \mathbf{B} & -\mathbf{B} & \\ & & \mathbf{I} - \mathbf{A} + \mathbf{B} & -\mathbf{B} \\ & & & \mathbf{I} - \mathbf{A} + \mathbf{B} \\ & & & & \cdots \end{pmatrix} \begin{pmatrix} \cdots \\ \mathbf{x}_{k-1} \\ \mathbf{x}_k \\ \mathbf{x}_{k+1} \\ \cdots \end{pmatrix} = \begin{pmatrix} \cdots \\ \mathbf{y}_{k-1} \\ \mathbf{y}_k \\ \mathbf{y}_{k+1} \\ \cdots \end{pmatrix} \tag{3}$$

The existence, convergence and computation of the inverse of the above matrix has been repeatedly discussed. The original exposition developed the infinite series, repeated in every row (and column) of the inverse and shown in the appendix. It also exposed the theoretical possibility of this series to diverge and determined the critical point where the matrix $\mathbf{I} - \mathbf{A} + \mathbf{B}$, standing in the diagonal, becomes singular and renders computation impossible.

The problems emerging with such a doubly infinite matrix can be gleaned already from the following simplified argument. Let us imagine the above hypermatrix as consisting of scalar matrices. Then the vector of summation, that is the vector $\mathbf{e} = (\dots 1, 1, \dots, 1, \dots)$, which has infinitely many unit elements, can be instantly seen as an eigenvector of the matrix, belonging to the (scalar) eigenvalue $1 - A$ (the scalar B being cancelled). The inverse of the matrix, if it exists, must have the same eigenvector, belonging to the reciprocal eigenvalue Q (also a scalar). Expressed in another way, the rows (and columns) of the inverse must sum up to Q.

On the other hand, a vector of the proportions $(\dots 1, \lambda, \lambda^2, \dots, \lambda^n, \dots)$, where the growth rate λ is computed from equation (1), is again an eigenvector, belonging this time to the eigenvalue zero. But the existence of a zero eigenvalue implies singularity, thus the doubly infinite matrix defies inversion.

In spite of these perplexing considerations the actual computations behaved well. Later, Petri (1972) proved that, by changing the time period, even an existing singularity or divergence can be removed and does not endanger the computation. Thus, the singularity of the matrix can be remedied but cannot be excluded *ab ovo*.

Notwithstanding the encouraging experience, the existence of negative elements in the inverse remained perplexing. Again, no actual computation resulted in negative outputs. It was also proven, by various methods, that the sum of any row of the inverse must add up to Q (as shown above), and as we know for the latter matrix, the Leontief inverse is always intrinsically positive.

Still the theoretical purport of any and every negative element in the inverse entails a situation, where by producing judiciously less, the economy may enjoy a higher amount of final consumption. (Or, vice versa, the consuming more may curb the total production required.) Both instances run against common sense, indeed, against all our ingrained economic wisdom.

Our task is, then, to review this problem, find arguments, and if we have to accept it, to find improvements, if it hinges only on a specific and particular set-up of the actual computation.

2. About Truncation

Although in a strict theoretical sense, that is mathematically, we are able to discuss and handle infinite matrices, the computer always has but a limited memory. Thus, if we arrange for the actual computation, it will be only a finite segment of the matrix that may be squeezed into the computer. We have to truncate the infinite sequence of rows and columns, both at the initial starting postion (in the upper left-hand corner) and at the final ending position (in the lower right-hand corner) to furnish the machine with a square matrix for inversion. Of course, practical exigencies also act as constraints. Although theoretical correctness would request an infinite time series of the envisaged final bills, actual and/or planned, we may only furnish a severely shortened vector of 10–20 years, at best.

Much depends now on the actual shape of truncation. If we inspect the matrix $\mathbf{I}-\mathbf{A}+\mathbf{B}$, standing in the diagonal, we notice that its inverse, taken separately, contains, more often than not, negative elements. If we now, in addition, truncate the lower right-hand corner to

$$\begin{pmatrix} \mathbf{I}-\mathbf{A}+\mathbf{B} & -\mathbf{B} & & \\ & \mathbf{I}-\mathbf{A}+\mathbf{B} & -\mathbf{B} & \\ & & \mathbf{I}-\mathbf{A}+\mathbf{B} & -\mathbf{B} \\ & & & \mathbf{I}-\mathbf{A}+\mathbf{B} \end{pmatrix} \tag{4}$$

then further trouble is unavoidable. Why? The matrices $\mathbf{B}$, appearing with negative signs in the first upper parallel to the diagonal, are necessary inputs for the next years. They represent the capital invested into the respective capacities needed to perform all the varied operations going on in the diverse branches of the economy. In opposition to this, we notice the same matrix $\mathbf{B}$ on the diagonal, but now positively signed. This stamps the latter to an output of the year considered. This set-up is a theoretically unobjectionable way to handle the productive capital that remains in existence during a longer series of years. It has been pioneered by Neumann, exploited by Sraffa and widely used in economic activity analysis.

According to this approach, capital is just a special kind of 'joint product' of the given year and may be lumped together with the yearly flows. This entails certain unwanted consequences, because it is impossible to handle any year in isolation. The productivity of the system hinges now not only on the flow inputs and outputs of the given year but also on the 'jointly produced' capital. It also depends on the possible difference of capital inputs and outputs of the neighbouring years. Thus, great care is required to keep these artificial (not real—just imaged) capital 'flows' (inputs and outputs) together.

If we truncate the theoretically infinite matrix to a square and finite one, we inadvertently cut off, in the last year, the negatively signed one of the two intertwined $\mathbf{B}$s. This is the $\mathbf{B}$ that duly belongs to the next year, but is now chopped away and thus disregarded. As the $\mathbf{B}$s must always come up in pairs, one with a positive and one with a negative sign, they usually cancel. Now, with

238 *A. Bródy*

truncation, this cancellation is made impossible. That is the reason why a matrix like $I-A+B$, itself the result of a truncation, may have negative elements, if inverted. It is an incomplete part of the whole and therefore may become singular or misbehave, etc.

In the original equation (1), there was only one B, acted upon by the difference (usually growth) of x total production. It has been equation (3) that substituted this difference with two separate x values, to be multiplied by two separate (possibly different, because dateable) Bs. Then, we additionally committed murder (by truncation) on the negatively signed B, therefore the remaining positive B will make us pay dearly, for having to miss its twin.

It ruins (distorts downward) the computation of the required output. In the final year, a strange burst of 'output' is produced that, under normal circumstances, cannot be extracted from the system. This output, Bx, is nothing less than all the stock invested into the economy. It cannot be considered as a *bona fide* final output of the last year. Even if we decide to stop production (and all economic activity) at the end of the year, we will be unable to sell all that capital on the market (and certainly not in the same year).

Summing up, by applying this form of truncation, we obtain an answer to a question, correct in itself, but not the one we intended to ask. Our original question sought a path of total production that furnishes the prescribed final bill. It remains implied, but unstated, that we presume business continuing as usual in the next year. We did not want to kill the system and were quietly assured that it would go on also after the final year of our computation, or forecast.

Instead, with the truncation as illustrated, we receive a doomsday answer. It represents the outputs that are needed for the same final bill of goods, if after the final day, we disband the economic system, consume everything, and neither produce final bills, nor anything else ever after. This is an interesting computation in itself, and is much less absurd than its sharp wording would suggest.

If we plan investment, we must plan scrapping. Investment appraisal and the appraisal, whether an ongoing project should continue with its usual operations or should be disbanded, are two separate and disjunct questions. Our indicators, computed with the above truncation, help to answer the second question. (I live in a country where, during its structural adjustment, such sharp questions do occur fairly often, after being thoroughly neglected in the four decades of Soviet-type planning.)

But we wanted to answer the first, original and implied question. It certainly requires an answer, as a matter of fact it happens to be the basic question of forecasting. It therefore commands universal interest. I propose the following set-up for answering it. Let us truncate the lower right-hand corner in a different way. There are various possibilities for doing this and additional considerations will be set out in the appendix. Here we go for the simplest variant, rendering the explanation straightforward:

$$\begin{pmatrix} I-A+B & -B & & \\ & I-A+B & -B & \\ & & I-A+B & -B \\ & & & I-A \end{pmatrix} \tag{5}$$

The matrix $I-A$ in the lower right-hand corner is always regular, its inverse is Q and so produces a well-behaved sequence, where the respective rows all add up to

Q, as the theory requests. Nevertheless, we neglected the problem of investments in the last year. Thus, we possibly still undercorrected and relapsed into 'simple reproduction' in the not openly envisaged future, by cancelling all the flows required for further growth.

What to do then with the expansion requirements, needed to augment the capacities for the subsequent year (and not yet considered in the suggested set-up)? My simplest proposal is to add them to the final bill of the last year. This seems to be the easiest way out of the conundrum, and the only actual economic decision that has to be taken for the not explicitly considered future, during the span of the years to which the computation addresses itself. This is a very simple modification but does, indeed, alter both the results and their trends characteristically, as our subsequent numerical example will show.

3. Doom and Growth

By luck, a 5-year chain already exhibits the essence and regularity of both set-ups. For the sake of transparency, a one-sector model is displayed, with $\mathbf{A} = 0.8$, hence $(\mathbf{I} - \mathbf{A}) = 0.2$, $\mathbf{Q} = 5$ and $\mathbf{B} = 1.8$. The Doomsday inverse, according to equation (4), carries the elements 0.5 in the diagonal (the reciprocal of $\mathbf{I} - \mathbf{A} + \mathbf{B}$) and the successive cells in the columns will be multiplied always by 0.9 (which is equal to $\mathbf{B}$ times the diagonal element).

The doom matrix

$$
\begin{pmatrix}
2 & -1.8 & & & \\
 & 2 & -1.8 & & \\
 & & 2 & -1.8 & \\
 & & & 2 & -1.8 \\
 & & & & 2
\end{pmatrix}
$$

and its inverse

$$
\begin{pmatrix}
0.5 & 0.45 & 0.405 & 0.3646 & 0.32805 \\
 & 0.5 & 0.45 & 0.405 & 0.3645 \\
 & & 0.5 & 0.45 & 0.405 \\
 & & & 0.5 & 0.45 \\
 & & & & 0.5
\end{pmatrix}
$$

The matrix for normal growth, where in the last year only the usual flow requirements are met, is shown below, together with its inverse.

The growth matrix

$$
\begin{pmatrix}
2 & -1.8 & & & \\
 & 2 & -1.8 & & \\
 & & 2 & -1.8 & \\
 & & & 2 & -1.8 \\
 & & & & 0.2
\end{pmatrix}
$$

and its inverse

$$
\begin{pmatrix}
0.50 & 0.45 & 0.405 & 0.3646 & 3.2805 \\
 & 0.5 & 0.45 & 0.405 & 3.645 \\
 & & 0.5 & 0.45 & 4.05 \\
 & & & 0.5 & 4.5 \\
 & & & & 5
\end{pmatrix}
$$

As we see, the proposed modification affects only the last column of the inverse, in every other respect it remains the same. This is generally true, even in the case of a disaggregated, multi-sectoral model. (The question is relegated to the appendix.) The change, furthermore, does not affect the inner regularity and proportions of the last column and only works with a different multiple in the two cases.

The partial equality of the two matrices and the deviation of only the last column may lead to a second, seemingly much more sophisticated, proposition for solving the problem of truncation. The two systems are treacherously indiscernible up to the last column. Thus, it seems to be feasible to compute a solution and then disregard its results for this last period. That is, if you want to forecast to 2000,

240   *A. Bródy*

then compute up to 2001 and drop the last year. Yet such an answer would be thoroughly incorrect. It is no better than the ridiculous advice given—jokingly—to railwaymen: if the last carriage rocks and clanks, unhook it. All right, you unhook it, but then you have again a last carriage that will start rattling, so you have to unhook it too ... and so on. Finally, you are left with no train whatever.

We verify this by the following computations. The row sums (these are total outputs producing the final bill $y = [1\ 1\ 1\ 1\ 1]$) will be surprisingly low and shrinking [2.0476 1.7195 1.355 0.95 0.5] for the doom inverse. We can see the devolution starting from the first year onwards, production collapses with an increasing speed. For the proposed normal growth inverse the row sums add up to [5 5 5 5 5] as they really should, considering the value of the Leontief-inverse $Q = 5$.

Let us now further illustrate a simple sequence, where we want to satisfy an exponentially increasing final bill. To be close to equilibrium, we may chose a near equilibrium, yearly 10%, increase of the final bill. We then obtain the following data:

Final bill y	1.0	1.1	1.21	1.331	1.4641
Doom path	2.4505	2.1672	1.7969	1.3243	0.73205
Growth path	6.7732	6.9702	7.1336	7.2540	7.3205

I believe only the data of the last row may be accepted as a realistic solution to the usual problem. The withering doom path resembles more the paths which the former Eastern Bloc countries trace after shock therapy.

As can be seen, neither solution satisfies the steady-state growth equation exactly. Indeed, no finite segment of the system (and its inverse) will ever admit the 'true' equilibrium for a solution. It is only the infinite (and therefore, strictly speaking, not computable) model which allows us to reach (or even start and maintain) a theoretical and complete equilibrium. We may be very clever in determining and elucidating the path of abstract equilibrium but we can hardly find a working and finite economic mechanism which would make it come about.

It is therefore appropriate to turn to the question of how such a system may actually move around a never exactly observable, computable or feasible equilibrium growth path. It never will be found on it but, again, it seldom deviates more than a few percentage points. If we speak about a country that is maladjusted and in deep disarray, we usually mean an economy where the quantities seem to be 10–20% off from a situation which economists would consider satisfactory. Prices, rents and wages may perhaps diverge somewhat more. Still, for the mathematical mind, this all remains subsumed under the category of 'small' perturbations 'near' equilibrium.

4. Cycles and Equilibrium

Accepting the sad fact of a blindfolded economy where the exigencies of a perfect equilibrium can never be met, we may ask how the minor and major discrepancies do actually work out. Goodwin (1953) originally proposed a theoretically very fruitful approach for the closed static variant of the Leontief model. It has been based on the simple and robust argument of Adam Smith. Excess demand augments prices whereas excess profits lead to an increase of supply and this keeps the economic motion close to its equilibrium. The skew-symmetric model, built around the system matrix $(\mathbf{A} - \mathbf{I})$ and its transposed negative, did theoretically and qualitatively explain the cycle behaviour around equilibrium.

Alas, the computed eigenvalues, the spectrum of the system matrix, did not account well for the cycle lengths observed in economic life. The positive semi-definite matrix, $\mathbf{G}$ (it is a so-called Gram matrix), that allows the computation of the squared frequencies of oscillation is

$$\mathbf{G} = (\mathbf{I} - \mathbf{A})^{T}(\mathbf{I} - \mathbf{A}) = \mathbf{I} - \mathbf{A}^{T} - \mathbf{A} + \mathbf{A}^{T}\mathbf{A}$$

We know that a positive matrix $\mathbf{A}$ has a dominant positive eigenvalue. This must equal 1, to render self-replacement possible. All the other eigenvalues of the matrix $\mathbf{A}$ congregate around zero and will be the smaller and the more densely packed, the more sectors the matrix has. Thus, the spectrum of the matrix $\mathbf{G}$ contains a single zero, signalling equilibrium self-replacement. To this zero, there belongs the (only) positive eigenvectors of the equilibrium proportions of prices (from the left hand) and quantities (from the right hand). All the other remaining eigenvalues scatter fairly densely around 1, and will be assigned to eigenvectors that are not unsigned—the various components of the possible periodic fluctuations.

The set-up thus establishes a wealth of $2\pi/1$, which is roughly 6-year, cycles around equilibrium. Our old-time friends, the 4-year inventory cycle and the close-to-10-year investment cycle, moreover, all the suspected longer swings, are clearly missing. Nevertheless, this is an important model, explaining the observed fluctuation in a simple and theoretically unobjectionable way, after Kalecki's efforts at higher mathematics. The basic theory is sound and coherent, but the numerical results clearly lack realism.

My own exercise, 20 years later, in Bródy (1972), based on the same idea (with some variations toward a logarithmic set-up, also borrowed from Goodwin's later work on cycles) exploited the matrix of the closed dynamic model. The findings have been reported to the Fifth International Conference. The advance towards a more realistic spectrum of frequencies has been but very slight. This model did produce a greater assortment for the timing of the computed swings. Still the frequencies did not cover the whole domain, then already investigated by diligent time-series analysis. Some of the better known periodicities did emerge but all the computations depicted unacceptably and unbelievably smooth paths for the economy.

In possession of the infinite dynamic set-up, detailed above, we can perhaps do better now and investigate the actual sortment of economic cycles, the total spectrum of a theoretically infinite economic system. 'Infinite' here means, of course, only 'not limited in time' and does not suggest or assume anything about the number of sectors or actors or markets in the economy.

Let us therefore start from more realistic assumptions for the aggregated model. The net surplus produced by an average contemporary economy is roughly about 10% of its turnover. Capital intensity, that is the capital–output ratio, can invariably be found around 3 years. Both quantities do undergo a heavy fluctuation of, say, $\pm 30\%$, whether we inspect cross-country or time-series data. Wanting to determine only orders of magnitude, we may just as well start with averages and then try to ascertain the disturbances caused by the fluctuation of our benchmark data.

242   *A. Bródy*

Thus, we will set up the computation with a value for $\mathbf{C} = \mathbf{I} - \mathbf{A} = 0.1$ and for the stock matrix $\mathbf{B} = 3$. The matrix of equation (3) is now

$$
\mathbf{H} = \begin{pmatrix} \cdots & & & \\ & \mathbf{C}+\mathbf{B} & -\mathbf{B} & \\ & & \mathbf{C}+\mathbf{B} & -\mathbf{B} \\ & & & \mathbf{C}+\mathbf{B} \\ & & & \end{pmatrix} = \begin{pmatrix} \cdots & & & \\ & 3.1 & -3 & \\ & & 3.1 & -3 \\ & & & 3.1 \\ & & & \cdots \end{pmatrix} \tag{6}
$$

This matrix, of course, has all its eigenvalues equal to 3.1. But if multiplied by it transpose, to compute the Gram matrix which yields the required squared frequencies, we find a well-known and interesting matrix, a so-called chain. The latter consists of a positive (and dominant) diagonal bordered by two negative parallels. Such chains have been already considered and thoroughly investigated in geodetic work. A chain matrix is the 'pre-computable' part of all and any network of field measurements (see Bodewig, 1959, parts III.C. and IV.B.14.). The simple structure of chains rendered geodetic calculus feasible, even relatively fast, already before the advent of the electronic computer.

To obtain the general structure of the chain, we have to compute only two of its elements: the one on the diagonal, and an adjacent negative. They will be endlessly repeated in succession. The diagonal element will be always $\mathbf{D} = 2(\mathbf{B}^2 + \mathbf{CB}) + \mathbf{C}^2$ and all off-diagonal elements always $\mathbf{F} = (\mathbf{B}^2 + \mathbf{CB})$, with a negative sign.

$$
\mathbf{H}^\mathsf{T}\mathbf{H} = \begin{pmatrix} \cdots & -\mathbf{F} & & \\ \mathbf{D} & -\mathbf{F} & & \\ -\mathbf{F} & \mathbf{D} & -\mathbf{F} & \\ & -\mathbf{F} & \mathbf{D} & \\ & & -\mathbf{F} & \cdots \end{pmatrix} = \begin{pmatrix} \cdots & -9.3 & & \\ 18.61 & -9.3 & & \\ -9.3 & 18.61 & -9.3 & \\ & -9.3 & 18.61 & \\ & & -9.3 & \cdots \end{pmatrix} \tag{7}
$$

This very simple structure already allows us to assess the limits of the spectrum by inspection and describe the possible economic cycles implied in the general set-up.

The maximal eigenvalue cannot surpass the column sums of the absolute values of the elements, that is 37.21. This value is fairly insensitive to the differences through time and space, mentioned above. We may compute it as $4(\mathbf{B}^2 + \mathbf{CB}) + \mathbf{C}^2$. Its square root, $2\mathbf{B} + \mathbf{C}$, somewhat larger than $2\mathbf{B}$, gives rise to cycle periods of $T \approx 2\pi/6$, that is to cycles of roughly 1-year duration.

Thus, many cycles· (strictly speaking an infinite amount of them, at least in theory) will be around 1 year, with but minor discrepancies in their length. Approximately 1.5-year cycles would be generated by a capital intensity of 2. If the capital–output ratio happens to be around 4, then the length of these swings would scatter slightly around 10 months. This is somewhat disturbing and far from trivial, because one would expect the length of swings to increase with increasing capital intensity.

The minimal eigenvalue will be $\mathbf{C}^2$, the square of the profit margin, a fairly stable magnitude, yielded as the algebraic sum of all the columns. It will give rise to a cycle length equal to $T \approx 2\pi/\mathbf{C}$, that is 6.28/0.1, approximately 60 years with a tolerance of ± 18 years. This resembles the famed Kondratiev cycle. It is again embarrassing to observe that this economic cycle of the longest accepted duration is not connected to capital intensities. Here it came up as the child of the flow matrix. Between these two limits of 1 and 60 years, we will find quite a few, not too sharply determined, cycles. All eigenvalues are separate but packed more densely around the shortest cycles. (The appendix quotes an exact equation for computing all the cycles.)

Finally, the infinite form may admit the well-known theoretical equilibrium value, with its computed growth rate of $C/B = 0.1/3 = 0.0333$ (which happens to be close to the observed secular rate of growth in the developed countries). In this instance, the symmetric form may have an eigenvalue of its square, leading to a cycle around $2\pi/0.033 \approx 190$ years. In all the finite approximations computed longer and longer cycle lengths were found when increasing the size of the model. Still the maximal cycle length remained below 200 years. With the truncation, proposed above, the maximal length then tended to overshoot 200 years.

Thus, one cannot yet rigorously claim the theoretical existence of a 200-year cycle. Both its possibility and presumed order of magnitude should be taken only as a first and hesitant conjecture. There are also the other disturbing interrelations, reported above, that cast a certain shadow on the findings, as described. But perhaps they still call attention to a field of possible research helpful in understanding those macro-relations that are anchored to the basic orders of magnitudes of the economic systems and are well reflected in all the input–ouput tabulations.

As a final point, I exhibit a time series that has been constructed in the following way. Starting from a 100×100 system, set up according to equation (6), all its frequencies have been computed. (The cycle lengths are again to be found in the appendix.) Then a time series is constructed by summing all the component cycles with unit amplitude, starting from the year zero. In Figure 1, the slice for the 'years' from 1900 to 2000 is presented.

I do not think this trajectory of virtual GDP resembles the path of any actual economy in the twentieth century. Nevertheless the trajectory does exhibit the usual shape of an economic time series in a general way. It is unsmoothed, jagged, unfathomable and probably not very predictable when its preparation is not known. And even if known, in a general way, there seems to be no way to estimate more than 5–10 coefficients (and wavelengths) from a 100-year sample. The

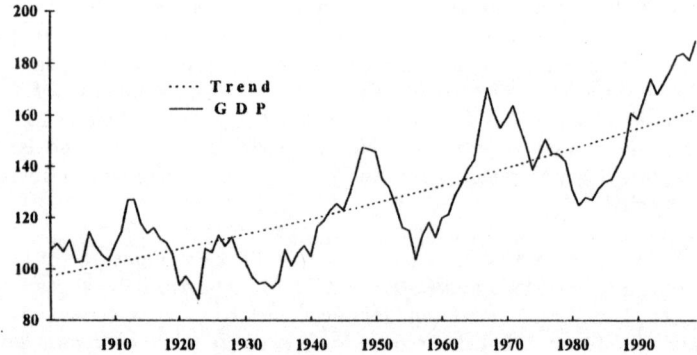

Figure 1. The 'years' 1900–2000.

244   A. Bródy

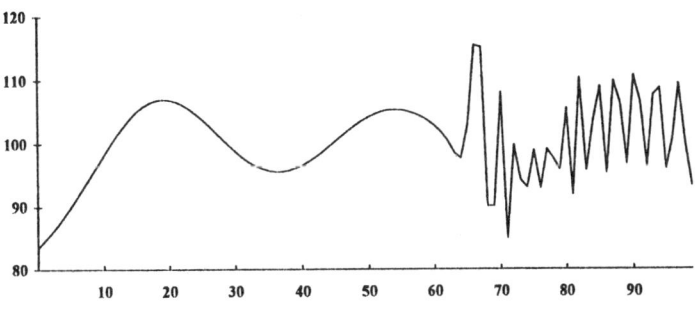

Figure 2. The first 100 'years'.

thoroughly unreliable and fake 'trend' is depicted as a teaser. The series is stationary and cannot have any trend.

Here, we have then a very simple system, neither chaotic, nor random. Seemingly an easy textbook exercise in all its constituent parts. The basic simplicity is complicated and marred only by the multiplicity of cycles. The number of distinct (but close) cycles happens to be very large in relation to the number of observations we have at our disposal. And I found no method yet to separate this exhibit from the path of a Brownian motion, a white noise or a chaotic attractor.

To emphasize how surprising the trajectory of such a system may be, Figure 2 shows the first 100 'years', where the simultaneous start of all the cycles produces a smooth path, for a while. This smoothness then suddenly disappears to give way to violent oscillations.

All this bewildering motion is strictly periodic. The above trajectories must certainly reappear after a while, once the starting point of all the cycles again meet. A strict return is secured only if the cycle lengths can be expressed in rational numbers. But even for irrational lengths, an approximate return with any predetermined accuracy, will take a finite time. Yet all returns, even an only very roughly approximate return will require a time span that, already for a finite, 100-sector model, may outlast the practical lifetime of the universe.

If now the above considerations are accepted, then we may have to modify the old economic wisdom of separating the growth paths into a trend, a cyclic and a random component. Cycles and random shocks are indiscernible in the above model and segments of a possible 200-year cycle may perhaps explain some of the phenomena, usually attributed to growth, or trend or drift.

In a later publication, I plan to return to the intriguing question of a singular or divergent system matrix of the form of equation (3), and also to the actual market movement around equilibrium and how this motion may be, at least theoretically, improved or made convergent.

References

Bodewig, E. (1959) *Matrix Calculus* (Amsterdam, North-Holland).

Bródy, A. (1972) An input–output model for the market, in: A. Brody & A. P. Carter (eds) *Input–Output Techniques* (Amsterdam, North-Holland), pp. 574–581.

Goodwin, R. (1953) Static and dynamic linear general equilibrium models, in: *Input–Output Relations, Proceedings of a Conference on Inter-Industrial Relations, Driebergen, Holland* (Leiden, Stenfert Kroese), pp. 54–87.

Leontief, W. W. (1953) Dynamic analysis, in: W. W. Leontief *et al.* (eds) *Studies in the Structure of the American Economy* (Oxford, Oxford University Press), pp. 53–90.

Leontief, W. W. (1970) The dynamic inverse, in: A. P. Carter & A. Bródy (eds) *Contributions to Input–Output Analysis* (Amsterdam, North-Holland), pp. 17–46.

Petri, P. (1972) Convergence and temporal structure in the Leontief dynamic model, in: A. Bródy & A. P. Carter (eds) *Input–Output Techniques* (Amsterdam, North-Holland), pp. 563–573.

Appendix

(1) Change in the inverse. According to the formulae of Sherman-Morisson and Bartlett (see Bodewig, 1959, pp. 38–41), if $A^{-1} = R$ and the element in the lower right-hand corner of matrix A is decreased by the amount d, then the inverse R will increase by a multiple β of the simple diad $R_{.n}R_{n.}$, formed from the last row and last column of the inverse.

As in our case the nth row of the inverse is empty, save its last element, only the last column of the inverse will change into another multiple of the former column.

The equation for β is given as $\beta = d/(1 - dr_{nn})$. Here r_{nn} stands for the lower right-hand corner element of the inverse. Thus, a multiple $r_{nn}d/(1 - dr_{nn})$ of the last row must be added to the last row. We decreased the original matrix by 1.8 and the corner element of the inverse has been 0.5, thus a multiple $0.9/(1 - 0.9) = 9$ of the original column must be added, making the last column tenfold its previous value.

The formula process remains correct also if the scalars are generalized to square matrices. See Bodewig (1959, I.3.14), and the Frobenius–Schur relation.

If we now return to the matrices of equation (4) and (5), we may compute the correct inverses by defining $R = (I - A + B)^{-1}$. If this inverse exists, then the doom matrix

$$
\begin{pmatrix}
I-A+B & -B & & \\
& I-A+B & -B & \\
& & I-A+B & -B \\
& & & I-A+B
\end{pmatrix}
\tag{4}
$$

has the inverse

$$
\begin{pmatrix}
R & RBR & (RB)^2R & (RB)^3R \\
& R & RBR & (RB)^2R \\
& & R & RBR \\
& & & R
\end{pmatrix}
\tag{4'}
$$

The growth matrix

$$
\begin{pmatrix}
I-A+B & -B & & \\
& I-A+B & -B & \\
& & I-A+B & -B \\
& & & I-A
\end{pmatrix}
\tag{5}
$$

246   *A. Bródy*

has the inverse

$$
\begin{pmatrix}
\mathbf{R} & \mathbf{RBR} & (\mathbf{RB})^2\mathbf{R} & (\mathbf{RB})^3\mathbf{Q} \\
 & \mathbf{R} & \mathbf{RBR} & (\mathbf{RB})^2\mathbf{Q} \\
 & & \mathbf{R} & \mathbf{RBQ} \\
 & & & \mathbf{Q}
\end{pmatrix}
\tag{5'}
$$

Both inverses can be checked by direct multiplication.

Now the hypermatrix (5) has a hypereigenvector of unit matrices $[\mathbf{I}\ \mathbf{I}\ \mathbf{I}\ \mathbf{I}]^T$, (the transposition is needed to make it a column hypervector). This belongs to the hypereigenvalue $\mathbf{I} - \mathbf{A}$. Therefore, its inverse must have its row sums equal to the reciprocal hypereigenvalue, that is $\mathbf{Q}$.

This exposition alerts us to the fact, that the truncation has to be addressed in a different way, if we compute prices.

(2) Variants of truncation. Let us consider a finite time horizon, extending from the period 1 to T. Then we may define two problems:

- *Doom scenario*: Determine that path of x from 1 to T that secures prescribed final outputs y, also for 1 to T, with $x_{T+1} = 0$.
- *Growth scenario*: Determine that path for x from 1 to T, that secures prescribed final outputs y, also for 1 to T, with $x_{T+1} = x_T$.

These two scenarios may be now expressed mathematically in a single but more general scenario by stipulating $x_{T+1} = \rho x_{T_1}$. This means that ρ is an arbitrary magnitude in the interval $[0, 1]$. $\rho = 0$ is equivalent to the doom scenario, $\rho = 1$ to the growth scenario, but it can assume any value in between. It may be interesting to investigate what happens if we try to push ρ over 1. The equilibrium growth rate, with $\rho > 1$, can be almost surely achieved. But how does this influence the computation and what sensible limits will be met in our effort to increase the size of ρ!

This argument instantly proves the underestimation by the inverse exhibited in equation (5´), mentioned in the main text.

(3) Eigenvalues of the chain $H^T H$. Bodevig (1959, p. 241) exhibited the eigenvalues of a general geodetic chain, designated here by $\Omega_n(2)$. The latter is an $n \times n$ chain with $+2$ in the diagonal and -1 in the upper and lower parallels. Its eigenvalues are set out in his equation (14.3a), and are

$$
\lambda = 4 \sin^2\{\pi m/(2n+2)\}, \qquad \text{for } m = 1, 2, \dots, n
$$

With n tending toward infinity, the series of computed values will be found in the interval extending from $4 \sin^2(0)$ to $4 \sin^2(\pi/2)$, that is from 0 to 4.

Our matrix $\mathbf{H}^T\mathbf{H}$ of equation (7) is identical to the same chain $\Omega_n(2)$, multiplied by $(\mathbf{B}^2 + \mathbf{CB})$, and with $\mathbf{C}^2$ added in the diagonal, that is $0.01\mathbf{E} + 9.3\Omega_n(2)$. (Here we designated the unit matrix by $\mathbf{E}$ instead of $\mathbf{I}$, to avoid confusion.)

Its eigenvalues therefore will cover the interval 0.01 to 37.21, as could be already inferred by inspecting the elements standing in an arbitrary column.

(4) Cycle lengths. The following data list the 100 cycle lengths, in years, of the chain discussed above and computed to four decimal digits. The matrix has been

Truncation and Spectrum of the Dynamic Inverse   247

set out in equation (7). The lower right-hand corner element has been reduced to 0.1.

251.1100	3.3289	1.7519	1.2731	1.0830
45.2600	3.1762	1.7151	1.2589	1.0777
29.0270	3.0376	1.6802	1.2453	1.0726
20.6340	2.9112	1.6471	1.2323	1.0679
15.8650	2.7956	1.6156	1.2199	1.0634
12.8470	2.6895	1.5857	1.2080	10593
10.7810	2.5917	1.5573	1.1966	1.0554
9.2829	2.5013	1.5302	1.1858	1.0519
8.1487	2.4177	1.5045	1.1754	1.0486
7.2614	2.3400	1.4799	1.1655	1.0456
6.5488	2.2676	1.4565	1.1560	1.0429
5.9643	2.2002	1.4341	1.1470	1.0404
5.4764	2.1371	1.4128	1.1383	1.0382
5.0632	2.0781	1.3925	1.1301	1.0363
4.7089	2.0227	1.3730	1.1223	1.0346
4.4018	1.9706	1.3544	1.1149	1.0332
4.1332	1.9217	1.3367	1.1078	1.0321
3.8964	1.8755	1.3197	1.1011	1.0312
3.6860	1.8320	1.3035	1.0947	1.0305
3.4980	1.7908	1.2879	1.0887	1.0302

[10]

INTERNATIONAL ECONOMIC REVIEW
Vol. 13, No. 2, June, 1972

RELATIVE STABILITY IN TWO TYPES OF DYNAMIC LEONTIEF MODELS*

BY K. TOKOYAMA AND Y. MURAKAMI[1]

1. ECONOMISTS ARE NOW FAMILIAR with Leontief's dynamic model

(1) $$[I - A]X(t) = B[X(t + 1) - X(t)]$$

where A is an input-output matrix, B is a stock-flow matrix and $X(t)$ is a vector of outputs in period t.[2]

R. Solow [3] clarified a stability condition of this system: The system (1) is relatively stable if and only if all the characteristic roots of $B^{-1}(I - A)$, other than the positive smallest root ρ_F, lie inside[3] a circle with the radius $1 + \rho_F$ centered at $(-1, 0)$ as shown in Figure 1-A. We may call the interior of this circle the relative stability zone of system (1).

A calculation making use of empirical data for Japan indicates that the system (1) is unstable;[4] that is, there exists at least one root outside the relative stability zone. Nevertheless, the actual Japanese economy seems to have clung to its balanced growth path for many years.

2. There is no doubt that the left-hand side of the equation (1) represents

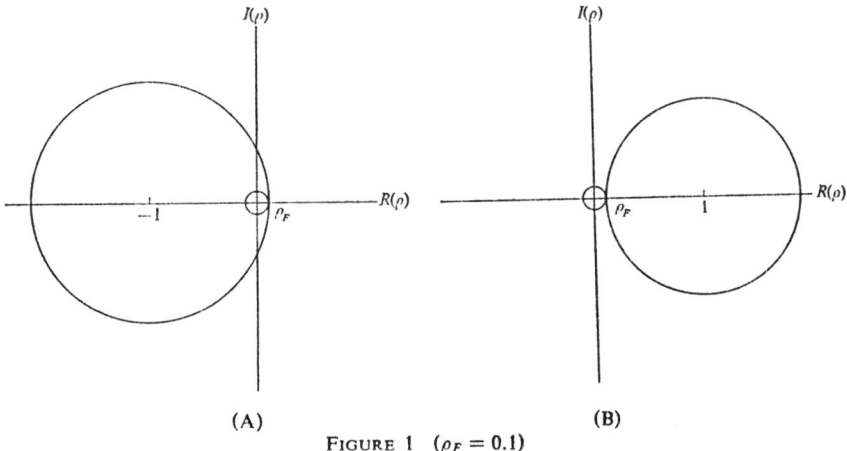

(A)   (B)

FIGURE 1 $(\rho_F = 0.1)$

* Manuscript received November 20, 1970; revised November 4, 1971.

[1] The authors are grateful to the members of the Tokyo Center for Economic Research, particularly, to Professors K. Inada and J. Tsukui. This work is partly sponsored by the Tokyo Center for Economic Research.

[2] As usual, we assume that A is indecomposable and satisfies the Hawkins-Simon condition, and that B is nonsingular.

[3] For convenience of presentation, we assume that there exists no other root than ρ_F on the boundary of stability zone and every root is simple.

[4] See Tsukui [4] or Murakami, Tokoyama and Tsukui [2].

current net output. On the other hand, there may be alternatives on the meanings of the right-hand side. If we assume that the right-hand term literally
stands for investment necessary for a future increase in output, then the equation (1) represents a planning model for dynamic allocation of resources rather
than a descriptive model explaining actual economy. In order to use the system
(1) as a descriptive model, we must replace $X(t + 1)$ by anticipated output
$X^*(t + 1)$ and introduce some additional assumption concerning expectations.

Expectations will, in general, be based on past actual changes in outputs.
Assuming linearity in this relation, we have an expectation function

$$X^*(t + 1) - X(t) = \sum_{i=1}^{T} A_i[X(t + 1 - i) - X(t - i)],$$

where A_i is an expectation matrix. Substituting this equation into (1), we get
a descriptive model

(I) $$[I - A]X(t) = \sum_{i=1}^{T} B_i[X(t + 1 - i) - X(t - i)],$$

where $B_i = BA_i$. We call this a backward-lag-type dynamic Leontief model.

In contrast with this backward-lag-type model, we may consider a generalization of the planning model. If the time lag of investment gestation is really
one period for every commodity, the system (1) may be thought of as an appropriate planning model. However, a gestation lag may not be confined to
one production period for some commodities. Moreover, lags may be different
from industry to industry. By incorporating these possibilities, the dynamic
Leontief model may be extended as follows:

(II) $$[I - A]X(t) = \sum_{i=1}^{T} B_i[X(t + i) - X(t - 1 + i)],$$

where B_i is a stock-flow matrix for those capitals which requires i periods for
their full gestation. We call this a forward-lag-type dynamic Leontief model.

3. For a special case of the backward-lag-type model, we can easily derive
a stability zone in a way similar to that used for model (1). If B_i is zero for
$i \neq 1$ in (I), we have

(2) $$[I - A]X(t) = B_1[X(t) - X(t - 1)].$$

In this case, the relative stability zone is the outside of a circle with the radius
$1 - \rho_F$ centered at $(1, 0)$ as shown in Figure 1-B. This case presents a striking
contrast to the case studied by Solow. Namely, as a model is turned from a
forward-type to a backward-type, the relative stability zone is inverted inside
out. Consequently, a descriptive model seems likely to be stable even when a
planning model is unstable. Our empirical data, in fact, bring out the stability
of the system (2), as against the instability of the system (1).

Our primary aim is to investigate whether this contrast persists in extended
cases.

4. The general cases (I) and (II) are complicated for formal analysis. As a

410   K. TOKOYAMA AND Y. MURAKAMI

first approximation to the general cases, we shall analyze the following simple extensions:

(3) $[I - A]X(t) = \lambda_1 B[X(t + 2) - X(t + 1)] + \lambda_2 B[X(t + 1) - X(t)],$

(4) $[I - A]X(t) = \lambda_1 B[X(t) - X(t - 1)] + \lambda_2 B[X(t - 1) - X(t - 2)],$

where $\lambda_1 + \lambda_2 = 1$[5] and $\lambda_i \geq 0$.

Equation (3) means that some part—$100\lambda_1$ percent—of a capital increment technically requires two production periods as a gestation lag, while the rest requires only one period.[6] Equation (4), on the other hand, states that the anticipated increase in output is a weighted average of the actual increases in outputs in the past two periods.[7]

We have the following propositions as to the existence of a balanced growth path and the stability of these models.

PROPOSITION 1-A. *The forward-lag-type dynamic Leontief model* (3) *has a unique balanced growth path which is identical with that of the ordinary model* (1). *The balanced growth factor* ν_F *is uniquely determined by* λ_i *and* ρ_F. ν_F *is greater than 1.*

PROPOSITION 1-B. *The backward-lag-type dynamic Leontief model* (4) *has a unique balanced growth path which is identical with that of the ordinary model* (1), *if and only if*[8]

either $\lambda_1 \geq 1 - 1/4\rho_F$ *in the case where* $\rho_F < 1/2$,

or $\lambda_1 > \rho_F$ *in the case where* $\rho_F \geq 1/2$.

If $\lambda_1 \geq \rho_F$, *the balanced growth factor* ξ_F *is uniquely determined by* λ_i *and* ρ_F, *while, if* $\lambda_1 < \rho_F$, *it depends not only on these parameters, but also on initial conditions.*[9] ξ_F *is greater than 1.*[10]

PROPOSITION 2-A. *The forward-lag-type dynamic Leontief model* (3) *is relatively stable, if and only if*

$$\lambda_1 \geq 1/2$$

[5] The condition $\lambda_1 + \lambda_2 = 1$ is not essential, because if $\lambda_1 + \lambda_2 \neq 1$, we can define B^* as $(\lambda_1 + \lambda_2)B$ to normalize λ_i.
[6] We may also consider another extension:
$$[I - A]X(t) = \lambda_1 B[X(t + 1) - X(t)] + \lambda_2 B[X(t) - X(t - 1)].$$
The treatment of system (3) is applicable to this case.
[7] The expectations are conservative. A series of expected outputs is determined by the difference equation $\Delta X^*(t) = \lambda_1 \Delta X^*(t - 1) + \lambda_2 \Delta X^*(t - 2)$, where steady growth is possible if and only if $\lambda_1 > 1$. Hence, the condition $\lambda_1 + \lambda_2 = 1$ means that future outputs are expected to fall into stagnation or show oscillation.
[8] In an actual economy, the existence condition seems to be satisfied, since usually $1 - 1/4\rho_F < 0$. ρ_F, in fact, is unlikely to exceed 0.25 as a maximal rate of economic growth per year. If we choose, as a unit of production period, more than one physical year, ρ_F may be over 0.25. In this case, however, more weight would be assigned to a current period in generating expectations, so that λ_1 would be larger and again the condition would be satisfied.
[9] ξ_F converges to a commom value independent of initial conditions as time elapses.
[10] We note that $\xi_F > 1$ even if $\lambda_1 < 1$; that is, actual economy is able to grow steadily at a positive rate even when expectations are so conservative that stagnations are foreseen.

DYNAMIC LEONTIEF MODELS 411

and all the characteristic roots of $B^{-1}(I - A)$ other than ρ_F lie inside[11] the quasi-cardioid G:

$$\left[R(\rho) + \frac{1}{4\lambda_1} \right]^2 + I(\rho)^2$$

$$= \left[\lambda_1 \nu_F^2 + \frac{\lambda_2 - \lambda_1}{4\lambda_1} \sqrt{4(2\nu_F^2 - 1)\lambda_1^2 + 4(2R(\rho) + 1)\lambda_1 + 1} \right]^2,[12]$$

where $R(\rho)$ and $I(\rho)$ are the real coordinate and the imaginary coordinate on a complex plane, respectively.

PROPOSITION 2-B. *The backward-lag-type dynamic Leontief model* (4) *is relatively stable if and only if*

$$\lambda_1 \leqq \rho_F \quad \text{for} \quad \lambda_1 < 1/2 \quad \text{or} \quad \lambda_1 > \rho_F \quad \text{for} \quad \lambda_1 \geqq 1/2$$

and all the characteristic roots of $B^{-1}(I - A)$ other than ρ_F lie outside[11] the quasi-cardioid G*:

$$\left[R(\rho) - \frac{1}{4\lambda_2} \right]^2 + I(\rho)^2$$

$$= \left[\lambda_2 \xi_F^{-2} + \frac{\lambda_1 - \lambda_2}{4\lambda_2} \sqrt{4(2\xi_F^{-2} + 1)\lambda_2^2 - 4(2R(\rho) + 1)\lambda_2 + 1} \right]^2.[13]$$

5. Relative stability zones for these two cases are shown in Figure 2. These extended cases also give evidence that the relative stability zone is inverted inside out and outside in, as a model is converted from a planning to a descrip-

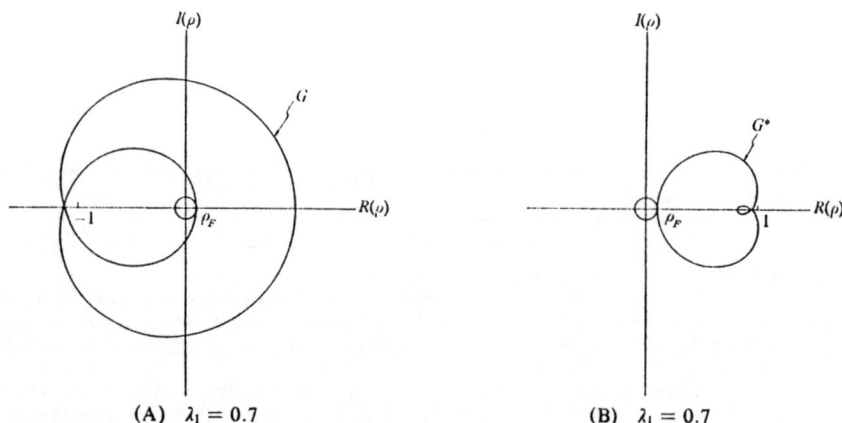

(A) $\lambda_1 = 0.7$ (B) $\lambda_1 = 0.7$

FIGURE 2 $(\rho_F = 0.1)$

[11] Sometimes, quasi-cardioid has two loops. "Inside" here means "inside an inner loop," while "outside" means "outside an outer loop." See Appendix.
[12] $\lambda_1 \neq 0$. If $\lambda_1 = 0$, the system (3) is reduced to (1).
[13] $\lambda_2 \neq 0$. If $\lambda_2 = 0$, the system (4) is reduced to (2).

412   K. TOKOYAMA AND Y. MURAKAMI

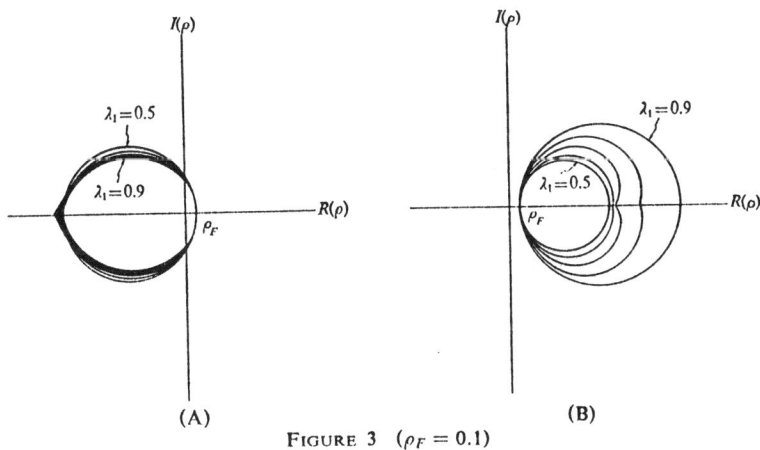

FIGURE 3 ($\rho_F = 0.1$)

tive type. The logical relation between the stability properties of these models is not fully clear-cut because of the existence of that region of λ_l where a model is unstable regardless of the distribution of characteristic roots. However, if λ_l is chosen so as not to fall into this region, then a descriptive model is much more likely to be relatively stable than a planning model, and if a planning model is stable, a descriptive one is necessarily so.

A change of lag parameter λ_l seems to have little effect upon the stability zone of model (3): and a delay of lag strengthens stability in the model (4), except when λ_l fall into the instability region, as shown in Figure 3. Therefore, without reversing the stability property, we can, for practical purposes, extend the first order difference systems to second order ones.[14]

Harvard University, U.S.A.
University of Tokyo, Japan

APPENDIX

PROOF OF PROPOSITION 1-B[15]. Rewrite (4) as

$$(\lambda_1 I - D^{-1})X(t) - (\lambda_1 - \lambda_2)X(t-1) - \lambda_2 X(t-2) = 0,$$

where $D = (I - A)^{-1}B$. From this, the characteristic equation of system (4) is

(A-1) $|[\lambda_1 \xi^2 - (\lambda_1 - \lambda_2)\xi - \lambda_2]I - \xi^2 D^{-1}| = 0,$

where ξ is a characteristic root of system (4). The equation $(A$-1) implies that the set of characteristic vectors of system (4) completely coincides with that of system (1) and, moreover, the relation

(A-2) $(\lambda_1 - \rho)\xi^2 - (\lambda_1 - \lambda_2)\xi - \lambda_2 = 0$

[14] See Eckaus and Parikh [1].
[15] We can prove proposition 1-A in a similar manner.

holds, where ρ is a characteristic root of D^{-1}. Therefore, the unique positive characteristic vector $X_F{}^{16}$ associated with the Frobenius root of D also gives the unique balanced growth path of the system (4), if and only if the equation $(\lambda_1 - \rho_F)\xi^2 - (\lambda_1 - \lambda_2)\xi - \lambda_2 = 0$ has a positive root.

If $\lambda_1 = \rho_F$, the equation has a real root, except when $\rho_F = 1/2$; if $\lambda_1 \neq \rho_F$, it has two real roots $(\xi_F' \geqq \xi_F'')$ when $1/4\lambda_2 \geqq \rho_F$. Then $\xi_F'\xi_F'' \gtrless 0$ iff $\rho_F \gtrless \lambda_1$; and if $\rho_F > \lambda_1$, $\xi_F' + \xi_F'' \lessgtr 0$ iff $\lambda_1 \gtrless 1/2$ and vice versa. From these, the first half of the proposition follows.

ξ_F' and ξ_F'' depend only upon ρ_F and λ_i. If $\lambda_1 > \rho_F$, ξ_F' is the only positive root which, in turn, gives the unique balanced growth factor ξ_F. If $\lambda_1 < \rho_F$, ξ_F'' is also positive so that ξ_F is given by the equation $[\xi_F' + c(\xi_F''/\xi_F')'\xi_F'']/[1 + c(\xi_F''/\xi_F')']$, where c is determined by initial conditions. In this case, ξ_F converges to ξ_F', since $\xi_F'' \leqq \xi_F'$. If $\lambda_1 = \rho_F < 1/2$, ξ_F is $(1 - \rho_F)/(1 - 2\rho_F)$.

The last assertion follows from a simple calculation.   Q.E.D.

PROOF OF PROPOSITION 2-A. The characteristic equation of system (3) is

(A-3) $|[\lambda_1\nu^2 - (\lambda_1 - \lambda_2)\nu - \lambda_2]I - D^{-1}| = 0$.

Its general solution can be expressed as $\Sigma(c_i'\nu_i'^t + c_i''\nu_i''^t)X_i$, where ν_i' and ν_i'' are roots of (A-3), X_i is a characteristic vector of D, and c_i' and c_i'' are determined by initial conditions. The balanced growth factor ν_F is given by the positive root ν_F' of (A-3) with which X_F is associated. Hence, the system (3) is relatively stable if and only if all the roots of (A-3) other than ν_F' are less than ν_F in modulus; that is, geometrically all the other roots lie in the interior of a circle C with the radius ν_F centered at origin.

From (A-3), we have

(A-4) $$\rho = \lambda_1\left(\nu + \frac{\lambda_2 - \lambda_1}{2\lambda_1}\right)^2 - \frac{1}{4\lambda_1} \ .$$

By this mapping, we transform the circled domain (the interior of C) on the ν-complex plane into a domain on the ρ-complex plane, which we call the relative stability zone of system (3).

LEMMA. *A complex function $w = (z + a)^2$ where a is real, transforms a circle $R(z)^2 + I(z)^2 = r^2$ on the z-plane into a closed curve on the w-plane whose equation is*

(A-5) $R(w)^2 + I(w)^2 = [r^2 + a\sqrt{2(r^2 + R(w))} - a^2]^2$,

or, in polar coordinate,

(A-6) $s^2 - 2(a^2\cos\theta + r^2)s + (r^2 - a^2)^2 = 0$,

where $R(w) = s\cos\theta$ and $I(w) = s\sin\theta$.

---

[16] The existence and the uniqueness of X_F are assured by the assumptions concerning D. See footnote 2) on p. 408.

414   K. TOKOYAMA AND Y. MURAKAMI

PROOF. From the complex function,

$$R(w) = R(z)^2 - I(z)^2 + 2aR(z) + a^2,$$
$$I(w) = 2I(z)(R(z) + a),$$
$$R(z)^2 + I(z)^2 = r^2.$$

Eliminating $R(z)$ and $I(z)$ from these equations, we have (A-5).   Q.E.D.

Figure A shows the image of circles for some parameters: (a) $|a| = 0.3$, $r = 0.2$ (b) $|a| = r = 0.3$ (c) $|a| = 0.3, r = 0.5$. If $r > |a|$, the image consists of two loops which we call an inner loop and an outer loop, respectively; but if $r < |a|$, it has only single loop. If $r = |a|$, (A-6) is reduced to $s = 2a^2(\cos\theta + 1)$; that is, the image becomes cardioid. We generally call such an image quasi-cardioid.

It is to be noted that: (i) $\partial s_1/\partial r > 0$ for all $r > 0$ and $\partial s_2/\partial r \gtreqqless 0$ iff $r \gtreqqless |a|$;[17] (ii) (A-6) continuously converges to $s = a^2$, as $r \to 0$, where $s_i(s_1 > s_2)$ are roots of (A-6).

Now, from the Lemma, the circle C is transformed by (A-4) into the quasi-cardioid G in the ρ-plane. Confine attention to the case where $\lambda_1 \geqq 1/2$, for otherwise the negative root ν_F'' with which X_F is associated is larger than $\nu_F'(=\nu_F)$ in modulus; that is, the system (3) is unstable. Then, $\nu_F > |(\lambda_2 - \lambda_1)/2\lambda_1|$. Hence, the quasi-cardioid G has two loops.

From properties (i) and (ii), the interior of the inner loop is the image of the circled domain, i.e., the relative stability zone of system (3). First, no point in the interior corresponds to points on the outside of C, because, as the circle expands from C, both the inner and outer loops of its image expand, since the

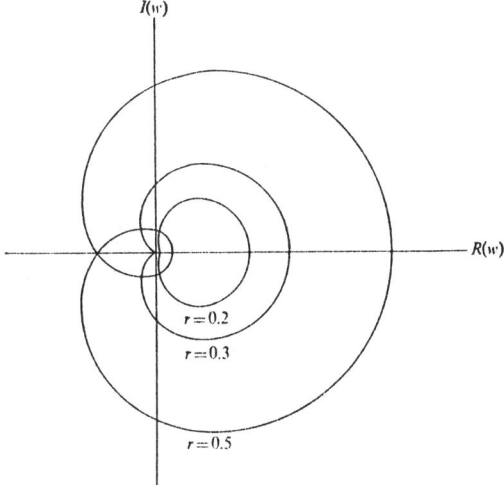

FIGURE A   ($|a| = 0.3$)

[17] $\partial s_i/\partial r = 2r[1 \pm \sqrt{a^2(\cos\theta + 1)} / \sqrt{a^2(\cos\theta - 1) + 2r^2}].$

radius of the expanding circle is greater than ν_F and, *a fortiori*, $|(\lambda_2 - \lambda_1)/2\lambda_1|$, so that $\partial s_i/\partial r > 0$ $(i = 1, 2)$. Second, any point in the interior corresponds to some point in the inside of C, because, as the circle contracts to the origin, its image continuously contracts to a point $(\lambda_1 - 1, 0)$ belonging to the interior.

Q.E.D.

PROOF OF PROPOSITION 2-B. The equation (A-2) defines the mapping which transforms the circle C^* with the radius ξ_F. This mapping can be regarded as a composed mapping:

(A-7a) $$\eta = 1/\xi \, ,$$

(A-7b) $$\rho = -\lambda_2\left(\eta + \frac{\lambda_1 - \lambda_2}{2\lambda_2}\right)^2 + \frac{1}{4\lambda_2} \, .$$

Hence, the image of C^* is the quasi-cardioid G^*. However, the stability zone of system (4) is the exterior of G^*, for (A-7a) transforms the interior of C^* into the exterior of a circle with the radius $1/\xi_F$.   Q.E.D.

REFERENCES

[1] ECKAUS, R. S. AND K. S. PARIKH, *Planning for Growth* (Cambridge: MIT Press, 1968).
[2] MURAKAMI, Y., K. TOKOYAMA AND J. TSUKUI, "Efficient Paths of Accumulation and the Turnpike of the Japanese Economy," in A. P. Carter and A. Brody eds., *Input-Output Techniques*, Vol. II of Applications to Input-Output Analysis (Amsterdam: North-Holland Publishing Company, 1970).
[3] SOLOW, R. M., "Competitive Valuation in a Dynamic Input-Output Systems," *Econometrica*, XXVII (January, 1959), 30–53.
[4] TSUKUI, J., "Application of a Turnpike Theorem to Planning for Efficient Accumulation: An Example for Japan," *Econometrica*, XXXVI (January, 1968), 172–186.

[11]

WHY SINGULARITY OF DYNAMIC LEONTIEF SYSTEMS DOESN'T MATTER

Ulrich Meyer

1. Introduction

A dynamic Leontief system is a dynamic input-output model described by

$$X(t) = AX(t) + B\Delta X(t) + Y(t) \tag{1}$$

In (1), X(t) is the vector of gross output for the n sectors of an economy in period t, Y(t) is the vector of final demand (excluding net investment) assumed to be exogenously given for every period throughout the paper, A and B are the nonnegative matrices of input-output respectively capital coefficients, and finally it is

$$\Delta X(t) = X(t + 1) - X(t).^1$$

If matrix B is nonsingular, the system (1) of difference equations is soluble for X(t + 1):

$$X(t + 1) = (I + B^{-1} (I - A)) X(t) - B^{-1} Y(t). \tag{2}$$

This forward recursive form shows that for any given inivital value X(0) there exists one and only one solution of (1) and further that the general solution is to be described with the aid of the eigenvalues and eigenvectors of $I + B^{-1} (I - A)$.

Unfortunately in empirical applications, the nonsingularity of B almost never holds. The most important reason for this fact is that there are some sectors which don't produce investment goods so that B contains some rows of zeros.[2] In such cases it is impossible to transform the system of difference equations (1) into its explicit form (2). Therefore the following questions arise:

— Do solutions of (1) exist at all?
— Does a solution of (1) exist for a given initial value?
— How is the general solution of (1) to be described?
— Do nonnegative solutions of (1) exist?

The present literature of the problem[3] provides answers mainly to the first of the above questions, whereas especially the economically so important fourth question was neglected.

This paper analyses all four questions. It is organized as follows: Section 2 and 3 treat the first two questions in two different ways. Sections 4 and 5 deal with the last two questions for homogeneous respectively inhomogeneous systems.

The main conclusion — leading to the title of the paper — is that singularity of B brings problems at most, if one tries to describe the time path of sectoral output levels out of a given initial value X(0) — a purpose which dynamic Leontief systems are not

---

[1] See, for instance, Schumann [13], p. 160 f or more specially for dynamic input-output models Meyer [9], p. 3 f.

[2] See Livesey [7], p. 537 for another more technical source of singularity of B.

[3] See Kendrick [3], Livesey [6] and [7], and Luenberger and Arbel [8].

181

suitable for. On the other hand, the statements concerning steady state solutions and moreover: nonnegative solutions are almost the same for regular as for singular capital coefficient matrices.

2. Existence of Solutions for Admissible Initial Values

For the purpose of simplicity, this and the next section treat only the case that singularity of B arises because of rows of zeros, that is, we assume

$$B = \begin{bmatrix} B_1 \\ O \end{bmatrix} \tag{3}$$

with an $r \times n$ — matrix B_1 of rank r (= rank of B), where r ($0 < r < n$) is the number of capital goods (among others) producing sectors.[4] System (1) may be written as

$$B\Delta X(t) = (I - A) X(t) - Y(t). \tag{4}$$

If the gross output $X(t)$ and thus the whole right hand side is given, (4) can be solved for the change in gross output $\Delta X(t)$. With (3) we can split (4) into the two systems of equations

$$B_1 \Delta X(t) = (I - A)_1 X(t) - Y_1(t) \tag{4.1}$$

$$O = (I - A)_2 X(t) - Y_2(t), \tag{4.2}$$

where the index 1 (respectively 2) means partitioned matrices or vectors consisting only of the first r (respectively the last n–r) rows of the original matrix or vector. Looking at (4.1) and (4.2) one immediately notices that not for every $X(t)$ there exists some solution $\Delta X(t)$ of (4), but only for those $X(t)$, which satisfy (4.2) (in which $\Delta X(t)$ doesn't appear at all). Economically this means that for sectors not producing capital goods the net output $(I - A)_2 X(t)$ must be equal to the final demand $Y_2(t)$. Vectors of gross output $X(t)$ satisfying (4.2) we will call admissible in this paper.[5]

If $X(t)$ is an admissible vector, the equation system (4) — which is equivalent to (4.1) in this case — is soluble for $\Delta X(t)$. According to the fact that we have only r (linear independent) equations and n unknowns, the solution is not unique but there exist n–r degrees of freedom in the choice of $\Delta X(t)$. For any solution $\ldots, X(t-1), X(t+1), \ldots$ of (4), now understood as system of difference equations, not only $X(t)$ must be admissible, but $X(t+1)$, too. So $\Delta X(t)$ must be choosen so that $X(t+1)$ also satisfies (4.2). With $X(t+1) = X(t) + \Delta X(t)$ this condition can be written as

$$-(I - A)_2 \Delta X(t) = (I - A)_2 X(t) - Y_2(t+1). \tag{5}$$

---

[4] For a general singular matrix B, not yet being of the form (3), one can reach this form by performing some „elementary row operations" on the whole system (1), see Luenberger and Arbel [8], p. 992. The results of sections 2 and 3, therefore, are valid for general singular matrices B, too. Statements about nonnegativity, however, are not invariant against such row operations. So we will drop assumption (3) in section 4 and 5, because there it would mean an essential loss of generality.

[5] For a matrix B not of form (3), one would, more generally, call admissible a vector $X(t)$, if it admits a solution of (4) (for the unknown variable $\Delta X(t)$).

(4.1) together with (5) yields a system of n equations for the determination of $\Delta X(t)$ out of a given $X(t)$:

$$\widetilde{B}\Delta X(t) = (I - A) X(t) - \widetilde{Y}(t) \qquad (6)$$

with

$$\widetilde{B} := \begin{bmatrix} B_1 \\ -(I - A)_2 \end{bmatrix}, \qquad \widetilde{Y}(t) := \begin{bmatrix} Y_1(t) \\ Y_2(t+1) \end{bmatrix}. \qquad (7)$$

The previous considerations can be summarized in the following proposition:

Proposition 1: (i) Every solution $X(t)$ of (1) is a solution of (6), too.

(ii) Every solution $X(t)$ of (6) with an admissible initial value $X(0)$ is a solution of (1), too.

For the system of difference equations (6) it is clear that the general solubility depends on the regularity of $\widetilde{B}$. So we have:

Proposition 2: The dynamic Leontief system (1) has a solution for any given time path $Y(t)$ and for any admissible initial value $X(0)$, if and only if $\widetilde{B}$, as defined in (7), is invertible. In that case the existing solution is unique.

The necessity of the condition in this proposition refers to the solubility of (1) for all possible time paths of $Y(t)$. For special developments of final demand (for instance in the case $Y(t) \equiv 0$ treated below) solutions exist without any assumption for $\widetilde{B}$.[6] On the other hand, regularity of $\widetilde{B}$ is by no means a very strong assumption: B_1 and $(I - A)_2$ being of full rank, singularity of $\widetilde{B}$ could arise only by a very unlikely linear dependence between the rows of B_1 with those of $(I - A)_2$. So, in the following we will suppose $\widetilde{B}$ to be regular.

Proposition 1 reduces the singular dynamic Leontief system (1) to the regular dynamic Leontief system (6), (with the restriction that only solutions of (6) with admissible $X(0)$ are also solutions of (1)[7]). The matrix $\widetilde{B}$ in (6), however, contains negative coefficients, so the condition of nonnegativity is violated, which would be necessary for the application of the theorem of Frobenius and Perron which usually is employed to solve dynamic Leontief systems.[8] Thus the method described in this section[9] is appropriate to get some evidence about the existence of pure mathematical solutions of singular dynamic Leontief systems, but it is less appropriate to derive results about the economically interesting, nonnegative solutions. Before turning to this problem in sections 4 and 5, we shall present another possibility to overcome the problem of singularity, due to Luenberger and Arbel [8].

3. Modelling Stocks of Capital Goods instead of Output Levels

The vector $Z(t)$ of stocks of the n commodities which are necessary as capital goods to produce the output $X(t)$ is described by

$$Z(t) = BX(t). \qquad (8)$$

---

[6] Similarly, for a final demand of the form $Y(t) = (1 + w)^t Y(0)$ (with an „adequate" growth rate w) a solution exists even if $\widetilde{B}$ is singular. See Meyer [9], p. 8–34.

[7] Notice, however, that for any solution of (6) at most the vector $X(0)$ might be not admissible; that means: even for a not admissible $X(0)$ the vector $X(1)$ computed by (6) – and, therefore, every vector $X(t)$, $t \geqslant 2$ – will be admissible. The reason for this fact is that the structural matrix of (6), $I + \widetilde{B}^{-1}(I - A)$, is only of rank r, as easily is seen by looking at the matrix $I + \widetilde{B}(I - A)^{-1}$, the last n–r rows of which consist only of zeros.

[8] See Meyer [9], for instance.

[9] Cf. Kendrick [3], Livesey [7], and Luenberger and Arbel [8].

Corresponding to (8), for the changes of stocks: $\Delta Z(t) = Z(t+1) - Z(t)$ one has:

$$\Delta Z(t) = B\Delta X(t). \tag{9}$$

Substitution of (9) in (4) yields

$$\Delta Z(t) = (I - A) X(t) - Y(t), \tag{10}$$

which means that the changes of the stocks of capital goods are equal to the amount of net production $(I - A) X(t)$ minus final demand $Y(t)$[10]. In the case of invertible B, substitution of

$$X(t) = B^{-1} Z(t) \tag{11}[11]$$

in (10) leads to a system of difference equations for $Z(t)$:

$$\Delta Z(t) = (I - A) B^{-1} Z(t) - Y(t). \tag{12}$$

(12) describes the time path of the stocks of capital goods corresponding to the time path of outputs of the Leontief system (1) or (4). The solutions of the system of difference equations for stocks of capital goods (12) correspond one to one to solutions of the system of difference equations for output levels (1) by virtue of the transformation (8) respectively (11).

Let us now come back to the case that the last $n-r$ commodities are not used as capital goods, i. e. that the matrix of capital coefficients is singular according to (3). To describe the changes of the stocks of capital goods then the first r rows of (10) are sufficient:

$$\Delta Z_1(t) = (I - A)_1 X(t) - Y_1(t). \tag{13}$$

On the other hand, as B^{-1} does not exist, it is impossible to deduce $X(t)$ only from $Z_1(t)$ like in transformation (11) respectively (8). Besides the condition

$$Z_1(t) = B_1 X(t), \tag{14.1}$$

now describing the connection between stocks of capital goods $Z_1(t)$ and output levels $X(t)$, the admissibility of $X(t)$, (cf. 4.2)) has to be taken in account:

$$Y_2(t) = (I - A)_2 X(t). \tag{14.2}$$

---

[10] Remember that in dynamic input-output analysis reinvestment usually is reckoned as intermediate input, included in the input-output coefficients a_{ij}.

[11] (11) means that the vector of stocks of capital goods $Z(t)$ determines the vector of output levels $X(t)$. Of course the stocks of capital goods in a certain sector determine the capacity of this sector and, therefore, in case of full capacity utilization — as is assumed throughout conventional dynamic input-output-analysis (for an exception see Meyer [9], part 2) — the output level of this sector. (11), however, says more: When the stocks of capital goods $Z(t)$ are given for the whole economy, the determination of sectoral output levels $X(t)$ with the aid of (11) implicitly means a certain distribution of these stocks to the sectors. Exactly if B is invertible, this distribution is feasible for any given $Z(t)$ in one and only one way.

Equations (14.1) and (14.2) uniquely determine the vector X(t), if we assume regularity of $\widetilde{B}$ as in section 2:

$$X(t) = \widetilde{B}^{-1} \begin{bmatrix} Z_1(t) \\ -Y_2(t) \end{bmatrix}. \tag{15)^{12}}$$

Substitution of (15) in (13) yields a system of difference equations of order r

$$\Delta Z_1(t) = (I - A)_1 \widetilde{B}^{-1} \begin{bmatrix} Z_1(t) \\ -Y_2(t) \end{bmatrix} - Y_1(t), \tag{16}$$

describing the time path of the stocks of capital goods $Z_1(t)$ just as (12) in the case of regular matrix B. The solutions of the system of difference equations for stocks of capital goods (16) correspond one to one to the solutions of the system of difference equations for output levels (1) by virtue of the transformation (14.1) respectively (15).

The Luenberger-Arbel-method, therefore, shows the following: If one describes an economy not by time paths of output levels, but by time paths of stocks of capital goods, in the case of a singular matrix of capital coefficients one gets "automatically" a system of difference equations of order $r < n$ without any singularity problem (under the weak assumption of a regular matrix $\widetilde{B}$). The time paths of (16) and (1) corresponding each other one to one, it becomes clear that the dynamic structure underlying the system (1) (of order n) is virtually only of order $r = \text{rank } B$.

4. Nonnegativity for the Homogeneous System

To get the general solution of the inhomogeneous system of difference equations (1) one has to analyze the corresponding homogeneous system. Beyond this, the homogeneous system can be interpreted as a closed input-output model by treating one of the n sectors as sector of private households producing the output "work" by means of the input "consumption".[13] In this sense, the solution of the homogeneous system is interesting by itself.

The homogeneous system of (1) may be written as

$$(I - A)^{-1} B \Delta X(t) = X(t). \tag{17}$$

Let be $\mu_1, \ldots, \mu_n$ the eigenvalues of $(I - A)^{-1} B$ with $\mu_1 \geqslant \ldots \geqslant \mu_n$. For every eigenvalue μ_i different from zero with corresponding eigenvector E_i the time path

$$X(t) = (1 + \frac{1}{\mu_i})^t E_i \tag{18}$$

represents a basic solution of (17). In the following we abandon the special assumption (3), but only assume rank $r < n$ for the matrix of capital coefficients B. Then the rank of $(I - A)^{-1} B$ is r, too, and it follows that $\mu_{r+1} = \ldots = \mu_n = 0$. For simplicity, we assume

---

[12] Considering only (14.1), there are many possible distributions (represented by vectors X(t)) of a given stock of capital goods of an economy $Z_1(t)$ to the several sectors. (15) says that there exists exactly one such distribution, which implies a net production $(I - A) X(t)$, the last n−r components of which are just equal to the given final demand $Y_2(t)$ in these sectors. Cf. the preceeding footnote.

[13] A model with completely endogenous final demand is a closed model, too. See for instance Schumann [13], p. 212 f. or Meyer [9], p. 68 f.

that the other r eigenvalues are different two by two and not equal to zero.[14] If, for $i = 1, \ldots, r$, we set $\lambda_i = 1/\mu_i$, the general solution of (17) is

$$X(t) = \sum_{i=1}^{r} \alpha_i (1 + \lambda_i)^t E_i. \tag{19}$$

So, contrary to the situation with regular B, the space of solutions of the system (17) is only of dimension $r = \text{rank } B$. This fact corresponds to the possibility, derived in the preceeding section, to reduce the order of the system of difference equations to r, and further it corresponds to the restriction of admissible initial values $X(0)$ through the $n-r$ equations (4.2) as presented in section 2.

To prepare the discussion of nonnegativity of solutions we show the following proposition, which holds for singular as for regular B.

Proposition 3: Let A be irreducible. The we have:
  (i) $\lambda_1 > 0$ and $E_1 > 0$
  (ii) None of the other eigenvectors $E_i, i = 2, \ldots, r$, is nonnegative.

Proof: From irreducibility of A it follows that $(I - A)^{-1}$ is strict positive.[15] Now, if B has a positive coefficient in each column, i. e. if each sector needs some capital goods for production, $(I - A)^{-1}B$ is strict positive, too, and the proposition follows directly from the theorem of Frobenius.[16]

Thus, the only case which has to be treated here is that of columns of zeros in B.[17] So let, in case after renumbering the sectors, the last s $(s > n-r)$ columns of B only consist of zeros. $(I - A)^{-1}B$ then may be written as

$$(I - A)^{-1} B = \begin{bmatrix} S^1 & O \\ S^2 & O \end{bmatrix}, \tag{20}$$

where S^1 is a quadratic, positive matrix of order n–s (which determines the dimensions of the other submatrices in (20). For $i = 1, \ldots, r$ let be $E_i = (E_i^1, E_i^2)$ a partition of eigenvector E_i corresponding to the partition (20). Then we have

$$(I - A)^{-1} BE_i = \begin{bmatrix} S^1 & O \\ S^2 & O \end{bmatrix} \begin{bmatrix} E_i^1 \\ E_i^2 \end{bmatrix} = \begin{bmatrix} S^1 E^i \\ S^2 E_i^1 \end{bmatrix} = \begin{bmatrix} \mu_i E_i^1 \\ \mu_i E_i^2 \end{bmatrix}. \tag{21}$$

The eigenvalues $\mu_1, \ldots, \mu_r$, therefore, are eigenvalues of S^1, too, with eigenvectors E_i^1.[18] Thus (ii) and the part $\lambda_1 = 1/\mu_1 > 0, E_1^1 > 0$ of (i) follow from the theorem of Frobenius applied to the positive matrix S^1. Finally, from $S^2 > 0$ we have $E_1^2 = \lambda_1 S^2 E_1^1 > 0$, which completes the proof.

In the following we shall assume A to be irreducible. Proposition 3 shows that then, with regard to the existence of nonnegative solutions, singularity of B doesn't matter: Just as in the case of regular B, for singular B there is virtually only one nonnegative solu-

---

[14] This assumption is always justified for empirical matrices. Moreover, proposition 3 will show that from irreducibility of A it follows $\mu_1 > 0$, the only essential part of the above assumption.

[15] Of course, for $(I - A)^{-1}$ to exist and to be nonnegative we have to assume — as usually in input-output analysis — that the maximum eigenvalue of A is less than one. See Takayama [14], p. 392, for instance.

[16] See for instance Gantmacher [2], p. 46 f. or Takayama [14], p. 372 f.

[17] One could regard this case of "production without capital" as economically irrelevant. The case is possible, however, if one of the sectors describes the "production" of private households in a closed model; see Brody [1], p. 43 f., for instance.

[18] Note that $E_i^1 \neq 0$ for $i = 1, \ldots, r$; for otherwise from (21) it would follow $E_i^2 = (1/\mu_i) S^2 E_i^1 = 0$.

tion, the basic solution (18) for $i = 1$, called balanced growth path, with λ_1 being the balanced growth rate.[19] If there is at least one i. e. $2, \ldots, r$ with

$$\left| 1 + \lambda_i \right| < 1 + \lambda_1, \tag{22}$$

the balanced growth path could be superposed by other basic solutions without the condition of nonnegativity (for all periods t) being violated. On the other hand, if (22) is not valid for all i. F. $\{2, \ldots, r\}$, the balanced growth path is not stable: every solution (19) with $\alpha_i \neq 0$ for all $i = 2, \ldots, r$ then runs into negative output levels of some sectors because of the negative elements in the eigenvectors $E_2, \ldots, E_r$.

While (as yet) no general theorems are known[20], whether or under which circumstances (22) is satisfied for all $i = 2, \ldots, r$, all empirical results of dynamic input-output models up to now unanimously show complete instability, i. e. that (22) is violated for all $i > 1$.[21] That means, that dynamic input-output models of type (17) — and more generally of type (1) — are not appropriate to describe the course of development of an economy out of an empirically given starting point $X(0)$ (which, even if it should be admissible, certainly would imply $\alpha_i \neq 0$ for all i in (19)).

Those questions dynamic input-output models are suitable for are related to the balanced growth path.[22] Balanced growth rate and balanced sector structure, however, for singular B exist just as in the case of regular B, and there are no differences in interpretation and computation.

5. Nonnegative Solutions of the Inhomogeneous System

In the sections 2 and 3 we asked for pure mathematical solutions. We saw that also in the case of a singular matrix of capital coefficients B for all possible time paths of final demand $Y(t)$ and for all admissible initial values $X(0)$ a solution of (1) exists (under a weak additional assumption: the regularity of $\tilde{B}$, cf. proposition 2).

Economically meaningful, however, are only nonnegative solutions. The existence of such solutions only depends on the condition that the given (nonnegative) final demand $Y(t)$ doesn't grow "to fast". Proposition 4 gives a precise meaning to this phrase. Notice that in this proposition, which is interesting for regular B, too, the invertibility of B doesn't play any role as in proposition 3 of the preceeding section.

Proposition 4: For $A \geqslant 0$, $B \geqslant 0$, and A irreducile, let be λ_1 the balanced growth rate of the homogeneous part of (1). Then we have:

(i) Necessary condition for the existence of a nonnegative solution of the dynamic Leontief system (1) is

$$\sum_{t = 0}^{\infty} \frac{Y(t)}{(1 + \lambda_1)^t} < \infty . \tag{23}$$

[19] This holds without any additional assumption like (3) or invertibility of $\tilde{B}$, as in the preceeding two sections. Only for a reducible matrix A some slight modifications must be made, for as Kogelschatz had shown, there exist nonnegative matrices A and B (A reducible) so that (17) has only the trivial solution (and (1), therefore, has only the particular solution). See Kogelschatz [4], p. 67, p. 84 f. and Meyer [9], p. 26–34.

[20] For some few theoretical considerations to the question of (in-) stability see Morishima [12], p. 635 f. and Meyer [9], p. 79–89.

[21] See Leontief [5], p. 5–15, p. 160 f, Tsukui [15], p. 178 f, and Meyer and Schumann [10], p. 20. All these papers, however, are relating to models with regular B; but results for singular matrices of capital coefficients will be very similar. Thus computations of the author for an 14-sector-input-output-model with singular B corresponding to the 12-sector-model in Meyer and Schumann [10], p. 13 f. (with regular B) discovered complete instability, too.

[22] For questions of the interpretation of dynamic input-output models see Meyer and Schumann [10], [11] and Meyer [9], p. 71–79, p. 100–102.

(ii) For every nonnegative solution $X(t)$ of (1) there exists a vector $\bar{\bar{X}}$ with:

$$X(t) < (1 + \lambda_1)^t \, \bar{\bar{X}} \quad \text{for all } t. \tag{24}$$

Proof: Define $\bar{X}(t) := X(t) / (1 + \lambda_1)^t$ and $\bar{Y}(t) := (I - A)^{-1} Y(t) / (1 + \lambda_1)^t \; [>0]$. Then (1) can be written as:

$$\bar{Y}(t) = (I + (I - A)^{-1} B) \bar{X}(t) - (1 + \lambda_1)(I - A)^{-1} B \bar{X}(t + 1). \tag{25}$$

Now, let be P the (row-) eigenvector of $(I - A)^{-1} B$ belonging to the Frobenius eigenvalue μ_1, so that $P(I - A)^{-1} B = \mu_1 P$. From proposition 3 (i), (formulated for row-vectors instead of column-vectors) it follows that $P > 0$.[23] Premultiplication of (25) with P yields:

$$P\bar{Y}(t) = (1 + \mu_1) P\bar{X}(t) - (1 + \mu_1) P\bar{X}(t + 1), \tag{26}$$

and by adding up (26) for the periods $\tau = 0, 1, 2, \ldots, t$ one gets:

$$P \sum_{\tau = 0}^{t} \bar{Y}(\tau) = (1 + \mu_1) P\bar{X}(0) - (1 + \mu_1) P\bar{X}(t + 1) \tag{27}$$

Now, if $X(t)$ is a solution of (1), which is nonnegative for all t, the two left hand side terms and the four right hand side terms of the above two equations (26) and (27) are nonnegative numbers. (26), therefore, reveals $P\bar{X}(t)$ to be a diminishing sequence, from which by positivity of P the existence of an $\bar{\bar{X}}$ with $\bar{X}(t) < \bar{\bar{X}}$ for all t can be deduced, proving part (ii) of the proposition. (27), on the other hand, shows that $P\sum_{\tau = 0}^{t} \bar{Y}(\tau)$ is less than $(1 + \mu_1) P\bar{X}(0)$ for all t, so proving part (i) of the proposition by use of positivity of P, again.

(23), a little bit laxly, can be said to be the condition that final demand $Y(t)$ has to grow more slowly than with the rate λ_1.[24] This condition is economically plausible, at once: λ_1 being the balanced growth rate of the homogeneous system says, which growth of outputs and stocks of capital is possible for an economy (the technology of which is described by the matrices A and B), if final demand is zero, that is, if the whole net output $(I - A) X(t)$ is disposable for purposes of investment. If net output $(I - A) X(t)$ has to meet a final demand greater than zero, the realizable growth will be smaller, of course. But then it is clear that in particular the final demand which has to be met may only grow less than with the rate λ_1.

The general solution of (1) is

$$X(t) = X^0(t) + \sum_{i = 1}^{r} \alpha_i (1 + \lambda_i)^t E_i \tag{28}$$

with λ_i and E_i as in the preceeding section and $X^0(t)$ being a particular solution. Besides the term $\alpha_1 (1 + \lambda_1)^t E_1$ at most the term $X^0(t)$ of the sum in (28) is nonnegative, and this term, if it is nonnegative, in consequence of proposition 4 (ii) grows more slowly than with the rate λ_1. Thus, all what has been said about the instability of the balanced growth path of the homogeneous system is valid for the nonnegative solutions of the inhomogeneous system, too.

Note that the reverse implications generally are not valid.

[23] It is this (and only this) implication the irreducibility of A is supposed for.
[24] Exactly, the following relations hold:
$Y(t) < (1 + w)^t \, \bar{Y}(t)$ for all t with $w < \lambda_1$
→ $\sum_{\tau = 0}^{\infty} Y(\tau) / (1 + \lambda_1)^{\tau} < \infty$ $[= (23)]$
→ $\lim_{\tau \to \infty} Y(\tau) / (1 + \lambda_1)^{\tau} = 0$

REFERENCES

[1] Bródy, A.: Proportions, Prices, and Planning. A Mathematical Restatement of the Labor Theory of Value. Amsterdam–London 1970.

[2] Gantmacher, F. R.: Matrizenrechnung Teil II. Spezielle Fragen und Anwendungen. 2. ber. Aufl., Berlin 1966.

[3] Kendrick, D.: On the Leontief Dynamic Inverse. Quarterly Journal of Economics, Vol. 86 (1972), S. 693–696.

[4] Kogelschatz, H.: Strukturänderungen und Wachstumsgleichgewichte. Input-Output–Theoretische Untersuchungen. Meisenheim am Glan 1977.

[5] Leontief, W.: General Numerical Solution of the Simple Dynamic Input-Output-System. In: Report on Research for 1953, Harvard Economic Research Project (without year).

[6] Livesey, D. A.: The Singularity Problem in the Dynamic Input-Output Model. International Journal of Systems Science, Vol. 4 (1972), S. 437–440.

[7] ... A Minimal Realization of the Leontief Dynamic Input-Output Model. In: Polenske, K. R. and Skolka, J. V. (eds.): Advances in Input-Output Analysis. Proceedings of the Sixth International Conference of Input-Output Techniques. Vienna, April 22–26, 1974. Cambridge/Mass. 1976.

[8] Luenberger, D. G. and Arbel, A.: Singular Dynamic Leontief Systems. Econometrica, Vol. 45 (1977), S. 991–995.

[9] Meyer, U.: Dynamische Input-Output-Modelle. Athenäum Ökonomie, Vol. 1. Königstein/Ts 1980.

[10] --- und Schumann, J.: Das dynamische Input-Output-Modell als Modell gleichgewichtigen Wachstums. Mit einem Anwendungsbeispiel für die Bundesrepublik Deutschland. Zeitschrift für die gesamte Staatswissenschaft, Band 133 (1977), S. 1–37.

[11] ... und ... Ansatze zur Wieterentwicklung des dynamischen Input-Output-Modells. In: Helmstädter, E. (ed.): Neuere Entwicklungen in den Wirtschaftswissenschaften. Schriften des Vereins für Socialpolitik, Gesellschaft für Wirtschafts- und Sozialwissenschaften, Neue Folge Band 98. Berlin 1978.

[12] Morishima, M.: Prices, Interest and Profit in a Dynamic Leontief System. Econometrica, Vol. 26 (1958), S. 358–380.

[13] Schumann, J.: Input-Output–Analyse. Berlin–Heidelberg–New York 1968.

[14] Takayama, A.: Mathematical Economics. Hindsale/Ill. 1974.

[15] Tsukui, J.: Application of a Turnpike Theorem to Planning for Efficient Accumulation: An example for Japan. Econometrica, Vol. 36 (1968), S. 172–186.

[12]

DYNAMIC INPUT-OUTPUT ANALYSIS WITH DISTRIBUTED ACTIVITIES

Thijs ten Raa*

Abstract—This paper offers a new approach to economic models in which activities take time. Departing from a standard economic model (Leontief's dynamic input-output model), we recast the activities from ordinary vectors into temporal distributions. In doing so, we preserve the formal structure and simplicity of the standard model. This is the secret of the power of our approach which asserts itself in the resolution of some open dynamic input-output problems. In particular, we are able to solve models with singular capital structures (i.e., singular derivatives coefficients matrices), unbalanced growth and different time profiles of investment or other production activities.

De cost gaet voor de baet uyt.
(The cost goes before the benefit.)

TEMPORALLY distributed activities are important. De Galan (1980, p. 217) ascribes labor market failure to, among other things, the sluggishness of certain adjustments which results from the fact that activities such as education take time. Furthermore, if one neglects the time used up in the production process, then one will generate too high growth rates as most dynamic economic models actually do. Yet little work has been done on modeling with distributed economic activities. Exceptions are input-output analysis with transit and production lags by Bródy (1965), or with investment lead times by Gladyshevskii and Belous (1978), Johansen (1978), and Zhuravlev (1982). But these studies are in the realm of balanced growth in which the structure of the problem is the same as in static input-output; Zhuravlev comes closest to our work by inclusion of turnpike results.

Temporally distributed activities will be considered single elements in a distribution space and be

Received for publication February 23, 1984. Revision accepted for publication August 6, 1985.

*Tilburg University.

I owe Wassily Leontief much for help throughout the study. I would like to thank Erik Thomas whom I consulted for the analysis. András Bródy, Duncan Foley, and the late Leif Johansen kindly commented on the first draft. I am grateful to Teun Kloek, Rick van der Ploeg, Albert Verbeek, and Ton Vorst for suggestions on the generalized inverse of the capital matrix. Harm Bart provided some useful references. The paper was presented at the fourth IFAC/IFORS Conference on the Modelling and Control of National Economies, Washington, D.C., June 17–19, 1983 and at the Econometric Society Winter 1985 meetings, New York City. Travel support by the Netherlands Organization for the Advancement of Pure Research (Z.W.O.) is gratefully acknowledged.

subjected to the calculus of distributions, which yields simple expressions for seemingly complicated equations involving lags and so on, and solutions to the distributed input-output models. It enables us to resolve open dynamic input-output problems, such as the solution of equations with singular capital structures and analysis of economies with different time profiles of investment or other production activities under conditions of unbalanced growth. It should be mentioned that the same approach is relevant for regional economic models as that of Leontief et al. (1977). Then economic activities are modeled as spatial distributions. This topic is the subject of ten Raa (1984). Similarly, our analysis of distributed activities may serve as a model for capital of circulation and the complete economic system as outlined by Foley (1982).

The organization of the present paper is as follows. Section I identifies the economic subjects of this study and develops the central theme: input-output profiles are considered single elements in a distribution space, a concept that is defined in the appendix. Section II analyzes the static input-output model with possibly continuously distributed activities. Section III widens the scope to the case of balanced growth. Section IV handles a pure dynamic model with a possibly singular capital structure. Section V solves the traditional dynamic input-output model. By synthesis of the treatment of continuity (section II) and invertibility (section IV), section VI analyzes the distributed dynamic input-output model. Section VII concludes the paper.

I. Productive Capital

Productive capital is divided into circulating capital and fixed capital (Marx, 1974, p. 158). Circulating capital is absorbed in production and consists of flows of goods. Fixed capital must merely be present when production takes place and consists of stocks of goods. Circulating and fixed capital are represented by, respectively, the input-output flow coefficients matrix A and the input-output stock coefficients matrix B, both of Leontief.

Circulating capital (A) is fluid, but it can be like water or like syrup. Some circulating capital, such as electricity, is absorbed immediately, but other circulating capital, such as minerals, must be treated during some time. Electricity is (super) fluid capital; minerals are working capital. (Super) fluid capital is, by definition, processed instantaneously; working capital is defined to be capital in the pipe line.

The same distinction can be made with regard to fixed capital (B). Some fixed capital, such as a stapler, is ready for immediate use, but other fixed capital, such as a transport container, must be present some time in advance. A stapler is instant capital; the container is advanced capital. Instant capital is fixed capital which can produce instantaneously, while advanced capital must be installed in advance, all by definition.

A good starting point for the incorporation of the production times in the circulating and fixed capital matrices A and B is Marx (1974, p. 239). For example, if input i's production time in sector j equals τ_{ij}, then we can write interindustry demand for i at time 0 as $\sum_j a_{ij} x_j(\tau_{ij})$ where $x(t)$ is the output vector at time t.

In general, the ith input requirement for one unit of sector j^{th} output is represented by an input profile on the past. We shall now introduce a powerful point of view. Giving up the idea of a_{ij} being some number altogether, we redefine an *input-output coefficient* as a nonnegative distribution on the nonpositive time axis. The width of its support (τ_{ij}) reflects the production time. This set-up obviously applies to capital stock coefficients as well. Then the width of the support of the distribution reflects the investment lead time.

II. Static Input-Output Analysis

An input-output flow coefficient a_{ij} is a *nonnegative* distribution with *nonpositive support*, where $i, j = 1, \ldots, n$ represent the sectors of the economy. The future and current flow requirements exercised by sector j—with *output* distribution x_j—on sector i at time t sum up to, heuristically,

$$\int_{s=-\infty}^{0} a_{ij}(s) x_j(t-s)\, ds,$$

abstracting from technical change. Summing over j, which may be done under the integral sign, we obtain interindustry demand for i at time t:

$$\int_{s=-\infty}^{0} \sum_{j=1}^{n} a_{ij}(s) x_j(t-s)\, ds.$$

The material balance for good i at time t between output and interindustry demand plus *final demand* z_i reads

$$x_i(t) = \int_{s=-\infty}^{0} \sum_{j=1}^{n} a_{ij}(s) x_j(t-s)\, ds + z_i(t).$$

Letting x, z and A denote the output and final demand vectors and the input-output flow coefficients matrix,

$$x(t) = \int_{s=-\infty}^{0} A(s) x(t-s)\, ds + z(t).$$

Invoking the notation for the convolution product (appendix), we obtain

$$x = A^* x + z. \tag{1}$$

Formulation (1) is free of integrability requirements. It holds for x and z n-dimensional vector distributions and A an $n \times n$ matrix distribution (nonnegative and with nonpositive support) over time in the sense of Schwartz (1957). The purpose of this section is to solve the *Leontief planning problem* of finding output x fulfilling (1) given final demand z.

Our input-output distribution a_{ij} is essentially the outgrowth of temporal disaggregation of a traditional input-output coefficient. Thus, summing over time we capture the traditional coefficient, now denoted $\int a_{ij}$. This expression is shorthand for $\langle a_{ij}, 1 \rangle$ (where $\int$ generalizes the Lebesgue-Stieltjes integral). We see that the traditional input-output matrix corresponds to $\int A$. This matrix is defined component-wise. Therefore, the well-known conditions for the producibility of final demand now apply to $\int A$:

ASSUMPTION. *Nonnegative matrix $\int A$ fulfills the Hawkins-Simon (1949) conditions.*

There are some well-known equivalent conditions. One is the condition that the *spectral radius is less than one*:

$$\rho\left(\int A\right) < 1. \tag{2}$$

The other is the *convergence* of the power expansion of the inverse of $I - \int A$:

$$\sum_{0}^{\infty} \left(\int A \right)^{k} < \infty. \tag{3}$$

We wish to derive that $\sum_{0}^{\infty} A^{*k}$ itself converges ($A^{*2} = A^{*}A$ and so on) and is a continuous functional. For then it is the *inverse distribution* of $I\delta - A$ (where δ is the Dirac distribution or unit point mass at the origin defined in the appendix). The latter is the operator in our equation (1) which consequently can be solved. Essentially, standard input-output results are confirmed for the more general case of distributed inputs.

PROPOSITION 1. *Let the above assumption be fulfilled. Then $\sum_{0}^{\infty} A^{*k}$ exists and is continuous. And for every z which is nonnegative and agrees with a bounded function near infinity, there is a solution x to (1) which is similar.*

Proof. See the appendix.

Remark. The assumed boundedness can be relaxed to hold just almost surely.

Example. A typical fully distributed input-output flow coefficient is $A(t) = \frac{1}{4}e^{t}\check{H}(t)$. Here $\check{H}$ is the *Heaviside function on the negative reals*, defined by $\check{H}(t) = 1$ for $t < 0$ and zero elsewhere. The assumption is fulfilled as the total mass of A is $\frac{1}{4}$. Now let us calculate $\sum_{0}^{\infty} A_{0}^{*k}$. For $t < 0$,

$$A^{*2}(t) = \int_{t}^{0} A(s)A(t-s) \, ds$$

$$= \frac{1}{16}\int_{t}^{0} e^{s}e^{t-s} ds = \frac{1}{16}e^{t}(-t).$$

And so on, for $t < 0$,

$$A^{*k}(t) = \frac{1}{4^k}e^{t}(-t)^{k-1} \Big/ (k-1)!$$

$$= \frac{1}{4}e^{t}\left(-\frac{1}{4}t\right)^{k-1} \Big/ (k-1)!.$$

In sum, for $t < 0$,

$$\sum_{0}^{\infty} A^{*k}(t) = \delta + \sum_{0}^{\infty} A^{*k+1}(t)$$

$$= \delta + \sum_{0}^{\infty} \frac{1}{4}e^{t}\left(-\frac{1}{4}t\right)^{k} \Big/ k!$$

$$= \delta + \frac{1}{4}e^{t}e^{-\frac{1}{4}t} = \delta + \frac{1}{4}e^{\frac{3}{4}t}.$$

For $t \geq 0$, $A^{*k}(t) = 0$. Thus the inverse operator is $\delta + \frac{1}{4}e^{\frac{3}{4}(\cdot)}\check{H}$.

III. Balanced Growth

An input stock coefficient b_{ij} is also a *nonnegative* distribution with *nonpositive support*. The future and current capacity expansion of sector j demands, heuristically,

$$\int_{s=-\infty}^{0} b_{ij}(s)\dot{x}_{j}(t-s) \, ds$$

of i at time t, where the dot denotes differentiation (see the appendix). These *investment* terms are separated from final demand. The material balance for good i at time t becomes

$$x_{i}(t) = \int_{s=-\infty}^{0} \sum_{j=1}^{n} \left[a_{ij}(s)x_{j}(t-s) \right.$$
$$\left. + b_{ij}(s)\dot{x}_{j}(t-s) \right] ds + z_{i}(t)$$

or

$$x = A^{*}x + B^{*}\dot{x} + z \tag{4}$$

which is free of integrability requirements. The purpose of this paper is to solve the Leontief planning problem for equation (4).

The remainder of this section is confined to the case of *balanced growth*:

$$z(t) = z(0)e^{gt}$$

and also

$$x(t) = x(0)e^{gt}.$$

PROPOSITION 2. *Let the assumption of section II be fulfilled. Consider balanced growth. Then there is a maximum growth rate $g^{*} > 0$ such that the following holds. For every z with $z(0)$ nonnegative and $0 \leq g < g^{*}$ there is a solution x to (4) with similar $x(0)$ and g.*

Proof. See the appendix.

IV. Pure Dynamics

In dynamic input-output analysis, as well as control theory, it is assumed that the matrix of coefficients of the first (vector) derivative is invertible. This practice constitutes a problem which manifests itself most pointedly in equation (4) of the last section if we neglect the nonderivative term and concentrate the derivative coefficients in the origin by putting $A = 0$ and $B = B_{0}\delta$, B_{0} an ordinary but possibly singular matrix. Then equation (4) becomes

$$x = B_{0}\dot{x} + z. \tag{5}$$

The standard technique is to write $\dot{x} = B_0^{-1}x - B_0^{-1}z$ and to proceed as usual. However, as Bródy (1974, p. 137) notes:

Yet the presence of the matrix $[B_0^{-1}]$ alerts us to further theoretical problems. First, B_0 itself can be singular in practice. If, say, two sectors have the same capital structure, then B_0, having two columns equal, will be singular, and if the capital structures are very similar, B_0 will be severely ill-conditioned. Furthermore, $[B_0^{-1}]$, if it exists at all, will have the economically meaningful growth rate, λ, as its eigenvalue of minimal modulus. Actual computation, then, will be dominated by other eigenvalues, and therefore be clumsy and inexact.

Another source of trouble is that some goods need no fixed capital or only to a minor extent. In such a case B_0 has zero or almost zero rows and, therefore, is singular or "severely ill-conditioned."

We shall overcome the singularity shortcoming of dynamic input-output analysis and control theory by deriving a more general solution to equation (5) which does not hinge on the invertibility of B_0. In other words, B_0's with zero eigenvalues must be facilitated. We shall proceed gradually and first admit only zero eigenvalues with a *complete* system of eigenvectors, that is, zero eigenvalues with a number of eigenvectors equal to the multiplicity of the zero eigenvalues. For then the role of B_0^{-1} can be played by a generalized inverse reminiscent of the one of Rao (1974), that is, any A_0 satisfying $B_0 A_0 B_0 = B_0$. The *form* of the generalized inverse is chosen such that equation (5) *can be solved* explicitly which will be done after the presentation and discussion of the definition. Surprisingly, Moore-Penrose generalized inverses do not work, in spite of suggestions in the literature. For example, Kendrick (1972) and Livesey (1973, 1976) make a number of full rank assumptions that implicitly rule out conditions such as capital structure similarity across sectors.

DEFINITION. *Let B_0 be a square matrix of which the zero eigenvalue has a complete system of eigenvectors. A generalized inverse of B_0 is a square matrix B_0^- such that $B_0^- B_0^2 = B_0$.*

Justification. Bring B_0 on *triangular form*

$$T\begin{pmatrix} J_1 & 0 \\ 0 & J_2 \end{pmatrix}T^{-1}$$

such that the *zero* eigenvalues are precisely arranged in the diagonal of J_1. J_1 and J_2 are upper triangular and all nonzero eigenvalues are displayed on the diagonal of J_2. T is the base transformation matrix. By the nature of B_0, J_1

may be assumed zero. This can be seen by taking the Jordan canonical form of B_0 which fulfills the described conditions on J_1 and J_2. Since the diagonal of upper triangular J_2 never vanishes, this matrix is invertible. The generalized inverse is now

$$B_0^- = T\begin{pmatrix} K & 0 \\ L & J_2^{-1} \end{pmatrix}T^{-1}$$

with K and L arbitrary matrices of appropriate size. This is easily verified:

$$B_0^- B_0^2 = T\begin{pmatrix} K & 0 \\ L & J_2^{-1} \end{pmatrix}T^{-1}T\begin{pmatrix} 0 & 0 \\ 0 & J_2^2 \end{pmatrix}T^{-1}$$
$$= T\begin{pmatrix} 0 & 0 \\ 0 & J_2 \end{pmatrix}T^{-1} = B_0.$$

Thus, the generalized inverse of B_0 exists but is not unique. The justification is rounded off by the next example which shows that B_0^- generalizes the inverse.

Examples. (1) B_0 regular. Then $B_0^- = B_0^{-1}$. (2) B_0 zero. Then B_0^- is arbitrary. (3) $B_0 = \begin{pmatrix} 1 & 0 \\ 0 & 0 \end{pmatrix}$. Then the Rao inverse defined in the introduction of this section is $\begin{pmatrix} a & b \\ 1-a & c \end{pmatrix}$. The Moore-Penrose inverse is obtained by putting $a = \frac{1}{2}$ and $b = c = 0$. Our B_0^- is obtained by putting $a = 1$. (4) $B_0 = \begin{pmatrix} 0 & 1 \\ 0 & 0 \end{pmatrix}$. Then $B_0^2 = 0$ and B_0^- is undefined. Indeed, B_0 does not fulfill the assumption: zero is the only eigenvalue, but there is no complete system of eigenvectors.

Equation (5) is now rewritten such that solving it amounts to inverting a distribution: $(I\delta - B_0\delta)*x = z$. The next proposition inverts the operator. The solution features the *Heaviside function on the negatives* $\check{H}$ which was defined by $\check{H}(t) = 1$ for $t < 0$ and zero elsewhere (section II, the example).

PROPOSITION 3. *Let B_0 be a square matrix whose zero eigenvalue has a complete system of eigenvectors. Then*

$$(I\delta - B_0\delta)^{*-1} = \check{H}\exp(B_0^- t)B_0^{-2}B_0 + \delta(I - B_0^- B_0).$$

Proof. See the appendix.

Examples. (1) B_0 regular. Then $B_0^- = B_0^{-1}$. Hence the inverse operator becomes $\check{H}\exp(B_0^- t)B_0^{-1}$. (2) B_0 zero. Then the inverse operator is $0 + \delta(I - 0) = \delta I$, as should be. (3) $B_0 = \begin{pmatrix} 1 & 1 \\ 0 & 0 \end{pmatrix}$. Then we may choose $B_0^- = I$. Hence the inverse operator becomes $\check{H}e'\begin{pmatrix} 1 & 1 \\ 0 & 0 \end{pmatrix} + \delta\begin{pmatrix} 0 & -1 \\ 0 & 1 \end{pmatrix}$.

Remarks. (1) In example 3 the arbitrary

$$B_0^- = \begin{pmatrix} 1 & b \\ 0 & c \end{pmatrix}.$$

But in the inverse operator,

$$\exp(B_0^- t)B_0^{-2}B_0 = \sum_0^\infty \frac{t^k}{k!}B_0^{-(k+2)}B_0$$

$$= \sum_0^\infty \frac{t^k}{k!}B_0^{-(k+1)}\begin{pmatrix} 1 & 1 \\ 0 & 0 \end{pmatrix}$$

$$= \sum_0^\infty \frac{t^k}{k!}\begin{pmatrix} 1 & 1 \\ 0 & 0 \end{pmatrix}$$

and

$$B_0^- B_0 = \begin{pmatrix} 1 & 1 \\ 0 & 0 \end{pmatrix},$$

i.e., the arbitrariness in B_0^- is immaterial in the sense that a and b do not show up in the inverse operator. In fact, it is easy to show that the inverse operator is unique. (2) The inverse in example 3 has a negative component. This means that there is *disinvestment*, in fact, of good 1 in sector 2. For further discussion see Leontief (1970).

Next we admit zero eigenvalues with an incomplete system of eigenvalues. B_0 can now be any square matrix. This complete generality has a price, however. It is no longer possible to express the inverse operator in sole terms of B_0. We now have to invoke its triangular form factors J_1, J_2 and T.

PROPOSITION 4. *Let* $B_0 = T\begin{pmatrix} J_1 & 0 \\ 0 & J_2 \end{pmatrix}T^{-1}$ *be the triangular form with diag* J_1 *zero and diag* J_2 *never vanishing. Then*

$$(I\delta - B_0\delta)^{*-1}$$

$$= T\begin{pmatrix} \sum_0^{n-1} \overset{(k)}{\delta} J_1^k & 0 \\ 0 & \check{H}\exp(J_2^{-1}t)J_2^{-1} \end{pmatrix}T^{-1},$$

where $\overset{(k)}{\delta}$ *is the* k^{th} *derivative of* δ, $k = 0, \ldots, n$, *and* n *is the size of* B_0 *or the number of sectors in the economy.*

Proof. See the appendix.

Example. $B_0 = \begin{pmatrix} 0 & 1 \\ 0 & 0 \end{pmatrix}$. Then $J_1 = B_0$, $J_2 = \varnothing$ and $T = I$. Hence the inverse becomes

$$\sum_0^1 \overset{(k)}{\delta} B_0^k = \delta I + \dot{\delta}B_0 = \begin{pmatrix} \delta & \dot{\delta} \\ 0 & \delta \end{pmatrix}.$$

V. Traditional Dynamics

In traditional input-output, production is instantaneous. The coefficients are concentrated in the origin: $A = A_0\delta$ and $B = B_0\delta$ with A_0 and B_0 matrices and δ the Dirac distribution (see the appendix). Equation (4) of section II reduces to the familiar dynamic input-output equation,

$$x = A_0x + B_0\dot{x} + z. \tag{6}$$

Although equation (6) is standard, its Leontief planning problem has not been solved yet, due to the B_0 singularity problems discussed in the last section. The next proposition does it. Recall that the Leontief planning problem was defined in section II as that of finding output x given final demand z. The connection with initial value problems will be discussed in section VI.

PROPOSITION 5. *Let the assumption of section II be fulfilled, i.e.,* A_0 *fulfills the Hawkins-Simon (1949) conditions. Let* B_0's *zero eigenvalues have a complete system of eigenvectors. Then for every* z *the solution to equation (6) is*

$$x = \left\{ \check{H}\exp[B_0^-(I - A_0)t]\right\}*B_0^-(I - A_0)$$

$$\times B_0^- B_0\sum_0^\infty A_0^k z + (I - B_0^- B_0)\sum_0^\infty A_0^k z.$$

Proof. See the appendix.

Remarks. (1) z may not grow too fast, for then x would become infinite. Formally, z must fulfill the convolution condition of Schwartz (1961). In fact, z must be tempered by a growth rate which is less than g^* of proposition 2. (2) The assumption on B_0 can be dropped. Then the solution is modified by applying proposition 4 instead of 3 in the derivation. (3) In the special case that B_0 is invertible, the solution reduces to

$$x = \check{H}\exp[B_0^-(I - A_0)t]*B_0^{-1}z.$$

This agrees with the literature, e.g., Bródy (1974, p. 136). (4) A discrete time formulation and solution to the problem yields Leontief's (1970) "Dynamic Inverse." The relation between the formulations, such as the bias involved, is discussed in ten Raa (1986).

VI. Distributed Dynamics

Last but not least we shall solve the Leontief planning problem for the full equation with distributed input-output coefficients of section III, reproduced here for convenience:

$$x = A^*x + B^*\dot{x} + z. \tag{4}$$

The technique will be factorization. The matrix distributions will be split into parts which are concentrated in the origin and parts away from the origin. The first parts will be subjected to proposition 4, the latter ones to a standard device of the theory of distributions. The procedure works provided that there is an intermediate time span over which the coefficients matrices are regular. Therefore, it is assumed that on some open interval $(\epsilon, 0)$, however small, A agrees with an integrable function and B with an absolutely continuous function. (This means that for all positive γ, there is a positive Δ such that

$$\sum_{k=1}^{m} \|B(t_k) - B(s_k)\| < \gamma$$

for every finite system of pairwise disjoint subintervals (s_k, t_k) of $(\epsilon, 0)$ with total length $\sum_{k=1}^{m}(t_k - s_k)$ less than Δ.) The assumption is met in applied econometrics where A and B have finite supports. We now have

PROPOSITION 6. *Let the assumption of section II be fulfilled. On some interval $(\epsilon, 0)$, let A be integrable and B absolutely continuous. Then for every z the solution x to the above equation is the convolution product of a locally integrable function, a multiple of the Dirac distribution and a distribution with support in the negatives, all with z. The expression for x is specified in the proof.*

Proof. See the appendix.

Remarks. (1) Remark 1 of section V applies. (2) A discrete time formulation and solution to the

problem is presented in ten Raa (1986) who also comments on the length of the industrial reporting period as compared to the time between purchase of input and production of output in terms of significance of distributed versus traditional input-output.

Example. Consider a simple economy with a fixed capital good 1 and a circulating capital good 2. For simplicity, let each sector require only one kind of capital. To keep the example interesting, let each sector require capital of the other. The circulating capital consumption by sector 1 is $1/3$ per unit of output, exponentially distributed. One unit of fixed capital is needed per unit of output in sector 2. Formally,

$$A(t) = \begin{pmatrix} 0 & 0 \\ 1 & 0 \end{pmatrix} \tfrac{1}{3} e^t \breve{H}(t)$$

and (7)

$$B = \begin{pmatrix} 0 & 1 \\ 0 & 0 \end{pmatrix} \delta.$$

A straightforward application of proposition 6 in the appendix shows that the solution to the Leontief planning problem for final demand z is given by the output path

$$x(t) = \begin{pmatrix} \tfrac{1}{4} z_1(t) + \tfrac{1}{4} \dot{z}_2(t) - \tfrac{3}{16} z_2(t) + \tfrac{3}{16} \int_{-\infty}^{0} e^{\frac{1}{4} s} z_1(t-s) \, ds + \tfrac{9}{64} \int_{-\infty}^{0} e^{\frac{1}{4} s} z_2(t-s) \, ds \\ \tfrac{3}{4} z_2(t) + \tfrac{1}{4} \int_{-\infty}^{0} e^{\frac{1}{4} s} z_1(t-s) \, ds + \tfrac{3}{16} \int_{-\infty}^{0} e^{\frac{1}{4} s} z_2(t-s) \, ds \end{pmatrix}. \tag{8}$$

Note that current and future values of final demand, z, determine output, x. Capital requirements are met by the appropriate past production levels, as indicated by the same formula for x. Should one desire a particular level of output and capital stock at, say, time zero, then the formula implicitly determines all feasible future paths of final demand, z, and their sustaining output paths, x. The selection of such a path of final demand z requires a behavioral rule or plan and goes beyond the scope of the present article. For an interesting discussion of this issue I refer to Leontief (1963).

VII. Conclusion

The new approach to economic models with temporally distributed activities, exemplified by distributed input-output analysis, consists of four steps. First, the standard, nondistributed economic model (Leontief's dynamic input-output model) is taken as the point of departure. Second, activities are reinterpreted as temporal distributions. Third, the ordinary product is replaced by the convolution product. Fourth, the consequent model is subjected to the calculus of distributions.

The approach offers a unifying and extending framework for the dynamic inverse of Leontief (1970) and also Bródy (1974), and for the distributed lag studies of Bródy (1965), Gladyshevskii and Belous (1978), Johansen (1978), and Zhuravlev (1982).

The application of the theory of distributions of Schwartz (1957) is novel and promising for economic science. This paper features the following results:

1. Solutions to dynamic economic models with singular capital structures.
2. Unbalanced growth solutions to the traditional dynamic input-output model.
3. Analysis of the dynamic input-output model with distributed activities.

APPENDIX

Distributions for Economists

Having reconsidered input-output coefficients, now being nonnegative distributions on the nonpositive time axis, it may be helpful to the nonmathematical reader to give a precise account of the concepts involved. Nonnegative distributions are essentially measures (Schwartz, 1957). Unsigned distributions are generalizations that cover basically all linear operators. So let us first recapitulate the concept of a measure and then generalize. Throughout this paper, time will be the underlying space.

A measure associates amounts of mass with subsets of the time axis. Thus, a measure can be viewed as a mapping from indicator functions to the reals. The indicator functions are "test" functions representing subsets of time. A measure is no arbitrary mapping defined on the test space of indicator functions, but must be nonnegative and additive, meaning that the measure of the sum of indicator functions that is still an indicator function equals the sum of the measures. It is possible to extend measures to the test space of continuous and bounded functions: First, the measure of a multiple of an indicator function is defined as the multiple of the measure of the indicator function itself. Second, the measure of a step function is the sum of the measures of the steps. And third, the measure of a continuous and bounded function is defined by a limit process of step functions. By the nonnegativity and additivity assumptions, a measure is a nonnegative linear operator on the test space of continuous and bounded functions.

A prime example is the *Dirac* measure, δ, that represents the unit point mass at the origin. Being a measure, it is defined by the value it associates with an *indicator function*, 1_I. Here I is a subset of the time axis and 1_I is defined by $1_I(t) = 1$ if $t \in I$

and $1_I(t) = 0$ if $t \notin I$. The value δ associates with 1_I could be denoted $\delta(1_I)$. However, since the argument itself is a function here, $\langle \delta, 1_I \rangle$ is more common notation. Measure δ is defined by $\langle \delta, 1_I \rangle = 1_I(0)$. In other words, if I contains the origin, then $\langle \delta, 1_I \rangle = 1 - I$ embodies one unit of mass—but if I does not contain the origin, then $\langle \delta, 1_I \rangle = 0 - I$ embodies no mass. The extension of δ to a continuous and bounded function, ϕ, is straightforward: $\langle \delta, \phi \rangle = \phi(0)$.

Measures have been defined on the wide class of continuous and bounded functions. A distribution is a generalization of a measure. In other words, there are more distributions than measures. This is obtained by defining distributions on a narrower class of test functions. At first sight this procedure seems paradoxical, but it is right. By requiring that operators are defined *only* on a smaller set of functions, one admits more of them, in other words, generalizes. Distributions are defined on the *test space* of infinitely differentiable functions with compact support. (The support of a function is defined as the closure of the set of points where the function is nonzero.) The test space is endowed with a natural topology that corresponds with uniform convergence of all derivatives. A *distribution* is formally defined as a continuous linear mapping from this test space to the reals (or sometimes the complex numbers).

Since measures are defined a fortiori on the narrow test space of infinitely differentiable functions with compact supports, they are distributions. Distributions also generalize locally integrable functions f. For such an f one can define the distribution T_f by $\langle T_f, \phi \rangle = \int f(t)\phi(t)\, dt$. A first manifestation of the flexibility of distributions is the possibility to define their *derivatives* no matter what. The definition of the derivative of a distribution T, $\dot{T}$, should generalize the derivative of, say, a continuously differentiable function, f. In other words, we want $\dot{T}_f = T_{\dot{f}}$. Now $T_{\dot{f}}$ is defined by

$$\langle T_{\dot{f}}, \phi \rangle = \int \dot{f}(t)\phi(t)\, dt = - \int f(t)\dot{\phi}(t)\, dt = -\langle T_f, \dot{\phi} \rangle.$$

(The integration by parts produced no residual term as ϕ has compact support.) This motivates the following definition of $\dot{T}$: $\langle \dot{T}, \phi \rangle = -\langle T, \dot{\phi} \rangle$.

The *convolution product* of two continuous functions, f and g, with compact supports is defined by

$$(f^*g)(t) = \int f(s)g(t - s)\, ds.$$

The definition of the convolution product of a distribution, T, and a test function, ϕ, should generalize; in other words, we want

$$T_f{}^*\phi = f^*\phi = \int f(s)\phi(t - s)\, ds = \langle T_f, \phi(t - \cdot) \rangle.$$

This motivates the definition of $T^*\phi$ as an infinitely differentiable function by

$$(T^*\phi)(t) = \langle T, \phi(t - \cdot) \rangle.$$

The definition of the convolution product can be generalized further to apply to two distributions, provided that a certain condition is fulfilled (Schwartz, 1961, p. 123). Elementary facts are $\delta^*T = T$ (in other words, δ is the unit element) and $\dot{S}^*T = S^*\dot{T}$. It is easy to check this for $T = T_\phi$. Then

$$(\delta^*\phi)(t) = \langle \delta, \phi(t - \cdot) \rangle = \phi(t - 0) = \phi(t),$$

while

$$\begin{aligned}(\dot{S}^*\phi)(t) &= \langle \dot{S}, \phi(t - \cdot) \rangle = -\langle S, [\phi(t - \cdot)]\dot{} \rangle \\ &= -\langle S, \dot{\phi}(t - \cdot) \cdot (-1) \rangle = \langle S, \dot{\phi}(t - \cdot) \rangle \\ &= (S^*\dot{\phi})(t).\end{aligned}$$

DYNAMIC INPUT-OUTPUT ANALYSIS   307

Distributions even generalize operations such as differentiation. The convolution product of δ and any distribution T yields $\delta * T' = \delta * \dot{T} = \dot{T}$. This device will take care of the investment term in the dynamic input-output equation. δ is a distribution, but not a measure (which must be nonnegative). This is why distributions are more convenient tools for dynamic input-output than measures. Moreover, in some cases distributions along with the convolution product form an algebra and equations can be solved by finding inverse distributions. This observation is the clue to the resolution of distributed input-output problems.

Before starting the main analysis, let me disclaim any rigor or comprehensiveness in this mathematical section. A referee suggested a better introduction, namely Lighthill (1964), as well as a more advanced and encyclopedic treatment: Gel'fand and Shilov (1967).

Proof of Proposition 1. To demonstrate existence of $\sum_0^\infty A^{*k}$ and its continuity in test functions, ϕ, we estimate, using nonnegativity,

$$\left\langle \sum_0^\infty A^{*k}, \phi \right\rangle \leq \left\langle \sum_0^\infty A^{*k}, \|\phi\|_\infty \right\rangle = \left\langle \sum_0^\infty A^{*k}, 1 \right\rangle \|\phi\|_\infty$$

$$= \int \left(\sum_0^\infty A^{*k} \right) \|\phi\|_\infty = \sum_0^\infty \left(\int A \right)^k \|\phi\|_\infty \tag{9}$$

where the last equality rests on the fact $\int (A^{*k}) = (\int A)^k$. (This fact will be established for $k = 2$, the further cases going by induction. The $(i, j)^{\text{th}}$ element of the left hand side matrix equals

$$\left[\int (A^{*2}) \right]_{ij} = \int \left[(A^{*2})_{ij} \right] = \left\langle (A^{*2})_{ij}, 1 \right\rangle$$

$$= \left\langle \sum_m a_{im} * a_{mj}, 1 \right\rangle$$

$$= \sum_m \left\langle a_{im}, \left\langle a_{mj}, 1 \right\rangle \right\rangle = \sum_m \left\langle a_{im}, \int a_{mj} \right\rangle$$

$$= \sum_m \left\langle a_{im}, 1 \right\rangle \int a_{mj} = \sum_m \int a_{im} \int a_{mj}$$

$$= \left(\int A \int A \right)_{ij} = \left[\left(\int A \right)^2 \right]_{ij},$$

the $(i, j)^{\text{th}}$ element of the right hand side.

By the convergence consequence, (3), of the assumption, the right hand side of (9) is finite. Consequently, the distribution on the left hand side, $\sum_0^\infty A^{*k}$ exists and is continuous in ϕ. To demonstrate the second part of the proposition, consider a distribution z which is nonnegative and near infinity agrees with a bounded function. Then $z = z' + z''$ with z' nonnegative and agreeing with a bounded function and with z'' nonnegative and support bounded from above. We shall show that, first,

$$x' = \left(\sum_0^\infty A^{*k} \right) * z'$$

is nonnegative and agrees with a bounded function, and second,

$$x'' = \left(\sum_0^\infty A^{*k} \right) * z''$$

is a bounded (i.e., finite total mass) nonnegative distribution with support bounded from above. Since $x = x' + x''$, this is enough. Nonnegativity is obvious. To demonstrate the boundedness of x', choose nonnegative locally integrable functions A_m that approximate $\sum_0^\infty A^{*k}$ from below and define $x_m = A_m * z'$. Then, by nonnegativity, $x_m \uparrow x'$, and, defining $\| \cdot \|_\infty$ of a vector or matrix component wise as a vector or matrix of the same order,

$$\|x_m\|_\infty \leq \|A_m\|_1 \|z'\|_\infty = \left\langle A_m, 1 \right\rangle \|z'\|_\infty$$

$$\leq \left\langle \sum_0^\infty A^{*k}, 1 \right\rangle \|z'\|_\infty = \int \left(\sum_0^\infty A^{*k} \right) \|z'\|_\infty$$

$$= \sum_0^\infty \left(\int A \right)^k \|z'\|_\infty$$

by the first part of the proof, (9). By the assumption and the principle of monotone convergence, x_m converges in the $\| \cdot \|_\infty$-norm. In fact, $\|x_m\|_\infty \uparrow \|x\|_\infty$ for our $x_m \uparrow x$. Taking the limit in our inequality we obtain $\|x\|_\infty \leq \sum_0^\infty (\int A)^k \|z'\|_\infty$. x'' is as desired since the supports of both $\sum_0^\infty A^{*k}$ and z'' are bounded from above so that these distributions fulfill the convolution condition of Schwartz (1961) and their convolution also has support bounded from above.   Q.E.D.

Proof of Proposition 2. Substituting the balanced growth expressions, equation (4) becomes

$$x(0) e^{gt} = (A + Bg)^* x(0) e^{gt} + z(0) e^{gt}$$

or, by definition of the convolution product (see the first section of this appendix),

$$x(0) e^{gt} = \left\langle A + Bg, x(0) e^{g(t-\cdot)} \right\rangle + z(0) e^{gt}$$

or, by linearity of distribution $A + Bg$,

$$x(0) e^{gt} = e^{gt} \left\langle (A + Bg) e^{-g(\cdot)}, x(0) \right\rangle + z(0) e^{gt}.$$

Dividing through we obtain

$$x(0) = A(g)^* x(0) + z(0) \tag{10}$$

with

$$A(g) = (A + Bg) e^{-g(\cdot)}. \tag{11}$$

(11) shows that for $g \geq 0$, $A(g)$ is a nonnegative distribution. It has nonpositive support. Thus $A(g)$ is an input-output matrix distribution. By the nonpositivity of the support, $\int A(g)$ is an increasing function of g. By a standard result on nonnegative matrices, spectral radius $\rho[\int A(g)]$ is a continuous function of g. By spectral radius consequence (2) of the assumption, $\rho[\int A(0)] < 1$. Ruling out the trivial case $A = B = 0$ (for which $g^* = \infty$ fulfills the proposition), $\rho[\int A(\infty)] = \infty$. By the intermediate value theorem there is a $g^* > 0$ such that $\rho[\int A(g^*)] = 1$. It follows that for $0 \leq g < g^*$, $\rho[\int A(g)] < 1$. By (2), $A(g)$ fulfills the Hawkins-Simon conditions and we may subject it to proposition 1. Hence for every $z(0)$ which is nonnegative there is a nonnegative solution to (10). The solution can be taken constant and denoted $x(0)$. It remains to justify that g^* is the maximum growth rate. This rests on the fact that for $g = g^*$, $\rho[\int A(g)] = 1$, which implies, by the theory of nonnegative matrices, that the condition—for every nonnegative $z(0)$ there is a solution $x(0)$ of

$$x(0) = \left[\int A(g) \right] x(0) + z(0) = A(g)^* x(0) + z(0)$$

—is violated. Consequently, in the statement of the proposition, g has to be strictly less than g^* indeed and any higher critical growth rate would invalidate the proposition.   Q.E.D.

Proof of Proposition 3. To prove that the expression in the statement of the Proposition is truly the inverse distribution, we multiply through by the operator, $I\delta - B_0\dot\delta$, to check that it yields the unit distribution, δI. Thus,

$$\left[\tilde{H}\exp(B_0^- t)B_0^{-2}B_0 + \delta(I - B_0^- B_0)\right]^*(I\delta - B_0\dot\delta)$$

$$= \tilde{H}\exp(B_0^- t)B_0^{-2}B_0 + \delta(I - B_0^- B_0)$$

$$- \left[\tilde{H}\exp(B_0^- t)\right]B_0^{-2}B_0^2 - (I - B_0^- B_0)B_0\dot\delta$$

$$= \tilde{H}\exp(B_0^- t)B_0^{-2}B_0 + \delta(I - B_0^- B_0)$$

$$- \tilde{H}\exp(B_0^- t)B_0^{-3}B_0^2 + \delta B_0^{-2}B_0^2 - (B_0 - B_0^- B_0^2)\delta$$

$$= \tilde{H}\exp(B_0^- t)B_0^{-2}(B_0 - B_0^- B_0^2)$$

$$+ \delta\left[I - B_0^-(B_0 - B_0^- B_0^2)\right] - (B_0 - B_0^- B_0^2)\delta$$

which equals δI for $B_0 - B_0^- B_0^2 = 0$.   Q.E.D.

Proof of Proposition 4. The left hand side of the statement of the Proposition equals

$$(I\delta - B_0\dot\delta)^{*-1}$$

$$= \left(I\delta - T\begin{pmatrix} J_1 & 0 \\ 0 & J_2 \end{pmatrix}T^{-1}\dot\delta\right)^{*-1}$$

$$= \left[T\left(I\delta - \begin{pmatrix} J_1 & 0 \\ 0 & J_2 \end{pmatrix}\dot\delta\right)T^{-1}\right]^{*-1}$$

$$= T\begin{pmatrix} I_1\delta - J_1\dot\delta & 0 \\ 0 & I_2\delta - J_2\dot\delta \end{pmatrix}^{*-1}T^{-1}$$

$$= T\begin{pmatrix} (I_1\delta - J_1\dot\delta)^{*-1} & 0 \\ 0 & (I_2\delta - J_2\dot\delta)^{*-1} \end{pmatrix}T^{-1}.$$

Since the diagonal of upper triangular J_2 never vanishes, this matrix is regular, and by proposition 3 (example 1),

$$(I_2\delta - J_2\dot\delta)^{*-1} = \tilde{H}\exp(J_2^{-1}t)J_2^{-1}.$$

Since the diagonal of upper triangular J_1 is zero, the nth power of this matrix is zero, and therefore,

$$\sum_0^{n-1}\overset{(k)}{\delta} J_1^k * (I_1\delta - J_1\delta) = \sum_0^{n-1}\overset{(k)}{\delta} J_1^k - \sum_0^{n-1}\overset{(k+1)}{\delta} J_1^{k+1}$$

$$= \overset{(0)}{\delta} J_1^0 - \overset{(n)}{\delta} J_1^n = \delta I_1$$

or

$$(I_1\delta - J_1\delta)^{*-1} = \sum_0^{n-1}\overset{(k)}{\delta} J_1^k.$$

Substitution of the two derived inverses yields the right hand side of the statement of the Proposition.   Q.E.D.

Proof of Proposition 5. The proof is organized as follows. First we rewrite equation (6) such that on the left hand side an operator applies to unknown x and on the right hand side there is known z. Then we find the inverse of the operator. Convoluting through with the inverse, the left hand side becomes x and the right hand side the convolution product of the inverse and z. This is the solution. Simplification finishes the proof. We differentiate (6) by parts (see the first section of this appendix) which, incidentally, makes the treatment of circulat-

ing and fixed capital uniform:

$$[(I - A_0)\delta - B_0\dot\delta]^*x = z.$$

We factorize the operator:

$$(I - A_0)\delta - B_0\dot\delta = (I - A_0)\left[I\delta - (I - A_0)^{-1}B_0\dot\delta\right].$$

Here we used the Hawkins-Simon conditions. These also yield that the B_0 property carries over to $(I - A_0)^{-1}B_0$. Proposition 3 inverts the operator:

$$\left[I\delta - (I - A_0)^{-1}B_0\dot\delta\right]^{*-1}(I - A_0)^{-1}$$

$$= \left\{\tilde{H}\exp\left[\left[(I - A_0)^{-1}B_0\right]^- t\right]\right.$$

$$\times\left[(I - A_0)^{-1}B_0\right]^{-2}(I - A_0)^{-1}B_0$$

$$+ \delta\left(I - \left[(I - A_0)^{-1}B_0\right]^-\right.$$

$$\left.\left.(I - A_0)^{-1}B_0\right)\right\}(I - A_0)^{-1}$$

where $[(I - A_0)^{-1}B_0]^-$ is the generalized inverse of $(I - A_0)^{-1}B_0$ which can also be written $B_0^-(I - A_0)$, by which the inverse operator becomes

$$\left[\tilde{H}\exp[B_0^-(I - A_0)t]B_0^-(I - A_0)B_0^- B_0\right.$$

$$\left.+ \delta(I - B_0^- B_0)\right]\sum_0^\infty A_0^k.$$

Convoluting with the right hand side, z, we obtain the solution,

$$x = \left\{\tilde{H}\exp[B_0^-(I - A_0)t]B_0^-(I - A_0)B_0^- B_0\right.$$

$$\left.+ \delta(I - B_0^- B)\right\}\sum_0^\infty A_0^k * z$$

$$= \left\{\tilde{H}\exp[B_0^-(I - A_0)t]B_0^-(I - A_0)B_0^- B_0\sum_0^\infty A_0^k\right\}*z$$

$$+ \delta(I - B_0^- B)\sum_0^\infty A_0^k * z$$

$$= \left\{\tilde{H}\exp[B_0^-(I - A_0)t]\right\}^*B_0^-(I - A_0)B_0^- B_0\sum_0^\infty A_0^k z$$

$$+ (I - B_0^- B)\sum_0^\infty A_0^k z.   \text{Q.E.D.}$$

Proof of Proposition 6. The organization of the proof is just as of the previous one. Thus, refer to the first paragraph of the proof of Proposition 5. By the assumption that A is integrable on $(\epsilon, 0)$, $A = A_0\delta + A_1 + A_2$ with A_0 a matrix, A_1 a locally summable function on $(-\infty, 0)$, and A_2's support in $(-\infty, \epsilon)$ for some negative ϵ. Here we use the fact that a nonnegative distribution concentrated in the origin must be a multiple of the Dirac distribution according to Schwartz (1957).

Similarly, $B = B_0\delta + B_1 + B_2$ with B_0 a matrix, B_1 absolutely continuous and B_2's support in $(-\infty, \epsilon)$. Through differentiation by parts (see the first section of this appendix), the equation becomes

$$(I\delta - A - \dot{B})^*x = z. \tag{12}$$

By substitution, the operator in (12) becomes

$$I\delta - A - \dot{B} = C_0 - C_1 - C_2 \tag{13}$$

with

$$C_0 = (I - A_0)\delta - B_0\dot{\delta} \tag{14}$$

the traditional dynamic input-output operator,

$$C_1 = A_1 + \dot{B}_1 \tag{15}$$

a locally integrable function on $(-\infty, 0)$, and

$$C_2 = A_2 + \dot{B}_2 \tag{16}$$

whose support is in $(-\infty, \epsilon)$. We factorize the operator, (13):

$$C_0 - C_1 - C_2 = C_0^*\left(I\delta - C_0^{*-1}{}^*C_1 - C_0^{*-1}{}^*C_2 \right). \tag{17}$$

Here

$$C_0^{*-1} = \left\{ \check{H}\exp[\,B_0^-(I - A_0)t\,]\,B_0^-(I - A_0)\,B_0^-\,B_0 \right.$$
$$\left. + \delta(I - B_0^-B_0) \right\} \sum_0^\infty A_0^k \tag{18}$$

(or a straightforward modification) by (14) and proposition 5 (remark 2); A_0 fulfills the Hawkins-Simon conditions by the assumption of section III and the fact $0 \le A_0\delta \le A$. In further factorizing, the operator, (17), becomes

$$C_0^*\left(I\delta - C_0^{*-1}{}^*C_1 \right)$$
$${}^*\left[I\delta - \left(I\delta - C_0^{*-1}{}^*C_1 \right)^{*-1}{}^*C_0^{*-1}{}^*C_2 \right]. \tag{19}$$

This makes sense and is invertible provided that the factors

$$I\delta - C_0^{*-1}{}^*C_1,$$

and

$$I\delta - \left(I\delta - C_0^{*-1}{}^*C_1 \right)^{*-1}{}^*C_0^{*-1}{}^*C_2$$

are invertible. By (18), C_0^{*-1} is the sum of an infinitely differentiable function on $(-\infty, 0)$ and a multiple of the Dirac distribution. Consequently its convolution product, with C_1 which is locally summable by (14), exists and is a locally summable function on $(-\infty, 0)$. By Schwartz (1961, p. 143) $I\delta - C_0^{*-1}{}^*C_1$, has an inverse which is the sum of the Dirac distribution and a locally integrable function C_1^- on $(-\infty, 0)$. The last factor of (19) now is

$$I\delta - \left(I\delta + C_1^- \right)^*C_0^{*-1}{}^*C_2,$$

where the remainder has support in $(-\infty, \epsilon)$ by virtue of C_2 as specified in (16). Consequently this factor has a power expansion inverse which is the sum of the Dirac distribution and a distribution C_2^- with support in $(-\infty, \epsilon)$. Thus the inverse of (19) becomes

$$\left(I\delta + C_2^- \right)^*\left(I\delta + C_1^- \right)^*C_0^{*-1}$$

with C_0^{*-1}, C_1^- and C_2^- given by (18) and the above text. Convoluting through this distribution with z yields the specific expression for x. To determine the nature of this solution, recall that C_0^{*-1} is, by (18), the sum of an infinitely differentiable function on $(-\infty, 0)$ and a multiple of the Dirac distribution, C_1^- is a locally integrable function on $(-\infty, 0)$, and C_2^- is a distribution with support in $(-\infty, \epsilon)$. Let us summarize this symbolically as

$$C_0^{*-1} \in C_-^\infty + D_0', \quad C_1^- \in L^1_{\text{loc}, -},$$

and

$$C_2^- \in D'_{(-\infty, \epsilon)}.$$

It follows that the inverse belongs to

$$\left(D_0' + D'_{(-\infty, \epsilon)} \right)^*\left(D_0' + L^1_{\text{loc}, -} \right)^*\left(C_-^\infty + D_0' \right).$$

This space can be written out as

$$D'_-{}^*C_-^\infty + \left(D_0' + D'_{(-\infty, \epsilon)} \right)^*\left(D_0' + L^1_{\text{loc}, -} \right)$$

or

$$C_-^\infty + \left(D_0' + L^1_{\text{loc}, -} \right) + D'_{(-\infty, \epsilon)}{}^*\left(D_0' + L^1_{\text{loc}, -} \right)$$

which is simply

$$L^1_{\text{loc}} + D_0' + D'_{(-\infty, \epsilon)}. \qquad \text{Q.E.D.}$$

Example. Consider the full input-output equation, (4), with A and B given by (7) of section VI. Then, in the proof of proposition 6,

$$A = A_0\delta + A_1 + A_2 = 0 + \begin{pmatrix} 0 & 0 \\ 1 & 0 \end{pmatrix}1/3e^{(\cdot)}\check{H} + 0$$

and

$$B = B_0\delta + B_1 + B_2 = \begin{pmatrix} 0 & 1 \\ 0 & 0 \end{pmatrix}\delta + 0 + 0,$$

so that (14), (15), and (16) reduce to

$$C_0 = I\delta - \begin{pmatrix} 0 & 1 \\ 0 & 0 \end{pmatrix}\dot{\delta},$$

$$C_1 = \begin{pmatrix} 0 & 0 \\ 1 & 0 \end{pmatrix}\tfrac{1}{3}e^{(\cdot)}\check{H},$$

$$C_2 = 0.$$

Consequently, the operator, (19), reduces to

$$\left[I\delta - \begin{pmatrix} 0 & 1 \\ 0 & 0 \end{pmatrix}\dot{\delta} \right]^*\left[I\delta - C_0^{*-1}{}^*\begin{pmatrix} 0 & 0 \\ 1 & 0 \end{pmatrix}\tfrac{1}{3}e^{(\cdot)}\check{H} \right]. \tag{19'}$$

The second factor of this operator, (19'), becomes by the example to proposition 4,

$$I\delta - \begin{pmatrix} \delta & \dot{\delta} \\ 0 & \delta \end{pmatrix}^*\begin{pmatrix} 0 & 0 \\ 1 & 0 \end{pmatrix}\tfrac{1}{3}e^{(\cdot)}\check{H}$$

$$= I\delta - \tfrac{1}{3}\begin{pmatrix} \dot{\delta} & 0 \\ \delta & 0 \end{pmatrix}^*e^{(\cdot)}\check{H}$$

$$= I\delta - \tfrac{1}{3}\begin{pmatrix} e^{(\cdot)}\check{H} - \delta & 0 \\ e^{(\cdot)}\check{H} & 0 \end{pmatrix}$$

$$= \begin{pmatrix} \tfrac{4}{3}\delta - \tfrac{1}{3}e^{(\cdot)}\check{H} & 0 \\ -\tfrac{1}{3}e^{(\cdot)}\check{H} & \delta \end{pmatrix}. \tag{20}$$

The inverse of this second factor, (20), is

$$\begin{pmatrix} \left[\tfrac{4}{3}\delta - \tfrac{1}{3}e^{(\cdot)}\check{H}\right]^{*-1} & 0 \\ \tfrac{1}{3}e^{(\cdot)}\check{H}^*\left[\tfrac{4}{3}\delta - \tfrac{1}{3}e^{(\cdot)}\check{H}\right]^{*-1} & \delta \end{pmatrix}$$

$$= \begin{pmatrix} \tfrac{3}{4}\left[\delta - \tfrac{1}{4}e(\cdot)\check{H}\right]^{*-1} & 0 \\ \tfrac{1}{4}e^{(\cdot)}\check{H}^*\left[\delta - \tfrac{1}{4}e^{(\cdot)}\check{H}\right]^{*-1} & \delta \end{pmatrix}$$

$$= \begin{pmatrix} \tfrac{3}{4}\left[\delta + \tfrac{1}{4}e^{\frac{3}{4}(\cdot)}\check{H}\right] & 0 \\ \tfrac{1}{4}e^{(\cdot)}\check{H}^*\left[\delta + \tfrac{1}{4}e^{\frac{3}{4}(\cdot)}\check{H}\right] & \delta \end{pmatrix}$$

$$= \begin{pmatrix} \tfrac{3}{4}\delta + \tfrac{3}{16}e^{\frac{3}{4}(\cdot)}\check{H} & 0 \\ \tfrac{1}{4}e^{\frac{3}{4}(\cdot)}\check{H} & \delta \end{pmatrix},$$

by the example to proposition 1 and the easily verifiable elementary fact, $e^{(\cdot)}\check{H} * e^{\frac{3}{4}(\cdot)}\check{H} = 4e^{\frac{3}{4}(\cdot)}\check{H} - 4e^{(\cdot)}\check{H}$. Convoluting through with the inverse of the first factor of (19') which is given by the example to proposition 4, we obtain the inverse operator related to (19'),

$$\begin{pmatrix} \frac{3}{4}\delta + \frac{3}{16}e^{\frac{3}{4}(\cdot)}\check{H} & 0 \\ \frac{1}{4}e^{\frac{3}{4}(\cdot)}\check{H} & \delta \end{pmatrix} * \begin{pmatrix} \delta & \delta \\ 0 & \delta \end{pmatrix}$$

$$= \begin{pmatrix} \frac{3}{4}\delta + \frac{3}{16}e^{\frac{3}{4}(\cdot)}\check{H} & \left[\frac{3}{4}\delta + \frac{3}{16}e^{\frac{3}{4}(\cdot)}\check{H}\right] * \delta \\ \frac{1}{4}e^{\frac{3}{4}(\cdot)}\check{H} & \left[\frac{1}{4}e^{\frac{3}{4}(\cdot)}\check{H}\right] * \delta + \delta \end{pmatrix}$$

$$= \begin{pmatrix} \frac{3}{4}\delta + \frac{3}{16}e^{\frac{3}{4}(\cdot)}\check{H} & \frac{3}{4}\delta + \frac{9}{64}e^{\frac{3}{4}(\cdot)}\check{H} - \frac{3}{16}\delta \\ \frac{1}{4}e^{\frac{3}{4}(\cdot)}\check{H} & \frac{3}{16}e^{\frac{3}{4}(\cdot)}\check{H} - \frac{1}{4}\delta + \delta \end{pmatrix}$$

$$\times \begin{pmatrix} \frac{3}{4}\delta & \frac{3}{4}\delta - \frac{3}{16}\delta \\ 0 & \frac{3}{4}\delta \end{pmatrix} + \begin{pmatrix} \frac{3}{16} & \frac{9}{64} \\ \frac{1}{4} & \frac{3}{16} \end{pmatrix} e^{\frac{3}{4}(\cdot)}\check{H}.$$

Convoluting through this distribution with z yields the specific expression for x, (8), posted in the example to proposition 6 in section VI.   Q.E.D.

REFERENCES

Bródy, A., "The Model of Expanding Reproduction," *Applications of Mathematics to Economics* (Budapest: Akadémiai Kiadó, 1965), 61–63.

———, *Proportions, Prices and Planning* (Budapest: Akadémiai, Kiadó and Amsterdam: North-Holland Publishing Company, 1974).

Foley, D. K., "Accumulation, Realization, and Crisis," *Journal of Economic Theory* 30 (2) (1982), 300–319.

Galan, C. de, "Gedifferentieerde Loonvorming," *Economisch Statistische Berichten* 65 (1980), 214–218.

Gel'fand, I. M., and G. E. Shilov, *Generalized Functions* (New York: Academic Press, 1967).

Gladyshevskii, A. I., and G. K. Belous, "Microeconomic Calculations of Distributed Lags in Capital Construc-

tion," *Matekon* 14 (3) (1978), 58–79.

Hawkins, D., and H. A. Simon, "Some Conditions of Macroeconomic Stability," *Econometrica* 17 (1949), 245–248.

Johansen, L., "On the Theory of Dynamic Input-Output Models with Different Time Profiles of Capital Construction and Finite Life-Time of Capital Equipment," *Journal of Economic Theory* 19 (2) (1978), 513–533.

Kendrick, D., "On the Leontief Dynamic Inverse," *Quarterly Journal of Economics* 86 (1972), 693–696.

Leontief, W., "When Should History be Written Backwards?" *The Economic History Review*, Second Series, 16 (1) (1963), 1–8.

———, "The Dynamic Inverse," in A. P. Carter and A. Bródy (eds.), *Contributions to Input-Output Analysis* (Amsterdam: North-Holland Publishing Company, 1970), 17–46.

Leontief, W., A. P. Carter, and P. A. Petri, *The Future of the World Economy* (New York: Oxford University Press, 1977).

Lighthill, M. J., *Introduction to Fourier Analysis and Generalized Functions* (Cambridge: Cambridge University Press, 1964).

Livesey, D. A., "The Singularity Problem in the Dynamic Input-Output Model," *International Journal System Science* 4 (1973), 437–440.

———, "A Minimal Realization of the Leontief Dynamic Input-Output Model," in K. R. Polenske and J. Skolka (eds.), *Advances in Input-Output Analysis* (Cambridge, MA: Ballinger Publishing Company, 1976), 527–541.

Marx, K., *Capital 2: The Process of Circulation of Capital* (New York: International Publishers, 1974).

ten Raa, Th., "The Distribution Approach to Spatial Economics," *Journal of Regional Science* 24 (1) (1984), 105–117.

———, "Applied Dynamic Input-Output with Distributed Activities," *European Economic Review* (1986).

Rao, C. R., *Linear Statistical Inference and Its Applications* (New York: John Wiley & Sons, 1974).

Schwartz, L., *Théorie des Distributions* (Paris: Hermann, 1957).

———, *Méthodes Mathématiques pour les Sciences Physiques* (Paris: Hermann, 1961).

Zhuravlev, S. N., "On Solutions to a Dynamic Input-Output Model with the Maximization of Consumption as the Criterion," *Matekon* 18 (3) (1982), 50–64.

[13]

Output and Investment for Exponential Growth in Consumption—The General Solution and Some Comments[1]

1. Stone and Brown [1] have obtained a relationship between q and e from the relationships

$$Bq = v + e \qquad \dots \dots \dots \dots \dots \quad (1)$$

$$v = K\Delta q \qquad \dots \dots \dots \dots \dots \quad (2)$$

and
$$Ee = (I + R)e \qquad \dots \dots \dots \dots \dots \quad (3)$$

where $B = I - A$ and

$$Ex_t = x_{t+1} \quad \text{and} \quad \Delta x_t = (E - 1)x_t,$$

q is the output vector, v the investment vector and e the consumption vector; A is the matrix of input-output coefficients, K is the matrix of capital output coefficients, R is the matrix of consumption-change and I is the unit matrix.

Here R is used in place of $\hat{r}$ used in the Stone and Brown paper to cover the case when R is not a diagonal-matrix, that is, when there is interconnected growth in the consumption of commodities.

Stone and Brown have considered only one particular solution of (1), (2) and (3) and not the general solution. In this note the general solution is obtained in Section 2 and the particular solution of Stone and Brown is generalized to the case when R is not necessarily diagonal and to the case of polynomial growth in consumption in Section 3.

In Section 4 it is shown that the Stone and Brown particular solution is the minimal solution which is non-negative for all t, except perhaps in certain exceptional cases.

2. The general solution of

$$Bq = v + e$$

$$v = K\Delta q \qquad \dots \dots \dots \dots \dots \quad (4)$$

and any given path of e is given by $q = Q + \bar{q}$ where $\bar{q}$ is any particular solution obtained from the three relations (4) and Q is the solution of

$$Bq = v$$

and
$$v = K\Delta q. \qquad \dots \dots \dots \dots \dots \quad (5)$$

[1] I am thankful to Mr. P. N. Mathur for helpful discussions.

Q is therefore given by

$$Q = (I + K^{-1}B)^t l$$

(K being assumed to be non-singular) where l is a vector of arbitrary constants.

Hence the general solution is given by

$$q = (I + K^{-1}B)^t l + \bar{q}. \qquad \qquad \ldots \ldots \ldots \ldots \quad (6)$$

If $q_0 = \bar{q}_0$ at $t = 0$

then $l = 0$ and $q = \bar{q}.$

$q_0 = \bar{q}_0$ implies that even the initial output is such as to just sustain the particular path of e after $t = 0$.

If $q_0 \neq \bar{q}_0$ then

$$q = \bar{q} + (I + K^{-1}B)^t (q_0 - \bar{q}_0) \qquad \ldots \ldots \ldots \ldots \quad (7)$$

If $q_0 < \bar{q}_0$, q will be less than $\bar{q}$ by $(I + K^{-1}B)^t \,|\, q_0 - \bar{q}_0 \,|$ and if $q_0 > \bar{q}_0$, q will be greater than $\bar{q}$ by $(I + K^{-1}B)^t (q_0 - \bar{q}_0)$.

Similar results for v also can be obtained.

For the solution to be economically meaningful q must be a non-negative vector. If, however, external assistance is allowed in the model, then the $-$ve q's indicate the need and direction of the external assistance. The question of a non-negative solution is taken up in Section 4. When $q = q_0$ at $t = 0$, the solution of (4) can also be obtained in the form

$$q = (I + K^{-1}B)^t q_0 - [K^{-1}e_{t-1} + (I + K^{-1}B)K^{-1}e_{t-2} + \ldots \quad (8)$$
$$+ (I + K^{-1}B)^{t-1}K^{-1}e_0]$$

as follows.

From the first two equations in (1) we have

$$\Delta q = K^{-1}Bq - K^{-1}e. \qquad \ldots \ldots \ldots \ldots \quad (9)$$

Treating this as a non-homogeneous difference equation in q and following the same method as for a non-homogeneous difference equation in one variable, we get the solution as in (8).

Following the method given in [3] of the Stone and Brown paper, a "forward" particular solution

$$\bar{q} = (B + K)^{-1} \sum_{\theta=0}^{\infty} [K(B + K)^{-1}]^{\theta} e_{t+\theta} \qquad \ldots \ldots \ldots \quad (10)$$

can be obtained provided

$$\underset{\varphi \to \infty}{\text{Lim}} \sum_{\theta=\varphi}^{\infty} [K(B + K)^{-1}]^{\theta} e_{t+\theta} = 0. \qquad \ldots \ldots \ldots \quad (11)$$

When

$$e_{t+\theta} = (I + R)^{\theta} e_t$$

(10) takes the form given in equation (17) of the Stone and Brown paper.

OUTPUT AND INVESTMENT—THE GENERAL SOLUTION   79

Since both (6) where $\bar{q}$ is given by (10), and (8) are solutions for $q = q_0$ at $t = 0$, both of them must be equivalent. It can easily be shown that they are so.

For if (6) and (8) are to be equivalent it is evident that the equality

$$(I + K^{-1}B)^t \bar{q}_0 = \bar{q} + [K^{-1}e_{t+1} \ldots + (I + K^{-1}B)^{t-1}K^{-1}e_0] \quad \ldots \ldots (12)$$

must hold for all t.

To prove that the equality (12) holds for all t consider the coefficient of e_{t+T} on the l.h.s.

It is given by

$$(I + K^{-1}B)^t(B + K)^{-1}[K(B + K)^{-1}]^{t+T}$$

$$= (I + K^{-1}B)^t(I + K^{-1}B)^{-1}K^{-1}(I + BK^{-1})^{-(t+T)}$$

since $$(B + K)^{-1} = (I + K^{-1}B)^{-1}K^{-1}$$

and $$K(B + K)^{-1} = (I + BK^{-1})^{-1}$$

$$= [I + K^{-1}B]^{t-1}[I + K^{-1}B]^{-(t+T)}K^{-1}$$

$$= (I + K^{-1}B)^{-(T+1)}K^{-1}$$

which is equal to the coefficient of e_{t+T} on the r.h.s. Hence the l.h.s. = r.h.s. and it follows that the forms (6) and (8) are equivalent. Since the form (8) does not involve the summation of an infinite series, it is convenient to use it when the value of q at $t = 0$ is given.

Stone and Brown have obtained a particular solution $\bar{q}$ when $Ee = (I + R)e$ which is valid even when R is not a diagonal matrix. It is evident that their particular solution for v and hence for that for q in part 2 of their paper would converge only if $(KB^{-1})^\theta R^\theta$ tends to 0 as $\theta \to \infty$ for which it is necessary and sufficient that the largest latent root of R should be less than the smallest latent root of BK^{-1} in modulus. When this condition is satisfied the solution is valid and is given by

$$\bar{v} = Me \quad \ldots \ldots \ldots \ldots \ldots \ldots \ldots (13)$$

and $$\bar{q} = B^{-1}(I + M)e$$

where $$M = \sum_{\theta=1}^{\infty} (KB^{-1})^\theta R^\theta.$$

If R is a diagonal matrix with r_i as the ith element $B^{-1}(I + M)e$ can be shown to be equivalent to

$$B^{-1} \sum_{i=1}^{n} (I - r_i KB^{-1})^{-1}E_i \quad \ldots \ldots \ldots \ldots \ldots (14)$$

where $E_i = \begin{pmatrix} o \\ \vdots \\ e_i \\ o \\ o \end{pmatrix}$, by rearranging the terms in the series.[1]

---

[1] Mathur [2] has also derived the particular solution in the form (14) in a different way and he has then shown that the form given by Stone and Brown, is equivalent to form in (14).

When R is not diagonal, $q = B^{-1}(I + M)e$ can be shown to be equivalent to

$$q = B^{-1} \sum_{i=1}^{n} (I - r_i KB^{-1})^{-1} L^{-1} I_i Le \qquad \dots \dots \dots \quad (15)$$

I_i being a matrix with 1 in the ith place on the diagonal and all other elements being zero, as follows, where L is the latent vector matrix of R and r_i are the latent roots of R.

Let $\qquad\qquad q' = Lq, \; v' = Lv, \; e' = Le$

and $\qquad\qquad LBL^{-1} = B' \text{ and } LKL^{-1} = K'$

Since L is the latent vector matrix of R

$$LR = \hat{r}L$$

where $\hat{r}$ is the diagonal matrix with r_i as the elements. Then we have

$$B'q' = v' + e'$$
$$v' = K'\Delta q'$$

and $\qquad\qquad \Delta e' = \hat{r}e'$

Hence, as before,

$$q' = (B')^{-1}(I + M')e'$$

where $\qquad\qquad M' = \sum_{i=1}^{\infty} (K'B'^{-1})^{\theta} \hat{r}^{\theta}$

or $\qquad\qquad q' = B'^{-1} \sum_{i=1}^{n} (I - r_i K'B'^{-1})^{-1} E'_i \qquad \dots \dots \dots \quad (16)$

where $\qquad\qquad E'_i = \begin{pmatrix} o \\ \vdots \\ e_i' \\ o \\ o \end{pmatrix} = I_i Le$

Substituting the values of q', B', K' and E'_i and simplifying the equation (16) reduces to (15).

Stone and Brown have also considered particular solutions when $E^{\theta}e = e$ or R is a zero matrix and when $E^{\theta}e = (I + R0)e$, and obtained them as

$$q = B^{-1}Ie \qquad \dots \dots \dots \dots \dots \dots \dots \quad (17)$$

and $\qquad\qquad q = B^{-1}(I + KB^{-1}R)e$ respectively.

Results (17) can be generalised to show that when

$$E^{\theta}e = \sum_{r=0}^{k} \frac{\theta \cdot (\theta - 1) \dots (\theta - r + 1)}{r!} R^r e \qquad \dots \dots \dots \quad (18)$$

where k is a +ve integer, the particular solution corresponding to (17) is given by

$$q = B^{-1}\left[\sum_{\theta=0}^{k} (KB^{-1})^{\theta} R^{\theta} \right] e. \qquad \dots \dots \dots \dots \quad (19)$$

When $k \to \infty$, e has exponential growth and the particular solution of q in (19) reduces to the particular solution of q in (8) corresponding to exponential growth.

OUTPUT AND INVESTMENT—THE GENERAL SOLUTION   81

4. The general solution of equations (1), (2) and (3) in Section 1 is given by

$$q = (I + K^{-1}B)^t(q_0 - \bar{q}_0) + \bar{q}$$

When $e_0 = 0$, $\bar{q} = 0$ and $\bar{q}_0 = 0$ and

$$q = (I + K^{-1}B)^t q_0.$$

Hence if $q_0 > 0$, $q > 0$, since the model envisages increasing output over time.[1]

Hence

$$(I + K^{-1}B)^t(q_0 - \bar{q}_0) \gtreqless 0$$

according as

$$q_0 \gtreqless \bar{q}_0.$$

Hence

$$q \gtreqless \bar{q}$$

according as

$$q_0 \gtreqless \bar{q}_0.$$

For large t, $(I + K^{-1}B)^t(q_0 - \bar{q}_0)$ is dominated by the terms in $(1 + \lambda)^t$ where $1 + \lambda$ is the latent root of $(I + K^{-1}B)$ with the largest modulus and with non-zero coefficients and since $(I + K^{-1}B)^t(q_0 - \bar{q}_0) > 0$ for all t when $(q_0 - \bar{q}_0) > 0$, the terms in $(1 + \lambda)^t$ must be positive. With the restrictions mentioned above on r_i [2] that

$$|r_i| < \lambda_1 \text{ for all } i$$

where λ_1 is the smallest (in modulus) latent root of $K^{-1}B$ or the reciprocal of the largest (in modulus) latent root of $B^{-1}K$ which is real and positive since $B^{-1}K$ is non-negative

$$|1 + r_i| < 1 + \lambda_1 \leqq |1 + \lambda|$$

Therefore for large t the terms in $(1 + \lambda)^t$ and hence $(I + K^{-1}B)^t(q_0 - \bar{q}_0)$ dominate q. Further $\bar{q}$ is non-negative which is evident from its form (13) if R is non-negative and in particular if R is diagonal with non-negative elements in the diagonal. Hence for q to be non-negative for all $t q_0 > \bar{q}_0$. When $q_0 \geq \bar{q}_0$, $q \geq \bar{q}$. Hence $\bar{q}$ is the minimal non-negative solution.[3]

Poona.   V. MUKERJI.

---

[1] (i) If $(I + K^{-1}B)^t l > 0$ when $l > 0$ for all l and for all t then $(I + K^{-1}B)$ is non-negative for all t. Hence $(I + K^{-1}B)$ is non-negative and $1 + \lambda$, is its dominant root which is real and positive and has a positive latent vector corresponding to it. It should be noted that the latent vector matrices of $(I + K^{-1}B)$ and of $B^{-1}K$ are the same.

(ii) If $(I + K^{-1}B)^t$ is not non-negative then $(I + K^{-1}B)l > 0$ for $l > 0$ for all t only when l which is $q_0 - \bar{q}$ in this case is proportional to the latent vector corresponding to $1 + \lambda_1$.
In both cases (i) and (ii) $q > \bar{q}$ according as $q_0 > q_0$.

(iii) When $(I + K^{-1}B)$ is not non-negative but $1 + \lambda_1$ is its only positive real root and has the largest modulus then for large t, $(I + K^{-1}B)l \gtreqless 0$ according as $l \gtreqless 0$ and $\bar{q}$ is still the minimal non-negative solution for large t. For small t if any element of q becomes −ve for any t then $q = \bar{q}$ has to be the only initial condition which is admissible if q is to be non-negative for all t. If, however, for small $t q$ remains +ve then $q > \bar{q}$ may not be true even when $q_0 > \bar{q}_0$ for small t. Some elements of q may be greater than those of $\bar{q}$ while the converse may be true for the other elements.

[2] If the conditions on r_i are not satisfied, Stone and Brown q is not a valid non-negative solution. It has to be investigated if there are valid non-negative solutions when these conditions are not satisfied.

[3] For the exceptional case when $\bar{q}$ may not be the minimal non-negative solution see (iii) footnote 1.

82   REVIEW OF ECONOMIC STUDIES

REFERENCES

[1]   Stone, Richard and Brown, J. A. C. " Output and investment for exponential growth
      in consumption ". *Review of Economic Studies*, June, 1962.

[2]   Mathur, P. N. " Output and investment for exponential growth in consumption—
      an alternative formulation: and derivation of their technological upper limits ".
      Review of Economic Studies, XXXX, 1964.

[3]   Leontief, W. W. "Lags and the Stability of the Dynamic Systems," *Econometrica*,
      Vol. 29, No. 4, October, 1961.

[14]

Stability of a Dynamic Input-Output System

Cumulative processes of inflation and changes in relative prices have been almost entirely neglected in discussions of the theory of economic growth. The neglect of relative prices may be attributed to the restriction of theoretical analysis to models involving only a single commodity, national output. The neglect of inflation and deflation is a consequence of confining analysis to equilibrium situations such as Harrod-Domar[1] steady growth equilibrium or the Cassell-vonNeumann evenly progressing economy.[2] While a study of the behavior of an economic system in equilibrium must be part of any complete theory of economic growth, the analysis of the inter-relationship of inflation and growth requires in addition a theory of disequilibrium describing the cumulative processes of expansion and contraction, inflation and deflation, which characterize the behavior of decentralized economic systems.

The purpose of this paper is to develop a theory of growth and inflation based on a multi-sector generalization of the familiar Harrod-Domar growth model, namely, Leontief's dynamic input-output system.[3] There is an interesting dual or price system corresponding to the model for output determination as Solow has demonstrated.[4] Unfortunately, there are serious obstacles in the way of any application of the dynamic input-output model and the corresponding price system to the analysis of inflation and economic growth. The first obstacle is that both the price system and the model of output determination are models for the determination of price and output levels in equilibrium. Specifically, it is assumed that profits are zero in each industry, or that all profits have reached some kind of long-run equality among industries. Changes in relative prices reflect changes in relative costs. In the theory of output determination, output levels are equal to the rates at which output is utilized. Changes in the level of output reflect changes in the level of demand. A second obstacle to application of this theory is a certain difficulty in maintaining the non-negativity of output levels and prices required for economic interpretation of the time-paths of price and output levels determined by the model. This difficulty is summarized in the dual stability theorem: If output levels can be guaranteed to remain

[1] Harrod, R., " An Essay in Dynamic Theory," *Economic Journal*, Vol. 49, No. 193, March, 1939, pp. 14-33.

————, *Towards a Dynamic Economics*, London, Macmillan, 1948.

Domar, E., " Capital Expansion, Rate of Growth, and Employment," *Econometrica*, Vol. 14, No. 2, April, 1946, pp. 137-47.

[2] Cassell, G., *The Theory of Social Economy*, New York, Harcourt Brace, 1924.

vonNeumann, J., " A Model of General Economic Equilibrium, " *Review of Economic Studies*, Vol. 13, No. 1, 1945-6, pp. 1-9.

[3] Leontief, W., " Dynamic Analysis," *Studies in the Structure of the American Economy*, ed. W. Leontief, New York, Oxford, 1953, pp. 53-92.

[4] Solow, R., " Competitive Valuation in a Dynamic Input-Output System," *Econometrica*, Vol. 27, No. 1, January, 1959, pp. 30-53; see the references listed there for previous discussion of a dual or price system corresponding to the dynamic input-output system.

[5] Jorgenson, D., "On a Dual Stability Theorem," *Econometrica*, Vol. 28 No. 4, October 1960, pp. 892-2

non-negative for any—meaningful—initial output levels (that is, output levels which are themselves non-negative), then prices must become negative for some meaningful initial price levels, and conversely.

To avoid dual instability, a number of re-interpretations of the basic model have been proposed. The basic idea underlying each of the attempts to re-interpret the dynamic input-output system and its dual is the same: the requirement that outputs must be equal to total utilization of the corresponding commodity and that prices must be equal to the corresponding costs must be relaxed. This alteration of the model is essential if the economic interpretation of the results is to be retained. However, while the system for which equalities between output and utilization and prices and cost hold exactly provides a determinate time-path of prices and quantities, the behavior of the system when inequalities are introduced can be determined only by adding further behavioral conditions to the system. One proposal is that the additional relations be obtained by invoking some explicit principle of maximization. The resulting theory may be interpreted as a model of optimal capital accumulation along the lines suggested by Dorfman, Samuelson, and Solow.[1] While this interpretation is appealing for applications of the dynamic input-output system to problems of planning, there is little evidence to suggest that such a theory of capital accumulation will be useful in descriptive studies. A second proposal is that the dynamic input-output system be supplemented by requiring that capital accumulation be irreversible.[2] This interpretation presents serious difficulties; the effect of irreversibility of capital accumulation on the formation of prices has nowhere been explored. Nevertheless, this approach provides descriptive realism and is not without promise.

In this paper a third re-interpretation of the model is suggested. Inequalities between output and utilization or prices and cost are held to define disequilibrium variables, each of which has a natural economic interpretation. For example, the difference between output and utilization of a given commodity may be interpreted as an excess supply of that commodity; similarly, the difference between price and cost for a commodity may be interpreted as profit per unit of the commodity sold. Classical theories of the business cycle have been based largely on the reactions of economic decision-makers to disequilibrium, that is, to excess demands and supplies on the one hand and profits and losses on the other.[3] When the classical reaction patterns are combined with technological relationships determining the character of equilibrium price and output levels, a complete and determinate theory of inflation and economic growth results. More specifically, disequilibrium analysis will be based on the theory of speculative stocks[4]: Entrepreneurs react to disequilibrium primarily through alteration of levels of investment in inventories and fixed capital equipment. Investment policies are determined by capital requirements dictated by three separate motives for the holding of stocks: For use in production or for transactions purposes, in anticipation of an increase in prices or for speculative purposes, and

[1] Dorfman, R., P. Samuelson, and R. Solow, *Linear Programming and Economic Analysis*, New York, McGraw-Hill, 1958.

[2] McManus, M., " Self-contradiction in Leontief's Dynamic Model," *Yorkshire Bulletin of Economic and Social Research*, Vol. 6, No. 9, May, 1957, pp. 1-21.
Leontief, *op. cit.*

[3] " Classical " is used here in the sense of " pre-Keynesian." The typical " classical " mechanism is Wicksell's cumulative process of inflation. For detailed references, see below, footnote 1, page 114.

[4] The theory of speculative stocks considered here is based on that of N. Kaldor, "Speculation and Economic Stability," *Review of Economic Studies*, Vol. 7, No. 1, October, 1939, pp. 1-27. Kaldor discusses in detail the microeconomic basis of the theory of speculative stocks and applies the theory to the stability of commodity markets and of aggregate income.

STABILITY OF A DYNAMIC INPUT-OUTPUT SYSTEM   107

to avoid risk or for precautionary purposes.[1] In the discussion that follows, the analysis is confined to investment policy as determined by holding of stocks for transactions and speculative purposes. As a consequence of the level of stocks held in the economy, prices for a commodity may rise or fall. In general the higher the level of stocks the less the price of a commodity will rise or the more its price will fall. This theory supplements the equilibrium relations in two important respects: First, the behavior of the system depends not only on the technological characteristics of the system, but also on the behavior of economic decision-makers in each of the sectors of the economy. Secondly, the complete system surmounts the difficulties associated with dual instability; by suitable restrictions on the initial values of the disequilibrium variables, the non-negativity of all economic variables is preserved.

To begin the analysis it is necessary to review the main facts about the dynamic input-output system and its dual. This review is followed by a discussion of the interaction of output and price determination through the adjustment of speculative stocks. Close attention is paid throughout to the non-negativity of output levels and prices and to the economic interpretation of disequilibrium.

The closed form of the dynamic input-output system with time continuous is given by the following set of simultaneous, first-order, differential equations:

$$x = Ax + B\dot{x},$$

where x is a vector of output levels; the ith component of x, x_i, is the level of output of the ith sector. The vector $\dot{x}$ is the set of rates of change of the output levels; the ith component, $\dot{x}_i = \dfrac{dx_i}{dt}$, is the rate of change of the level of output in the ith sector. The matrices A and B are input-output and stock-flow matrices, respectively. The typical element of A, say a_{ij}, is the amount of the ith output required by the jth industry as input for production of one unit of its own output. The typical element of B, say b_{ij}, is the amount of the ith output required as a stock by the jth industry for each unit of its own output. For the case in which there is a single output, the dynamic input-output system reduces to the familiar Harrod-Domar growth model. The input-output matrix, A, corresponds to the marginal propensity to consume and the stock-flow matrix, B, corresponds to the accelerator coefficient or " relation ". In the closed version of the dynamic input-output model, households are treated as one of the sectors of the model; households have labor and property services as output and consumer goods as input. For a more detailed inter-pretation of the model of output determination, the classic work of Leontief may be consulted.[2]

To begin the discussion of the dual or price system, let us denote by p_i the price of the ith output and by ρ the rate of interest; let $\dot{p}_i = \dfrac{dp_i}{dt}$ be the rate of change of the price of the ith input. Suppose first that prices are constant and equal to the cost of

---

[1] The classification of motives for holding of stocks follows K. Arrow, " Historical Background," *Studies in the Mathematical Theory of Inventory and Production*, ed. K. Arrow, S. Karlin, and H. Scarf, Stanford, Stanford University Press, 1958, pp. 3-15. Arrow follows Keynes' classification of the motives for holding money stocks in the *General Theory*, pp. 170-1, 195-6.

[2] Leontief, *op. cit.*

production, including the price of variable inputs *and* interest on capital. Then p_i, the price of the *i*th output, is given by:

$$p_i = \Sigma_j \, a_{ji} \, p_j + \rho \, \Sigma_j \, b_{ji} \, p_j, \qquad (i = 1, 2 \ldots n).$$

The first of the two sums is the current cost of production; a typical element of this sum, $a_{ki} \, p_k$, is the price of the *k*th commodity multiplied by the amount of that commodity required for production of one unit of the *i*th commodity. The second sum is total interest charges on stocks; to compute these charges, the sum of all stock values is multiplied by the rate of interest. A typical element of the sum of stock values, say $b_{ki} \, p_k$, is the price of the *k*th commodity multiplied by the amount of that commodity held by the *i*th sector for production of one unit of the *i*th commodity. Using matrix notation, this version of the dual may be written in the form:

$$p = A' \, p + \rho \, B' \, p,$$

where p is a vector with elements p_i, ρ is a scalar, and A', B' are the transposed matrices corresponding to A, B. Now suppose that prices are permitted to change; if prices rise, holders of stocks benefit from appreciation in the value of stocks held; if prices fall, holders of stocks suffer losses on depreciation in the value of stocks. If each price is equal to cost of production, including variable costs, interest charges, and depreciation on the value of stocks held, p_i, the price of the *i*th commodity, is given by:

$$p_i = \Sigma_j \, a_{ji} \, p_j + \rho \, \Sigma_j \, b_{ji} p_j - \Sigma_j \, b_{ji} \, \dot{p}_j.$$

The first two sums correspond to current costs of production and interest charges, as before. The third sum represents the return to the holder of stocks on the appreciation of stocks. If prices are rising, the change in value is added to revenue (or subtracted from cost). If prices are falling the change in value is added to cost (subtracted from revenue). A typical element of this sum, $b_{ki} \, \dot{p}_k$, is the time-rate of change of the value of the *i*th stock due to appreciation of the price of the corresponding commodity. An alternative interpretation of this term is perhaps more familar: Suppose r_i is the own-rate of interest on the *i*th commodity:[3]

$$r_i = \frac{dp_i}{dt} \, / \, p_i, \qquad (i = 1, 2 \ldots n).$$

Then the typical element may be written:

$$b_{ki} \, \dot{p}_i = \frac{\dot{p}_i}{p_i} \, b_{ki} \, p_i = r_i \, b_{ki} \, p_i.$$

Employing matrix notation two alternative versions of the dual to the dynamic input-output system are as follows:

$$p = A'p + \rho B'p - B'\dot{p},$$
$$= A'p + \rho B'p - B'Rp,$$

where $\dot{p}$ is a vector with elements $\dot{p}_i$, R is a diagonal matrix with elements r_i, and the remaining terms are defined as before.

---

[3] Own-rates were introduced into economic literature by P. Sraffa, "Dr. Hayek on Money and Capital," *Economic Journal*, Vol. 42, No. 165, March, 1932, pp. 42-53.

STABILITY OF A DYNAMIC INPUT-OUTPUT SYSTEM 109

The dynamic input-output system and its dual may be solved by putting each in normal form:

$$\dot{x} = B^{-1} (I-A) \, x,$$

$$\dot{p} = [-(B')^{-1} (I-A') + \rho I] \, p.$$

At the outset of the discussion of the solutions to this set of simultaneous differential equations, it is convenient to assume that the rank of the matrices B and $I-A$ is equal to the order of the output and price systems. In this case B^{-1} exists and $B^{-1} (I-A)$, $(B')^{-1}$ $(I-A')$ are non-singular. If this condition is not satisfied initially, the order of the system can be reduced until the condition is satisfied by eliminating variables and equations. In effect, it is assumed that such a reduction has already taken place. Secondly, it is convenient to assume that the matrix $(I-A)^{-1}B$ is indecomposable in the sense of Debreu and Herstein.[1] It is a simple matter, of little economic interest, to generalize the results given below to the decomposable case. Under the conditions stated, there is a unique positive set of output proportions and a unique positive set of relative prices which satisfy the dynamic input-output system and its dual. Existence of such solutions is implied by the non-negativity of $(I-A)^{-1}B$ and $B'(I-A')^{-1}$ provided that A is an input-output matrix. Uniqueness of such solutions is a consequence of the indecomposability of these two matrices. Secondly, since the two matrices have the same characteristic values, the characteristic value of the dynamic input-output system associated with the unique positive set of output proportions, that is, the rate of growth of the system in long-run equilibrium, corresponds to a characteristic value of the price system associated with the equilibrium relative prices. The latter may be interpreted as the equilibrium commodity own-rate of interest for all commodities. The equilibrium commodity own-rate is equal to the money rate of interest less the rate of growth of the system.

The unique equilibrium output proportions are globally stable if and only if the initial output levels lie in the subspace spanned by characteristic vectors of $B^{-1}(I-A)$ less than the long-run equilibrium rate of growth in real part. Similarly, the equilibrium relative prices are globally stable if and only if the initial price levels lie in the subspace spanned by characteristic vectors of $[-(B')^{-1}(I-A] + \rho I]$ associated with characteristic values less than the long-run equilibrium commodity own-rate of interest in real part. These facts are an immediate consequence of the following theorem on relative stability:

A characteristic solution to a system of linear differential equations with constant coefficients is relatively stable in the large if and only if all characteristic roots of the system have real parts less than the real part of the characteristic root associated with the solution in question.[2] By the dual stability theorem, these conditions cannot be satisfied for both the dynamic input-output system and its dual for any non-negative initial price and output levels. To retain the economic interpretation of price and output variables, it is necessary to relax the assumption that outputs are strictly equal to requirements for current production and desired capital accumulation and that prices are strictly equal to the costs of production.

If the requirements of strict equality of output to utilization and price to cost are relaxed, we may introduce disequilibrium variables, corresponding to the excess (or deficiency)

---

[1] Debreu, G. and I. Herstein, " Non-negative Square Matrices," *Econometrica*, Vol. 21, No. 4, October, 1953, pp. 597-607. This terminology is not standard. In the theory of Markov chains, " irreducible " is used in place of Debreu and Herstein's " indecomposable."

[2] For proof, see D. Jorgenson, *op. cit.*

REVIEW OF ECONOMIC STUDIES

of output over utilization and price over cost of production. Where ξ_i is the excess of the ith output over current utilization of the ith commodity, we have:

$$\xi_i = x_i - \sum_j a_{ij} \, x_j - \sum_j b_{ij} \, \dot{x}_j, \qquad (i = 1, 2 \ldots n),$$

or where ξ is a vector with components ξ_i:

$$\xi = x - Ax - B\dot{x}.$$

Similarly, where π_i is the excess of the ith price over cost of production, we have:

$$\pi_i = p_i - \sum_j a_{ji} \, p_j - \rho \sum_j b_{ji} \, p_j + \sum_j b_{ji} \, \dot{p}_j, \qquad (i = 1, 2 \ldots n),$$

or where π is a vector with components π_i:

$$\pi = p - A'p - \rho B'p + B' \dot{p}.$$

The disequilibrium variables for output are flow variables; since excess supply results in the accumulation of inventories and excess demand in decumulation of inventories and excess demand in decumulation, it is useful to introduce disequilibrium variables corresponding to excessive or deficient stocks. Where s is a vector of stocks of each commodity held through the economy, stocks are equal to ordinary technical requirements when

$$s = Bx.$$

Let ψ be a vector of excess stocks; then:

$$\psi = s - Bx.$$

But, by definition, output is current utilization plus accumulation of stocks:

$$x = Ax + \dot{s},$$

so that:

$$x = Ax + B\dot{x} + \psi,$$

and we have the fundamental stock-flow identity of the disequilibrium system:

$$\dot{\psi} = \xi,$$

the rate of change in excess stocks is equal to the excess supply of the corresponding commodity.

The problem for disequilibrium theory is this: What governs the time-path of the disequilibrium variables? A hypothesis based on the investment decisions of participants in the market for each commodity will be discussed. The hypothesis combines investment for speculative and transactions purposes with a market mechanism by which stocks in excess of required levels result in a decline in prices. The interaction of market price formation and decisions to hold stocks generates a cumulative process of disequilibrium, similar in form to the cumulative processes of accumulation and decumulation or inflation and deflation of classical theories of the business cycle.

To begin the discussion of disequilibrium theory for the dynamic input-output system we recall first that the output in any industry is equal to current utilization of the corresponding commodity plus increments to stock holdings. Using the notation introduced in the previous section, we have for each sector:

STABILITY OF A DYNAMIC INPUT-OUTPUT SYSTEM 111

$$x_i = \sum_j a_{ij} x_j + \dot{s}_i, \qquad\qquad (i = 1, 2 \ldots n).$$

If the accumulation of stocks is for transactions purposes (inventories) or for productive investment (fixed capital), change in holdings of stock may be divided into two parts: the accumulation required for expansion of output plus (or minus) an amount related to the excess of current stocks over equilibrium stocks. It is simplest to assume that the adjustment of accumulation for excessive or deficient stocks already in hand is proportional to the excess or deficiency. If stocks held are in excess of desired stocks, investment will be reduced; if stocks are held less than technical requirements investment will be increased. Under these assumptions the rate of change of stocks of the ith commodity held throughout the economy is given by:

$$\dot{s}_i = \sum_j b_{ij} x_j + h_i (s_i - s_i^+), \qquad\qquad (i = 1, 2 \ldots n),$$

where s_i^+ is the desired stock and s_i is the actual stock held of the ith commodity.[1] The constant of proportionality between investment and excess stocks, h_i, must be negative. Using matrix notation, the system of equations governing investment behavior is given by

$$x = Ax + B\dot{x} + H (s - s+),$$

Where H is a diagonal matrix with negative elements h_i along the main diagonal.

This disequilibrium adjustment mechanism is closely related to the flexible accelerator of Goodwin.[2] The second component of the rate of change of stocks held is proportional to the difference between actual and desired levels of stock. A similar disequilibrium mechanism for inventory investment has been discussed by Mills.[3] A good deal of empirical evidence for the validity of the flexible accelerator mechanism as a theory of fixed investment has been assembled by Chenery and Koyck.[4] The validity of the mechanism as a theory of inventory investment has been substantiated empirically by the recent study of Darling.[5] In the flexible accelerator theory of investment, desired stocks are usually determined by requirements for transactions or productive purposes alone. If holding of stocks for speculative purposes is significant, the stocks which entrepreneurs desire to hold are no longer equal to technical requirements alone. Desired stocks may be separated into two parts: Those required for transactions and productive purposes and those held in anticipation of an increase in the price level. Investment is equal to technical requirements plus (or minus) an amount which is proportional to the difference between actual and desired stocks. In addition to this theory of investment, the complete model includes a disequilibrium mechanism which describes the adjustment of price levels to costs and to stocks held in excess of technical requirements.

---

[1] A similar but not identical mechanism is discussed by H. Rose, "The Possibility of Warranted Growth," *Economic Journal*, Vol. 69, No. 274, June, 1959, pp. 313-33. Further discussion of the flexible accelerator is contained in: D. Jorgenson, "Growth and Fluctuations, a Causal Interpretation," *Quarterly Journal of Economics*, Vol. 74, No. 3, August, 1960, pp. 416-36. For discussion of some alternative mechanisms, see J. D. Sargan, "The Instability of the Leontief Dynamic Model," *Econometrica*, Vol. 26, No. 3, July, 1958, pp. 381-92.

[2] Goodwin, R., "Secular and Cyclical Aspects of the Multiplier and Accelerator," *Income, Employment and Public Policy*, essays in honour of A. H. Hansen, New York, Norton, 1948, pp. 108-32.

[3] Mills, E., "Expectations, Uncertainty, and Inventory Fluctuations," *Review of Economic Studies*, Vol. 22, No. 1, 1954-5, pp. 15-22.

[4] Chenery, H., "Overcapacity and the Acceleration Principle," *Econometrica*, Vol. 20, No. 1, January, 1953, pp. 1-28.
Koyck, L., *Distributed Lags and the Theory of Investment*, Amsterdam, North-Holland, 1954.

[5] Darling, P., "Manufacturer's Inventory Investment, 1947-58," *American Economic Review*, Vol. 49, No. 5, December, 1959, pp. 950-62.

To begin the discussion let us denote the desired stock of the ith commodity by s_i^+. As before technical requirements are given by the stock-flow coefficients; it is simplest to assume that speculative holdings of a commodity are proportional to the difference between current price and expected or long-run normal price for the commodity. Then if desired stock is equal to technical requirements plus speculative holdings we have:

$$s_i^+ = \sum_j b_{ij} x_j + n_i (p_i - p_i^+), \qquad (i = 1, 2 \ldots n),$$

where p_i^+ is the long-run equilibrium price level and is equal to the cost of production, that is:

$$p_i^+ = \sum_j a_{ji} p_j + \rho \sum_j b_{ji} p_j - \sum_j b_{ji} \dot{p}_j, \qquad (i = 1, 2 \ldots n),$$

and n_i is a negative constant of proportionality. This constant may be referred to as the *coefficient of speculative stocks* by analogy with Kaldor's elasticity of speculative stocks.[1] The coefficient of speculative stocks may be defined as the rate of change in the desired level of stocks with respect to a change in the difference between current and long-run equilibrium prices. This coefficient is negative since holdings of stocks decrease as the margin of current price over long-run equilibrium price increases. The flexible accelerator mechanism for determination of the level of investment in the ith commodity discussed above, is given by:

$$\dot{s}_i = \sum_j b_{ij} \dot{x}_j + h_i (s_i - s_i^+), \qquad (i = 1, 2 \ldots n),$$

where h_i is a negative constant; if desired stock is determined solely by technical requirements the constants h_i may be interpreted as rates of growth in stocks held in excess of technical requirements; this interpretation is not valid if desired stocks include stocks held for speculative purposes.

Combining the flexible accelerator theory of investment with the theory of speculative stocks, where stocks are held for both transactions and speculative purposes, we have for each commodity:

$$\dot{s}_i = \sum_j b_{ij} \dot{x}_j + h_i [s_i - \sum_j b_{ij} x_j - n_i (p_i - p_i^+)],$$

or, using matrix notation throughout:

$$\dot{s} = B\dot{x} + H[s - Bx - N(p - p+)],$$

where N is a diagonal matrix with elements n_i along the main diagonal. Combined with the original dynamic input-output model given by:

$$x = Ax + \dot{s},$$

this gives the following theory for determination of the level of output:

$$x = Ax + B\dot{x} + H[s - Bx - N(p - p+)].$$

In addition to the relationship between investment and opportunity for speculative gain, the complete system must include a description of the market mechanism by which changes in the gap between current and long-run normal prices are related to the level of stocks held in excess of requirements for transactions and productive purposes. If

---

[1] Kaldor, *op. cit.*, p. 7.

STABILITY OF A DYNAMIC INPUT-OUTPUT SYSTEM 113

holdings of stocks are in excess of ordinary technical requirements, the gap between prices and costs will decline; if such stocks are negative the gap between prices and costs will increase. If it is assumed that the price-cost gap will decline in proportion to the quantity of speculative stocks held, this relationship may be given the following form:

$$\dot{p}_i = \dot{p}_i^+ + m_i \left(s_i - \sum_j b_{ij} x_j\right).$$

The rate of change of prices is equal to the rate of change of costs (long-run normal prices) less an amount which is proportional to the speculative stock holdings. The constant of proportionality, m_i, must be negative. These constants will be referred to as *coefficients of speculative profits*. The coefficient of speculative profits for a given commodity may be defined as the rate of change of changes in profits with respect to changes in the level of stocks in excess of technical requirements. In matrix notation this mechanism is given by:

$$\dot{p} = \dot{p}+ + M(s - Bx).$$

The complete system is composed of the market mechanism for price formation, the theory of investment given by the flexible accelerator and the theory of speculative stocks, and by the dynamic input-output system and its dual. The complete system consists of the following sets of differential equations:

$$
\begin{aligned}
x &= Ax + B\dot{x} + \psi, \\
p &= A'p + \rho B'p + B'\dot{p} + \pi, \\
\dot{\psi} &= H[s - Bx - N(p - p^+)], \\
\dot{p} &= \dot{p}+ + M(s - Bx).
\end{aligned}
$$

Substituting ψ for $s-Bx$ and π for $p-p+$, the system may be written in normal form as follows:

$$
\begin{bmatrix} \dot{x} \\ \dot{p} \\ \dot{\psi} \\ \dot{\pi} \end{bmatrix}
=
\begin{bmatrix}
B^{-1}(I-A) & 0 & B^{-1}H & -B^{-1}HN \\
0 & (-B')^{-1}(I-A'-\rho B') & 0 & (B')^{-1} \\
0 & 0 & H & -HN \\
0 & 0 & M & 0
\end{bmatrix}
\begin{bmatrix} x \\ p \\ \psi \\ \pi \end{bmatrix}.
$$

This system is decomposable and possesses a causal interpretation in the sense of Orcutt, Simon, and Wold.[1] Price and output levels are influenced by the level of stock holdings in excess of technical requirements and by the level of profit and stock holdings in excess of desired stocks, respectively. However, the rate of change of excess stocks and profits is not affected by current output and price levels. If prices are equal to costs and stocks are equal to technical requirements the complete system reduces the dynamic input-output system and its dual:

---

[1] Orcutt, G., "Actions, Consequences and Causal Relations," *Review of Economics and Statistics*, Vol. 34, No. 4, November, 1952, pp. 305-13.

Simon, H., "Causal Ordering and Identifiability," *Studies in Econometric Method*, ed. W. Hood and T. Koopmans, New York, Wiley, 1953, pp. 49-74.

Wold, H., "A Generalization of Causal Chain Models," *Econometrica*, Vol. 28, No. 2, April, 1960, pp. 443-63, and the references listed there.

Strictly speaking, the model discussed is causal only in the "vector sense" of Simon.

$$\dot{x} = B^{-1}\,(I{-}A)\,x,$$

$$\dot{p} = (-B')^{-1}\,(I{-}A' - \rho B')\,p.$$

When speculative profits and losses are just balanced by corresponding losses and profits in operation, price movements are governed by technological considerations alone. Speculative stocks are zero and all investment is in accord with the increase in technical requirements. Output levels are also determined by purely technological considerations. So long as there are no speculative stock holdings and speculative profits and losses are just balanced by losses and profits in operations, prices follow a course which is independent of the movement of output levels and vice-versa. In the following discussion the dynamic input-output system and its dual will be referred to as the *equilibrium part* of the complete system. It should be observed that a second type of reduction of the system is possible. If the coefficient of speculative stocks for each commodity is set equal to zero the output system and the associated disequilibrium mechanism together reduce to the simple version of the flexible accelerator discussed by Goodwin.

To characterize the behavior of the complete dynamic input-output system, it is necessary to discuss two separate, and essentially unrelated, questions of stability. First, to retain the economic interpretation of the output variables it is required that they be non-negative for any non-negative initial levels of output; similarly, prices must be non-negative for any non-negative initial price levels. A necessary condition for non-negativity is that the unique positive equilibrium output proportions and relative prices be stable among the solutions of the equilibrium system. An immediate consequence of the causal interpretation of the complete system is that the stability of the system depends on the relative stability of the equilibrium part and the disequilibrium part of the system, where the disequilibrium part consists of the relations governing the development of excess stocks and profits together. This is easily verified by observing that characteristic values of the complete system are simply the characteristic values of the equilibrium and disequilibrium parts, separately. From this observation it is immediately clear that if macro-economic stability is assured, stability of the equilibrium part of the system is equivalent to the condition that all characteristic values of the disequilibrium part are less than the smaller of the two numbers: the equilibrium rate of growth and the equilibrium own-rate of interest. This result on relative stability is an immediate consequence of the theorem on relative stability given above.

The *disequilibrium part* of the system generates cumulative processes of inflation (or deflation) of profit levels and accumulation (or decumulation) of stocks in excess of technical requirements. The form of the disequilibrium part reveals that the cumulative process is self-sustaining: Deficient stocks raise profits. Profits depress desired stock-holding levels and thereby generate investment decisions which result in changes in the level of stocks held. These changes affect the level of profits and the chain of causation is renewed. Such cumulative processes are familiar from classical theories of the business cycle, perhaps best exemplified by the cumulative process of inflation discussed by Wicksell.[1] To analyze the cumulative process generated by holdings of speculative stocks and market price reactions to such holdings, we differentiate the flexible accelerator to obtain:

$$\dot{\psi} = H\,\psi - HN\,\dot{\pi}.$$

But $\dot{\pi}$ is determined by the market mechanism as follows:

$$\dot{\pi} = M\,\psi.$$

[1] Wicksell, K., *Interest and Prices*, London, Macmillan, 1936.
——, *Lectures on Political Economy*, Vol. II, London, Routledge, 1935.

STABILITY OF A DYNAMIC INPUT-OUTPUT SYSTEM   115

Combining these two disequilibrium mechanisms we obtain the relation:

$$\dot{\psi} = H\psi - HNM\,\psi.$$

The characteristic values of the system have the form:

$$\frac{h_i \pm \sqrt{h_i^2 - 4h_i\, m_i\, n_i}}{2},$$

where h_i, m_i, and n_i are diagonal elements of the matrices H, M, and N. Since h_i, m_i are negative numbers and n_i is a positive number, all characteristic values of the disequilibrium part are negative and all complex characteristic values have a negative real part, equal to the corresponding value of h_i.

The cumulative process generated by disequilibrium will exhibit two characteristic modes of behavior. Each disequilibrium variable will either decline exponentially or oscillate with steadily diminishing amplitude. The rate of diminution of the amplitude of fluctuations will increase with any increase in the constants h_i, the proportion between stocks in excess of desired stocks and investment. Similarly, the rate of decline in exponentially declining excess stocks will increase with any increase in these parameters. Where the disequilibrium path involves oscillations the rate of decline in amplitude will be unaffected by the size of the coefficients of speculative stocks and speculative profits. However, the rate of decline of exponentially decreasing components of excess stocks and profits will be reduced by any increase in these coefficients. In general, the effect of speculation is either to reduce the rate at which the system would approach equilibrium if no speculation were to take place or to give rise to oscillations which are damped at the same rate as the disequilibrium variables decrease when no speculation takes place. If the system is macro-economically stable, the equilibrium system is stable relative to the disequilibrium system if the money rate of interest is at least as great as the rate of growth. Provided that this condition is satisfied, the presence of speculation will not make a system unstable if the system is stable with no speculation.

To assure macro-economic stability, it is required that initial profits and excess stocks be consistent with the requirement that long-run equilibrium output proportions and relative prices be relatively stable within the output and price systems, respectively. Beginning with the equilibrium part of the complete system alone, let the matrix of characteristic vectors of this system be represented by:

$$\begin{bmatrix} X_1 & X_2 & 0 \\ 0 & P_1 & P_2 \end{bmatrix}$$

where X_1, P_1 are associated with characteristic values of $B^{-1}(I-A)$ and $(-B'^{-1}(I-A'-\rho B')$ less than the long-run equilibrium rate of growth and smaller than the money rate of interest less the equilibrium rate of growth in real part, respectively, together with the long-run equilibrium output proportions and the equilibrium relative prices, respectively. Then X_2, P_2 are associated with characteristic values greater than these quantities in real part together with complex roots with real part equal to these quantities in real part. Then we have:

$$\begin{bmatrix} X_1 & X_2 & 0 \\ 0 & P_1 & P_2 \end{bmatrix} \begin{bmatrix} a_1 \\ a_2 \\ b_1 \\ b_2 \end{bmatrix} = \begin{bmatrix} x(0) \\ p(0) \end{bmatrix}$$

where a_2 and b_2 are vectors of zeros, by macro-economic stability. But then, for the complete system, let the matrix of characteristic vectors be represented by:

$$
\begin{bmatrix}
X_1 & X_2 & 0 & Y_{11} & Y_{12} \\
0 & P_1 & P_2 & Y_{21} & Y_{22} \\
0 & 0 & & Z_{11} & Z_{12} \\
0 & 0 & & Z_{21} & Z_{22}
\end{bmatrix}
\begin{bmatrix}
a_1 \\ 0 \\ b_1 \\ 0 \\ c \\ d
\end{bmatrix}
=
\begin{bmatrix}
x(0) \\ p(0) \\ \psi(0) \\ \pi(0)
\end{bmatrix}
$$

so that c and d may be calculated from the equations:

$$Y_{11}c + Y_{12}d = x(0) - X_1a_1,$$
$$Y_{21}c + Y_{22}d = p(0) - P_1b_1,$$

The constants c and d may be used to compute the initial values of $\psi(0)$ and $\pi(0)$ and these initial values, together with the initial values of prices and outputs, determine the behavior of the complete system.

In this paper we have constructed a model of inflation and economic growth based on the dynamic input-output system and its dual and the theory of speculative stocks. The theory has a causal interpretation as follows: The complete model may be decomposed into two parts, an equilibrium part composed of the dynamic input-output system and its dual, and a disequilibrium part composed of a model of cumulative inflation or deflation and expansion or contraction based on the theory of speculative stocks. Changes in prices and outputs are affected by the level of profits and excess stocks; but changes in excess stocks and profits are not determined by price and output levels but comprise a self-generating cumulative process of the type familiar from the classical theory of the business cycle. The casual interpretation of the complete system reduces the problem of stability to that of the relative stability of equilibrium and disequilibrium parts.

There are many directions in which this theory could be generalized. First, stocks desired for precautionary motives were omitted from the analysis. In order to combine speculation with trading in futures contracts, it would be necessary to analyze precautionary holdings as well as transactions and speculative holdings of stocks. Secondly, alternative assumptions about the formation of expectations of future prices could be adopted rather than the hypothesis examined here, that expected price is equal to the long-run normal price, which is equal to the cost of production. Finally, it would be of interest to deal explicitly with the problem of the irreversibility of accumulation of fixed capital equipment.

The main conclusions of this study are as follows. First, the investment is determined by capital requirements, steady growth output proportions and equilibrium relative prices are stable within the complete system, provided that the money rate of interest is at least equal to the equilibrium rate of growth. This conclusion may be verified when capital requirements are determined by transactions motives alone and remains true when capital requirements are determined by both transactions and speculative motives. The chief consequence of speculative activity is to generate damped oscillations in speculative stocks and profits or to slow the approach to equilibrium which would take place if no speculative investment were undertaken.

Berkeley, California.   DALE W. JORGENSON.

[15]

Econometrica, Vol. 31, No 4 (October, 1963)

NUMERICAL SOLUTION OF A MODIFIED LEONTIEF DYNAMIC SYSTEM FOR CONSISTENT FORECASTING OR INDICATIVE PLANNING[1]

By Clopper Almon

This paper presents a modified version of the Leontief dynamic input-output system, a method for numerically solving this system, and an illustrative application to the American economy. The modifications of the original dynamic input-output system [4] are five:

1. The flow coefficients are not assumed to be constant but may have linear trends, which are assumed to be known in advance.

2. Consumer demands depend upon population and the real wage rate. (Government expenditure and population growth are exogenous.)

3. Substitution of capital for labor is allowed by a Cobb-Douglas function in each industry. These functions allow the productivity of *new* capital to increase exponentially.

4. Investment results not only from the growth of output, but also from the substitution of capital for labor as the wage goes up and the productivity of new capital increases. A delay between the time money is spent for new capital and the time the capital becomes operative can be easily introduced, though it has been used in the illustrative application.

5. The growth path of the wage rate is adjusted so that the resulting final demands give rise to outputs which provide full employment for an exogenously determined labor force. The effects of possible price changes are not considered.

The resulting system was originally intended for consistent forecasting, that is, for making forecasts such that, if they are accepted by business, then the production, investment, and employment decisions based on them cause them to come true and yield full employment. I should think that the system might also be useful in indicative planning as it is practiced, for example, in France.

Section 1 describes the model more fully. Section 2 explains the solution method, the core of which is the expansion $(I - U)^{-1} = I + U + U^2 + U^3 + \ldots$, where U is a differential operator. Section 3 reports results obtained with a ten-sector illustrative model based on American data. Though this application was intended as a test and illustration of the method, rather than as a quantitative study of the American economy, there is enough resemblance between the model and the economy that the results are not

---

[1] Computations reported here were done at the Massachusetts Institute of Technology Computation Center, Cambridge, Massachusetts.

666   CLOPPER ALMON

uninteresting. The model was computed for the period 1953–1961 under two assumptions about the rates of productivity increase, so that the effect of these rates on the solution could be ascertained. In this application, the solution procedure worked well and the results seem entirely reasonable.

1. THE MODEL

1.1. We assume that the matrix, A, of static input-output coefficients is determined solely by time, t. In the illustrative application, a linear dependence is assumed:

(1) $$A(t) = A_1 + A_2 t,$$

where A_1 and A_2 are constant, known matrices. The general solution method, however, makes no rigid assumption about the form of the dependence.

1.2. Final demand is composed of government demand, exports, and consumer demand. The first two are considered to be known functions of time. The last is found by multiplying the number of consumers, which is a known function of time, by the consumption per consumer, which is assumed to depend only upon w, an index of the real wage rate.[2] Thus, F, the vector of final demands, depends only on w and t, time:

(2) $$F = F(t,w).$$

Again, the general method of solution makes no rigid assumption about the form of $F(t,w)$. In the illustrative model, $F(t,w)$ is of the form $F(t,w) = F_1 + F_2 t + (w(t) - 1)(F_3 + F_4 t)$, where $F_1, \ldots, F_4$ are constant vectors and $w(0) = 1$. This function results from assuming linear trends for exports, government spending, and the number of consumers, while per capita consumption of each commodity is assumed to be a linear function (with intercept) of the wage rate. Of course, time trends in consumers' demand, independent of $w(t)$, could also be included. Only minor changes would be required to have per capita expenditure determined by any other form of Engel curve or even to use a recursively defined function such as the Stone-Rowe system [6]. The income tax rate could also be considered variable in the determination of disposable income so that the effect of various tax policies on the course of $w(t)$ necessary for full employment could be studied.

1.3. The equation relating expenditure on plant and equipment to output, the wage rate, and the rate of increase of productivity is derived from the assumption that business will minimize the labor and capital cost of pro-

---

[2] The wage-rate index will be assumed below to be the same in all industries, and this common index will be identified with the $w(t)$ used here. This identification involves a slight error if wage levels are different in industries with different rates of growth of employment, I know of no simple alternative, however.

A MODIFIED LEONTIEF SYSTEM   667

ducing the output given by the forecast. For this derivation, we must specify the production function and the way it is affected by productivity changes.

Output of industry j, X_j, is related to the capital, K_j, and employment E_j, in the industry by the function:

(3) $$X_j = \alpha_j E_j^{\,a_j} K_j^{1-a_j} ,$$

where α_j and a_j are constants. In the measure of capital used for K, machines made in different years are counted according to their marginal products, not according to their marginal cost. Thus, a 1961 model loom may cost its manufacturer no more in labor and materials than did the 1960 model. But because of an improved design, it may be worth 1.05 times as much to the textile manufacturer. If one 1960 loom has a value of 1.00 in K, then a 1961 loom has a value of 1.05. In this case, we would say that the rate of productivity increase, v, was five per cent per year.

It appears, however, that, in the usual series of investment, measured in constant dollars, both model looms would count equally. Such a series *is* appropriate for measuring the output of an input-output industry. For if each unit of output has approximately the same amount of materials in it regardless of its productivity, the coefficients in the A matrix will tend to remain approximately constant. But clearly the constant-dollar series must be modified for use in the production function. Namely, if v is the rate of increase of productivity, and d is the depreciation rate, then from a series, $I(t)$, of gross investment in constant dollars, we derive the series for $K(t)$ as follows:[3]

$$K(t) = \int_{-\infty}^{t} e^{v\tau . d(t-\tau)} I(\tau) d\tau ,$$

where we have dropped the industry subscript for simplicity. We shall use this relation in its differentiated form

(4) $$\dot{K} = e^{vt} I(t) - dK .$$

We can now proceed to determine the relation between expenditure on plant and equipment and output, the wage rate, and the rate of productivity change. In line with the assumption of fixed prices, we assume a fixed cost of funds ϱ. Now the fact that the productive value of capital in constant dollars is increasing at the rate v may also be expressed by saying that the price (in constant dollars) of a unit of K is declining at the rate v. Setting the

---

[3] This formulation of technological change is equivalent to that of Solow [5]. The rate v, here corresponds to $\lambda/(1-\alpha)$ in his notation.

price of capital at 1 when $t = 0$, the price at time t is e^{-vt}. Business is there-fore assumed to minimize the sum of its labor and capital costs, $w(t)E(t) +$ $\varrho e^{-vt}K(t)$, subject to the constraint (3). Forming the appropriate Lagrangian expression, minimizing with respect to E and K, using the two resulting equations to eliminate the Lagrangian multiplier and then using (3) to eli-minate E, the desired level of capital in industry j at time t is found to be

$$(5) \qquad\qquad K_j(t) = C_j X_j(t) w(t)^{a_j} e^{a_j v_j t} .$$

Here C_j is the desired capital-output ratio at $t = 0$, and $w(t)$ is the index of the wage rate. This index is assumed to be same for all industries. Differentiating (5) with respect to time, using (4) to eliminate $\dot{K}_j$ from the result, and then applying (5) to eliminate K_j gives

$$(6) \qquad I_j(t) = C_j w^{a_j} e^{-b_j v_j t} (\dot{X}_j + (a_j \frac{\dot{w}}{w} + (a_j v_j + d_j)) X_j ,$$

where $b_j = 1 - a_j$. This equation gives the total amount of spending by the jth industry in constant dollars. It may be broken down into demands for the outputs of the various capital producing industries by multiplying by a certain vector which we may call B_j^*. Let $B_j = C_j B_j^*$ and $B = [B_1, \ldots, B_n]$, that is, element b_{ij} of the matrix B shows, for $t = 0$, how much of the produce of industry i is needed as capital by industry j in order for the latter to increase its output by one unit. Then the vector of total investment demands for the output of each industry is

$$(7) \qquad\qquad \text{Inv}\ (t) = BG_1(t,w)X(t) + BG_2(t,w)DX(t) ,$$

where: $G_1(t,w)$ is a diagonal matrix with the jth diagonal element being

$$e^{-b_j v_j t} (a_j w^{-b_j} \dot{w} + (a_j v_j + d_j) w^{a_j}) ,$$

$G_2(t,w)$ is a diagonal matrix with the jth diagonal element being $e^{-b_j v_j t} w^{a_j}$, $X(t)$ is the vector of outputs, and D is the differential operator d/dt.

Notice that this investment equation is based upon the assumption that capital is at all times—including the initial moment—optimally adjusted for the full-employment level of output. Since this assumption may be violated by the actual initial capital stocks, an initial lull or spurt of capital investment may occur. This lull or spurt is not accounted for in this model. In my empirical work so far, this problem has not appeared quantitatively important. I point out, however, that the difficulty does exist.

1.4. The complete system of balance equations for the economy is now

$$(8) \quad X(t) = A(t)X(t) + BG_1(t,w)X(t) + BG_2(t,w)DX(t) + F(t,w) ,$$

plus the full employment equations

$$\sum_{j=1}^{n} E_j(t) \equiv E(t) = L(t) ,$$

A MODIFIED LEONTIEF SYSTEM   669

where $L(t)$ is the exogenously known labor force. Using (5) to eliminate K_j from (3) and solving for E_j gives

$$E_j = C'_j X_j w^{-b_j} e^{-b_j v_j t},$$

where C'_j is a constant. Hence (9) may be written as

(10) $\qquad \displaystyle\sum_{j=1}^{n} C'_j X_j w^{-b_j} e^{-b_j v_j t} = E(t) = L(t).$

Equations (8) and (10) comprise $n + 1$ equations in the $n + 1$ unknown functions, $X_1(t), \ldots, X_n(t)$, and $w(t)$. We may say that for a growth pattern to be in equilibrium it must satisfy these equations. They must be regarded, however, only as constraints on the movement of equilibrium outputs and cannot be used to explain how the system behaves starting from an arbitrary initial point. For given a course of $w(t)$ and an arbitrary $X(0)$ and $F(0,1)$, all elements of (8) are determined except $DX(0)$. That is, we would have to determine the growth rates of the outputs in a way such that the accelerator investment would just use up the residual outputs left over from the other uses. Such a way of determining $DX(0)$ makes no economic sense, and, starting from most initial points, leads to bizarre growth patterns with some industries growing thousands of per cent a year while others have negative outputs (see [2]).

The next section, however, presents a method of finding a solution of (8) and (10) which is quite sensible economically. It may be argued that if $A(t)$, $G_1(t,w)$, and $G_2(t,w)$ are constant, then all the non-bizarre solutions will converge, probably quickly, to this solution. I see no reason to doubt that the same result is essentially true for the non-constant case.

2. THE METHOD OF SOLUTION

Observe that $X(t)$ enters (8) linearly while $w(t)$ enters nonlinearly. This circumstance suggests the following approach:

a. Choose a particular functional form for w, say $w(t) = w(t,p)$, where p is a vector of the parameters in the wage functions.

b. Make an initial guess for p, say p^0.

c. With $w(t) = w(t,p^0)$, solve (8) for $X(t)$.

d. Use (10) to calculate $E(t)$.

e. Vary p so as to bring $E(t)$ as close as possible to $L(t)$.

Several forms of $w(t,p)$ were tried, but only the results with polynomials e.g., $w(t) = 1 + p_1 t + p_2 t^2 + p_3 t^3$, are reported below. Steps b and d need no explanation; this section is concerned chiefly with Steps c and e.

Suppose now that $w(t)$ is specified; let us consider a method of performing

Step c, that is, of finding a solution of (8). G_1, G_2, and F are now simply functions of t, and we may rewrite (8) as

$$(11) \qquad [I - A(t) - BG_1(t)]X(t) - BG_2(t)DX(t) = F(t) .$$

Let $\hat{t}$ be the midpoint of the range over which we are forecasting, and multiply both sides of (11) by $[I - A(\hat{t}) - BG_1(\hat{t})]^{-1}$, writing the result as

$$(12) \qquad\qquad [P(t) - Q(t)D]X(t) = R(t) ,$$

where P, Q, and R are defined by comparison with (11). Since

$$P(t) = [I - A(\hat{t}) - BG_1(\hat{t})]^{-1} [I - A(t) - BG_1(t)] ,$$

$P(\hat{t}) = I$, and in general, $P(t)$ should not be far from I. This fact will speed the convergence of an iterative process to be described in a moment; this accelerated convergence is the reason for the multiplication of (11) by the inverse.

Now multiplying (12) through by $P(t)^{-1}$ gives

$$[I - P(t)^{-1}Q(t)D]X(t) = P(t)^{-1}R(t) ,$$

or

$$X(t) = [I - P(t)^{-1}Q(t)D]^{-1}P(t)^{-1}R(t) .$$

Denoting by U the differential operator $P(t)^{-1}Q(t)D$, we apply to the inverse on the right the expansion

$$(I - U)^{-1} = I + U + U^2 + U^3 + \ldots ,$$

and get

$$(13) \quad X(t) = P(t)^{-1}R(t) + P(t)^{-1}Q(t)D[P(t)^{-1}R(t)]$$
$$+ P(t)^{-1}Q(t)D[P(t)^{-1}Q(t)DP(t)^{-1}R(t))] + \ldots \quad .$$

It may be readily verified by substitution in (12) that if this series converges it is a solution of (12) and, therefore, of (8). The economic interpretation of (13) is that the first term gives what output would be if there were no accelerator investment. The second term adds the accelerator investment resulting from the growth in the first-term component of output. The third term adds the accelerator investment resulting from the growth in the second-term component of output, and so on. In practice, of course, it is necessary to truncate the series, and I have stopped with the three terms shown here. The accuracy of the solution may be directly ascertained by substitution in equation (12).

Since we do not have an analytic expression for $P(t)^{-1}$, the differential operator, D, in (13) must be interpreted as a numerical differentiation operator. This fact suggests that we divide up the interval over which we are forecasting by a number of equally spaced points, t_1, t_2, ..., t_T, and proceed as follows:

A MODIFIED LEONTIEF SYSTEM 671

a. Calculate $P(t_i)^{-1} R(t_i)$ for $i = 1, \ldots, T$. For each t_i, this calculation is most easily accomplished by applying the Seidel method[4] to solve the equations $P(t) Y_1(t) = R(t)$. Since $P(t)$ differs but little from I, the Seidel process converges rapidly. The function $Y_1(t)$ is now the first right hand term of (13).

b. Apply to the series $Y_1(t_i)$, $i = 1, \ldots, T$, a numerical differentiation operator, D, to obtain the derivative series $\dot{Y}_1(t_i)$. Then for each t_i solve the equations $P(t_i) Y_2(t_i) = Q(t_i) \dot{Y}_1(t_i)$ by the Seidel method to obtain the function $Y_2(t)$, the second term on the right of (13).

c. Apply the numerical differentiation operator to $Y_2(t)$, obtaining $\dot{Y}_2(t)$ and solve $P(t) Y_3(t) = Q(t) \dot{Y}_2(t)$ by the Seidel method for $Y_3(t)$, the third term on the right of (13).

d. The approximate solution of (8) is then $\tilde{X} = Y_1 + Y_2 + Y_3$. Its accuracy is checked by substitution into (12), a process which again requires numerical differentiation.

The reader may rightfully question the convergence of the series (13). I cannot prove that it would, in theory, converge; and, in computing as outlined above, it certainly will not. For after taking four or five terms we would find ourselves differentiating a function which is essentially a rounding error, multiplying the result by a matrix with a norm of about 3, differentiating the result, and so on. The result would clearly be explosive. On the other hand, if only three or four terms are taken, their sum, $\tilde{X}$, may be very close to a solution of (11) in the sense that if $\tilde{X}$ is substituted for X in (11), the two sides are nearly equal. Since the difference between the two sides has a clear economic meaning, the excess of production over use of each product, we can judge directly the usefulness of $\tilde{X}$ as a solution to (11). This numerical check then, rather than theoretical considerations, is advanced as the test of the worth of the series (13).

In my computing so far, I have used a five-point numerical differentiation operator, though a three-point operator would probably have been sufficiently accurate. If it is desired to introduce lags in investment, so that investment by industry i at time t depends upon its rate of growth at $t + \tau_i$, this lag may be easily incorporated by changing the weights used in the numerical differentiation. Each industry could have its own set of weights. My own view is that, since the growth paths turn out to be almost linear, the inclusion of lags is not likely to make much difference.

The method used to vary the wage parameters to obtain full employment, Step e in the above list, is based on the method of least squares as used in regression analysis. The approach is to form the function

$$S(p) = \sum_{i=1}^{T} [L(t_i) - E(t_i,p)]^2 ,$$

---

[4] See any numerical analysis book.

672   CLOPPER ALMON

and to vary p so as to minimize $S(p)$. Here $E(t_t,p)$ is the value of E computed from (10) when $w(t)$ and $X(t)$ are calculated using $p = (p_1, \ldots, p_m)$ for the parameters of the wage rate. Now write

$$S(p^o + \Delta p) \approx \sum_{t=1}^{T} [L(t_t) - (E(t_t,p) + E_{P_1^o}(t_t,p^o)\Delta p_1 + \cdots$$

$$+ E_{P_m}(t_t,p^o)\Delta p_m)]^2 .$$

where $E_{P_j}(t_t,p^o)$ are finite approximations of $\delta E(t_t,p^o)/\delta p_j$.

Minimizing the expression on the right with respect to $\Delta p_1, \ldots, \Delta p_m$ is just a standard regression problem. Letting (Δp^o) denote the solution of this problem, the next guess of p is $p^1 = p^o + (\Delta p^o)$. The process may then be repeated to get p^2, p^3, etc.

With cubic and quartic polynomials for the wage rate, this procedure worked efficiently, and it was not necessary to go beyond p^2. The time paths of the various $E_{p_j}(t,p)$ were sufficiently different that there was no difficulty in the inversion of the cross-products matrix.[5]

3. AN APPLICATION

This section reports the results of applying the solution method just described to the system presented in Section 1. The model is a ten-sector representation of the American economy between July, 1953 and April, 1962, a period of eight and three-quarters years. The interval extends from the mid-point of the first year after the Korean mobilization to the most recent date for which output data were available at the time of writing. At the terminal date, most industries were at record levels of output. The purposes of the application were, first, to test the efficiency and accuracy of the solution procedure and, second, to see whether the model could reflect the main features of the economy well enough to be a useful tool for consistent forecasting and indicative planning.

Descriptions of all input data except the A_2 matrix, which shows changes in the static input-output coefficients, and the v vector of rates of productivity increases are found in [1] and will not be repeated here. No information

---

[5] The method of steepest descent was also tried for minimizing $S(p)$, but it worked very poorly. Apparently the surface of $S(p)$ had valleys with steep sides but gradually descending "creeks" at the bottom. The steepest descent method would get into the creek, but could not find the direction down the valley to the minimum. Probably the method failed because finite differences had to be used to approximate the partials of $S(p)$. Since the "step" used in making the approximations would, in one direction, reach up on to the steep sides, the approximate gradient always came out almost perpendicular to the wall rather than running down the valley to the minimum.

A MODIFIED LEONTIEF SYSTEM 673

RESULTS OF 8-3/4 YEAR FORECAST
FROM MID-1953 TO APRIL, 1962

Industry	(1) V	(2) Forecast: V = Col(1), 1953 = 100	(3) Actual: 1953 = 100	(4) Forecast: V = 1.5 Col (1), 1953 = 100	(5) Annual Rate: V = Col (1)	(6) Annual Rate: V = 1.5 Col (1)	(7) % Error 1953: V = Col (1)	(8) % Error 1962: V = Col (1)	(9) % Error, 1953: V = 1.5 COL (1)	(10) % Error 1962: V = 1.5 Col (1)
Agric., Food, Textiles, Apparel	.07	129	125	136	3.0	3.5	.041	.024	.098	.039
Services	.00	136	128	145	3.5	4.2	.024	.011	.139	.012
Paper Printing, Furniture, Lumber	.06	133	133	145	3.3	4.3	.049	.016	.318	.009
Chemicals	.07	164	176	174	5.7	6.4	.072	.032	.319	.040
Fuel and Electricity	.08	143	146	155	4.2	5.0	.043	.021	.234	.025
Transportation Equipment	.07	127	130	134	2.7	3.3	.018	.004	.133	.004
Machinery	.07	126	130	138	2.6	3.8	.207	.105	1.320	.109
Construction, Fab. Metal Prod.	.01	126	122	141	2.7	4.0	.111	.049	.610	.050
Primary Metals	.06	116	112	127	1.7	2.8	.122	.062	.899	.056
Transportation	.01	128	116	135	2.8	3.4	.045	.022	.266	.024
Wage Rate	—	128	124	135	2.9	3.4				

from the period after 1957 was used in the determination of this part of the input data. "Full employment" was taken to be attained at three per cent unemployment.

All rows of A_2 were assumed to be zero except the Chemicals and the Primary Metals rows. All elements in the Chemicals row of A were assumed to increase proportionately, and all elements of the Primary Metals row were assumed to decrease proportionately. Data up through 1960 were used in determining the amount of increase or decrease. A few rough calculations suggested that v for all manufacturing was about .07. This figure and some general impressions on the differences among industries led to the v vector shown in column (1) of the accompaning table. Since Solow's calculations [6] give a value of v for the whole economy of .10, approximately fifty per cent greater than the average of column (1), the model was also computed using a v-vector fifty per cent larger than that shown. For each industry, the index of output for April, 1962 with 1953 = 100 is shown in column (2) for the original v and in column (4) for the increased v. Columns (5) and (6) show the annual growth rates implied by these indexes. Column (3) contains, for comparison, indexes of the actual growth of the American economy. The average output in 1953 is taken as 100 in these indexes. Columns (7)–(10) are for the evaluation of the accuracy of the solution method. The approximate solution of (12) given by the first three terms of (13), $\tilde{X}(t)$, was substituted into (12) and the discrepancy, $\delta(t)$,

$$\delta(t) = P(t)\tilde{X}(t) - R(t) - Q(t)D\tilde{X}(t) ,$$

was calculated. Since $P(t) \approx I$, these descrepancies are, roughly speaking, the excesses of production over use.[6] In the table, they are expressed as a per cent of production. Columns (7) and (8) pertain to the run with the first v; columns (9) and (10), to the run with the increased v. The first column of each pair shows the discrepancies in 1953; the second column, those for 1962.

Performance of the Solution Method

By using a cubic wage function,

$$w(t) = 1 + .0364t - .00068t^2 + .0002t^3 ,$$

for the version with the original v, and a quartic,

$$w(t) = 1 + .0147t + .00569t^2 = .000435t^3 + .00012t^4 ,$$

for the version with the larger v, a course of employment was obtained which

---

[6] The exact excesses, ε, could have been found by solving by the Seidel method the equations $P(t)\varepsilon(t) = \delta(t)$. Since this additional calculation would have made the economic interpretation more clearcut, it probably would have been worthwhile. But it could hardly effect the general conclusion to be drawn from the size of $\delta(t)$.

A MODIFIED LEONTIEF SYSTEM   **675**

differed from "full employment" by less than one tenth of one per cent in any year. In both runs, the greatest deviations were in the first and second years; after the third year, the deviations were less than one twentieth of one per cent. It was not possible to attain this close a fit with a cubic in the version with the large v. As mentioned before, these values for the wage parameters were the second calculated guess, i.e., p^2 in the above notation. Since p^2 differed little from p^1, it did not seem worthwhile to go further.

With a given set of wage parameters, the IBM7090 computer calculated outputs at three month intervals for a ten year period in approximately 22 seconds. Improvements in the program could probably reduce this time by one third. The time required for such a run is proportional to the number of intervals. For a given number of intervals, it is asymptotically proportional to the square of the number of sectors, not to the cube, as is the time for matrix inversion. The present program could accommodate problems of up to about seventy sectors.

Varying the length of interval made very little difference in the course of outputs. Six month intervals and three month intervals gave practically the same answers.

The discrepancies shown in columns (7)–(10) of the table show that the errors in solution were greatest in the capital goods industries, as was to be expected. Judging from the behavior of the last term taken in the series expansion of $(I - U)^{-1}$, an additional term would have diminished these discrepancies. At present, the discrepancies are insignificant by the end of the period, and, indeed, at their worst, they are hardly important. It is difficult to imagine that the machinery industry would be seriously inconvenienced by producing, for one year, 1.32 per cent more than the output for which its capital and labor are optimal. Just why the errors started large at the beginning of the period and decreased, I do not know; on other runs, they started small and increased slightly.

On balance, it is my impression that the solution method and the present machine program, while they leave room for improvement, are definitely useable for serious work.

Comparison of Forecast with Actual Growth

Comparison of columns (2) and (3) of the table show that the run using the v vector in column (1) gave a forecast which is quite compatible with the actual course of events. Note that the variable coefficients in the Chemicals and the Primary Metals rows produced marked results, Chemicals having an index of 164, Metals only 116. Even so, comparison with the actual indexes suggests that the rate of change of the coefficients should have been slightly larger.

The real wage rate (compensation per full-time equivalent employee deflated by the consumer price index) actually increased 3 per cent less than did the forecast; consequently, the two principal consumer goods industries, (1) Food and Clothing, and (2) Services, also increased less than the forecast, the first 3 per cent less, the second 6 per cent less. The fact that these industries, which employ half the labor force, were operating at less then forecast output agrees well with the fact that there was unemployment of 5.5 per cent in April, 1962 rather than the 3.0 allowed by the forecast. Two capital goods industries, Machinery and Transportation Equipment, were, on the other hand, producing a little above the forecast level, as might be expected, since April, 1962 fell in the upswing of a business cycle. Construction, however, was below forecast. This disparity between Machinery and Construction is probably due to the particular nature of the 1962 recovery and does not show a long-run trend. In the expansion of 1959 and 1960 the situation was reversed: Construction was higher than forecast, and Machinery was lower.

The relatively rapid rate of growth of the Fuel and Electricity industry was, at least in the model, the result of consumer demand for its output having a large derivative with respect to income. The greatest difference between actual and forecasted outputs occurred in Transportation. This difference may be largely due to the shortcomings of the "actual" index, which is based on ton-miles and passenger-miles in the various carriers where available, or the gap may indicate a need for declining coefficients in the Transportation row of the A matrix or in that row of the B matrix.[7]

In general it appears, at least to my optimistic eye, that is possible for the model to reflect the technology of the economy well enough to be of practical value in consistent forecasting or indicative planning.

Effects of Productivity Change

Comparison of columns (3) and (4) of the table shows that the larger v gave forecasts not only considerably in excess of the amounts actually produced in 1962, but also exceeding the amounts which could conceivably have been produced had there been only three per cent unemployment. Though most of this gap is no doubt attributable to an unrealistically large v, part of it may be the result of capital having grown less than it could have had resources not been left idle by recessions.

The long-range results may be seen from the table; a comparison of the complete course of the two forecasts for the wage rate and selected industries is shown in the accompanying graphs. Two results stand out. First, in nine

---

[7] A referee points out that Johansen [3, Section 8.8] had a similar experience with this sector.

A MODIFIED LEONTIEF SYSTEM   677

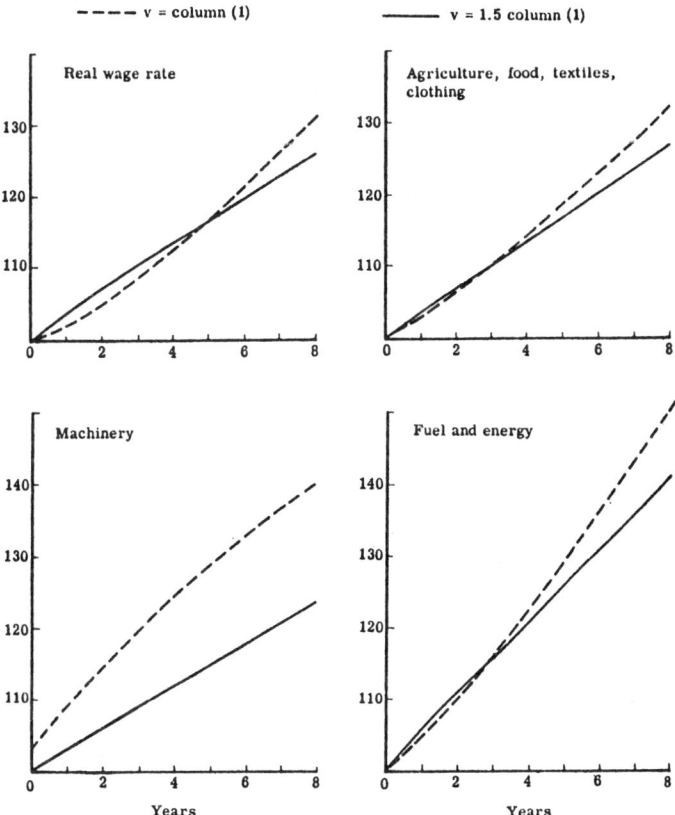

FIGURE 1—Effects of Different Rates of Productivity Increase

years the forecasts diverged markedly. Secondly, in the first few years there was little difference between the forecasts for consumer goods, but for capital goods they diverged most rapidly during this period. (At the initial point, the forecasts were almost identical in all industries; the largest gap, in Machinery, was three per cent of output.)

The first result was to be expected; the second may call for a bit of explanation. With the original v, relatively little investment was induced by the decline in the effective price of capital, the $a_j v_j$ term in (6). Consequently, a high value of $\dot{w}(0)$ was necessary to stimulate enough investment to give "full employment." The high value of $\dot{w}$ promoted investment by making final demand grow rapidly and encouraging substitution of capital for labor. As time went on, however, the large increase in consumer demand relative to productivity made it necessary to diminish the rate of growth of the wage

678   CLOPPER ALMON

rate. With the high value of v exactly the reverse was the case. In the fifth year, the wage rates were equal in the two forecasts. If the annual rates of growth of the wage rates are compared for *just* the last five years, it is seen that the fifty per cent increase in v caused a thirty per cent increase in these growth rates rather than the twenty per cent increase shown by the overall figures in the table.

This behavior of the wage rate produced the effects noted above. It appears, then, that even for short-range forecasts of capital goods production it is necessary to have an accurate v-vector. For consumer goods the exact value of v becomes important only in the range beyond four of five years.

Harvard University

REFERENCES

[1] ALMON, C.: "Consistent Forecasting in a Dynamic Multisector Model," Technical Report No. 4 of the Center for Research in Management Science, University of California, Berkeley, 1961.

[2] ———: "Consistent Forecasting in a Dynamic Multisector Model," *Review of Economics and Statistics*, May, 1963. (A revision of parts of [1].)

[3] JOHANSEN, L.: *A Multi-Sectoral Model of Economic Growth*, Amsterdam, North Holland, 1960.

[4] LEONTIEF, W. W.: *Studies in the Structure of the American Economy*, New York, Oxford, 1953.

[5] SOLOW, R.: "Investment and Technical Progress" in K. Arrow *et al.*, *Mathematical Methods in the Social Sciences 1959*, Stanford, Stanford University Press, 1960.

[6] STONE, J. R. N., AND D. A. ROWE: "The Durability of Consumers' Durable Goods," *Econometrica*, April, 1960, pp. 407–16.

[16]

A DYNAMIC INPUT-OUTPUT MODEL
WITH ASSURED POSITIVE OUTPUT (*)

F. Duchin and D. B. Szyld (**)

Institute for Economic Analysis, New York University

1. INTRODUCTION

Most of the empirical work to date making use of the input-output (IO) approach has been carried out within the context of the static model in which the levels of all categories of final demand including investment are exogenously fixed. The static IO model, through the matrix of technical coefficients, A (or the so-called Leontief inverse, $(I - A)^{-1}$), represents the interdependency among all the producing sectors of the economy. Any set of outputs computed on the basis of this matrix will be consistent with respect to the levels of activity of all individual sectors at any given time. These properties account for the frequent use of the static IO model.

The dynamic IO model extends these properties to include the determination of the sectoral production and accumulation of capital goods through a multi-sectoral accelerator formulation. The composition and amount of each sector's demand for capital goods per unit increase of its own output is determined by its detailed technical requirements, represented by a column in the capital coefficients matrix, B. The characteristic advantage of the input-output formulation in the dynamic case is that it imposes intertemporal consistency simultaneously for all sectors between the specific capital items produced and delivered in one period and increments of output that in subsequent periods will be available for use.

(*) Research supported in part by National Science Foundation Grant PRA-8012844.

(**) Second author is now at the Department of Computer Science, Duke University.

— 270 —

The mathematical properties of the dynamic model have been extensively studied but the model has not been used in empirical work because it produces implausible results. This paper indicates the nature of the difficulties, describes the new formulation (first used in (Leontief and Duchin, 1986)), and presents some empirical results. Hopefully this work will stimulate the transition from a static toward a dynamic framework for applied input-output analysis.

2. HISTORICAL DEVELOPMENT

The dynamic input-output model was formulated by Leontief in 1949 (Leontief, 1953). He represented investment as the rate of change in required capital stocks, with a vector differential equation of the form

$$x - Ax - B\dot{x} = y \qquad (1)$$

where x is the vector of outputs, A is the matrix of input requirements on current account, B is the matrix of capital requirements, and y is the vector of non-investment final demand. Leontief exhibited the form of the solution of equation (1) in the case where the components of y are exponentials (Leontief, 1953, pp. 59-65), and (Iverson, 1954) for the first time produced numerical solutions of such systems of up to 21 differential equations describing the U.S. economy in terms of 21 interrelated sectors.

Leontief eventually formulated the model in terms of difference equations with dated technical matrices reflecting structural change in the economy (Leontief, 1970):

$$x_t - A_t x_t - B_{t+1}(x_{t+1} - x_t) = y_t . \qquad (2)$$

Equation (2) is intended to be solved for the set of vectors of output, consistent with the given time sequence of technical matrices and final demand requirements. In theoretical work the system is « closed », that is, non-investment final demand is assumed to consist only of personal consumption, and households are treated like any other sector with consumption as its input requirements. In addition, it is assumed that no technical change takes place. Under these circumstances, equation (2) reduces to:

$$x_t - Ax_t - B_{t+1}(x_{t+1} - x_t) = 0 . \qquad (3)$$

— 271 —

A minimal condition for an economically meaningful solution is the existence of a set of nonnegative vectors of output x_t satisfying equation (3). It is well known that when the model is solved forward in time, a set of nonnegative solutions exists only if the initial conditions lie on the so-called « balanced growth path »; conditions for the existence of a balanced growth path are discussed in (Szyld, 1985). Actual values for initial conditions will rarely exactly satisfy this constraint.

The fact that negative outputs will typically be generated follows from the implicit requirement in equation (2) or (3) that the entire physical productive capacity be utilized (i.e., full capacity utilization), which involves both perfect foresight of future stock requirements and the « reversibility » [1] of the capital stock. To solve this dilemma by assuring the irreversibility of capital already in place, a « multi-phase process » was suggested (Leontief, 1953) according to which capital stocks are increased only when output grows. In (Uzawa, 1956) this process was represented by replacing the term $B\dot{x}$ in equation (1) by $B \cdot \max(\dot{x}, 0)$. Uzawa was able to prove the existence under certain conditions of solutions to this formulation of the dynamic model. The introduction of this nonlinearity amounted to allowing for unused capacity when output is falling.

While this approach appeared promising, Leontief and others (Leontief, 1953; Dorfman, Samuelson and Solow, 1958) were concerned about possible contradictions in switching between this regime when output is falling and the full capacity utilization required when output is rising. This potential problem is not encountered if one (realistically) abandons the requirement of full capacity utilization even when output is growing. If output and capacity are not defined to be identical, then the model must provide for the determination not only of output but also of a particular, sectoral pattern of capacity utilization. This is the approach taken in the present formulation; see (Jorgenson, 1961) for a rather different generalization of the Leontief model also involving the difference between actual and desired stocks.

In the present work we introduce the notion of an investment plan for expansion in each sector. We assume that the effective expansion of a sector's capacity may require several time periods, in which case expansion plans must be formulated and their implementation begun this amount of time in advance. The amount of planned expansion depends upon future sectoral production as anticipated when the plan is formulated.

---

[1] The stock is said to be reversible if capital in place but not in use in a particular sector is freely transferable to other uses within the economy. This occurs when elements of $(x_{t+1} - x_t)$ or $\dot{x}$ in equations (1)-(3) are negative.

— 272 —

Once in place, the plan is adhered to even if the sector's circumstances change. If adequate capacity is already in place, no expansion plan is implemented. These assumptions are explicitly represented in the following section.

Another difficulty that arises in solving equation (2) or (3) for x_{t+1} in terms of x_t is the need to invert the capital matrix B. While most theoretical work is carried out at a level of abstraction at which it is assumed that the B matrix is invertible, the fact is that the matrix is invariably singular, with rows of zeros corresponding to sectors that do not produce durable (or stockable) goods. It has proved possible (under certain assumptions) to solve the system within the balanced growth framework despite the singularity of the B matrix (Livesey, 1973, and 1976; Luenberger and Arbel, 1977; Meyer, 1982); but these results have not been used to solve empirical problems in part because of the other difficulties described earlier, notably the assumption of full capacity utilization. Solutions to the model we have devised are obtained at each time step without requiring inversion of the B matrices.

Implicit in the formulation of equations (2) and (3) is the assumption that the capital goods needed to increase a sector's productive capacity between periods t and $t + 1$ are produced during period t. The algebraic representation of different gestation periods for different capital goods was introduced by (Johansen, 1978) who also demonstrated the existence of a balanced growth path solution for the model he presented, without technological change. The question was further studied by (Åberg and Persson, 1981), and a similar concept had been used by (Belen'kii, Volkonskii and Pavlov, 1973-75) and (Volkonskii, 1975-76). Our formulation also allows for different lag structures.

Realistic closure of the model for households is unfortunately not achieved simply by adding a row and a column to the IO matrices and remains an open problem in input-output work. In addition, it is not useful in empirical work to ignore production absorbed by government purchases and international trade. For these reasons the dynamic model described in this paper is still « open ».

As in the case of the static model, a dual price equation can be written for the dynamic IO model; the price system is not treated in this paper.

3. THE NEW FORMULATION

Our objective was to design a dynamic input-output model with which it would be possible to study demand for labor and capital under alterna-

— 273 —

tive assumptions about future technological change in the United States. Once a model of the type represented by equation (2) is solved for the vectors of outputs for period t, $x(t)$ ([2]), the vectors of employment requirements by occupation are easily obtained.

In the present formulation, the investment term in equation (2) is replaced by expressions formulated in accordance with the following considerations:

> Once capacity is in place, it need not be fully utilized and is not reversible.
>
> In each time period, expansion decisions are made for each sector based on recent past growth rates, and capital goods are ordered. Some capital goods must be delivered several periods before the new facility of which they are part can effectively add to the investing sector's capacity.
>
> Replacement investment is explicitly represented, separately from expansion.

We introduce two additional (vector) variables:

$c(t)$ output capacity during period t,

$o(t)$ increase in productive capacity between periods $t - 1$ and t

and we define $c(t) = c(t - 1) + o(t)$. If, for sector i, $c_i(t) > x_i(t)$, capacity is under-utilized; if $c_i(t) < x_i(t)$, it is overutilized ([3]).

A sector's future capacity requirements are projected several periods in advance, independent of the capacity in place. For that reason we also introduce the vector $c^*(t)$ of projected capacity requirements for (future) period t and define the increase in capacity in sector i as:

$$o_i(t) = \max \left[0, c_i^*(t) - c_i(t - 1) \right].$$

([2]) In this section, time is represented by the letter t in parentheses rather than as a subscript. We reserve the use of subscripts to denote the specific components (e.g., sectors) of a vector. Equation (2), for example, becomes

$x(t) - A(t)x(t) - B(t + 1)[x(t + 1) - x(t)] = y(t)$.

([3]) Over- and under-utilization are relative to a presumed state of exactly full capacity utilization. Base year rates of capacity utilization are specified in the initial conditions and the concept in the model follows whatever definition of full capacity utilization is used in their derivation.

— 274 —

Thus if $c_i(t-1) \geqslant c_i(t)$ then $o_i(t) = 0$, no new output capacity is needed, and $c_i(t) = c_i(t-1)$. Otherwise, the change in capacity, o, is the increase needed to achieve the projected capacity requirement, c^*.

The investment term in period t could now be written as $B(t+1) \cdot o(t+1)$, implying that investment goods required to increase the capacity in period $t+1$ are produced and delivered one period earlier. In fact, we recognize that different types of capital goods may have to be delivered two or more periods earlier. We denote by τ_{ij} the lag between the period when a capital item is produced (by sector i) and the period in which it effectively adds to the capacity of sector j and by τ_j the maximum lag for any capital good required by sector j, i.e., $\tau_j = \max_i \tau_{ij}$.

Planned capacity expansion in sector j will require τ_j periods for its realization and thus will need to be formulated at least τ_j periods in advance. We make the provisional simplifying assumptions that τ_{ij} and τ_j are the same for all capital-using sectors j. Following (Johansen, 1978, p. 515) we denote as τ_i the lag for capital goods produced by sector i and $\tau = \max_i \tau_i$.

The investment term now becomes

$$\sum_{\theta=1}^{\tau} B^0(t) o(t+\theta)$$

where the (ij)-th entry of $B^0(t)$, $b_{ij}^0(t)$, is the amount of capital produced in period t by sector i to increase the capacity of sector j by one unit in period $t+\theta$ [4]. Of course, $b_{ij}^0(t) = 0$ for $\theta > \tau_i$.

Future capacity, $c^*(t+\tau)$, planned τ periods in advance, is based on output levels in the last completed period and recent past changes in output. In order to prevent the generation of excessive expansion in times of rapid growth, likely to be followed by a long period of under-utilization, a sector-specific maximum admissible annual rate of expansion of capacity, δ_i, is imposed. (Only the sector's expansion investment and not its output is potentially constrained by δ_i.) This results in the following expression:

$$c_i^*(t+\tau) = \min \left[1 + \delta_i, \frac{x_i(t-1) + x_i(t-2)}{x_i(t-2) + x_i(t-3)} \right]^{\tau+1} x_i(t-1). \tag{4}$$

---

[4] These capital coefficient matrices $B^0(t)$ are related to $B(t+1)$ of equation (2) by

$$B(t+1) = \sum_{\theta=1}^{\tau} B^0(t+\theta-1).$$

— 275 —

We can now write the whole model and solve for $x(t)$ for each period from t_0 through the final period t_T. The initial conditions must specify values for

$$c(t_0),$$ (IC)

$$c^*(t),\ t = t_0 + 1, \dots, t_0 + r - 1,$$

$$x(t),\ t = t_0 - \tau, \dots, t_0 - 1.$$

Given these initial conditions, we compute o and c, in that order, for periods $t_0 + 1$ through $t_0 + \tau - 1$. For each period in turn ($t = t_0, \dots, t_T$) we next solve for $c^*(t + \tau)$ using (4). We then compute the future additions to capacity

$$o(t + \tau) = \max\,[0,\ c^*(t + \tau) - c(t + \tau - 1)]$$ (5)

and update the capacity,

$$c(t + \tau) = c(t + \tau - 1) + o(t + \tau).$$ (6)

Replacement investment is represented as

$$R(t)x(t)$$

where the (ij)-th entry of the replacement matrix $R(t)$ is the amount of capital goods produced by sector i and held by sector j that must be replaced in order for sector j to produce a unit of output during period t. We can now solve for $x(t)$ from

$$[I - A(t) - R(t)]x(t) = \sum_{\theta=1}^{\tau} B^\theta(t)o(t + \theta) + y(t).$$ (7)

Inversion of the B matrices is clearly not at issue in this formulation. Thus equation (2) has been replaced by equations (4)-(7).

Finally, labor requirements by occupation during period t are obtained as

$$e(t) = L(t)x(t)$$

where the (qj)-th element of $L(t)$ is the amount of labor of occupation q required to produce a unit of output of sector j during period t.

— 276 —

4. ANALYSIS OF THE MODEL

The new formulation (4)-(7) maintains many aspects of the inter-temporal, inter-sectoral consistency of the original formulation (2) while assuring the existence of positive solutions. Furthermore, under certain conditions the new formulation reduces to the original one; that is, it is a true generalization of Leontief's dynamic input-output model.

In this section we first show that the new formulation of the dynamic model produces nonnegative solutions if the corresponding static model does. We then show that the new model has a balanced growth solution and that it coincides with that of Leontief's dynamic model. Finally, we point out certain characteristics of the model that will require additional refinement in future work.

Proposition 1: If for each period t, 1) non-investment final demand $y(t)$ is such that the solutions $x^s(t)$ of the static input-output model (^{5}),

$$[I - A(t) - R(t)]x^s(t) = y(t), \tag{8}$$

are nonnegative and 2) the matrices $A(t) + R(t)$ satisfy the Hawkins-Simon condition (Hawkins and Simon, 1949), then for any set of initial conditions (IC), there exists a unique set of nonnegative solutions $x(t)$ to the model (4)-(7).

Remark 1: If $y(t)$ is nonnegative, condition 1) is obviously satisfied if 2) is. The Hawkins-Simon condition assures positive output only in the case of nonnegative $y(t)$. Note, however, that $y(t)$ generally includes negative components corresponding to sectors whose net imports exceed domestic final demand.

Remark 2: After a transformation, if necessary, to an appropriate set of units, the column sums of $A(t) + R(t)$ are less than unity if we (realistically) assume that each sector's outlays for replacement are covered by its value-added. Then the Hawkins-Simon condition, which is generally applied only to A, is satisfied also by $A + R$ (see (Berman and Plemmons, 1979, p. 134)).

Proof of Proposition 1: From equation (5), the vectors of additions to capacity $o(t + 0)$ are always nonnegative. Since the matrices $B^0(t)$

(^{5}) The superscript s, for static, is added here to avoid confusion with the solutions of (4)-(7).

— 277 —

are also nonnegative, so is the product $B^0(t)o(t+\theta)$. Under 2) of the hypothesis, $[I-A(t)-R(t)]^{-1}$ exists and is nonnegative; see, e.g. (Berman and Plemmons, 1979). Thus, $z(t)$, the solution of

$$[I-A(t)-R(t)]z(t) = \sum B^0(o(t+\theta))$$

is nonnegative. The solution of (4)-(7), $x(t)$, is

$$x^s(t) + z(t) \qquad (Q.E.D.).$$

Remark 3: The proof of Proposition 1 is independent of the form of equation (4). In other words, for any (admittedly arbitrary) formulation determining future desired capacity, it is assured that the model (4)-(7) has nonnegative solutions.

Consider now a special case of (4)-(7), obtained by assuming a uniform one year lag and no replacement [6]. In other words consider the model

$$c_i^*(t+1) = \left[\frac{x_i(t-1) + x_i(t-2)}{x_i(t-2) + x_i(t-3)}\right]^2 x_i(t-1), \tag{4'}$$

$$o(t+1) = \max[0, c^*(t+1) - c(t)], \tag{5'}$$

$$c(t+1) = c(t) + o(t+1), \tag{6'}$$

$$[I-A(t)]x(t) = B^1(t)o(t+1) + y(t). \tag{7'}$$

Since the model (4')-(7') is a special case of (4)-(7), Proposition 1 is valid: given *any set* of nonnegative initial conditions $x(0)$, $x(-1)$, $x(-2)$, $c(1)$, there exists a unique set of nonnegative solutions $x(t)$, $t > 0$. In particular, the statement holds for expression (4') of which (4) is the generalization for $\tau > 1$.

Expression (4') is of a form which ensures that if the initial conditions $x(0)$, $x(-1)$, $x(-2)$ and $c(1)$ are on the balanced growth path and full capacity utilization is assumed for the first period, then the solutions $x(t)$ for all subsequent time periods will also be on the balanced growth path, perfect foresight is achieved in the « planning » process, and full capacity utilization is maintained. The following proposition, which can be proved by recursion in a straightforward manner, formalizes these concepts.

---

[6] One can assume that replacement is included in the A matrix.

— 278 —

Proposition 2: Consider the model (4')-(7') with $y(t) \equiv 0$ and no technological change. Denote by v the Frobenius eigenvector of the non-negative matrix $(I - A)^{-1}B$ and by $\lambda > 0$ the corresponding eigenvalue. If

$$x(0) = \alpha v, \qquad x(-1) = v^{-1}\alpha v, \qquad x(-2) = v^{-2}\alpha v$$

and

$$c(1) = v\alpha v,$$

where $v = (1 + \lambda)/\lambda$, then $x(t) = c^*(t) = c(t) = v^t\alpha v$ for $t > 0$.

Note that the solution for $x(t)$ given in Proposition 2 is a balanced growth solution and that it is the same as the balanced growth solution to the corresponding Leontief model.

In theoretical work with equations (1)-(3), replacement investment is assumed to be included with current account requirements in the A matrix. The A matrix used by the analyst in empirical work, however, is the current account matrix prepared by a government statistical office which by convention does not include replacement requirements. The explicit designation of an R matrix in the new model, (4)-(7), assures that in empirical work the production of replacement capital will not be overlooked. In the present treatment all replacement investment, whether it preserves or modernizes the existing stock, is assumed to be proportional to output and to be productive, without a lag, in the period of delivery—just as in the Leontief model. There is clearly a need in future work for a more refined conceptual representation of replacement with preservation of capacity linked to the composition and age of the existing stock while the decision to modernize the existing stock is linked to cost comparisons among technological alternatives.

While the new formulation realistically permits the underutilization of existing capacity, the present version of the model does not automatically preclude its overutilization either. This can occur in cases where output has grown faster than anticipated, although it is a self-limiting process since the rapid growth will trigger new expansion plans which will tend to eliminate capacity overutilization. Overutilization of capacity may be realistic in cases, for example, where it is feasible to employ an additional work shift. In other cases, it may be more realistic to satisfy the additional demand through increased imports. With the present formulation, the researcher has to reject as infeasible a scenario that produces unrealistic overutilization of capacity in one or more sectors.

— 279 —

5. RESULTS

The dynamic input-output model described in equations (4)-(7) was constructed and computations were carried out on the basis of A, R, B, and L matrices and vectors of non-investment final demand y, assembled for the years between 1963 and 1977 and projected for the years through 1990. The classification schemes involved 89 sectors and 53 occupational categories. In addition, values were estimated for sectoral lags, τ_i, and sectoral ceilings on annual anticipated rates of real growth of output, δ_i. These data and the specified initial conditions are documented in (Leontief and Duchin, 1986, Chapters 2-6 and Appendices A and B, and Leontief and Duchin, 1985, Chapter 4). The purpose of this section is to analyze some of the results obtained with this model. Additional computations were made using the same database and the familiar formulation of the static input-output model, equation (8), for benchmark years $t = 1963$, 1967, 1972, 1977 and 1990 ([7]).

The values of output of sector i, $x_i(t)$, according to equations (4)-(7) will in all cases be at least as large as the corresponding solutions of equation (8), $x_i^s(t)$, since the former include two components not accounted for in the static solution: *a*) deliveries by sector i of capital goods to all sectors j to expand the capacity of sector j at time $t + \tau_i$ and *b*) deliveries by sector i of goods and services on capital or current account required for the production of all deliveries of capital goods, produced by any sector k, for purposes of expansion. Since final demand is defined to exclude expansion investment, the solutions of equation (8) include no production contributing either directly or indirectly to expansion.

A small sample of the results are plotted in the accompanying figure for illustration. These graphs show output levels for years between 1963 and 1990 for two representative sectors, Plastics and Synthetic Materials (SIC 2821-4) ([8]) and Optical and Photographic Equipment (SIC 383, 385-6). Output according to the static model is plotted for benchmark years and interpolated for interventing years (dotted line). The difference between the solutions of the dynamic and static models is divided (by the hashed line) into two portions: the direct production of capital goods for expansion (called *a*) above) and the indirect contributions (called *b*)).

According to the graphs (which are representative of those obtained

---

([7]) These are chosen as benchmark years because official 10 tables have been compiled for 1963, 1967, 1972, and 1977 and matrices were projected for 1990.
([8]) Standard Industrial Classification.

for all 89 sectors), the behavior of the dynamic model for past years appears to be acceptably close to actual output.

In the case of sectors which do not produce capital goods, like Plastics and Synthetic Materials, the entire difference between the static and dynamic results is the indirect contribution to the production of capital for expansion. For Optical and Photographic Equipment, most of the difference in output corresponds to the direct delivery of capital goods for expansion.

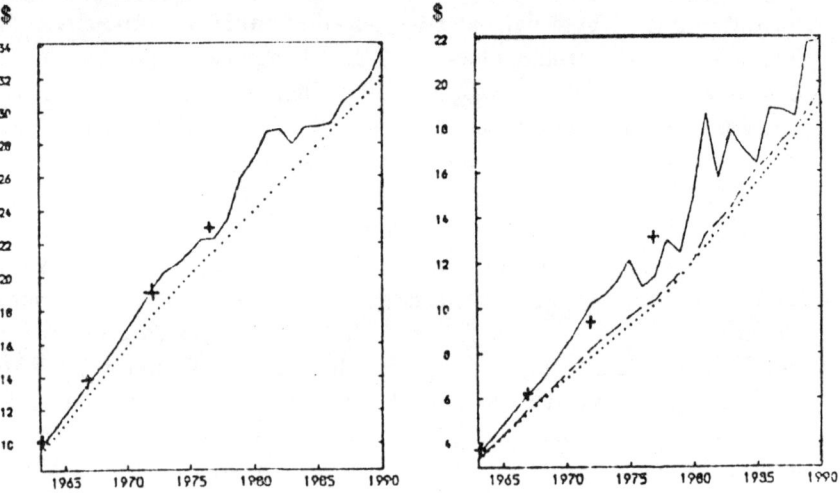

Output of Plastics and Synthetic   Output of Optical and Photographic
Materials (SIC 2821-4)   Equipment (SIC 383, 385-6)

* Vertical axes are measured in billions of dollars, 1979 prices.

The dotted line corresponds to the static model and the solid line to the dynamic model. The difference between the two is divided by the hashed line into two portions: the area above the hashed line corresponds to direct deliveries of capital goods for expansion; the remaining area corresponds to indirect inputs to expansion. In the case of Plastics, the hashed and solid lines coincide.

The cross represents actual output in benchmark years. Note that the vertical axes have different units in the two graphs.

6. CONCLUSIONS

This paper describes a new formulation of the dynamic input-output model that relaxes some of the constraints of the original formulation to permit a realistic empirical implementation. The new model uses the concept of a sectoral expansion plan to determine future desired capacity. Capital goods must be produced a variable number of periods before

— 281 —

they effectively add to planned capacity. Once in place, capacity need not be fully utilized and is not reversible. If the lag is uniformly assumed to be one year and if capacity and output must be identical, the new formulation has a balanced growth solution identical to that of the old.

Some of the results obtained with the new model are presented and compared with both actual outputs and results obtained with a static input-output model. The new formulation makes it possible to analyze the direct and the indirect contribution of each sector to the overall expansion of the economy.

REFERENCES

Åberg M. and Persson H.: « A note on a closed input-output model with finite life-times and gestation lags », *Journal of Economic Theory*, 24 (1981), 446-452.
Belen'kii V.Z., Volkonskii V.A. and Pavlov N.V.: « Dynamic input-output models in planning and price calculations and economic analysis », *Matekon* (Ekonomika i matematicheskie), 10-11 (1973-73), 74-101.
Berman H. and Plemmons R.: *Nonnegative Matrices in the Mathematical Sciences*, New York: Academic Press, 1979.
Dorfman R., Samuelson P.A. and Solow R.M.: *Linear Programming and Economic Analysis*, New York, Mc Graw-Hill, 1958.
Hawkins D. and Simon H.: « Some conditions of macroeconomic stability », *Econometrica*, 17 (1949), 245-248.
Iverson K.E.: « Machine solutions of linear differential equations — Applications to a dynamic economic model », Ph. D. Thesis, Applied Mathematics, Harvard University, 1954.
Johansen L.: « On the theory of dynamic input-output models with different time profiles of capital construction and finite life-time of capital equipment », *Journal of Economic Theory*, 19 (1978), 513-541.
Jorgenson D.W.: « Stability of a dynamic input-output system », *Review of Economic Studies*, 28 (1961), 105-116.
Leontief W.: « Dynamic Analysis », in: *Studies in the Structure of the American Economy*, ed. W. Leontief and others, New York, Oxford University Press, 1953; reprinted White Plains, N.Y., International Arts and Science Press, 1977, pp. 53-90.
Leontief W.: « The dynamic inverse », in: *Contributions to Input-Output Analysis*, ed. A.P. Carter and A. Brody, Amsterdam, North Holland Publishing Co., 1970, pp. 17-43; reprinted in W. Leontief: *Essays in Economics, Volume Two*, White Plains, N.Y., M.E. Sharpe, 1977.
Leontief W. and Duchin F.: « Automation, the changing pattern of U.S. exports and imports, and their implications for employment », prepared under National Science Foundation grant PRA 83-11407, March 1985.
Leontief W. and Duchin F.: *The Future Impact of Automation on Workers*, New York, Oxford University Press, 1986.
Livesey D.A.: « The singularity problem in the dynamic input-output model », *International Journal of Systems Science*, 4 (1973), 437-440.
Livesey D.A.: « A minimal realization of the Leontief dynamic input-output model », in: *Advances in Input-Output Analysis*, Proceedings of the Sixth International Conference in Input-Output Techniques, Vienna, April 22-26, 1974, ed. Karen Polenske and Jiri Skolka, Cambridge, Mass., Ballinger Publishing Co., 1976, pp. 527-541.
Luenberger D.G. and Arbel A.: « Singular dynamic Leontief systems », *Econometrica*, 45 (1977), 991-995.

— 282 —

Meyer U.: « Why singularity of dynamic Leontief systems doesn't matter », *Input-Output Techniques*, Proceedings of the Third Hungarian Conference on Input-Output Techniques, 3-5 November 1981, Budapest, Statistical Publishing House, 1982, pp. 181-189.

Szyld D.: « Conditions for the existence of a balanced growth solution for the Leontief dynamic input-output model », *Econometrica*, forthcoming, 1985.

Uzawa M.: « Note on Leontief's dynamic input-output system », *Proceedings of the Japan Academy*, 32 (1956), 79-82.

Volkonskii V.A.: « Industry price level and the norm of effectiveness in the system of optimal planning », *Matekon* (Economica i matematicheskie), 12 (1975-76), 28-46.

[17]

Structural Change and Economic Dynamics, vol. 1, no. 2, 1990

PRACTITIONERS' CORNER:

MICRO-ELECTRONICS AND EMPLOYMENT: A DYNAMIC INPUT–OUTPUT STUDY OF THE WEST GERMAN ECONOMY[1]

PETER KALMBACH[1] AND [2]HEINZ D. KURZ

1. INTRODUCTION

The present paper summarizes the theoretical model elaborated and the applied work carried out by the research unit 'Technologischer Wandel und Beschäftigung' at the University of Bremen.[2] The purpose of the study was to investigate the impact of the diffusion of micro-electronic-based new technologies on the volume and composition of employment in the West German economy.

The structure of the paper is as follows. Section 2 describes the method of enquiry adopted and relates our approach to others to be found in the literature. Section 3 gives a brief outline of the dynamic input–output model underlying our investigation; emphasis is on the formulation of private investment demand and on the treatment of the process of diffusion of the new methods of production. Section 4 provides a summary of the findings obtained in a series of simulation runs. Section 5 draws some conclusions and indicates some directions for further research.

2. THE METHOD

The general method adopted in our approach may be described in terms of the following passage taken from Hicks: 'We compare two alternative paths that extend into the future. Along one of those paths some new "cause" is not operating; along the other it is. The difference between the paths is the effect of that cause. The difference itself extends over time, so that there are "short-run" and "long-run" effects. But merely to distinguish between short-run and long-run is not sufficient; it is the *whole* of the difference between the paths which is the effect of the cause' (Hicks, 1983, p. 109; Hicks's emphasis).

Address: [1] University of Bremen, FRG; [2] University of Graz, FRG.
[1] We thank Reiner Franke and an anonymous referee for helpful comments on an earlier draft of this paper.
[2] Financial support by the *Stiftung Volkswagenwerk* is gratefully acknowledged. For a full account of the various aspects of the investigation undertaken, see the research unit's final report (Kalmbach *et al.*, 1989); for a brief discussion of the dynamic input–output model, see Kattermann and Kurz (1988).

More specifically, it is our aim to provide an analytical framework within which innovation-induced labour displacement and compensation can be consistently discussed. It deserves to be stressed that we are not interested in forecasting the time profile of employment in the West German economy until the year 2000. We are rather concerned with simulating exclusively those employment effects that accompany the diffusion of a new, well-defined micro-electronic-based 'best-practice technique' (*bpt*) in the West German economy. Factors other than those related to the diffusion process are not taken into account; they are considered 'frozen in'.

We use the scenario technique. In particular, we distinguish between transitions of the economy from the 'old' to the 'new' technique characterized by different speeds of the diffusion process. The reference scenario, which serves as a baseline, is taken to be the one in which no further change in the methods of production takes place. This generates a time path of employment with which we compare those paths that involve a more or less rapid diffusion of the new *bpt*. The new *bpt* itself is taken to be immutable, that is, we do not enter into speculations about further developments of technological knowledge. (Forecasts of the evolution of new technological patterns have not proved to be very reliable in the past.) The identification of the going *bpt* was a major task of our research project and involved the evaluation of a vast literature on modern technology, branch studies, and expert interviews.

The use of a dynamic input–output model in which final demand is partly endogenized is motivated as follows. First, in order to take into account both the primary and the secondary effects of technological change on output and employment, an *inter-industry* approach is indispensable. Secondly, the fact that the diffusion process takes time necessitates a *dynamic* analysis. Thirdly, technological change is generally associated with structural change; the latter is partly reflected in changes in the composition of output, an explanation of which would require the *endogenization* of final demand. It is worth mentioning that the approach chosen allows the modelling of both capital accumulation and de-cumulation in different sectors. Hence the model under consideration is able to deal with growing as well as with declining industries.

Our study exhibits several limitations, the two most important ones of which are the following. First, the model is essentially formulated in terms of quantities and does not adequately deal with (relative) prices and income distribution. Secondly, the endogenization of final demand is accomplished in a very rudimentary manner only. In particular, we were not able, in the time given, to model the impact of technological change in the domestic economy on the latter's export (and import) performance. Hence an important argument pro compensation could not be fully examined. However, it is possible to approach this problem from a different perspective: the model allows us to study the effects of exogenous variations of export demand. Therefore, it may be used to answer the question to what extent exports would have to be stimulated by the diffusion process in order to effectuate full compensation, which the other factors may have been unable to bring about. In a second step of the analysis one would then have

MICRO-ELECTRONICS AND EMPLOYMENT   373

to investigate whether the required expansion of exports is probable, given the technological dynamism to be observed in the major competing countries. This consideration draws attention to the obvious fact that in open economies the employment effects of technological change cannot be ascertained in terms of approaches that try to isolate the domestic economy from what is going on in the rest of the world. What is needed is a model of interdependent economies which would allow us to study the impact of differences in the domestic diffusion speeds on the economic performances of the system as a whole and its constituent parts.

Our approach bears some relationship to the models by Meyer and Schumann (1978), Meyer (1980), Duchin and Szyld (1985), and Leontief and Duchin (1986). It was particularly the latter study of the future impact of automation on employment in the US economy which inspired us to embark on a similar research project for the West German economy. However, we deemed it useful to explore a theoretical approach which differs from the one employed by Leontief and Duchin in a variety of respects. In particular, we thought that the 'core' of the model, the formulation of private investment behaviour, should and could be improved in order to overcome the model's following 'unrealistic' features:[3] (i) the model does not allow declining industries which, however, are often an important aspect of structural change; (ii) the growth rates of output are extremely high in some periods and extremely low in others; (iii) because of high output growth the expansion of productive capacity, over long periods of time, is limited by exogeneously given maximum growth rates only; (iv) fluctuations in the degree of utilization of productive capacity are very pronounced; (v) although there is cyclical and even quite regular behaviour, e.g. in the growth rates, the cycles are too long, i.e. some twenty years.

In what follows we provide a brief sketch of the characteristic features of our model. Emphasis is on the formulation of investment behaviour.

3. THE DYNAMIC INPUT–OUTPUT MODEL

3.1. *Desired Capacity*

As regards the modelling of investment demand, a two-step decision hypothesis is assumed. First, entrepreneurs are taken to form expectations about future demand. Secondly, as to the capacities required to match these levels of demand, entrepreneurs are taken to decide in each period how much of the expected output is to be provided by means of the 'old' and the 'new' (*bpt*) technique, respectively. By these two steps (and by summing up over sectors) we arrive at a vector of investment demand ('by origin').

Each sector j of the economy ($j = 1, 2, \ldots, n$) is assumed to have at its disposal one or two single product methods of production each of which is characterized by fixed coefficients of production. The coefficients of what will be called the old and the new technique will be indicated by superscripts I and II,

---

[3] It should be noted that the formulation of private investment demand is to a large extent responsible for the dynamic behaviour of the model and thus the 'empirical findings' of the simulation runs.

374 PETER KALMBACH AND HEINZ D. KURZ

respectively. Thus, in an otherwise conventional notation, a_{ij}^m and l_{kj}^m ($i, j = 1, 2, \ldots, n$; $k = 1, 2, \ldots, s$; $m = I, II$) represent the amounts of circulating means of production, i, and different kinds of labour, k, required per unit of output of the different commodities, j, if technique m is adopted. Similarly, the b_{ij}^m designate the requirements of stocks of durable capital goods per unit of capacity in sector j under technique m.

In the course of time technique II will gradually replace technique I. The going level of diffusion of the new technique in sector j in period t is given by the parameter $\alpha_j(t)$, $0 \leqslant \alpha_j(t) \leqslant 1$, which is a measure of the relative weight of the new technique. The 'average' coefficient $a_{ij}(t)$ is determined by

$$a_{ij}(t) = [1 - \alpha_j(t)]a_{ij}^I + \alpha_j(t)a_{ij}^{II}. \tag{1}$$

Similarly for the other coefficients.

The weights $\alpha_j(t)$ are scenario parameters given from outside the system. We shall consider altogether twenty-one periods from $t = 0$ to $t = 20$. The diffusion process is characterized by the time paths of the $\alpha_j(t)$. We shall, for simplicity, assume linear time curves (starting with $\alpha_j(0) = 0$), which may be considered crude approximations to logistic time curves. These curves are fully described for each sector once the time span T_j needed for the diffusion process to be completed is given. We shall treat T_j as an exogenous parameter and put

$$\alpha_j(t) = \min\{1, t/T_j\}. \tag{2}$$

One of the questions addressed in our investigation is how different T_j affect the time paths of the state variables, in particular output and employment.

We assume a uniform implementation lag of investment of two periods. Hence, at the beginning of period t the capacities of period $t+2$ will be decided. (The corresponding investment demand is assumed to be divided in equal proportions among the two periods.) The desired capacities in period $t+2$, $K_j^*(t+2)$, are seen to depend on two kinds of considerations, a long-run and a short-run consideration.

The *long-run* orientation is expressed by sectoral trend rates of growth, $gKTr_j(t)$. Between $t+1$ and $t+2$ capacity $K_j(t+1)$ should grow at this rate (since by hypothesis all demands for capital goods can be realized, $K_j(t+1)$ is already known for certain at date t). Let $K_j^1(t+2)$ designate the corresponding planning magnitude, i.e.

$$K_j^1(t+2) = [1 + gKTr_j(t)]K_j(t+1). \tag{3}$$

The trend rates of growth are determined by the following error-adjustment process

$$gKTr_j(t) = (1 - \text{Lam } Tr_j)gKTr_j(t-1) + \text{Lam } Tr_j \cdot gx_j(t-1), \tag{4}$$

where $gx_j(t-1) = [x_j(t-1) - x_j(t-2)]/x_j(t-2)$ is the last rate of output growth actually experienced, and Lam Tr_j ($0 < \text{Lam } Tr_j < 1$) is a weighting parameter.

According to the *short-run* planning approach sector j orientates his decision to expected sales and tries to correct present over- or underutilization of productive

MICRO-ELECTRONICS AND EMPLOYMENT 375

capacity. Using the weight Lam X_j ($0 < \text{Lam } X_j < 1$), the sector on the basis of the last two rates of growth of output actually experienced ascertains the 'expected' rate of growth, $gx \text{ Exp}_j(t-1)$, i.e.

$$gx \text{ Exp}_j(t-1) = \text{Lam } X_j \cdot gx_j(t-1) + (1 - \text{Lam } X_j) \cdot gx_j(t-2). \tag{5}$$

Thus, expected demand for period $t+2$ is given by $[1 + gx \text{ Exp}_j(t-1)]^3 \cdot x_j(t-1)$. The corresponding capacity depends on the sector's views as to the 'normal' degree of utilization, $u \text{ Norm}_j = x_j / K_j$. If expectations were fulfilled, the capacity at the beginning of period $t+2$

$$K^a := [1 + gx \text{ Exp}_j(t-1)]^3 \cdot x_j(t-1)/u \text{ Norm}_j \tag{6}$$

would involve normal utilization. It seems to be sensible to postulate a maximum rate of growth as regards this aspects of firms' capacity adjustment policy

$$K^b := [1 + gk \text{ Max}_j] \cdot K_j(t+1). \tag{7}$$

The impact of sales can thus be formulated as follows

$$K_j^2(t+2) = \min\{K^a, K^b\}. \tag{8}$$

The 'compromise' between $K_j^1(t+2)$ and $K_j^2(t+2)$ may be represented in terms of the weight Wght $K_j(t)$ ($0 \leqslant \text{Wght } K_j(t) \leqslant 1$)

$$K_j^*(t+2) = [1 - \text{Wght } K_j(t) \cdot K_j^1(t+2) + \text{Wght } K_j(t) \cdot K_j^2(t+2). \tag{9}$$

The weights are not rigid but depend on the 'dispersion' of the two rates of growth of output observed in the preceding two periods,

$$\text{Disp } Gx_j(t-1) := |gx_j(t-1) - gx_j(t-2)|, \tag{10}$$

and on a fixed so-called 'risk aversion parameter', Rho_j, which is assumed to be non-negative. We specify

$$\text{Wght } K_j(t) = 1/[1 + \text{Rho}_j \cdot \text{Disp } Gx_j(t-1)]. \tag{11}$$

The short-run alternative $K_j^2(t+1)$, that is, Wght $K_j(t) = 1$, will thus either be chosen if the last two rates of growth of sales are the same, or if $\text{Rho}_j = 0$. With an increase in dispersion, given a positive Rho_j, the weight shifts in favour of the long-run alternative $K_j^1(t+2)$. We should like to add that this device of capacity planning can give rise to rather cyclical behaviour, already in a one-sector stationary economy without technical change (see Franke and Weghorst, 1988).

3.2. Private Investment Demand

Once the desired capacities $K_j^*(t+2)$ have been ascertained, the corresponding stocks of capital goods and hence investment demand can be determined. Let $K_j^{m*}(t+2)$ denote that part of sector j's capacity which is planned to be provided in terms of technique m ($m = I, II$). We have

$$K_j^{II*}(t+2) = \alpha_j(t+2)K_j^*(t+2)$$
$$K_j^{I*}(t+2) = [1 - \alpha_j(t+2)]K_j^*(t+2). \tag{12}$$

376 PETER KALMBACH AND HEINZ D. KURZ

Associated with the capacities $K_j^{m^*}(t+2)$ are the capital stocks $S_{ij}^{m^*}$ which sector j has to have at its disposal at the beginning of period t. Clearly,

$$S_{ij}^{m^*}(t+2) = b_{ij}^m K_j^{m^*}(t+2) \quad m = I, II. \tag{13}$$

Before proceeding with the determination of investment requirements a few additional premises underlying our model should be mentioned. First, we shall assume that the installation of the desired capacities is always possible; this, however, does not necessarily imply that the relevant capital goods will always be available in the right proportions. Secondly, it will be assumed that within a given sector partly used capital goods can be transferred costlessly between techniques, whereas transfer between sectors and foreign trade in used capital goods are ruled out. Thirdly, the wear and tear of fixed capital items (in efficiency units) is described by means of the parameters δ_{ij} $(0 < \delta_{ij} < 1)$, which are not affected by variations in capital utilization.

In order to change the stocks $S_{ij}^m(t+2)$ to the planned levels $S_{ij}^{m^*}(t+2)$, investment of the amount

$$I_{ij}^m(t+2) = S_{ij}^{m^*}(t+2) - (1 - \delta_{ij})S_{ij}^m(t+1) \quad m = I, II \tag{14}$$

is necessary. The magnitudes I_{ij}^m can be positive, negative, or nil. A negative value signifies that a part of the existing stock will be rendered idle or will be transferred to the other technique, provided there is a need for the capital good under consideration. Total investment requirement of good i in sector j is given by

$$I_{ij}(t+2) = \max\{0, I_{ij}^I(t+2) + I_{ij}^{II}(t+2)\} \tag{15}$$

Taking into account the assumption concerning the implementation lag and the temporal distribution of investment, total private gross investment in capital good i in period t amounts to

$$\mathrm{Inv}_i^{Pr}(t) = [\Sigma_j I_{ij}(t+1) + \Sigma_j I_{ij}(t+2)]/2. \tag{16}$$

Equation (16) does not yet give private investment demand for domestically produced investment goods, $z^{Pr}(t)$. For its determination imports have to be taken into account and adjustments have to be made because of the different price concepts underlying input–output tables and capital stock accounts. The various (tedious) operations may be summarized by a mapping Φ^{Pr}, i.e.

$$z^{Pr}(t) = \Phi^{Pr}[\mathrm{Inv}^{Pr}(t)]. \tag{17}$$

Actual capital stocks at the beginning of period $t+2$, $S_{ij}^m(t+2)$, can now be readily derived from these magnitudes. We omit the precise formulation (because of a lack of space). As has been mentioned above, these stocks need not coincide with the desired stocks, $S_{ij}^{m^*}(t+2)$; however, they never fall short of the latter. Finally, from the capital stocks installed in each sector we can derive the sectors' realized capacities embodied in the two techniques, $K_j^I(t+2)$ and $K_j^{II}(t+2)$. Obviously,

$$K_j^m(t+2) = \min\{S_{ij}^m(t+2)/b_{ij}^m; b_{ij}^m > 0\}, \quad m = I, II \tag{18}$$

Total capacity of sector j is accordingly given by

$$K_j(t+2) = K_j^I(t+2) + K_j^{II}(t+2). \tag{19}$$

3.3. *Other Components of Final Demand*

As to the treatment of private consumption demand, government expenditures, and export demand a few remarks must suffice. Underlying our formulation of private consumption demand is a simple econometric model. The vector of consumption goods demanded by households in period t is taken to be an affine function of sectoral gross outputs in the preceding period. Basically, a disaggregated Keynesian consumption function is used with different marginal propensities to consume and different values for autonomous consumption.

Total government expenditures are taken to be a fixed proportion of gross domestic product of the preceding period, both on the reference path and the various diffusion paths. The share of the government sector is assumed to be equal to a weighted average of its historical values in the years 1973–86. However, we assumed that the composition of government expenditures remains the same only on the reference path, while on the diffusion paths there is a shift in favour of investment expenditures and among these in favour of certain expenditures in equipment (office machines, electronic equipment, etc.). This shift will be larger the shorter the total time needed in the government sector to accomplish the transition to the new technologies.

Export demands form the only autonomous demand component of the model. Therefore they determine (on average and in the long run) the pace of growth of the economy. We start from empirical values of exports and their growth rates. The latter will, however, be reduced in the course of the dynamic process. More precisely, we assume that the growth rates will steadily fall to one-half of their previous levels over the first ten periods, and then remain constant. This drop in growth rates is assumed to reflect, however imperfectly, the loss in international competitiveness due to 'technological inertia' on the reference path. This pattern of the slow down of export growth was in fact taken to apply also to most of the diffusion scenarios we studied. This is not meant to imply that we think, contrary to what has been said above, that the diffusion of micro-electronic-based new technologies has no impact on exports (and, via import substitution, on imports). It rather means that we lack hypotheses about this impact which can be relied on with sufficient confidence. However, as has been indicated in Section 2, the model allows us to ascertain the stimulus to exports that would be required in order to bring about full compensation which the other compensatory factors may have been unable to effectuate.

4. SOME RESULTS OF OUR INVESTIGATION

4.1. *Empirical Basis*

Before summarizing a few of our findings it seems to be useful to give some information about the empirical basis of our investigation. As it is shown in the

378 PETER KALMBACH AND HEINZ D. KURZ

presentation of the model, the old and the new technique are described in terms of the coefficients a_{ij}^I, l_{kj}^I, b_{ij}^I and a_{ij}^{II}, l_{kj}^{II}, b_{ij}^{II}, respectively. The input coefficients of the old technique are derived from a commodity x commodity table for 1980. It distinguishes between fifty-one commodity groups and is a slightly aggregated version of the input–output table published by the Statistisches Bundesamt.

With respect to the labour coefficients we had to decide which criterion of disaggregation serves best our purpose and which degree of disaggregation should be applied—both decisions of course being constrained by the availability of reliable statistical information. We decided to differentiate between several *activities* performed in the production process, a distinction which in our opinion has some advantages compared with other criteria of disaggregation employed in other studies (for example, in the investigation of the Austrian Institute of Economic Research, 1981). The empirical basis for this disaggregation is mainly the micro census. In contrast to the Leontief–Duchin study our degree of disaggregation is much lower; we distinguish between eight different activities only, whereas Leontief and Duchin specified fifty-three different occupations. Our procedure was not dictated by the micro census which, in principle, allows a higher degree of disaggregation. But it is a consequence of our approach that not only for the technique in existence but for the *bpt*, too, the labour coefficients had to be determined. The results of research work carried out by industrial sociologists show convincingly that there are considerable degrees of freedom for labour organization with respect to the use of new technologies. Hence, the determination of the columns of *bpt* labour coefficients inevitably involves some hypothesis about the dominant labour organization. As the distinction of many activities would require more specific information about the labour organization related to the *bpt*, we deemed it useful to distinguish between rather broad categories only. There is a single exception to this rule: concerning activities connected with electronic data processing the differentiation is more detailed.

As to the capital coefficients the denominators are sectoral capacities and not volumes of output. Estimates of the normal degree of capacity utilization provided by Deutsches Institut für Wirtschaftsforschung (DIW) were used in this context. The capital stocks, that is, the magnitudes entering the numerators, are derived from capital stock data which have been made available by the Ifo-Institut. As the Ifo-Institut estimated the stocks in existence of different capital goods on an industry basis, a transformation into a commodity x commodity table had to be accomplished. The capital stock data are constructed according to the so-called user concept: since leasing has grown in importance, from the point of view of production it appears to be superior to associate the capital stock with the user and not the owner.

Much more cumbersome than the description of the prevailing technique was, of course, the task of ascertaining the *bpt*. The information collected is derived from different sources: branch studies, case studies, studies about the diffusion of specific micro-electronic-based technologies, and expert interviews. Limitations of time and manpower made it necessary to concentrate only on a subset of the fifty-one commodity groups, i.e. those which we considered to be most important in respect to the use of micro-electronic-based technology: mechanical engineer-ing, office machine production, road vehicle construction, ship building, electrical engineering, cellulose, paper and cardboard production, printing, wholesale trade, retail trade, mail and communication, credit institutions, insurance, the software branch and other services, education and science, and health services. For the other groups solely the introduction of micro-electronic-based office automation is taken into account. But it has to be admitted that even for the commodity groups which have been investigated in greater detail, the information was often not conclusive and sometimes even contradictory. Nevertheless we had to form an opinion about which coefficients of the *bpt* could justly be considered to be different from the existing ones and to what extent. It goes without saying that we were engaged in a lot of guesswork.

4.2. *Main Findings*

As it has already been mentioned, we were interested in the differences between the *reference scenario* and various *diffusion scenarios*. The first is characterized by a technique which is 'frozen in', whereas the diffusion scenarios exhibit different speeds of diffusion. It has been assumed that the speed of diffusion is uniform across all commodity groups; however, we have also investigated the effects of different speeds for special groups which in the past exhibited marked differences in regard to diffusion of micro-electronic-based technology.

First, we compare the reference scenario with what is called the *standard diffusion scenario* (S1). The latter is characterized by the assumption that there is a linear increase in the diffusion parameter $\alpha(t)$ and that the diffusion is completed after twenty-one periods, which is the last period considered ($\alpha(20) = 1$).

The results obtained will be presented in aggregated form which distinguishes between six commodity groups. We computed the average yearly deviations for selected variables between reference and diffusion scenario after a couple of years ($t = 5, 10, 15, 20$). The percentages of deviation for output are shown in the following table.

As Table 1 shows there is a positive difference in output between standard

TABLE 1. *Deviations of Yearly Average* Output *Between S1 and Reference Path* (*Six-Sector Aggregation Level*)

	$t = 5$ Diff. in %	$t = 10$ Diff. in %	$t = 15$ Diff. in %	$t = 20$ Diff. in %
Agriculture, forestry	−0.19	0.41	0.67	0.85
Energy, water, mining	−0.32	0.89	1.41	1.75
Manufacturing	0.29	1.96	2.19	2.67
Construction	−0.18	9.16	11.17	12.28
Services	−0.05	1.71	2.77	3.68
State	−2.22	−2.80	−2.37	−1.61
Total economy	−0.18	1.62	2.24	2.91

($T = 20$; uniform α)

380 PETER KALMBACH AND HEINZ D. KURZ

diffusion scenario and reference scenario, which in the last period considered ($t = 20$) has reached a yearly average of 2.9 per cent.[4] In contrast to opinions often expressed, the output-increasing effects connected with the diffusion of new technologies are not very pronounced at the beginning of the diffusion process; indeed, after six periods ($t = 5$) the difference shows a small negative percentage. (We may mention in this context that, perhaps unexpectedly, the *average* capital coefficient associated with the *bpt* is smaller than the one of the old technique.) It is especially in the second sub-period that output on the diffusion path gains relatively to the reference scenario.

This becomes more obvious if we plot the respective paths of output, growth rates of output, and capacity utilization. Figure 1 shows that in the reference scenario there is a marked decrease in the growth rate of aggregate output beginning in $t = 6$ and that capacity utilization continues its downward trend, whereas in the diffusion scenario both growth rates and capacity utilization increase. Clearly, it is this difference in economic performance which is

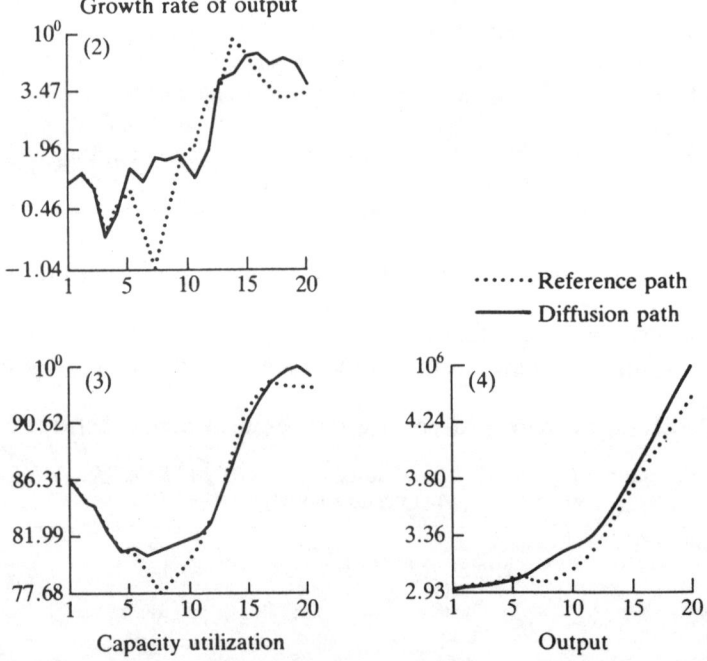

FIG. 1. Total economy (reference path and S1).

---

[4] The average deviation here and in what follows is always to be interpreted as the arithmetic mean of all (positive and negative) deviations in the years included. The deviation in the last year considered normally exhibits, of course, a different percentage of deviation. For example, the output in the standard diffusion scenario for $t = 20$ is 11.5 per cent above the output of the reference scenario.

MICRO-ELECTRONICS AND EMPLOYMENT 381

responsible for the assessment that in respect to output the diffusion path, all in all, is superior. Because of the cyclical behaviour still making itself felt, there is in this respect no clear-cut dominance: we have periods, in which the diffusion path exhibits higher growth rates than the reference path, but for other periods the reverse constellation holds good. (For this reason time averages seem to be more informative.)

The output differences in the aggregated sectors deserve a brief additional comment. It came as a surprise to us that it is construction which exhibits the largest positive difference, because our investigation of *bpt* generally indicated a lower construction coefficient. Obviously, this effect is more than compensated by the output-stimulating effects due to the diffusion process. The remarkable performance of the construction sector can be explained as follows. First, in 1980, the starting period of our investigation, productive capacity in construction was small, reflecting the low levels of investment during the prolonged slump of the seventies. The performance in the eighties and nineties therefore reflects to a certain extent a catch-up process of the construction sector. Secondly, the structural change implied by the diffusion of micro-electronic-based new technologies involves a shift in favour of those sectors with above average construction coefficients. These sectors, e.g. mail and communication, expand much more rapidly than the rest of the economy and thus spur construction. Clearly, the more rapid is the diffusion process the more the construction sector benefits from this sectoral shift.[5]

Next, let us look at employment. The aggregated results are contained in Table 2. As the last row of the table shows, the output-stimulating effects of diffusion compared with the reference scenario are, for the economy as a whole, too weak to compensate the negative employment effect induced by the predominantly declining coefficients (in particular the reduction of labour coefficients). Average yearly employment under the presently discussed diffusion regime is about 3 per cent lower than in the reference scenario. This result is obtained on the

TABLE 2. *Deviations of Yearly Average* Employment *Between S1 and Reference Path* (*Six-sector Aggregation Level*)

	t = 5 Diff. in %	t = 10 Diff. in %	t = 15 Diff. in %	t = 20 Diff. in %
Agriculture, forestry	−0.21	0.38	0.62	0.79
Energy, water, mining	−0.72	−0.08	−0.16	−0.38
Manufacturing	−1.03	−0.54	−1.74	−2.80
Construction	−0.26	9.01	10.94	11.96
Services	−2.06	−2.19	−3.13	−4.55
State	−3.82	−5.72	−6.74	−7.65
Total economy	−1.72	−1.26	−2.04	−3.01

(T = 20; uniform α)

[5] It should be noted here that the result reported in Fig. 2 and Table 4 below that production activities do not lose much on S1 is closely related to the brisk expansion of construction.

382 PETER KALMBACH AND HEINZ D. KURZ

assumption that export-stimulating effects as well as input-substitution effects of diffusion are absent. Since it seems probable that such effects do in fact exist, the negative employment effect of diffusion is overestimated.

On the other hand, there is some reason to believe that it is underestimated. If we have again a look at construction we are taught that it is the group with the highest positive employment effect. But this partly reflects only the fact that construction belongs to the commodity groups where nothing but the influence of office automation on *bpt* was studied. If the introduction of new technologies should have further and mainly coefficient-reducing effects, this would be reflected in a smaller difference.

The relatively large labour displacement in the state sector is the combined result of two factors at work on the diffusion path: first, there is the assumed change in the composition of public expenditures to the detriment of labour intensive public consumption; secondly, there is the labour-saving effect of the introduction of the new technologies in the state sector. Of these two factors the first can be seen to be the more important one.[6]

It is a characteristic feature of our approach that it is possible to change assumptions in respect to speed of diffusion, uniformity, or differences in the sectoral speeds of diffusion, export performance, etc., and to study the effects of those changed conditions. It suffices to give a single example of the underlying scenario idea: we studied both the effect of a higher (uniform) and that of a lower speed of diffusion on employment. Table 3 reproduces the employment differences in the cases where the diffusion process is assumed to be completed after fifteen (S2) or after thirty years (S3), respectively.

It can be seen that with a faster diffusion (S2) there is connected a smaller negative employment difference than in the standard diffusion scenario. The contrary is true for a lower speed of diffusion (S3). It is remarkable that construction, which exhibits a positive difference in the comparison of the standard diffusion scenario or S2 with the reference scenario, now in $t = 15$ and

TABLE 3. *Deviations of Yearly Average Employment Between S2/S3 and Reference Path (Six-sector Aggregation Level)*

	S2				S3			
	$t = 5$ Diff. in %	$t = 10$ Diff. in %	$t = 15$ Diff. in %	$t = 20$ Diff. in %	$t = 5$ Diff. in %	$t = 10$ Diff. in %	$t = 15$ Diff. in %	$t = 20$ Diff. in %
Agriculture, forestry	−0.27	0.49	1.73	2.32	−0.19	0.13	−0.59	−1.34
Energy, water, mining	−0.93	−0.11	1.24	1.60	−0.57	−0.28	−1.77	−3.22
Manufacturing	−1.08	−0.39	−0.74	−1.88	−1.02	−1.10	−3.40	−5.04
Construction	1.13	13.71	22.37	25.48	−2.27	1.04	−6.95	−9.58
Services	−2.73	−3.06	−2.47	−2.85	−1.41	−1.58	−4.09	−6.89
State	−6.43	−9.24	−8.10	−6.93	−1.22	−1.43	−3.34	−5.93
Total economy	−2.30	−1.76	−0.85	−0.98	−1.23	−1.11	−3.68	−5.92

$(T = 15;$ uniform $\alpha)$ $(T = 30;$ uniform $\alpha)$

[6] This becomes obvious when S1 will be compared with the other two scenarios S2 and S3 below.

MICRO-ELECTRONICS AND EMPLOYMENT 383

$t = 20$ has the largest negative difference. The results mentioned last partly confirm and partly contradict the suppositions formulated more than fifty years ago by Lederer (1981). Confirmed is his view that technical progress (or in our case diffusion) can go along with lower employment. Yet our findings don't support the view that an acceleration of technical progress (diffusion) of necessity aggravates the employment problem.

Up to now, we have considered only differences in employment in general without taking into account the different activities to which labour is allocated. As was mentioned, with the exception of electronic data-processing activities we distinguish only between rather general categories; for example, all production activities are lumped together. Restricting ourselves to the comparison between the standard diffusion scenario and the reference scenario, we present the results in Fig. 2. (Attention should be given only to differences and not to absolute values.)

The results in general confirm common opinions: traditional activities lose in importance on the diffusion path compared with the reference scenario. The only surprising result is that the number of persons allocated to production activities is slightly higher on the diffusion path if the twenty-one periods are taken together. However, for $t = 20$ there is a small negative difference (-0.9 per cent compared with -5.3 per cent for total employment).

For the last period under consideration ($t = 20$) we have in addition decomposed the employment differences in the eight activities subject to the criterion how differences in demand, A- and L-coefficients between the two scenarios in $t = 20$ contributed to the total percentage difference in each activity. Since in the diffusion scenario under discussion the technique in $t = 20$ is identical with bpt, we can split up the employment differences (in obvious notation) as follows:

$$L^{II}x^{II} - L^{I}x^{I} = L^{II}(I - A^{II})^{-1}[y^{II} - y^{I}] + L^{II}[(I - A^{II})^{-1} - (I - A^{I})^{-1}]y^{I}$$
$$+ [L^{II} - L^{I}](I - A^{I})^{-1}y^{I}$$

The result (differences in percentage points) are summarized in Table 4.

The table shows that the positive difference in final demand between S1 and the reference scenario in $t = 20$ has positive effects on the employment of all activities, although the percentages differ. In general, the difference in the A-coefficients contributes to a positive employment effect (exception: services which are not connected with data processing), too, but their contribution is considerably smaller. The effect of the difference in labour-coefficients is, as it was to be expected, negative on total employment, but as the column for the eight activities shows this is the net result of positive and negative effects in respect to separate activities.

In $t = 20$ total employment under the diffusion regime is 5.3 per cent below the employment of the reference scenario. Without the compensation effects of demand and A-coefficients, the difference would be 10.5 per cent. Hence we have to conclude, with all the reservations necessitated by the limitations of our analysis, that there are compensating mechanisms at work, but that they are too weak to bring about full compensation of the labour displacement effect.

384   PETER KALMBACH AND HEINZ D. KURZ

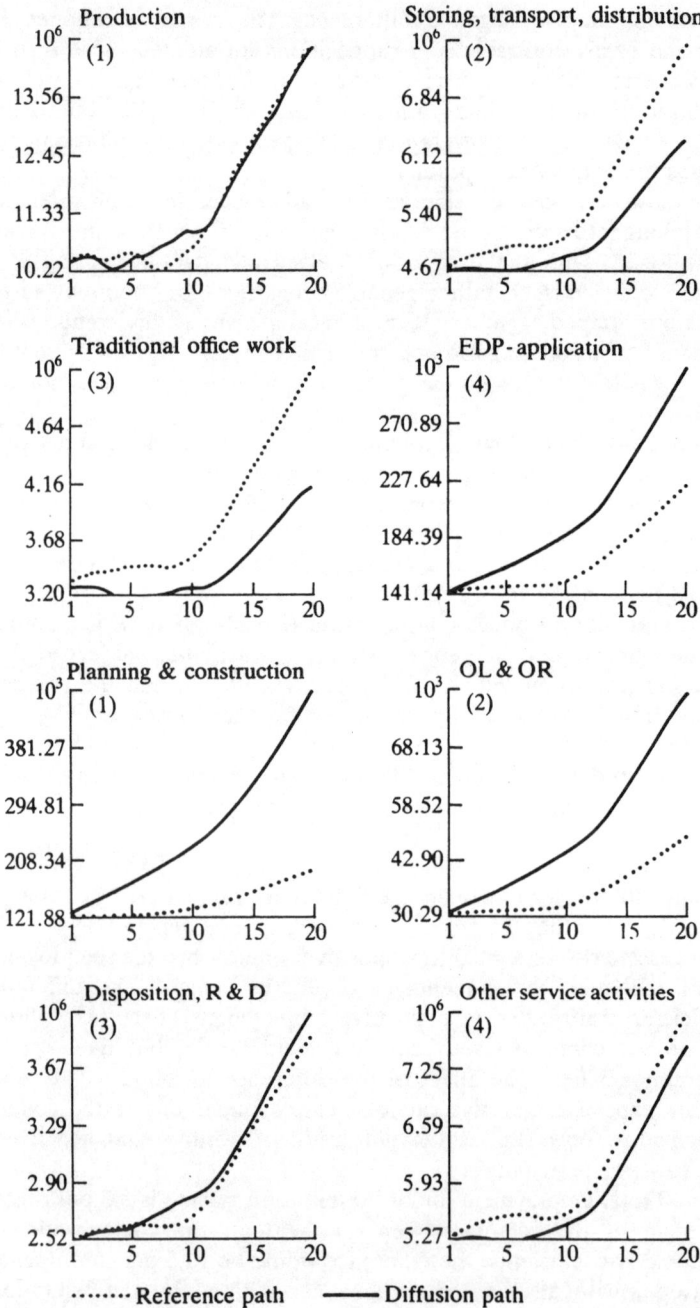

FIG. 2. Employment (activities) on reference path and S1.

TABLE 4. *Components of Employment Effects (%), Reference Path and S1 in t = 20*

	Demand	A-matrix	Labour coefficient	Total
Production	5.81	0.20	−6.56	−0.92
Storing, transport, distribution	6.33	0.79	21.29	−15.65
Traditional office activities	5.67	0.25	−23.90	−19.38
EDP-application	6.17	0.78	31.30	40.48
Planning and construction	6.74	1.63	123.81	142.78
OL and OR	5.99	0.96	56.56	67.52
Disposition, R & D	5.87	0.53	−2.22	4.06
Other service activities	3.67	−0.13	−7.80	−4.55
Total	5.47	0.30	−10.51	−5.34

$(T = 20;$ uniform $\alpha)$

5. CONCLUSIONS AND INDICATIONS FOR FURTHER RESEARCH

It goes without saying that our investigation does not claim to have solved the time-honoured problem under consideration. As it was mentioned above, our approach is subject to criticisms both from the point of view of economic theory and the empirical analysis carried out. In terms of theory, attention focused on investment demand whereas the endogenization of other important components of final demand was done in an extremely provisional way. In particular, it would be of considerable interest to study distributional effects on consumption and the influence of new products on consumption patterns (a conceptually difficult task in an input–output framework). The main weakness of our approach and therefore the part where further research seems to be most required is the treatment of foreign trade. For economies like that of the Federal Republic of Germany with remarkable shares of exports and imports there are good reasons to expect that exports and imports may differ considerably *vis-à-vis* different diffusion paths. An appropriate endogenization of export and import performance would lead to a substantial improvement of our analysis.

As far as the empirical aspect is concerned several limitations of our study have been mentioned which should be overcome by further research. First, the *bpt* should be investigated for all sectors and not only for a sub-group as it is the case in our study. Secondly, it seems worthwhile to study not only the effect of diffusion but of future improvements in technology, i.e. to take into account that the *bpt* itself is changing over time. In principle, this can be incorporated into our approach but we abstained from pursuing this route, given the data situation. Perhaps this route could be followed successfully in a 'joint venture' of engineers and economists. Thirdly, we think our approach would gain considerably if some sectors could be disaggregated. In the traditional classification of input–output table producers of old and new technologies are lumped together in one and the same sector. This has, of course, the consequence that important information is lost. Since sectors like 'engineering' or 'office and data-processing machines' include producers of old and new technologies we are not able to study the shifts between these sub-categories but only the net effect of increase and decline which

386 PETER KALMBACH AND HEINZ D. KURZ

takes place in these heterogeneous sectors. The statistical information available to us prevented us from disaggregating the most important producer sectors according to the principle mentioned. With an improved statistical basis this route is worth pursuing.

REFERENCES

AUSTRIAN INSTITUTE OF ECONOMIC RESEARCH (1981). *Mikroelektronik. Anwendungen, Verbreitung und Auswirkungen am Beispiel Österreichs*, edited by the Austrian Ministry of Science and Technology. Vienna and New York, Springer-Verlag.
HICKS, J. R. (1983). *Classics and Moderns. Collected Essays on Economic Theory*, vol. III. Oxfod, Basil Blackwell.
DUCHIN, F. and SZYLD, D. (1985). 'A Dynamic Input–Output Model with Assured Positive Outputs', *Metroeconomica*, 37, pp. 269–82.
FRANKE, R. and WEGHORST, W. (1988). 'Complex Dynamics in a Simple Input–Output Model without the Full Capacity Utilization Hypothesis', *Metroeconomica*, 40.
KALMBACH, P. *et al.* (1989). *Mikroelektronik und Beschäftigung. Eine Untersuchung der Auswirkungen des Einsatzes programmgesteuerter Arbeitsmittel unter Verwendung eines dynamischen Input–Output-Modells*. Abschlußbericht der Forschungsgruppe 'Technologischer Wandel und Beschäftigung', Bremen.
KATTERMANN, D. and KURZ, H. D. (1988). 'Technological Change and Employment', in P. Flaschel and M. Krüger (eds.), *Recent Approaches to Economic Dynamics*. Frankfurt and New York, Peter Lang.
LEDERER, E. (1981). *Technischer Fortschritt und Arbeitslosigkeit*, originally published in 1938. Frankfurt, Europäische Verlagsanstalt.
LEONTIEF, W. and DUCHIN, F. (1986). *The Future Impact of Automation on Workers*. New York, Oxford University Press.
MEYER, U. (1980). *Dynamische Input–Output-Modelle*. Königstein, Athenäum.
—— and SCHUMANN, J. (1978). 'Ansätze zur Weiterentwicklung des dynamischen Input–Output-Modells', in E. Helmstädter (ed.), *Neuere Entwicklungen in den Wirtschaftswissenschaften*. Berlin, Duncker & Humblot.

[18]

A linear programming system analyzing embodied technological change*

Anne P. CARTER

Harvard University

At the Third International Conference on Input-Output Techniques in September, 1961, two of us, Professor Mathur and myself, presented papers (see MATHUR 1963 and CARTER 1963) suggesting that structural change be introduced into dynamic input-output models, under the assumption that given new techniques are capital embodied. At that time, very little was known about new-technology input structures, nor did we have any clear picture of how rapidly input-output structures change in general. Hence, it was not possible for either of us to appraise the relevance or the merits of this approach in analyzing the operation of the economy as a whole. Mathur, whose primary emphasis was theoretical, had to restrict his implementation to a hypothetical example, where United States input-output structure for 1947 represented 'best practice' structures to be adopted in new capacity for the Indian economy in all sectors. My own emphasis was operational, but empirical coverage was very limited indeed. The study was restricted to analysis of detailed cross-section and time-series materials for two relatively homogeneous 4-digit Standard Industrial Classification industries: tin cans, and ball and roller bearings.

The informational bottleneck is still serious, and the present paper does not begin to eliminate it. For the United States, and no doubt for most other countries as well, there still is no comprehensive map-

---

* The author wishes to thank Brookes Byrd and William Benz for assistance:

ping of input structures associated with the newest or 'best practice' techniques in each sector. This is easily understandable: the basic data-gathering work required to describe new-technology structures, and to render them compatible with existing input-output conventions and classifications, is enormous, and the information is not normally generated by our established statistical systems. Until the value of using such information is better accepted, it is difficult to justify the effort involved. Thus, we find ourselves in an awkward position: unable to appraise the practical value of the embodiment hypothesis because the data for testing are not available; unable to justify gathering the data because the evidence about the approach is so fragmentary.

The present paper contributes some gross evidence about the value of this type of approach in analyzing the performance of the economy as a whole, but the informational basis is still very weak. Essentially, we compute a statistical approximation to coefficients representing new techniques, and introduce embodied technical change into the system, using these crude estimates to represent the latest technology.

1. The basic model

Many facets of the embodiment question can be analyzed without employing a full-fledged dynamic model. For present purposes, a relatively simple, linear programming model was used. It differs from the conventional, static input-output model in only three major respects:
(1) Instead of a single structure, each sector is assigned two alternative structures, one representing the observed average input-output structure prevailing in a particular base period, and the other representing a new technological layer.
(2) Capital is required for the creation of any new capacity, whether for net expansion or replacement. Capital coefficients govern the expansion of capacity with either old or new techniques. A ceiling, equal to the total volume of investment actually observed in a given time interval, is placed on the sum total of gross investment, i.e., on total expenditures on plant and equipment, in the entire economy. Fixing total investment limits the amount of replacement that can take place, and thus the rate of transition from old to newer technology.

(3) The problem is defined as one of delivering a given *increment* to final demand by means of *changes* in the levels of various activities throughout the economy. These changes may increase the levels of production with new input structures, and increase or decrease the levels of production with older input structures. Let

A^n = a matrix of new-technology input coefficients,

A^t = a matrix of average input-output structures, i.e., of conventional input-output coefficients, observed for some base period,

ΔX^n = a vector of increments to output levels associated with the new-technology input structures,

ΔX^t = a vector of increments to output with old-technology input structures, and

ΔY = a vector of increments to final demand.

The basic balance equation is

$$(I - A^n)\Delta X^n + (I - A^t)\Delta X^t \geq \Delta Y. \tag{1}$$

The vector ΔX^t is composed of positive elements, representing additions to capacity with old-technology structure, and negative elements representing retirements of old capacity. (Retirements will include a minimal 3 per cent allowance for wear and tear, discussed below.) Distinguishing increases in old-technology capacity from retirements, we partition the vector ΔX^t into two positive subvectors ΔX^{t+}, containing all the positive elements; and ΔX^{t-}, containing all the negative elements of ΔX^t, i.e., $\Delta X^{t+} - \Delta X^{t-} = \Delta X^t$. We assume that new-technology capacity will not be retired during the time interval considered, and so ΔX^n is not partitioned. Thus, all elements of ΔX^n must be positive or zero. Eq. (1) can now be written in the form

$$(I - A^n)\Delta X^n + (I - A^t)\Delta X^{t+} - (I - A^t)\Delta X^{t-} \geq \Delta Y. \tag{2}$$

Increases in capacity with either 'old' or 'new' input structure are permitted, subject to the limit on total investment in the economy. This constraint is specified by

$$B^n \Delta X^n + B^t \Delta X^{t+} \leq \varkappa, \tag{3}$$

80   ANNE P. CARTER

where B^n and B^t are vectors of capital coefficients associated with new and old techniques, respectively; and $\varkappa$ is the given total amount of gross new investment available to the system over the period studied. For each interval, the total investment ceiling is actual expenditure on plant and equipment in the American economy summed from the base year through the year before the terminal year of the interval. Retirement of capacity is assumed not to release capacity for other sectors, and no terms involving ΔX^{t-} appear in eq. (3).

Let L^n and L^t be vectors of labor coefficients with new and old techniques. An objective function,

$$L^n \Delta X^n + L^t \Delta X^{t+} - L^t \Delta X^{t-} = \text{minimum}, \qquad (4)$$

is specified. For simplicity, we assume that labor is the only primary factor in the objective function. However, it is not difficult to introduce a weighted sum of labor and capital charges in place of straight labor inputs in the objective function.

Eqs. (2), (3), and (4) are the core of the linear programming model. It chooses an optimal mix of input structures, under conditions of embodied technical change, subject to an overall investment ceiling. Initial capacities are characterized by old (i.e., by initial average) technology. Given a specified increment to the bill of goods ΔY and the total lump of investment over the time period, the system selects that combination of activity levels, with new and old techniques, that minimizes total labor costs. Were there no limit on total investment, the system could choose *any* combination of new and old techniques. Depending on the relative advantages of individual new and old structures, each sector would either replace its entire capacity or leave it intact with old structures. Increments to capacity would have matching new or old structures. The amount of available investment, however, limits achievement of this 'unlimited' optimum. Provided that capacity requirements for supplying the given increment to final demand are met, investment will be allocated to replace capacities where the labor-saving advantages of new techniques are greatest. Two additional sets of constraints, eqs. (5) and (6), complete the specification of the system. Initial capacity limits the amount of scrappage of old capacity that can take place in each sector. For most sectors, it is probably more realistic to impose replacement ceilings of less than 100 per cent of initial capacity. Initial capacity actually consists of many technological layers, some of them very similar, if not identical, to the best practice techniques. Thus, in reality, the labor saving achieved by replacing old with new capacity in most sectors decreases as more and more capacity is replaced. In principle, of course, this condition calls for further disaggregation of each sector's initial input structure. Lacking the data for this, we imposed ceilings on the scrappage rates of all sectors. Thus, the set of constraints,

$$\Delta X^{t-} \leq \gamma X^{t},\tag{5}$$

was imposed, where X^{t} represents initial capacities and γ is a constant. γ was varied experimentally within a range equivalent to 6 to 9 per cent per annum.

Minimal scrappage rates were also set to allow for physical attrition and retirements incidental to the needs of changing product mix and geographical relocation of capacity, not explicitly introduced in the model:

$$\Delta X^{t-} \geq \alpha X^{t},\tag{6}$$

where α is the minimal scrappage rate, equivalent to 2, and then 3, per cent per annum.

Beyond the specification of eq. (5) and eq. (6), no *a priori* distinction between investment for expansion and replacement was made. Where the new technique is advantageous, its capacity is likely to expand. If this expansion of capacity is compensated by reductions in old capacity it is 'replacement'. Otherwise, it is 'expansion'. Whether a sector expands or replaces depends on the demand for its output and, thus, on final demands and activity levels for other sectors. Except for eq. (6), we do not prejudge whether a particular addition to capacity will turn out to be an expansion or a replacement. It is determined by the simultaneous workings of the entire system. *Ex ante*, an individual producer may distinguish between replacement and expansion of his facilities. If he finds no market for the output of a portion of his capacity, however, what he may have intended to be expansion will turn out, *ex post*, to be replacement.

82   ANNE P. CARTER

2. *Empirical implementation*

The basic data used to implement and test this system consisted of the
set of 1947 and 1958 input-output matrices, rendered comparable
through joint research efforts of the Harvard Economic Research Project and the U.S. Department of Commerce, Office of Business Economics (see VACCARA and SIMON 1968; and CARTER 1967); an estimated
1961 bill of goods from the Office of Business Economics; capital
coefficients from the NATIONAL PLANNING ASSOCIATION (1965), HENDER-
SON et al. (1953), and other special studies at the Harvard Economic
Research Project; labor coefficients derived from worksheet information furnished by the U.S. Department of Labor Interagency Growth
Project; investment and capital stock information from the U.S. DE-
PARTMENT OF COMMERCE (1957), (1947, 1954, 1958), and (1949 through
1957). All data were price adjusted to a 1958 basis.

To implement the system, eqs. (2) through (6), it was necessary first
to estimate the new-technology parameters A^n and L^n, input-output
flow coefficients and labor coefficients to represent the newer technological layers. Ideally, one would wish to have the best practice coefficients estimated directly, from sample information, as described in
MIERNYK (1969), or based on technological judgment as described in
KOMIYA (1959) or CARTER (1953, 1957). While Miernyk has estimated
sets of best practice coefficients for individual regions, there is nothing
approaching a complete set of direct estimates of new-technology structures for the United States as a whole. Rough statistical approximations
had to be used instead. Incremental coefficients were computed as
estimates of these new-technology parameters. In effect, incremental
coefficients are generated by running the model of embodied technological change 'in reverse'. They represent what the coefficients for
new technology *must have been*, in order to produce the changes in
input structure actually observed over the period 1947–1958, with given
sectoral investments and assuming capital embodiment. This method,
clearly, is crude, and can give only very rough estimates of best-practice
structures. The incremental coefficient matrix was derived as follows:
Each 1958 flow coefficient a_{ij}^{58} was viewed as a weighted average of 1947
(a_{ij}^{47}) and new-technology (a_{ij}^n) coefficients:

$$a_{ij}^{58} = a_{ij}^n w_j + a_{ij}^{47} (1 - w_j).$$

Hence, each incremental coefficient could be estimated from observed 1947 and 1958 coefficients and the weights w_j;

$$a_{ij}^n = [a_{ij}^{58} - a_{ij}^{47} (1 - w_j)]/w_j, \qquad (7)$$

where w_j is the proportion of 1958 output characterized by new-technology input structure in industry j. The weight w_j is approximated by the proportion of 1958 capacity installed during the period 1947–57 inclusive. This, in turn, is roughly equal to the ratio of gross new investment over the period, to gross capital assets at the end of the period,

$$w_j = \sum_{t=47}^{57} e_j^t / k_j^{58}, \qquad (8)$$

where e_j^t is sector j's annual expenditures on new plant and equipment, and k_j^{58} is the value of its gross capital assets in 1958. Incremental labor coefficients l_j^n were computed similarly to a_{ij}^n. The 1947 and 1958 matrices are not entirely comparable, cell-by-cell, and the rigid assumption of embodiment for all change is not correct. Changes may, in fact, be tied to investment for some elements of a column and not for others. Thus, there were bound to be some terms in the incremental coefficient matrix that did not make good technological sense. Actually, the computed incremental matrix did not contain many apparent technological 'monstrosities'. One across-the-board refinement of these estimates was imposed: when negative coefficients appeared in the incremental matrix, they were replaced by positive coefficients arbitrarily valued at fifty per cent of the 1958 coefficient. This adjustment affected only 25 cells with 1958 coefficients equal to or greater than 0.005, and should introduce no serious biases into the computations.

This single set of incremental coefficients, inferred from the observed 1947–1958 coefficient changes, represents new-technology structures for the entire period 1947–1961 in our computations. Coefficients representing average technology in the base year are simply observed input-output coefficients for that base year. The linear programming problem was computed for three different time intervals: 1947–58, 1947–61, and 1958–61. For the first two intervals, 1947 input-output,

84

ANNE P. CARTER

TABLE 1

Computed increases and decreases in activity levels with old- and new-technology input structures, 1947–58 (tens of millions of 1958 dollars)

Industry	Base year output X^{47}	$\Delta X^{t-} \leq 0.66 X^{47}$ Increases (ΔX^n or ΔX^{t+})	$\Delta X^{t-} \leq 0.66 X^{47}$ Decreases (ΔX^{t-})	$\Delta X^{t-} \leq 0.88 X^{47}$ Increases (ΔX^n or ΔX^{t-})	$\Delta X^{t-} \leq 0.88 X^{47}$ Decreases (ΔX^n)	$\Delta X^{t-} \leq 1.00 X^{47}$ Increases (ΔX^{t+} or ΔX^{t-})	$\Delta X^{t-} \leq 1.00 X^{47}$ Decreases (ΔX^{t-})
7 Food products	4829	2908†	1609	2878†	1609	2865†	1609
8 Tobacco	533	403	355*	506	474*	250	177
9 Textiles	2256	2261	1503*	2815	2004*	3074	2255*
10 Wood	764	568	509*	208	254	207	254
11 Furniture	353	362	235*	436	314*	478	353*
12 Paper products and containers	872	706†	290	690†	290	657†	290
13 Printing and publishing	973	949	648*	619	324	610	324
14 Chemicals	1172	2071	781*	2369	1041*	2508	1171*
15 Petroleum refining	1046	1048	370*	1022	348	1020	348
16 Rubber and plastic products	503	375	167	390	167	413	167
17 Leather	407	276	271*	373	361*	415	407*
18 Glass and glass products	198	84	66	81	66	76	66
19 Stone and clay products	450	479	150	469	150	466	150
20 Iron and steel manufacturing	2151	452†	716	433†	716	429†	716
21 Nonferrous metals manufacturing	754	406	251	366	251	390	251

LINEAR PROGRAMMING SYSTEM OF ANALYSIS

#	Sector							
22	General metalworking	1493	1395	995*	835	497	872	497
23	Engines and turbines	167	188	111*	232	148*	256	166*
24	Farm machinery and equipment	237	172	158*	219	210*	243	237*
25	Construction and mining machinery	309	208	205*	96	102	95	102
26	Industrial machinery	1153	413†	384	425†	384	444†	384
27	Office and computing machines	92	227	61*	251	81*	262	91*
28	Household and service industry mach.	442	453	294*	552	392*	599	441*
29	Electric apparatus	585	533	390*	659	520*	718	585*
30	Communication eq. and electronic comp.	315	805	210*	886	280*	919	315*
31	Batteries, X-ray and engine electric eq.	141	64	47	63	47	60	47
32	Motor vehicles and others	2289	1908	1525*	1706	1342*	1087	762
33	Aircraft and parts	251	1248	167*	1313	223*	1346	251*
34	Instruments and clocks	202	298	134*	344	179*	366	201*
35	Optical and photographic equipment	89	129	59*	148	79*	158	89*
36	Misc. manufacturing prod.	389	404	259*	489	346*	308	162*

† Identifies sectors where Δx_j^{t+} rather than Δx_j^{t} have non-zero values.
* Identifies sectors where $\Delta x_j^{t-} > 0.33 x_j^{47}$.

TABLE 2

Computed increases and decreases in activity levels with old- and new-technology input structures, 1947–61
(tens of millions of 1958 dollars)

Industry	Base year output X^{47}	$\Delta X^t \leq 0.70X^{47}$ Increases (ΔX^n or ΔX^{t+})	$\Delta X^t \leq 0.70X^{47}$ Decreases (ΔX^{t-})	$\Delta X^t \leq 0.84X^{47}$ Increases (ΔX^n or ΔX^{t+})	$\Delta X^t \leq 0.84X^{47}$ Decreases (ΔX^{t-})	$\Delta X^t \leq 1.00X^{47}$ Increases (ΔX^n or ΔX^{t+})	$\Delta X^t \leq 1.00X^{47}$ Decreases (ΔX^{t-})
					Computed changes in activity levels		
7 Food products	4829	3636†	2028	3617†	2028	3598†	2028
8 Tobacco	533	477	373*	541	448*	615	533*
9 Textiles	2256	2717	1578*	3075	1894*	3473	2255*
10 Wood	764	620	534*	320	320	313	320
11 Furniture	353	416	247*	463	296*	517	353*
12 Paper products and containers	872	948†	366	955†	366	946†	366
13 Printing and publishing	973	1143	680*	1161	698*	868	408
14 Chemicals	1172	2578	820*	2747	984*	2967	1171*
15 Petroleum refining	1046	1540	732*	1260	439	1255	439
16 Rubber and plastic products	503	510	211	512	211	521	211
17 Leather	407	291	285*	351	342*	422	407*
18 Glass and glass products	198	122	83	123	83	121	83
19 Stone and clay products	450	756	295*	640	189	632	189
20 Iron and steel manufacturing	2151	753†	903	716†	903	703†	903

LINEAR PROGRAMMING SYSTEM OF ANALYSIS   87

21	Nonferrous metals manufacturing	754	798	527*	525	316	484	316
22	General metalworking	1493	1659	1044*	1842	1253*	1213	626
23	Engines and turbines	167	185	116*	209	140*	241	166*
24	Farm machinery and equipment	237	162	166*	194	199*	228	237*
25	Construction and mining machinery	309	218	216*	263	259*	124	129
26	Industrial machinery	1153	575†	484	563†	484	569†	484
27	Office and computing machines	92	313	64*	329	76*	347	91*
28	Household and service industry mach.	442	552	309*	612	370*	685	441*
29	Electric apparatus	585	629	409*	709	491*	802	585*
30	Communication eq. and electronic comp.	315	1090	220*	1145	264*	1203	315*
31	Batteries, X-ray and engine electric eq.	141	91	59	89	59	89	59
32	Motor vehicles and others	2289	2454	1601*	2804	1922*	2714	1848*
33	Aircraft and parts	251	1030	175*	1074	211*	1120	251*
34	Instruments and clocks	202	370	141*	401	169*	433	201*
35	Optical and photographic equipment	89	152	62*	164	74*	179	89*
36	Misc. manufacturing products	389	470	272*	527	327*	586	389*

† Identifies sectors where Δx^{t+}_j rather than Δx^n_j have non-zero values.

* Identifies sectors where $\Delta x^{t-}_j > 0.33 x^t_j$.

88   ANNE P. CARTER

labor, and capital coefficients represented the initial technology; while in the third case, initial technology was represented by 1958 coefficients. To repeat, new technology was represented, in all three cases, by the incremental coefficients based on observed 1947–58 changes. 1958 capital coefficients were assumed to represent capital requirements with incremental technology, too.

Increments to final demands ΔY were computed directly from observed final demand vectors for the years in question, while total expenditures on plant and equipment were summed from Census of Manufactures time series. Since reliable capital expenditures estimates were not available to fit the 83-order input-output classification, it was necessary to aggregate to a new 36-order scheme for these computations. This classification is shown in tables 1, 2, and 3. It gives relatively good detail for manufacturing sectors, but had to be heavily aggregated in non-manufacturing. Therefore the levels of investment in non-manufacturing sectors were taken as given: optimizing computations were restricted to allocating total manufacturing investment among the manufacturing sectors only. For the non-manufacturing sectors (sectors 1–6, not mentioned in the tables), capital coefficients were set equal to zero.

Several variants of the basic model were computed for each of the three intervals, 1947–58, 1947–61, and 1958–61. For 1947–58 and 1947–61, minimal decumulation was set at 33 and 42 per cent (3 per cent per annum) of initial capacity. These variants differed only in the arbitrary ceiling imposed on the amount of initial capacity that each sector was permitted to replace. Thus, for 1947–58, alternative upper limits of 55, 66, 77, 88, and 99 per cent (5 to 9 per cent per annum) of initial capacity were imposed on each sector's decumulation. Similarly, for 1947–61 the alternative upper limits were 70, 84, and 100 per cent of base-year capacity. While the observed total volume of investment in manufacturing was well in excess of requirements to cover a three per cent per annum minimal replacement for 1947–58 and 1947–61, total investment in manufacturing for the interval 1958 through 1961 barely covered 2 per cent per annum replacement. Thus, the minimal decumulation level of 6 per cent (2 per cent per annum) for each sector was the largest that could be imposed for the 1958–61 period.

TABLE 3

Computed increases and decreases in activity levels
with old- and new-technology input structures, 1958–61
(tens of millions of 1958 dollars)

Industry	Computed changes in activity levels $\Delta X^{t-} \leq 0.21 X^{58}$		Base year output
	Increases $(\Delta X^n \text{ or } \Delta X^{t+})$	Decreases (ΔX^{t-})	X^{58}
7 Food products	704†	382	6386
8 Tobacco	90	34	592
9 Textiles	549	172	2872
10 Wood	93	48	832
11 Furniture	69	28	473
12 Paper products and containers	261†	78	1309
13 Printing and publishing	243	74	1261
14 Chemicals	563	140	2347
15 Petroleum refining	254	104	1734
16 Rubber and plastic products	130†	40	684
17 Leather	24	22	398
18 Glass and glass products	32	12	214
19 Stone and clay products	163	44	751
20 Iron and steel manufacturing	251†	114	1911
21 Nonferrous metals manufacturing	112	54	919
22 General metalworking	325	118	1996
23 Engines and turbines	4	12	220
24 Farm machinery and equipment	0	18*	244
25 Construction and mining machinery	19	18	308
26 Industrial machinery	139†	72	1227
27 Office and computing machines	93	12	222
28 Household and service industry machinery	114	32	566
29 Electric apparatus	118	42	730
30 Communication eq. and electronic components	329	50	852
31 Batteries, X-ray and engine electric equip.	22	8	153
32 Motor vehicles and others	637	158	2652
33 Aircraft and parts	62	272*	1269
34 Instruments and clocks	84	20	350
35 Optical and photographic equipment	28	8	152
36 Misc. manufacturing products	82	30	531

† Identifies sectors where Δx_j^{t+} rather than Δx_j^n have non-zero values.
* Identifies sectors where $\Delta x_j^{t-} > 0.33 x_j^{47}$.

3. Results of the computations

The results of the computations are summarized in tables 1, 2, and 3, and in figs. 1–6. Each table shows gross additions to, and retirements of, capacity, computed for a single interval under specified assumptions. In effect, they show how investment is rationed. The few sectors where the computation chose old technology over new, for expansion of capacity, i.e., where ΔX_j^{t+} was non-zero, are identified by a plus sign. These are sectors where incremental technology, as estimated here, brought net disadvantage as compared with the technology of the base

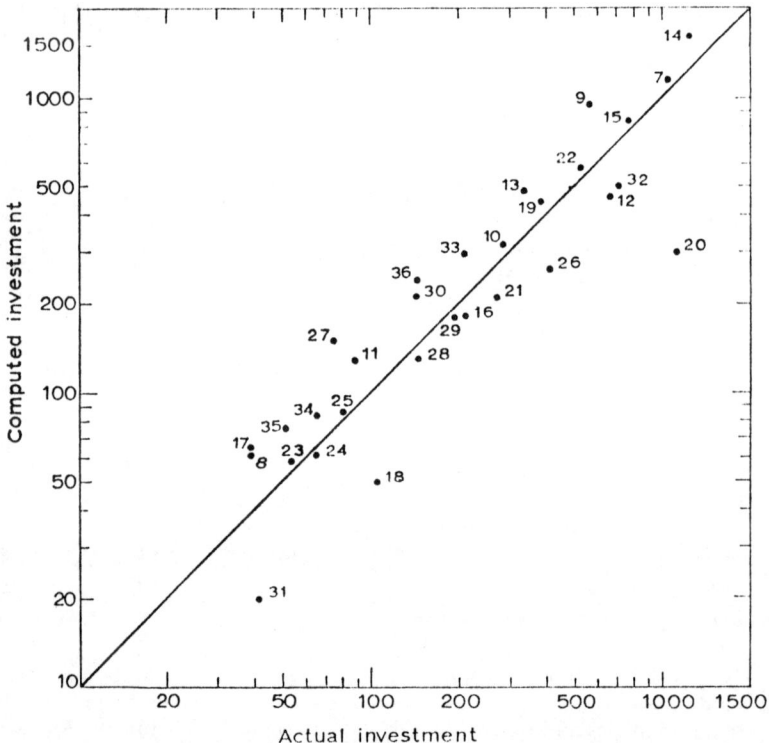

Fig. 1. Comparison of estimated and actual gross investment by 36-order manufacturing sectors, 1947–1958, in tens of millions of 1958 dollars. (The names of the sectors are given in tables 1–3.)

year, when used in combination with the structures chosen for other sectors. The apparent superiority of old over new technologies for these sectors is rooted in the details of 1947–58 changes, which cannot be explored in depth here. CARTER (1967) surveys and explains some of these developments. An asterisk in the retirements column identifies industries that decumulated old capacity more than the minimum. The optimizing procedure tends, of course, to allocate as much investment as possible to those sectors where new technology has the greatest labor-saving advantage over old. Retirement of old capacity has higher

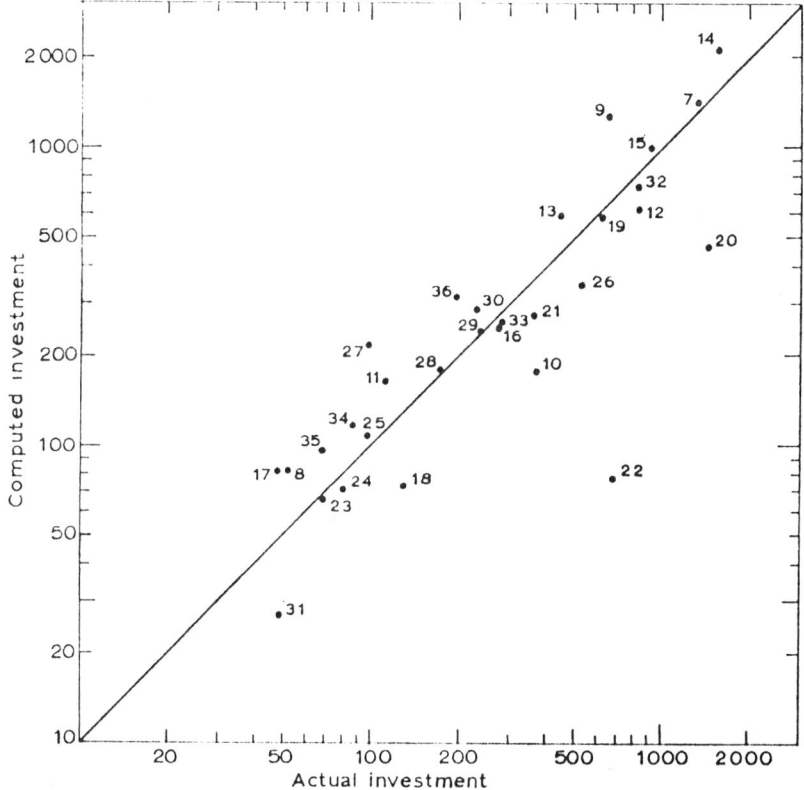

Fig. 2. Comparison of estimated and actual gross investment by 36-order manu-facturing sectors, 1947–1960, in tens of millions of 1958 dollars. (The names of the sectors are given in tables 1–3.)

priority in textiles, chemicals, and the various electrical and service machinery sectors than it does in early metalworking, motor vehicles, wood products, or food and tobacco. With higher sectoral replacement ceilings, retirements tend to be concentrated in relatively fewer sectors. Note that aggregation poses problems here. With very fine specification of both new and old structures, one could very likely see

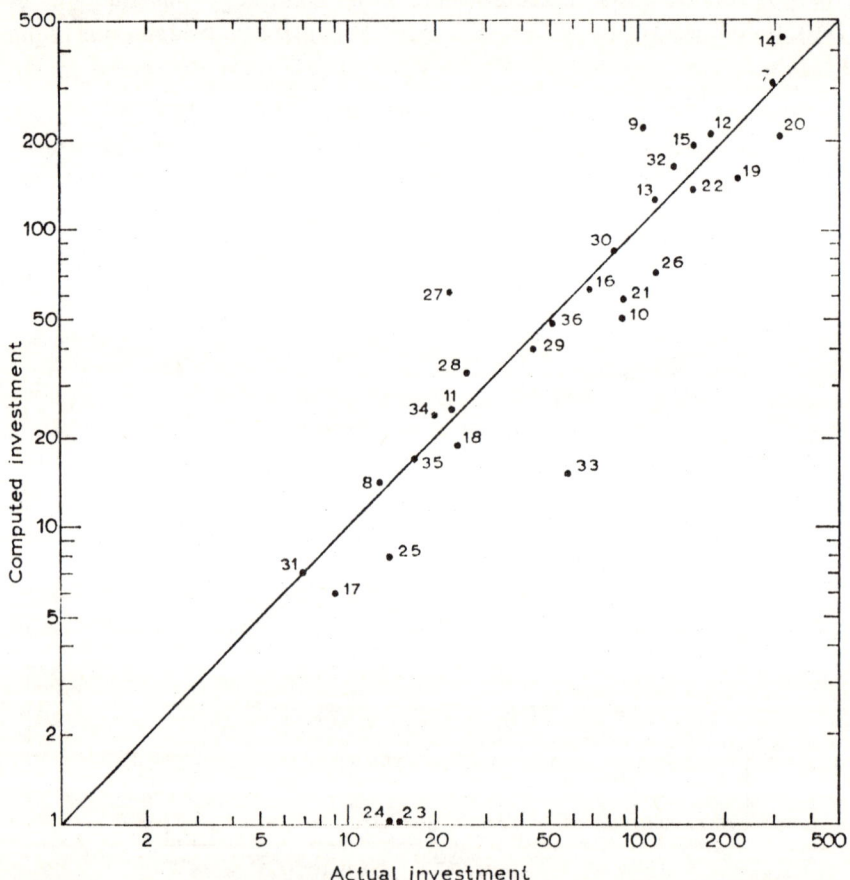

Fig. 3. Comparison of estimated and actual gross investment by 36-order manufacturing sectors, 1958–1960, in tens of millions of 1958 dollars. (The names of the sectors are given in tables 1–3.)

some high (low) ranking opportunities in areas where the average advantage of new structures is low (high). Thus, in reality, there are some profitable innovative opportunities in sectors where new techniques are on the whole unimpressive, and *vice versa*.

Figs. 1–6 give more details of how the system performed. Figs. 1, 2, and 3 are comparisons of computed with actual gross investment, i.e., gross additions to capital stock, in each sector. The results shown in these charts were all based on annual decumulation ceilings of 6 per cent. The minimal rates of annual decumulation of capacity were 3 per cent for the 1947–58 and 1947–61 periods, and 2 per cent for the 1958–61 period.

The right-hand quadrants of figs. 4, 5, and 6 show total employment requirements as estimated in the computations, and actual employment in the terminal year, for each sector. The left-hand quadrants are comparisons of actual employment in the final year with employment required to produce the bill of goods of the last year with intermediate input and labor coefficients of the *base* year. Thus, the left-hand quadrant of each graph tells what error is introduced into industry employment estimates by reliance on obsolete input-output and labor coefficients; the right-hand quadrant shows what error remains when embodied technical change updates these coefficients in our present linear programming model.

The figures can speak for themselves. Estimated labor requirements based on obsolete coefficients are almost always larger than actual labor requirements: hence, the clustering of points below the 45-degree line in the left-quadrant graphs. When embodied technical change is introduced with the linear programming system, there is no very clear tendency to over- or under-estimate labor requirements: points tend to lie about equally above and below the 45-degree line.

4. Conclusions

On the whole, figs. 1–3 show that the estimated allocation of investment among sectors is not unreasonable when lower and upper limits are placed on the scrappage of initial capacity. Over the periods studied, an accelerator, plus a 3 to 6 per cent annual replacement rate for

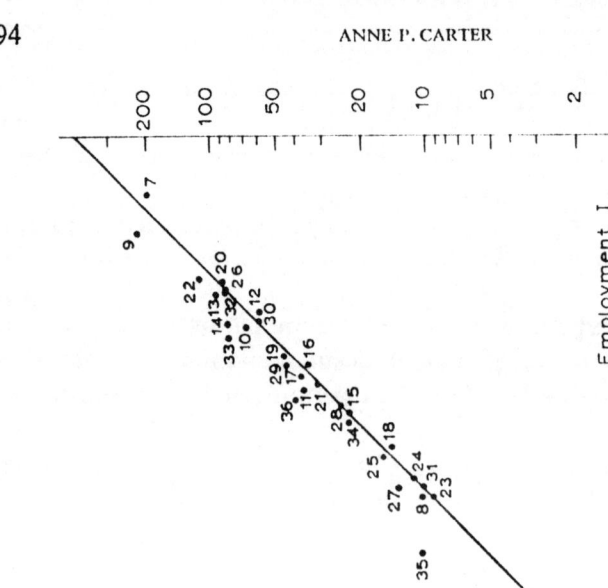
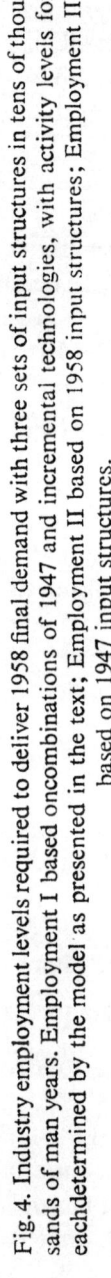

Fig. 4. Industry employment levels required to deliver 1958 final demand with three sets of input structures in tens of thousands of man years. Employment I based oncombinations of 1947 and incremental technologies, with activity levels for eachdetermined by the model as presented in the text; Employment II based on 1958 input structures; Employment III based on 1947 input structures.

LINEAR PROGRAMMING SYSTEM OF ANALYSIS 95

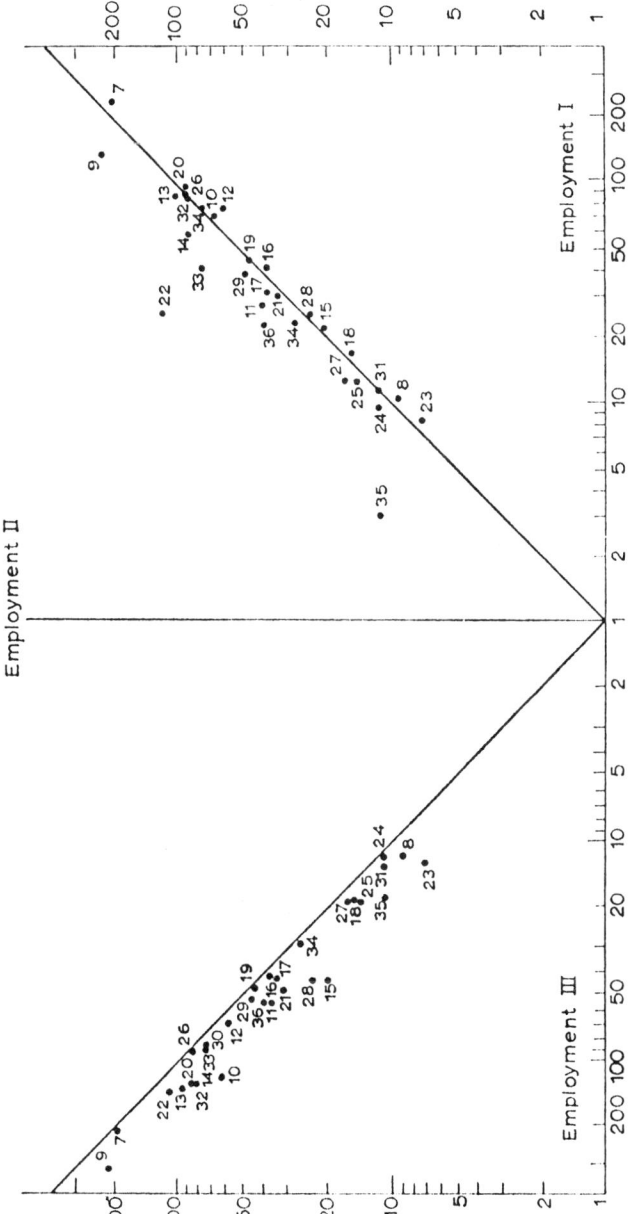

Fig. 5. Industry employment levels required to deliver 1961 final demand with three sets of input structures in tens of thousands of man years. Employment I based on combinations of 1947 and incremental technologies, with activity levels for each determined by the model as presented in the text; Employment II based on 1961 input structures; Employment III based on 1947 input structures.

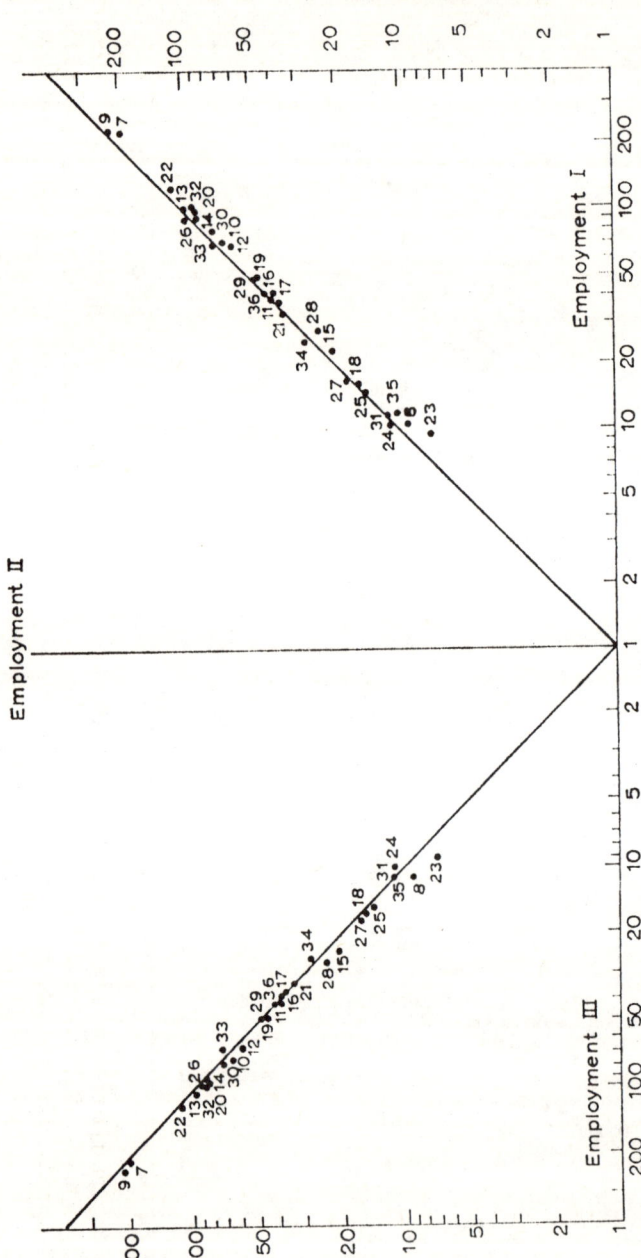

Fig. 6. Industry employment levels required to deliver 1961 final demand with three sets of input structures in tens of thousands of man years. Employment I based on combinations of 1958 and incremental technologies, with activity levels for each determined by the model as presented in the text; Employment II based on 1961 input structures; Employment III based on 1958 input structures.

initial capacity, gives a fair approximation of the distribution of new investment among manufacturing sectors. Some question of the consistency of the input-output and capital coefficients with investment data still remains. For it appears that observed investment is quite sufficient to cover the postulated 3 per cent per year lower limit on scrappage in the earlier periods, 1947–58 and 1947–61, and to permit additional replacement in many sectors where it was economically warranted. It is not clear why, over the 1958–61 interval, observed gross investment in manufacturing was barely sufficient to permit 2 per cent annual replacement of initial capacity, with a small amount left over for replacement in only two sectors. Most likely, the data are at fault.

Comparison of input structures with new and old technologies serves to establish a hierarchy of advantages of replacement opportunities among different sectors, but the overall level of investment is predetermined in this system. Thus, any estimates of new-technology structures that preserve the same ranking of advantages of new over old structures among industries, will yield approximately the same distribution of investment. In a more dynamic formulation, investment levels themselves would depend on the development paths of capital-producing industries and their suppliers.

The use of incremental coefficients to represent new-technology structures is a special kind of trend extrapolation, where change in coefficients is made proportional to investment, rather than to time. The basic weakness of any extrapolation, with present data limits, is that it rests on only two observations, a coefficient for 1947, and the corresponding coefficient for 1958. With so little information, there is not much sense in trying to demonstrate that one type of extrapolation gives 'better results' than another. The long-run advantage of the method described here is that it permits us to make use of better new-technology information as it becomes available. When reliable new-technology coefficients are estimated, they can be substituted for the makeshift incremental coefficients. In forecasting future input-output structures, data-gathering resources should be devoted to the search for reasonable estimates of such new-technology structures. Mutually consistent rates of adoption of the new technologies may then be computed according to the system just presented.

98   ANNE P. CARTER

References

CARTER (Grosse), A.P., 1953, The technological structure of the cotton textile industry. *In:* W.Leontief et al. Studies in the Structure of the American Economy (Oxford University Press, New York)

CARTER, A.P., 1957, Capital coefficients as economic parameters: the problem of instability. *In:* National Bureau of Economic Research, Studies in Income and Wealth *19*, Problems of Capital Formation (Princeton University Press, Princeton)

CARTER, A.P., 1963, Incremental flow coefficients for a dynamic input-output model with changing technology. *In:* T.Barna (ed.) Structural Interdependence and Economic Development (St. Martin's Press, New York)

CARTER, A.P., 1967, Changes in the structure of the American economy, 1947 to 1958 and 1962. Review of Economics and Statistics *49*, 209–224

HENDERSON, J.M., 1953, Estimates of the capital structure of American industries. 1947. Harvard Economic Research Project (unpublished)

KOMIYA, R., 1959, Technological progress and the production function in the United States steam power industry. *In:* Harvard Economic Research Project, Report on Research for 1958–1959 (unpublished)

MATHUR, P.N., 1963, An efficient path for the technological transformation of an economy. *In:* T.Barna (ed.) *op. cit.*

MIERNYK, W.H., 1970, Sampling techniques in making regional industry forecasts. *In:* A.P.Carter and A.Brody (eds.) Contributions to Input-Output Analysis (North-Holland Publishing Co., Amsterdam)

NATIONAL PLANNING ASSOCIATION, 1965, Capacity Expansion Planning Factors (National Planning Association, Washington)

U.S. DEPARTMENT OF COMMERCE (Bureau of the Census), 1957, Special Survey MCD-11 (U.S. Government Printing Office, Washington)

U.S. DEPARTMENT OF COMMERCE (Bureau of the Census), Census of Manufactures. 1947, 1954, 1958 (U.S. Government Printing Office, Washington)

U.S. DEPARTMENT OF COMMERCE (Bureau of the Census), Annual Survey of Manufactures, 1949 through 1957 (U.S. Government Printing Office, Washington)

VACCARA, B.N. and N.W.SIMON, 1968, Factors affecting the postwar industrial composition of real product. *In:* National Bureau of Economic Research, Studies in Income and Wealth *32*, The Industrial Composition of Income and Product (Columbia University Press, New York)

[19]

JOURNAL OF ECONOMIC THEORY **19**, 513–533 (1978)

On the Theory of Dynamic Input–Output Models with Different Time Profiles of Capital Construction and Finite Life-Time of Capital Equipment

LEIF JOHANSEN*

Institute of Economics, University of Oslo, Blindern, Oslo, Norway

Received August 22, 1978

1. BACKGROUND

There exists a well developed theory of "classical" or standard dynamic input-output models with uniform construction or gestation periods for all sectors and types of capital equipment, and with infinite durability of capital. In practice different construction periods are very important, ranging from, say, one year up to some seven or eight years. For some sectors finite durability of capital equipment is also important, although, for many purposes, perhaps less so than the differences in constructions period. In practical planning dynamic input-output models with different construction periods seem to have been used mainly in Eastern Europe, but examples can also be found in some developing countries. Experience particularly in Eastern Europe suggests that the length of the construction periods is of considerable importance for the growth potential of an economy. In this paper we shall be concerned particularly with the growth aspect, although construction periods are obviously important also for the generation of possible cycles.

In addition to the formulation of the dynamic system in terms of quantities of inputs and outputs, we shall also study the corresponding price system. In connection with the more complicated dynamic pattern in the present context, it will be elucidating to consider the price version of the input-output model as a system of equations representing investment calculations rahter than equations representing price fixation on the basis of cost calculations.

As far as possible we shall exploit results for the simplest case of a dynamic input-output model. For convenience we put down the equations for this model.

Let there be n sectors, and let x_{it} and y_{it} represent total output and final demand for sector i in period t. Let a_{ij} be the current input coefficients

---

* I am greatly indebted to H. Persson and M. Åberg of the University of Gothenburg for their valuable comments and cooperation in the elaboration of this paper.

514   LEIF JOHANSEN

and b_{ij} be the coefficients for capital stock produced in sector i and used in sector j. The ordinary input-output equations are then

$$x_{it} - \sum_{j=1}^{n} a_{ij}x_{jt} - \sum_{j=1}^{n} b_{ij}(x_{j,t+1} - x_{jt}) = y_{it} \qquad (i = 1,...,n). \qquad (1.1)$$

In order to study the growth possibilities in such a system, it is useful to study first the corresponding homogeneous system, i.e. the system for which all $y_{it} = 0$. For this system we have a balanced growth path with a growth rate λ, i.e. a growth path at which

$$x_{it} = x_i(1 + \lambda)^t \qquad (1.2)$$

where the composition of output $x_1,...,x_n$ and the growth rate λ must satisfy the following equations:

$$x_i - \sum_{j=1}^{n} a_{ij}x_j - \lambda \sum_{j=1}^{n} b_{ij}x_j = 0 \qquad (i = 1,...,n). \qquad (1.3)$$

The value of λ is determined as the real positive root of the equation

$$|I - A - \lambda B| = 0 \qquad (1.4)$$

where I is the unit matrix, A is the matrix of a_{ij} and B is the matrix of b_{ij}.

The value of λ represents the growth potential of the economy in the sense that it is the growth rate which is achievable if all outputs are used as inputs into production again (as current input and investment). If there is some non-productive consumption, represented by $y_{it} > 0$, then the growth rate will be some proportion of λ determined by the savings ratio.

The price equations corresponding to this system is

$$p_i = \sum_{j=1}^{n} p_j a_{ji} + r \sum_{j=1}^{n} p_j b_{ji} \qquad (i = 1,...,n) \qquad (1.5)$$

where $p_1,...,p_n$ are prices and r is the interest rate. The value of r is determined by an equation similar to (1.4), and we have $r = \lambda$. This equality represents the fact that the rate of interest is equal to the rate at which capital is able to grow if all outputs are ploughed back as productive inputs.

For some purposes it is useful to have the following formula for the change in λ (and r) when the coefficients a_{ij} and b_{ij} are changed:

$$d\lambda = - \frac{\sum_{i,j}(p_i x_j da_{ij} + \lambda p_i x_j db_{ij})}{\sum_{i,j} p_i b_{ij} x_j} \qquad (1.6)$$

This formula can be derived very simply by differentiating the equations in (1.3), multiplying the resulting equations by p_i, taking the sum over i, and finally using Eq. (1.5). (A. Bródy [2] uses this formula for assessing the consequences for numerical computations of λ of errors in the data for a_{ij} and b_{ij}. However, the formula also has important economic interpretations, giving directly the consequences for the growth rate — and the interest rate — of various sorts of combined changes in the coefficients of the input-output system.)

Eq. (1.3) and (1.4) above were written down for the case of a closed model, i.e. the case in which the elements y_{it} in (1.1) are zero. If we interpret the elements y_{it} in (1.1) as consumption, then we could again study the growth rate under proportional growth, i.e. growth in which all elements of output and consumption grow at the same rate. Then the growth rate will be equal to the investment or savings ratio multiplied by the intrinsic growth rate λ determined by (1.4), when the investment or savings ratio is calculated in terms of total income and total consumption evaluated by means of the equilibrium prices determined by the price equations (1.5). For an elaboration of this observation, see L. Johansen [6].

The equations of the model as written above do not specify labour explicitly. The model could be conceived as a pure capital accumulation model, with labour abundance, or one may in a well-known way interpret one sector, say number n, as a labour sector, defining the coefficients on the row $a_{n1},..., a_{nn}$ as labour input coefficients, and the column coefficients $a_{1n},..., a_{nn}$ as consumption requirements per unit of work. The price p_n would then be the minimum wage rate necessary to cover the corresponding consumption expenditures. (If we interpret sector n in this way, and still have final demand items $y_{1t},..., y_{nt}$, then these items are final demand categories in excess of necessary consumption, for instance interpreted as consumption out of non-wage income.)

This remark on the treatment of labour applies also to the more general model set out in the following sections.

2. The Model with Different Time Profiles for Capital Construction and Finite Life-Time of Capital Equipment

Let b_{ij} represent the amount of capital equipment produced in sector i and needed per unit of output in sector j, as before. However, we now decompose b_{ij} into elements $b_{ij1}, b_{ij2},..., b_{ijT}$ such that

$$b_{ij1} + b_{ij2} + \cdots + b_{ijT} = b_{ij}.$$

Here $b_{ij\theta}$ is input in capital construction which must be delivered θ periods before the piece of production capacity, of which it is a part, is to be ready for use, for $\theta = 1,..., T$. T is accordingly the longest gestation period, and the distribution of b_{ij} over $b_{ij1}, ..., b_{ijT}$ gives the time profile of this particular input into capital construction. We could of course introduce T'_{ij} for the longest gestation period for deliveries belonging to b_{ij}. However, we get a simpler notation system by using T for the longest gestation period for the whole system, implying that $b_{ij\theta} = 0$ for $\theta > T_{ij}$.

On the output side we let capacity created in sector i in a certain period last for S_i periods. In other words, the capacity remains constant for S_i periods, and then suddenly drops to zero. It is possible to extend the model so as to cover also more general cases (and this has recently been done by M. Åberg and H. Persson [8]).

In setting out the quantity equations for this model it is convenient to write down separately equations for output and equations for changes in capacity. As above we let x_{it} represent output from sector i in period t. We let production capacity in the same sector in the same period be K_{it}, so that $x_{it} \leq K_{it}$. Furthermore, production capacity to be completed so as to be ready for use in period t will be denoted by k_{it}. This is a gross concept, representing net addition to capacity as well as replacement investment. Instead of (1.1) we now have the following equations for output:

$$x_{it} - \sum_{j=1}^{n} a_{ij} x_{jt} - \sum_{\theta=1}^{T} \sum_{j=1}^{n} b_{ij\theta} k_{j,t+\theta} = y_{it} \qquad (i = 1,..., n). \qquad (2.1)$$

The double sum in this formulation represents deliveries to capacity which is to be ready for use 1, 2,..., T periods ahead.

Total capacity in period t is determined as total capacity in the preceding period, $t - 1$, plus gross addition to capacity, k_{it}, minus capacity which is becoming obsolete in period t, which is the same as capacity created S_i periods earlier, i.e. $k_{i,t-S_i}$. This gives the following equation

$$K_{it} = K_{i,t-1} + k_{it} - k_{i,t-S_i} \qquad (i = 1,..., n). \qquad (2.2)$$

We now want to study balanced growth paths with full capacity utilization, i.e. we assume

$$x_{it} = K_{it} \qquad (i = 1,..., n) \qquad (2.3)$$

so that

$$x_{it} = x_{i,t-1} + k_{it} - k_{i,t-S_i} \qquad (i = 1,..., n). \qquad (2.4)$$

Our system now consists of (2.1) and (2.4) with x_{it} and k_{it} as variables.

We again study the homogeneous system and consider especially the possibility of proportional growth in all sectors. This requires both output and capacity creation to grow at the same rate, i.e.

$$x_{it} = x_i(1 + \lambda)^t, \; k_{it} = k_i(1 + \lambda)^t \qquad (i = 1,..., n). \qquad (2.5)$$

Inserting this in Eq. (2.1) and (2.4) we obtain, after cancellation of the factor $(1 + \lambda)^t$:

$$x_i - \sum_{j=1}^{n} a_{ij}x_j - \sum_{\theta=1}^{T} \sum_{i=1}^{n} b_{ij\theta}k_j(1 + \lambda)^\theta = 0, \qquad (2.6)$$

$$x_i = x_i(1 + \lambda)^{-1} + k_i - k_i(1 + \lambda)^{-S_i}. \qquad (2.7)$$

We can now use Eq. (2.7) to express k_i in terms of x_i. (We assume throughout that $\lambda > 0$.) Inserting the resulting expression into (2.6) we have

$$x_i - \sum_{j=1}^{n} a_{ij}x_j - \lambda \sum_{j=1}^{n} \left[\sum_{\theta=1}^{T} b_{ij\theta} \frac{(1 + \lambda)^{S_j + \theta - 1}}{(1 + \lambda)^{S_j} - 1} \right] x_j = 0. \qquad (2.8)$$

This system of equations is comparable to (1.3) for the standard dynamic input-output model. It reduces to this form if $T = 1$ and $S_j \to \infty$. Then the sum in brackets in (2.8) contains only one element which tends to b_{ij1} when $S_j \to \infty$.

For the further consideration of system (2.8) it is convenient to introduce a sort of total capital coefficients defined (for $\lambda \neq 0$) by

$$b_{ij}^* = b_{ij}^*(\lambda) = \sum_{\theta=1}^{T} b_{ij\theta} \frac{(1 + \lambda)^{S_j + \theta - 1}}{(1 + \lambda)^{S_j} - 1}. \qquad (2.9)$$

We write $b_{ij}^*(\lambda)$ to signify that these are functions of the growth rate λ. With these symbols introduced the system (2.8) can be written as

$$x_i - \sum_{j=1}^{n} a_{ij}x_j - \lambda \sum_{j=1}^{n} b_{ij}^*(\lambda)x_j = 0. \qquad (2.10)$$

Corresponding to the determination of λ by (1.4) in the standard case λ is now to be determined by

$$| I - A - \lambda B^*(\lambda)| = 0 \qquad (2.11)$$

where $B^*(\lambda)$ is the matrix of the coefficients defined by (2.9) as functions of λ.

The introduction of the "coefficients" $b_{ij}^*(\lambda)$ is useful because it makes the system similar to the system for the standard case, the "only" difference being that the constant matrix B in the standard case is replaced by a matrix $B^*(\lambda)$ whose elements depend on λ. One step in the same direction is taken in papers by V. Z. Belenkii et al. [1] and by V. A. Volkonskii [7] who introduce similar coefficients which reflect the time profiles of capital construction. They are somewhat more general in that they assume different growth rates for different sectors, but less general in that they do not allow for different durabilities. On the other hand W. F. Gossling [3, 4] uses a similar type of "coefficients" to reflect replacement needs in the case of finite durabilities of capital equipment, but does not allow for different time profiles of capital construction.

Some further comments on the economic interpretation of the "coefficients" $b_{ij}^*(\lambda)$ will be given in section 4.

The system now described will determine a unique value of the growth rate λ. If we are able to solve (1.4) numerically for λ, then it will also be a simple matter to solve (2.11), at least approximately, by iteration or interpolation. Some further observations on these aspects are given in the appendix notes.

From the formulation just given one can see the direction of the effect of the time profiles introduced in the present formulation of the dynamic input-output model. Consider first the capital construction profile. Suppose that we have the correct solution for a special set of profiles. Then increase the production or gestation periods by shifting some parts of the total coefficients b_{ij} towards longer lags, keeping the totals fixed as given by $b_{ij} = \sum_0 b_{ij0}$. If we calculate $b_{ij}^*(\lambda)$ for the new profile of construction periods, but with the old value of λ, then it follows from (2.9) that the values of $b_{ij}^*(\lambda)$ will increase, i.e. the elements of the matrix $B^*(\lambda)$ in (2.11) will increase. The old value of λ does then no longer satisfy Eq. (2.11), and the new correct value must be lower than the previous one. (The formal proof is given in section 5.) In other words, extentions of construction periods diminish the growth rate.

Consider next the durabilities of capital equipment S_j. If some S_j is increased, then all $b_{ij}^*(\lambda)$ for this j decline, for the initially given value of λ. Then this value of λ does no longer satisfy (2.11), and the new solution for λ will give a higher value than the previous one. In other words, increases in the durability of capital equipment increase the growth rate.

3. PRICES, INTEREST RATE, AND INVESTMENT PROFITABILITY

In the standard case the price of the dynamic input-output model can be written down in the form (1.5), simply as current input cost plus an interest rate applied to the value of capital stock in each sector. In the case of different construction periods and finite lifetime of capital equipment this cannot be done so simply, because we cannot write down a simple expression for the value of capital per unit of output as done by $\sum_j p_j b_{ji}$ in (1.5). It seems better to approach the price problem via the investment profitability calculations. The equilibrium requirement now is that the present value of investment outlays and the present value of future revenue achieved by establishing a piece of production capacity in a sector should be in balance.

Now consider sector i. For the comparison of present value of outlays with the present value of revenues it is immaterial to which point if time we refer the various items by discounting. We consider the point of time at which a piece of capacity is being completed and ready for use. For establishing a capacity of one unit in sector i we must invest an amount $\sum_j p_j b_{ji1}$ one period earlier, an amount $\sum_j p_j b_{ji2}$ two periods earlier, etc. The value of this stream of investment outlays, calculated at the point of time when the capacity is completed, will be

$$\sum_{\theta=1}^{T} \sum_{j=1}^{n} p_j b_{ji\theta}(1+r)^\theta. \tag{3.1}$$

When the capacity has been installed, it will produce one unit of output per period for S_i periods, beginning with the immediately commencing period. The revenue earned per period will be $(p_i - \sum_j p_j a_{ji})$, so that the present value of the stream of revenues will be

$$\left(p_i - \sum_{j=1}^{n} p_j a_{ji}\right)\left[1 + \frac{1}{1+r} + \left(\frac{1}{1+r}\right)^2 + \cdots + \left(\frac{1}{1+r}\right)^{S_i-1}\right] \tag{3.2}$$

$$= \frac{(1+r)^{S_i} - 1}{r(1+r)^{S_i-1}}\left(p_i - \sum_{j=1}^{n} p_j a_{ji}\right).$$

Equilibrium now requires that (3.1) and (3.2) be equal:

$$\sum_{\theta=1}^{T} \sum_{j=1}^{n} p_j b_{ji\theta}(1+r)^\theta = \frac{(1+r)^{S_i} - 1}{r(1+r)^{S_i-1}}\left(p_i - \sum_{j=1}^{n} p_j a_{ji}\right). \tag{3.3}$$

This formula can be reorganized so as to make it comparable with the formulas for the volume system. We obtain

$$p_i - \sum_{j=1}^{n} p_j a_{ji} - r \sum_{j=1}^{n} p_j \left[\sum_{\theta=1}^{T} b_{ji\theta} \frac{(1+r)^{S_i+\theta-1}}{(1+r)^{S_i} - 1}\right] = 0. \tag{3.4}$$

This is comparable with (2.8). Introducing the notations from (2.9) we can write the equations as

$$p_i - \sum_{j=1}^{n} p_j a_{ji} - r \sum_{j=1}^{n} p_j b_{ji}^*(r) = 0 \tag{3.5}$$

corresponding to (2.10). For the determination of the rate of interest r this yields the same equation as for the determination of the growth rate λ in the volume system, i.e.

$$|I - A - rB^*(r)| = 0. \tag{3.6}$$

This means that we have the rate of interest equal to the growth rate, i.e. $r = \lambda$, just as for the standard system set out in the introductory section.

We may conclude as follows: By requiring present value calculations for investments to be in balance, we have obtained a system of price equations which stand in relation to the volume equations in exactly the same way as for the price equations in the standard dynamic input-output model. We have also obtained a way of representing the generalized system, allowing for different time profiles of capital construction and finite life-time of capital equipment, which is exactly the same as for the standard system, except for the fact that we have to replace the constant capital input coefficients b_{ij} by "coefficients" $b_{ij}^*(\lambda)$ or $b_{ij}^*(r)$ which are not constant, but depend on the growth rate or the rate of interest.

4. ALTERNATIVE DERIVATION OF THE PRICE EQUATIONS

As already pointed out we do not have a simple measure of capital value, independent of the rate of interest, in the present model. Furthermore, if we consider a piece of production capacity through its history, it will begin to increase in value from the first investment; it will reach the maximal value at the point of time when it is ready for use, and from then on decline in value towards the expiration of its life-time. Under these circumstances we cannot build up a price equation from the cost side by taking costs into account simply by multiplying capital value by the rate of interest. This is why we preferred the investment calculation point of view used in preceding section.

However, as an alternative it is possible to build up the price equations from cost considerations by using an annuity method of calculating interest charges and amortization. We then write the price equations in the form

$$p_i = \sum_{j=1}^{n} p_j a_{ji} + D_i \tag{4.1}$$

where D_i represents capital costs.

We now interpret D_i as a constant amount every year over the life-time of the capacity such that its present value is equal to the investment made. The value of capital invested per unit of capacity in sector i, calculated at the point of time when the capacity is ready for use, is

$$J_i = \sum_{\theta=1}^{T} \sum_{j=1}^{n} p_j b_{ji\theta} (1 + r)^\theta. \tag{4.2}$$

Accordingly we get the following relation between D_i and J_i :

$$D_i \left[1 + \frac{1}{1 + r} + \cdots + \left(\frac{1}{1 + r} \right)^{s_i - 1} \right] = J_i, \tag{4.3}$$

which gives

$$D_i = \frac{r(1+r)^{S_i-1}}{(1+r)^{S_i} - 1} J_i \, .\tag{4.4}$$

If we combine this with (4.2) and insert in (4.1), then we get precisely the price equations (3.4).

If we add the amounts D_i over the life-time of the equipment, then we get more than J_i. We can consider D_i as covering both amortization and interest charges. The essential thing is that the total annuity is worth J_i, but we might consider D_i as made up of a declining interest charge and an increasing amortization amount, according to the "constant total annuity" principle of amortization (see e.g. J. Lesourne [5, pp. 248–49]).

We may conclude this section by giving yet another interpretation which is perhaps less convincing as a representation of cost accounting, but which may nevertheless be of interest because of the light it sheds on the interpretation of the capital coefficients $b_{ij}^*(\lambda)$ or $b_{ij}^*(r)$.

Consider first a breakdown of the investment J_i defined by (4.2) according to sectors of origin j, i.e. consider

$$p_j \sum_{\theta=1}^{T} b_{ji\theta}(1+r)^{\theta-1}.\tag{4.5}$$

This is the value of capital produced in sector j which must be invested in sector i per unit of output from sector i. (As a minor deviation from (4.2) we have here calculated the value of the investment at the point of time of the last input into the project, i.e. one period before it is actually used. This is the reason for the exponent $\theta - 1$ instead of θ. In the present context this provides a better connection with previous formulas.) However, the capacity created lasts only for S_i periods. Thus, if we want to sustain the production of one unit of output from sector i for an indefinite time, then this investment must be repeated every S_i period. In this sense we may say that the capital requirement for capital produced by sector j and used in sector i, per unit of output from sector i, will be

$$p_j \sum_{\theta=1}^{T} b_{ji\theta}(1+r)^{\theta-1} \left[1 + \left(\frac{1}{1+r}\right)^{S_i} + \left(\frac{1}{1+r}\right)^{2S_i} + \cdots \right]\tag{4.6}$$

$$= p_j \left[\sum_{\theta=1}^{T} b_{ji\theta}(1+r)^{\theta-1} \right] \frac{1}{1 - (1+r)^{-S_i}} = p_j b_{ji}^*(r).$$

The last equality follows by a simple reorganization of formula (2.9). According to this, total capital value per unit of output in sector i in the sense now given will be

$$\sum_{j=1}^{n} p_j b_{ji}^*(r),\tag{4.7}$$

522   LEIF JOHANSEN

and the last term in the price equation (3.5) can be interpreted as interest
on this extended capital concept.

Comparing the two approaches presented in this section, we may say
that there is a choice between two viewpoints: We may consider capital
costs as consisting of interest and amortization on existing capital equipment,
or, we may consider capital costs as consisting of interest on the extended
capital concept which is the present value of the stream of investments
necessary to sustain a constant flow of output when an investment has to be
repeated at certain intervals corresponding to the finite durability of capital
equipment.

5. EVALUATION OF ALTERNATIVE TECHNIQUES

For the standard dynamic input-output model we have formula (1.6)
for the effects of changes in the technological coefficients on the growth rate.
We now seek a similar expression for the present case with different time
profiles of capital construction and finite life-time of capital equipment. In
connection with (1.6) we described how this formula could be derived by
simple differentiation. If we apply the same procedure to formula (2.10)
and use the price equations (3.5), then we get

$$d\lambda = -\frac{\sum_{i,j}(p_i x_j \, da_{ij} + \lambda p_i x_j \, db_{ij}^*(\lambda))}{\sum_{i,j} p_i b_{ij}^*(\lambda) \, x_j}. \tag{5.1}$$

In this formula the differential $db_{ij}^*(\lambda)$ must be evaluated so as to be expressed
in terms of changes in the basic coefficients $b_{ij\theta}$. We must then also take into
account that $db_{ij}^*(\lambda)$ depends on $d\lambda$. We have

$$db_{ij}^*(\lambda) = \sum_{\theta=1}^{T} \frac{\partial b_{ij}^*(\lambda)}{\partial b_{ij\theta}} \, db_{ij\theta} + \frac{\partial b_{ij}^*(\lambda)}{\partial \lambda} \, d\lambda \tag{5.2}$$

where $b_{ij}^*(\lambda)$ is defined by (2.9). (We use partial differentiation of $b_{ij}^*(\lambda)$ since
$b_{ij}^*(\lambda)$ is a function of all $b_{ij\theta}$ as well as of λ, although we have for simplicity
not indicated this explicitly in the notations.)

The partial derivatives of $b_{ij}^*(\lambda)$ with respect to $b_{ij\theta}$ are seen immediately
from (2.9). The derivative with respect to λ can also be written down on the
basis of (2.9), but does not simplify in any very convenient way. We therefore
retain it as $\partial b_{ij}^*(\lambda)/\partial \lambda$. Then we get

$$d\lambda = -\frac{\sum_{i,j}(p_i x_j \, da_{ij} + \lambda p_i x_j \sum_{\theta=1}^{T}[(1+\lambda)^{S_j+\theta-1}/((1+\lambda)^{S_j}-1)] \, db_{ij\theta})}{\sum_{i,j}(p_i b_{ij}^*(\lambda) \, x_j + \lambda p_i (\partial b_{ij}^*(\lambda)/\partial \lambda) \, x_j)}.$$

$$\tag{5.3}$$

The denominator in this expression can be shown to be positive. For this purpose introduce

$$\tilde{b}_{ij}(\lambda) = \lambda b_{ij}^*(\lambda).$$

(5.4)

Using the definition (2.9) this can be written as

$$\tilde{b}_{ij}(\lambda) = \sum_{\theta=1}^{T} b_{ij\theta}(1+\lambda)^\theta \Big/ \sum_{\tau=0}^{S_j-1}(1+\lambda)^{-\tau}$$

(5.5)

from which it is easily seen that

$$\frac{\partial \tilde{b}_{ij}(\lambda)}{\partial \lambda} > 0.$$

(5.6)

On the other hand, we have

$$\frac{\partial \tilde{b}_{ij}(\lambda)}{\partial \lambda} = b_{ij}^*(\lambda) + \lambda \frac{\partial b_{ij}^*(\lambda)}{\partial \lambda}.$$

(5.7)

Then the positivity of the denominator in (5.3) follows.

The direction of the change in the growth rate by changes in the coefficients will accordingly be determined by the sign of the numerator. Thus, if we have a technological change affecting the input coefficients in a certain sector j, then the effect on λ is determined by the sign of

$$\sum_{i=1}^{n} p_i \, da_{ij} + \lambda \sum_{i=1}^{n} p_i \sum_{\theta=1}^{T} \frac{(1+\lambda)^{S_j+\theta-1}}{(1+\lambda)^{S_j}-1} \, db_{ij\theta},$$

(5.8)

or, if we prefer, by the sign of

$$\frac{(1+r)^{S_j}-1}{r(1+r)^{S_j-1}} \sum_{i=1}^{n} p_i \, da_{ij} + \sum_{i=1}^{n} p_i \sum_{\theta=1}^{T}(1+r)^\theta \, db_{ij\theta}.$$

(5.9)

In this expression the first term is the present value (referring to the point of time when a piece of capacity is ready for use) of the changes in current input costs over the coming S_j periods, and the second term is the present value of the changes in investment costs. If the expression is positive, the value of the growth rate λ will decline, and vice versa. Thus, the effect of a change in technology on the growth rate can be indicated by a present value calculation of the implied cost changes, using the equilibrium prices and the equilibrium rate of interest. From this criterion it is clear, as pointed out before, that a change in the time profile of capital construction which shifts some capital input from a longer to a shorter gestation lag, while keeping the total capital input as defined by $\sum_\theta b_{ij\theta}$ constant, will increase the growth rate. However, for the exact numerical evaluation of the effect one must use the full expression (5.3).

6. THE MODEL WITH POSITIVE CONSUMPTION DEMAND. SAVINGS AND GROWTH

We now return to the model as given by (2.1)–(2.4) with positive final, non-productive demand, i.e. $y_{it} \geq 0$ for $i = 1,..., n$, and $y_{it} > 0$ for at least some i. We shall refer to y_{it} as consumption. (As already suggested, if there is a labour sector among $1,..., n$, then y_{it} could be interpreted as consumption out of non-wage income.)

When there is positive consumption, then the growth rate will no longer be the $\lambda = r$ previously considered. We now consider proportional growth of production and consumption at a rate γ. Inserting this and arranging the equations in the same way as we did in section 2, we now get

$$x_i - \sum_{j=1}^{n} a_{ij} x_j - \gamma \sum_{j=1}^{n} b_{ij}^*(\gamma) x_j = y_i \qquad (i = 1,..., n) \qquad (6.1)$$

where $b_{ij}^*(\gamma)$ corresponds to $b_{ij}^*(\lambda)$ as defined by (2.9), only with the growth rate λ replaced by γ.

The system (6.1) is no longer homogeneous in $x_1,..., x_n$, and γ cannot be found by an equation like (2.11). Something must also be added in order to make the problem of finding γ determinate. This missing element must clearly be related to the saving or investment proportion in the economy. By inspection of (6.1) it seems plausible that, if we keep $x_1,..., x_n$ normalized to a certain level, and then increase consumption $y_1,..., y_n$, then the proportions between $x_1,..., x_n$ will have to be readjusted, and γ will have to be reduced in order to make the equations hold. (From (5.4–6) we know that $\gamma b_{ij}^*(\gamma)$ decreases if γ decreases.) The increase in consumption as compared with the level of production, means a reduced investment proportion. Accordingly, we should expect a higher consumption proportion to be associated with a lower rate of growth γ. To make these considerations more precise we have to bring the prices into the picture. We then use the equilibrium prices and the rate of interest as determined in section 3.

For simplicity we introduce the following notations:

$$v_i = p_i - \sum_{j=1}^{n} p_j a_{ji} = \text{gross value added per unit of output in sector } i \text{ (profits if there is a labour sector among } 1,..., n);$$

$$V = \sum_{i=1}^{n} v_i x_i = \text{total gross value added;}$$

$$C = \sum_{i=1}^{n} p_i y_i = \text{value of total consumption;}$$

$$J = V - C = \text{value of gross investment.}$$

Now multiply Eq. (6.1) by price p_i and take the sum over i. This gives

$$J = V - C = \gamma \sum_{i=1}^{n} \sum_{j=1}^{n} p_i b_{ij}^*(\gamma)\, x_j .\tag{6.2}$$

On the other hand, multiply through the equations in (3.5) — the equations determining the equilibrium prices and the interest rate — by x_i and take the sum over i. This gives

$$V = r \sum_{i=1}^{n} \sum_{j=1}^{n} p_i b_{ij}^*(r)\, x_j .\tag{6.3}$$

Combining (6.2) and (6.3) we get for the growth rate γ:

$$\gamma = \frac{J}{V}\, rR \quad \text{where} \quad R = R(r, \gamma) = \frac{\sum_{i,j} p_i b_{ij}^*(r)\, x_j}{\sum_{i,j} p_i b_{ij}^*(\gamma)\, x_j} .\tag{6.4}$$

This expression consists of the gross investment quota J/V (investment in proportion to profits if there is a labour sector among $1,...,n$) multiplied by the rate of interest r which reflects the productivity of capital, corrected by a term $R = R(r, \gamma)$ which in general depends on both r and γ and on prices and output composition.

For the standard case $S_j = \infty$ and $T = 1$, $b_{ij}^*(r)$ and $b_{ij}^*(\gamma)$ both reduce to a constant $b_{ij1} = b_{ij}$. Then the proportion to the right in (6.4) is identically equal to unity and we have

$$\gamma = \frac{J}{V}\, r \qquad \text{(for } S_j = \infty \text{ and } T = 1).\tag{6.5}$$

In this case there is no scrapping or depreciation. J/V is the investment proportion in total income, and the growth rate is the product of this investment proportion and the rate of interest r, which reflects capital productivity. Three points are worth observing in this connection.

    1.   The formula just given corresponds to the classical growth formula for one-sector models.

    2.   In deriving this growth formula we have used the equilibrium prices in calculating the value of gross investment J and total value added V. Accordingly, it appears that these equilibrium prices serve excellently in performing the aggregation, since (6.5) is an exact formula under the conditions stated when J and V are calculated by means of the equilibrium prices, i.e. there is no aggregation error.

    3.   An interesting corollary of this result is a *dynamic non-substitution theorem*. If there is a choice between different techniques in the various sectors and we want to maximize the growth rate γ under a fixed investment proportion J/V, then we should use the production techniques which maximize

the intrinsic growth rate $\lambda = r$. Criteria for this maximization follow from the methods of evaluation of alternative techniques given in section 5. The non-substitution aspect of this is that the technologies thus determined should be used regardless of the composition of consumption. (This non-substitution interpretation has been elaborated in L. Johansen [6].)

When the conditions stipulated for (6.5) do not hold, then the proportion to the right in (6.4) is variable. We may trace the connection between the gross investment quota J/V and the growth rate γ in the following way. Consider the system (6.1) and keep $y_1, \ldots, y_n$ fixed. For a given value of γ we can then solve the system for $x_1, \ldots, x_n$. (If we like we could require a normalization of $x_1, \ldots, x_n$ and readjust the level of $y_1, \ldots, y_n$.) By inserting the given value of γ and the resulting $x_1, \ldots, x_n$ into (6.4) we can calculate the implied gross investment quota J/V. By repeating this calculation for different values of γ we can trace a curve relating J/V and γ. For $\gamma = r$ it is clear that there is no room for $y_1, \ldots, y_n > 0$, so at this end we have $\gamma = r$ and $J/V = 1$. At the other end we have $\gamma = 0$. This case needs a special treatment since the definition (2.9) of $b_{ij}^*(\gamma)$ is not valid for this case. Clearly $b_{ij}^*(\gamma) \to \infty$ as $\gamma \to +0$. On the other hand, for the case $\gamma = 0$ we could replace $\gamma b_{ij}^*(\gamma)$ by

$$\bar{b}_{ij}(0) = \frac{1}{S_j} \sum_{\theta=1}^{T} b_{ij\theta} \tag{6.6}$$

which follows from (5.5). We then get from (6.2) and (6.3)

$$\frac{J}{V} = \sum_{i,j} p_i \frac{\sum_\theta b_{ij\theta}}{S_j} x_j \Big/ r \sum_{i,j} p_i b_{ii}^*(r) x_j \qquad \text{for} \quad \gamma = 0. \tag{6.7}$$

In other words, we have a positive gross investment quota for a zero growth rate, which is of course as it should be.

The fact that $\gamma b_{ij}^*(\gamma)$ increases with γ (see (5.6)) suggests that there is a positive association between γ and J/V. We have

$$\sum_{i,j} p_i [\gamma b_{ii}^*(\gamma)] x_j = \frac{J}{V} r \sum_{i,j} p_i b_{ii}^*(r) x_j \, ,$$

and for the increasing γ the left hand side would tend to increase while prices, r and $b_{ij}^*(r)$ remain the same. However, this consideration is not quite sufficient to establish a monotonous positive association since the composition of output $x_1, \ldots, x_n$ in general changes with the growth rate. It only establishes a presumption for normal cases.

The natural idea now is, of course, to introduce the concepts of *net* investment and *net* income and try ot establish an equation like

$$\gamma = \frac{\text{Net investment}}{\text{Net income}} \cdot r = sr = s\lambda \tag{6.8}$$

where net investment is gross investment J minus depreciation, net income is gross value added V minus depreciation, and s is introduced for the rate of saving out of net income. In fact, when r and γ are determined as explained before, then equation (6.8) can be shown to hold as a consequence of reasonable definitions of the concepts involved.

In order to see this it is necessary to introduce the notion of total value of existing capital. We write this as $K_t(r)$ for period t, and $K(r)$ for the base point of time. Since each piece of capital now lives through a history with a construction period of, in general, more than one time unit, and a productive life with gradually declining remaining life-time, the value of capital cannot be calculated independently of the rate of interest. This is signified by the notations just given. The value of capital will, of course, also depend upon prices, but this is true also for the standard case.

We may now define net income as

$$\text{Net income} = rK(r), \tag{6.9}$$

i.e. as the product of the interest rate and the value of capital stock. The rationale of this is that the rate of interest is equal to the intrinsic growth rate λ as shown before. This means that, if nothing is extracted for consumption, then the value of total capital stock would increase by $\lambda K_t(r) = rK_t(r)$ from one period to the next, and income is defined as the value which can be extracted from the system without reducing total wealth.

If we now introduce

$$I = \text{value of total net investment,}$$

and use C for consumption as introduced above, then the concepts should satisfy the following equation

$$C + I = rK(r). \tag{6.10}$$

Furthermore, since we are studying proportional growth at a rate γ, we must also have

$$I = \gamma K(r). \tag{6.11}$$

According to the definition of the rate of saving we have

$$I = rK(r) - C = srK(r). \tag{6.12}$$

From (6.11) and (6.12) follows (6.8) as sought for.

It follows from this development that the comments made in connection with (6.5) for the standard case also hold for the general case, including the "dynamic non-substitution theorem". In deriving these results for the general case, we have only used some reasonable requirements which the

528   LEIF JOHANSEN

definitions of the aggregated concepts ought to satisfy, in addition to the fact that $r = \lambda$ is the rate at which wealth will increase if nothing is extracted for consumption. We have not yet shown in detail how the various concepts could be calculated. However, they are implied by the formulas we have already given.

Let D be total depreciation (at the base point of time). Then the net investment quota involved in (6.8) is $s = (J - D)/(V - D)$. Then (6.4) and (6.8) together imply

$$\frac{J}{V} R = \frac{J - D}{V - D} \tag{6.13}$$

where $R = R(r, \gamma)$ is defined in (6.4). This gives the following expression for depreciation, when we also use (6.4) to eliminate V:

$$D = J \frac{1 - R}{1 - (\gamma/r)}. \tag{6.14}$$

Net income will be

$$V - D = V \frac{1 - (\gamma/rR)}{1 - (\gamma/r)}. \tag{6.15}$$

From the definitional requirement (6.9) we have for the value of capital stock

$$K(r) = \frac{V}{r} \frac{1 - (\gamma/rR)}{1 - (\gamma/r)} \tag{6.16}$$

from which net investment according to (6.11) will be

$$I = V \frac{\gamma}{r} \frac{1 - (\gamma/rR)}{1 - (\gamma/r)} = J \frac{R - (\gamma/r)}{1 - (\gamma/r)} \tag{6.17}$$

where the last equality uses (6.4). It is easily seen that this is the same as $J - D$ as calculated from (6.14).

In the formulas above γ/rR should be replaced by J/V as given by (6.7) for the case of $\gamma = 0$.

The use of the formulas given above should perhaps be recapitulated. Suppose we want to calculate the growth rate corresponding to a given net investment quota. We must then first solve the price system and get the interest rate r (equal to the intrinsic growth rate λ). Then the growth rate γ follows simply from (6.8). Having established the growth rate γ we can use (6.1) to find output composition $x_1, ..., x_n$ for a given consumption composition $y_1, ..., y_n$. (We can normalize either the level of output or the level of consumption.) Having now both prices and outputs, r and γ, we can calculate $R = R(r, \gamma)$ according to the definition in (6.4). Value added V and gross investment J follow easily from the definitions, and then the other aggregated magnitudes, i.e. total depreciation D, net income $(V - D)$, the value of capital stock $K(r)$, and net investment follow from (6.14–17).

APPENDIX: NOTES ON THE SOLUTION OF THE CHARACTERISTIC EQUATION

The characteristic equation determining the intrinsic growth rate of the dynamic input-output model was given in section 2 in the following form

$$|I - A - \lambda B^*(\lambda)| = 0 \tag{A.1}$$

where the elements of the matrix $B^*(\lambda)$ are given by (2.9) in the text.

In this appendix we shall present some observations on the solution of (A.1). We are only interested in real and positive solutions. Furthermore, we shall exploit as far as possible what is known about the standard case in which we have a constant matrix B instead of $B^*(\lambda)$.

In order to study the existence and possible uniqueness of the solution of equation (A.1), it is convenient to introduce an additional variable z and replace (A.1) by the following system in two equations and two variables, λ and z:

$$|I - A - zB^*(\lambda)| = 0, \tag{A.2}$$

$$z = \lambda. \tag{A.3}$$

From (A.2) we may consider z as a function of λ, $z = g(\lambda)$. (It is known that there will exist one real positive solution z to (A.2) for a given λ if A is productive and irreducible, which we shall assume.) The function will be continuous for $\lambda > 0$ since z will be a continuous function of B^* and B^* is a continuous function of λ.

Let us first consider the case in which all $S_j = \infty$. Then we have

$$b_{ij}^*(\lambda) = \sum_{\theta=1}^{T} b_{ij\theta}(1 + \lambda)^{\theta-1}. \tag{A.4}$$

Then $b_{ij}^*(\lambda)$ is an increasing function of λ for all i, j for which some $b_{ij0} > 0$ for some $\theta > 1$; otherwise $b_{ij}^*(\lambda)$ is constant.

Now consider first $\lambda = 0$ in (A.2). The value $\lambda = 0$ raises no special problems in this case since $b_{ij}^*(\lambda)$ is well defined by (A.4) also for $\lambda = 0$. Then the system is the same as

$$|I - A - zB| = 0 \tag{A.5}$$

in which B is the matrix of

$$b_{ij} = \sum_{\theta=1}^{T} b_{ij\theta}. \tag{A.6}$$

530   LEIF JOHANSEN

This is the same as the characteristic equation of a dynamic input-output model of the standard type for which all investments in a project have been compressed into one period. For this system there exists one real positive solution z, i.e. we have $g(0) > 0$. If we now increase λ, then some or all elements of $B^*(\lambda)$ will increase while none will decline. It is then known that the value of the solution z to (A.2) will decline. (This also follows from (1.6).) Accordingly $g(\lambda)$ is a declining function of λ. It follows from this that there will exist one unique solution for λ in (A.1) corresponding to the unique solution for z and λ in (A.2–3) as illustrated in figure 1.

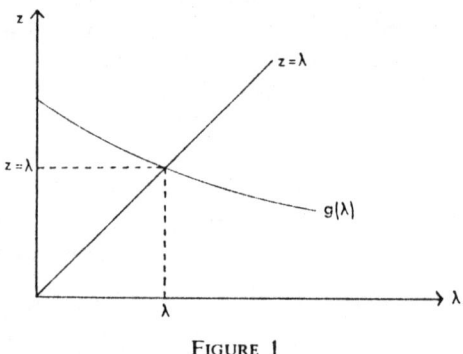

FIGURE 1

If we now go back to the general case in which we have $b_{ij}^*(\lambda)$ given by (2.9), then the reasoning will be more complicated. For a very small value of λ the value of $b_{ij}^*(\lambda)$ will be very large, and it will approach infinity as $\lambda \to +0$. It follows from this that $g(\lambda)$ will now tend to zero as $\lambda \to 0$. In other words, for very small values of λ, $g(\lambda)$ is an increasing function of λ. On the other hand, if we go on increasing λ, then sooner or later all $b_{ij}^*(\lambda)$ for which $b_{ij\theta} > 0$ for some $\theta > 1$ will start increasing, and then $g(\lambda)$ will be a declining function of λ. (This effect will dominate the effect of those $b_{ij}^*(\lambda)$ for which $b_{ij\theta} = 0$ for $\theta > 1$, since these $b_{ij}^*(\lambda)$ will tend to constants as λ increases.)

In this case the solution may be as illustrated in figure 2. In order to secure the existence of a solution $\lambda > 0$ in this case, the curve for $g(\lambda)$ must not lie below the line $z = \lambda$ throughout. In order to see when this will hold it is useful to rewrite Eq. (A.2) into the form

$$\left| I - A - \left(\frac{z}{\lambda}\right) [\lambda B^*(\lambda)] \right| = 0 \tag{A.7}$$

or

$$| I - A - \rho \tilde{B}(\lambda)| = 0 \text{ where } \rho = \frac{z}{\lambda} \tag{A.8}$$

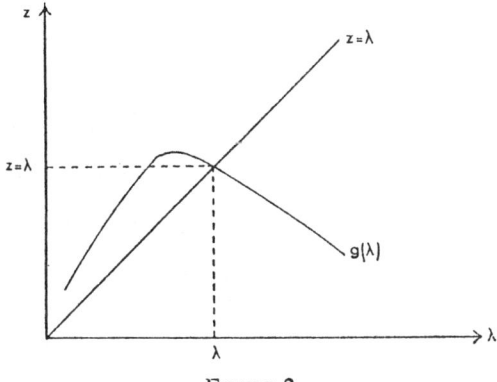

FIGURE 2

and where $\tilde{B}(\lambda) = \lambda B^*(\lambda)$ has positive elements defined by (5.4–5). It was also observed by (5.6) that the elements of $\tilde{B}(\lambda)$ increase with the value of λ, and at least some of them increase strictly. From these facts follows that ρ is a strictly declining function of λ.

From (5.5) we see that, when $\lambda \to 0$ the elements $\tilde{b}_{ij}(\lambda)$ tend towards

$$\tilde{b}_{ij}(0) = \frac{1}{S_j} \sum_{\theta=1}^{T} b_{ij\theta} \tag{A.9}$$

which are purely physical characteristics: investments of various sorts regardless of gestation periods, divided by the life-time of capital in the sector. ρ is a continuous function of the elements $\tilde{b}_{ij}$ and will tend towards a value ρ_0 determined by

$$| I - A - \rho_0 \tilde{B}(0)| = 0 \tag{A.10}$$

when λ tends to zero.

Now let us see what this means in connection with figure 2. If ρ_0 determined by (A.10) is $\rho_0 < 1$, then we will never get a solution $\lambda > 0$ since the function $g(\lambda) = z = \rho\lambda$ then starts from the origin by being below the ray $z = \lambda$, and will not intersect it for any $\lambda > 0$ since ρ is a declining function of λ. On the other hand if $\rho_0 > 1$, then $g(\lambda)$ will be above $z = \lambda$ in the figure immediately to the right of the origin, and since we know that $g(\lambda)$ will eventually decline, there will exist a solution $\lambda > 0$.

As a byproduct of this line of reasoning we also see that the solution for λ is unique. Since $\rho = z/\lambda$ is the slope of the ray from the origin to a point on the curve $z = g(\lambda)$ in figure 2, if there is an intersection between $z = \lambda$ and $z = g(\lambda)$ for some $\lambda > 0$, there cannot be another intersection to the right of the first one.

The treatment of the existence and uniqueness problem given above is partly influenced by the mathematical treatment of a generalized model by

532   LEIF JOHANSEN

M. Åberg and H. Persson [8]. They approach the problems in a somewhat different way, but their approach suggested the crucial role of the fact that the elements $\lambda b_{ij}^*(\lambda)$ increase with λ.

We saw above that the existence of a solution $\lambda > 0$ depends on the existence of a solution $\rho_0 > 1$ to Eq. (A.10). Introducing $\sigma = \rho_0 - 1$ we can write the equation as

$$| I - (A + \tilde{B}(0)) - \sigma \tilde{B}(0)| = 0. \tag{A.11}$$

We now have a solution $\lambda > 0$ if there is a positive solution for σ in (A.11). Such a solution exists if $A + \tilde{B}(0)$ is a productive matrix in the usual input-output sense. The interpretation of $A + \tilde{B}(0)$ is straightforward: it consists of the current input-output coefficients in A plus capital coefficients summed over gestation lags and averaged out over the life-time of capital equipment in the sector concerned, see (A.9).

From the formulation (A.2–3) it is clear that there would be no difficulty in solving the present problem numerically if we are able to solve the characteristic equation for the standard case of a constant matrix B. A natural idea is to solve the equations iteratively, i.e. to start with an initial guess about the value of λ, say λ_0, insert this in (A.2) and solve for z, next insert this value for λ and solve again for z, and so on. This would generate λ_0, λ_1, λ_2,..., λ_q,... according to

$$| I - A - \lambda_{q+1} B^*(\lambda_q)| = 0 \qquad (q = 0, 1, 2,...). \tag{A.12}$$

This process would probably converge in most cases, but there seems to be nothing in what has been demonstrated above which shows that it will always converge from any initial guess λ_0. However, even if the process (A.12) should not work well, it would be easy to find the solution with any desired degree of accuracy by calculating the value of z for selected values of λ and then proceed by interpolations.

REFERENCES

1. V. Z. BELENKII, V. A. VOLKONSKII, AND N. V. PAVLOV, Dynamic input-output models in planning and price calculations and economic analysis, *Matekon* **10** (1973–74), 74–101.
2. A. BRÓDY, "Proportions, Prices and Planning," Akadémiai Kiadó, Budapest, and North–Holland, Amsterdam, 1970.
3. W. F. GOSSLING, "Productivity Trends in a Sectoral Macroeconomic Model," Input-Output Publishing Company, London, 1972.
4. W. F. GOSSLING, Relative prices and wages-bills, under steady growth-rates, *in* "Capital Coefficients and Dynamic Input–Output Models" (W. F. Gossling, Ed.) Input–Output Publishing Company, London, 1975.

DYNAMIC INPUT–OUTPUT MODELS 533

5. J. LESOURNE, "Economic Analysis and Industrial Management," Prentice–Hall, Englewood Cliffs., N.J., 1963.

6. L. JOHANSEN, The rate of growth in dynamic input-output models: some observations along lines suggested by O. Lange and A. Bródy, in "Jahrbuch der Wirtschaft Osteuropas," Band 4, pp. 69–88, Günter Olzog Verlag, Munich, 1973.

7. V. A. VOLKONSKII, Industry price levels and the norm of effectiveness in the system of optimal planning, *Matekon* **12** (1975), 28–46.

8. M. ÅBERG AND H. PERSSON, "A Dynamic Nonlinear Closed Input-Output Model," Working Paper, Department of Economics, University of Gothenburg, to appear.

Part III
Multiplier Analysis, Extended IO-Models and Demographic Accounting

[20]

THE MULTIPLIER AS MATRIX

THE great attraction of the Keynesian system is its simplicity, which is, at the same time, its danger and its limitation. I propose to indicate how we may relax its cruder aggregative aspects without too hopelessly complicating matters. To accomplish this step we naturally turn to the Leontieff matrix as an adequately simple representation of general equilibrium. Yet it is generically different from the Keynesian system by being homogeneous, *i.e.*, the proportions are unique, but the scale of the whole system may be any multiple of the correct proportions. Only a small change is required to transform the one into the other, but it is just this small change which is necessary to study the short run generation and propagation of income.

The generalisation of the Keynesian system proceeds perfectly naturally in two directions. If we extend his concept of a marginal propensity to consume of less than one, to all other industries, we get a matrix multiplier with extraordinary formal analogies with the simple multiplier. To counterbalance the increased complexity, there is a much richer, more complete result. Even though a matrix multiplier should prove too difficult in practice, it yields considerable clarification of principle, for by taking a broader standpoint, it shows more clearly the meaning and limitations of the Keynesian multiplier.

The compound-matrix multiplier may be broken down into a kind of simple multiplier for each sector. Correspondingly we must have given not only total investment but also its distribution by industry. These sector multipliers may be sorted out in such a way, by a change of variables, that there exist n separate and independent multipliers of exactly the same form and simplicity as the Keynesian multiplier. Or again we may develop a single, massive multiplier which applies to all transactions instead of income alone, and which is a weighted mean of all sector multipliers.

The second direction of generalisation is the dynamical one. It is fairly generally agreed that Keynes was wrong to maintain rigidly the notion of a purely static multiplier. Granted the existence of lags in the flow of payments, we find that usually only one lag is assumed, specifically the one between income and consumption. The obvious extension is to admit a lag between

income and expenditure for every industry as well. This leads
to a dynamical-matrix multiplier which again shows an almost
complete formal analogy with the simple multiplier. Although
still a crude simplification, such a system does make a first step
towards a realistic picture of the actual circular flow of payments
in an economy. Any money spent is propagated with an unex-
pected slowness through the succeeding sectors even though any
individual sector lag is short, and this aspect of the mechanism
tallies with the observed sluggishness of the economy in response
to spending programs.

The consequence of many short lags cannot be demonstrated
exactly, because the result is not one long lag but a distributed
lag, and this is derived for the particular case of consumption in
order that it may be compared with the usual assumption of a
single lag. As a result of the slow, staggered filtering of payments through the mechanism, their effects may get out of step
in such a way as to create oscillations of any magnitude or duration. Thus the introduction of many lags leads to qualitatively
different behaviour from that of the dynamical Keynesian multiplier. It is a remarkable fact that the dynamical-matrix
multiplier can be shown to have necessarily an oscillatory element
in its behaviour.

We may first consider in simplified form how Keynes modified
the older approach, in order to see how, pursuing the same line
of development, we can best modify his own.

Let us represent an economy by

$$
\begin{array}{cccccccc}
 & Y_{12} + & \cdots\cdots\cdots\cdots\cdots\cdots & + Y_{1n} & = & {}_R Y_1 \\
 & & & & + & & + \\
Y_{21} & \cdot\ + & \cdots\cdots\cdots\cdots\cdots\cdots & + Y_{2n} & = & {}_R Y_2 \\
+ & + & \cdot & & + & & + \\
\vdots & \vdots & & \cdot & \vdots & & \vdots \\
 & & & \cdot & + & & \vdots \\
+ & + & & \cdot\ Y_{n-1,n} & + & \\
Y_{n1} + & Y_{n2} + & \cdots\cdots\cdots + Y_{n,n-1} & \cdot & = & {}_R Y_n \\
\| & \| & & \| & & \| \\
{}_e Y_1 + & {}_e Y_2 + & \cdots\cdots\cdots\cdots\cdots + {}_e Y_n & = & PT
\end{array}
$$

(1)

These symbols stand for money quantities and Y_{ij} means Y units
of the product of i industry sold to j industry (or better sector,
since it need not be homogeneous or indeed an industry at all,
e.g., the Government). Although it is not strictly necessary, it is
helpful to assume a closed economy for simplicity. ${}_R Y_j$ is the

total revenue from the sale of j's product; $_eY_i$ is the total expenditure made at the same time by sector i. Again merely for simplicity we lump all the owners of factors of production into one sector n and call it households.

If we add all sales (rows) we get $\overline{PT}$, total transactions. If we add all of the expenditures (columns) we get also PT. The sum of outlays is identically equal to the sum of all receipts, since we merely add the same things in different order. This is a peculiarly trivial tautology, completely devoid of empirical content, but not altogether useless since it is sometimes ignored.

This system is very general : it need not be stationary, and it may be analysed statically or dynamically. The tautology I shall call Say's Law of the First Kind, without necessarily implying that it correctly represents that much disputed proposition of J. B. Say. Here it takes visible form in the fact that every element in the matrix of the system is necessarily at once in a column (a purchase) and in a row (a sale). Every sale is a purchase, or supply is also demand. Any attempt to narrow and sharpen the law involves an empirical element, and hence cannot be stated as self-evident and necessarily true. Yet the wider version is not useless. Keynes implicitly accepted it, for his multiplier argument (and the equality of savings and investment) rests upon it.

That it is so may easily be demonstrated from equations (1). The sum of the columnar sums is equal to the sum of the row sums so that

(2) $\quad _RY_n - {}_eY_n = ({}_eY_1 - {}_RY_1) + ({}_eY_2 - {}_RY_2) + \ldots\ldots$
$$+ ({}_eY_{n-1} - {}_RY_{n-1}).$$

Savings (absorptions of purchasing power by households) equals investment (injections of purchasing power by firms). Since all the terms on the right-hand side need not have the same sign, we are naturally led to a generalisation : the algebraic sum of injections (an absorption being a negative injection) in a closed economy is zero.

(3) $$\sum_{i=1}^{n} ({}_eY_i - {}_RY_i) = 0.$$

If we assume that consumption is linear in income we get

(4) $\quad _RY_n = \dfrac{1}{1-\alpha}[b + ({}_eY_1 - {}_RY_1) + \ldots + ({}_eY_{n-1} - {}_RY_{n-1})],$

where α is the marginal propensity to consume and b the consumption independent of income, and thus we get the multiplier in the usual form. The income must be the multiplier value of the elements of expenditure not out of receipts. These are, for

540   THE ECONOMIC JOURNAL   [DEC.

households, the constant expenditures which are not determined by the level of income. For firms they are the excesses of expenditures over revenues, for the most part net investment, but not necessarily. For example, they may arise merely because of change, *e.g.*, the spending of yesterday's receipts to-day. They may be dividends paid out of past not current earnings, or conversely there may be net investment going on even though expenditures exactly equal receipts. Treating the government as a sector, relief payments not tax financed, would be an injection though certainly not investment.

In this system the rows, $_R Y_i$, need not equal the columns, $_\bullet Y_i$. If the equality of corresponding rows and columns be assumed, then we have what I shall call Say's Law of the Second Kind. It is clearly not in general true. Thus if sector i arbitrarily increases its outlay (column i), it does not follow (in fact it is almost certain *not* to follow) that its receipts (row i) will increase by a like amount. Yet for all sectors taken together it is necessarily so, and hence the total system is in a kind of neutral equilibrium with respect to total transactions.

In the early chapters of the *General Theory*, Keynes attacked Say's Law of the Second Kind. Starting with all transactions, he cancels out inter-firm transactions and leaves national income. He then states that Say implies that the income generated is exactly equal to net (of inter-firm) output. Hence money available to spend and spent on output is equal to the money value of output identically, with the consequence that the level of aggregate money output is indeterminate. If the nth sector is the total factor market, the proposition disputed by Keynes would be that the nth row is necessarily equal to the nth column. Obviously it may be so or it may not be so, but there is no necessity for it to be so, and hence it cannot be enunciated as a general law. It is almost never true for modern capitalist society, because the factor owners do not consume all they earn.

To illustrate the point and lay the basis for further analysis, let us take a stationary state and make a static analysis of it, assuming given and fixed prices and production coefficients. The system may be written as :

$$(5) \quad \begin{bmatrix} -1 & a_{12} \cdots\cdots\cdots a_{1n} \\ a_{21} & -1 \\ \vdots & & \vdots \\ \vdots & & \vdots \\ \vdots & -1 & a_{n-1,n} \\ a_{n1} & a_{n2}\cdots a_{n,n-1} & -1 \end{bmatrix} \begin{Bmatrix} y_1 \\ \vdots \\ \vdots \\ \vdots \\ \vdots \\ y_n \end{Bmatrix} = \begin{Bmatrix} 0 \\ \vdots \\ \vdots \\ \vdots \\ \vdots \\ 0 \end{Bmatrix}$$

where the a's are the coefficients and the y's the rates of money outputs or sales.[1] Under these restrictive conditions Say's Law of the Second Kind holds, each sector disburses exactly its receipts, and the sum of the elements in any one column of the matrix of (5) is zero. If all firms act thus, all households do too by virtue of Say's Law of the First Kind, for if we add all the equations, the first $n - 1$ columns annul themselves, so that we get

$$(6) \qquad - (1 - \sum_{i=1}^{n-1} a_{in})y_n = 0.$$

Hence, if we have any income at all, the marginal propensity to consume, $\alpha = \Sigma a_{in}$, must equal unity, so that y_n the level of income is indeterminate. Consequently the matrix has a rank of $n - 1$ and the solutions are

$$(7) \qquad \begin{Bmatrix} y_1 \\ \vdots \\ y_n \end{Bmatrix} = C \begin{Bmatrix} y_1{}^* \\ \vdots \\ y_n{}^* \end{Bmatrix}$$

where C is arbitrary and y^* is any set of values which satisfies (5). The proportions are unique, but the general level is arbitrary. Such a system is a simple example of the doctrine which Keynes attacked.

The " classical " economists knew, of course, that the whole of income was not necessarily spent, but they satisfied the Law of the Second Kind by including a capital market which achieved the result. A preponderance of opinion has followed Keynes in denying that the interest rate is able to accomplish so difficult a task. Therefore we cannot assume that households automatically disburse all their receipts, and we must assume a marginal propensity to consume of less than one. For equations (5) this means that the rank of the matrix is raised to n and that any solution other than zero must be due to the inhomogeneous elements (the injections). There is a great deal of empirical evidence, summarised in Allen and Bowley, *Family Expenditure*, for approximately linear consumption terms, so that we might write the nth column as

$$(8) \qquad \begin{matrix} a_{1n}y_n & + & b_{1n} \\ \vdots & & \vdots \\ a_{n-1,n}y_n & + & b_{n-1,n} \\ & -1 & \end{matrix}$$

---

[1] The a's may be obtained by dividing all the elements of any column by its element along the principle diagonal (the sector output) thus obtaining the input ratios. The array of coefficients is the Leontieff matrix, where all intra-industry sales are ignored, and where prices are absorbed into the technical coefficients. Cf. *The structure of the American Economy, 1919–1929*, Cambridge, 1941.

or summing

$$(9) \qquad - (1 - \alpha_n)y_n + \sum_{i=1}^{n-1} b_{in}$$

where the one represents the negative expenditure which is the income of the factor owners. This is a linear consumption function with a constant marginal propensity to consume, $\alpha = \Sigma a_{in}$. Likewise, we know that firms do not merely disburse what they receive, but they sometimes disburse more and sometimes less. In principle at least, we may separate the injections from the passive current account, which would be the only one in a stationary state. Calling net injections b, we may write any column j as

$$(10) \qquad \begin{matrix} a_{1j}y_j + b_{1j} \\ \vdots \quad \vdots \\ a_{nj}y_j + b_{nj} \end{matrix}$$

and summing, the stationary elements annul themselves, so that we get

$$\sum_{i=1}^{n} b_{ij}$$

for the net injections or sources of spending. Households or firms may either be sources or sinks of the flow of funds, though by Say's Law they cannot all be the one or the other at the same time. We may now rewrite our equations (5) as

$$(11) \qquad \begin{bmatrix} \ \\ \ a \ \\ \ \end{bmatrix} \begin{Bmatrix} \ \\ y \\ \ \end{Bmatrix} = - \begin{Bmatrix} \sum_j b_{1j} \\ \vdots \\ \sum_j b_{nj} \end{Bmatrix}$$

This inhomogeneous system is consistent, since the augmented matrix has the same rank as the unaugmented, and it therefore has a solution, and that solution is unique. This solution is the multiplier value of the total injections. It is convenient to add all the other rows to the last row, which makes an equivalent system with the same solution as (11).

$$(12) \qquad \begin{bmatrix} -1 & a_{12} & \cdots\cdots\cdots & a_{1n} \\ a_{21} & -1 & & \\ \vdots & & & \vdots \\ \vdots & & & \vdots \\ a_{n-1,1} & a_{n-1,2} & \cdots -1 & a_{n-1,n} \\ 0 & 0 & 0 & -(1-\alpha_n) \end{bmatrix} \begin{Bmatrix} y_1 \\ \vdots \\ \vdots \\ \vdots \\ y_n \end{Bmatrix} = - \begin{Bmatrix} \sum_j b_{1j} \\ \vdots \\ \vdots \\ \sum_j b_{n-1,j} \\ \sum_i \sum_j b_{ij} \end{Bmatrix}$$

By thus isolating the lowest diagonal element, we are able to solve for national income, y_n, without solving for all the other variables.

$$(13) \qquad y_n = \frac{\sum_{ij} b_{ij}}{1 - \alpha_n}.$$

This shows quite clearly the basis for the Keynesian method of treating income and its intimate connection with Say. By virtue of applying Say's Law of the Second Kind to firms but refusing to do so to households, he was enabled to separate out national income and make an important and difficult problem easily soluble.

The Statical Matrix Multiplier

The simplicity of the Keynesian method is perhaps justification enough. Yet it is worth while raising the question of the soundness of applying Say's Law of the Second Kind to firms. It is well known that firms tend to absorb funds at some times and to inject them at others. There are the phenomena of internal financing, of the failure to disburse earnings, of heavy fixed charges and of the payment of dividends above current earnings. Although these actions may be legally imputed to households, none the less the decisions and determining factors lie in the industries. In fact, there is a considerable body of evidence for linear total cost functions (over a considerable range) with a high positive intercept. Or to put it another way, marginal cost is constant and well below price. In view of these facts it would be wise to drop the, admittedly highly convenient, technique of equating current receipts and expenditures.

In accord with this hypothesis we must change the typical element in the equations from $a_{ij}y_j$ to $a_{ij}y_j + b_{ij} + \beta_{ij}(t)$ where the b_{ij} are the fixed outlays and the β_{ij} are the outlays not explained by the level of output. The fixed costs or outlays are, of course, variable in the long run, but have undoubtedly considerable constancy in the short run, and it is for this case only that the multiplier is useful. The Leontieff data are not sufficient to determine the two constants a_{ij} and b_{ij}. What is necessary is to have two (at least) levels of output which are not distinguished by differences in prices or technology, or other equivalent supplementary information.

Adding all the coefficients in any column j, we get

$$- (1 - \sum_i a_{ij}), \; i \neq j,$$

and calling $\sum a_{ij}$ the marginal propensity to spend, α_j, we see that in effect we have a kind of multiplier (or as it would be better to call it, a divider) for each sector. In the case of industries the α_j is approximately the same thing as marginal cost, and hence we may base our assumption of a constant marginal propensity of less than one on the evidence for marginal costs that are constant and less than price over a considerable range.

In order to simplify notation, b_{ij} and β_{ij} may be lumped together and called injections, b_{ij}. Also they may be taken as constants, since variable injections may be considered as a series of different constant injections, each of which lasts for a short time only. It is helpful, to emphasise the extraordinary formal analogy between the Keynesian and the matrix multiplier, to rewrite equations (11) as

$$(14) \qquad \Big[I - a\Big]\{y\} = \Big\{\sum_j b_{ij}\Big\}$$

where a is redefined to be the same as before except for the omission of the units along the principle diagonal, and where I is the unit matrix analogous to unity in scalar algebra. The solution then is

$$(14a) \qquad \{y\} = \Big[I - a\Big]^{-1}\Big\{\sum_j b_{ij}\Big\}$$

which says that the list or vector of transactions is equal to the matrix multiplier value of the vector of injections, *i.e.*, specified not only as to total amount but also by sector in which they are spent. It yields much richer results than the Keynesian multiplier as well as more accurate and useful ones.[1] Unfortunately it also removes multiplier calculations from the sphere of the ordinary economist, who can afford neither research staff nor elaborate calculating machinery.

Adding all the equations to the last one in (14), we get

$$(15) \quad (1 - \alpha_1)y_1 + (1 - \alpha_2)y_2 + \ldots\ldots + (1 - \alpha_n)y_n = \sum_{ij} b_{ij},$$

which may be rewritten as

$$\left(\frac{\sum_i (1 - \alpha_i)y_i}{\sum_i y_i}\right)\sum_i y_i = \sum_{ij} b_{ij}.$$

Hence

$$(15a) \qquad \sum_i y_i = \sum_{ij} b_{ij} \bigg/ \frac{\sum_i (1 - \alpha_i)y_i}{\sum_i y_i},$$

or

total transactions = weighted average multiplier × total injections.

[1] This point is demonstrated in some detail, though in a slightly different context, by the Bureau of Labour Statistics study, *The Structure of the American Economy under Full Employment Conditions*.

The Dynamical Matrix Multiplier

The more important consequences of considering the whole economy rather than the national income alone, come when we consider, as is obviously necessary, a dynamical structure. In the previous section we have imputed a marginal propensity to spend of less than unity to all sectors rather than merely to households. In this section we shall investigate the implications of assuming lags in the circulation of money throughout all sectors rather than in households alone, as is the assumption in the simple income-expenditure lag usually incorporated in multiplier analysis.

The problem is somewhat more complicated in the case of firms than in that of households. In place of putting current inputs as linearly dependent on the current rate of sales or outputs, we may assume that they are linearly dependent on the current rate of fabrication. For this we need the Frisch sausage-grinder function, which gives a precise answer to the old economic problem : at what rate will meat be being ground at any time if there has been a varying rate of input ? [1] Assuming that production starting is equal to current sales, $s(t)$, and calling the fabrication period 2θ, we have

$$y(t) = \int_{t-2\theta}^{t} \frac{s(\tau)}{2\theta} \, d\tau \approx s(t - \theta),$$

by taking the mid-point of a function over a short stretch of time as the best approximation to its average value. But the sales at time t of any industry are the inputs of its products by all the other sectors, hence a typical row becomes

$$a_{i1}y_1(t) + b_{i1} + \ldots\ldots\ldots + a_{in}y_n(t) + b_{in} = y_i(t + \theta_i).$$

Consequently equations (14) become [2]

$$(16) \qquad \left[I \right] \left\{ y(t+\theta) \right\} - \left[a \right] \left\{ y(t) \right\} = \left\{ \sum_j b_{ij} \right\}.$$

I shall now make the assumption that all the lags θ_i are the same and measure time in these uniform unit-lag periods. The more complicated, and realistic, case of unequal lags may be solved in principle, but the gains in simplicity are great from taking them

---

[1] Cf. his " Propagation and Impulse Problems " in *Economic Essays in Honour of Gustav Cassel*, London, 1933.

[2] It is worth noting that if we interpret this system more broadly as a technological, rather than merely as a payments, matrix, we have the simplest possible dynamical general interdependence system. It would then be interpreted as, to-day's output gives rise to to-morrow's input. As such, it is a first step in dynamic analysis or economic planning. It is, however, only a first step, since it gives no explanation of investment, nor does it take account of its effects.

all to be equal.   (16) is exactly analogous to the ordinary lagged multiplier and may be formally solved in the same elementary way by using it as a recurrence relation which gives rise to a geometric series, in this case a matric geometric, or Neumann as it is sometimes called, series.   Letting the simple symbol stand respectively for square and column matrices, we have

$$y(1) = b + ay(0),$$

where $y(0)$ is any given initial transactions vector.

$$y(2) = b + a[b + ay(0)] = b + ab + a^2y(0).$$
$$(17) \quad y(3) = b + ab + a^2b + a^3y(0)$$
$$\vdots$$
$$y(t) = [I + a + a^2 + \ldots\ldots + a^{t-1}]b + a^ty(0).^{[1]}$$

Thus y consists of a steady-state part due to the constant injections and a transient or variable part due to the n arbitrary initial sector rates of production.

Exactly as in the case of the simple multiplier, there arises the question of whether or not this approaches a limit as time progresses.   We say that this matrix-power series converges if, given

$$h(t) = I + a + a^2 + a^3 + \ldots\ldots + a^{t-1},$$

$h(t) \longrightarrow H$ as $t \longrightarrow \infty$.   This means that every element in h converges to a scalar limit in the ordinary sense.   Post-multiplying by a,

$$h(t)a = a + a^2 + a^3 + \ldots\ldots + a^t,$$

and adding I to both sides

$$h(t)a + I = I + a + a^2 + a^3 + \ldots\ldots + a^t,$$
$$= h(t) + a^t.$$

Therefore

$$h(t)[I - a] = I - a^t.$$

If as $t \longrightarrow \infty$, $h(t) \longrightarrow H$, then $a^t \longrightarrow 0$ and

$$(18) \qquad\qquad H = [I - a]^{-1},$$

so that

$$y(t) \longrightarrow [I - a]^{-1}b \text{ as } t \longrightarrow \infty.$$

Consequently we find that the dynamical-matrix multiplier has the static value as a limit, if a limit exists, in the case of continued constant injections.   By a similar argument we find that a single set of injections generates a total result equal to the multiplier value.   Equations (17) have perfectly determinate solutions, even if the geometric series is not convergent but no multiplier exists

[1] I have had the privilege of reading an unpublished manuscript of Mr. Tun Thin, in which he uses this device.

(as is also true in simple Keynesian analysis). The question of convergence is of considerable practical and theoretical interest. A sufficient condition may be stated as follows : this series converges—and hence a matrix multiplier exists—if every sector has a marginal propensity to spend of less than one. Thus our condition is exactly parallel to the condition on the marginal propensity to consume in the simple multiplier. If each sector exactly disburses receipts for all levels of output we get a pure propagator analogous to the quantity theory of money, since it implies that all marginal propensities are always one exactly. This conclusion fits our intuition that if each sector always disburses all its receipts, nothing will ever disappear (no leaks or sinks of purchasing power), and hence there is no tendency for the system to run down, or to approach a level if there are constant injections. On the other hand, we feel that obviously if no sector ever disburses quite all of any added revenue, then a dollar injected will eventually exhaust all its effects, direct and indirect.

Such intuitions are vital in suggesting results, but they are not conclusive and may, indeed, be quite false. Fortunately, our hypothesis is not difficult to prove. Call any element in the matrix $[a]^t$, $a_{ik}^{(t)}$ and let $\sum\limits_{k=1}^{n} | a_{ik}^{(t)} | = z_i$. If M is an upper bound for all n of the z_i, then

$$| a_{ik}^{(t)} | \leqslant M^t$$

for $i, k = 1, 2, 3, \ldots \ldots \ldots n$, and all t. This follows from the fact that any row or column may be considered as a vector, and for any vector its magnitude or length is less than or equal to the sum of its components. The inner product of any two such vectors is, by the Schwarz inequality, less than or equal to the product of their magnitudes. Then by induction on t we get the above inequality, and in addition that

$$\sum\limits_{k=1}^{n} | a_{ik}^{(t)} | \leqslant M^t.$$

But by hypothesis—all marginal propensities less than one—M is less than one for all n sectors. Hence the elements in the matrix all tend to zero as t tends to infinity and the sum of the geometric series goes to a finite limit.[1]

---

[1] I have followed the proof given in Courant und Hilbert, *Methoden der Mathematischen Physik*, Berlin, 1931, p. 16 n. Cf. also Prof. Leontieff, " Computational Problems Arising in Connection with Economic Analysis of Interindustrial Relations," *The Annals of the Computational Laboratory of Harvard University*, vol. XVI, p. 174.

To proceed systematically with the difference equations (16) we first try a particular solution of the inhomogeneous system. Trying a column of constants $\{Y^*\}$ we find that it is a solution if

(17) $Y^* = [I - a]^{-1}b$

or, in other words, the particular solution of the inhomogeneous system is the statical multiplier value of the constant injections. Then we seek the general solution of the associated homogeneous equations

(18) $Iy(t + 1) - ay(t) = 0.$

By substitution it is found that solutions of the form

$$\{y\} = \left\{\begin{matrix} Y_1 \\ \vdots \\ Y_n \end{matrix}\right\} \lambda^t$$

are the required ones. To state it another way, we seek those values of λ and y which satisfy

(19) $[I\lambda - a]y(t) = 0.$

This system has only non-null solutions if the matrix $[I\lambda - a]$ is singular, the necessary and sufficient condition for which is the vanishing of the determinant of the matrix. This last gives us the characteristic equation of degree n in λ with n roots and hence n columns of y each with one arbitrary constant.

The most illuminating way to regard the matrix equation (17) is that given the matrix a, which represents the structure of the economy, we seek those transactions vectors, and the corresponding λ's, which a transforms into other vectors proportionate to them, since

$$ay = \lambda y.$$

The vectors which a transforms in this way are called its *character-istic* or *latent vectors*, and they are determined only as to proportions, being arbitrary to the extent of a multiplicative constant (for which reason they are sometimes called characteristic or eigen rays). To each such vector there corresponds just one *characteristic number*, λ, there being in all n different ones, the n *latent roots* of the matrix a. $[I\lambda - a]$ is called the *characteristic matrix* of a, and $|I\lambda - a| = \Delta(\lambda) = 0$ is known as its *characteristic equation*. By the celebrated Cayley-Hamilton theorem a satisfies its own characteristic equation, *i.e.*, $\Delta(a) = 0$. This equation may be factored into the same components as the corresponding scalar function, hence

$$[I\lambda_1 - a][I\lambda_2 - a] \dots \dots \dots [I\lambda_n - a] = 0.$$

Throughout I shall assume that all the roots λ_i are distinct. No empirical matrix like a can give rise to repeated latent roots, because more accurate observations could always, in principle, be made revealing that the roots were not exactly equal. Repeated roots, or degeneracy, can only arise by definition, in the statement of the problem or in distinguishing the boundary of a region. Given the fact that there are n distinct latent roots, then there exists an $n \times n$, non-singular, square matrix h such that

(20) $$ hah^{-1} = c $$

where c is diagonal with the n distinct roots along the principle diagonal.[1] c is unique, and canonical, except for the order in which the λ's occur on the diagonal.

This transformation of similarity (or collineation) may be applied to our problem with striking results. Transform y by h, thus

(20a) $$ \eta = hy. $$

Applying (20a) to (18),

$$ ah^{-1}\eta(t) = h^{-1}\eta(t + 1), $$

or

(18a) $$ hah^{-1}\eta(t) = c\eta(t) = \eta(t + 1) $$

where c is diagonal. In the new co-ordinates, η, the variables are independent of one another ("uncoupled") and we have n simple, separate first-order-difference equations :

(18a) $\eta_i(t + 1) = \lambda_i\eta_i(t)$, $i = 1, 2, \ldots\ldots\ldots n$,

which are obviously satisfied by the n simple solutions

(18b) $$ \eta_i = N_i\lambda_i^t, $$

with the n arbitrary constants N_i. These are called normal co-ordinates, and by their use we see that there are in our system n modes of behaviour, all independent of one another, any one or all of which may be excited at any one time. This fact is a direct, though scarcely obvious, consequence of the linearity of the system, and it is known as Daniel Bernoulli's Principle of the Superposition of Motions.[2] The matrix a can also be reduced to canonical form if it has repeated roots or a rank less than n, but the form is no longer so simple.

The latent roots along with the transformation matrix h determine the possible behaviour types of the system. Since a is

[1] Cf. Birkhoff and MacLane, *Modern Algebra*, New York, 1946.

[2] Cf. E. T. Whittaker, *Analytical Dynamics*, fourth edition, New York, 1944, p. 186.

not symmetric, these roots may be real or complex. If all the roots are real and positive, the system is non-oscillatory. If any of the roots are real and negative, there may be oscillations of period two. If any of the roots are complex there will be longer-period oscillations; indeed *oscillations of any length are possible on the basis of the multiplier mechanism alone.* Whether real or complex, if all the roots have a modulus greater than one, then the system is dynamically unstable, and correspondingly it is definitely stable if all the moduli are less than one. If some are greater and some less, it is not definitely stable or unstable, but its behaviour depends upon which of the modes of motion happen to be excited.

Not only may this system exhibit oscillatory behaviour—it must do so.[1] To prove this we may proceed in the following way. The characteristic polynomial of the matrix a is

$$| \lambda I - a | = k_0 + k_1 \lambda + \ldots \ldots \ldots + k_{n-1}\lambda^{n-1} + (- 1)^n\lambda^n,$$

where $k_0 = | a |$, and $k_{n-1} = \pm (a_{11} + a_{22} + \ldots \ldots \ldots + a_{nn})$ and is called the trace of a. But in our matrix all the diagonal elements are zero so that the trace is identically zero. There exists, however, a diagonal matrix similar to a with a's latent roots along the diagonal. Since similar matrices have the same characteristic polynomial and hence the same trace,

$$\lambda_1 + \lambda_2 + \ldots \ldots \ldots + \lambda_n = 0.$$

Therefore all the latent roots of a cannot be real and positive with the result that one or more of the natural modes of motion of our payments system must be oscillatory. If this root (or roots) is real and negative, it will give rise to a cycle of two lags in duration, but if it has an imaginary part, the period may be of any length.

The transformation into diagonal form makes it simple to discuss the question of convergence of the matrix multiplier infinite series. Any power series is easily investigated because

$$c = hah^{-1},$$
$$c^2 = hah^{-1}hah^{-1} = ha^2h^{-1},$$
$$\vdots$$
$$c^k = ha^kh^{-1},$$

and in general

$$hf(a)h^{-1} = f(hah^{-1}) = f(c).$$

Therefore, calling the geometric matric series $f(a)$, we have for (17)

$$y = f(a)b + a^ty(0),$$

[1] I am indebted to Mr. Robert Solow for perceiving this remarkable result.

and transforming variables by the proper collineation, h, so that $\eta = hy$ and $\xi = hb$, we get

(17a) $$\eta = hf(a)h^{-1}\xi + a^t h^{-1}\eta(0),$$

But $$hf(a)h^{-1} = f(hah^{-1}) = f(c),$$

where c is canonical with the latent roots of a along the principle diagonal. But

(21)
$$[f(c)] = \begin{bmatrix} f(\lambda_1) & 0 & \cdots\cdots\cdots\cdots & 0 \\ 0 & f(\lambda_2) & & \vdots \\ \vdots & & & \vdots \\ \vdots & & f(\lambda_{n-1}) & 0 \\ 0 & \cdots\cdots\cdots\cdots & 0 & f(\lambda_n) \end{bmatrix}$$

Hence $f(c)$ converges if the geometric series of each of its roots converges separately. Therefore the necessary and sufficient condition for the existence of a matrix multiplier is that $|\lambda_i| < |$ for all i, and this is the same as the condition that the entire system be definitely, dynamically stable, which is as it should be.[1] Correspondingly the statical multiplier can be handled with utmost simplicity, although this simplicity is somewhat more apparent than real. From (14) we have

(14a) $$h[I - a]h^{-1}\eta = \xi,$$

or

(14b) $$[I - c]\eta = \xi,$$

or

(14c)
$$\begin{bmatrix} 1-\lambda_1 & 0 & \cdots\cdots\cdots\cdots & 0 \\ 0 & 1-\lambda_2 & & \vdots \\ \vdots & & & \vdots \\ \vdots & & 1-\lambda_{n-1} & 0 \\ 0 & \cdots\cdots\cdots\cdots & 0 & 1-\lambda_n \end{bmatrix} \begin{Bmatrix} \eta_1 \\ \vdots \\ \vdots \\ \vdots \\ \eta_n \end{Bmatrix} = \begin{Bmatrix} \xi_1 \\ \vdots \\ \vdots \\ \vdots \\ \xi_n \end{Bmatrix},$$

or

(14d)
$$\begin{Bmatrix} \eta_1 \\ \vdots \\ \vdots \\ \vdots \\ \vdots \\ \vdots \\ \eta_n \end{Bmatrix} = \begin{bmatrix} \dfrac{1}{1-\lambda_1} & 0 & \cdots\cdots\cdots\cdots & 0 \\ 0 & \dfrac{1}{1-\lambda_2} & & \vdots \\ \vdots & & & \vdots \\ \vdots & & \dfrac{1}{1-\lambda_{n-1}} & 0 \\ 0 & \cdots\cdots\cdots & 0 & \dfrac{1}{1-\lambda_n} \end{bmatrix} \begin{Bmatrix} \xi_1 \\ \vdots \\ \vdots \\ \vdots \\ \vdots \\ \vdots \\ \xi_n \end{Bmatrix}.$$

Therefore in normal co-ordinates each sector is a kind of multiplier value of the corresponding constant injections. This result holds

---

[1] It is also possible to define convergence conditions for the more complicated case of repeated roots. Cf. Turnbull and Aitken, *The Theory of Canonical Matrices*, London, 1945, pp. 73–4.

formally regardless of convergence, but, exactly as in the case of the simple multiplier, it makes no sense unless the dynamical-multiplier series is convergent.

It is possible to consider any variable injections in terms of step-wise approximations. For a stable system we may write general solution as

$$(22) \qquad \begin{Bmatrix} y_1(t) \\ \vdots \\ y_2(t) \end{Bmatrix} = \begin{bmatrix} a \end{bmatrix}^t \begin{Bmatrix} Y_1 \\ \vdots \\ Y_n \end{Bmatrix} + \begin{bmatrix} I - a \end{bmatrix}^{-1} \begin{Bmatrix} b_1 \\ \vdots \\ b_n \end{Bmatrix},$$

where $Y_1 \ldots \ldots Y_n$ are arbitrary constants and $b_1 \ldots \ldots b_n$ the total injections by sector. If the system has been in equilibrium and b is changed to $b + \Delta b$, we get

$$\begin{Bmatrix} y(0) \end{Bmatrix} = \begin{bmatrix} I - a \end{bmatrix}^{-1} \begin{Bmatrix} b \end{Bmatrix},$$

and

$$\begin{bmatrix} a \end{bmatrix}^0 = \begin{bmatrix} I \end{bmatrix}.$$

Hence

$$\begin{bmatrix} I - a \end{bmatrix}^{-1} \begin{Bmatrix} b \end{Bmatrix} = \begin{Bmatrix} Y \end{Bmatrix} + \begin{bmatrix} I - a \end{bmatrix}^{-1} \begin{Bmatrix} b \end{Bmatrix} + \begin{bmatrix} I - a \end{bmatrix}^{-1} \begin{Bmatrix} \ \ \end{Bmatrix}.$$

Therefore

$$(23) \qquad \begin{Bmatrix} Y \end{Bmatrix} = - \begin{bmatrix} I - a \end{bmatrix}^{-1} \begin{Bmatrix} \Delta b \end{Bmatrix}.$$

The solution may then be written as

$$(24) \quad \begin{Bmatrix} y(t) \end{Bmatrix} = \begin{bmatrix} I - a \end{bmatrix}^{-1} \begin{Bmatrix} b + \Delta b \end{Bmatrix} - \begin{bmatrix} a \end{bmatrix}^t \begin{bmatrix} I - a \end{bmatrix}^{-1} \begin{Bmatrix} \Delta b \end{Bmatrix},$$

which states that the transactions vector commences at its previous value and moves by some complicated path to the new matrix-multiplier value as given by the first term (the second term goes to zero with the lapse of time).

Total Transactions

Likewise we may discuss the behaviour of total transactions in the dynamical system. Writing

$$\begin{Bmatrix} y(t + 1) \end{Bmatrix} \quad \text{as} \quad \begin{Bmatrix} y(t) \end{Bmatrix} + \begin{Bmatrix} \Delta y(t) \end{Bmatrix}$$

we may restate (16) as

$$(16a) \qquad \begin{bmatrix} I - a \end{bmatrix} \begin{Bmatrix} y \end{Bmatrix} = \begin{Bmatrix} b \end{Bmatrix} - \begin{Bmatrix} \Delta y \end{Bmatrix}$$

or as

$$(16b) \qquad \begin{Bmatrix} y \end{Bmatrix} = \begin{bmatrix} I - a \end{bmatrix}^{-1} \begin{Bmatrix} b - \Delta y \end{Bmatrix}$$

which says that the transactions vector is always equal to the matrix-multiplier value of injections less absorptions (or plus injections if Δy is partially or wholly negative) due to the motion of the system itself. Premultiplying (16a) by

$$\begin{bmatrix} 1 & 0 & 0 & \ldots \ldots & 0 \\ 0 & 1 & & & \vdots \\ \vdots & & & & \vdots \\ 0 & & & 1 & 0 \\ 1 & 1 & \ldots \ldots & 1 & 1 \end{bmatrix}$$

and considering only the last row, we have

(25) $$\sum_i \Delta y_i = \sum_i b_i - \sum_i (1 - \alpha_i) y_i,$$

which states that the rate of change per unit time of total transactions is equal to aggregate injections (" investment ") less aggregate absorptions (" savings "). Here also there is an exact analogy with the simple multiplier.

The Lag in the Flow of Payments

One of the many uses which may be made of the dynamic-matrix multiplier is to illuminate the question of what is the nature and magnitude of the lag in the income flow in a society. The answer is that there is no *one* lag but many, endlessly compounded. If we follow the path of a dollar injected we find that in the following period some fraction (which fraction depends on the payments structure of the particular industry) only will again become income. Some part of the balance will go to other industries, which in turn will do the same, and so on *ad infinitum*. Therefore there is no simple income–expenditure lag as ordinarily assumed in multiplier analysis, but rather there is a distributed lag that spins out the consequences of any disturbance much longer than any inspection of industry or consumer lags by themselves would lead us to expect.

Thus in an aggregative model with a single lag we are led to speak of " days " or " weeks " or at most " months," which would give rise to such short dynamical adjustments that they might well be neglected. Indeed, this is the only rational reason which can be given to support Keynes's refusal to make the multiplier explicitly dynamical in its form. But the moment we compound these short lags we get something like an equivalent lag that is much longer and certainly not negligible. Therefore if we wish to make aggregative analysis as a simple, though crude, approximation to reality, we must insert a fictitious lag that looks much longer than the observable constituent lags. The evidence from the income velocity of money is that the order of magnitude of the equivalent or average lag is three or four months.

It is important to make some qualitative estimates of the effect of introducing many lags, although exact comparison is impossible, since there is no actual, single lag to compare with the lag in the simple multiplier. From (25) we have

$$\Delta y_1 + \Delta y_2 + \ldots\ldots\ldots + \Delta y_n = - \sum_i (1 - \alpha_i) y_i,$$

whereas if we have only a single-households lag,

$$\Delta y_n{}^* = - \sum_i (1 - \alpha_i) y_i.$$

Practically without exception, total transactions, national income and the other sector outputs move up and down together. Therefore all the Δ's will tend to be of the same sign, and hence we must divide the same quantity of motion into n parts. Consequently, the rate of change of national income will be very much slower than a single-lag mechanism would lead us to expect. To be more precise, corresponding to each latent root there is a solution, and for each solution all the sectors preserve fixed ratios to one another through any motion. Hence we may rewrite (25) as

(25a) $(k_1 + k_2 + \ldots\ldots\ldots + k_{n-1} + 1)\Delta y_n = - \sum_i (1 - \alpha_i) y_i$

where the k's are the given and constant ratios, which are all or nearly all positive because of the tendency of all the sectors to move in sympathy. Hence

(26) $\dfrac{\Delta y_n}{\Delta y_n{}^*} = \dfrac{1}{k_1 + k_2 + \ldots\ldots\ldots k_{n-1} + 1} < 1,$

and, in fact, it is likely to be very much less than one, indicating that the multiple-lag system is markedly less stable than the simple one.

The point is that the money filters through this complicated machine in many steps and very slowly. But this is not all; the money does not move in step, but some becomes income again and some does not until later, and some never does. As a result the scattered parts of a single injection may get out of step, and there arises the possibility of qualitatively different behaviour, *e.g.*, oscillation. The nature of the solutions is determined by the roots of the characteristic equation of the matrix. Since it is an empirical fact that this matrix is not even approximately symmetrical, there is no necessity for it to have real roots. There is also, however, no necessity for it to have complex roots, but a simple numerical example will easily demonstrate the possibility. Barring a negative marginal propensity to consume, the simple multiplier cannot oscillate but must go unswervingly to its appointed end.

I have stated that instead of one long lag we have a type of distributed lag. It has sometimes been supposed that consumption depends on income according to some sort of distributed lag, but this is made as an hypothesis. From the dynamical-matrix multiplier we may show that it is so and also exactly in what way. Taking from (16) the purely dynamical part, we have

$$\left[\,a\,\right]\left\{y(t)\right\} = \left\{y(t+1)\right\}.$$

We may partition it conformably into

$$(27) \quad \left[\begin{array}{c:c} g & c \\ \hdashline f & 0 \end{array}\right]\left\{\begin{array}{c} y_m(t) \\ \hdashline y_n(t) \end{array}\right\} = \left\{\begin{array}{c} y_m(t+1) \\ \hdashline y_n(t+1) \end{array}\right\},$$

from which we get

$$\left\{y_m(t+1)\right\} = \left\{c\right\}y_n(t) + \left[\,g\,\right]\left\{y_m(t)\right\},$$

$$= \left\{c\right\}y_n(t) + \left[\,g\,\right]\left\{c\right\}y_n(t-1) + \left[\,g\,\right]^2\left\{y_m(t-1)\right\},$$

$$(27a) \qquad \vdots$$

$$= \left[\sum_{s=0}^{s=i}\left[\,g\,\right]^s y_n(t-s)\right]\left\{c\right\} + \left[\,g\,\right]^{i+1}\left\{y_m(t-i)\right\}.$$

Because a converges, g will do so even more rapidly. Therefore the last term on the right-hand side disappears as we let i increase without limit. We wish to know how present consumption depends on past income. The list of current consumer purchases is $\left\{c\right\}y_n(t)$, and from (27) we have, indicating a row matrix by $<\quad>$,

$$(27b) \qquad <f>\left\{y_m(t)\right\} = y_n(t+1).$$

Therefore the consumer purchases at any time, $t+2$, are given by

$$(28) \qquad \left\{c\right\}<f>\left[\sum_{s=0}^{\infty}\left[\,g\,\right]^s y_n(t-s)\right]\left\{c\right\},$$

in which all the elements are given constants with the exception of the incomes for all previous time. Consequently we find that present consumption depends in a perfectly definite, and in principle derivable, way on all previous income, *i.e.*, there is a distributed lag involved in the consumption function.

R. M. GOODWIN

Harvard University.

[21]

INTERINDUSTRY ANALYSIS AND THE STRUCTURE OF INCOME-DISTRIBUTION (*)

by Kenichi Miyazawa and Shingo Masegi,
Yokohama Municipal University

I. - INTRODUCTION

In the usual interindustry analysis, consumption demand as part of final demand is treated as an exogenous variable, so that the usual Leontief matrix multiplier analysis lacks the multiplier process *via* the consumption function customarily found in the Keynesian Model. In the usual procedure, in order to treat consumption demand as an *endogenous* variable in the Leontief system, the household sector is transferred to the processing sectors, and is regarded as an industry whose output is labor and whose inputs are consumption goods. But the correct procedure in dealing with consumption is not to regard it as a fictitious production activity but to introduce the Keynesian consumption function on a disaggregated form. To this end, we have formulated the matrix multiplier combining Leontief's propagation process and the Keynesian propagation process, using the Leontief inverse multiplied by the *subjoined inverse matrix*, showing the effect of endogenous changes in the consumption demand (¹).

Nevertheless, this procedure does not always treat adequately the interrelation between the interindustrial and consumption structures, because the consumption structure depends on the structure of income-distribution which regulates the consumption pattern, made up, as it is, of the expenditure behavior of various income-groups.

In this paper, we shall try to introduce the process of income distribution and expenditure into the input-output system. If we term the income multiplier incorporating income-distribution-factors the « Kalecki multiplier » (²), our task is to combine the Leontief output multiplier and the Kalecki multiplier in its disaggregated and generalized form.

(*) *The work of putting this paper into English was financed by the Ford Foundation as part of a project for promoting the translation of Japanese economic studies.*
(¹) See K. Miyazawa [4], especially Section IV and V.
(²) M. Kalecki [3], Chap. 5.

— 90 —

II. - Interindustry Analysis, and the Process of Distribution and Expenditure of National Income

1) *The Leontief Multiplier, Keynesian Multiplier and Kalecki Multiplier.*

At the outset, in order to summarize our problem, we will give a brief macro-numerical example of the model to be developed later. In the usual input-output model, final demand f (= consumption C + investment $I = 10$) determines the level of output X *via* the input coefficient $a = R/X = 3/4$ (where R = intermediate inputs), i. e.

			$\bar{f}$	total
R		C	I	X
	30	8	2	40

Y {
| W | 6 |
| P | 4 |
}

total X 40

$$X = \frac{1}{1-a}\,\bar{f} = \frac{1}{1-3/4}\cdot 10 = 40.$$ This is a macrocosmic expression of the Leontief output multiplier as a matrix. But consumption C is originally induced by the income Y (= wage W + profit $P = 10$). The consumption coefficient is $c = C/Y = 8/10$, so that the Keynesian income multiplier equation is $Y = \dfrac{1}{1-c}\,I = \dfrac{1}{1-8/10}\cdot 2 = 10.$ Thus the output-determination in the input-output model for consumption demand as an endogenous variable is given as

$$X = \frac{1}{1-a}\,\bar{f} = \frac{1}{1-a}\cdot\frac{1}{1-c}\cdot I \qquad (1)\;(^1)$$

Of course the income-multiplier $\dfrac{1}{1-c}$ only holds for a particular income-distribution pattern. Let $d_1 = W/Y$ and $d_2 = P/Y$ denote the relative share of wages and profit, respectively, $c_1 = C_w/W$ and $c_2 = C_p/P$ the propensity to consume of laborers and capitalists, respectively, then we have the generalized Kalecki income multiplier $\dfrac{1}{1-c} = \dfrac{1}{1-(c_1d_1 + c_2d_2)}$, which incorporates the income-distribution factors $(^2)$.

$(^1)$ This macro-multiplier (or its disaggregated form) is derived more convincingly by tracing the propagation process from the initial injections, see K. Miyazawa [4].

$(^2)$ If we put $c_1 = 1$, $0 < c_2 < 1$, we have Kalecki's own formulation $\dfrac{1}{1-c} = \dfrac{1}{(1-d_1)(1-c_2)}$ as a special case of the above expression. If we put $c_1 = 1$, $c_2 = 1/2$, then we have $Y = \dfrac{1}{1-(c_1d_1 + c_2d_2)}\,I =$

$= \dfrac{1}{1-(6/10 + 1/2\cdot 4/10)}\cdot 2 = 10$ or $Y = \dfrac{1}{(1-d_1)(1-c_2)}\cdot I = \dfrac{1}{1-6/10}\cdot$

$\cdot\dfrac{1}{1-1/2}\cdot 2 = 10.$

— 91 —

For a comparison with the Leontief system, let $v = Y/X = 1 - a$ denote the value-added ratio, and $v_1 = W/X$, $v_2 = P/X$ the value-added ratios of wage-income and profit-income, respectively, then the output-determination can be formulated as

$$X = \frac{1}{1-a}\bar{f} = \frac{1}{1-a}\cdot\frac{1}{1-(c_1d_1 + c_2d_2)}\cdot I \qquad (2)$$

$$= \frac{1}{1-a}\frac{1}{1-\dfrac{c_1v_1 + c_2v_2}{1-a}}\cdot I \qquad (3)$$

This equation (3) is the macro-counterpart of the matrix multiplier which we will develop next.

2) *Generalization of the Input-Output Model.*

The value-added sector in the interindustry model is not only divided into n industry-groups along the column, but also divided into r income-groups along the row as shown in the above macro-numerical example. Let us express the income of kth group earned from jth industry as Y_{kj} $(j = 1, ..., n; k = 1, ..., r)$; this $v \times n$ income-formation shows the most generalized pattern of income-distribution. Corresponding to this income-distribution pattern, consumption demand E_{ik} is also defined as consumption for ith commodity by the kth income-group $(i = 1, ..., n; k = 1, ..., r)$. Then the coefficients of our model is given as in Table 1.
We write

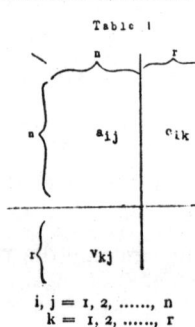

Table 1

$i, j = 1, 2, ..., n$
$k = 1, 2, ..., r$
$(n > r)$

A = the $n \times n$ matrix of input coefficients a_{ij},
V = the $r \times n$ matrix of value-added ratios $v_{kj} = Y_{kj}/X_j$,
C = the $n \times r$ matrix of consumption coefficients $c_{ik} = E_{ik}/Y_k$
where X_j is jth industry's output, and Y_k is kth income-group's income. Let

X = a column vector of output,
f_c = a column vector of consumption demand,
f = a column vector of final demand other than consumption,
then the input-output system is

$$X = AX + f_c + f \qquad (2.1)$$

The consumption function of our model can be written as follows:

— 92 —

$$f_c = CVX = \sum_{k=1}^{r} c^{(k)} v^{(k)} X = \sum_{k=1}^{r} c_{ik} v_{kj} X_j \qquad (2.2) \ (^1)$$

where $c^{(k)} = (c_{1k}, c_{2k}, ..., c_{nk})'$ is a column vector and $v^{(k)} = (v_{k1},$
$v_{k2}, ..., v_{kn})$ is a row vector.
Substituting the consumption function (2.2) in (2.1), we get

$$[I - A - CV] X = f \qquad (2.3)$$

Solving (2.3) for X, we obtain

$$X = [I - A - CV]^{-1} f \qquad (2.4)$$

Further, if we write the Leontief inverse $[I - A]^{-1} = B$, we can show that the inverse matrix in (2.4) is converted into the form: the Leontief inverse B multiplied by the inverse $[I - CVB]^{-1}$ which shows the effects of endogenous changes in consumption demand of the household sectors, i. e.,

$$[I - A - CV]^{-1} = [\{I - CV (I - A)^{-1}\} (I - A)]^{-1}$$
$$= B [I - CVB]^{-1} \qquad (2.5)$$

We can term the inverse $[I - CVB]^{-1}$ the *subjoined inverse matrix* showing the effect of endogenous changes in each income-group's consumption expenditure. This matrix multiplier equation (2.5) corresponds perfectly to the macro-multiplier (3) in the above (^{2}). This formula (2.5) distinguishes the inverse reflecting consumption activity from the inverse reflecting production activity. But if the consumption coefficients and value-added ratios are not as stable as the input coefficients, it is desirable that the « subjoined inverse » be converted into a form which can be easily computed and revised. By the development of such a practical computation formula, we can also introduce the theoretical relation of the inter-income group activity. Let us write

$$VBC = L = (l_{kv}) \qquad k = 1, ..., r$$
$$K = (I - L)^{-1} = (k_{kv}) \qquad v = 1, ..., r$$

Then, as shown in the next section, we can prove that:

$$B [I - CVB]^{-1} = B [I + CKVB] \qquad (2.6)$$

(^{1}) Instead of (2.2), if we add the non-homogenous terms to the consumption function, c_{ik} becomes marginal coefficients. In this case, we can treat the non-homogenous terms as included in f.

If we define some $c^{(k)}$ which is the capitalist group's coefficient as « propensity to consume *plus* propensity to invest », our model formally contains the problem of an induced investment.

(^{2}) If we put $r = 1$ in (2.5), i. e., if we do not distinguish the income-groups, the equation (2.5) coincides with the formula which we have derived previously (see [4] p. 63), and it corresponds perfectly to the macro-multiplier (1) in the above.

--- 93 ---

In practical problems, since r is very much smaller than n, the $r \times r$ matrix K is very easily computed. Then, if we already have the numerical table for B, we can renew the subjoined inverse whenever necessary ([1]).

II. - The relationship of inter-income-groups and the multi-sector income multiplier

1) *The Coefficients of Inter-income-groups and the Propagation Process.*

Next, we must work out (i) the proof of the formula (2.6), and (ii) the economic meaning of the matrices L and K.

(i) can be attempted in various ways ([2]), but we have selected the method which traces the propagation process by the initial injections, since this method may at the same time reveal the economic meaning of the matrices L and K.

Denoting by m the numerical order of the propagation, we get

$$X_1 = Bf \qquad (3.1)$$

$$X_m = BCVX_{m-1} \qquad (m \geq 2)$$

Hence,

$$X_m = (BCV)^{m-1} Bf = BC\,(VBC)^{m-2}\,VBf$$

$$= BC\,L^{m-2}\,VBf \qquad (3.2)$$

Thus,

$$X = \sum_{m=1}^{\infty} X_m = Bf + BC\left(\sum_{m=2}^{\infty} L^{m-2}\right) VBf \qquad (3.3)$$

Hence, if the term $\sum\limits_{m=2}^{\infty} L^{m-2}$ (i. e. $\sum\limits_{m=0}^{\infty} L^m$) is convergent ([3]),

---

([1]) Our model can be easily extended for an open economy with foreign trade.

([2]) For example, we can prove the theorem that:

Theorem: P : the $n \times r$ matrix, Q : the $r \times n$ matrix, I_r, I_n : the unit matrices of r and n order, respectively, then we have

$$(I_n - PQ)^{-1} = I_n + P\,(I_r - QP)^{-1}\,Q \qquad (*)$$

Proof: Put $\quad Y = (I_r - QP)^{-1}$

then $\quad Y\,(I_r - QP) = I_r$

$PY\,(I_r - QP)\,Q = PQ$

$PYQ\,(I_n - PQ) = PQ$

$I_n - PYQ\,(I_n - PQ) = I_n - PQ$

$I_n = (I_n + PYQ)\,(I_n - PQ)$

$\therefore (I_n - PQ)^{-1} = I_n + PYQ = I_n + P\,(I_r - QP)^{-1}\,Q$

In this theorem, putting $P = C$, $Q = VB$ in the equation (*), we obtain our formula (2.6).

([3]) The convergence conditions of our model will be examined in Section IV.

— 94 —

$$X = B \left[I + C \left(I - L \right)^{-1} VB \right] f$$
$$= B \left[I + CKVB \right] f \tag{3.4}$$

This result coincides perfectly with (2.6).

The matrix $L = VBC$ may be interpreted as a set of coefficients which show the interrelationship between income-groups in the process of propagation resulting from each income-group's consumption expenditure. In order to prove this point, we take the νth income group as representative and trace its consumption expenditure effect on another kth income group's income.

Bf	$v^{(\nu)} Bf$	$c^{(\nu)} v^{(\nu)} Bf$
→	→	→
increase of output in each industry	increase of income in ν th group	increase of consumption in ν th group
$\boxed{1}$	$\boxed{2}$	$\boxed{3}$

$Bc^{(\nu)} v^{(\nu)} Bf$	$v^{(k)} Bc^{(\nu)} v^{(\nu)} Bf$
→	→ ...
increase of output in each industry due to the consumption of the ν th group	increase of income in kth group due to additional income of the ν th income group
$\boxed{4}$	$\boxed{5}$

Thus the element of L , i. e. $l_{k\nu}$, can be written as

$$l_{k\nu} = v^{(k)} Bc^{(\nu)} = \frac{v^{(k)} Bc^{(\nu)} v^{(\nu)} Bf}{v^{(\nu)} Bf} = \frac{\boxed{5}}{\boxed{2}} \tag{3.5}$$

That is, the coefficient $l_{k\nu}$ shows how much income in the kth income-group is generated by the expenditure from 1 unit of additional income in the νth income-group. Thus we can term L the «matrix of inter-income-group coefficients», and K «the interrelational multiplier in the income groups».

A proposition arises in connection with the matrix of inter-income-group coefficients: the column sums of the matrix L equal the total consumption coefficients of each income group, i. e.

$$j_r L = j_r VBC = j_n \left(I - A \right) BC = j_n C \tag{3.6}$$

where j_n and j_r are row vectors of the n and r order whose elements all equal 1.

2) *The Income Multiplier as a Matrix.*

We can also derive the income multiplier as a matrix as distinguished from the output multipler as a matrix in (3.4).

Denote by Y the column vector whose elements are incomes of r income groups, then,

$$Y = VX = VB \, (I + CKVB) \, f = (I + VBCK) \, VBf$$

$$= (I + LK) \, VBf \tag{3.7}$$

It is easily verified that $I + LK = K$ (because $I = [I - L] \, K = K - LK$), so we have

$$Y = KVBf \tag{3.8}$$

We can designate matrix KVB as the *multi-sector income multiplier* which shows the income formation in each income-group.

This multi-sector income multiplier is a distinguishing characteristic of our model. In the usual input-output analysis which regards consumption demand as exogenous, the outputs of various industries have different values depending the proportions of final demand, but as far as the value-added sector is concerned income has the same value as final demand and does not depend the proportions of final demand. On the contrary, as shown in (3.8), in our model incomes (both total income and group incomes) have different values depending the proportions of final demand and this is because our model takes into account the structure of income distribution.

This conclusion can not be obtained by the introduction of endogenous consumption structure without distribution-pattern. The reason for this is as follows. If we do not distinguish the income-groups, i. e. if we put $r = 1$, the matrix V becomes the row vector, and correspondingly, matrix C becomes the column vector. If we write them v and c respectively, then

$$L = VBC = v \, Bc = j \, (I - A) \, Bc = jc = c$$

$$(= \text{Keynesian macro-propensity to consume})$$

$$\therefore \, K = (I - L)^{-1} = \frac{1}{1 - c}$$

So the income multiplier equation (3.8) becomes

$$Y = KVBf = \frac{1}{1 - c} \, v \, Bf = \frac{1}{1 - c} \, jf = \frac{1}{1 - c} \, f_0 \, . \tag{3.9}$$

where $f_0 = f_1 + f_2 + \dots + f_n$. This multiplier coincides exactly

--- 96 ---

with the Keynesian multiplier and income equals $\dfrac{1}{1-c}$ × (final demand) regardless of the proportions of f [1].

Further, if we regard consumption demand as an exogenous variable as is usual, the income multiplier equation becomes

$$Y = VB\bar{f} = vB\bar{f} = j\bar{f} = \bar{f}. \tag{3.10}$$

and income equals final demand irrespective of the proportions of final demand. Thus, in order to conclude that the values of income differ depending on the proportions of final demand, it is necessary to introduce not only the structure of consumption demand but also the structure of income distribution.

3) *Structure of the Propagation Process.*

Now, we return to the output propagation equation (3.3). Equation (3.3) can be interpreted as incorporating the propagation process from the income-formation side. But the same propagation process also can be observed from the consumption side or the production side. The three aspects of the propagation process are (a) the income-formation side $(VBC = L)$

$$X = Bf + BC \left[I + VBC + (VBC)^2 + \ldots \right] VBf$$
$$= Bf + BC \left[I - L \right]^{-1} VBf \tag{3.11}$$

(b) the consumption expenditure side (CVB)

$$X = B \left[I + CVB + (CVB)^2 + \ldots \right] f$$
$$= B \left[I + C (I - L)^{-1} VB \right] f \tag{3.12}$$

(c) the production side (BCV)

$$X = \left[I + BCV + (BCV)^2 + \ldots \right] Bf$$
$$= \left[I + BC (I - L)^{-1}V \right] Bf \tag{3.13}$$

It is interesting that in all cases we can obtain the computation formula (2.6) by projecting the propagation process into the income-formation side $L = VBC$. Instead, if we derive the sum of the geometrical progression from the consumption side (CVB) or the production side (BCV), we do not obtain the computation formula (2.6) directly but the equation (2.5) which is the product of two inverse

---

[1] The output multiplier corresponding to this case will be

$$X = B \left[I + \frac{1}{1-c}\, cj \right] f$$

and this coincides with the results in our previous paper. See [4], p. 63.

matrices.   This means that the income-formation side has a homogenous character, and contrasts strikingly with the heterogenous characters of production activity and consumption activity.

One other point regarding the propagation process should be explained.   Equations (3.11)-(3.13) assume a propagation process in which the entire process is a succession of separate two-step movements: in the first, the propagation from the production side is represented entirely by the effect of matrix B, and in the next step, the propagation occurs on the income-formation and consumption expenditure sides.   But instead of this assumption, we may also assume another possible process in which the propagation occurs simultaneously in all three sides, i. e., production, distribution and expenditure.   In the latter case, instead of equation (3.11)-(3.13), the propagation equation may be rewritten as follows:

$$X = f + (A + CV) f + (A + CV)^2 f + \dots \qquad (3.14)$$

We write $A + CV = Q$, and, if we assume the term $\sum\limits_{m=0}^{\infty} Q^m$ to be convergent, we have

$$X = [I - Q]^{-1} f = [I - A - CV]^{-1} f \qquad (3.15)$$

which coincides with (2.4).   By formulae (2.5) and (3.4), we get

$$X = B [I - CVB]^{-1} f = B [I + CKVB] f .$$

Thus, the two propagation cases, i. e. the case of (3.11)-(3.13) and the case of (3.14), have the same sum, but obviously the *truncated multiplier* in the case of (3.11)-(3.13) has a larger value than the truncated multiplier in the case of (3.14).   We turn next to the analysis of the convergence conditions in those two cases.

IV. - The convergence conditions of the model

So far, we have assumed the existence of a meaningful solution, $X \geqq 0$, for our fundamental equation, $X = AX + CVX + f$, $(f \geqq 0)$, i. e., we assumed the existence of $(I - A - CV)^{-1} = = (I - Q)^{-1} \geqq 0$ and of $K = (I - L)^{-1}$.   In order to treat these problems and their relationships, we will first review the properties of the Leontief-type matrices as preparation for developing the convergence conditions of our model.

1) *The Properties of Leontief-type matrices.*

For non-negative square matrices in general, the following properties are well known:

[I] Let a be a $n \times n$ non-negative matrix. Then the conditions 1°-4° below are equivalent.

— 98 —

$1°$ $\displaystyle\sum_{m=0}^{\infty} a^m$ converges

$2°$ All characteristic roots of a are less in absolute value than 1.

$3°$ $I - a$ is non singular and $(I - a)^{-1}$ is non-negative

$4°$ For any non-negative vector f, the equation $(I - a)\, x = f$ has a unique non-negative solution.

For Leontief-type matrices, i. e. non-negative matrices with no column-sums greater than 1, Woodbury gives the following lemma (^{1}):

[II] Let a be Leontief-type and $I - a$ nonsingular. Then the equation $(I - a)\, x = f$ has a unique non-negative solution.

From the propositions [I] and [II] we obtain

Lemma 1. Let a be Leontief-type. $\displaystyle\sum_{m=0}^{\infty} a^m$ converges if and only if $I - a$ is nonsingular.

Now, we may transform a into the form (4.1) below by some permutation matrix P

$$P^{-1}\,\underline{a}\,P \;=\; \begin{pmatrix} A_1 & A_{12} & \cdots\cdots & A_{1k} \\ & A_2 & \cdots\cdots & A_{2k} \\ & & \ddots & \vdots \\ 0 & & & A_k \end{pmatrix} , \qquad (4.1)$$

where A_1, A_2, ..., A_k are indecomposable square submatrices, and $k \geq 2$ or $k = 1$ depending on whether or not a is decomposable.

Then we may improve another proposition of Woodbury's (^{2}).

[III] Let a be Leontief-type. A necessary and sufficient condition that for any non-negative vector f, the equation $\underline{(I - a)\, x = f}$ have a non-negative solution is that at least one of the column sums be less than 1 for some column in each submatrices A_1, A_2, ..., A_k in (4.1).

Based on [I], another form of [III] is obtained by replacing the paragraph underlined in [III] with « all characteristic roots of a be less in absolute value than 1 », which we call [III'].

(^{1}) M. A. Woodbury [6], p. 353, Lemma 3.2.
(^{2}) M. A. Woodbury [6], p. 357, Corollary 3.6, where the condition is stated as follows: « at least one of the column sums be less than 1 for some column in each *block of columns* of the matrix ».

— 99 —

Solow's Theorem asserts that the condition of [III'] is a sufficient one [1]. We can see that it is necessary, too [2].

A different form of [III] or [III'], more convenient for our purpose, is

Lemma 2. [3]. Let a be Leontief-type.

(1°) If all column-sums are less than 1, $\sum\limits_{m=0}^{\infty} a^m$ converges.

(2°) If all column-sums are equal to 1, $\sum\limits_{m=0}^{\infty} a^m$ diverges.

(3°) In case some column-sums are equal to 1 and some less than 1, $\sum\limits_{m=0}^{\infty} a^m$ converges if and only if a is not decomposable into the following form (by some simultaneous permutation of rows and columns):

$$\begin{bmatrix} A^{(1)} & A^{(12)} \\ 0 & A^{(2)} \end{bmatrix}, \quad \begin{array}{l} \text{where all column-sums of } A^{(1)} \\ \text{are equal to } 1 \end{array} \tag{4.2}$$

The assertions of (1°), (2°) in this proposition have nothing to do with the decomposability of a, and as for (3°) also the general decomposability does not matter but only the particular one.

To be precise, the condition in (3°) includes two cases: The case where a is indecomposable and the case where a is decomposable but not into the form (4.2).

Now, let us return to our model. We may assume that the matrices A, V and C in the preceding sections have the following properties [$p1$]-[$p4$].

---

[1] R. Solow [5], p. 36, Theorem 1 and p. 38, Corollary.
[2] Proof of the necessity of the condition in [III'].
We show that (i) implies (ii) below.
 (i) All characteristic roots of a are less in absolute value than 1.
 (ii) Each A_1, A_2, ..., A_k has at least one column-sum less than 1.
 Suppose that the condition (ii) does not hold. Then all column-sums of some A_i are equal to 1. For m-dimensional vector $j = (1, 1, ..., 1)$, m being the degree of A_i, $jA_i = 1_j$, i. e. 1 is a characteristic root of A_i. As the characteristic roots of A_1, A_2, ..., A_k are also that of a, 1 is a characteristic root of a, unlike (i).

[3] Proof of Lemma 2.
(1°), (2°) and the necessity of the condition in (3°) are immediately evident from [III'] and [I]. (As to (1°), (2°), see also R. Solow [5], p. 32, p. 37).

Sufficiency of the condition in (3°): Suppose that $\sum\limits_{m=0}^{\infty} a^m$ diverges. Then, by [III'], a must be decomposable and, for some A_i in (4.1), all column-sums are equal to 1. If $i = 1$, put $A_1 = A^{(1)}$. If $i \neq 1$, A_{1i}, ..., $A_{i-1,i}$ are all zeromatrices (otherwise, at least one column-sum in the i-th block of columns of a must be greater than 1). Hence we can remove A_i in (4.1) to the upper left corner by some simultaneous permutation of rows and columns, without losing the character of the form (4.1).
Then we put $A_i = A_n^{(1)}$.
In either case, a is decomposable into the form (4.2).

— 100 —

$$[p1] \quad \sum_{i=1}^{n} a_{ij} + \sum_{k=1}^{r} v_{kj} = 1 \qquad (j = 1, 2, ..., n)$$

$$[p2] \quad \sum_{k=1}^{r} v_{kj} > 0 \quad \text{or} \quad \sum_{i=1}^{n} a_{ij} < 1 \quad (j = 1, 2, ..., n)$$

$$[p3] \quad \sum_{j=1}^{n} v_{kj} > 0 \qquad (k = 1, 2, ..., r)$$

$$[p4] \quad 0 < c_k \leqq 1 \qquad (k = 1, 2, ..., r), \quad \text{where} \quad c_k = \sum_{i=1}^{n} c_{ik}$$

These assumptions are reasonable from an economic point of view. (A generalization of [p1] is to be examined later).

Then, the existence of $B = (I - A)^{-1}$ is guaranteed by [p2] (See Lemma 2 1°). As A, V and C are non-negative, $n \times n$, $r \times n$ and $n \times r$, matrices, $VBC = L = (l_{kj})$ and $A + CV = Q = (q_{ij})$ are also non-negative, $r \times r$ and $n \times n$, respectively; and the following equalities hold:

Lemma 3. (1°) $\sum_{k=1}^{r} l_{kj} = c_j$ $\qquad (j = 1, 2, ..., r)$

(2°) $\sum_{i=1}^{n} q_{ij} = 1 - \sum_{k=1}^{r} (1 - c_k) v_{kj}$ $\qquad (j = 1, 2, ..., n)$

From the equalities and [p4]:

Corollary. L and Q are Leontief-type.

2) *Convergence conditions in the model.*

We can now consider the convergency of the propagation in our model.

Theorem 1. The convergency of $\sum\limits_{m=0}^{\infty} L^m$ coincides with that of $\sum\limits_{m=0}^{\infty} Q^m$.

Proof. Consider first $R = CVB$. As $j_n C \leqq j_r$, $j_n R = j_n CVB \leqq$ $\leqq j_r VB = j_r (I - A) B = j_n$. Thus, R is also Leontief-type. Since $I + R ... + R^m = I + C (I + L + ... + L^{m-1}) VB$. The convergency of $\sum L^m$ and that of $\sum R^m$ are equivalent. Next, from Lemma 1, $\sum R^m$ and $\sum Q^m$ converge if and only if $|I - R| \neq 0$ and $|I - Q| \neq 0$, respectively.

And, since $I - Q = I - A - CV = (I - CVB)(I - A)$, $|I - Q| = |I - R| \cdot |I - A|$, where always $|I - A| \neq 0$. Hence $|I - Q| \neq 0$ and $|I - R| \neq 0$ are equivalent. This means that $\sum Q^m$ converges if and only if $\sum R^m$ converges, and therefore if and only if $\sum L^m$ converges.

A simultaneous permutation of rows and columns in A, as a change of the order of industry groups, induces a permutation of the

— 101 —

columns in V and that of the rows of C. On the other hand, a permutation of rows in V, as a change of the order of income groups, induces a permutation of columns in C, and conversely. For brevity, we call the former I-permutation and the latter II-permutation.

Then, as a convergence condition of $\Sigma\, Q^m$, we have:

Theorem 2. Let $c_k = \sum_{i=1}^{n} c_{ik}$ $\quad (k = 1, ..., r)$ be the total propensities to consume of income groups.

(1^0) If all $c_1, ..., c_r$ are less than 1, then $\Sigma\, Q^m$ converges.

(2^0) If $c_1 = ... = c_r = 1$, then $\Sigma\, Q^m$ diverges.

(3^0) In case some of c_k $(k = 1, ..., r)$ are equal to 1 and some less than 1, $\Sigma\, Q^m$ converges if and only if A, V and C are not decomposable by any II- and I- permutation simultaneously into the following form:

$$A = \begin{bmatrix} A_1 & A_{12} \\ \hline 0 & A_2 \end{bmatrix}, \qquad C = \begin{bmatrix} C_1 & C_{12} \\ \hline 0 & C_2 \end{bmatrix} \qquad (4.3)$$

$$V = \begin{bmatrix} V_1 & V_{12} \\ \hline 0 & V_2 \end{bmatrix},$$

where $0 < h < n$, $0 < s < r$, and all column-sums of C_1 are equal to 1.

Proof.   From Lemma 3, (2^0), $\quad \sum_{i=1}^{n} q_{ij} = 1\quad$ if and only if

$$(1 - c_k)\, v_{kj} = 0 \qquad (k = 1, ..., r) \tag{i}$$

(1^0) $c_k < 1$ $(k = 1, ..., r)$: Suppose that there exists a number j such that $\sum_{i=1}^{n} q_{ij} = 1$. Then, $v_{1j} = ... = v_{rj} = 0$ from (i). This contradicts $[p2]$. Hence, $\sum_{i=1}^{n} q_{ij} < 1$ for all j, and therefore $\Sigma\, Q^m$ converges (Lemma 2, 1^0).

(2^0) $c_1 = ... = c_r = 1$: As the equations (i) hold for all j,

$$\sum_{i=1}^{n} q_{ij} = 1 \ (j = 1, ..., n).$$ Thus, $\Sigma \, Q^m$ diverges from Lemma 2 (2^0).

(3^0) A simultaneous permutation of Q induces a I-permutation of A, V and C only, and conversely. A II-permutation leaves Q unchanged. Therefore $\Sigma \, Q^m$ converges, from Lemma 2. (3^0), if and only if Q is not decomposable by any I-permutation of A, V and C, into the following form:

$$\begin{array}{c} \overset{h}{\overbrace{}} \\ h\left\lgroup \begin{array}{c|c} Q_1 & Q_{12} \\ \hline 0 & Q_2 \end{array} \right\rgroup \end{array}$$

where all column-sums of Q_1 are (ii)

equal to 1, $0 < h < n$

We shall prove that Q is decomposable into (ii) if and only if A, V and C is decomposable into the form (4.3).

Let Q be decomposed into (ii). By a suitable II-permutation, without changing Q, we may take

$$c_1 = ... = c_t = 1 , \ c_{t+1} , \ ..., \ c_r < 1 \qquad (0 < t < r) \qquad \text{(iii)}$$

As all column-sums of Q_1 are equal to 1, we have, from (i) and (iii),

$$v_{kj} = 0 \qquad (k = t + 1 , \ ..., \ r : j = 1 , \ ..., \ h) \qquad \text{(iv)}$$

Again, from the form (ii), $q_{ij} + \sum_{k=1}^{r} c_{ik} v_{kj} = 0$

$(i = h + 1 , \ ..., \ n; \quad j = 1 , \ ..., \ h)$.

As all terms on the left-hand sides of these equations are non-negative,

$$a_{ij} = 0 \qquad (i = h + 1 , \ ..., \ n; \quad j = 1 , \ ..., \ h) \qquad \text{(v)}$$

$$c_{ik} v_{kj} = 0 \qquad (i = h + 1 , \ ..., \ n; \quad j = 1 , \ ..., \ h; \ k = 1 , \ ..., r) \quad \text{(vi)}$$

We may take, if necessary, after transforming by some II-permutation, the first s rows of V such as $v_{kj} > 0$, for $k = 1 , \ ..., \ s$ and for some j_k $(1 \leq j_k \leq h)$, and

$$v_{kj} = 0 \qquad (k = s + 1 , \ ..., \ t; \quad j = 1 , \ ..., \ h) \qquad \text{(vi)}$$

Here $0 < s \leq t < n$, from [p2] and (iv). Then, from (vi),

$$c_{ik} = 0 \qquad (i = h + 1 , \ ..., \ n; \quad k = 1 , \ ..., \ s) \qquad \text{(vii)}$$

The last II-permutation changes the order of columns in C, but only among the first t columns. Hence (iii) remains valid. And, as A is unchanged, so is (v). From (iv), (iv'), (v) and (vii), we conclude that A, V and C are decomposable into the form (4.3).

The converse is obvious and the proof is completed.

— 103 —

The condition in (3°) of this theorem contains the following two cases: (a) A is indecomposable, (b) A is decomposable, but not into (4.3) together with V and C simultaneously.

As a consequence we see

Corollary 1. In the case where some c_1, ..., c_r are equal to 1 and some less than 1, ΣQ^m converges if A is indecomposable.

So we can deal with Kalecki's Model as a particular case of Corollary 1, where $n = 1$, $r = 2$.

According to Theorem 1, we have another

Corollay 2. The convergence condition of ΣQ^m given in Theorem 2 is also that of ΣL^m.

Further, from [1] follows

Corollary 3. A necessary and sufficient condition that, for any $f \geqq 0$, the equation $(I - Q) X = f$ has a non-negative solution coincides with the convergence condition given in Theorem 2.

The zero parts of A, V and C in (4.3) may be larger, but not as large as V_2 and C_1 vanish, on the ground of [p3], [p4].

Further, we may adopt a more general assumption than [p1]:

$$[p1'] \qquad \sum_{i=1}^{n} a_{ij} + \sum_{k=1}^{r} v_{kj} \leqq 1 .$$

Then, the possibility of divergence of ΣQ^m becomes more limited:

(1°) in Theorem 2 remains true, but (2°) no longer holds. As for (3°), the given condition is a sufficient, but not a necessary one ([1]).

([1]) One case represented by assumption [p1'] is an open economy with foreign trade. As shown Section III, in the case of a *closed* economy with no foreign trade, the conclusion that income has different values depending on the proportion of final demand can be only derived by introducing the structure of income distribution, but in the case of an *open* economy with foreign trade the same conclusion can be derived without introducing the distribution structure, because the coefficients on the production side enter into the income-formation process through imports. See K. Miyazawa [4].

REFERENCES

[1] DEBREU G. and HERSTEIN I. N.: *Non-negative Square Matrix*, « Econometrica », Vol. 21, No. 4, Oct. 1953.
[2] HERSTEIN I. N.: *Comments on Solow's Structure of Linear Models*, « Econometrica », Vol. 20, No. 4, Oct. 1952.
[3] KALECKI M. - *Theory of Economic Dynamics*, 1954.
[4] MIYAZAWA K.: *Foreign Trade Multiplier, Input-Output Analysis and the Consumption Function*, « Quarterly Journal of Economics », Vol. 74, No. 1, Feb. 1960.
[5] SOLOW R.: *On the Structure of Linear Models*, « Econometrica », Vol. 20, No. 1, Jan. 1952.
[6] WOODBURY M. A.: *Properties of Leontief-type Input-Output Matrices*, in *Economic Activity Analysis*, ed. by O. Morgenstern, 1954.

[22]

The Economic Journal, **89** *(December* 1979), 850–873
Printed in Great Britain

ACCOUNTING AND FIXED PRICE MULTIPLIERS IN A SOCIAL ACCOUNTING MATRIX FRAMEWORK*

This paper is concerned with the relationships between output, factor demands and income, and the decomposition of these relationships into separate effects as suggested by the structure of a social accounting matrix representation of the flows between them. Since output, factor and the non-government institutions sector (households and companies) are all disaggregated in the system to be examined, it follows that the analysis is concerned not only with output levels and the level of factor and household incomes, but also with the structure of production, the distribution of factor incomes, and the distribution of disposable income both among households and between them and the corporate sector. This is the first sense in which this paper is concerned with decomposition, and it makes the point that the distribution of income and the structure of production are inextricably interwoven.

The closed-loop character of the present formulation implies that the incomes of production activities, factors and institutions are all derived from injections into the economy via a multiplier process. This multiplier is a matrix $\mathbf{M}$ which can be expressed as the product of three multiplier matrices $\mathbf{M_1}$, $\mathbf{M_2}$ and $\mathbf{M_3}$. The first of these captures the effects of transfers within the economy, for example, the distribution of profits from companies to households, and the transfers of goods between activities, which are the essence of input–output. The other matrices $\mathbf{M_2}$ and $\mathbf{M_3}$ capture the consequences of the circular flow of income within the economy. Matrix $\mathbf{M_3}$ shows the full circular effects of an income injection going round the system and back to its point of origin in a series of repeated (and dampening) cycles. In contrast, $\mathbf{M_2}$ captures the cross-effects of the multiplier process whereby an injection into one part of the system has repercussions on other parts. These cross-effects correspond to open-loop effects and hence to the recent class of models, such as that of Maton, Paukert and Skolka (1978), which trace the effects of some exogenous changes in income distribution on output and employment, with no allowance for the effects in the reverse direction of changes in output and employment on the distribution of income. The decomposition of $\mathbf{M}$ into component parts is the second sense in which the paper is concerned with decomposition.

The first perspective on decomposition is illustrated in Section I by means of a simplified social accounting matrix (SAM) for Sri Lanka in 1970. This shows balanced accounts for factors, production activities, households and com-

* The views expressed are those of the authors and do not necessarily reflect views of the World Bank. We are particularly grateful to Charles Blitzer and Sherman Robinson for comments on an earlier draft, and to Sir Richard Stone for his general support of the line of work reported in this paper. Particular contributions due to him are acknowledged in the text. Also we wish to thank Kenshi Ohashi for computational assistance.

panies set in the broader framework of a full national accounting system. Section II then explores the structure of these accounting balances in terms of a multiplier matrix and its decomposition into transfer, open-loop and closed-loop effects.[1] An additive version of the decomposition due to Stone (1978*a*) is also presented.

The multipliers discussed in Section II of the paper are referred to as accounting multipliers. Their data base is the SAM observed for 1970 and their role is simply to represent the accounting balances of the SAM in a novel way which gives some insights into economic structure. With the accounting multipliers as a starting point, it is then possible to move on, in Section III of the paper, to consider the potentially more interesting case of multipliers due to income effects in a fixed price model. The argument shows that these fixed price multipliers are strictly analogous to the accounting multipliers. The only difference arises from extensive use of marginal expenditure propensities in the fixed price case, while the accounting multipliers are built up from the average expenditure propensities which can be calculated directly from the SAM. Thus the fixed price multipliers can be interpreted as having a data base which is the initial SAM now complemented by estimates of income elasticities when the latter differ from unity. Our pedagogic procedure of presenting accounting multipliers first, and then the fixed price multipliers, makes it possible to bring out the implications of income elasticity effects, such as Engel's law, within a fixed price system. Indeed, following the decomposition of the fixed price multiplier matrix in Section IV, we are able to show that the differences between this matrix and the accounting multiplier matrix can themselves be represented as a multiplicative matrix effect which is dependent on income elasticities which differ from unity.

The empirical results presented in Section V illustrate the various components of fixed price multipliers and alternative ways of deriving them. The results show how the estates sector in Sri Lanka is relatively isolated within the economy because its linkages with other sectors are slight. The results also show the extent to which input–output calculations underestimate the linkages between producing sectors in comparison with the case where the full circular flow of incomes is taken into account. More generally, the anatomy of the economy in terms of income and production structures, and their interdependence, is captured by the various multiplier matrices discussed in this paper.

The inclusion of different types of households in the present formulation distinguishes the approach from standard closed-loop Leontief systems and allows the distribution of income to be brought into the picture. The inclusion of factors as well as households implies that the present formulation extends the structure of accounting balances as set out by Quesnay (1758) and the previous closed-loop multiplier formulations which have been developed within

---

[1] This aspect has been treated previously by us in Pyatt, Roe *et al.* (1977), Chapter 4. However, there is an error in the exposition with respect to the treatment of indirect taxes, which is removed in the present paper. The multiplier decomposition has also been applied in Bell, Devarajan, Hazell and Slade (1976) and Stone (1978*a, b*).

Table 1

A Social Accounting Matrix for Sri Lanka in 1970 (Rs. 10⁶)

Receipts	Factors of production (1) — Labour Urban	Labour Rural	Capital Estate	Capital Private	Capital Public	Household current accounts (2) Urban	Rural	Estate	Corporate current accounts (3) Private	State	Production activities: commodity groups (4) Tea and rubber	Other agric.	Food process.	Other manuf.	Mining & constr.	Services	Government curr. accts. (5)	Consolidated cap. accts. (6)	Indirect taxes (net) (7)	Rest of world (8) Commodity trans.	Other	Totals
Endogenous accounts																						
(1) Factors of production																						
Labour																						
Urban	—	—	—	—	—	—	—	—	—	—	16	154	32	187	59	1225	—	—	—	—	—	1673
Rural	—	—	—	—	—	—	—	—	—	—	133	1171	54	243	123	1460	—	—	—	—	—	3184
Capital																						
Estate	—	—	—	—	—	—	—	—	—	—	615	34	10	2	4	46	—	—	—	—	—	711
Private	—	—	—	—	—	—	—	—	—	—	143	1736	141	586	924	2201	—	—	—	—	—	5731
Public	—	—	—	—	—	—	—	—	—	—	—	—	16	77	22	72	—	—	—	—	—	187
(2) Household current accts.																						
Urban	1673	—	—	799	—	—	—	—	434	—	—	—	—	—	—	—	92	—	—	—	6	3004
Rural	—	3184	—	3356	—	—	—	—	204	—	—	—	—	—	—	—	153	—	—	—	6	6903
Estate	—	—	711	61	—	—	—	—	7	—	—	—	—	—	—	—	6	—	—	—	6	791

Continued Overleaf

Table 1 Continued

Account	(1)	(2)	(3)	(4)	(5)	(6)	(7)	(8)	(9)	(10)	(11)	(12)	(13)	(14)	(15)	(16)	(17)	(18)	(19)	(20)	(21)	Totals
(3) Corporate curr. accts.	—	—	—	—	—	—	—	—	—	—	—	—	—	—	—	—	—	—	—	—	—	
Private	—	—	—	—	—	—	—	—	—	—	—	—	—	—	—	—	—	—	—	—	—	1402
State	—	—	—	—	—	—	—	—	—	—	—	—	—	—	—	—	—	—	—	—	—	481
(4) Production activities:																						
commodity groups																						
Tea and rubber	—	—	—	—	—	14	56	6	—	—	—	—	8	2	2	−30	—	—	—	1180	—	1238
Other agric.	—	—	—	1294	—	404	1199	169	—	—	166	7	66	45	20	78	—	—	—	108	—	3568
Food process.	—	—	—	—	—	275	1065	138	—	—	11	—	188	40	26	90	—	—	—	152	—	2019
Other manuf.	—	—	—	—	—	341	904	112	—	—	121	248	490	210	66	75	—	—	—	164	—	2887
Mining & constr.	—	—	—	—	—	2	6	1	—	—	—	236	5	58	92	1595	—	—	—	19	—	2014
Services	—	—	—	—	—	875	1933	208	74	56	120	251	234	230	1371	154	—	—	—	490	—	5996
Exogenous accts.																						
(5) Government curr. accts.	—	—	—	—	—	332	119	—	236	152	—	—	—	—	—	—	75	44	—	—	—	2346
(6) Consolidated cap. accts.	—	—	—	—	—	520	808	11	505	329	—	—	—	—	—	—	382	41	—	—	—	2596
(7) Indirect taxes (net)	—	—	—	—	—	34	72	3	37	35	76	416	80	205	29	270	—	—	—	131	—	1388
(8) Rest of world																						
Commodity trans.	—	—	—	—	—	207	741	143	87	92	199	368	77	202	43	364	−279	—	—	—	—	2244
Other	—	—	—	—	—	—	—	—	—	—	—	—	—	—	—	—	36	—	—	—	—	165
Totals	1673	3184	711	5731	187	3004	6903	791	1402	481	1238	3568	2019	2887	2014	5996	2346	2596	1388	2244	165	

Source: Adapted from Pyatt, Roe *et al.* (1977).

his accounting framework.[1] While the data source for the present analysis is perhaps the first to give detailed accounts on a disaggregated basis for factors, households and activities,[2] subsequent studies have begun or been completed which achieve comparable tabulations.[3] In parallel with this effort, a great many studies are forthcoming which model simultaneously the behaviour of factor markets, production structure, and income distribution.[4] However, the published models do not have an explicit accounting structure and are heavily concerned with mechanisms for determining prices endogenously. The fixed price multipliers discussed here take prices as exogenous, while our accounting multipliers are clearly implicit in all closed models. By making them explicit, and then moving on to a simple fixed price model, we hope to provide some of the missing links between the sophisticated experimental models now being developed and the simple input–output, semi-input–output and macro-models which remain the basis of actual planning methods.

I. THE SOCIAL ACCOUNTING MATRIX

Table 1 sets out a social accounting matrix (SAM) which provides the numerical base for subsequent empirical illustrations. In reading this table it is important to keep in mind the convention that entries are to be read as receipts for the row account in which they are located, and expenditures or outlays for their column account. The SAM is square because each account has both receipts and expenditures; and the row and column sums for a given account must be equal because all income must be accounted for by an outlay of one type or another. Eight groups of accounts are shown, some of which are further disaggregated. The partitioning of the eight groups into endogenous and exogenous accounts is discussed following an explanation of the flows depicted in Table 1.[5]

Factors of production receive income from domestic production (shown as the intersection of accounts in row block 1 with column block 4) which in turn is distributed to households and companies (rows 2, 3 intersecting with column 1), and as net factor income payments abroad (row 8 intersecting with column 1).

---

[1] The distinguishing feature of Quesnay's *Tableau Economique* from the present perspective is that value added in different production activities is paid directly to households of various types as opposed to being routed to them via a set of factor accounts. This simplified approach is also adopted in Desai (1961) and in a model of Iran (Pyatt *et al.* (1972)) which is of the fixed-price multiplier genre. In a recent note, Stone (1978*b*) has applied the analysis of accounting multipliers in this paper to Quesnay's *Tableau*.

[2] See Pyatt, Roe *et al.* (1977). This study distinguishes 18 types of labour and 3 of capital; 21 household groups; two types of companies and 48 different production activities.

[3] Pyatt and Round (1977) compare the Sri Lanka study with the social accounting basis of the Iran study referred to in a previous footnote and a subsequent investigation in Swaziland (Pyatt, Round *et al.* 1974). A recent conference reported on continuing work in the Philippines and Saudi Arabia, while results for Botswana (Greenfield, 1978), Malaysia (Pyatt and Round, 1978), and the United Kingdom (Stone, 1978*a*) were also presented.

[4] Recent publications include Adelman and Robinson (1978), Dervis and Robinson (1978), and Gupta (1977). Unpublished work sponsored by the World Bank's Research Program, includes that of Taylor, Bacha, Cardosa and Lysy on Brazil (forthcoming), and Ahluwalia and Lysy on Malaysia.

[5] See Pyatt, Roe *et al.* (1977) for a more detailed description of the accounting structure.

Factor incomes received by households include wages, unincorporated business profits, and rent on dwellings (row 2, column 1); but households also receive distributed profits from the corporate sector (2, 3), and transfers from government (2, 8), before arriving at total household income. Similarly, corporate enterprises receive factor incomes in the form of gross profits (3, 1), as well as current transfers from government (3, 5). Government income is derived from direct tax payments and other transfers by households (5, 2), corporate enterprises (5, 3) and from the rest of the world (5, 8), as well as intra-government transfers (5, 5), together with net indirect tax payments (5, 7) shown as a receipt from a special indirect tax account. The expenditures on domestically produced commodities are shown in the row of account 4. They include outlays by households (4, 2), government (4, 5), investment (4, 6), and the rest of the world (4, 8), as well as intermediate transactions between production activities (4, 4). Indirect taxes on all of these expenditures, and purchases of imported goods, are shown as separate outlays by the various spending units. They are received in row 7 by the account for (net) indirect taxes, and in row 8 by the rest of the world revenue account. Finally, outlays on domestic investment (column 6) are matched by domestic and foreign savings (row 6) where the latter (5, 8) is the final balancing item in the rest of the world accounts.

An important feature to note is that factors, institutions and activities are all disaggregated in Table 1, so that the SAM captures the distribution of factor incomes as well as their level. It also shows the distribution of income among household types.

To move from a SAM to a model structure requires that each account should be designated as endogenous or exogenous. The accounts in Table 1 have been ordered so that the endogenous accounts occupy the leading rows and columns of the SAM. This is shown schematically in Table 2. The notation to be used in subsequent discussion is given with this table, as are a number of accounting relationships, equations (1) to (11), which follow directly from the SAM structure. Equation (1) states that transactions between endogenous accounts, denoted by matrix $\mathbf{N}$, can be expressed as the product of a square matrix, $\mathbf{A}_n$, of average propensities to consume and a vector of endogenous incomes, $\mathbf{y}_n$. Similarly (2) equates leakages, $\mathbf{L}$, with the product of a non-square matrix, $\mathbf{A}_l$, of average propensities to leak and the endogenous incomes, $\mathbf{y}_n$. It is important to note that since $\mathbf{N}$, $\mathbf{L}$ and $\mathbf{y}_n$ are observed in a SAM such as Table 1, the matrices $\mathbf{A}_n$ and $\mathbf{A}_l$ can be obtained directly. Equations (3) and (4) express the accounting relationship by which endogenous incomes are determined. Equations (5) and (6) have the same role with respect to incomes of the exogenous accounts, $\mathbf{y}_x$. Equation (7) sums expenditures (columns) of the endogenous accounts. It implies that, for these accounts, row and column sums will be equal provided equation (8) holds, i.e. provided column sums of $\mathbf{A}_n$, plus those of $\mathbf{A}_l$, add to unity in all cases. Equation (9) expresses column sums for exogenous accounts. The requirement that these be equal to row sums (equation (6)) yields equation (10). Finally, an implication of (10) is obtained in (11), which states that, in aggregate, injections into the system must equal leakages.

Table 2

Notation and Accounting Balances: Equations (1) to (11)

Receipts	Expenditures		Totals
	Endogenous accounts	Exogenous accounts	
Endogenous accounts	$N = A_n \hat{y}_n$ (1)	X	$y_n = n + x$ (3)
			$= A_n y_n + x$ (4)
Exogenous accounts	$L = A_l \hat{y}_n$ (2)	R	$y_x = 1 + Ri$ (5)
			$= A_l y_n + Ri$ (6)
Totals	$y'_n = (i'A_n + i'A_l)\hat{y}_n$ (7)	$y'_r = i'X + i'R$ (9)	
	$\therefore i' = i'A_n + i'A_l$ (8)	$\therefore A_l y_n - X'i = (R - R')i$ (10)	$\lambda'_a y_n = x'i$ (11)

$A_n = N\hat{y}_n^{-1}$ = matrix of average endogenous expenditure propensities.
$A_l = L\hat{y}_n^{-1}$ = matrix of average propensities to leak.
$Ni = n$ = vector of row sums of $N = A_n y_n$.
$Xi = x$ = vector of row sums of X.
$Li = 1$ = vector of row sums of $L = A_l y_n$.
$\lambda'_a = i'A_l$ = vector of column sums of A_l, i.e. the vector of aggregate average propensities to leak.
N = matrix of SAM transactions between endogenous accounts.
X = matrix of injections from exogenous into endogenous accounts.
L = matrix of leakages from endogenous into exogenous accounts.
R = matrix of SAM transactions between exogenous accounts.

From equation (4) and the definition of 1 it follows that

$$y_n = (I - A_n)^{-1}x = M_a x \qquad (12)$$

and

$$1 = A_l (I - A_n)^{-1}x = A_l M_a x \qquad (13)$$

provided that $(I - A_n)^{-1}$ exists. This inverse is the accounting multiplier matrix M_a which relates endogenous incomes y_n to injections, x. The existence and decomposition of M_a are discussed in the next section.[1] Meanwhile it can be noted that the linkage between injections and leakages as given by equation (13) satisfies the requirement[2]

$$i'A_l M_a = \lambda'_a M_a = i' \qquad (14)$$

or, in words, that each injection is ultimately accounted for by one or more leakages.

In deriving the matrix M_a it has been assumed that the accounts for factors, households, companies and production activities are endogenous. The corresponding exogenous accounts are therefore those for government current expenditure, investment,[3] indirect taxes and international transactions. Injections, X, therefore include current transfers to households and companies both from government and the rest of the world, plus the demands placed on production activities through government consumption, investment and exports. Direct and indirect taxes, savings, imports and income transfers abroad constitute the leakages.[4]

[1] Tabular results of M_a and $A_l M_a$ are available on request from the authors.
[2] This follows from $i' = i'(A_n + A_l) = i'A_n + \lambda'_a$
 $= \lambda'_a(I - A_n)^{-1} = \lambda'_a M_a$.
[3] To obtain Tinbergen's semi-input–output model as a special case of our analysis, it would be necessary to endogenise investment in the non-traded goods sector(s).
[4] It can be noted that if model formulation was to specify the import and indirect tax content of government expenditure, investment and exports, then this would imply that some elements of R were determined as a function of X. The equation (11) would now be sufficient to determine the balance of trade, government savings, and the current account deficit on the balance of payments.

II. DECOMPOSITION OF ACCOUNTING MULTIPLIERS

From equation (4) it follows that for any matrix $\tilde{\mathbf{A}}_n$ of the same size as $\mathbf{A}_n$ and such that $(\mathbf{I}-\tilde{\mathbf{A}}_n)^{-1}$ exists, we can write

$$
\begin{aligned}
\mathbf{y}_n &= \mathbf{A}_n\mathbf{y}_n+\mathbf{x} = (\mathbf{A}_n-\tilde{\mathbf{A}}_n)\mathbf{y}_n+\tilde{\mathbf{A}}_n\mathbf{y}_n+\mathbf{x} \\
&= (\mathbf{I}-\tilde{\mathbf{A}}_n)^{-1}\,(\mathbf{A}_n-\tilde{\mathbf{A}}_n)\mathbf{y}_n+(\mathbf{I}-\tilde{\mathbf{A}}_n)^{-1}\,\mathbf{x} \\
&= \mathbf{A}^*\mathbf{y}_n+(\mathbf{I}-\tilde{\mathbf{A}}_n)^{-1}\,\mathbf{x}.
\end{aligned}
\tag{15}
$$

Multiplying throughout by $\mathbf{A}^*$ and substituting for $\mathbf{A}^*\mathbf{y}_n$ on the right-hand side of equation (15) now gives

$$
\mathbf{y}_n = \mathbf{A}^{*2}\mathbf{y}_n+(\mathbf{I}+\mathbf{A}^*)\,(\mathbf{I}-\tilde{\mathbf{A}}_n)^{-1}\,\mathbf{x}.
$$

Similarly, multiplying both sides of (15) by $\mathbf{A}^{*2}$ and substituting for $\mathbf{A}^{*2}\mathbf{y}_n$ in this last expression, we get

$$
\begin{aligned}
\mathbf{y}_n &= \mathbf{A}^{*3}\mathbf{y}_n+(\mathbf{I}+\mathbf{A}^*+\mathbf{A}^{*2})\,(\mathbf{I}-\tilde{\mathbf{A}}_n)^{-1}\,\mathbf{x} \\
&= (\mathbf{I}-\mathbf{A}^{*3})^{-1}\,(\mathbf{I}+\mathbf{A}^*+\mathbf{A}^{*2})\,(\mathbf{I}-\tilde{\mathbf{A}}_n)^{-1}\,\mathbf{x}
\end{aligned}
\tag{16}
$$

provided that $(\mathbf{I}-\mathbf{A}^{*3})^{-1}$ exists.

Comparison of (16) with (12) shows that the above algebra has decomposed the accounting multiplier matrix $\mathbf{M}_a$ into the product of three separate matrices. This decomposition is quite general. It can become informative by reference to the structure of $\mathbf{A}_n$ and choosing an $\tilde{\mathbf{A}}_n$ accordingly. Specifically, we can write

$$
\mathbf{A}_n = \begin{bmatrix} 0 & 0 & \mathbf{A}_{13} \\ \mathbf{A}_{21} & \mathbf{A}_{22} & 0 \\ 0 & \mathbf{A}_{32} & \mathbf{A}_{33} \end{bmatrix}
\quad\text{and}\quad
\tilde{\mathbf{A}}_n = \begin{bmatrix} 0 & 0 & 0 \\ 0 & \mathbf{A}_{22} & 0 \\ 0 & 0 & \mathbf{A}_{33} \end{bmatrix}
\tag{17}
$$

so that $\mathbf{A}^*$ defined by equation (15) can be written

$$
\mathbf{A}^* = \begin{bmatrix} 0 & 0 & \mathbf{A}_{13}^* \\ \mathbf{A}_{21}^* & 0 & 0 \\ 0 & \mathbf{A}_{32}^* & 0 \end{bmatrix}
\quad\text{where}\quad
\begin{cases} \mathbf{A}_{13}^* = \mathbf{A}_{13} \\ \mathbf{A}_{21}^* = (\mathbf{I}-\mathbf{A}_{22})^{-1}\,\mathbf{A}_{21} \\ \mathbf{A}_{32}^* = (\mathbf{I}-\mathbf{A}_{33})^{-1}\,\mathbf{A}_{32} \end{cases}
\tag{18}
$$

and where the partitioning of $\mathbf{A}_n$ (and of $\tilde{\mathbf{A}}_n$ and $\mathbf{A}^*$) corresponds to the separate accounts in the SAM for factors, the endogenous institutions (households and companies), and production activities.

At this point in the argument it is worth noting that the three-part decomposition of $\mathbf{M}_a$ in (16) does not require the three-way partitioning of matrix $\mathbf{A}_n$ as in (17): $\mathbf{A}_n$ can be partitioned into as many (or few) sets of accounts as one wishes. Similarly, there is nothing special from a mathematical perspective in choosing to end the sequence of substitutions which leads to equation (16) after three steps. Further substitutions are possible, and the general result is

$$
\mathbf{y}_n = (\mathbf{I}-\mathbf{A}^{*k})^{-1}\,(\mathbf{I}+\mathbf{A}^*+\mathbf{A}^{*2}+\ldots+\mathbf{A}^{*(k-1)})\,(\mathbf{I}-\tilde{\mathbf{A}}_n)^{-1}\,\mathbf{x}.
$$

Our choice of three partitions for $\mathbf{A}_n$, and the decision to end the chain of successive substitutions after three steps ($k=3$) derives from the structure of the SAM in Table 1 and this structure derives in turn from the conceptual framework of economics. Thus the particular application of the mathematics which is illuminating in our context is to have three partitions of $\mathbf{A}_n$, corresponding to factors, endogenous institutions, and production activities; and to choose $k = 3$ not simply because there are three partitions, but because with this particular trio of partitions, three steps in the sequence of substitutions corresponds to one complete cycle in the circular flow of income within the economy.

Further reference to the SAM (Table 1) shows that with the chosen partitioning of $\mathbf{A}_n$, its zero sub-matrices are indeed empty blocks within the accounts. The non-zero sub-matrix $\mathbf{A}_{13}$ reflects payments from activities to factors; $\mathbf{A}_{21}$ corresponds to the mapping of incomes from factors to households and companies; and the non-zero elements of $\mathbf{A}_{32}$ record the average propensities with which different types of households consume the goods produced by the various production activities. Sub-matrix $\mathbf{A}_{22}$ captures current transfers between endogenous institutions and in our example is restricted to the distribution of dividends and interest to households. Sub-matrix $\mathbf{A}_{33}$ shows the transactions between activities, i.e. inter-industry flows.

With these conventions we now define

$$\mathbf{M}_{a1} = (\mathbf{I} - \tilde{\mathbf{A}}_n)^{-1}; \ \mathbf{M}_{a2} = (\mathbf{I} + \mathbf{A}^* + \mathbf{A}^{*2}); \ \mathbf{M}_{a3} = (\mathbf{I} - \mathbf{A}^{*3})^{-1} \qquad (19)$$

with the implication from (12) and (16) that

$$\mathbf{M}_a = \mathbf{M}_{a3} \mathbf{M}_{a2} \mathbf{M}_{a1}. \qquad (20)$$

Equations (17)–(19) imply, first, that $\mathbf{M}_{a1}$ is a block diagonal matrix with successive diagonal elements given by $\mathbf{I}$, $(\mathbf{I} - \mathbf{A}_{22})^{-1}$ and $(\mathbf{I} - \mathbf{A}_{33})^{-1}$. They also imply that

$$\mathbf{A}^{*2} = \begin{bmatrix} 0 & \mathbf{A}_{13}^* \mathbf{A}_{32}^* & 0 \\ 0 & 0 & \mathbf{A}_{21}^* \mathbf{A}_{13}^* \\ \mathbf{A}_{32}^* \mathbf{A}_{21}^* & 0 & 0 \end{bmatrix} \text{ so that } \mathbf{M}_{a2} = \begin{bmatrix} \mathbf{I} & \mathbf{A}_{13}^* \mathbf{A}_{32}^* & \mathbf{A}_{13}^* \\ \mathbf{A}_{21}^* & \mathbf{I} & \mathbf{A}_{21}^* \mathbf{A}_{13}^* \\ \mathbf{A}_{32}^* \mathbf{A}_{21}^* & \mathbf{A}_{32}^* & \mathbf{I} \end{bmatrix} \qquad (21)$$

and that $\mathbf{M}_{a3}$ is also block diagonal with successive diagonal elements given by

$$(\mathbf{I} - \mathbf{A}_{13}^* \mathbf{A}_{32}^* \mathbf{A}_{21}^*)^{-1}, \quad (\mathbf{I} - \mathbf{A}_{21}^* \mathbf{A}_{13}^* \mathbf{A}_{32}^*)^{-1} \quad \text{and} \quad (\mathbf{I} - \mathbf{A}_{32}^* \mathbf{A}_{21}^* \mathbf{A}_{13}^*)^{-1}.$$

The structure of $\mathbf{M}_{a2}$ and $\mathbf{M}_{a3}$ derives from that of $\mathbf{A}^*$. From (18) it can be observed that the pattern of zero and non-zero cells of $\mathbf{A}^*$ corresponds to a circular permutation matrix of size 3×3. Accordingly, if $\mathbf{y}_n$ is partitioned compatibly with $\mathbf{A}_n$, then the structure of equation (15) implies that the partitions of $\mathbf{y}_n$ are related to each other as points on a closed loop. In Fig. 1 these points are shown schematically as the corners of a triangle. Matrix $\mathbf{A}^*$ represents the mapping from one partition of $\mathbf{y}_n$ to another. Starting from any corner of the triangle, three steps in this mapping brings one back to the starting point. Hence the structure of $\mathbf{A}^*$ implies that our formulation contains a closed-loop system which is the algebraic statement of the circular flow of income, e.g. from activities to factors to institutions; and then back to activities in the form

Input–Output Analysis I

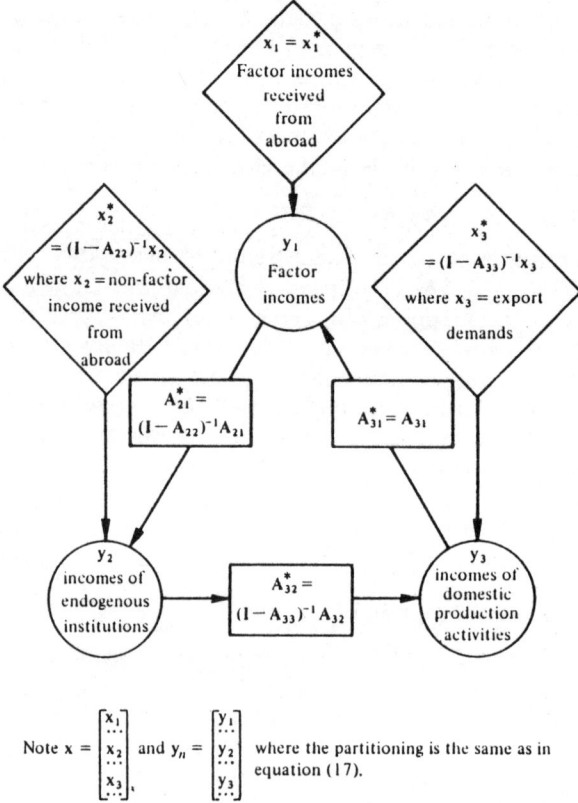

Note $x = \begin{bmatrix} x_1 \\ \cdots \\ x_2 \\ \cdots \\ x_3 \end{bmatrix}$, and $y_n = \begin{bmatrix} y_1 \\ \cdots \\ y_2 \\ \cdots \\ y_3 \end{bmatrix}$ where the partitioning is the same as in equation (17).

Fig. 1. The closed-loop structure of accounts as defined by equations (15), (17) and (18).

of consumption demand. This structure explains why $\mathbf{M}_{a3}$ is block diagonal and justifies referring to this matrix as the closed-loop or circular multiplier matrix.

Matrix $\mathbf{M}_{a1}$ is also block diagonal as previously noted. It captures the effects of one group of accounts on itself through direct transfers and is independent of the closed-loop nature of the system. Since there are no direct transfers between factors, the first diagonal block of $\mathbf{M}_{a1}$ is simply an identity matrix. The second diagonal block captures the multiplier effect resulting from direct transfers between institutions $(\mathbf{I} - \mathbf{A}_{22})^{-1}$. The third diagonal block similarly refers to the multiplier effect of inter-industry transfers $(\mathbf{I} - \mathbf{A}_{33})^{-1}$, which is the Leontief inverse. Matrix $\mathbf{M}_{a1}$ can be referred to as the transfers multiplier.

If $\mathbf{M}_{a1}$ and $\mathbf{M}_{a3}$ are block diagonal, all effects between partitions of $\mathbf{y}_n$ must be captured by $\mathbf{M}_{a2}$. This matrix is therefore referred to as the cross-effects matrix or alternatively as the open-loop multiplier matrix. This terminology can be justified by considering the implications of one partition of $\mathbf{y}_n$ for the others. Take as an example the effect of household and company incomes on both factor incomes and production. This is an open-loop system and equivalent to breaking the closed loop by setting $A_{21} = 0$, i.e. the effect of factor incomes on the incomes of institutions is ignored. From (18) it is apparent that A_{21}^* is now zero, so that all terms in M_{a3} and M_{a2} which involve A_{21}^* will be zero. This implies that M_{a3} will now be an identity matrix. From (21), certain cells of M_{a2} will also be zero. But the columns of M_{a2} which refer to households and companies will be unaltered. These columns show the impact of incomes in the second partition of y_n (endogenous institutions) on factor incomes (the first partition) and activity incomes (the third partition) in an open-loop system.

So far the discussion has assumed that the matrices M_{a1}, M_{a2} and M_{a3} exist and that it is legitimate to describe them as multiplier matrices in the sense that each has elements which are not less than the corresponding elements of an identity matrix. To justify this it can be noted that the matrix A_n is semi-positive.[1] It follows that M_a will be a multiplier matrix if it exists.

Mathematical conditions for the existence of M_a can obviously be postulated.[2] If A_n is a semi-positive indecomposable matrix, then M_a will exist if no column sum exceeds unity and at least one column sum is strictly less than unity. Expression (8) supports the former conditions, and we have only to guarantee a leakage from some accounts for M_a to exist, providing of course that A_n is indecomposable. It is of interest to note that since $(A_n - \tilde{A}_n)$ can be viewed as a circular permutation matrix then A_n is certainly 'block' indecomposable of order 3. But this is not a sufficient condition for A_n to be indecomposable in the general sense.

The existence of M_a is enough to ensure the existence of M_{a1}. This can be shown by first noting that $\tilde{A}_n$ is a semi-positive, completely decomposable matrix. If the conditions on the column sums hold for the existence of M_a then they will hold for the existence of M_{a1}, since $\tilde{A}_n$ is contained within A_n. Furthermore, M_{a1} will be a multiplier matrix. It also follows from (16) and (17) that A^* will be semi-positive if M_{a1} exists. Hence from (21) M_{a2} will exist and will be a multiplier matrix. Finally, from (20), since M_a, M_{a2} and M_{a1} all exist, then M_{a3} must also exist because it is bounded by finite matrices on both sides. Moreover, A^{*3} is semi-positive, so that M_{a3} is also a multiplier matrix.

A final remark on the existence of these multiplier matrices is to note that they essentially depend upon the designation of at least one exogenous account with at least some injection into, and hence some leakage from, the endogenous accounts which remain. This ensures at least one element of λ_a is positive.

To provide a useful way of presenting the results of our decomposition, Stone (1978a) has proposed an additive form of equation (20), namely.

$$M_a = I + (M_{a1} - I) + (M_{a2} - I)M_{a1} + (M_{a3} - I)M_{a2}M_{a1} \qquad (22)$$

so that elements of M_a are accounted for by (i) the initial injection; (ii) the net contribution of transfer multiplier effects; (iii) the net contribution of open-

[1] This is always possible in a SAM since a negative element in the *i*th row, *j*th column can be set equal to zero and balance restored by adding a positive element of the required size in the *j*th row, *i*th column.

[2] These are generally discussed in a particularly relevant context by Lancaster (1968), pp. 94–5.

loop or cross-multiplier effects; and (iv) the net contribution of circular or closed-loop multiplier effects.[1] To illustrate this form of the decomposition requires results for the product matrix $\mathbf{M}_{a2}\mathbf{M}_{a1}$ in addition to the details of $\mathbf{M}_a$.[2]

III. FIXED-PRICE MULTIPLIERS

The accounting multipliers described in Section II are interesting for the information they contain on the structure of an economy as revealed by a SAM. However, because they are accounting multipliers they cannot be interpreted directly as measures of the effects of changes in injections into the economy on the levels of endogenous incomes. For this latter purpose we need to know how different economic agents behave in response to changes. In this and subsequent sections, we shall be concerned with the behaviour which generates the expenditure patterns of endogenous accounts under the assumption that prices remain fixed when income is altered. Since prices may in fact change, the multipliers obtained under this assumption are referred to as fixed-price multipliers.

Under the assumption that prices are fixed, it follows from the accounting balance equation (3) that

$$dy_n = d\mathbf{n} + d\mathbf{x} \tag{23}$$
$$= \mathbf{C}_n dy_n + d\mathbf{x} \tag{24}$$
$$= (\mathbf{I} - \mathbf{C}_n)^{-1} d\mathbf{x} = \mathbf{M}_c d\mathbf{x} \tag{25}$$

and similarly that

$$d\mathbf{l} = \mathbf{C}_l dy_n \tag{26}$$
$$= \mathbf{C}_l(\mathbf{I} - \mathbf{C}_n)^{-1} d\mathbf{x} = \mathbf{C}_l \mathbf{M}_c d\mathbf{x}. \tag{27}$$

The result (23) is obtained by taking the total differential of (3). Equation (24) then follows from the fact that, if prices are fixed, the vector $\mathbf{n}$ of incomes received by endogenous accounts, as a result of expenditures by these same accounts, can be a function of $\mathbf{y}_n$ but otherwise is constant. Hence (24) follows from (23) if the (i, j)th element of matrix $\mathbf{C}_n$ is the partial derivative of the ith element of $\mathbf{n}$ with respect to the jth element of $\mathbf{y}_n$. In this sense $\mathbf{C}_n$ is a matrix of marginal propensities to consume. If $(\mathbf{I} - \mathbf{C}_n)^{-1}$ exists, then equation (25) shows how elements of $\mathbf{y}_n$ change as a result of changes in injections. Similarly, the matrix $\mathbf{C}_l$ in equation (26) is a matrix of marginal propensities to leak; and equation (27) shows how leakages change as a result of injections.

Equations (25) and (27) are analogous to equations (12) and (13). Consequently, under the condition that the matrix $\mathbf{C}_n$ is non-negative, $\mathbf{M}_c$ is a multiplier matrix, to be referred to as the fixed-price multiplier matrix. Matrices

---

[1] The arrangement (22) is applied in Stone (1978a) to a decomposition $\mathbf{M}_a = \mathbf{M}_{a2}\mathbf{M}_{a3}\mathbf{M}_{a1}$ so that, in comparison with (20), the order of $\mathbf{M}_{a2}$ and $\mathbf{M}_{a3}$ is inverted. This alternative ordering was used in Pyatt, Roe *et al.* (1977), chapter 4. It is easily checked that both orderings are legitimate. However, the ordering adopted in (20) is perhaps to be preferred since it corresponds to the progression from transfer effects to open-loops to closed-loop models.

[2] Tabular results are available on request from the authors. It can be noted that, since $\mathbf{M}_{a1}$ is block diagonal, it follows from the structure of $\mathbf{M}_{a2}$ defined in (21) that setting off-diagonal blocks of $\mathbf{M}_{a2}\mathbf{M}_{a1}$ equal to zero reduces this product to the matrix $\mathbf{M}_{a1}$.

Table 3

Estimates of the Matrices $\mathbf{M}_c$ and $\mathbf{C}_1\mathbf{M}_c$ Derived from Tables 1 and 4

	Origin of injection															
	(1) Factors of production					(2) Household curr. accts.			(3) Corporate curr. accts.		(4) Production activities: Commodity groups					
	Labour			Capital												
Endogenous accounts	Urban	Rural	Estate	Private	Public	Urban	Rural	Estate	Private	State	Tea and rubber	Other agric.	Food process.	Other manuf.	Mining & constr.	Services
(1) Factors of production																
Labour																
Urban	1·19	0·25	0·28	0·20	—	0·19	0·25	0·28	0·10	—	0·26	0·26	0·24	0·24	0·25	0·41
Rural	0·34	1·47	0·58	0·37	—	0·34	0·47	0·58	0·18	—	0·58	0·74	0·60	0·40	0·45	0·62
Estate	0·01	0·02	1·03	0·02	—	0·01	0·02	0·03	0·01	—	0·52	0·03	0·03	0·02	0·02	0·03
Capital																
Private	0·55	0·76	0·94	1·60	1·00	0·55	0·76	0·94	0·29	—	0·88	1·16	0·98	0·73	1·14	0·98
Public	0·02	0·03	0·03	0·02	1·00	0·02	0·03	0·03	0·01	—	0·03	0·03	0·03	0·05	0·04	0·04
Sub-total	2·12	2·53	2·86	2·21	—	2·12	1·53	1·86	0·58	—	2·26	2·21	1·88	1·44	1·90	2·08
(2) Household curr. accts.																
Urban	1·31	0·41	0·49	0·54	—	1·31	0·41	0·49	0·47	—	0·45	0·51	0·45	0·40	0·49	0·62
Rural	0·68	1·94	1·16	1·37	—	0·68	1·94	1·16	0·50	—	1·13	1·46	1·21	0·86	1·16	1·23
Estate	0·02	0·03	1·04	0·04	—	0·02	0·03	1·04	0·02	—	0·53	0·04	0·04	0·02	0·03	0·04

Continued Overleaf

Table 3 Continued

(3) Corporate curr. accts.																
Private	0·14	0·19	0·23	0·39	—	0·14	0·19	0·23	1·07	—	0·22	0·28	0·24	0·18	0·28	0·24
State	0·02	0·03	0·03	0·02	1·00	0·02	0·03	0·03	0·01	1·00	0·03	0·03	0·03	0·05	0·04	0·04
Sub total (2+3)	2·17	2·60	2·95	2·36	1·00	2·17	2·60	2·95	2·07	1·00	2·35	2·32	1·97	1·50	2·00	2·17
(4) Production activities: commodity groups																
Tea and rubber	0·01	0·01	0·02	0·01	—	0·01	0·01	0·02	*	—	1·01	0·01	0·01	0·01	0·01	0·01
Other agriculture	0·38	0·59	0·84	0·46	—	0·38	0·59	0·84	0·21	—	0·62	1·53	1·09	0·38	0·41	0·45
Food processing	0·22	0·38	0·52	0·29	—	0·22	0·38	0·52	0·13	—	0·38	0·31	1·28	0·27	0·26	0·28
Other manufactures	0·42	0·62	0·64	0·48	—	0·42	0·62	0·64	0·22	—	0·63	0·54	0·48	1·53	0·59	0·50
Mining and constr.	0·01	0·01	0·02	0·01	—	0·01	0·01	0·02	0·01	—	0·01	0·01	0·01	0·01	1·14	0·02
Services	0·72	0·86	0·97	0·70	—	0·72	0·86	0·97	0·35	—	0·83	0·75	0·69	0·58	0·76	1·73
Sub-total	1·75	2·47	3·00	1·95	—	1·75	2·47	3·00	0·92	—	3·48	3·16	3·56	2·77	3·17	3·19
Exogenous accounts																
(5) Government curr. accts.	0·26	0·15	0·16	0·19	0·32	0·26	0·15	0·16	0·27	0·32	0·15	0·17	0·15	0·13	0·17	0·18
(6) Institutions cap. accts.	0·43	0·44	0·38	0·46	0·68	0·43	0·44	0·38	0·56	0·68	0·35	0·42	0·37	0·30	0·39	0·41
(7) Indirect taxes (net)	0·13	0·17	0·19	0·14	—	0·13	0·18	0·19	0·07	—	0·20	0·16	0·18	0·27	0·20	0·18
(8) Rest of world																
Commodity transactions	0·16	0·22	0·25	0·17	—	0·16	0·22	0·25	0·08	—	0·28	0·22	0·28	0·28	0·22	0·21
Other	0·01	0·02	0·02	0·04	—	0·01	0·02	0·02	0·02	—	0·02	0·03	0·02	0·02	0·03	0·02
Sub-total	1·00	1·00	1·00	1·00	1·00	1·00	1·00	1·00	1·00	1·00	1·00	1·00	1·00	1·00	1·00	1·00

$\mathbf{C}_n$ and $\mathbf{C}_l$ will have column sums which add to unity and $\mathbf{M}_c$ will exist under conditions analogous to those for the existence of $\mathbf{M}_d$. Hence, given estimates of the matrices $\mathbf{C}_n$ and $\mathbf{C}_l$, both the fixed-price multiplier, $\mathbf{M}_c$, and the matrix of marginal leakages, $\mathbf{C}_l \mathbf{M}_c$, can be calculated. These matrices are illustrated in Table 3 using data for Sri Lanka which are discussed below.

To go further, we need to consider data sources for $\mathbf{C}_n$ and $\mathbf{C}_l$. This can be done with reference to Table 1, which shows that the outlays of factor incomes primarily generate incomes for the endogenous domestic institutions. The table shows that all urban labour income accrues to urban households. Thus the first column of $\mathbf{C}_l$ is zero, and all elements of the first column of $\mathbf{C}_n$ are also zero except the element in the row for urban households, which is one. Thus the sum of the first column of $\mathbf{C}_l$, plus that for $\mathbf{C}_n$ also, is unity as it must be. The second, third and fifth columns of $\mathbf{C}_n$ and $\mathbf{C}_l$ are similarly obtained. For the fourth column, there are five different recipients of the income which accrues to private capital. The proportions in which they receive this income will depend on who owns private capital. And if the structure of ownership can be taken as given, then there is no reason to assume other than that increments of income will be distributed in the same proportions as the shares observed in the SAM. On these grounds, columns of $\mathbf{C}_n$ and $\mathbf{C}_l$ which refer to factor outlays are estimated by assuming that marginal and average propensities are the same.

For marginal and average propensities to be equal requires income elasticities of particular expenditures to be unity. This is clearly not true for household expenditures, and Table 4 sets out the marginal propensities which have been assumed. It is to be noted that the income elasticities of demand for imports are unusually low. This is partly because consumer imports in Sri Lanka include imports of the staple foods, rice and wheat, and partly because the observed cross-section elasticity has been lowered in recognition of the restrictions on imports which applied at that time.

For companies, marginal allocations of income have been assumed to be equal to the average allocations implied by Table 1. This is in default of any better basis for deciding how corporate taxation, savings and distribution policy might be responsive to changes in corporate income.

It has also been assumed that the allocation of total costs for production activities is the same at the margin as on average. The best way to justify this is as follows. First, the assumption of fixed prices would be reasonable if inter-industry technology follows Leontief assumptions so that there are no scale effects, and prices are fixed for given indirect tax rates if import prices are fixed and factor costs per unit of output are constant. These assumptions would make elements of $\mathbf{A}_l$ and $\mathbf{C}_l$ the same in the corresponding columns for production activities, with a similar equivalence of those elements of $\mathbf{A}_n$ and $\mathbf{C}_n$ which refer to inter-industry transactions. With respect to factor payments, profits will have a constant share if value-added price, i.e. value added per unit of output, is set as a constant mark-up over labour costs per unit of output. Labour costs per unit of output will be constant if labour is paid at fixed piece rates. Alternatively, it can be assumed that wage rates are fixed and the average product of labour is constant. This alternative assumption is necessary

Table 4

Household Average and Marginal Expenditure Propensities, Sri Lanka, 1970

	Urban		Rural		Estate	
	Average	Marginal	Average	Marginal	Average	Marginal
Endogenous						
(4) Production activities: commodity groups						
Tea and rubber	0·005	0·002	0·008	0·006	0·008	0·006
Other agriculture	0·134	0·080	0·174	0·134	0·214	0·241
Food processing	0·092	0·059	0·154	0·149	0·174	0·246
Other manufactures	0·114	0·122	0·131	0·204	0·142	0·156
Mining and construction	0·001	0·001	0·001	0·001	0·001	0·001
Services	0·291	0·315	0·280	0·311	0·263	0·302
Sub-total	0·637	0·579	0·748	0·805	0·802	0·952
Exogenous						
(5) Government current account	0·111	0·164	0·017	0·022	—	0·010
(6) Institutions capital account	0·173	0·209	0·117	0·135	0·014	0·015
(7) Indirect taxes (net)	0·011	0·020	0·010	0·014	0·004	0·005
(8) Rest of world						
Commodity transactions	0·069	0·028	0·107	0·024	0·181	0·018
Other	—	—	—	—	—	—
Sub-total	0·364	0·421	0·251	0·195	0·199	0·048

Source: Pyatt, Roe *et al.* (1977), Chapter 5.

if labour incomes are to be assumed proportional to employment levels. It implies that the economy is working below capacity in all sectors. With these assumptions it is not unreasonable to assume prices fixed and that columns of $\mathbf{C}_n$ which relate to activities can be estimated by columns of $\mathbf{A}_n$.

In aggregate, the above arguments imply that $\mathbf{A}_n$ is equal to $\mathbf{C}_n$ (and similarly for $\mathbf{A}_l$ and $\mathbf{C}_l$) except for the data in Table 4. These arguments also illustrate the fact that to estimate $\mathbf{C}_n$, and hence $\mathbf{M}_c$, it is only necessary to estimate a SAM and those income elasticities which are different from unity.

IV. DECOMPOSITIONS OF THE FIXED-PRICE MULTIPLIERS

A further implication of the discussion in the previous section is that the patterns of zero and non-zero entries in partitions of $\mathbf{C}_n$ and $\mathbf{A}_n$ are the same. Hence the fixed-price multiplier matrix can be decomposed into a transfer effects multiplier, $\mathbf{M}_{c1}$; an open-loop multiplier matrix, $\mathbf{M}_{c2}$; and a closed-loop multiplier matrix, $\mathbf{M}_{c3}$. Furthermore, these effects can be expressed multiplicatively as

$$\mathbf{M}_c = \mathbf{M}_{c3}\mathbf{M}_{c2}\mathbf{M}_{c1} \tag{28}$$

or in Stone's additive form[1]

$$\mathbf{M}_c = \mathbf{I} + (\mathbf{M}_{c1} - \mathbf{I}) + (\mathbf{M}_{c2} - \mathbf{I})\mathbf{M}_{c1} + (\mathbf{M}_{c3} - \mathbf{I})\mathbf{M}_{c2}\mathbf{M}_{c1}. \tag{29}$$

With prices fixed, the differences between corresponding elements of $\mathbf{M}_a$ and $\mathbf{M}_c$ must be due to income effects. This can be formalised by writing from (24)

$$dy_n = \mathbf{C}_n dy_n + d\mathbf{x} \tag{24}$$

$$= (\mathbf{C}_n - \mathbf{A}_n)dy_n + \mathbf{A}_n dy_n + d\mathbf{x} \tag{30}$$

$$= (\mathbf{I} - \mathbf{A}_n)^{-1}[(\mathbf{C}_n - \mathbf{A}_n)dy_n + d\mathbf{x}]$$

$$= \mathbf{M}_a(\mathbf{C}_n - \mathbf{A}_n)dy_n + \mathbf{M}_a d\mathbf{x}$$

$$= [\mathbf{I} - \mathbf{M}_a(\mathbf{C}_n - \mathbf{A}_n)]^{-1} \mathbf{M}_a d\mathbf{x}$$

$$= \mathbf{M}_y \mathbf{M}_a \, d\mathbf{x} \tag{31}$$

where

$$\mathbf{M}_y = [\mathbf{I} - \mathbf{M}_a(\mathbf{C}_n - \mathbf{A}_n)]^{-1} \tag{32}$$

and

$$\mathbf{M}_y \mathbf{M}_a = \mathbf{M}_c. \tag{33}$$

Thus the income effects can be captured in a matrix $\mathbf{M}_y$ which transforms the accounting multiplier matrix $\mathbf{M}_a$ into a fixed-price multiplier matrix $\mathbf{M}_c$. However, $\mathbf{M}_y$ itself is not a multiplier matrix because, as can be seen from (32), elements of $\mathbf{M}_y$ can be negative since elements of $\mathbf{C}_n$ can be less than the corresponding elements of $\mathbf{A}_n$, i.e. income elasticities can be less than one. In our example, the matrix $\mathbf{M}_y$ is particularly simple. Since only households have income elasticities which differ from one, it is only in the columns for households that $\mathbf{M}_y$ differs from an identity matrix.

---

[1] Tabular results are available on request from the authors.

V. EMPIRICAL RESULTS

A number of general points as well as particular features of the Sri Lanka economy in 1970 can be illustrated from the empirical results. Of the general features it can be noted from Table 3 that the columns for factors contain little information that is not included in the detail for institutions. With respect to labour, this is partly because there is a one-to-one relationship between types of labour and types of household, and partly because the basic SAM shown as Table 1 does not record any transfers between household types. Similarly, for public capital, all income goes directly to state corporations. From there it all leaks out immediately from the endogenous accounts, so that the columns for public capital and state corporations have a particularly simple structure.

Diagonal blocks of matrices $M_{a2}M_{a1}$ and $M_{c2}M_{c1}$ record the non-zero elements of the transfer matrices M_{a1} and M_{c1}. Given our assumptions, these are identical. Results for the simple Leontief inverse indicate that inter-industry linkages are weak in Sri Lanka except for the dependence of 'Other agriculture' on demands from 'Food processing'. In contrast, Table 3 shows that much stronger linkages are involved when the full circular flow illustrated in Fig. 1 is taken into account.

A general feature of Table 3 is the relative constancy of the multipliers along rows of the tables. For example, an injection of 100 units into any activity other than Services results in a fixed-price multiplier effect on Services which lies within the relatively narrow range of 58 to 83 units. The implication is that second- and third-order effects are largely independent of the structure of demand.[1]

This homogeneity of higher-order effects is important for the structure of employment and income distribution. Table 3 shows that whichever activity might be expanded, Urban labour income expands by 24 to 26 per cent of the size of the injection, unless the injection is into Services, where the multiplier is 0·41. Similarly, over the range of six activities, the multiplier for Rural wage income lies between a low of 0·40 (for Other Manufactures) and 0·74 (for Other Agriculture). For Estate Labour there is an exception to this rule: an injection into Tea and Rubber has a multiplier of 0·52 for Estate Labour but otherwise is 0·01, 0·02 or 0·03.

This general pattern of results is the consequence of linkages within the economy, or the lack of them, as seen through the original choice of SAM classifications in Table 1. The estate sector and the activity 'Tea and rubber' are largely independent of what goes on elsewhere in the economy, while other sectors are much more closely integrated.

Table 5 sets out some examples of the particular method of decomposition which is described in this paper. The format shows the additive decomposition of fixed price multipliers in the last four columns, and of the accounting multipliers in the first four columns. The central column then shows the income

---

[1] A similar phenomenon is observed by Stone (1978a) for the United Kingdom. It can be traced back through the structure of the multipliers to the fact that different household types have similar expenditure patterns.

Table 5

Illustrations of Multiplier Decomposition

Account in which injection originates	Account affected by the injection	Accounting multiplier effects						Income effects, $(M_y - I) M_a$	Fixed-price multiplier effects				
		Initial Injection, I	Transfer effects, $M_{a1} - I$	O-L effects, $(M_{a3} - I) M_{a1}$	C-L effects, $(M_{a2} - I) M_{a3} M_{a1}$	Sub-total, M_a			Sub-total, M_c	C-L effects, $(M_{c2} - I) M_{c3} M_{c1}$	O-L effects, $(M_{c3} - I) M_{c1}$	Transfer effects, $M_{c1} - I$	Initial injection, I
(1) Tea and rubber	Tea and rubber	100	2	—	2	102	1		101	1	—	2	100
(2)	Other agriculture	—	1	—	59	61	1		62	60	—	1	—
(3)	Food processing	—	—	8	32	33	5		38	37	8	—	—
(4)	Urban households	—	—	25	31	39	6		45	37	25	—	—
(5)	Rural households	—	—	50	78	103	10		113	88	50	—	—
(6)	Estate households	—	—	—	3	53	*		53	3	—	—	—
(7) Other agriculture	Other agriculture	100	5	—	57	162	−9		153	48	—	5	100
(8)	Food processing	—	—	—	31	32	−1		31	30	—	—	—
(9)	Other manufactures	—	4	—	36	40	14		54	50	—	4	—
(10)	Urban households	—	—	17	31	48	3		51	34	17	—	—
(11)	Rural households	—	—	68	77	145	1		146	78	68	—	—
(12)	Estate households	—	—	2	2	4	*		4	2	2	—	—

Continued overleaf

Table 5 Continued

	Services					Urban households				
(13) Other agriculture	2	—	52	54	-9	45	43	—	—	—
(14) Food processing	1	—	29	30	-2	28	27	—	—	—
(15) Other manufactures	5	31	34	39	11	50	45	—	5	—
(16) Urban households	—	52	29	60	2	62	31	—	—	—
(17) Rural households	—	1	71	123	*	123	71	—	—	—
(18) Estate households	—	*	3	4	*	4	3	—	—	—
(19) Tea and rubber	—	—	1	1	*	1	*	1	—	—
(20) Other agriculture	—	22	31	53	-15	38	24	14	—	—
(21) Food processing	—	11	17	28	-6	22	15	7	—	—
(22) Other manufactures	—	16	22	37	5	42	25	17	—	—
(23) Services	—	33	36	69	3	72	37	35	—	—
(24) Urban labour	—	9	10	19	*	9	10	9	—	—
(25) Rural labour	—	17	21	38	-4	34	19	15	—	—
(26) Estate labour	—	1	1	2	-1	1	*	1	—	—
(27) Urban households	100	—	32	132	-1	131	31	—	—	100
(28) Rural households	—	—	77	77	-9	68	68	—	—	—
(29) Estate households	—	—	3	3	-1	2	2	—	—	—

* Absolute value less than 1.
O–L, Open-loop. C–L, Closed loop.

effects that link accounting and fixed-price multipliers, given the assumed fixed-price model.

The first three rows of Table 5 show the decomposition of an injection of 100 units into the tea and rubber sector on itself. There are virtually no multiplier effects since tea and rubber are not large items in endogenous expenditures for any group. In Table 4, tea is shown to be an inferior good, and this fact leads to a fixed-price multiplier that is smaller than the accounting multiplier. In contrast, the second and third rows of Table 5 show that an injection into Tea and Rubber has a transfer effect on the sectors Other Agriculture and Food Processing which derives from the input–output inverse $(I - A_{33})^{-1}$. Also, there are substantial closed-loop effects: the extra income in Tea and Rubber is spent in ways which result, through the closed-loop, in extra demands on Other Agriculture and Food Processing. These extra demands are larger with the fixed-price multipliers than with the accounting multiplier. This is because, in Table 4, leakages are a decreasing fraction of income for the estate households who are the main element in the first link of the multiplier chain which starts with an injection into Tea and Rubber.

The next three rows of Table 5 (rows 4 to 6) show how households are affected by injections into Tea and Rubber. The open-loop effects primarily benefit estate households. But the lack of linkage of this sector to the rest of the economy implies negligible closed-loop effects for them: the closed-loop effects essentially benefit urban and rural households. The closed-loop effects are again greater according to the fixed-price model than they are according to the accounting multipliers.

Rows 7 to 12 of Table 5 show similar results for an injection into the production sector Other Agriculture. Engel's Law as captured in Table 4 is now sufficiently strong for the fixed-price multipliers to be less than the accounting multipliers in rows 7 and 8. In row 9, the fact that Other Manufactures are superior goods leads to a relatively large increase in the multiplier as we move from M_a to M_c. It can be noted that the closed-loop effects on household incomes in rows 10 to 12 are very similar to those in rows 4 to 6 and in rows 16 to 18. Similarly, the closed-loop effects on other activities in rows 7 to 9 are essentially replicated when the initial injection is into Services, as in rows 13 to 15, or into Tea and Rubber, as in rows 2 and 3.

In Table 4, leakages in aggregate are a declining fraction of income for rural and estate households, largely because of the food composition of Sri Lanka imports. The results for urban households in rows 19 to 29 of Table 5 are therefore more typical of what might be found in economies with a higher degree of self-sufficiency in basic foods and where institutions like Sri Lanka's free rice rations are non-existent. These last examples show that the fixed-price multipliers are smaller than accounting multipliers as a general result. Exceptions are for the superior elements of demand, viz. Other Manufactures and Services. It is to be noted that an injection into the Urban Household sector does next to nothing for the Estate sector, but the impact on rural activities and incomes is considerable.

VI. CONCLUSIONS

In this paper we have been concerned with the structure of simple models from various perspectives. From one perspective we have been concerned with the sequential extension of models from a simple Leontief input–output base, to open-loop models, and hence to closed loops. The novelty here is to consider simultaneously the three possible open-loop models in a triangular system, and to show how the multiplier matrix for a model at one stage in this chain of development is obtained as the product of a new multiplier matrix and the multiplier matrix which maintained at the previous stage. This illustrates how complexity in model formulation can be built up sequentially. More innovative is our separate recognition of factors, institutions and activities, with each being disaggregated into several types so that household income distribution, the structure of production and the factoral distribution of income are all interwoven in the scheme.

From another perspective, the analysis here illustrates the approach to model building which starts with a SAM and hence with the structure of an economy at some base date.[1] The accounting multipliers described here give insight into the anatomy of this structure in terms of transfer effects and the full circular and cross-effects between different parts of the economy, corresponding to the circular flow of income which characterises the multiplier process. Our analysis shows that this decomposition of structure can be derived directly from accounting balances. An integral part of it is to show how the structure of production and income distribution are interrelated, and how they derive from the structure of exogenous demand and the distribution of assets.

The analysis also shows the extent to which initial structure is important in determining the impact of changes in demand. Under the assumption that prices are fixed, incremental changes will follow a different pattern to that of the accounting balances only in so far as income elasticities for the outlays of endogenous accounts differ from their average value of unity.

The fixed-price multipliers discussed here represent only a single step beyond the structure of accounting balances. Subsequent steps could embrace the interaction of price changes and shifts in exogenous demand, including variations in the exchange rate and in factor prices. Similarly, investment demands might be modified in the light of savings patterns, capacity utilisation and the flow of funds. These and other developments could, in principle, be built on the foundations laid in this paper, which therefore constitute a beginning. But the starting point and the first step are important. The way they are formulated here is in terms of the accounting structure of the circular flow of income and its modification by allowing for income effects. These already cover a wide class of models in actual use, which our analysis extends by embracing the distribution of income among different types of households and the structure of asset ownership, both among these household types and between them and other

---

[1] This is, of course, the tradition of the Cambridge Growth Project. See Cambridge, Department of Applied Economics (1962–74).

institutions. Thus, for example, our results on fixed-price multipliers could have been presented as the results of a model with the following specifications: (i) Leontief technology for intermediate inputs, with complementary imports at prices which are set exogenously; (ii) Cobb–Douglas production functions, with firms setting prices as a constant mark-up on material costs and hiring factors so as to minimise variable costs; (iii) wages set so as to clear labour markets; and (iv) household consumption patterns given by linear expenditure systems. Such assumptions are among the variants with which the results in Table 3 are consistent. It seems to us much more helpful to see these results for what they are, namely, a SAM structure modified by allowing consumer demand elasticities to be different from unity. Not least, this brings out the importance of structure, as given by the SAM, in determining results, and the incremental adjustments which follow from allowing behaviour to be different at the margin from what it is on average.

Development Research Centre, World Bank GRAHAM PYATT
University of Warwick JEFFERY I. ROUND

Date of receipt of final typescript: February 1979

REFERENCES

Adelman, I. and Robinson, S. (1978). *Income Distribution Policy in Developing Countries: A Case Study of Korea.* Oxford University Press.
Bell, C., Devarajan, S., Hazell, P. and Slade, R. (1976). 'A social accounts analysis of the structure of the Muda regional economy.' (Mimeo) Development Research Center, World Bank.
Cambridge, Department of Applied Economics (1962–74). *A Programme for Growth*, vols. 1–12. Chapman and Hall.
Dervis, K. and Robinson, S. (1978). 'The foreign exchange gap, growth and industrial strategy in Turkey: 1973–1983.' World Bank Staff Working Paper no. 306, The World Bank, Washington, D.C.
Desai, P. (1961). 'A short-term planning model for the Indian economy.' *Review of Economics and Statistics*, vol. 43, no. 2, pp. 193–200.
Greenfield, C. C. (1978). 'The 1974/75 social accounting matrix for Botswana.' Paper presented at World Bank Conference on Social Accounting Methods in Development Planning, Cambridge, UK, 16–21 April, 1978.
Gupta, S. (1977). *A Model for Income Distribution, Employment, and Growth: A Case Study of Indonesia.* World Bank Occasional Paper no. 24, Johns Hopkins University Press.
Lancaster, K. J. (1968). *Mathematical Economics.* Macmillan, London.
Maton, J., Paukert, F. and Skolka, J. (1978). *Redistribution of Income Patterns of Consumption and Employment: A Case Study for the Philippines*, ILO, Geneva.
Pyatt, G. with J. Bharier, R. M. Lindley, R. Mabro and Y. Sabolo (1972). 'Methodology for macroeconomic projections.' (Mimeo.) Comprehensive Employment Strategy Mission to Iran, Working Paper no. 12, Geneva.
—— and Roe, A. R. with R. M. Lindley, J. I. Round and others (1977). *Social Accounting for Development Planning: with Special Reference to Sri Lanka.* Cambridge University Press.
—— and Round, J. I. *et al.* (1974). 'Swaziland as perceived in a social accounting framework.' Unpublished report prepared for the Swaziland Government.
—— and Round, J. I. (1977). 'Social accounting matrices for development planning', *Review of Income and Wealth*, Series 23, No. 4, pp. 339–64.
—— —— (1978). 'The distribution of income and social accounts: a study of Malaysia in 1970.' (Mimeo), Development Research Center, World Bank.
Quesnay F. (1758). *Tableau Economique.* Reproduced in facsimile with an introduction by H. Higgs by the British Economic Society, 1895.

Stone, J. R. N. (1978a). 'The disaggregation of the household sector in the national accounts.' Paper presented at World Bank Conference on Social Accounting Methods in Development Planning, Cambridge, UK, 16–21 April 1978.

—— (1978b). 'Multipliers for Quesnay's Tableau.' Paper prepared for World Bank Conference on Social Accounting Methods in Development Planning, Cambridge, UK, 16–21 April 1978.

[23]

Macroeconomic Structure and Computable General Equilibrium Models

Sherman Robinson, *University of California, Berkeley*

David W. Roland-Holst, *Mills College*

Economy-wide analysis can be undertaken within three different accounting frameworks: (1) the national income and product accounts, which focus on balance among macroaggregates; (2) the input–output accounts, which focus on intermediate flows and on the sectoral composition of production and demand; and (3) the social accounting matrix (SAM), which provides a framework incorporating both national income and product as well as input–output information. All three of these frameworks have been used to develop fixed coefficient, linear multiplier models. Keynesian multipliers at the macro level have multisectoral counterparts in the input–output model and "multi-institutional" counterparts in SAM-based models. These linear multiplier models tend to be completely demand driven and do not incorporate supply constraints or substitution possibilities. Computable general equilibrium (CGE) models have been developed which capture nonlinear substitution possibilities and multisectoral supply–demand interactions, and also incorporate macro variables and mechanisms for achieving balance among aggregates. "Marginal" multipliers can be derived for CGE models using the Jacobian matrix of partial derivatives at a given equilibrium. This paper develops an approach to analyzing Jacobian multipliers from a CGE model that decomposes macro, sectoral, and institutional linkages in a SAM framework. We give an illustration of SAM–multiplier decomposition using a small CGE model of the United States.

1. INTRODUCTION

Economics has long struggled with problems of reconciling analysis at different levels of aggregation. Macroeconomic models, based on national income and product accounts, focus upon problems of achieving balance among aggregates. A second approach, input–output analysis, has traditionally focused on intermediate flows and on the sectoral composition of production and demand. More recently, computable general equilibrium (CGE) models have been developed that are Walrasian and multisectoral, but that also

---

Address correspondence to Sherman Robinson, Department of Agriculture and Resource Economics, University of California, Berkeley, CA 94720.

Journal of Policy Modeling 10(3):353–375 (1988)   353
© Society for Policy Modeling, 1988   0161-8938/88/$3.50

incorporate macro variables and mechanisms for achieving balance among aggregates. CGE models rely on the social accounts framework and the social accounting matrix (SAM) to capture national income and product as well as input–output information. The advent of these models has intensified the study of macroeconomic "closure," or the reconciliation of the macroeconomic and multisectoral perspectives.

Fixed coefficient, linear multiplier models have been used in all three of these frameworks. Keynesian multipliers at the macro level have multisectoral counterparts in the input–output model and "multi-institutional" counterparts in SAM-based models. These linear multiplier models tend to be completely demand driven and do not incorporate supply constraints or substitution possibilities. In practice, they are usually based on average coefficients computed from accounting data, although it has long been recognized that, could they be estimated, marginal coefficients would be more congruent with the underlying economic theory.

It is possible to compute marginal multipliers with CGE models using the Jacobian matrix of partial derivatives at a given equilibrium. This Jacobian matrix provides a linear local approximation of the responsiveness of the endogenous variables in the model to changes in the exogenous variables. A multiplier model based on such approximate marginal coefficients can provide a convenient way to analyze the causal chains by which exogenous forces work their way through the economic system.

This paper develops an approach to analyzing Jacobian multipliers that decomposes macro, sectoral, and institutional linkages in a SAM framework. First the Jacobian multipliers and associated decomposition for a theoretical CGE model are discussed, then linkage decompositions in a SAM-based macromodel. Finally, we give an illustration of the multiplier decomposition and macro linkages with a small CGE model of the United States.

2. MULTIPLIERS FROM COMPUTABLE GENERAL EQUILIBRIUM MODELS

The main objective of the proposed methodology is to analyze the complex linkages among economic agents that are characteristic of a general equilibrium system. These linkages are components of an elaborate network of price-mediated market interactions. For this discussion, we use a very general specification of a CGE

GENERAL EQUILIBRIUM MODELS 355

model which takes the form of a continuously differentiable function

$$y = F(x,y), \tag{1}$$

where y denotes a vector of endogenous variables and x denotes a vector of exogenous variables.[1]

Starting from an equilibrium, the dependence of the endogenous variables upon the exogenous variables can be analyzed by total differentiation:

$$dy = D_x F(x,y)dx + D_y F(x,ydy). \tag{2}$$

Solving this equation yields the multiplier model

$$
\begin{aligned}
dy &= [I - D_y F(x,y)]^{-1} D_x F(x,y)dx \\
&= [I - D_y F(x,y)]^{-1} \Delta x \\
&= M \Delta x,
\end{aligned}
\tag{3}
$$

where $\Delta x = D_x F(x,y)dx$. This multiplier model captures the equilibrium dependence of the endogenous variables upon one another as well as upon exogenous shocks. It is common in policy analysis to focus attention upon a subset of the endogenous variables of immediate interest. Such a partial approach ignores indirect linkages involving other endogenous variables and may not adequately capture equilibrium relationships.

To assess the significance of these omitted linkages, consider a partition of the endogenous variables into two sets, a vector y denoting those variables of interest and z consisting of the remaining endogenous variables. The multiplier expression above must now be derived from the simultaneous equations

$$dy = D_{yx} F(x,y,z)dx + D_{yy} F(x,y,z)dy + D_{yz} F(x,y,z)dz \tag{4}$$

$$dz = D_{zx} F(x,y,z)dx + D_{zy} F(x,y,z)dy + D_{zz} F(x,y,z)dz, \tag{5}$$

where, for example, $D_{yx} F(x,y,z) = D_{yx}$ denotes the matrix of partial derivatives $[\delta y_i/\delta x_j]$. These multipliers take the form

$$
\begin{aligned}
dy &= [I - (D_{yy} + D_{yz}(I - D_{zz})^{-1} D_{zy})]^{-1} \\
&\quad [D_{yx} + D_{yz}(I - D_{zz})^{-1} D_{zx}] \, dx = M_y \Delta x
\end{aligned}
\tag{6}
$$

---

[1] A general equilibrium model, of course, can be specified under far weaker assumptions; however, these assumptions are required to support the Jacobian analysis and are characteristic of nearly all applied CGE models.

$$dz = [I - (D_{zz} + D_{zy}(I - D_{yy})^{-1}D_{yz})]^{-1}$$
$$+ [D_{zx}(I - D_{yy})^{-1}D_{yx}]dx \qquad (7)$$
$$= M_z\Delta x.$$

The matrix M_y above represents the multiplier term of immediate interest. It is apparent, however, that this matrix is generally not equivalent to its restricted counterpart $[I - D_{yy}]^{-1}$, which ignores general equilibrium linkages working through other endogenous variables.

To illustrate the role of omitted endogenous variables, consider a standard input–output or SAM multiplier model. Assume that y consists of quantity variables, and z represents prices. The standard input–output or SAM multipliers consist of $[I - D_{yy}]^{-1}$ and ignore any linkages that work through variations in prices. Such linkages are represented by the off-diagonal blocks D_{yz} and D_{zy} in equation 6 above. Such models are used to analyze the impact of quantity shocks, thus assuming D_{zx} is zero (e.g., there is no direct effect on prices). In this case, an examination of the expression for dy indicates that the omitted endogenous variables (i.e., prices) can safely be ignored if either D_{yz} or D_{xy} equals zero. That is, the shock does not affect prices or changes in prices do not affect real variables. The traditional assumption is that prices are fixed (hence the term fixed-price multipliers).

3. MODELING MACROECONOMIC LINKAGES IN A SAM FRAMEWORK

3.1. A SAM-Based Macroeconomic Model

To focus discussion on macroeconomic and sectoral structure, consider now a partition of the endogenous variables based on the social accounting matrix (SAM). The basic aggregate macroeconomic accounts are represented by five balance equations

$$Y = C + Z + G + E - M \qquad (8)$$
$$Y = C + S^H + T \qquad (9)$$
$$Z = S^H + S^G + F \qquad (10)$$
$$S^G = T - G \qquad (11)$$
$$F = M - E, \qquad (12)$$

where Y = GNP, C = consumption, Z = investment, G = government expenditure, E = exports, M = imports, S^H = household savings, T = taxes, and F = balance of trade. These macro equations can be grouped into a macro SAM as in Figure 1. The entry A represents total intermediate flows, which are netted out of the macro balance equations. A SAM is always square, with the receipt row and ex-

GENERAL EQUILIBRIUM MODELS 357

		Expenditures			
Receipts	(1)	(2)	(3)	(4)	(5)
1. Suppliers	A	C	Z	G	E
2. Households	Y	0	0	0	0
3. Capital Account	0	S^H	0	S^G	F
4. Government	0	T	0	0	0
5. Rest of the World	M	0	0	0	0

Figure 1. A macroeconomic social accounting matrix.

penditure column for each account balancing. Thus any economic model based on the SAM satisfies Walras' Law. The five equations above state the summing up properties of the SAM; column sums equal row sums.

3.2. SAM Multipliers

Multiplier modeling is an area of SAM applications undergoing rapid expansion.[2] Following the approach of input–output models, a linear multiplier model can be constructed by assuming that all the expenditure (column) coefficients in the SAM are constant. Since the SAM is square and the columns sum into unity, the resulting coefficient matrix is singular. In terms of equation 6 above, no exogenous variables x have yet been defined and D_{yy} is a singular matrix. The standard approach is to partition the SAM by designating some accounts as exogenous. This generates a full-rank submatrix D_{yy} of SAM coefficients. The corresponding D_{yx} matrix consists of columns representing newly exogenous accounts. The omitted rows for these accounts define additional variables, still endogenous, whose links with the other endogenous variables have been broken. In effect, D_{yz} has been defined as zero by choice of the exogenous variables. In most applications, it has been customary to designate capital accounts, government, and the rest of the world as exogenous, while sectoral production, factor returns, and household incomes are designated as endogenous. In the present case, capital accounts are kept endogenous to capture the role of the savings–investment balance in the determination of national income,[3] whereas sectoral government expenditure and exports are

---

[2] For examples, see Pyatt and Round (1985) and Stone (1981).

[3] This convention is used in Robinson and Roland-Holst (1987), where it is argued that this closure corresponds to revealed macro policy since about 1980.

treated as exogenous. Sectoral government revenue and imports remain endogenous but are omitted from the multiplier analysis; they are treated as "leakages" from the SAM model. No linkage is directly modeled for these accounts.[4]

The remaining, endogenous variables for this model consist of sectoral sales, incomes by household, and total savings. The variables are categorized as

$$y = [Y^s, Y'', Z] \text{ and } x = [G, E]. \tag{13}$$

These modeling conventions lead to the linear, constant coefficient multiplier model

$$dy = M \, dx \tag{14}$$
$$= (I - S)^{-1},$$

where the matrix S corresponds to the column-normalized coefficients of the SAM tableau in Figure 1.

3.3. Decomposition of Macro Effects

The macro effects captured by the multiplier matrix can be decomposed into various elements reflecting different types of linkages in the economy.[5] The endogenous accounts are partitioned into two groups. The first includes factor and product markets, the real side of the economy, and consists of supplier and household accounts. The first partitioned square block on the main diagonal represents physical production, income generation, and the feedback through household consumption expenditure. The second group captures financial flows and, in this case, consists only of the capital account, representing the loanable-funds market which channels savings into demand for investment goods. These conventions lead to the additive decomposition

$$S = S_1 + S_2 = \begin{bmatrix} A & C & 0 \\ Y & 0 & 0 \\ 0 & 0 & 0 \end{bmatrix} + \begin{bmatrix} 0 & 0 & Z \\ 0 & 0 & 0 \\ 0 & S'' & 0 \end{bmatrix}, \tag{15}$$

where the letters A, Y, and so on now denote coefficient matrices. After some algebraic manipulation,[6] equations 14 and 15 yield a decomposition of the SAM multipliers as

---

[4]There is of course a macro consistency linkage since the model is based on normalized column coefficients.

[5]See again Pyatt and Round (1985) and Stone (1981).

[6]See Robinson and Roland-Holst (1987) for details.

GENERAL EQUILIBRIUM MODELS 359

$$dy = M\,dx = M_3 M_2 M_1 dx, \qquad (16)$$

where

$$M_1 - \begin{bmatrix} \mu_1 & (I-A)^{-1}C\mu_2 & 0 \\ Y\mu_1 & \mu^2 & 0 \\ 0 & 0 & I \end{bmatrix} \qquad (17)$$

$$M_2 = \begin{bmatrix} I & 0 & \mu_1 Z \\ 0 & I & Y\mu_1 Z \\ 0 & S'' & I \end{bmatrix} \qquad (18)$$

$$M_3 = \begin{bmatrix} I & \mu_1 Z S'' \lambda_1 & 0 \\ 0 & \lambda_1 & 0 \\ 0 & 0 & \lambda_2 \end{bmatrix} \qquad (19)$$

The μ and λ terms denote reduced-form multiplier linkages for the real and financial sides of the endogenous economy, namely

$$\mu_1 = [I - (A + CY)]^{-1} \qquad (20)$$

$$\mu_2 = [I - Y(I-A)^{-1}C]^{-1} \qquad (21)$$

$$\lambda_1 = [I - Y\mu_1 Z S'']^{-1} \qquad (22)$$

$$\lambda_2 = [I - S''Y\mu_1 Z]^{-1}. \qquad (23)$$

The first two terms represent Keynesian income and expenditure multipliers. For example, in a model with one sector, one household, and no interindustry flows or imports ($A = M = 0$ and $Y = 1$); these terms are very familiar as $\mu_1 = \mu_2 = 1/(1-\text{MPC})$, where MPC is the marginal propensity to consume. The second pair of terms denotes the closed-loop multipliers acting through the savings–investment balance. These represent processes that are also quite Keynesian in nature, but they are omitted from multiplier studies when capital accounts are made exogenous.

In models with many sectors and household categories, the factor matrices of the decomposition capture complex production–income–consumption–savings–investment linkages. While the multiplicative decomposition elucidates the pattern of transmission linkages in the macroeconomy, net multiplier effects of exogenous shocks are better assessed with an additive decomposition of the form[7]

---

[7]This additive decomposition is similar to one proposed by Pyatt and Round (1979) and Stone (1981), but they decompose total rather than net multipliers.

$$dy - dx = (M - I)dx = [N_1 + N_2 + N_3]dx, \tag{24}$$

where $N_1 = (M_1 - I)$, $N_2 = (M_2 - I)M_1$, and $N_3 = (M_3 - I)M_2 M_1$.

4. MACROECONOMIC LINKAGES IN A CGE FRAMEWORK

To develop a macroeconomic framework that takes fuller account of equilibrium relationships, we can combine the CGE model of section 2 with the social accounting variables of section 3 above. This allows direct comparison between general equilibrium and Keynesian multiplier estimates. Consider the subset of endogenous variables representing the macro variables of section 3, that is $y = [Y^S, Y^H, Z]$, and the multiplier model of equation 6 above, namely

$$\begin{aligned} dy &= D_{yx}F(x,y,z)dx + D_{yy}F(x,y,z)dy + D_{yz}F(x,y,z)dz \\ &= [I - (D_{yy} + D_{yz}(I-D_{zz})^{-1}D_{zy})]^{-1} \\ &\quad [D_{yx} + D_{yz}(I-D_{zz})^{-1}D_{zx}]dx \\ &= M\Delta x \\ &= (I-J)^{-1}\Delta x. \end{aligned} \tag{25}$$

In terms of the macroeconomic endogenous variables, the Jacobian J corresponds to the average expenditure coefficients of the linear model of equation (15):

$$J = D_{yy} + D_{yz}(I-D_{zz})^{-1}D_{zy} = \begin{bmatrix} A & C & Z \\ Y & H & K \\ S^s & S^h & S^z \end{bmatrix}, \tag{26}$$

where

- A denotes an "activity" matrix of marginal intermediate input requirements,
- C is a consumption matrix of sectoral marginal consumption propensities for each household group,
- Z is a vector of sectoral marginal investment coefficients,
- Y is a matrix of sectoral marginal value added coefficients (one category per household group),
- H is a matrix of marginal interhousehold transfers,
- K is a matrix of marginal "financial income" coefficients,

S^S, S^H are vectors of marginal savings rates, and
S^Z is a scalar representing gross financial flows.[8]

The matrix decomposition of M now follows precisely as in the previous section.[9] Important differences can be expected to arise between the Keynesian and CGE multiplier matrices and their components. Differences in the M matrices result largely from the nature of the underlying models: demand-driven Keynesian versus general equilibrium. These fall into two major categories. First, differences in the qualitative response of the models will lead to significant qualitative differences in the impacts of exogenous forces. The lack of supply constraints in the Keynesian case and the imposition of relatively elaborate equilibrium constraints in the other case lead to quite different direct and indirect effects, as will be seen in the numerical example of the next section.

A second, generally less significant source of divergence between the estimates is the higher degree of linkage complexity in the CGE model. Most SAM-based multiplier studies assume (and indeed rely upon) systematic sparsity in expenditure-income linkages. These are apparent in the SAM tableau of the macromodel in Figure 1. Note that the counterpart for the CGE model, the matrix J above, will generally be completely dense. The CGE linkages can be seen in Figure 2, a summary of the reduced-form macro multiplier terms. As is apparent from the example in Figure 2, the financial multiplier term, λ_{ij}, reflects extremely complex interactions. Despite this apparent complexity, however, the magnitude of their overall effect is small in full employment responses to exogenous shocks. This is demonstrated in the example of the next section.

5. AN APPLICATION TO THE UNITED STATES ECONOMY

This section presents an empirical example of the modeling and decomposition methods discussed above. The results reported here are based upon a CGE model of the U.S. economy. The model was im-

---

[8] In a model with disaggregated financial accounts, S^Z represents financial flows across accounts. In the present, single account specification, it is unity.

[9] It should be noted here that although this technique begins with general equilibrium information in the form of the matrix J, the decomposition calculations rely on linear, constant coefficient relationships and thus the decomposition itself is an approximation of the true Jacobian multiplier components.

Multiplier	SAM Model	CGE Model
μ_{11}	$[I - (A+CY)]^{-1}$	$[I - (A + C(I-H)^{-1}Y]^{-1}$
μ_{12}	$(I - A)^{-1}C\mu_2$	$(I - A)^{-1}C\mu_2$
μ_{21}	$Y\mu_1$	$(I - H)^{-1}Y\mu_1$
μ_{22}	$Y\mu_1 C$	$[I - (H + Y(I-A)^{-1}C]^{-1}$
λ_{11}	$[I - Y\mu_1 ZS^H]^{-1}$	

$$\{I - (\mu_{11}Z + \mu_{12}K)\mu_{33}(S^S + [S^{H-1}$$
$$(\mu_{21}Z + \mu_{22}K)\mu_{33}S^H]^{-1}(\mu_{21}Z + \mu_{22}K)\mu_{33}S^H)]\}^{-1}$$

Figure 2. Own-effect macro multiplier terms compared.

plemented with the generalized algebraic modeling system (GAMS)[10] and calibrated to data for 1982. This model was then used to generate the SAM in Table 1, which represents expenditure and income flows for 10 productive sectors, three household groups classified by income level, capital accounts, government, and the rest of the world. This SAM is produced by the CGE model for its base solution values and reconciles the observed 1982 input–output accounts with national income and product accounts for the same year.

Table 2 contains the generalized inverse multiplier matrix corresponding to the SAM (as in equation 14 above). These multipliers represent the (supply) unconstrained effects of exogenous injections upon sectoral sales, household incomes, and savings. A one-dollar injection to (column) agent i generates a total multiplier effect for (row) agent j of m_{ij}. These multipliers have been treated extensively elsewhere[11] and will not be elaborated here. They represent a natural disaggregation of their Keynesian counterparts, measuring demand-driven income generation in the absence of any capacity constraints.

A different perspective on the effects of exogenous shocks is provided by the results in Table 3. This table contains the Jacobian multiplier matrix derived in equation 25 above. Actual calculation of the Jacobian was done by numerical perturbation of the CGE model, with respect to the exogenous variables, around the base equilibrium solution.[12] The elements here correspond in a one-to-one manner to those in Table 2.

The most arresting feature of the Jacobian multiplier matrix is the prevalence of negative elements. It is traditional to view the multiplier

---

[10]See Meeraus (1985).

[11]See Robinson and Roland-Holst (1987).

[12]A more extensive discussion of the method is given in the Appendix.

363

Table 1. Social Accounting Matrix for the United States (1982, billions)

	1	2	3	4	5	6	7	8	9	10	11	12	13	14	15	16	Total
1 Dairy & Meat	12.9	2.1	0.6	53.4	0.1	0.0	0.0	0.0	0.1	1.6	1.8	2.7	1.8	0.4	0.4	0.2	78.0
2 Grains	21.5	4.9	0.2	19.6	0.1	0.0	0.0	0.0	0.1	0.9	0.1	0.4	0.4	-0.4	6.8	17.5	72.1
3 Other Agriculture	2.4	2.2	2.9	18.5	0.5	0.0	1.5	0.0	0.8	6.5	3.3	5.4	4.6	-0.2	1.1	1.8	51.4
4 Light Consumer	14.4	0.2	0.9	178.2	19.7	10.3	22.9	6.4	23.3	79.1	66.4	118.1	96.3	6.0	21.2	27.6	691.1
5 Basic Int	2.4	13.3	5.9	58.1	357.5	85.0	99.0	19.9	15.3	154.4	22.9	44.8	35.0	0.3	23.9	55.9	993.9
6 Capital Goods	0.8	1.0	0.7	3.8	18.4	128.1	22.0	7.7	2.0	28.1	9.9	29.2	31.0	132.5	69.3	80.2	564.9
7 Construction	0.6	0.9	1.0	4.1	16.5	3.0	0.6	0.6	5.1	58.6	0.0	0.0	0.0	228.4	80.3	0.0	399.8
8 Electric	0.1	0.3	0.1	2.8	2.4	14.8	3.7	7.2	2.9	18.1	11.5	26.2	24.0	4.7	13.1	15.4	147.5
9 Whl & Ret Trade	5.1	4.8	2.9	39.6	35.3	31.1	41.6	7.4	66.2	75.4	89.2	175.3	171.3	29.1	17.7	19.3	811.3
10 Services	6.0	4.7	3.3	70.6	120.1	53.3	52.4	14.1	172.8	382.9	234.3	403.3	384.7	14.0	416.5	130.5	2463.5
Industry Total	66.3	34.5	18.7	448.7	570.6	325.7	243.6	63.3	288.6	805.6	439.5	805.4	749.1	414.9	650.5	348.4	6273.2
11 Low 40% HH	0.8	3.1	2.3	15.1	23.0	13.6	12.1	4.2	35.9	121.7	0.0	0.0	0.0	0.0	210.0	-0.2	441.15
12 Med 40% HH	2.7	8.6	7.4	61.1	81.5	66.0	56.3	19.8	155.3	445.4	0.0	0.0	0.0	0.0	115.1	-0.5	1018.7
13 High 20% HH	3.3	11.7	9.2	67.1	95.8	66.3	57.6	20.1	164.7	515.0	0.0	0.0	0.0	0.0	63.2	-0.5	1073.4
HH Total	6.8	23.4	18.9	143.3	200.2	145.9	126.0	44.0	355.9	1082.0	0.0	0.0	0.0	0.0	388.3	-1.2	2533.6
14 Capital Acct	1.9	9.8	5.6	21.0	46.8	4.3	6.9	1.9	36.2	230.2	-18.8	56.9	97.4	0.0	-92.0	6.6	414.9
15 Government	2.3	4.3	3.6	34.4	60.3	28.1	23.3	7.9	139.3	263.8	20.7	156.5	226.9	0.0	183.2	-24.4	1129.9
16 Rest of World	0.7	0.1	4.6	43.7	116.0	61.0	0.0	30.4	-8.7	81.8	0.0	0.0	0.0	0.0	0.0	0.0	329.4
Total	78.0	72.1	51.4	691.1	993.9	564.9	399.8	147.5	811.3	2463.5	441.5	1018.7	1073.4	414.9	1129.9	329.4	10681.0

364

Table 2. SAM Multipliers

	1	2	3	4	5	6	7	8	9	10	11	12	13	14	Average
1 Dairy & Meat	1.289	0.089	0.062	0.175	0.043	0.044	0.055	0.044	0.049	0.052	0.071	0.060	0.053	0.054	0.153
2 Grains	0.406	1.115	0.038	0.107	0.026	0.026	0.033	0.026	0.029	0.031	0.042	0.036	0.031	0.031	0.141
3 Other Agriculture	0.091	0.067	1.091	0.074	0.027	0.027	0.037	0.026	0.032	0.034	0.045	0.038	0.034	0.033	0.118
4 Light Consumer	0.727	0.449	0.426	1.771	0.391	0.400	0.504	0.398	0.447	0.460	0.626	0.534	0.475	0.482	0.578
5 Basic Int	0.777	0.906	0.726	0.729	2.044	0.776	0.952	0.668	0.561	0.657	0.685	0.624	0.577	0.853	0.824
6 Capital Goods	0.342	0.373	0.330	0.298	0.297	1.545	0.366	0.300	0.287	0.326	0.307	0.322	0.319	0.734	0.439
7 Construction	0.314	0.349	0.312	0.273	0.267	0.230	1.267	0.210	0.266	0.312	0.254	0.272	0.274	0.807	0.386
8 Electric	0.084	0.089	0.079	0.080	0.071	0.104	0.091	1.116	0.081	0.087	0.106	0.099	0.092	0.105	0.163
9 Whl & Ret Trade	0.661	0.638	0.572	0.592	0.502	0.538	0.651	0.484	1.599	0.562	0.740	0.659	0.618	0.676	0.678
10 Services	1.434	1.408	1.283	1.357	1.254	1.257	1.458	1.142	1.460	2.421	1.863	1.578	1.463	1.421	1.486
Industry Totals	6.124	5.483	4.918	5.456	4.922	4.946	5.413	4.413	4.812	4.941	4.740	4.223	3.935	5.195	4.966
11 Low 40% HH	0.189	0.203	0.185	0.176	0.160	0.162	0.187	0.150	0.186	0.193	1.177	0.156	0.145	0.179	0.246
12 Med 40% HH	0.715	0.741	0.696	0.689	0.615	0.665	0.755	0.612	0.747	0.744	0.690	1.611	0.571	0.723	0.755
13 High 20% HH	0.813	0.858	0.794	0.769	0.693	0.725	0.830	0.668	0.823	0.836	0.771	0.681	1.636	0.793	0.835
HH Totals	1.717	1.801	1.675	1.634	1.468	1.552	1.772	1.429	1.756	1.773	2.638	2.448	2.351	1.695	1.837
14 Capital Acct	0.434	0.498	0.431	0.377	0.354	0.311	0.371	0.288	0.373	0.424	0.338	0.387	0.398	1.353	0.453

365

Table 3. Jacobian Multipliers

	1	2	3	4	5	6	7	8	9	10	11	12	13	14	Average
1 Dairy & Meat	1.089	-0.100	-0.049	0.089	-0.008	-0.012	-0.008	-0.012	-0.017	-0.015	0.005	0.002	-0.002	-0.016	0.068
2 Grains	0.296	0.828	-0.037	0.053	-0.005	-0.007	-0.005	-0.008	-0.010	-0.009	0.002	0.000	-0.002	-0.010	0.077
3 Other Agriculture	0.005	-0.031	0.535	0.010	-0.007	-0.011	-0.008	-0.011	-0.013	-0.011	-0.003	-0.005	-0.006	-0.012	0.031
4 Light Consumer	-0.114	-0.476	-0.305	1.007	-0.037	-0.049	-0.016	-0.059	-0.092	-0.079	0.084	0.060	0.038	-0.073	-0.008
5 Basic Int	-0.290	-0.103	-0.297	-0.307	0.731	-0.221	-0.179	-0.282	-0.511	-0.472	-0.378	-0.340	-0.335	-0.112	-0.221
6 Capital Goods	-0.131	-0.061	-0.140	-0.145	-0.098	0.994	-0.096	-0.079	-0.178	-0.194	-0.146	-0.056	-0.019	0.472	0.009
7 Construction	-0.045	-0.056	-0.074	-0.012	0.021	0.014	0.993	0.022	0.006	-0.028	-0.012	0.097	0.145	0.868	0.139
8 Electric	-0.018	-0.003	-0.022	-0.018	-0.015	0.005	-0.014	0.662	-0.024	-0.024	-0.004	0.006	0.009	0.046	0.042
9 Whl & Ret Trade	0.014	0.041	-0.088	-0.007	0.007	0.013	0.039	-0.058	0.869	-0.092	0.125	0.127	0.127	0.032	0.082
10 Services	-0.027	0.110	-0.188	-0.041	0.040	-0.007	0.000	-0.148	-0.082	0.696	0.344	0.255	0.232	-0.214	0.069
Industry Total	0.780	0.149	-0.664	0.629	0.630	0.719	0.706	0.026	-0.051	-0.226	0.017	0.148	0.188	0.981	0.288
11 Low 40% HH	-0.028	-0.015	-0.048	-0.006	0.007	0.014	0.012	-0.023	-0.009	0.002	0.998	0.000	0.001	-0.145	0.054
12 Med 40% HH	-0.109	-0.210	-0.119	0.004	-0.011	0.075	0.063	0.021	0.047	0.031	0.027	1.034	0.038	-0.184	0.050
13 High 20% HH	-0.113	-0.125	-0.142	-0.010	0.005	0.070	0.058	-0.037	0.006	0.018	0.008	0.017	1.022	-0.371	0.029
HH Total	-0.250	-0.349	-0.309	-0.012	0.001	0.159	0.133	-0.038	0.044	0.051	1.033	1.051	1.061	-0.699	0.134
14 Capital Acct	-0.123	-0.242	-0.163	-0.009	0.039	0.063	0.060	-0.023	0.080	-0.038	0.000	0.220	0.318	1.772	0.140

as a beneficent process by which the rewards of economic activity are spread throughout the economy. Even though these rewards are spread unevenly (see Table 2), the Keynesian multipliers generally register an incremental gain for all agents as a result of a transfer to any one. Such an expansive and benign view of the process of income generation may be justifiable from a demand-driven, fixed-price perspective. In a more general economic setting, however, capacity constraints and the price responses they activate will cause more complex adjustments in the equilibrium level and composition of output and income.

The qualitative features of the Jacobian multipliers reveal much about the equilibrium effects of exogenous shocks. It should be borne in mind that, with respect to a full employment equilibrium, an exogenous demand injection does not represent a windfall, but a contending claim on limited resources. Sometimes the adjustments in response to the shock will be beneficial to a given agent. This is the case for each direct recipient of an injection. As the diagonal elements in Table 2 indicate, the final effect on the original recipient is usually less than the initial injection. This contrasts with the Keynesian case, where the first round gains are always augmented by the asymptotic cycles of expenditure and income. The values for original recipients vary considerably, but in no case is the exogenous injection immiserising (i.e., $m_{ii} < 0$).[13]

To further contrst the general attributes of the two matrices, note the highly variegated nature of the Jacobian effects with respect to the origin of the shock. The columns of the SAM multiplier matrix are very similar except in their diagonal elements, indicating that the final net effect on a given agent is generally independent of the origin of the injection to the endogenous economy. This is definitely not the case with the Jacobian multipliers, which exhibit significant quantitative and qualitative differences based on origin of the shock. The difference apparently arises from the constant coefficients assumption. Maintaining constant expenditure patterns under a variety of exogenous shocks yields, in the demand-driven estimates of Table 2, an inevitable similarity in the pattern of outcomes.

Despite the positivity of the diagonal effects, about 60 percent of the elements in the Jacobian multiplier matrix are negative. These elements indicate detrimental effects upon others resulting from an exogenous (final demand) transfer to the Ith (column) agent. These effects operate through an elaborate system of market linkages and are

---

[13]Bearing in mind the country under study, note that this result may not generalize to others.

GENERAL EQUILIBRIUM MODELS   367

difficult to anticipate, but they can be interpreted in individual cases by reference to the equilibrium adjustment process. The prevalence of negative elements does not indicate the contentious nature of the underlying market mechanisms, however, and detailed analysis of individual cases supports this view.

Among the productive sectors, Jacobian multiplier relations are determined by direct (forward and backward) and indirect linkages. Strong backward linkages are generally beneficial, as in the case of the grains sector (2) benefiting ($m_{21} = 0.296$) from expansion in the dairy and meat sector (1). This is the largest positive cross-effect among industries. Forward linkages are generally detrimental to the forward industry (e.g., $m_{12} = -0.100$), since the new (exogenous) demand "appropriates" part of the output and drives up prices in the forward industry's input market.[14] A consistent example of this in the present case is the light consumer goods sector (4), which includes all processed food (see Table 1), and is adversely affected by new exogenous demand for any of the agricultural sector's output (row 4). Demand-side stimulus for the light consumer goods sector, however, is beneficial to all its agriculture suppliers (column 4). These results contrast sharply with the sign symmetry of the SAM multiplier estimates.

One might be tempted to generalize the above reasoning about forward and backward linkages, concluding for example that a sector with extensive forward linkages would benefit from injections to almost any sector. The basic intermediates sector appears to be a consistently significant benefactor in the demand-driven model (row 5 of Table 2) for just this reason, but the Jacobian multipliers give the opposite result. This apparent contradiction arises from the second component of intersectoral equilibrium linkages, competition for factors and intermediates. As has already been mentioned, the original recipient of the demand-side injection is induced to "appropriate" or bid away inputs from a full employment economy, and this will generally shrink output in other sectors that compete for these inputs. Extensive forward linkages for the basic intermediates sector are actually its own undoing. This industry's output is essential to expansion of all other industries (row 5, Table 1), but it is also the single largest consumer of its own output. Thus the forward linkage is outweighed by the appropriation effect, and it will inevitably be forced to shrink in the wake of the expanding sector.

---

[14]A concrete example of this would be higher beef prices resulting from government grain purchases for sale to the Soviet Union.

It is apparent from these few examples that sectoral equilibrium multipliers differ in important respects from their Keynesian counterparts. Although certain linkage relationships give rise to the beneficial interactions predicted by demand-driven models, capacity and resource limitations create a kind of commodity market crowding out, with price and substitution effects that can work to the disadvantatge of many agents.

Jacobian multipliers for households also require detailed inspection. The magnitudes of these multipliers are traceable to income and consumption effects. More significant is the role of the two sources of income, labor and capital services, and their price behavior in response to the exogenous shock. Low-income households are primarily labor owners, and the expansion of low-wage (agricultural) sectors in which they are extensively employed is detrimental to them. By contrast, the expansion of low-rental-rate sectors (agriculture again) is detrimental to high-income households. Middle-income households have mixed results. In the first five sectors, where they are underrepresented, their losses are generally between the low- and high-income groups. In the next five sectors, where they are more extensively represented, their gains exceed those of the other two groups.

The interhousehold multipliers are noteworthy in two respects. First, they exhibit large diagonal values. This is due to the concentration of their consumption in sectors in which they experience positive income effects. This type of linkage is discernable in the SAM consumption multipliers (columns 11–13), but is not accurately reflected in the sectoral income multipliers (rows 11–13) because wages and rentals are assumed constant. It is readily apparent in the corresponding Jacobian consumption and income multipliers, however. Also of interest in the interhousehold submatrix are the off-diagonal effects. Consumption effects dominate again in the adjustment process, and there are consequently no detrimental interhousehold linkages, although the beneficial effects are rather negligible.[15]

A detailed analysis of the multiplier decompositions developed in the previous sections is beyond the scope of this paper. A few comments are in order, however, regarding the composition of multiplier effects, especially as it differs bertween the SAM and Jacobian estimates. Table 4 represents a summary measure of the role of own-

---

[15]Again, these results may not generalize to a country with a large subsistence consumption population.

369

Table 4. SAM Own-Effect Shares of Net Multipliers, $(M_1 - I)_{ii}/(M - I)_{ii}$

	1	2	3	4	5	6	7	8	9	10	11	12	13	14
1 Dairy & Meat	94	78	72	91	67	72	73	74	70	67	81	75	70	0
2 Grains	98	90	74	92	69	73	74	75	71	69	82	75	71	0
3 Other Agriculture	88	82	88	87	68	72	75	73	71	69	82	75	71	0
Agri Average	93	83	78	90	68	72	74	74	71	68	82	75	71	0
4 Light Consumer	79	60	64	83	68	72	74	74	70	67	81	74	70	0
5 Basic Int	65	65	63	67	79	75	75	73	58	59	69	61	57	0
6 Capital Goods	31	27	29	31	35	69	45	48	30	29	40	35	32	0
7 Construction	18	15	18	18	21	19	17	18	16	19	21	15	13	0
8 Electric	60	56	57	63	61	77	68	81	64	62	75	70	66	0
9 Whl & Ret Trade	67	61	62	68	65	71	72	70	69	62	77	71	68	0
Industry Ave	53	48	49	55	55	64	59	61	51	50	61	54	51	0
10 Services	68	63	65	71	70	74	73	73	73	69	81	74	71	0
Sectoral Ave	67	60	59	67	60	67	65	66	59	57	69	62	59	0
11 Low 40% HH	70	68	69	72	71	75	74	75	74	71	75	67	64	0
12 Med 40% HH	68	64	67	71	69	75	74	75	73	70	74	66	63	0
13 High 20% HH	69	66	68	71	70	75	74	75	73	70	74	67	63	0
Househld Ave	69	66	68	71	70	75	74	75	73	70	74	67	63	0
14 Capital Acct	0	0	0	0	0	0	0	0	0	0	0	0	0	0

effects in the overall SAM multipliers.[16] This matrix consists of elements of the first component matrix of the additive net own effects, $N_1 = M_1 - I$, divided by the corresponding elements of the net overall multiplier matrix, $M - I$. These ratios measure the percentage of the total multiplier effect accounted for by own effects. Table 5 represents the corresponding measures for the Jacobian multipliers. In the latter case, most entries are positive, indicating that own effects operate in the same direction as overall effects (be these positive or negative). A negative entry indicates that the two effects are countervailing, which is impossible in the SAM case but plausible in a general equilibrium context.

Note the generally smaller entries in Table 4. This indicates the greater importance of open- and closed-loop effects, that is, the operation of the savings–investment balance, in the demand-driven, Keynesian model. In the Jacobian case, by contrast, own-effects account for almost everything (the few very large numbers result from very small denominators). This implies that, in an economy without excess capacity, most of the burden of adjustment to exogenous demand stimulus is borne by the commodity and factor markets, without recourse to new investment opportunities.

It should be noted in closing that the two types of multipliers studied here represent extreme cases. The Keynesian model behind the SAM multipliers assumes that supply is perfectly elastic and can accommodate new demand without imposing any tradeoffs on society. The Jacobian multipliers in the present example are, by contrast, obtained with respect to full employment equilibrium in a neoclassical, flexible-price CGE model. Between these two cases is a continuum of specifications of partial excess capacity and price rigidities. Each of these can be expected to yield differing information about the nature of bilateral income linkages in the economy, as will the application of these methods to a wider variety of countries. Another observation concerns the treatment of trade effects, which is an area of considerable interest in both U.S. modeling and elsewhere. What has been said throughout this discussion about the effects of exogenous government injections could have been said as well about export-induced effects. This only requires more detailed consideration of Armington specifications and terms of trade features.

---

[16]See Robinson and Roland-Holst (1987) for details.

371

Table 5: Jacobian Own-Effect Shares of Net Multipliers, $(M_1 - I)_{ij}/(M - I)_{ij}$

	1	2	3	4	5	6	7	8	9	10	11	12	13	14
1 Dairy & Meat	99	102	103	100	96	95	93	102	96	102	100	225	−70	0
2 Grains	100	101	102	100	96	95	94	102	96	102	100	0	−7	0
3 Other Agriculture	85	105	100	99	96	96	95	101	96	102	100	68	62	0
Agri Average	94	103	102	100	96	95	94	102	96	102	100	98	−5	0
4 Light Consumer	104	102	102	95	96	95	84	102	96	102	100	115	135	0
5 Basic Int	103	115	103	100	99	98	98	101	99	101	100	96	94	0
6 Capital Goods	75	−5	69	98	111	383	116	92	112	95	100	205	541	0
7 Construction	−35	−111	−8	62	11	−115	536	151	−589	33	100	−11	−7	0
8 Electric	82	−131	80	99	107	70	111	100	109	96	100	11	4	0
9 Whl & Ret Trade	116	111	97	98	91	91	97	99	101	99	100	97	96	0
Industry Ave	74	13	74	92	86	104	174	107	−12	88	100	86	144	0
10 Services	155	73	110	103	112	−8	1905	102	88	102	100	110	117	0
Sectoral Ave	88	46	86	95	91	90	323	105	30	93	100	92	97	0
11 Low 40% HH	136	234	128	113	149	136	142	108	27	−62	100	0	2694	0
12 Med 40% HH	112	112	114	77	63	109	110	89	118	87	100	167	186	0
13 High 20% HH	123	141	124	119	263	119	121	113	389	57	100	367	406	0
Household Ave	123	162	122	103	158	121	124	103	178	27	100	178	1095	0
13 Capital Acct	0	0	0	0	0	0	0	0	0	0	0	0	0	113

6. CONCLUSIONS

This paper presented a framework for reconciling macroeconomic aggregates, input–output accounts, the social accounting matrix, and a computable general equilibrium model. The resulting CGE-based macroeconomic structure was then implemented to study disaggregated multiplier relationships from two perspectives. For the same macro variables, multiplier matrices were computed from the SAM accounts and by Jacobian differentiation of the CGE model. The SAM multipliers correspond to a demand-driven, Keynesian model of excess capacity and fixed-price response to an exogenous stimulus. The Jacobian multipliers, however, correspond to the adjustment of a general equilibrium model from one full employment equilibrium to another. These differences in initial conditions and adjustment properties lead to quite important quantitative and qualitative differences in the derived multiplier effects. Most notable among these differences is the prevalence of negative effects in the Jacobian multiplier process. The standard feature of the fixed-price models—benefits of new demand being transmitted throughout the economy—is sharply contradicted in an economy with resource limitations and flexible prices, even to the extent that total income may decrease in response to some injections. These results reaffirm the importance of considering general equilibrium effects in the evaluation of economic policy.

APPENDIX: METHODS OF JACOBIAN COMPUTATION

Jacobian matrices provide the underlying information for implementing the differential methods described above. To obtain them from a CGE model, two principal methods are available. The first, following Johansen (1960), obtains an analytic Jacobian from a linearized approximation of the CGE model. The second method, which has been used on an ad hoc basis by a number of researchers,[17] evaluates derivatives numerically by computing solutions of the CGE model under perturbations of the exogenous variables.

A large literature has developed around the Johansen method.[18] In this approach, a log linearization of the structural equations is used in place of the original nonlinear specification to evaluate changes in equilibrium given changes in exogenous variables (including policy

---

[17]Most recently, Adelman, Roland-Holst, and Sarris (1986).

[18]See Dixon et al. (1982) for an up-to-date application and comprehensive introduction.

GENERAL EQUILIBRIUM MODELS 373

variables). The Johansen log linear Jacobians serve as locally approximate representations of an original structural specification, $y = F(x,y)$. In general, this system will be highly nonlinear, and a reduced-form derivation like $y = G(x)$ may not be readily obtainable by analytical methods. Instead of approaching the problem directly, define

$$v = \log[x] \qquad (A1.1)$$

$$u = \log[y] = \log[F(x,y)] = f(v,u), \qquad (A1.2)$$

and given $du = \hat{x}^{-1}dx$, consider the differential

$$
\begin{aligned}
du &= D_u f(v,u)du + D_v f(v,u)dv \\
&= D_u f(v,u)\hat{x}^{-1}dx + D_v f(v,u)\hat{y}^{-1}dy \qquad (A1.3) \\
&= \hat{x}^{-1}dx.
\end{aligned}
$$

Derivatives of the logarithmic expression $f(v,u)$ will generally be feasible to evaluate analytically, leading to a reduced-form system

$$dx = [I - \hat{x}D_u f(v,u)\hat{x}^{-1}\hat{x}D_v f(v,u)\hat{y}^{-1}dy \qquad (A1.4)$$

for the original variables.

Consider an alternative, strictly numerical technique. To use this method, the CGE model under consideration must be evaluated at an equilibrium $y = F(x,y)$. At this point, Jacobians with respect to the arbitrarily chosen vectors x and y can be generated, one row at a time, by perturbation of the exogenous variables. For the ith exogenous variable x_i, for example, the corresponding i^{th} row of the Jacobian is evaluated by recomputing an equilibrium

$$\ddot{y} = F(x + \Delta x_i, \ddot{y}), \qquad (A1.5)$$

where Δx_i denotes a perturbation[19] of the ith component of x. From the corresponding adjusted endogenous variables $\ddot{y}$, the ith row of the Jacobian is given by the elements

$$[\delta_{ij}] = \left[\frac{(\ddot{y} - y)_j}{\Delta x_i} \right] = \left[\frac{\Delta y_j}{\Delta x_i} \right]. \qquad (A1.6)$$

Carrying out this operation for all k components of x gives a complete set of rows. Notice that the Jacobian calculated by this method correspond not simply to $D_y F(x,y)$, but to the complete reduced form

---

[19]Optimal choice of perturbations or step sizes is still an open question.

374   S. Robinson and D.W. Roland-Holst

$$[I - D_yF(x,y)]^{-1}D_xF(x,y)d\dot{x}, \tag{A1.7}$$

which has already been adjusted to first-level exogenous effects for induced endogenous responses. This can be a convenience or a liability, depending upon the intended analysis.

What are the relative merits of the two methods?[20] The principal virtue of the Johansen method is its exactitude. It gives an analytical local representation of the relevant Jacobians. This can be useful if the model is highly sensitive to perturbations. The Johansen method also has the ability directly to decompose the endogenous and exogenous Jacobian factor matrices, which can be useful. The principal drawback of this method is its lack of operational flexibility. Although the x and y variables can be chosen arbitrarily for a given structural specification, the analytical work required to carry through the log–linear reduced-form calculations can be considered for a large model. This high fixed cost creates a natural reluctance to examine a wide variety of alternative endogenous and exogenous variable systems.

The numerical method obviates the need for extensive analytical work by simulating derivatives under direct equilibrium perturbations. Any independent variable in the structural specification can be designated and perturbed. After the equilibrium is recomputed, any endogenous variables can be designated as dependent and their differential adjustment normalized to yield the desired derivative estimates. This approach is attractive for experimental work with an automated model, which can be quickly and easily re-evaluated. The principal drawbacks of the method are its approximate and composite properties. The question of accuracy is not yet well studied in this context, but the literature on numerical analysis can be expected to yield some insights. The fact that the Jacobians calculated by this method include reduced-form endogenous effects can be a hindrance to those who want to study purely endogenous linkages or first-round exogenous effects, but judicious choice of exogenous variables can isolate these effects.

REFERENCES

Adelman, Irma, Roland-Holst, David W., and Sarris, Alexander (1986) Adjustment Under Uncertainty With Computable General Equilibrium Models. Department of Agricultural and Resource Economics, Working Paper No. 400. Berkeley: University of California.

Dixon, Peter B., Parmenter, B.R., Sutton, J., and Vincent, D.P. (1982) *ORANI: A Multisectoral Model of the Australian Economy*. Amsterdam: North-Holland.

---

[20]Powell (1981) discusses the attributes of the Johansen method in a broader setting.

GENERAL EQUILIBRIUM MODELS 375

Meeraus, A. (1985) An Algebraic Approach to Modeling, *Journal of Economic Dynamics and Control*, 5(1):81–108.

Powell, Alan A. (1981) The Major Streams of Economy-Wide Modelling: Is Rapproachement Possible? In *Large Scale Econometric Models: Theory and Practice* (Kmenta and Ramsey, Eds.). Amsterdam: North-Holland.

Pyatt, Graham, and Round, Jeffery I. (1979) Accounting and Fixed-Price Multipliers in a Social Accounting Framework, *Economic Journal* 89(356):850–873.

Pyatt, Graham, and Round, Jeffery I. (1985) *Social Accounting Matrices: A Basis for Planning*. Washington, D.C.: World Bank.

Robinson, Sherman, and Roland-Holst, David W. (1987) Modeling Structural Adjustment in the U.S. Economy: Macroeconomics in a Social Accounting Framework. Department of Agricultural and Resource Economics, Working Paper No. 440. Berkeley: University of California.

Stone, J.R.N. (1981) *Aspects of Economic and Social Accounting*, Monograph No. 126. Geneve: Librairie Droz.

[24]

The use of a social accounting matrix for comparative static equilibrium modelling

CHRISTIAN LAGER

5.1 INTRODUCTION

The intention of this chapter is to explain the interactions between production, income generation, income distribution and consumption within a comparative static equilibrium model using multiplier analysis. The chapter consists of four parts: the first – theoretical – part demonstrates how the aggregate Keynesian income multiplier can be disaggregated into Goodwin's (1949) matrix multiplier. In the second part input/output data and national account data are arranged within a social accounting framework which enables static equilibrium multiplier analysis. Thirdly, the model is explained which combines Leontief's production multiplier with disaggregated income multipliers of the Kalecki–Kaldor–Pasinetti type (see Kalecki, 1965; Kaldor, 1960; Pasinetti, 1965). The industrial production relations are described by linear homogenous production functions. Consumption is explained by a stepwise linear expenditure model. Finally, the first results of the model are discussed.

5.2 FROM SMALL TO LARGE (I) – DISAGGREGATION OF THE KEYNESIAN INCOME MULTIPLIER[1]

In a closed economy with one single production sector and one single consumption sector, the interactions between exogenous (autonomous) final demand and income can be defined by the well known Keynesian income-multiplier $(1 - c)^{-1}$,

---

[1] Discussions on disaggregating the Keynesian multiplier can be found in Miyazawa (1976) and in Gosh (1984).

76   *Use of a social accounting matrix*

where c represents the marginal propensity to consume. One of the disadvantages of Keynes macro-approach is the unexplained instability of this multiplier.

Post-Keynesian models do not treat c as a constant but disaggregate the household sector into different groups (workers and capitalists for instance). If each group (k) of households has a different propensity of consumption (c_k) then the aggregate propensity depends on the distribution of income and can be calculated as a weighted average of the (micro) consumption coefficients of all income groups. The weights (w_k) are the shares of the income of a group k in total income. The income multiplier of a closed economy with one single production sector and n different consumption sectors is then given by $(1 - \sum c_k w_k)^{-1}$.

The problem left aside so far is to explain the distribution of income – the income shares. The primary distribution of income[2] is determined by the mode of production (technologies) of the producers and – giving up the assumption of a single production sector – the share of industries' output in total production. In the following we will make use of a Leontief model which is a simple but adequate tool to describe a multi-industry economy. Using the IO format not only for production but also for income generation we write the balance equations for industrial outputs and for household income simultaneously.

$$\begin{bmatrix} X & K \\ V & 0 \end{bmatrix} i + \begin{bmatrix} f \\ g \end{bmatrix} = \begin{bmatrix} q \\ y \end{bmatrix} \tag{5.1}$$

where X = matrix of intermediate deliveries of the dimension industry by industry
     K = matrix of (income-related) consumption of the dimension industry by household groups
     V = Matrix of (production-related) income of the dimension household group by industry
     f = vector of exogenous final demand for industrial output
     g = vector of exogenous income by household groups
     q = vector of industries output
     y = vector of household income by household groups
     i = unit vector (to sum up a matrix)
     0 = zero matrix (vector)

If we introduce constant IO coefficients for intermediate and primary inputs,

$$A = X\hat{q}^{-1} \qquad L = V\hat{q}^{-1} \tag{5.2}$$

where ^ denotes the diagonalization operator so that $\hat{q}$ yields a square matrix with the elements of vector q in the diagonal (all other elements are zero)

$$C = K\hat{y}^{-1} \tag{5.3}$$

we can solve the enlarged Leontief system by inversion:

$$\begin{bmatrix} I - A & -C \\ -L & I \end{bmatrix}^{-1} \begin{bmatrix} f \\ g \end{bmatrix} = \begin{bmatrix} q \\ y \end{bmatrix} \tag{5.4}$$

[2] For the moment we assume that there exists no income redistribution mechanism and that income is generated and spent in the same units.

where

$$\begin{bmatrix} (I-A) & -C \\ -L & I \end{bmatrix}^{-1} = \begin{bmatrix} B(I-CLB)^{-1} & BC(I-LBC)^{-1} \\ LB(I-CLB)^{-1} & (I-LBC)^{-1} \end{bmatrix} = \begin{bmatrix} M_{II} & M_{IH} \\ M_{HI} & M_{HH} \end{bmatrix} = M$$

(5.5)

I = identity matrix

$B = (I - A)^{-1}$, the common Leontief inverse

The inverse M is the disaggregated matrix counterpart of the aggregate Keynesian income multiplier and gives the volume of production or income generated by an exogenous injection of one unit (exogenous) final demand or income respectively.

Analysing the reduction properties of the matrix multiplier we will first obtain the Kalecki–Kaldor–Pasinetti multiplier and finally derive the Keynesian multiplier.

The matrix M_{HI} specifies the amount of income generated in households by an exogenous injection of one unit final demand for products. The sum over the columns (iM_{HI}) gives total income generation. If we reduce the system to one single producer, (iM_{HI}) reduces to

$$\sum_k l_k \frac{1}{1-a} \left(1 - \sum_k c_k l_k \frac{1}{1-a} \right)^{-1}$$

where a = share of intermediate use in total output (costs)

l_k = share of primary inputs (income) generated by the kth household group

Since intermediate deliveries and primary inputs equal total outputs,

$$\sum_k l_k + a = 1$$

and since the shares of income of a group k in total income are defined by

$$w_k = \frac{l_k}{\sum_k l_k}$$

the matrix multiplier M_{HI} reduces to

$$\left(1 - \sum_k c_k w_k \right)^{-1}$$

which deviates from the Kalecki–Kaldor–Pasinetti multiplier only by taking exogenous income into account.

Further reduction of the system by aggregation of household groups consequently yields the Keynesian multiplier $(1 - c)^{-1}$.

The specification of the matrix multiplier system derived above neglects the following problems:

• It is not clearly specified whether the coefficients defined by equations (5.2) and (5.3) are real or nomial shares or in other words whether the production

78   *Use of a social accounting matrix*

functions of industries or utility functions of households are of the Leontief type
or of the Cobb–Douglas type.

- There exists no government, no income redistribution mechanism through
  direct or indirect taxes or transfers.
- A closed economy without foreign trade is supposed.
- The assumption that income is generated and spent by the same unit is
  unrealistic. No redistribution mechanism between income-generating factors
  and income-spending units is considered.

In order to elaborate a workable and realistic model, these crude assumptions will
be abandoned in the following section.

5.3 FROM SMALL TO LARGE (II) – DISAGGREGATION OF THE NATIONAL ACCOUNTS

The development of economic multiplier analysis goes hand in hand with the
disaggregation of national accounts (NA). Basic NA consists of four accounts:

(a) The *production account* shows production costs and disposition of outputs.
    For a one-sector economy intermediate outputs are cancelled and therefore
    value added equals final demand plus exports minus imports.
(b) The *income account* shows income generation and disposition of income
    (consumption and savings).
(c) The *capital (formation) account* balances the finance of capital (savings) and
    the formation of capital (net investment and net addition to stocks).
(d) The *foreign sector account* shows imports and exports.

The statistical information given by these four accounts enables aggregate
multiplier analysis. A disaggregated matrix multiplier analysis as mentioned above
requires a further breakdown of the production and income accounts.

Breaking down the production account by industry branches and the income
account of private households by income groups yields a social accounting matrix
(SAM)[3] (see Table 5.1).

The *disaggregated production account* is equal to an IO table and shows in the
rows the deliveries of domestic producers to other branches (intermediate use) and
to final use which consists of consumption of private households and government
as well as of investment, addition to stocks and of exports. The columns represent
the cost structures of industries. Intermediate purchases of domestic products are
subdivided into branches of origin and are separated from intermediate purchases
of foreign goods. Completing the cost structures of industries, the common primary
input categories (wages and salaries, indirect taxes, operating surplus and
consumption of fixed capital) are distinguished.

---

[3] The social accounting matrix concept was introduced by Stone (1961) and further developed and used
by Stone (1978), Pyatt and Round (1979) and Maton, Paukert and Skolka (1979).

Table 5.1 Scheme of a social accounting matrix

Income of \ Expenditures of	Industries	Individuals	Households	Government	Producers	Accumulation	Exports	Totals
Industries	Intermediate demand		Private consumption	Consumption		Investment and stocks	Exports	Total uses
Individuals	Wages and salaries			Transfer income	Profit income		Net transfers from abroad	Gross income of individuals
Households		Contribution of individuals to households income						Disposable income of households
Government	Indirect taxes	Direct taxes	Value added tax		Profit income			Government income
Producers	Profits							Profits
Accumulation	Fixed capital consumption		Savings	Savings			Net capital transfers	Source of capital formation
Imports	Intermediate demand							Total imports
Totals	Total costs	Outlays of Individuals	Outlays of Households	Government expenditures	Profits	Capital formation	Total exports	

80   *Use of a social accounting matrix*

Following recent NA practice (see UN, 1968), the income *account* is subdivided
into three main categories: government, producers and private households.
Government receives indirect taxes from industries, value-added tax from
consumers and direct taxes from earners of income. This income is spent on
governmental consumption, transfers (e.g. pensions) and savings. Profits generated
in production processes are distributed among profit earners. In order to elaborate
a social accounting framework which adequately supports matrix multiplier
analysis, the income account of private households ought to be disaggregated
into socioeconomic groups. One of the major problems in constructing an SAM
is that income of private households is generated and spent by different units.
While income is received by individuals (wages, salary and profit earners,
pensioners) and also partly spent by individuals (direct taxes, contribution to
social security funds), the consumption and saving decision are made by
households. Thus we have subdivided the income account of private households
into two accounts.

The *income account of individuals* balances gross income and shows wages
and salaries received from industrial branches, transfers from government, profit
income and net transfers from abroad. Gross income is spent by individuals for
direct taxes. The residual disposable income is then distributed among households.
The *income account of households* balances disposable income originating from
individual contributions. Disposable income of households is then spent on
consumption of domestic and foreign products, on consumption abroad, on
value-added tax and finally on savings. This subdivision of the income account
enables us to disaggregate accounting for individuals and households by different
socioeconomic groups. In our case individuals are clustered into 18 groups of
gross income, while households are grouped into 5 classes of disposable income.
The mode of socioeconomic disaggregation depends on the question to be
answered by the model. Individuals might be clustered by age, earning groups,
race, profession, education, etc. Households might be disaggregated into family
structure (number of dependents), family size, income-group, etc.

5.4 A COMPARATIVE STATIC EQUILIBRIUM MODEL BASED ON A SOCIAL ACCOUNTING MATRIX AND ITS USE FOR MULTIPLIER ANALYSIS

Given the structure of an SAM it is straightforward to construct a static
equilibrium model which might serve different purposes:

(a) Multiplier analysis enables the study and comparison of various policy
    scenarios. Implications of changing government expenditures, changing
    income redistribution policies and differing tax systems may be analysed.
(b) The model might also be used to achieve macroeconomic consistency and to
    identify discrepancies in economic plans and projections.

A *comparative static equilibrium model*   81

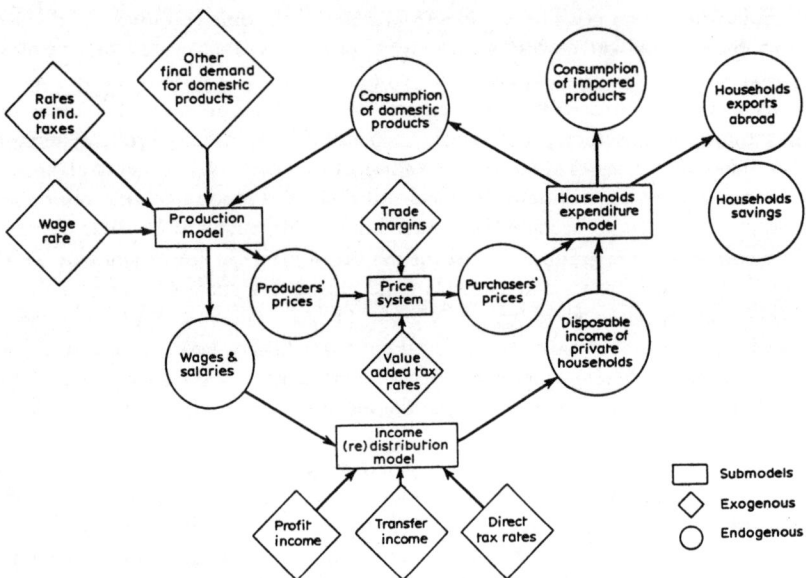

Figure 5.1 Flow chart of the model.

Figure 5.1 presents a schematic overview of the model and describes the interactions between income-generation, income-redistribution and income-spending mechanisms. Consequently the model consists of three submodels.

5.4.1 Production

The *production model* is characterized by simple linear homogeneous Leontief production functions defined by constant real IO coefficients (A^d, A^m) of intermediate inputs:

$$A^d = X^d \hat{q}^{-1} \qquad (5.6)$$

$$A^m = X^m \hat{q}^{-1} \qquad (5.7)$$

where X^d = matrix of intermediate deliveries of domestic products
X^m = matrix of intermediate deliveries of imported products
$\hat{q}$ = diagonalized vector of industries' gross outputs (q)

and constant coefficients for wages and salaries at constant prices (L^*):

$$L^* = W\hat{q}^{-1} \qquad (5.8)$$

where W = matrix of wages and salaries by (receiving) individual income groups and by industry branches

82　　　　　　　　　*Use of a social accounting matrix*

Following Kalecki (1971), profits and capital costs are calculated as a mark-up over variable costs. Producers' prices are immediately given by the dual production model:

$$\mathbf{p}^d = (\mathbf{p}^m \mathbf{A}^m + \mathbf{p}^l \mathbf{L}^* + \mathbf{t}^q)(\mathbf{I} + \hat{\mathbf{r}})[\mathbf{I} - (\mathbf{A}^d + \hat{\mathbf{t}}^v)(\mathbf{I} + \hat{\mathbf{r}})]^{-1} \tag{5.9}$$

where　$\mathbf{p}^d$ = row vector of domestic producers' price indices by industry branches

$\mathbf{p}^m$ = row vector of import price indices by industry branches

$\mathbf{p}^l$ = row vector of wage rate indices by income groups of individuals

$\mathbf{t}^q$ = vector of rates of indirect taxes levied on output quantities by industry branches

$\mathbf{t}^v$ = vector of rates of indirect taxes levied on output values by industry branches

$\hat{\mathbf{r}}$ = vector of mark-up coefficients for capital costs and profits by industry branches

5.4.2 Consumption

The *consumption model* is based on utility functions of the Cobb–Douglas type, or more precise on linear expenditure systems.[4] It is assumed that each household class has committed or necessary purchases (γ) and savings. These purchases are not affected by changes in income or price levels. Once these quantities have been purchased and committed savings have been carried out, the residual income is allocated in fixed proportions (β).

Because only demand for domestic production is relevant to the model, we define the linear expenditure model for consumers demand for domestic products:

$$\hat{\mathbf{p}}^* \mathbf{K}^d = \boldsymbol{\beta}^d \hat{\mathbf{y}} - \boldsymbol{\beta}^d \hat{\mathbf{y}}^0 + \hat{\mathbf{p}}^* \boldsymbol{\gamma}^d \tag{5.10}$$

where

$$\mathbf{p}^* = \mathbf{p}^d (\mathbf{I} + \hat{\mathbf{b}})(\mathbf{I} + \hat{\mathbf{h}})$$

and

$$\mathbf{y}^0 = \mathbf{p}^d \boldsymbol{\gamma}^d + \mathbf{p}^m \boldsymbol{\gamma}^m + \mathbf{s}^0$$

where　　$\mathbf{p}^*$ = vector of purchasers price indices

$\mathbf{K}^d$ = matrix of household consumption at constant producers' prices; industry branches by income groups of households

$\boldsymbol{\beta}^d$ = matrix of marginal (nominal) propensities for consumption of domestic products; industry branches by household groups

$\mathbf{y}^0$ = vector of values of total committed or necessary expenses by household groups

$\boldsymbol{\gamma}^d, \boldsymbol{\gamma}^m$ = matrix of necessary purchases of domestic ($\boldsymbol{\gamma}^d$) and imported products ($\boldsymbol{\gamma}^m$) by industry branches and household groups

$\mathbf{s}^0$ = vector of committed savings by household groups

---

[4] The linear expenditure system was introduced by Samuelson (1947), Klein and Rubin (1948), and Stone (1954) and was used also by Deaton (1975).

b = vector of value-added tax rates by industry branches
h = row vector of trade margins by industry branches

Final demand of households for domestic products is then given by

$$K^d = C\hat{y} + K^* \tag{5.11}$$

where matrices C and K^* are defined by

$$C = \hat{p}^{d^{-1}}(I + \hat{b})^{-1}(I + \hat{h})^{-1}\beta^d$$

$$K^* = \gamma^d - C\hat{y}^0$$

The parameters β and γ of the linear expenditure model were not estimated by econometric techniques but were calculated from cross-section data assuming that committed or necessary purchases or savings of each income group (k) equals actual purchases or savings of next lower income class $(k-1)$. Thus we obtain a stepwise linear engel-profile (engelcurve) and so the LES might be called a stepwise linear expenditure system.

5.4.3 Income redistribution

The submodel which determines the *income redistribution* mechanism is rather simple: primary income distribution – or more precise, wages and salaries – are given by the production model. Total disposable income of individuals is determined by

$$v = Lq + v^r$$
$$L = (I - \hat{t})\hat{p}L^* \tag{5.12}$$

where   v = total disposable income of individuals by gross classes of individuals
   t^1 = vector of rates of direct taxes levied on wages and salaries by gross income classes of individuals
   v^r = exogenous disposable income (profits, pensions, other transfers and other indirect taxes) by classes of individuals

In the next step the total disposable income of individuals is distributed among households:

$$Dv = y \tag{5.13}$$

where D = matrix of shares of contributions of individual income to a certain household group in total individual income

Given these three sets of models we write the three balance equations (for industrial output, for individual income and for household's income) simultaneously by the partitioned matrix equation:

$$\begin{bmatrix} A^d & 0 & C \\ L & 0 & 0 \\ 0 & D & 0 \end{bmatrix} \begin{bmatrix} q^d \\ v \\ y \end{bmatrix} + \begin{bmatrix} K^*i + f^d \\ v^r \\ 0 \end{bmatrix} = \begin{bmatrix} q^d \\ v \\ y \end{bmatrix} \tag{5.14}$$

84   *Use of a social accounting matrix*

which immediately yields the solution

$$
\begin{bmatrix} (I-A^d) & 0 & -C \\ -L & I & 0 \\ 0 & -D & I \end{bmatrix}^{-1} \begin{bmatrix} K^*i + f^d \\ v^r \\ 0 \end{bmatrix} = \begin{bmatrix} q^d \\ v \\ y \end{bmatrix}
\tag{5.15}
$$

The disaggregated matrix multiplier is obtained by partitioned inversion of the coefficient matrix on the left-hand side of equation (5.15).

	Industries	Individuals	Households
Industries	$B(I-CDLB)^{-1}$	$(BCD(I-LBCD)^{-1}$	$BC(I-DLBC)^{-1}$
Individuals	$LB(I-CDLB)^{-1}$	$(I-LBCD)^{-1}$	$LBC(I-DLBC)^{-1}$
Households	$DLB(I-CDLB)^{-1}$	$D(I-LBCD)^{-1}$	$(I-DLBC)^{-1}$

where $B = (I-A^d)^{-1}$, the Leontief inverse.

In this model the multiplier is not constant but depends on the price and tax system.

The labour coefficients (L) used in the multiplier system are influenced by exogenously given variable wage rates (p^l) and by rates of direct taxes (t^l) levied on wages and salaries. The consumption coefficients depend on rates for value added tax and producers' prices. Through producers' prices the consumption coefficients vary also with rates for indirect taxes, import duties, wage rates, and import prices. The effect of changing wage rates is of interest: if wage rates increase the multiplier becomes larger by increasing labour coefficients (L). But this effect is partly cancelled by an inflationary effect of decreasing consumption coefficients (C) which depend on reciprocal producer prices, which in turn depend on wage rates. Sensitivity analysis of changing exogenous variables entering the matrix multiplier might clarify these effects but is not covered in this chapter.

The matrix multiplier might be interpreted as follows:

B   the well-known Leontief inverse yields *production effects* generated by injections of exogenous final demand without taking income effects into account

LB   gives income of individuals generated by the production effects

DLB   gives households' income generated by these production effects

CDLB   yields additional injections of endogenous final demand generated by exogenous injections

BCDLB   *additional production effects* generated by exogenous final demand and first round effects of endogenous injections through income multiplier mechanism

$B(CDLB)^2$ *additional production effects* generated by exogenous, first-round and second-round effects

Summing all the production effects we obtain a von Neumann series which converges to our Multiplier $B(I-CDLB)^{-1}$. All other multipliers might be derived in the same way.

5.5 PRESENTATION OF SOME RESULTS

Table 5.2 presents the production effects of an exogenous injection of 100 Austrian schillings (AS) in all branches for three selected industries (food and beverages, non-metallic mineral industry, manufacturing of metals) and total effects for all sectors. Total production effects (column III) are subdivided into 'pure production effects' (column I) which neglects endogenized injections originating from income multiplier effects, and 'additional production effects originating from income multiplier effects' (column II). In general the analysis covered in Table 5.2 demonstrates that the simple Leontief multiplier accounts for approximately two-thirds of total production effects (minus initial injections). The additional production effects originating from the introduction of the income multiplier mechanism account for only one-third of total effects. While the pure production effects caused by injections in manufacturing sectors are much higher than the additional effects, the latter are important for injections in the labour-intensive service sectors.

Table 5.3 shows production effects caused by exogenous injections of income by types of households. An exogenous increase of income of 100 AS of poor households (column I) generates demand for (and consequently production of) agricultural products (11.16 AS), food and beverages (20.52 AS), trade margins (18.34 AS) and housing (13.58 AS). An increase of income in rich households (column V) generates relatively more production in textiles, minerals, oils and metal products. In general a 100 AS injection in poor households generates a 120 AS production while the same injection in rich households produces an increase of production of around 85 AS which is less than the initial injection. The reason is that poor households spend more income than they earn (negative savings), and produce a relatively higher demand for products which are produced in Austria (agro-food production, textiles) while rich households save their money, spend more abroad and generate a relatively higher demand for foreign products (cars, fuel). The medium income-class (column III) generates the largest production effect. Though the medium households have lower consumption ratios than the poor households, group III generates more production than Groups I and II. This effect can be explained by the stability of the distribution of labour in each industry.[5] In most industries many more medium-paid workers are employed than well-paid directors or low-paid workers (part-time workers,

---

[5] The stability of the distribution of labour is designed by a set of constant labour coefficients. The constancy of the labour/output ratios is a somehow unrealistic assumption (an increase of output does not require more directors) and will be eliminated in further model versions by using more flexible production functions for value added components.

Table 5.2 Production effects of an exogenous injection of 100 AS in final demand

Exogenous injections / Branches	3. Food			8. Oil			11. Metal products			All-sectors			
	I	II	III	I	II	III	I	II	III	I	II	(*)	III
Agriculture and forestry	10.16	1.49	11.65	4.37	0.96	5.30	5.96	1.15	7.11	148.98	14.34	(22.6)	163.32
Mining	0.14	3.07	3.21	4.62	2.40	7.02	8.55	3.08	11.63	165.96	36.18	(35.4)	202.14
Food, beverages & tobacco	122.02	2.48	124.50	3.17	1.64	4.81	5.57	1.99	7.56	196.79	24.46	(20.2)	221.25
Textiles and wearing apparel	0.41	3.66	4.07	1.59	2.15	3.74	3.53	2.55	6.08	156.01	32.26	(36.5)	188.27
Wood	1.93	3.47	5.40	2.47	2.14	4.61	7.88	2.53	10.41	181.92	31.82	(27.9)	213.74
Paper	0.95	2.95	3.90	2.60	2.12	4.72	5.12	2.66	7.78	171.98	31.91	(30.7)	203.89
Chemicals	0.45	2.43	2.88	1.84	1.74	3.58	4.43	2.20	6.63	163.23	26.21	(29.3)	189.44
Oil	0.26	0.88	1.16	134.40	0.65	135.05	5.02	0.82	5.84	157.58	9.73	(14.5)	167.31
Non-metallic minerals	0.19	3.14	3.33	5.69	2.19	7.88	7.81	2.66	10.47	175.87	32.52	(30.0)	208.39
Basic metal products	0.11	2.78	2.89	3.49	1.99	5.48	13.39	2.46	15.85	168.95	29.72	(30.1)	198.67
Manufacture of metals	0.08	2.95	3.03	1.44	2.01	3.45	116.76	2.44	119.20	154.45	29.99	(35.5)	184.44
Energy	0.09	1.61	1.70	12.73	1.31	14.06	7.02	2.73	8.75	141.69	19.84	(32.2)	161.53
Construction	0.13	3.62	3.39	1.60	2.20	3.80	8.88	2.67	11.55	160.60	32.74	(35.1)	193.34
Trade	0.16	3.32	3.48	1.88	2.13	4.01	3.39	2.62	6.01	144.10	32.10	(42.1)	176.20
Hotels, restaurants	2.67	2.86	5.53	3.07	1.62	4.69	3.16	1.91	5.07	157.07	24.74	(30.2)	181.81
Transportation	0.11	4.61	4.72	5.15	3.08	8.23	6.75	3.64	10.39	156.91	46.16	(44.2)	202.07
Finance, insurance, real estate	0.11	2.06	2.17	0.79	1.46	2.25	1.91	1.86	3.77	143.32	22.02	(33.7)	165.34
Other services	1.16	6.70	7.86	1.59	3.03	3.22	4.30	4.19	8.49	147.74	55.33	(53.7)	203.07
General government services	0.00	5.19	5.19	0.00	3.70	3.70	0.00	4.73	4.73	100.00	55.63	(100.0)	155.63
Average	102.17	3.10	105.27	104.87	2.06	106.93	106.44	2.52	108.81	157.53	30.88	(34.9)	188.41

Column I: pure production effects, $B = (I - A^d)^{-1}$
Column II: additional production effects originating from endogenized injections; $B(I - CDLD)^{-1} - B$
Column III: total production effects; $B(I - CDLB)^{-1}$
(*) Share of additional production effects (column II) in total production effects minus initial injection.

Presentation of some results   87

Table 5.3 Production effects of an exogenous increase of 100 AS of disposable income of households (in AS)
(Multiplier matrix BC (I-DLBC)$^{-1}$

| I/O branches | *Groups of disposable income of households** | | | | |
	I	*II*	*III*	*IV*	*V*
1. Agriculture and forestry	11.16	7.86	8.19	3.48	3.81
2. Mining	0.68	0.36	0.12	0.07	0.15
3. Food, beverages and tobacco	20.52	15.54	17.11	5.78	3.64
4. Textiles and wearing apparel	5.29	6.74	5.72	4.91	4.71
5. Wood	2.00	3.06	2.84	1.96	2.93
6. Paper	2.69	2.41	2.62	1.78	1.74
7. Chemicals	3.53	2.98	3.12	1.89	2.01
8. Oil	4.34	6.86	8.69	5.47	5.16
9. Non-metallic minerals	0.91	0.81	1.02	0.63	0.60
10. Basic metal products	1.04	1.16	1.48	0.93	1.23
11. Manufacture of metals	6.13	7.49	9.90	5.73	9.57
12. Energy	4.61	3.42	3.86	2.26	2.14
13. Construction	2.76	3.09	3.50	2.39	1.80
14. Trade	18.34	19,07	20.65	12.30	15.87
15. Hotels, restaurants	3.46	4.83	3.58	4.20	3.81
16. Transportation	8.31	8.43	6.09	5.51	5.63
17. Finance, insurance, real estate	13.58	12.99	14.82	12.33	12.50
18. Other services	7.66	8.17	5.25	4.90	6.21
19. General government services	2.85	2.85	2.78	2.53	2.87
Total	119.89	118.12	121.34	79.05	86.33

* Annual average income of households (in 1000 AS):
Group I 55
Group II 96
Group III 155
Group IV 231
Group V 377

Table 5.4 Income effects of 100 AS exogenous injection of households income on households income

| Receiving household groups | *Injections in household groups* | | | | | |
	I	*II*	*III*	*IV*	*V*	*Total*
I	100.631	0.673	0.591	0.441	0.527	102.86
II	2.283	102.535	2.215	1.661	1.952	110.74
III	9.329	9.718	108.972	6.431	7.497	141.95
IV	11.141	11.301	10.967	107.552	8.812	149.77
V	5.654	5.654	5.829	3.990	104.580	125.75
Total	129.180	129.881	128.574	120.075	123.368	126.21

88 *Use of a social accounting matrix*

apprentices, etc.). Therefore any exogenous injection will generate more income in the medium-income classes than in high- or low--income classes.

This is also demonstrated in Table 5.4 where income effects of a 100 AS exogenous injection in income are shown. The table reads as follows: A 100 AS injection in household group II generates an income of 0.67 AS in group I, 102.54 AS in group II, 9.72 AS in group III, and so on, so that effective demand in group II creates a total increase in income of about 130 AS. Injections in the first two groups generate more income than injections in richer households. On the other hand, an increase of 100 AS in all household groups produces significantly less income in the first two groups and more income in the medium and rich household groups. Poor households generate more indirect income than they receive while rich households receive more than they generate. This unfair redistribution of income towards medium and rich households is caused by the above-mentioned rigidity of the distribution of labour used in the industries and therefore partly cancels out government redistribution efforts.

REFERENCES

Deaton, A. (1975) *Models and Projections of Demand in Post-war Britain,* Chapman and Hall, London.

Goodwin, R. (1949) The multiplier as a matrix. *Economic Journal,* 59(4), 537–55.

Gosh, A. and Sengupta, A. (1984) Income distribution and the structure of production in an IO-framework, *Proceedings of the Seventh International Conference on Input–output Techniques,* UN, New York.

Kaldor, N. (1960) *Essays on Value and Distribution,* Duckworth, London.

Kalecki, M. (1965) *Theory of Economic Dynamics,* Allen & Unwin, London.

Kalecki, M. (1971) *Selected Essays on the Dynamic of the Capitalist Economy,* Cambridge University Press.

Klein, L. and Rubin, H. (1948) A constant utility index of the cost of living, *Review of Economic Studies,* 15(1), 84–7.

Maton, J., Paukert, F. and Skolka, J. (1979) Income distribution by size, structure of the economy and employment: a comparative study for four Asian countries. Paper presented to the Seventh International Conference on Input–Output Techniques, Innsbruck.

Miyazawa, K. (1976) Input–Output analysis and the structure of income distribution. *Lecture Notes in Economics and Mathematical Systems,* Vol. 116, Springer-Verlag, Berlin–Heidelberg–New York, pp. 2–21.

Pasinetti, L. (1962) Role of profit and income distribution in relation to the role of economic growth. *Review of Economic Studies,* 29, 267–79.

Pyatt, G. and Round, J. (1979) Accounting and fixed prices multiplers in a social accounting framework. *Economic Journal,* 89(4), 850–73.

Richter, J. (1981) Strukturen und Interdependenzen der österreichischen Wirtschaft. *Schriftenreihe der Bundeskammer der gewerblichen Wirtschaft,* no. 41, Vienna.

Samuelson, P. (1947) Some implications of linearity. *Review of Economic Studies,* 15(1), 88–90.

Sawyer, M. (1982) *Macroeconomics in Question: The Keynesian-monetarist Orthodoxies and the Kaleckian Alternative,* Wheatsheaf, Brighton.

Skolka, J. (1984) Input–output anatomy of changes in employment structure in Austria between 1964 nd 1976. *Empirica,* 11(2), 205–33.

References   89

Stone, R. (1954) Linear expenditure systems and demand analysis: an application to the
pattern of British demand. *Economic Journal*, 64(4), 511–27.

Stone, R. (1961) *Input–Output and National Accounts*, OECD, Paris, 1961.

Stone, R. (1978) The disaggregation of the household sector in the national accounts, Paper
presented at the World Bank SAM Conference in Cambridge, England, 16–21 April 1978.

UN (1968) *A System of National Accounts*, Series F, No. 2, Rev. 3, New York.

[25]

© *International Regional Science Review*, Vol. 13, Nos. 1 & 2, pp. 27-49, 1990

Extended Input-Output Models:
Progress and Potential

Peter W. J. Batey

Department of Civic Design
University of Liverpool
Liverpool L69 3BX United Kingdom

Adam Z. Rose

Department of Mineral Economics
Pennsylvania State University
University Park, Pennsylvania 16802 USA

ABSTRACT This article presents a critical survey of research on extended input-output models, emphasizing recent developments in demographic-economic and socio-economic analysis. Basic principles of model design and construction are reviewed, by reference to a representative selection of extended models. Two research themes — labor market analysis and income distribution — are pursued in greater detail as examples of the directions of current work. A comparison is made between extended models and social accounting matrices. The closing section contains a discussion of the prospects for future research.

1. Introduction

Until comparatively recently, most applications of regional input-output analysis have been confined to studies of interindustry linkages. They have analyzed primarily the output and employment effects of an exogenous increase in regional spending, but for the most part they have failed to consider the relationships between these developments in the regional economy and other elements in a regional system: population, transportation, energy, environment, etc.

The picture is rapidly changing, as new ways are found to expand the range of input-output applications. One area in which substantial progress has been made is demographic-economic analysis, where the focus is the effects of changes in population levels and structure upon a regional economy, and vice versa. Another is socioeconomic analysis, where the focus is the interactive effects of income status and economic activity. These two areas comprise what is known as extended input-output analysis. Analysis using extended models is notably broader than in conventional input-output models, and typically includes the study of household income and consumption, and the interactions among various institutions, income distribution, migration, labor force participation, employment and unemployment, and industrial output.

To achieve this, input-output models are embedded within a larger modeling framework. Wegener (1986) has identified two basic kinds of modeling frameworks: unified models in which one algorithm or system of equations is used to model both demographic and economic subsystems, and composite models in which specialized, and hence different, submodels are used for each subsystem. This review will focus on the first type, in the form of a unified extended input-output model expressed as a simultaneous equation system.

The purpose of this article is to provide a critical survey of the more important conceptual work on extended input-output models. Space limitations preclude the authors from mentioning other valuable theoretical contributions, as well as most of the important empirical work. Extended input-output analysis has become a major area of research, and the articles by Madden and Trigg, and Oosterhaven and Dewhurst in this volume provide good illustrations of the scope and direction of current work.

The article has five main sections. Section 2 outlines some basic principles in designing and constructing more broadly based input-output models. Sections 3 and 4 examine two research themes as illustrations of the directions of current work. Section 3 explores the potential of extended models in labor market analysis, including the effects of migration and the relationship between labor demand and labor supply, while section 4 explores the important question of income distribution. Section 5 contains a comparison of extended models and social accounting matrices. Section 6 then concludes with a discussion of the prospects for future research.

2. Extended Input-Output Analysis: Some Basic Concepts

Here the aim is to demonstrate, in conceptual terms, the relationships among some representative extended models. This shall be done by analyzing progressively more elaborate models, indicating the various choices that are open to the model builder in designing an operational model. The emphasis is on demographic extensions, but many of the principles are also applicable to other extensions.

The task of extending regional input-output models to include fuller coverage of household characteristics has been formalized by Batey and Weeks (1989) as a simple, four-stage process of elaboration. Each state builds on the previous one, as can be seen from figure 1 which summarizes the main variables and relationships embodied in the four models.[1]

The sequence starts with the simple, one-region static model in which household consumption is an element of final demand and household income a component of primary inputs. Model 1 measures

---

[1] The process is a flexible one and the model builder may omit certain stages. For variants on the forms of the model described here, see Batey and Weeks (1987a) and Batey, Dewhurst, and Jensen (1988).

direct and indirect effects of a change in final demand, but not the effect of a change in industrial output on household income and expenditure. In other words, it ignores the induced effect of household spending. It can measure certain demographic effects by multiplying the Leontief inverse by appropriate vectors of coefficients; one may obtain some indication of employment and inmigration in this way.

The standard way to model household induced effects is to enlarge the model by adding a single row and column to the matrix of interindustry coefficients, to represent household income and expenditure, respectively. This makes the household sector endogenous.[2] Model 2 shows the implications: household income and consumption now form a closed loop and there is positive feedback to output.

Several criticisms have been levelled at this form of model. Batey and Weeks (1989) and Blackwell (1978) point out that it assumes all households have the same wage rate and consumption propensities. What is more, it implicitly assumes the propensities apply solely to employed households. Consumption by unemployed households, if it is considered at all, is exogenous final demand. The model also does not indicate explicitly the source of newly-employed workers: are they local residents or are they inmigrants? By implication, before becoming employed, these workers had no impact upon the economy, and so in figure 1 it is assumed that all additional household income is, in fact, received by inmigrant workers and, in this example, none of the extra payments are made to the existing work force.

Over twenty years ago Miernyk et al. (1967) addressed the issue of a linear and homogeneous consumption function in detail in a classic study of the impact of the space program upon Boulder, Colorado. Building on work completed earlier, but published later by Tiebout (1969), Miernyk and his colleagues divided growth in personal income into two types: extensive and intensive. Extensive growth represented an increase in output and employment without any increase in per capita income. Intensive growth occurs as a result of increases in productivity. Inmigrants are assumed to receive the same wage rates as indigenous workers (extensive income) and any additional income is identified as intensive income, reflecting increases in the productivity of indigenous workers.

Indigenous and inmigrant workers are also assumed to have different consumption propensities. The Boulder model assumed new residents consume with average propensity, and there was a separate marginal propensity out of increased per capita incomes. It assumed linearity by dividing existing workers into a number of income groups, each with a different propensity to consume. Madden and Batey

---

[2] Model 1 is also known as the open or open-loop input-output model. Subsequent models represent ways to close the model to a wider scope of economic and demographic activity, i.e., to calculate the effects of such activity endogenously.

FIGURE 1

FUNCTIONAL RELATIONSHIPS FOR

SELECTED EXTENDED INPUT–OUTPUT MODELS

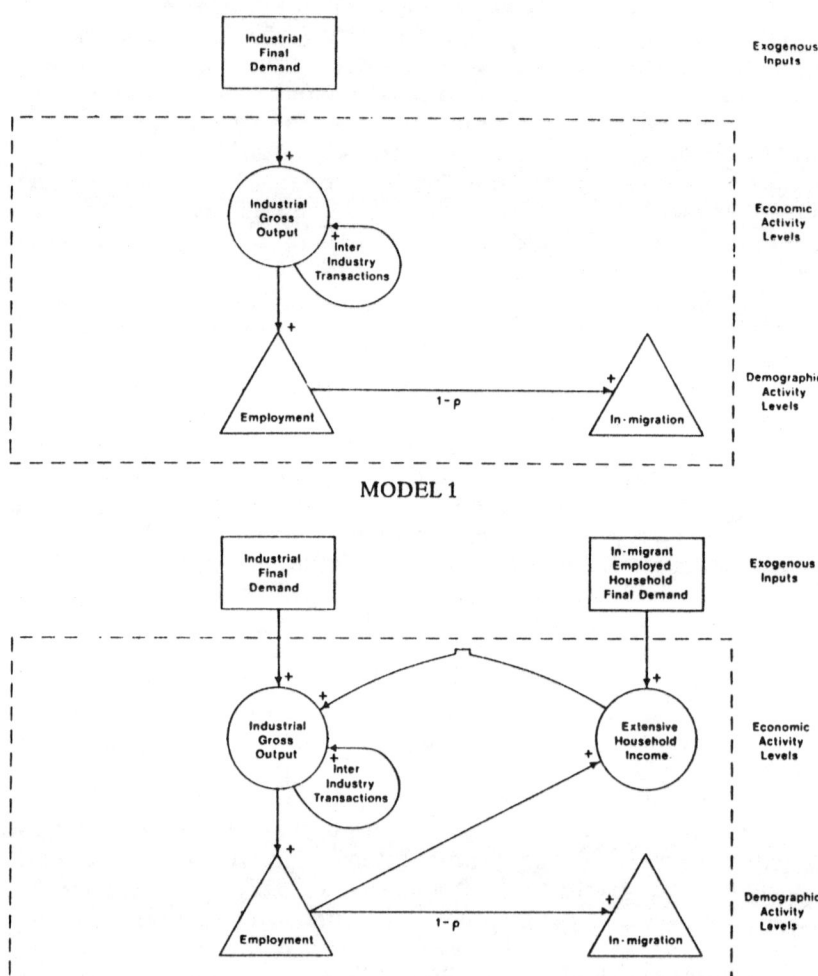

(1983) showed that this quasi-nonlinear relationship between income and consumption can be incorporated within a linear equation system.

The resulting model is shown as model 3 in figure 1. Its application has been quite rare, the two best known examples being the Boulder study and Blackwell's study of Cork, Ireland. Two main reasons account for its relative neglect. The first concerns problems of measurement, particularly of estimating intensive income. The

FIGURE 1 (Continued)

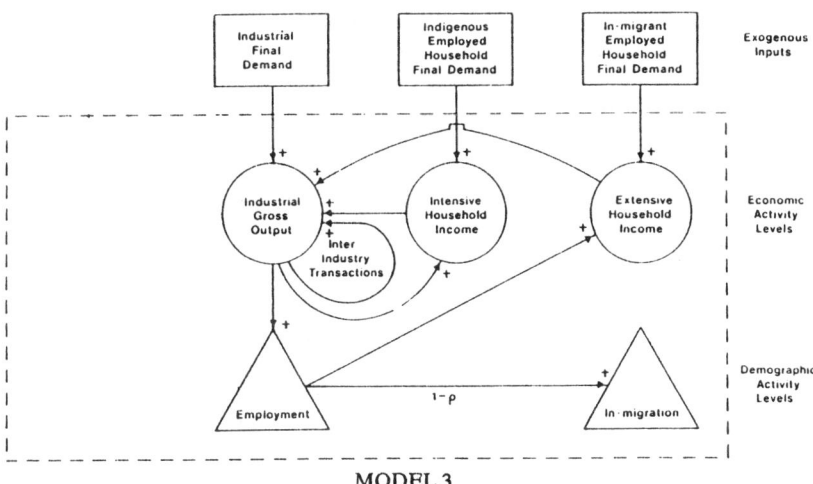

MODEL 3

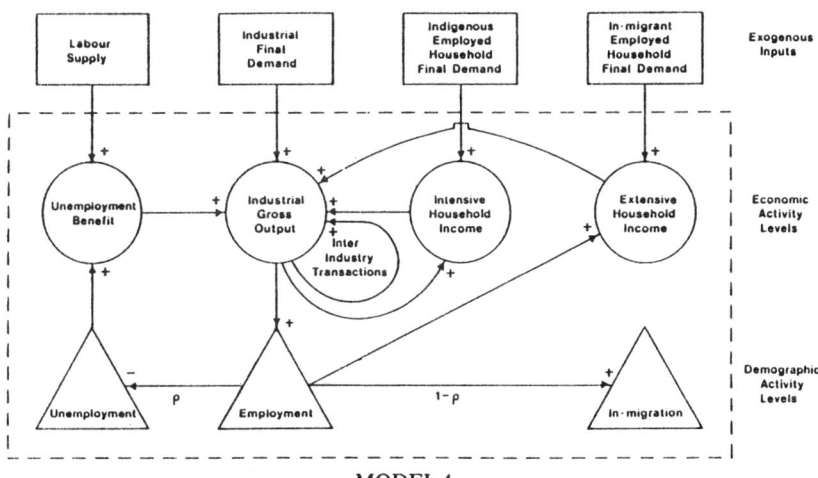

MODEL 4

residual method, favored by Miernyk and Blackwell, can lead to absurd results for individual sectors, and at no point is a satisfactory explanation given of whether inmigrant workers can be expected to benefit from the same additional wage payments as indigenous workers. The technical problems that arise in reformulating the model to take this into account are discussed in detail by Dewhurst and Jensen (1988).

The second reason for dismissing model 3 in empirical applications concerns the impact multipliers. Comparisons between the multipliers and the equivalent ones from a conventional model suggest that the differences are only slight. So far these comparisons have been restricted to the Boulder and Cork studies, but they do raise questions whether the disaggregation is worthwhile (Batey, Madden, and Weeks 1987; Batey and Weeks 1989).

Model 3 is probably best suited to circumstances where one expects rapid regional growth and a shortage of suitable local workers. It is clearly less applicable in declining regions with substantial pools of unemployed workers. It is useful, therefore, to consider an extension that models income and consumption of unemployed households explicitly, shown as model 4 in figure 1.

Model 4 has several features worth noting. Employment vacancies are filled by a combination of unemployed indigenous workers and inmigrants. A parameter, ρ, determines the precise mix for each industrial sector or groups of sectors. Unemployed workers receive a fixed monetary benefit and have different consumption propensities from their employed counterparts. For every vacancy filled by an unemployed indigenous worker, there is a corresponding reduction in the number of unemployed and consumption by the unemployed. Therefore, figure 1 shows a negative feedback loop linking employment, unemployment, unemployment benefits, and industrial gross output, along with the positive loop associated with the earlier extension of the basic input-output model.

As a summary of the four models, consider the effects measured by each. Model 1 measures direct and indirect effects and enables the user to assess the consequences of interindustry linkages. Model 2 measures direct, indirect, and extensive (or possibly total) induced effects; model 3 measures direct, indirect, and intensive and extensive induced effects; and model 4 measures direct, indirect and intensive, extensive, and redistributive induced effects. Here redistributive income, a term first used by Blackwell (1978), refers to the relative shift in income experienced by unemployed workers as they move into employment, and vice versa.

Algebraic Representation of Extended Models

In a series of articles, Batey and Madden (1981, 1983) have outlined the use of activity-commodity frameworks as a consistent and systematic means of extending input-output models. Such frameworks are represented as systems of blocks of simultaneous equations and the standard format is very straightforward: a square matrix of coefficients is postmultiplied by a vector of activity levels (unknowns), and the result is set equal to a vector of known constraints (inputs). The inverse of the matrix of coefficients allows a determinate solution.[3]

---

[3] A model with a rectangular matrix is possible. The solution method may be either by linear programming or the construction of a generalized inverse, depending on whether the model has more equations than unknowns, or vice versa. Optimization applications of the activity-commodity framework are discussed in Madden and Batey (1983).

Consider an example. Equation (1) represents an extended model that has three types of households: employed, unemployed, and inmigrant. It conforms to the model of Strathclyde described in Batey and Weeks (1987b).

$$
\begin{bmatrix}
I - A & -h_c^e & -h_c^r & -s \cdot h_c^u & 0 \\
-h_r^a(I - \hat{\rho}) & 0 & 0 & 0 & 0 \\
-h_r^a \cdot \hat{\rho} & 1 & 1 & 0 & 0 \\
\ell\hat{\rho} & 0 & 0 & 1 & 0 \\
-\ell(I - \hat{\rho}) & 0 & 0 & 0 & I
\end{bmatrix}
\cdot
\begin{bmatrix}
x^1 \\
x_H^e \\
x_H^r \\
u \\
m
\end{bmatrix}
=
\begin{bmatrix}
d_1 \\
d_H^e \\
d_H^r \\
p \\
0
\end{bmatrix}
\qquad (1)
$$

where $I - A$ is a square matrix, consisting of an identity matrix minus a Leontief technical coefficient matrix A; h_c^e is a column vector of consumption propensities for employed households; h_c^r is a column vector of average household consumption propensities for previously unemployed workers; h_u^c is a column vector of consumption propensities for unemployed households; s is a scalar equal to the unemployment benefit rate; h_r^r is a row vector of average employment income coefficients, divided into two components: $h_r^a(I - \hat{\rho})$ = income payments to inmigrant workers (extensive income), and $h_r^a \cdot \hat{\rho}$ = income payments to previously unemployed workers; ℓ is a row vector of employment to gross output ratios; x_1 is a column vector of industrial gross outputs; x_H^e is a scalar equal to the level of extensive household income received by inmigrants; x_H^r is a scalar equal to the level of redistributive income received by previously unemployed workers; u is a scalar equal to the unemployment level (number of workers); m is a column vector of levels of inmigration by sector (number of workers); d_1 is a column vector of industrial final demands by sector; d_H^e is a scalar equal to exogenous income payable to inmigrant employed households; d_H^r is a scalar equal to exogenous income payable to previously unemployed workers; and p is a scalar equal to the level of labor supply.

Several important points can be made about this framework. The first concerns the structure of the matrix of coefficients. By convention, interindustry technical coefficients are stored in the top left-hand quadrant, and the remaining entries are required by the extensions of the basic interindustry model. The second, third, and fourth rows and columns contain income and consumption coefficients for the three types of household. Employed households and unemployed households have opposite signs, reflecting the positive and negative feedback loops referred to earlier.

A valuable feature of activity-commodity frameworks is that the units of measurement can be varied. Whereas in a conventional Leontief model all activity levels are expressed in monetary units, the extended model of (1) has a mixture of monetary and demographic units.[4] The first three entries in the activity level vector are monetary values, while the last two entries are numbers of people, in this case numbers of unemployed and migrant households. This has particular benefits in the calculation of multipliers, since it is possible to estimate the consequences of unit changes in demographic variables (see Batey and Madden 1983 and Madden and Batey 1986 for a detailed analysis).

As a general rule, when (1) is used to assess impacts, the input variables on the right-hand side will be expressed as changes, and so the activity level variables will also measure changes. The only exception is in the fourth block. It is convenient here to think of p (labor supply) as the number of unemployed in the region before the impact, and of u as the number that remains unemployed after the impact.

Equation (1) can be used to examine two main kinds of impacts. One is a change in final demand, d_1; the second is a change in labor supply (p) due either to migration or to a change in participation rates. The general effect of the second kind can be seen in the flow diagram for model 4 in figure 1. The increment of new workers is assumed initially to be unemployed and receiving unemployment benefits. Consumption of this benefit increases industrial output and employed household income, and leads to further increases in industrial output. It also leads to an additional increment of jobs that absorbs some of the new workers and attracts a number of new induced migrants.

3. Labor Market Analysis

During the last five years there has been increasing recognition of the value of extended input-output models in the analysis of labor markets. Several strands of work can be identified in this field and here two of them will be examined. For detailed treatment of a third area, the modeling of spatial interaction within an extended model, see Madden (1985).

The Treatment of Migration

Extended models seem to have considerable potential in assessing the impact of interregional migration. Section 2 demonstrated that a comparatively simple extended model given by (1) could be used to study the effects of autonomous migration, where movement of workers occurs independently of economic conditions such as the existence of specific job vacancies. We were able to simulate this form

---

[4] The only significant difference between this model and a Leontief input-output system is the presence of positive coefficients in some off-diagonal cells of the matrix. Certain combinations of parameter values can lead to negative coefficients in the inverse, causing economically infeasible solutions. However, detailed sensitivity analysis has suggested that this problem only arises when parameter values are extreme (Batey and Weeks 1987b).

of migration by changing the labor supply input variable, and, because the activity-commodity framework was able to accommodate a mixture of measurement units, we also were able to examine the impact of this change upon other variables (industrial gross output, employment, and unemployment).

Suppose, that, instead of migration being autonomous, inmigrant workers are entering the study region to take up particular jobs. In this case, their impact may be tested either by increasing industrial final demands (see van Dijk and Oosterhaven 1986 who represent the effect of the inmigrant workers by a vector of consumption), or by converting the employed inmigrants' consumption into a single figure inserted as an increase in employed household final demand. However, there is a need to avoid double counting. One of the effects of a change in final demand (household or industrial) is to induce migration endogenously, via the $(I - \hat{\rho})$ term. Since this migration (and the consumption associated with it) should already have been taken into account as part of final demand, an adjustment is necessary within the extended model. In their model of the northern Netherlands, van Dijk and Oosterhaven (1986) overcame this problem by adding a further equation which served to moderate the effects of migration, removing the influence of induced migration. This additional equation forms a negative feedback loop, similar to the unemployment equation in model 4.

However, there are other ways in which migration might occur. As long as inmigration is assumed to be generated by job availability alone, there can be no unemployed inmigrants. It is more realistic to suggest that inmigration is a function not merely of shifts in labor demand, but of the changing size of the local economy in a wider sense. Batey and Madden (1988) have modeled a simple pull relationship between industrial gross output and inmigration. Their model represents an advance on earlier ones, in that it permits flows of employed and unemployed workers to be treated explicitly and as a direct response to local economic conditions. Furthermore, it is not difficult to adapt the model for a multiregion system so that both push and pull factors can be taken into account.

To take these refinements a step further, consider a specific example of migration of unemployed workers. The expansion of coal mining in a small town in a rural region is a good case in point (Phibbs 1989). As mine workers move into the region to take up job vacancies, they likely will be accompanied by other household members who will be added to the labor force and have an impact upon the local economy, even though many of them remain unemployed.

Phibbs has developed an iterative procedure to take the effects of dependent migrants into account. It refines the relationship between demographic change and service employment, generally neglected in most extended input-output models. Building on Phibbs' earlier work (1985), Batey and Madden (1988) represented dependent migrants in an activity-commodity framework. They assumed that the proportion of unemployed migrants is a function of the demographic category (age, sex, skill type) of a key migrant. As yet, the only operational version of this model is based on hypothetical data. Nevertheless, its data requirements are fairly modest and ought not to present a serious obstacle to its widespread implementation in the future.

The Internal Workings of Regional Labor Markets

One serious weakness of most extended models is the primitive way in which the regional labor market is modeled. At best there is a simple matching of labor supply and labor demand, assuming that some workers may be indigenous and others inmigrants. There has been very little consideration of the relationship between the economically active and inactive components of the regional population, of the mechanism by which job vacancies are filled, or of the transmission effect that is felt elsewhere in the local labor market when a job is offered to a worker from a particular demographic category.

A notable exception is the work of van Dijk and Oosterhaven (1986), whose model of the Northern Netherlands, designed to estimate the impact of migrants' expenditure, is perhaps the most ambitious of all operational extended input-output models. The activity-commodity framework for this model is given as:

$$
\begin{array}{cc}
\begin{array}{c} (28) \\ \end{array} & \begin{array}{c} (28) \\ \end{array} \quad \begin{array}{ccc} (1) & (1) & (1) \end{array}
\end{array}
$$

$$
\begin{array}{c}
(1) \\ (21) \\[4pt]
(22) \\ (23) \\ (24)
\end{array}
\left[
\begin{array}{cc|ccc}
I - A & 0 & -q^w & -q^u & -q^n \\
-\hat{L} & \mathbf{I - T} & 0 & 0 & 0 \\ \hline
-(c^q)\hat{W}\hat{L} & 0 & 1 & 0 & 0 \\
0 & 0.80(c^{qu})\hat{W}\hat{T}^u & 0 & 1 & 0 \\
0 & 12227(t^n) & 0 & 0 & 1
\end{array}
\right]
\begin{array}{c}
\Delta x \\ v \\[4pt]
\Delta c^w \\ \Delta c^u \\ \Delta c^n
\end{array} \qquad (2)
$$

$$
= \left[
\begin{array}{c}
\Delta f_{ex} \\
\Delta v_{ex} - \hat{P}^w e_{t-1} \\
\Delta c^w_{ex} - (c^q)^{\mathsf{T}} \hat{W} \hat{P}^w e_{t-1} \\
\Delta c^u_{ex} \\
\Delta c^n_{ex}
\end{array}
\right]
$$

where Δx is an N-dimensional vector of changes in sectoral gross output; A is an $N \times N$ vector of interindustry technical coefficients; q^w is an N-dimensional vector of consumption coefficients related to employed workers; Δc^w is the changes in total consumption from employed worker income; q^u is an N-dimensional vector of consumption coefficients related to (previously employed) unemployed workers; Δc^u is the change in total consumption from unemployed worker income (related to former wage rate); q^n is an N-dimensional vector of consumption coefficients related to inactive (subsistence level) benefits; Δc^n is the change in total consumption from unemployed worker income (subsistence level); Δf_{ex} is an N-dimensional vector of changes in final demand (the consumption demand of inmigrants); $\hat{L}$ is an N-dimensional diagonal matrix of marginal employment-gross output ratios; T is an N × N matrix of transition probabilities of people leaving industry i to take up jobs in industry j; v is an N-dimensional vector of the total number of vacancies that may be filled during the period under consideration; Δv_{ex} is an N-dimensional vector of exogenous changes in v; $\hat{P}^w$ is an N-dimensional diagonal matrix of increases in labor productivity; e_{t-1} is an N-dimensional vector of base-year employment levels in each industry; $\hat{W}$ is an N-dimensional diagonal matrix of average gross labor incomes, by industrial sector; Δc_{ex}^w is the consumption change originating from changes in exogenous incomes of workers; c^{qu} is an N-dimensional vector of consumption propensities for the unemployed (these depend on the level of the former unemployment benefits $[0.80\ \hat{W}]$ and so they are larger than c^q); Δc_{ex}^u is the consumption change originating from exogenous changes in numbers of unemployed or exogenous income changes of the unemployed; and t^n is an N-dimensional vector of transition probabilities for regional industry, corresponding to n, the number of economically inactive persons who receive subsistence level benefits.

The van Dijk-Oosterhaven model is in fact a sophisticated development of (1), discussed earlier. Batey and Weeks (1987a) have shown four principal differences between the two models. They are: (1) the incorporation of vacancy chains simulating the probabilities of workers leaving one industry and taking up employment in another industry; (2) the treatment of changes in labor productivity; (3) the inclusion of separate consumption propensities for workers in each industrial sector, reflecting differential wage rates; and (4) the inclusion of unemployment benefits that are directly related to the previous wage rate of a worker, as well as fixed rate benefits that apply to the economically inactive.

From a theoretical perspective, the vacancy chain submodel, located in the second row of the coefficients matrix in (2), is a highly desirable enhancement of the extended model. However, it is not clear that this feature has any marked effects upon model performance.

Changes in labor productivity are specified as exogenous and introduced via the constraints vector for explicit time periods. This is an interesting development and represents an alternative to the endogenous treatment of intensive income discussed earlier in relation to the Boulder model. It has the virtue of being a direct method of testing clearly specified hypotheses, e.g., on the amount of overtime worked, in a way that is impossible in the usual intensive income extended model.

The inclusion of disaggregated consumption propensities is an important innovation that could usefully be adopted more widely. A set of propensities, c_q, defines the proportion of a worker's employment income that is consumed locally, i.e., within the regional economy. However, instead of specifying a single proportion applicable to all employed workers, the van Dijk-Oosterhaven model includes separate propensities, one for each industrial sector. The corresponding column in the model contains a normalized vector of consumption proportions, q_w.

Relating unemployment benefits to a previous wage rate is clearly a response to social security regulations in the Netherlands, and is unlikely to be relevant to most applications in other countries.

Despite its sophistication, the van Dijk-Oosterhaven model has limitations. Recognizing this, Oosterhaven and Folmer (1985) have suggested a number of possible further refinements. The chief ones are making the modeling framework interregional and adding a top-down econometric model as a means of forecasting exogenous variables.

There is a further area of elaboration that justifies attention. Particularly in declining regions, many industrial sectors may be operating well below full labor capacity. The local impacts of an exogenous stimulus may be comparatively slight since some sectors may simply make more efficient use of the existing labor force. This will have the general effect of reducing multipliers.

Batey and Weeks (1987a) have described a procedure that incoporates spare labor capacity in a modified version of (1). The procedure requires the specification of the level of spare capacity in each sector and the translation of these into thresholds for input variables. Only when these thresholds are exceeded does the model begin to measure positive impacts in industrial gross output, household income, and employment. Lai (1987) has made some progress in developing an operational version of the spare capacity model to assess the impact of constructing a large tidal barrage in Merseyside.

4. Income Distribution

Extending the input-output model to analyze the size distribution of income involves an obvious modification. Just as one disaggregates the economy into sectors, it is natural to disaggregate factor payment recipients by income bracket. Still, it was not until the 1970s that research began in earnest on this subject.[5] The primary impetus was a concern by researchers and policymakers that income gains from

---

[5] The credit for the first application of input-output analysis to income distribution is owed to Alfred Conrad (1955). Although Conrad refers to an input-output framework, his model aggregates production to a single sector and involves a cumbersome solution algorithm. Also dating back to the 1950s many empirical tables began to disaggregate income payments into functional shares (labor vs. capital-related income). The emphasis of this article, however, is on the size distribution of personal income, i.e., disaggregation by income brackets.

economic development should be widespread. The obstacle to overcome all along, however, was a lack of necessary data. It is not difficult
to identify the sector of a buyer of a firm's output, but the income
bracket of a recipient of a factor payment is another matter. Still, in
less than two decades, much progress has been made in advancing
the theoretical basis for and the construction of input-output models
of income distribution.

Conceptual Considerations

With one exception, all of the extended models of income
distribution of the 1970s failed to establish any explicit theoretical
basis for their specification. There are more than a dozen major
alternative theories of income distribution (see summaries by Sahota
1978; Atkinson 1983), but input-output formulations barely mentioned them. They were put forth as if they contained an inherent
theory of distribution, or were compatible with any of several alternative theories. However, upon further scrutiny, the only way the
basic input-output model can explain the size distribution of personal
income is via economic structure. That is, the relative prominence
of income brackets differs across sectors, and hence changes in the
mix of gross output will alter the overall distribution.[6] At the same
time, most of the major income distribution theories (ability, individual
choice, human capacity) would appear to be at odds with this
framework.

The major conceptual work on income distribution in input-
output analysis is Miyazawa's (1968, 1976), though it has been
independently replicated to a degree by Ghosh and Sengupta (1984).
This work demonstrates the equivalence between the Cambridge
theory, or Keynes-Kaldor model, of income distribution and the
extended input-output model that disaggregates both payments and
consumption by income bracket. The Cambridge theory is based on
the feature that factor income and consumption propensities differ
significantly between social classes, and that various external stimuli
have differential direct effects on these classes, which are then further
refracted through the multiplier process.[7] The dualism theory of
distribution at the heart of the work by Ahluwalia and Chenery
(1974) is an extension of this concept into the area of social accounting,
with the distinctions between urban and rural populations, or modern
and backward sectors. According to both theories the capital accumulation process has the effect of altering input, income, and consumption coefficients over time, so that the complete theory would
be best addressed by a dynamic extended model.

---

[6] Economic structure has long been demonstrated to be a major determinant of
income distribution (see, e.g., Denison 1954). Rose, Stevens, and Davis (1988) have
argued that it is likely to be one of the major determinants in impact studies.

[7] The focus of the Cambridge model is on functional shares, but Miyazawa shows
how it can readily be transformed to personal income and more than two classes.

Open-Loop Models

In the mid-1970s, several researchers independently formulated extended input-output income distribution models (see Miyazawa 1976; Golladay and Havemen 1976; Paukert, Skolka, and Malton 1976; and Rose 1977). The major motivation of these models was the disaggregation of the payments sector by income class of recipient, thus transforming the typical value-added row into a matrix. Each element of the matrix is a fixed coefficient, v_{ki}, that represents the amount of income going to recipients in income bracket k per unit of gross output of good i.

An open-loop income distribution model can be defined as one in which there are direct and indirect impacts on income distribution, but no feedback (induced) effect through consumption demand (differentiated according to income or otherwise). A typical version (e.g., Weiskoff 1976; Rose 1977) can be illustrated by first defining: X_j is the gross output of industry j; X_{ij} is the amount of output of industry i used in producing good j; Y_{ki} is the amount of income received by group k from industry i; A is the n × n (sector) matrix of technical coefficients $a_{ij} = x_{ij}/X_j$; V is the m (income group) × n matrix of income coefficients $v_{ki} = Y_{ki}/X_i$; F_j is the final demand for good j; and Y_k is the income of recipient group k.

The model is one of simultaneous determination of income generation and distribution, where the vector of income by class is given by:

$$Y = VX \tag{3}$$

or, since $X = BF$, where $B = (b_{ij}) = (I - A)^{-1}$, the reduced form equation is:

$$Y = VBF. \tag{3a}$$

A development stimulus, for example, would affect income distribution through a change in final demand, F, and/or the inclusion of a new production sector that would yield an augmented inverse, B^*, of the original transaction table, viz:

$$Y = VB^* \, \Delta F. \tag{4}$$

A vector representing the distribution of income returns from a unit change in final demand in a given sector, $\Delta f_j = 1$, is given by:

$$\Delta Y_k = \Sigma_{i=1}^{m} v_{ki} b_{ij}^* \qquad k = 1 \ldots m, \tag{5}$$

where the subscript j refers to the sector in which the initial stimulus takes place.

Rose, Nakayama, and Stevens (1982) refer to (5) as the distributional impact vector. A separate vector can be obtained for each sector and used to calculate the associated Gini coefficient of income changes. The Gini coefficients can then be ranked in the manner of conventional output, employment, and income multipliers to see which sectors yield the most equitable changes in returns.

Closed-Loop Models

The closed-loop model incorporates the feedback effect of income differentiated consumption. In the prime example, the Miyazawa (1968, 1976) model, income distribution bridges the gap between the Leontief interindustry production process and the Keynesian income propagation process. Changes in the product mix alter the distribution of income, which in turn alters the pattern of consumption, which then further alters the interindustry mix, and so on. Each subsequent round is smaller than the previous one, and thus the end result is some finite multiple of the original income change.

The Miyazawa model can be expressed mathematically as follows:

$$X = AX + CVX + F, \tag{6}$$

where X is a vector of gross output (n × 1); A is a matrix of technical production coefficients (n × n); C is a matrix of personal consumption coefficients disaggregated by income class (n × m); V is a matrix of factor payment coefficients disaggregated by income class (m × n); and F is a vector of final demand minus personal consumption (n × 1).

The solution to the model can be stated in either of the following ways:

$$X = (I - A - CV)^{-1}F \tag{6a}$$

$$= B(I - CVB)^{-1}F, \tag{6b}$$

where the term $B = (I - A)^{-1}$ is the standard open Leontief inverse. The inverse in (6a) is a standard closed inverse, with the exception of the income disaggregation, and represents total multiplier effects. In contrast, (6b) distinguishes the indirect and induced aspects of these disaggregation effects. Miyazawa refers to the matrix $(I - CVB)^{-1}$ as the subjoined inverse, which depicts the effects of induced changes in each income group's consumption. This matrix is multiplied by the open inverse, B, which depicts the effects of exogenous stimuli.

The solution equation to the Miyazawa system can be expressed as:

$$X = B(I + CKVB)F, \tag{7}$$

where

$$K = (I - L)^{-1}, \text{ and } L = VBC.$$

Both K and L are (m × m) matrices focusing explicitly on the distributional aspects of the income propagation process. More specifically, Miyazawa defines L as the interrelational multiplier of income groups. Each coefficient of L shows the direct increase in the income of one group as a result of the expenditure from an additional unit of income by another group. Each coefficient of K shows the total (direct, indirect, and induced) increase in the income of one group as a result of the expenditure from an additional unit of income by another group. The interrelational multiplier is a very powerful concept, in that it provides a concise numerical tabulation of the interdependence between income groups, just as the standard output, income, and employment multipliers reflect the interdependence between economic sectors. Note that in the more general sense, the units of analysis can be regarded as regions rather than income brackets, thus transforming the model to one representing trade within an interregional system. This version of the model and some of the partitioned solutions bear a striking similarity to earlier work by Miller (1966).

Further Extensions

There has long been concern over the assumption of linear homogeneous relationships in input-output models. One can cope with problems of technological change involving primary factors or changes in taste involving consumption by using numerous standard ways of addressing the problem, most of which involve changing coefficients over time. One can cope with non-linearities associated with scale economies or technical substitution by distinguishing marginal and average coefficients. For impact studies it would be preferable to use marginal propensities to consume and analogous marginal income payment coefficients. These incremental multiplier models are explored further by Pyatt and Round (1979) and Robinson and Roland-Holst (1988), but otherwise do not differ in structure from the basic Miyazawa formulation. A model incorporating consumption non-linearities has also been made operational by Henry and Martin (1984).

Another extension involves the analysis of the number of persons who gain or lose from a policy. Such information is especially valuable in a public choice context, one in which public participation (e.g., a public hearing or referendum) is involved, and the sheer numbers of people affected each way are important. The data can be used to better inform parties at interest about how each will be affected, to predict the outcome of a formal vote, or to gauge public support for a policy in general. Several positive economic measures of distributional impacts have been put forward by Rose, Stevens, and Davis (1988).

Other extensions include still different demarcations of the basic unit of analysis. These include Batey and Madden's (1983) research on interrelational multipliers between occupational categories, Rose and Beaumont's (1988) regionalization of interrelational multipliers,

Rose, Stevens, and Davis's (1988) incorporation of institutional variables in distributional analysis, and socioeconomic demarcations of
social accounting matrices (e.g., Bell, Hazell, and Slade 1982).

5. A Comparison of Extended Input-Output Tables and Social Accounting Matrices

In the last decade there has been an explosion of research on
what are known as social accounting matrices. Interestingly, much of
this work has been undertaken by researchers outside the formal
input-output field (see, e.g., Pyatt and Roe 1977; Eckaus, McCarthy,
and Mohle-Eldin 1981; Bell, Hazell, and Slade 1982; Pyatt and Round
1985; de Melo 1988; and Round 1989). Although space limitations
preclude a review of social accounting matrices, an issue that has
recently become the focus of strong debate will be addressed: what
is the relationship between social accounting matrices and input-
output models, or, more specifically, are the two forms distinct?

The formalization of the social accounting matrix concept is
attributable to Sir Richard Stone (1961), as an outgrowth of his work
on national income accounting. Stone was a leader in developing the
System of National Accounts, which has served as a major data base
for both social accounting matrices and input-output tables throughout the world. However, there is a major difference between the
system of national accounts and social accounting matrices. While
both place an emphasis on income account balances, in the former
households are a single sector, while in the latter they are typically
disaggregated. In fact, the impetus for social accounting matrices is
the same as the impetus for extending input-output models to analyze
income distribution.

The comparison begins with two alternative definitions of social
accounting matrices: ". . . an accounting record for a whole economy
(not just transactions among producers), although not all entries will
be considered in the same detail" (Bulmer-Thomas 1982, 1); and
". . . a simple and efficient way of representing this fundamental law
(for every income there is a corresponding outlay or expenditure) . . . in square matrix form" (Pyatt 1988, 327-29).

These definitions are remarkably similar to the definition of an
input-output table.[8] Unfortunately, they do not adequately convey a
difference in emphasis between the two model forms — the social
accounting matrix's focus is on the interaction among various components of the socioeconomic system. The social accounting matrix
thus can be thought of as an extension of the basic input-output

---

[8] The term table is emphasized because, just as in the case of input-output tables,
social accounting matrices themselves are not a model, but simply a system of
accounts. In order to transform either into a model, some fundamental assumption
or specification of functional relationships is required. In most cases, linear homogeneity is assumed for the account relationships.

Input–Output Analysis I

table's focus on producer-producer relations to the broader realm of institutions, defined by Pyatt and Roe (1977) in this context as "entities having the legal right of ownership and hence being able to accumulate and provide services." Interestingly, from the standpoint of the previous sections, households are considered a type of institution in most social accounting matrices and are often disaggregated according to income type or social/spatial status.

Is there then a difference between social accounting matrices and input-output tables? The answer begins by examining polar cases of the two models. On the one hand, there is the basic input-output table with only a single row and column for households and no special features for institutional accounts in general. This model is comprehensive with respect to production accounts, but fails to include flows (taxes and transfer payments) between households, government, foreign earnings, etc. On the other hand, there is a most basic social accounting matrix with only a single (aggregated) production sector. This model is comprehensive with respect to income accounts, but fails to capture interindustry transactions. Even though both tableaus are double-entry arrays of accounts, they are clearly distinct in their emphasis and scope.

The confusion arises, however, because most theoretical and empirical versions of the two frameworks are not polar cases, but really mixed cases of remarkable similarity. Closed-loop income distribution models (e.g., Miyazawa 1976) contain a disaggregated and often complete set of income accounts. Most social accounting matrices have input-output tables embedded in them. Moreover, mathematical solutions from models generated by the two tableaus, whether polar or not, are virtually identical. Thus, many of the limitations of the standard input-output model referred to by social accounting matrix researchers have been overcome by work on extended models, which have also anticipated some of the so-called new social accounting matrix contributions. At the same time, the social accounting matrix literature contains many unique contributions that should prove useful to input-output research (see, e.g., Pyatt 1988).

6. Future Prospects

Extended input-output models now have a well-established niche within the regional modeling field and a considerable body of experience has been built up based on a range of applications. Ten years ago the picture was quite different: the building of extended models was still in its infancy and most models could be regarded merely as research tools. Applications were comparatively rare and model development tended to proceed in a rather disjointed fashion. There was little evidence that when a model was constructed to meet the needs of a particular study any account was taken of earlier experience in similar kinds of exercises.

This article has shown that model construction has become much more systematic. It has demonstrated that considerable progress has been made in the design and representation of model structure and in understanding the technical properties of models. All of this means that the model builder is now faced with a much clearer set of choices when constructing a model for a given region.

Despite these recent advances, considerable potential remains for model development and refinement. A good example concerns demographic-economic models, where there has been an increasing awareness of the rather crude way in which household structure has been modeled (Hynes and Jackson 1988; Madden 1988; Jackson and Hynes 1988). Most applications have taken an oversimplified view of household structure, making rigid assumptions about the numbers and mix of employed workers in a household, and generally neglecting the degree of interaction between different kinds of households. The time may be ripe for a more fundamental examination of this issue, perhaps by returning to the more ambitious demographic-economic modeling schemes advanced by Schinnar (1976) and Stone (1981).

Another promising line of inquiry concerns the treatment of space. So far most progress has been made in terms of interregional modeling and the article by Madden and Trigg in this volume provides a useful illustration of the benefits of this approach. Equally valid, however, is the modeling of geographical sub-areas within regions, taking explicit account of commuting flows and shopping trips. Some indication of what can be achieved is provided by Macgill's (1977) integration of the Leontief and Garin-Lowry models, and by Madden's (1985) multi-zonal extended input-output model of Nordrhein-Westfalia. Broadbent's (1973) pioneering work on activity-commodity frameworks contains a number of useful ideas about how spatial interaction models can be embedded within an extended model.

Finally, a number of studies are beginning to show the benefits of combining some of the principles of extended models and social accounting matrices. Trigg (1987) has demonstrated how the model of Stone and Weale (1986) embodies a relatively simple extended model and, in this volume, Madden and Trigg show a refinement that allows a much more realistic representation of interregional demographic and economic interaction.

Input-output income distribution models are being applied to an increasing number of important regional issues (e.g., tax incidence analysis, structural transformation of economies, transboundary pollution policy), thereby adding impetus to further research. On a conceptual level, the most pressing need is the incorporation of more explanatory variables of income distribution. These include effects of changing factor payment rates, demographic variables (age, family size, etc.), and stochastic elements. Perhaps more important are dynamic factors dealing with human capital and technological change.

Recent work by Leontief (1986) has provided the groundwork for future efforts.

The importance of dynamic elements is well-stated by Henry and Martin (1984), who provide an example of the likely different results of static and dynamic analyses of income distribution. In current models, upper income brackets contribute relatively much less to overall income formation and to the lot of the poor because of the former's high savings rates. These savings, however, are the source of the investment that transforms the economy and contributes greatly to economic growth. This process definitely has a very positive effect on total income in the long run, though whether it leads to any significant increase in the low level of trickle-down effects found by Rose and Beaumont (1988) or Civardi and Lenti (1988) remains to be seen.

The key need in this area is model construction. There is a dearth of primary data on income distribution on a multisector basis, especially at the regional level. Consumer expenditure data are not yet available for regions and the national data files are especially cumbersome. No doubt the sensitivity of issues revolving around income distribution are a major reason for the lack of data. However, it is possible to make much more data available, while still maintaining non-disclosure requirements. The data provided by the Internal Revenue Service in the United States (including "sterilized" sample files) could readily be expanded and regionalized.

Interregional (and international) applications of these models should expand in number as awareness of the spread of social, environmental, and energy problems grows. Ironically, Miyazawa's (1976) empirical work on income distribution multipliers was done in an interregional context. The conceptual formulation translates directly from a disaggregation of factor payment recipients by income bracket to recipients by region. Some of the recent work on social accounting matrices even enhances this conceptual base, but research is still needed on the combination of inter-bracket and interregional analysis.

The most problematic aspect of interregional income distribution analysis again, however, is on the empirical side. Transboundary income flows have often been neglected in both regional and interregional models. Recently, Rose and Stevens (1988) have pointed out that this results in an implicit "no cross-payments" assumption associated with intermediate transactions, and then have demonstrated that it results in a serious overstatement of regional multipliers. Some progress has been made in collecting data on commuter flows but complete resolution of this problem will be difficult because it involves obtaining data on absentee ownership of land and the spatial delineation of stock portfolios. Still, it is crucial to the accurate assessment of the impacts of public policy on both total income and its distribution.

References

Ahluwalia, S., and H. Chenery. 1974. A model of distribution and growth. In *Redistribution with growth*, eds. M. Ahluwalia, C. Bell, J. Duloy, and R. Jolly. London: Oxford University Press.

Atkinson, A. B. 1983. *The economics of inequality*. 2d ed. London: Oxford.

Batey, P. W. J., and M. Madden. 1981. Demographic-economic forecasting within an activity-commodity framework: Some theoretical considerations and empirical results. *Environment and Planning A* 13: 1067-83.

Batey, P. W. J., and M. Madden. 1983. The modelling of demographic-economic change within the context of regional decline: Analytical procedures and empirical results. *Socio-Economic Planning Sciences* 17: 315-28.

Batey, P. W. J., M. Madden, and M. J. Weeks. 1987. Household income and expenditure in extended input-output models: A comparative theoretical and empirical analysis. *Journal of Regional Science* 27: 341-56.

Batey, P. W. J., and M. J. Weeks. 1987a. *A comprehensive extended input-output model: Theoretical development and an empirical example.* Liverpool: University of Liverpool Department of Civic Design, Working Note 55.

Batey, P. W. J., and M. J. Weeks. 1987b. An extended input-output model incorporating employed, unemployed, and inmigrant households. *Papers of the Regional Science Association* 62: 93-115.

Batey, P. W. J., J. H. L. Dewhurst, and R. C. Jensen. 1988. On a general purpose demo-economic extended input-output model for Australian regions. *Australian Journal of Regional Studies* 3: 99-151.

Batey, P. W. J., and M. Madden. 1988. The treatment of migration in an extended input-output modelling framework. *Ricerche Economiche* 42: 344-56.

Batey, P. W. J., and M. J. Weeks. 1989. The effects of household disaggregation in extended input-output models. In *Frontiers of input-output analysis: Commemorative papers*, eds. R. E. Miller, K. R. Polenske, and A. Z. Rose. New York: Oxford, forthcoming.

Bell, C., P. Hazell, and R. Slade. 1982. *Project evaluation in regional perspective*. Baltimore: Johns Hopkins University Press.

Blackwell, J. 1978. Disaggregation of the household sector in regional input-output analysis: Some models specifying previous residence of workers. *Regional Studies* 12: 367-77.

Broadbent, T. A. 1973. Activity analysis of spatial-allocation models. *Environment and Planning A* 5: 673-91.

Bulmer-Thomas, V. 1982. *Input-output analysis in developing countries*. New York: John Wiley and Sons.

Civardi, M., and R. Lenti. 1988. The distribution of personal income at the sectoral level in Italy. *Journal of Policy Modeling* 10: 453-68.

Conrad, A. 1955. The multiplier effect of redistributive public budgets. *Review of Economics and Statistics* 37: 160-73.

de Melo, J., ed. 1988. SAM-based models: A symposium. *Journal of Policy Modeling* 10.

Denison, E. F. 1954. Income types and the size distribution. *American Economic Review* 44: 254-69.

Dewhurst, J. H. L., and R. C. Jensen. 1988. A non-linearity problem in an extended input-output model. St. Lucia: University of Queensland, Department of Economics, mimeographed.

Eckaus, R. S., F. D. McCarthy, and A. Mohle-Eldin. 1981. A social accounting matrix for Egypt, 1976. *Journal of Development Economics* 9: 183-203.

Ghosh, A., and A. Sengupta. 1984. Income distribution and the structure of production in an input-output framework. In *Proceedings of the seventh international conference on input-output techniques*. New York: United Nations.

Golladay, F., and R. Haveman. 1976. Regional and distributional effects of a negative income tax. *American Economic Review* 66: 629-41.

Henry, M., and T. Martin. 1984. Estimating income distribution effects on regional input-output multipliers. *Regional Science Perspectives* 12: 33-45.

Hynes, M., and R. W. Jackson. 1988. Demographics in demo-economic models: A note on the basic activity-commodity framework. *Environment and Planning A* 20: 1531-36.

Jackson, R. W., and M. Hynes. 1988. Demographics in demographic-economic models: A reply to Madden. *Environment and Planning A* 20: 1543-45.

Lai, A. T. C. 1987. An extended input-output model and its application in assessing the impact of the Mersey Barage. Liverpool: University of Liverpool, Department of Civic Design, mimeographed.

Leontief, W. 1986. Technological change, prices, wages, and rates of return on capital in the U.S. economy. In *Input-output economics.* 2d ed., ed. W. Leontief. New York: Oxford University Press.

Macgill, S. M. 1977. The Lowry model as an input-output model and its extension to incorporate full intersectoral relations. *Regional Studies* 2: 337-54.

Madden, M. 1985. Demographic-economic analysis in a multi-zonal region: A case study of Nordrhein-Westfalen. *Regional Science and Urban Economics* 15: 517-40.

Madden, M. 1988. Demographics in demographic-economic models: Notes on two activity-commodity frameworks. *Environment and Planning A* 20: 1537-42.

Madden, M., and P. W. J. Batey. 1983. Linked population and economic models: Some methodological issues in forecasting, analysis, and policy optimization. *Journal of Regional Science* 23: 141-64.

Madden, M., and P. W. J. Batey. 1986. A demo-economic model of a metropolis. In *Population structures and models,* eds. R. Wood and P. Rees. London: Allen and Unwin.

Miernyk, W. H., E. R. Bonner, J. H. Chapman, Jr., and K. Shellhammer. 1967. *Impact of the space program on a local economy: An input-output analysis.* Morgantown: West Virginia University Library.

Miller, R. E. 1966. Interregional feedback effects in input-output models: Some preliminary results. *Papers of the Regional Science Association* 17: 105-25.

Miyazawa, K. 1968. Input-output analysis and interrelational income multipliers as a matrix. *Hitotsubashi Journal of Economics* 18: 39-58.

Miyazawa, K. 1976. *Input-output analysis and the structure of income distribution.* Berlin: Springer-Verlag.

Oosterhaven, J., and H. Folmer. 1985. An interregional labor market model incorporating vacancy chains and social security. *Papers of the Regional Science Association* 58: 141-55.

Paukert, F., J. Skolka, and J. Malton. 1976. Redistribution of income patterns, consumption, and employment. In *Advances in input-output analysis,* eds. K. Polenske and J. Skolka. Cambridge: Balinger.

Phibbs, P. J. 1985. Estimating regional input-output multipliers in Australia. Ph.D. dissertation, University of New South Wales.

Phibbs, P. J. 1989. Demographic-economic impact forecasting in nonmetropolitan regions. In *Advances in regional demography,* eds. P. Congdon and P. W. J. Batey. London: Belhaven.

Pyatt, G. 1988. A SAM approach to modeling. *Journal of Policy Modeling* 10: 327-52.

Pyatt, G., and A. Roe. 1977. *Social accounting for developing planning with special reference to Sri Lanka.* Cambridge: Cambridge University Press.

Pyatt, G., and J. Round. 1979. Accounting and fixed price multipliers in a social accounting framework. *Economic Journal* 89: 850-73.

Pyatt, G., and J. Round. 1985. *Social accounting matrices: A basis for planning.* Washington, D.C.: The World Bank.

Robinson, S., and D. Roland-Holst. 1988. Macroeconomic structure and computable general equilibrium models. *Journal of Policy Modeling* 10: 353-75.

Rose, A. Z. 1977. *The economic impact of geothermal energy development.* Riverside, CA: University of California, Dry Lands Research Institute.

Rose, A. Z., B. Nakayama, and B. H. Stevens. 1982. Modern energy regional development and income distribution. *Journal of Environmental Economics and Management* 9: 149-64.

Rose, A. Z., and P. Beaumont. 1988. Interrelational multipliers for income distribution in West Virginia. *Journal of Regional Science* 28: 461-75.

Rose, A. Z., and B. H. Stevens. 1988. Transboundary income flows in regional input-output models. Paper presented at the Conference on the Construction and Use of Regional Input-Output Models, Alpine Lake Resort, WV.

Rose, A. Z., B. H. Stevens, and G. E. Davis. 1988. *Natural resource policy and income distribution.* Baltimore: Johns Hopkins University Press.

Round, J. I. 1989. Decomposition of input-output and economy-wide multipliers in a regional setting. In *Frontiers of input-output analysis*, eds. R. Miller, K. Polenske, and A. Z. Rose. New York: Oxford.

Sahota, G. 1978. Theories of personal income distribution: A survey. *Journal of Economic Literature* 16: 1-55.

Schinnar, A. P. 1976. A multi-dimensional accounting model for demographic and economic planning interactions. *Environment and Planning A* 8: 455-75.

Stone, R. 1961. *Input-output and national accounts.* Paris: Organisation for Economic Co-operation and Development.

Stone, R. 1981. The relationship of demographic accounts to national income and product accounts. In *Social accounting systems: Essays on the state of the art*, eds. F. T. Juster and K. C. Land. New York: Academic Press.

Stone, R., and M. Weale. 1986. Two populations and their economies. In *Integrated analysis of regional systems*, eds. P. W. J. Batey and M. Madden. London: Pion.

Tiebout, C. M. 1969. An empirical regional input-output projection model: The state of Washington, 1980. *Review of Economics and Statistics* 51: 334-40.

Trigg, A. 1987. The spatial and distributional impact of government spending: A social accounts approach. Ph.D. dissertation, University of Liverpool.

van Dijk, J., and J. Oosterhaven. 1986. Regional impacts of migrants' expenditures: An input-output vacancy chain approach. In *Integrated analysis of regional systems*, eds. P. W. J. Batey and M. Madden. London: Pion.

Wegener, M. 1986. Integrated forecasting models of urban and regional systems. In *Integrated analysis of regional systems*, eds. P. W. J. Batey and M. Madden. London: Pion.

Weiskoff, R. 1976. Income distribution and export promotion in Puerto Rico. In *Advances in input-output analysis*, eds. K. Polenske and J. Skolka. Cambridge: Balinger.

[26]

EFFECTIVE DEMAND IN A "CLASSICAL" MODEL OF VALUE AND DISTRIBUTION: THE MULTIPLIER IN A SRAFFIAN FRAMEWORK*

by

HEINZ D. KURZ†

Universität Bremen

I INTRODUCTION

According to Keynes, "the initial novelty" of the *General Theory* "lies in my maintaining that it is not the rate of interest, but the level of income which ensures equality between saving and investment" (Keynes, 1937, p. 250). This idea is developed in terms of the multiplier analysis in Chapter 10 of the *General Theory*[1]. However, even though Keynes stresses that a proper treatment of the employment and income effects of a given level of investment presupposes (at least) a two-sectoral framework of the analysis, differentiating between investment and consumption industries (see, for example, Keynes, 1936, pp. 116-17), he nevertheless discusses the problem within the framework of a single-commodity world, making only passing reference to the more general case. Keynes's procedure has been adopted by most macrotheorists and has led to the predominance of an approach to the problem of employment and output as a whole that neglects intersectoral relations of production and thus the structural aspect of the problem under consideration.

The one-commodity model in macroeconomics is generally legitimized in terms of its simplicity. Caution is in place, however, because there is no

---

*Manuscript received 15.3.84; final version received 6.6.84.

†I should like to thank R. Franke, G. Harcourt, P. Kalmbach, D. Kattermann, U. Krause, S. Parrinello, N. Salvadori, an anonymous referee and, in particular, Ian Steedman for helpful suggestions and comments on a preliminary draft of this paper, an English version of which was prepared during a most useful stay at the Faculty of Economics and Commerce, University of Rome. The support of the University of Rome is gratefully acknowledged.

[1]As is well known, the conception of the multiplier was first introduced into economic theory by Kahn (1931).

reason to suppose that the results derived in such a framework carry over to the multi-commodity case. With respect to the multiplier analysis this has been demonstrated a long time ago by Goodwin (1949) and Chipman (1949/50), later on by Schwartz (1961, Lecture 8), and more recently by Morishima (1976, Chapter 9). The latter arrived at the result that there are two cases where there is no need to disaggregate the economy into its individual industries. The first is where the marginal propensities to consume of workers equals that of capitalists; the second is where the wages-profits ratio is uniform across all consumption industries (*ibid.*, p. 271). Since both assumptions appear to be highly unrealistic, it seems appropriate to reformulate the principle of the multiplier in a multisectoral framework.

In contrast to the existing work in that direction, the reformulation presented in this paper is based on a "Classical" type of approach to the theory of value and distribution (see Sraffa, 1960), i.e., it will be assumed that the sectoral rates of profit and the technical conditions of production are given, so that the wage rate and the system of relative prices can also be taken as given. (We have, in other words, a particular fixprice economy.)[2] The assumption of given and constant rates of profit and prices is to some extent justified by the supposition that there are no capacity or labour limitations to the multiplier process. That is to say, only "unemployment equilibria" will be considered. More specifically, in what follows the principle of the multiplier will be discussed in static terms within the framework of an n-sectoral linear model of single-product industries and homogeneous labour as the only primary input. Although it is hardly deniable that "cases of joint production . . . form the general rule, to which it is difficult to point out any clear or important exceptions" (Jevons, 1965, p. 198); that labour *is* heterogeneous; and that in addition to labour there may exist other primary factors which constrain the short-period multiplier expansion, these assumptions will be retained throughout the main part of the argument. In fact, they prove sufficient to serve the purpose of the present article, i.e., to pour (some) water into the wine of traditional macroeconomics. Moreover, for the sake of simplicity, the analysis will be conducted in terms of a closed economy without a state. The consumption patterns and the savings propensities associated with the only two types of income, wages and profits, will be taken as given and constant. Finally, following Keynes's procedure in

2Whereas the present model is primarily concerned with the multiplier relationships between capitalists and workers, the papers by Goodwin (1949) and Chipman (1949/50) extend Keynes's concept of a marginal propensity to spend less than one to all sectors (or industries) of the economy. Their point of departure is the Leontief matrix of money quantities. Furthermore, these papers investigate the implications of assuming lags in the circulation of money, i.e., deal with the conditions for dynamic stability.

Effective Demand in a "Classical" Model, etc.   123

Chapter 10 of the *General Theory*, investment demand in value terms will be treated as autonomous. It deserves mentioning, however, that essentially the same argument developed in this paper applies to other autonomous or quasi-autonomous components of aggregate demand, such as autonomous consumption demand, public expenditure and, in particular, foreign demand. Thus the range of applicability of the general argument of this paper is wider than it may seem at first sight.

The structure of the paper is as follows. In Section II the matrix multiplier is derived and is demonstrated to depend on the technical conditions of production, income distribution, i.e., the set of sectoral profit rates, the consumption patterns and the propensities to save out of wages and profits. The Keynes and Kaldor multipliers are shown to be but special cases of this more general formulation. Section III contains an analysis of the income and employment levels associated with a *given* volume of (net) investment in price terms (or in terms of labour embodied). It is demonstrated that these levels generally depend on the *physical* composition of investment demand. A corollary of this finding, that *prima facie* looks counterintuitive, reads that an *increase* in the volume of investment could be associated with a *decrease* in the level of total employment (and income). Furthermore, it is shown that the income effect (but not the employment effect) is independent of the physical composition of investment, if the savings propensities are equal. In the concluding Section IV some possible generalizations of the approach are sketched.

II THE MATRIX MULTIPLIER IN A "CLASSICAL" MODEL OF VALUE AND DISTRIBUTION

We start with an exposition of the distribution and price aspect, the quantity aspect and the expenditure aspect of the simple economy under consideration. In accordance with the usual Keynesian macroeconomic approach, we shall carry out the analysis in terms of vertically integrated magnitudes, such as net national income, net investment, net savings, etc. (On the notion of vertical integration, see Pasinetti, 1980, Chapter 2.)

Distribution and Prices

In the case of single-product industries the system of prices is given by

$$\mathbf{P} = \mathbf{P}\mathbf{A}\,(\mathbf{I} + \hat{\mathbf{r}}) + w\mathbf{l}, \qquad\qquad \ldots\ldots(1)$$

where $\mathbf{P}$ is the row vector of the n prices, $\mathbf{A}$ is the quadratic, semi-positive, indecomposable and productive matrix of the coefficients of production, $\mathbf{I}$ is the identity matrix, $\mathbf{l}$ is the row vector of direct labour inputs per unit of output, $\hat{r}$ is the diagonal matrix of the sectoral rates of profit $r_i \geqslant 0, i = 1,$ $2, \ldots, n$, and w is the wage rate. Subtracting $\mathbf{PA}$ on both sides of (1) and post-multiplying by the Leontief inverse matrix $(\mathbf{I} - \mathbf{A})^{-1}$ we arrive at

$$\mathbf{P} = \mathbf{PA}\hat{r}\,(\mathbf{I} - \mathbf{A})^{-1} + w\,\mathbf{1}\,(\mathbf{I} - \mathbf{A})^{-1} \qquad \ldots\ldots(2\text{a})$$

or

$$\mathbf{P} = \mathbf{P}\tilde{\mathbf{H}} + w\Lambda, \qquad \ldots\ldots(2\text{b})$$

where

$$\tilde{\mathbf{H}} = \mathbf{A}\hat{r}\,(\mathbf{I} - \mathbf{A})^{-1} \text{ and } \Lambda = \mathbf{1}\,(\mathbf{I} - \mathbf{A})^{-1}.$$

Since, in general, $\mathbf{A}\hat{r} \neq \hat{r}\mathbf{A}$, in the case of differentiated profit rates we cannot make use of Pasinetti's $\mathbf{H}$ matrix, i.e., the matrix of the means of production that are needed directly and indirectly per unit of output;[3] Λ is the row vector of vertically integrated labour coefficients, i.e., of quantities of labour embodied per unit of output.

It is well known that for a given (and feasible) set of non-negative sectoral rates of profit the above price system has a positive solution that is determined up to a scalar multiple (see, e.g., Grillo, 1976). The choice of a standard of value eliminates this degree of freedom. Keynes proposes to express all value magnitudes in terms of *wage-units* (1936, p. 41), i.e., puts $w = 1$; he thus implicitly adopts Adam Smith's *labour-commanded* measure. We shall follow Keynes and express all prices in terms of units of labour commanded, i.e., start from the price system

$$\mathbf{p} = \mathbf{p}\tilde{\mathbf{H}} + \Lambda. \qquad \ldots\ldots(3)[4]$$

Let us now turn to the quantity aspect of our simple economy.

Quantities

The quantity side is described by the open Leontief system

$$\mathbf{x} = \mathbf{Ax} + \mathbf{y}, \qquad \ldots\ldots(4\text{a})$$

where $\mathbf{x}$ is the column vector of gross outputs of the different industries and $\mathbf{y}$ is the column vector of net outputs. In what follows $\mathbf{y}$ will be conceived as the vector of effective final demand. In a closed economy without public sector this demand is composed of consumers' demand $\mathbf{c}$ and investment demand $\mathbf{i}$; the former is made up of consumption demand out of wages $\mathbf{c}_w$ and out of profits $\mathbf{c}_p$. Hence

$$\mathbf{y} = \mathbf{c} + \mathbf{i} = \mathbf{c}_w + \mathbf{c}_p + \mathbf{i}. \qquad \ldots\ldots(5)$$

(5) inserted into (4a) gives

[3]In the case of a uniform rate of profit we would have
$$\mathbf{P} = (1 + r)\,\mathbf{PA} + w\mathbf{l} \qquad \ldots\ldots(1')$$
and thus
$$\mathbf{P} = r\mathbf{PH} + w\Lambda, \text{ where } \mathbf{H} = \mathbf{A}\,(\mathbf{I} - \mathbf{A})^{-1}. \qquad \ldots\ldots(2\text{b}')$$

[4]In what follows we shall assume throughout that the *real* wage rate in terms of some given bundle of commodities is positive.

$$x = Ax + c_w + c_p + i \qquad \qquad \dots\dots(4b)$$

and solved for x

$$x = (I - A)^{-1} y = (I - A)^{-1} (c_w + c_p + i). \qquad \dots\dots(6)$$

The volume of employment L associated with an effective demand y is determined by

$$L = lx = l (I - A)^{-1} y = \Lambda y. \qquad \qquad \dots\dots(7)^5$$

Let us now turn to the expenditure aspect.

Expenditures

Wages and profits, both measured in terms of labour commanded, can either be saved or spent on consumption goods. Let s_p be the savings ratio out of profits and s_w out of wages, where $1 \geqslant s_p$, $s_w \geqslant 0$ and s_p and s_w are not both zero. In addition, we shall assume that the non-saved parts of income will be used to buy consumption baskets, whose commodity composition is fixed. However, the consumption pattern out of wages is supposed to be different from the consumption pattern out of profits.[6] Let the standard consumption baskets associated with the two types of income be u_w and u_p respectively, where $u_w \neq u_p$.

Upon these specifications we can immediately turn to the question of what determines the physical composition of total consumption demand. Of course, for a given set of sectoral rates of profit (and thus a given price system) and a given vector of net outputs y or gross outputs $x = (I - A)^{-1}y$, total wages amount to

$$W = lx = \Lambda y \qquad \qquad \dots\dots(8)$$

and total profits to

$$\Pi = pA\hat{f}x = p\tilde{H}y. \qquad \qquad \dots\dots(9)$$

---

[5]The relationship expressed by (6) can also be formulated by means of matrix H. From (6) we have

$$Ax = A (I - A)^{-1}y = Hy$$

and because of (4a)

$$x = (I + H)y = (I + H) (c_w + c_p + i).$$

Hence the volume of employment is given by

$$L = l (I + H)y.$$

[6]By this token the famous Kaldor/Pasinetti problem of workers being profit receivers in the case where $s_w > 0$ is bypassed. As is well known, in the latter case a distinction has to be made between the distribution of income between wages and profits and the distribution of income between workers and capitalists. Obviously, if it is assumed that the consumption patterns relate to wages and profits and not to workers' income *vs.* capitalists' income, for the purpose of the present study no question arises as to the ownership of capital and thus the distribution of profits between workers and capitalists. However, anyone who finds the above assumption hard to swallow may as well start from the premise that workers do not save at all; in this case the general argument of the present paper still holds good.

Total consumption demands out of wages and profits are accordingly given by

$$C_w = (1 - s_w)\, \Lambda \mathbf{y} \qquad\qquad \dots\dots(10)$$

and

$$C_p = (1 - s_p)\, \mathbf{p}\tilde{\mathbf{H}}\mathbf{y} \qquad\qquad \dots\dots(11)$$

respectively.

Dividing (10) and (11) by the prices of the respective standard consumption baskets, i.e., $\mathbf{pu}_w$ and $\mathbf{pu}_p$, gives the numbers of these baskets that can be bought by C_w and C_p. Thus consumption demands out of wages and out of profits, in physical terms, amount to

$$\mathbf{c}_w = \frac{C_w}{\mathbf{pu}_w}\,\mathbf{u}_w = \frac{(1 - s_w)\,\Lambda\mathbf{y}}{\mathbf{pu}_w}\,\mathbf{u}_w \qquad\qquad \dots\dots(12)$$

and

$$\mathbf{c}_p = \frac{C_p}{\mathbf{pu}_p}\,\mathbf{u}_p = \frac{(1 - s_p)\,\mathbf{p}\tilde{\mathbf{H}}\mathbf{y}}{\mathbf{pu}_p}\,\mathbf{u}_p \qquad\qquad \dots\dots(13)$$

respectively.

Finally, we introduce the Keynesian premise, according to which investment demand is taken as autonomous

$$\mathbf{i} = \mathbf{i}^{aut}. \qquad\qquad \dots\dots(14)$$

We are now in a position to derive the (static) matrix multiplier.

The Multiplier

Substituting (12), (13) and (14) into (5) and bracketing out $\mathbf{y}$ leads to

$$\left[\mathbf{I} - \frac{(1 - s_w)}{\mathbf{pu}_w}\,\mathbf{u}_w\,\Lambda - \frac{(1 - s_p)}{\mathbf{pu}_p}\,\mathbf{u}_p\mathbf{p}\tilde{\mathbf{H}}\right]\mathbf{y} = \mathbf{i}^{aut}. \qquad\qquad \dots\dots(15)$$

In the Appendix it is shown that, given the assumptions of the present model, the matrix in equation (15) is non-singular and its inverse is semi-positive. Hence

$$\mathbf{y} = \mathbf{M}\mathbf{i}^{aut}, \qquad\qquad \dots\dots(16)$$

where

$$\mathbf{M} = \left[\mathbf{I} - \frac{(1 - s_w)}{\mathbf{pu}_w}\,\mathbf{u}_w\,\Lambda - \frac{(1 - s_p)}{\mathbf{pu}_p}\,\mathbf{u}_p\mathbf{p}\tilde{\mathbf{H}}\right]^{-1}. \qquad\qquad \dots\dots(17)$$

As was to be expected from the assumptions of the present model, the matrix multiplier depends on

1. the technical conditions of production ($\mathbf{A}$ and $\mathbf{l}$);
2. the set of sectoral profit rates ($\hat{\mathbf{r}}$);
3. the savings ratios out of wages and profits (s_w and s_p); and
4. the respective consumption patterns ($\mathbf{u}_w$ and $\mathbf{u}_p$).

In general terms,

$$\mathbf{M} = \mathbf{M}\,(\mathbf{A},\, \mathbf{l},\, \hat{\mathbf{r}},\, s_w,\, s_p,\, \mathbf{u}_w,\, \mathbf{u}_p). \qquad\qquad \dots\dots(18)$$

We can now distinguish between several special cases. First, there is the case of a uniform savings ratio s, in which (17) becomes

$$\mathbf{M^*} = \left[\mathbf{I} - (1-s) \left\{ \frac{1}{\mathbf{pu}_w} \mathbf{u}_w \, \Lambda + \frac{1}{\mathbf{pu}_p} \mathbf{u}_p \mathbf{p}\tilde{\mathbf{H}} \right\} \right]^{-1}. \quad \text{...(19)}$$

This may be called the *Keynesian* case. Clearly, even in this case the matrix multiplier is not only a function of a "psychological propensity", but depends also on the technique in use, the ruling rates of profit, the associated price vector and the consumption patterns.

If a uniform consumption pattern **u** obtains, we get

$$\mathbf{M^{**}} = \left[\mathbf{I} - \frac{1}{\mathbf{pu}} \mathbf{u} \left\{ \mathbf{p} - (s_w\Lambda + s_p\mathbf{p}\tilde{\mathbf{H}}) \right\} \right]^{-1}. \quad \text{......(20)}$$

This may be called for short the *Kaldorian* case.

The combination of a uniform savings ratio and a uniform consumption pattern leads to

$$\mathbf{M^{***}} = \left[\mathbf{I} - \frac{(1-s)}{\mathbf{pu}} \mathbf{up} \right]^{-1}. \quad \text{......(21)}$$

Finally, there is the familiar work-horse of traditional macroeconomic theory, i.e., the one-commodity model, in which the vectors **u** and **p** become scalars. In this most special of all special cases (17) simplifies to

$$M^{****} = s^{-1}. \quad \text{......(22)}$$

Let us now turn to a discussion of the "effects" of a given net investment on employment and income as a whole.

III   THE EMPLOYMENT EFFECT AND THE INCOME EFFECT

As in Keynes's multiplier analysis, in the present model consumption plays a purely passive role; the active element in the system is investment. Investment triggers off a process of income generation that, *via* income distribution and the ensuing effective demand for consumption goods, leads to a level of national income such that the savings forthcoming at this level are equal to investment. Given investment demand in physical terms, $\mathbf{i}^{aut}$, equation (16) determines the corresponding net social product in physical terms, **y**, that satisfies the $I = S$ condition.

We must now distinguish between the *employment effect* and the *income effect* of a physically specified investment demand **i**. The former is given by

$$L = \Lambda\mathbf{y} = \Lambda\mathbf{M}\mathbf{i}, \quad \text{......(23)}$$

whilst the latter is given by

$$Y = \mathbf{p}\mathbf{y} = \mathbf{p}\mathbf{M}\mathbf{i}. \quad \text{......(24)}$$

Accordingly, the employment effect measures the quantity of *labour embodied* in the net social product, whereas the income effect measures the quantity of *labour commanded* by the net social product. An important feature of the model consists in the fact that because of (8) the ratio between the two is equal to the *share of wages* Ω, i.e.,

$$\Omega = \frac{W}{Y} = \frac{\Lambda \mathbf{y}}{\mathbf{p}\mathbf{y}} = \frac{L}{Y} = \frac{\text{employment effect}}{\text{income effect}}. \qquad \ldots\ldots(25)$$

Before turning to the general case, there are three special constellations that deserve mention: first, the case where there are no produced means of production ($\mathbf{A} = 0$); secondly, the case with zero rates of profit ($\hat{\mathbf{r}} = 0$); and, finally, the case in which $\mathbf{p}\mathbf{A}\hat{\mathbf{r}}$ and $\mathbf{1}$ are proportional. Whilst in the former two cases $\mathbf{p} = \Lambda$ and $Y = L$, in the latter $\mathbf{p}$ is proportional to but greater than Λ and thus Y exceeds L. For obvious reasons these cases are not very interesting from the point of view of the present investigation.

The General Case

In general, $\mathbf{p}$ is neither equal nor proportional to Λ: relative prices, measured in terms of labour commanded, deviate from relative quantities of labour embodied in the different commodities. In what follows we shall demonstrate the dependence of the income and employment effects and of the ratio between the two, i.e., the share of wages, on the physical composition of investment demand by means of a simple two-sector example. It will be assumed that neither of the two commodities is a single-purpose good, i.e., positive quantities of both commodities may be contained both in the vector of investment demand $\mathbf{i}$ and in the vector of consumption demand $\mathbf{c}$. Moreover, the analysis is carried out on the assumption that $r_j > 0$ for at least one j ($j = 1, 2$) and $\mathbf{p} > \Lambda$ and in addition that

$$\frac{p_1}{p_2} > \frac{\Lambda_1}{\Lambda_2}. \qquad \ldots\ldots(26)$$

For the sake of comparison we start from the premise of a given *value* of investment demand in price terms

$$\bar{I} = \mathbf{p}\mathbf{i} = p_1 i_1 + p_2 i_2 \ (i_j \geqslant 0, j = 1, 2), \qquad \ldots\ldots(27)$$

and ask what are the employment and income levels associated with alternative semi-positive vectors $\mathbf{i}$ that satisfy (27).

The problem can be illustrated by means of a quantity diagram, in which the axes represent the quantities of the two commodities. In Fig. 1 the line connecting $\mathbf{i}^\oplus$ and $\mathbf{i}^\ominus$ is the *investment budget line* (27); its slope is equal to the price ratio p_1/p_2. To each of these possible physical specifications of investment demand there corresponds *via* (16) a particular vector of net social product $\mathbf{y}$. The line connecting all possible realizations of $\mathbf{y}$ may be called the *real net social product line*. (It is the locus of all linear combinations of $\mathbf{y}^\oplus$ and $\mathbf{y}^\ominus$.) In addition, Fig. 1 contains a bundle of *iso-income lines* Y^q,

$$Y^q = \mathbf{p}\mathbf{y}^q, \qquad (q = \oplus, \S, \ominus, \ldots) \qquad \ldots\ldots(28)$$

and a bundle of *iso-employment lines* L^q,

$$L^q = \Lambda \mathbf{y}^q. \qquad (q = \oplus, \S, \ominus, \ldots) \qquad \ldots\ldots(29)$$

Obviously, through each quantity combination $\mathbf{y}^q = (y_1^q, y_2^q)'$ of the real social product there passes an iso-income and an iso-employment line which indicate the corresponding levels of total income and total employment.[7]

Fig. 1 demonstrates that a given and *constant* value of investment $\overline{I}$, whose physical composition is notionally varied from $i^{\oplus}$ to $i^{\ominus}$, is associated with *varying* levels of total net income and total employment: income falls from $Y^{\oplus}$ to $Y^{\ominus}$ and employment from $L^{\oplus}$ to $L^{\ominus}$. There is therefore not "*the*" investment multiplier as traditional macroeconomic textbooks maintain.

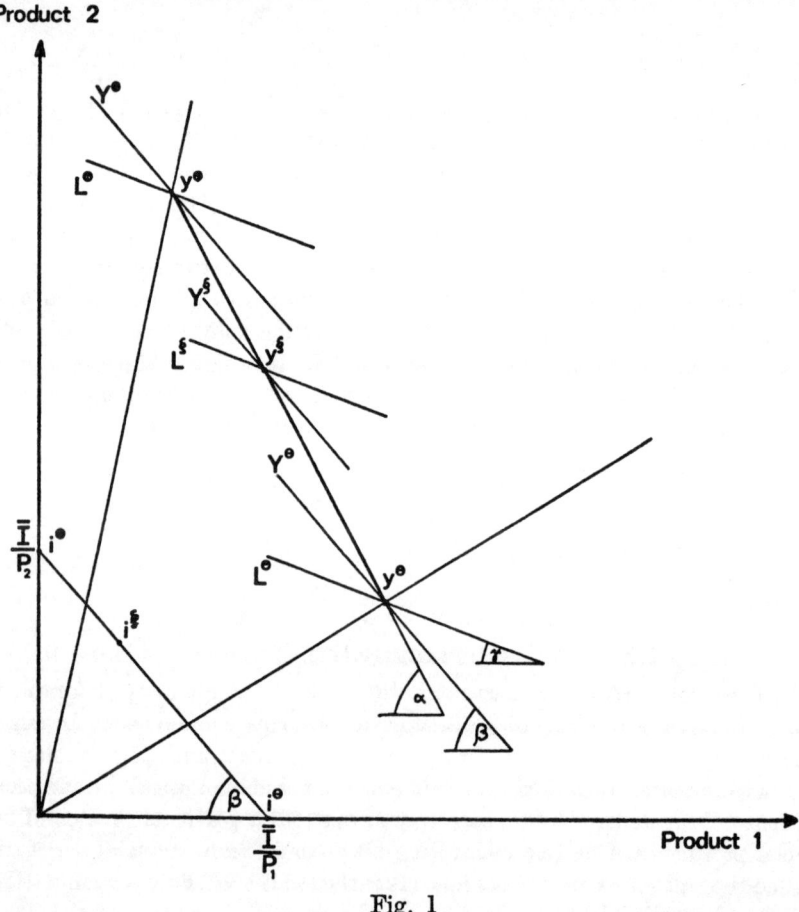

Fig. 1

[7]As regards the slope of the real net social product line (α) relative to the slope of the iso-income lines (β) and the slope of the iso-employment lines (γ) (according to (26) $\beta > \gamma$), a little calculation shows that in the case where $s_p > s_w$ we have $\alpha > \beta > \gamma$.

Two remarks are in place. First, with $s_p > s_w$ total income and employment always vary in the *same* direction. (Contrary movements of the two variables are tied to the constellation $s_p < s_w$.) Secondly, the fact that these variations are equidirectional does not imply, of course, that the ratio between the two variables remains constant. Rather $\Omega = W/Y = L/Y$ in general depends on the physical composition of investment. In other words, despite the fact that the sectoral *rates* of profit are fixed, the share of wages Ω and thus the *share* of profits $\pi \equiv 1 - \Omega$ are indeterminate unless investment demand is fully specified in physical terms. This means, on the other hand, that a change in relative shares is not of necessity indicative of a change in the overall level or the structure of the sectoral profit rates.

To conclude this section, it should be noticed that essentially the same investigation can be carried out starting from the premise of a *given* value of investment in terms of labour embodied, or what Kahn (1931) in his original formulation of the multiplier called "primary employment", i.e.,

$$L_I = \Lambda \mathbf{i}. \qquad \qquad \dots\dots(30)$$

Clearly, a given value of L_I is compatible with a range of different physical compositions of investment demand which are generally associated with different levels of total employment

$$L = \Lambda \mathbf{M} \mathbf{i}$$

and thus "secondary employment", i.e.,

$$L - L_I = \Lambda \left(\mathbf{M} - \mathbf{I} \right) \mathbf{i}. \qquad \qquad \dots\dots(31)$$

Kahn defines the ratio of secondary to primary employment, i.e., $(L - L_I)/L_I$, as "a measure of these 'beneficial repercussions' that are so often referred to" (1931, p. 173). Obviously, for a given L_I this measure is not unequivocal. (A similar reasoning applies to the income effects that are associated with a given volume of primary employment.)

Investment and Employment

A corollary of the above argument reads that an *increase* in the volume of investment in price terms, or an increase in primary employment, could be associated with a *decrease* in the volume of total employment (or total net income). This, at first sight somewhat paradoxical, result is illustrated by means of Fig. 2 with respect to investment demand in price terms. If the physical composition of the smaller investment demand I_1 happens to be such that the corresponding net social product is $\tilde{\mathbf{y}}$, total employment will be L_1, which is larger than the level of employment L_2 associated with the net social product $\hat{\mathbf{y}}$ that is generated by the particular physical composition of the larger investment demand I_2.

Product 2

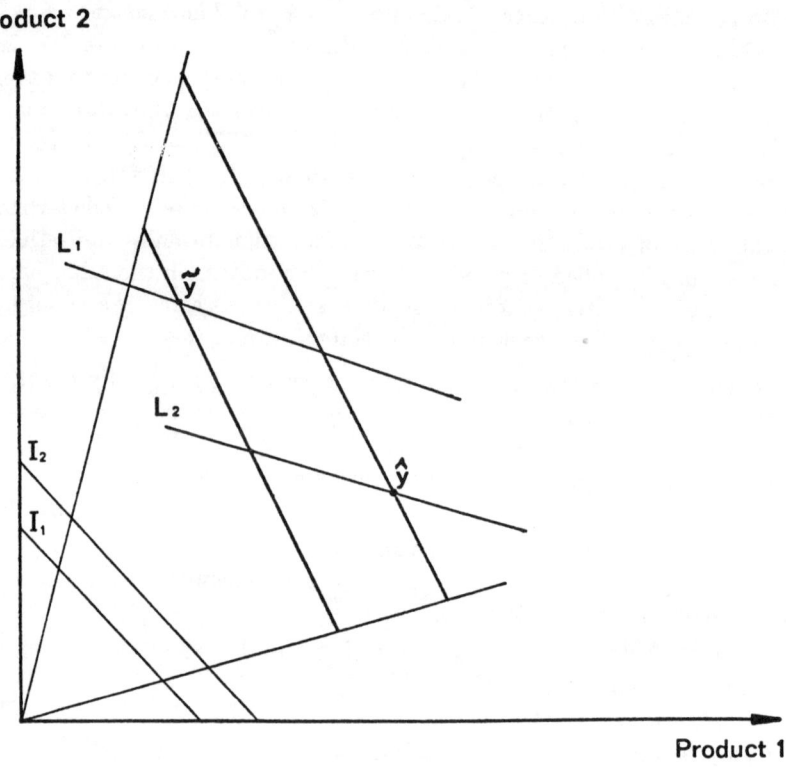

Fig. 2

Clearly, this constellation cannot occur if the commodity vector of the larger investment I_2 is at least as great as the commodity vector of the smaller investment I_1, i.e.,

$$I_2 = \mathbf{p i}_2 > I_1 = \mathbf{p i}_1 \text{ and } \mathbf{i}_2 \geqslant \mathbf{i}_1.$$

Finally, it should be noted that the view, occasionally expressed in economic policy discussions, according to which the employment effect of investment (or some other component of effective demand) is the greater, the greater is the *direct* labour intensity in the production of the goods demanded, cannot generally be sustained. It is in fact the vector Λ and not $\mathbf{l}$ that is of interest in this connection. Since relative prices, in general, deviate from relative quantities of labour embodied, the employment effect of a given investment in price terms is the greater, the greater is the quantity of labour that is necessary, directly and indirectly, in the production of the investment goods demanded.

The "Keynesian" Case

Let us now briefly investigate one of the special cases mentioned in Section II. Because of its overwhelming importance in the literature we choose the case of a uniform savings ratio which was referred to above as the "Keynesian" case. There, total savings in terms of labour commanded are equal to sY. Hence in equilibrium we have

$$Y = \frac{1}{s}\bar{I}. \qquad\qquad\qquad\qquad ......(32)$$

Product 2

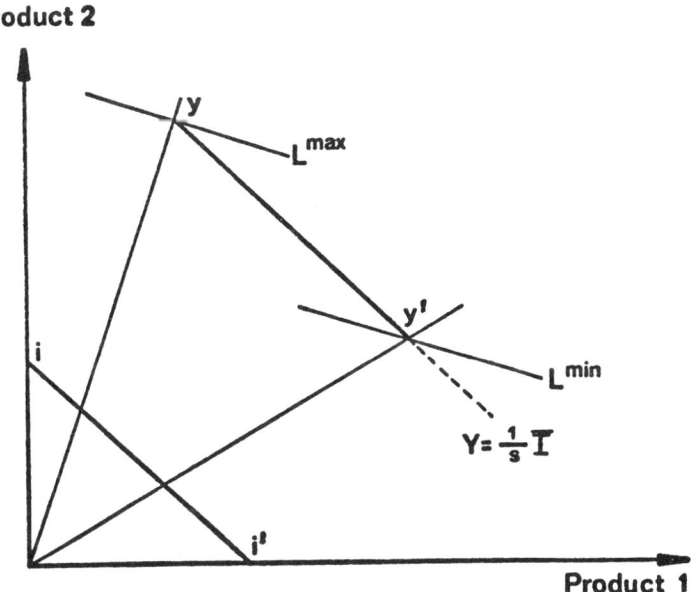

Fig. 3

Fig. 3 illustrates this case. Its characteristic feature consists of the fact that the slope of the real net social product line yy' is equal to that of the investment budget line ii' and the iso-income lines. It follows that the income effect of a given volume of investment in price terms is independent of the latter's physical composition. This is not true with respect to the employment effect and thus the share of wages $\Omega = L/Y$: they both depend on i. Moreover, it should be noticed that the income effect can be determined already on the basis of a knowledge of the savings ratio and the volume of investment, whilst without additional information about Λ and $\mathbf{M}^*$ and thus the technical conditions of production, the set of sectoral profit rates and the consumption patterns, *nothing* definite can be said about the employment effect, even if investment demand is physically specified.

Only if, in addition, prices $\mathbf{p}$ and quantities of labour embodied Λ are proportional, both a unique income level and a unique employment level are associated with a given volume of investment in price terms (a given primary employment).

Changes in Some of the Matrix Multiplier's Determinants

We may now ask how the employment and income effects associated with a given investment in physical terms are affected by hypothetical changes in two of the matrix multiplier's determinants, i.e., the savings ratios and the consumption patterns. (The effects of changes in the methods of production and in income distribution, i.e., $\hat{\mathbf{r}}$, are more difficult to ascertain and are left out due to a lack of space.)

A *ceteris paribus* change in either of the savings ratios produces essentially the same result as in the single-commodity framework. A rise in the savings ratios leads to a fall in at least one component of the vector of net social product, and no component rises. Hence in the present model, where $\mathbf{p}$ and Λ are strictly positive, both total income and total employment will be smaller. It goes without saying that if the change in one (or both) of the savings ratios is accompanied by a variation in the physical composition of investment demand, the composition effect dealt with in Section III may counteract and even offset this former effect.

The impact of the consumption patterns can be demonstrated by means of an example. Let us assume for simplicity that the *ceteris paribus* change in the jth consumption pattern $(j = w, p)$ is neutral with respect to the total price of the elementary commodity bundle, i.e., taking two vectors $\mathbf{u}_j^0$ and $\mathbf{u}_j^1$ $(\mathbf{u}_j^0 \neq \mathbf{u}_j^1)$, $\mathbf{p}\mathbf{u}_j^0 = \mathbf{p}\mathbf{u}_j^1$ by assumption. This need not imply of course that the two vectors of commodities "embody" the same quantity of labour, i.e., in general $\Lambda\mathbf{u}_j^0 \neq \Lambda\mathbf{u}_j^1$. Consequently, a change in $\mathbf{u}_j$ that is associated with a rise (fall) in the respective quantity of labour embodied leads to a higher (smaller) volume of total employment. (A similar argument can be developed with respect to the income effect, starting from the premise $\Lambda\mathbf{u}_j^0 = \Lambda\mathbf{u}_j^1$.)

IV SOME EXTENSIONS

If the assumption of single products gives way to that of universal joint production, it cannot be excluded that due to an *increase* in certain components of the vector of net production (the other components being kept unchanged) "we shall find that as a result the aggregate quantity of labour employed by society has indeed been *diminished*" (Sraffa, 1960, p. 60). This is the consequence of the well-known fact that in joint production systems the vector of quantities of labour embodied in the different commodities Λ may exhibit negative elements (see Steedman, 1977). Moreover, in this case with strictly positive prices p we may have contrary movements of the employment and income effects despite $s_p > s_w$.

With different qualities of labour it is not only total employment that is of interest, but also the quantities of employment of the different qualities of labour. Clearly, changes in the physical composition of a given volume of investment in price (or in labour)[8] terms in general entail not only changes in employment as a whole but also changes in the employment of the various kinds of labour. Moreover, with labour of different kinds available in fixed amounts in the short period, different physical specifications of investment demand will generally result in different degrees of employment and, perhaps, pose the problem of bottlenecks to the multiplier expansion.

Finally, additional primary factors, such as land of different qualities, may be taken into consideration. In general, this implies the problem of the choice of technique, since a greater quantity of a product that directly or indirectly uses such a factor may be produced either by means of an intensified use of a given quality of such a factor or by the simultaneous use of different qualities of the factor (see Sraffa, 1960, Chapter XI). It can be shown that even "small" changes in the physical composition of investment demand may entail "large" and possibly "paradoxical" changes in the system of relative prices and the division of income among wages, profits and rents. Furthermore, it can be demonstrated that even without joint production proper a rise in some components of effective demand (the other components being kept unchanged) may be accompanied by a reduction in total employment (see Kurz, 1979).[9]

V CONCLUSION

This paper has shown, in terms of a simple linear model of the production of commodities by means of commodities, that there is no such thing as

[8] In the case of heterogeneous labour, to start from a given volume of investment in labour terms presupposes that differences in quality have been previously reduced to equivalent differences in quantity. Following Sraffa's procedure (1960, p. 10), the reduction can be carried out on the basis of the given wage structure.

[9] Clearly, it is not only primary factors which may limit the short-period multiplier process. Capacity and the stocks of raw materials, semi-finished and finished goods must be considered too (*c.f.* Hicks, 1974, p. 14).

Effective Demand in a "Classical" Model, etc.   **135**

"*the*" multiplier. Rather the multiplier effects depend on the technical conditions of production, income distribution, consumption patterns and the physical composition of investment, as well as on savings ratios and the aggregate volume of investment. This is demonstrated both in price (investment/income) terms and in labour (primary/secondary employment) terms *à la* Kahn. In particular, it is shown that a larger volume of investment could be associated with smaller levels of total income and employment.

APPENDIX

In this Appendix it will be proved that the matrix $(I - N)$ in equation (15) is non-singular and its inverse M is semi-positive, given the following two assumptions:

(i) $0 \leqslant r_j < \dfrac{1 - \sum\limits_i a_{ij}}{\sum\limits_i a_{ij}}$ for all $j = 1, 2, \ldots, n$, and $r_j > 0$

for at least one j. (Furthermore, in accordance with our discussion in Section III, we shall assume that $pA\hat{r}$ and 1 are not proportional.)

(ii) $0 \leqslant s_w, s_p \leqslant 1$ and s_w and s_p are not both zero and not both unity.

Proof: From (i) it follows that all row sums of matrix $A (I + \hat{r})$ are strictly less than one. Hence the maximum eigenvalue of $A (I + \hat{r})$ too is strictly less than one (*c.f.* Nikaido, 1968, p. 108) and the price equation

$$p = pA (I + \hat{r}) + 1$$

has a strictly positive solution. From this and condition (ii) it follows that the matrix

$$N = \frac{(1 - s_w)}{pu_w} u_w \Lambda + \frac{(1 - s_p)}{pu_p} u_p p\tilde{H}$$

is semi-positive. It is sufficient to prove that $\lambda < 1$ for the maximum eigenvalue $\lambda = \lambda (N)$ of N. We may assume $\lambda \neq 0$, and by the Perron-Frobenius theorem there exists a left-hand eigenvector $v \geqslant 0$ associated with λ. Since $p = p\tilde{H} + \Lambda$, we have

$$\lambda v = vN = (1 - s_w) \frac{vu_w}{pu_w} \Lambda + (1 - s_p) \frac{vu_p}{pu_p}(p - \Lambda).$$

Hence $v = \alpha\, p + \beta\Lambda$ with real numbers α, β, which can be calculated as follows. Putting $\theta_i = (\Lambda\, u_i)/(pu_i)$, where $i = w, p$, we obtain

$$\lambda (\alpha p + \beta\, \Lambda) = (1 - s_w)\, \alpha\, \Lambda + (1 - s_w)\, \beta\theta_w\Lambda + (1 - s_p)\, \alpha\, (p - \Lambda)$$
$$+ (1 - s_p)\, \beta\theta_p\, (p - \Lambda).$$

Since prices are positive and $p = p\tilde{H} + \Lambda \geqslant \Lambda$, $0 \leqslant \theta_i \leqslant 1$. Now, by comparison of the coefficients of p and Λ we obtain

$$\begin{bmatrix} \lambda - (1 - s_p) & - (1 - s_p)\, \theta_p \\ - (s_p - s_w) & \lambda - (1 - s_w)\, \theta_w + (1 - s_p)\, \theta_p \end{bmatrix} \begin{bmatrix} \alpha \\ \beta \end{bmatrix} = \begin{bmatrix} 0 \\ 0 \end{bmatrix}.$$

Since $\mathbf{v}$ is not the zero-vector, α and β cannot both be zero and therefore the determinant on the left-hand side must be zero. Thus

$$\lambda^2 - [(1 - s_p)(1 - \theta_p) + (1 - s_w)\theta_w]\lambda + (1 - s_p)(1 - s_w)(\theta_w - \theta_p) = 0.$$

Being a real solution of this quadratic equation it turns out that $\lambda < 1$ iff

$$1 - [(1 - s_p)(1 - \theta_p) + (1 - s_w)\theta_w] + (1 - s_p)(1 - s_w)(\theta_w - \theta_p) > 0.$$

This inequality is equivalent to

$$s_p[1 - (1 - s_w)\theta_w] + s_w(1 - s_p)\theta_p > 0,$$

which is satisfied since, according to (ii), s_w and s_p are not both zero.

REFERENCES

Chipman, J. S. (1949/50). "The Multi-Sector Multiplier", *Econometrica*, Vol. XVIII, No. 4, pp. 355-374.

Goodwin, R. M. (1949). "The Multiplier as Matrix", *Economic Journal*, Vol. LIX, No. 4, pp. 537-555.

Grillo, M. (1976). "Introduzione di saggi del profitto differenti in uno schema di interdipendenze settoriali", *Giornale degli Economisti e Annali di Economia*, Vol. XXXV, No. 2, pp. 201-208.

Hicks, J. R. (1974). *The Crisis in Keynesian Economics*, Oxford, Oxford University Press.

Jevons, W. S. (1871). *The Theory of Political Economy*, London, Macmillan; reprinted 1965, New York, Kelly.

Kahn, R. (1931). "The Relation of Home Investment to Unemployment", *Economic Journal*, Vol. XLI, No. 2, pp. 173-198.

Keynes, J. M. (1936). *The General Theory of Employment, Interest and Money*, London, Macmillan.

———————— (1937). "Alternative Theories of the Rate of Interest", *Economic Journal*, Vol. XLVII, No. 2, pp. 241-252.

Kurz, H. D. (1979). "Wahl der Technik und Arbeitswertlehre in einem einfachen Modell mit zwei originären Faktoren", *Jahrbuch für Sozialwissenschaft*, Vol. XXX, No. 1, pp. 27-51.

Morishima, M. (1976). *The Economic Theory of Modern Society*, Cambridge, Cambridge University Press.

Nikaido, H. (1968). *Convex Structures and Economic Theory*, New York, Academic Press.

Pasinetti, L. L. (Ed.) (1980). *Essays on the Theory of Joint Production*, London, Macmillan.

Schwartz, J. T. (1961). *Lectures on the Mathematical Method in Analytical Economics*, New York, Gordon and Breach.

Sraffa, P. (1960). *Production of Commodities by Means of Commodities*, Cambridge, Cambridge University Press.

Steedman, Ian (1977). *Marx after Sraffa*, London, N.L.B.

[27]

INPUT-OUTPUT AND DEMOGRAPHIC ACCOUNTING: A TOOL FOR EDUCATIONAL PLANNING

RICHARD STONE

Introduction

We are all familiar with the idea of accounting for sums of money, of arranging transactions expressible in terms of money in a system of interlocking statements in each of which total incomings are equal to total outgoings. We know that in a closed system of n accounts the entries are not unrelated but are connected by $n - 1$ independent accounting identities, and that further arithmetical identities appear if we give separate symbols to the totals in the accounts. By adopting an accounting habit of thought, therefore, we force ourselves to keep in mind a number of inescapable connections between the concepts we use, connections which must as far as possible carry through into any measurements we make of the empirical correlates of these concepts. Within an accounting framework we can build models in the certain knowledge that these connections will be respected. Input-output analysis is the most obvious example of this kind of model-building.

There is, however, no reason why the application of accounting ideas should be restricted to concepts expressible in terms of money; concepts expressible in any other homogeneous unit will do equally well. In this paper elementary accounting ideas will be applied to demography, with its obvious unit the individual human being, and to education, with its equally obvious unit the student. The point of this exercise is to present in an orderly manner the vast mass of material relating to human resources. If we wish to plan our educational system in a rational way, we need first of all an integrated body of demographic information which will enable us to trace the flows of individuals with various characteristics into various activities, to show in detail the structure of the population at any one time, and to project into the future the way in which this structure can be expected to change under the impact of individual choice, or may be required to change if certain social and economic aims are to be achieved.

In an earlier article [1] I set out a model of the educational system which brought together the human inputs into the system, namely the flows of

---

[1] Stone, Richard, "A Model of the Educational System", *Minerva*, III, 2 (Winter, 1965), pp. 172–186.

students through its various branches, and the economic inputs, namely the costs of the teachers, buildings and equipment needed to carry out the functions of these branches. But I did not place clearly in focus the common accounting structure appropriate to both types of input, nor the formal similarity but essential difference of the models appropriate to each type. Here I try to repair these defects. First I discuss economic input-output and describe an accounting structure leading to a model which, given the usual assumption of fixed input coefficients, allows for time-lags in production. I then establish a formally identical structure for demographic flows and show that in this case the appropriate model is obtained by fixing the output coefficients, thought of as transition probabilities, rather than the input coefficients. Finally I indicate what the categories in a demographic matrix should be, with particular reference to educational categories.

Economic Input-Output

In economic input-output analysis the productive system is divided into a number of branches, or industries. Each industry is defined as producing a particular product or group of products, which constitutes its output. Within a given time-period, this output has two main destinations: it can either be absorbed at once by the productive system as an intermediate input, to be used in the fabrication of some other product; or it can flow out of the system as final product. Final product in its turn has three destinations: most of it goes to satisfy the demands of consumers; some goes to replace and extend the capital equipment of industries; and a small part does not leave the system altogether but forms a stock of products, some unfinished, which will flow back into production for intermediate use in the future. Producing goods and services for final use is the principal function of the industries. In order to perform this function, each industry, besides the materials, fuels and business services which constitute its intermediate inputs, needs the services of labour and capital. These, the primary inputs, flow into production from outside the productive system.

This in a nutshell is the economic system as seen from the point of view of input-output analysis. The purpose of this type of analysis is to study the interdependence of the industries and their connections with the other parts of the economy. If we want to apply input-output theory to the study of a particular economy we must of course bring imports and exports into the picture. But in what follows I shall ignore foreign trade, which would raise complications irrelevant to the object of this paper, and shall consider only a closed economy.

Before setting out the basic input-output model, let us look at the facts that have to be modelled. These are the inputs and outputs that flow within a given time-period between the branches of production and between these branches and the rest of the economy, which we may designate collectively as non-production. The whole set of flows and their totals can conveniently be arranged in a table, or matrix, with outputs in the rows and inputs in the columns. The entries in this table can be expressed in terms of money, in which case each row-and-column pair can be regarded as an account which balances: the revenues realised from the sale of the outputs are equal to the cost of the inputs. Reduced to its simplest terms, such a table can be represented as follows:

TABLE I

A Simple Economic Accounting Matrix

	Production	Non-production	Total
Production	W	f	q
Non-production	y'	O	$y'i$
Total	q'	$i'f$	

In this table the row and column for production are to be thought of as divided into many rows and columns, equal in number to the industries we wish to distinguish. The symbol W denotes a submatrix of intermediate product-flows between the industries: the element at the intersection of row j, say, and column k, say, of this submatrix shows the amount of the product of industry j absorbed by industry k during the period to which the table relates. Continuing along the first row of the table, the symbol f denotes a column vector of final products: the jth element of f shows the amount of final product made by industry j. And the symbol q denotes a column vector of total outputs: the jth element of q shows the total output of industry j. If we add together all the elements in a row of W and add on the corresponding element of f, we obtain the corresponding element of q.

Turning now to the first column of the table, we can see the costs that make up the value of output. Part of these consists of the costs of intermediate inputs, the elements of W, and the remainder consists of the costs of primary inputs, represented by the elements of the row vector y'. If we add together the elements of W and y' by columns we obtain the elements of q', which is simply a row vector with the same elements as q.

368   RICHARD STONE

The static, open input-output model for a closed economy is based on two premises. The first is the arithmetical identity which tells us that the total output of a period is absorbed either in intermediate or in final uses; that is

$$q \equiv Wi + f \tag{1}$$

where i denotes the unit vector, so that Wi denotes the row sums of W. The second is an assumption about the technology of production, which says that the inputs of intermediate products are related in fixed proportions to the output into which they enter; that is

$$W = A\hat{q} \tag{2}$$

where the circumflex on $\hat{q}$ means that the vector q is spread out to form a diagonal matrix; and where A denotes a matrix of input-output coefficients in which the element at the intersection of row j and column k measures the amount of input j needed to make one unit of output k.

The simplest input-output model comes from substituting for W from (2) into (1). Thus

$$\begin{aligned} q &= A\hat{q}i + f \\ &= Aq + f \\ &= (I - A)^{-1}f \end{aligned} \tag{3}$$

where I denotes the unit matrix and $(I - A)^{-1}$ is usually called the matrix multiplier because it is the matrix analogue of the scalar multiplier which plays such an important part in Keynes' theory of income determination. Since each industry needs primary inputs in addition to intermediate inputs, the column sums of A are less than one. As a consequence, A is convergent: A^{θ} approaches the null matrix as θ increases, with the result that $(I - A)^{-1} \equiv (I + A + A^2 + A^3 + ...)$ has finite elements. From this identity we can see that the outputs needed to meet final demand, f, can be divided into three parts: If, the production of f itself; Af, the inputs needed directly to produce f; and $(A^2 + A^3 + ...)f \equiv A^2(I - A)^{-1}f$, the inputs needed indirectly to produce f.

The model given in (3) is termed " open " because it does not generate all its variables but depends for its solution on a variable, f, which must be estimated exogenously. Its purpose is to enable us to calculate the amount of total output, q, which must be produced in order to satisfy a given level of final demand, f; and hence to work out what would happen to q if f were to change.

But this model is much too simple. Among other things, it implies that all the intermediate product used this year is made in the course of the year. We know, however, that part of the final product of any period goes to form a stock of intermediate products for use in the succeeding period; in other words, that f includes additions to stocks and work in progress. From this it

INPUT-OUTPUT AND DEMOGRAPHIC ACCOUNTING   369

follows that some of this year's W must have been part of last year's f; in other words, that some of the intermediate product used this year must have been made last year. In order to deal explicitly with this time-lag, therefore, we must treat additions to stocks and work in progress as a separate entity and think of exogenous final product as composed only of consumption goods and capital equipment.

With this modification in mind, let us consider a productive system in which all the intermediate product used this year was made last year and in which all the intermediate product made this year will be used next year, so that provision must be made in advance for any expected change in final demand. This state of affairs is shown in Table II below.

TABLE II

An Economic Accounting System with Simple Time-Lags

		Production			Non-production	Total
		Last year	This year	Next year		
Production	Last year		W			
	This year			ΛW	e	q
	Next year					
Non-production			y'			
Total			q'			

In this table production is divided into three periods, last year, this year and next year, but the table is filled in only for this year. The intermediate product absorbed this year, W, is shown as coming from last year, and the intermediate product made this year, ΛW, is shown as carried forward to next year. The symbol Λ denotes the lag operator (often written as E) which advances by one time-unit the variable to which it is applied. In a growing economy any difference between ΛW and W represents an excess of products made over products used, that is to say represents stockbuilding. The symbol e, therefore, denotes final product redefined to exclude stockbuilding.

The model of this situation is built up from two elements:

$$q \equiv \Lambda Wi + e \tag{4}$$

corresponding to (1); and

$$\Lambda W = A\Lambda\hat{q} \tag{5}$$

corresponding to (2). By substitution we see that in this case

$$\begin{aligned} q &= A\Lambda\hat{q}i + e \\ &= A\Lambda q + e \\ &= (I - A\Lambda)^{-1}e \end{aligned}$$

$$= \sum_{\theta=0}^{\infty} A^{\theta}\Lambda^{\theta}e \tag{6}$$

In the third row of (6) the solution is expressed as a dynamic matrix multiplier, that is a multiplier which combines the lag operator Λ with the parameter A; this device is of great convenience in giving formal expression to the solution of more complicated cases.[2] Its effect can be seen in the fourth row of (6), where Λ^{θ} advances the variable to which it is applied by θ time-units, so that $\Lambda^{\theta}e$ represents the value of e in θ years' time; thus this year's output, q, is no longer given simply in terms of this year's final demand but in terms of a weighted sum of present and future demands, the weights tending to zero with time. This result is easily obtained by applying successive values of Λ^{θ} to the second row of (6) and substituting these values in the preceding equation of the series.

The second row of (6) can also be written as

$$q = Aq + A\Delta q + e \tag{7}$$

where $\Delta \equiv \Lambda - 1$. Here the productive system is explicitly represented as: (i) replacing, for use next year, the intermediate product, Aq, which it is using up for current production and which was carried forward from last year; (ii) adding to stock a supplementary amount, $A\Delta q$, needed to sustain the increment of output from this year to next year; and (iii) satisfying this year's final demand for consumption goods and capital equipment, e. If we put $f = A\Delta q + e$, then (7) becomes the same as (3).

Let us now get a bit nearer to the real world and consider a system which gets this year's supplies of intermediate product partly from last year's production and partly from this year's, and produces intermediate product partly this year and partly for the next; but what it must consume within a year and what it can carry forward from one year to the next is rigidly determined. This state of affairs is shown in Table III on the following page.

---

[2] University of Cambridge, Department of Applied Economics, *A Computable Model of Economic Growth*, p. 80. No. 1 in *A Programme for Growth*. General Editor: Richard Stone. (London: Chapman and Hall, 1962.)

INPUT-OUTPUT AND DEMOGRAPHIC ACCOUNTING 371

TABLE III

An Economic Accounting System with Partial Time-Lags

		Production			Non-production	Total
		Last year	This year	Next year		
Production	Last year		W^{**}			
	This year		W^{*}	ΛW^{**}	e	q
	Next year					
Non-production			y'			
Total			q'			

Here the intermediate product absorbed this year is divided into two parts, W^{**}, which was made last year, and W^{*}, which is made this year. Also, the intermediate product made this year is partly absorbed this year, W^{*}, and partly carried forward for use next year, ΛW^{**}. Otherwise Table III is the same as Table II.

The model of this situation is built up from three elements. First, the arithmetical identity

$$q \equiv W^{*}i + \Lambda W^{**}i + e \qquad (8)$$

and, second and third, the technical assumptions

$$W^{*} = A^{*}\hat{q} \qquad (9)$$

and

$$W^{**} = A^{**}\hat{q} \qquad (10)$$

where $A^{*} + A^{**} = A$. From these we obtain

$$
\begin{aligned}
q &= A^{*}q + A^{**}\Lambda q + e \\
&= (I - A^{*})^{-1}(A^{**}\Lambda q + e) \\
&= (I - A^{*})^{-1}A^{**}\Lambda q + (I - A^{*})^{-1}e \\
&= \{I - [(I - A^{*})^{-1}A^{**}\Lambda]\}^{-1}(I - A^{*})^{-1}e \\
&= (I - A^{*})^{-1}\{I - [A^{**}(I - A^{*})^{-1}\Lambda]\}^{-1}e
\end{aligned}
$$

$$= (I - A^{*})^{-1}\sum_{\theta=0}^{\infty}[A^{**}(I - A^{*})^{-1}]^{\theta}\Lambda^{\theta}e \qquad (11)$$

corresponding to (6

By analogy with (7), the first row of (11) can also be written as

$$q = A^*q + (A^{**}q + A^{**}\Delta q) + e$$
$$= (A^* + A^{**})q + A^{**}\Delta q + e$$
$$= Aq + A^{**}\Delta q + e \tag{12}$$

which is the same as (7) except that the matrix of current coefficients, A, and the matrix of stockbuilding coefficients, A^{**}, are different.

Like (7), the statement expressed in (12) presupposes perfect foresight: in each year the amount of intermediate product made but not used is precisely equal to the needs of the succeeding year which cannot be met from that year's production. Its purpose is to illustrate a particular dynamic scheme, not to suggest that the real world is in a perpetual state of equilibrium.

Many things could be done to improve this simple model. For example, in the same way as the model generates the necessary amount of stock-building, it could be made to generate the necessary amount of fixed capital investment, leaving only consumption to be estimated exogenously. But such elaborations are not relevant to my present purpose, which is to show that an identical accounting framework and a very similar analysis can be used to describe and model demographic flows.

Demographic Input-Output

If we want to apply input-output methods to the analysis of demographic flows, the first thing to do is to define our categories in terms of the social, as opposed to the economic, system. Thus the unit, instead of being the pound, will be the human individual; and the main categories within which these units will be grouped, instead of being industries and products, will be age-groups and, within age-groups, activities or occupations. I shall say more about these categories in the next section, but first let us be clear about the flow equations of the system and their solution.

We can see that Table II provides the basic accounting framework in its simplest dynamic form; all that is necessary is to reinterpret the symbols. If we think of total output, q, as the total population of a country during a given period; of intermediate product, W, as the surviving part of this population; of final output, e, as deaths and emigrations; and of primary inputs, y, as births and immigrations; then we can rewrite the table more appropriately as Table IV.

In this table the sources of p', the population vector, are partly the survivors from last year, the elements of $\Lambda^{-1}S$, and partly the births and immigrations of this year, the elements of b'. Correspondingly, the destinations of p are partly the survivors into next year, the elements of S, and partly the deaths and emigrations of this year, the elements of d. If we sum the

INPUT-OUTPUT AND DEMOGRAPHIC ACCOUNTING   373

TABLE IV

A Demographic Accounting Matrix

		Our country			Elsewhere	Total
		Last year	This year	Next year		
Our country	Last year		$\Lambda^{-1}S$			
	This year			S	d	p
	Next year					
Elsewhere			b'			
Total			p'			

elements of the matrix S across the rows, we obtain a vector of the living population at the end of the year, that is $Si \equiv p - d$.

In order to build from Table IV a demographic model analogous to the economic model we built from Table II, we must reverse the roles of inputs and outputs. In the economic model it was assumed that while output patterns change with changes in final demand, the input patterns in the different industries are fixed. In the demographic case it seems more reasonable to make the opposite assumption, namely that input patterns may change with changes in the number of births and immigrations, but that the output patterns, or transition probabilities, for the different age-groups and activities are fixed: if out of 1,000 science graduates aged 21, say, 500 go on to further training, 300 get jobs in industry, 100 go into teaching, 50 become civil servants and 50 emigrate or die, we assume that if the number of science graduates aged 21 were 1,200, then 600 of them would go on to further training, 360 would get jobs in industry, 120 would go into teaching, 60 would become civil servants and 60 would emigrate or die.

This assumption means that instead of fixing the coefficients by columns, as we did in the economic model, we must fix them by rows. Also, since the determining variable is no longer the vector of final demands but the vector of primary inputs, we must take the building blocks for our model not from this year's row, as we did in the case of production, but from this year's column: we must ignore S and d and concentrate on $\Lambda^{-1}S$, b' and p'. In manipulating these variables, however, we shall find it convenient to transpose them, that is turn b' and p' into column vectors so that they become b and p, and interchange the rows and columns of S so that it becomes S'. Then we can write, corresponding to (4) and (5),

$$p \equiv \Lambda^{-1}S'i + b \qquad (13)$$

and

$$\Lambda^{-1}S' = C\Lambda^{-1}\hat{p} \qquad (14)$$

where $\Lambda^{-1}S'i$ denotes the column sums of $\Lambda^{-1}S$ written out as a column vector; and C denotes a matrix of transition probabilities (or output coefficients). By substituting for $\Lambda^{-1}S'$ from (14) into (13), we obtain

$$p = C\Lambda^{-1}p + b \qquad (15)$$

corresponding to the second row of (6). But whereas in (6) the coefficient matrix is applied to the future, in (15) it is applied to the past: the intermediate constituent of q is determined by next year's needs; the intermediate constituent of p is determined by last year's performance.

It is interesting to note here that Ghosh has considered a static economic model based on row rather than column coefficients, which he terms an allocation model.[3] Broadly speaking, his idea is that practical limits are set to the use of resources partly by input coefficients and partly by output (allocation) coefficients. In the context of production he does not press the claims of the allocation model very strongly; but given a dynamic form, this model seems to find a natural application in the context of demography.

From (15) we can calculate what the composition of p is likely to be in τ years' time. If we apply the operator Λ to (15), substitute for p into the new equation from (15), carry out this operation $\tau - 1$ times and apply Λ to the final equation of the series, we obtain

$$\Lambda^{\tau}p = \sum_{\theta=0}^{\tau-1} C^{\theta}\Lambda^{\tau-\theta}b + C^{\tau}p \qquad (16)$$

corresponding to the last row of (6). Equation (16) expresses the numbers in the various categories of the population (the elements of p) τ periods hence in terms of the present numbers and of all future births and immigrations up to and including those taking place in period τ. Like its economic counterpart, A, the matrix C has non-negative elements. Also, since people die at all ages, its column sums are less than one, so that C^{τ} approaches zero as τ increases. In fact, since people cannot become younger, C is upper-triangular and $C^{\tau}p = \{0, 0, ..., 0\}$ if τ exceeds the human life-span.

We can now compare the economic and demographic models. The last row of (6) shows output levels this year expressed in terms of present and

[3] Ghosh, A., *Experiments with Input-Output Models* (Cambridge University Press, 1964), pp. 111–118.

future values of e: present output depends on present and future demand. By contrast, (16) shows the future population in terms of its present value and of future values of b: future output depends on present and future supply. The solution of the economic model is based on the assumption that the input patterns, the elements of A, remain constant over time; by contrast, the solution of the demographic model is based on the assumption that the transition probabilities, or output patterns, the elements of C, remain constant over time.

These two points of contrast raise two important practical questions. First, how are we to estimate the future values of e in one case and of b in the other? Second, if we want to allow for changes in the coefficients, whether of inputs or of outputs, as in the real world we should, how can we introduce such changes in our models?

An answer to the first question for the economic model will be found in *Exploring* 1970 [4] and in my paper with Alan Brown and D. A. Rowe.[5] For the demographic model, if we are prepared to ignore for the time being the highly erratic element of immigration and concentrate on births, we can invoke a well-known piece of population mathematics [6] to express future values of p simply in terms of its present value, as follows.

Since it is reasonable to relate the number of births of either sex to the age composition of the female population, consider a vector of the female population grouped by year of age, f^* say, ranging from birth to the end of the female reproductive span. Then consider a matrix, H say, whose rows and columns are equal in number to the elements of f^*: the first row of H contains the rates at which females are born to females of different ages; the diagonal below the leading diagonal contains the survival rates of females at the different ages; all the other elements of H are zero. From this we can write

$$\Lambda^\theta f^* = H^\theta f^* \qquad (17)$$

Now consider another matrix, J say, whose rows are equal in number to the elements of p and whose columns are equal in number to the elements of f^*: the top left-hand corner of J contains a one; the rest of the first row contains the rates at which males are born to females of different ages; all the other elements of J are zero. From this we can write

$$\Lambda^{\tau - \theta} b = JH^{\tau - \theta} f^* \qquad (18)$$

where the first element of J picks out the first element of $H^{\tau - \theta} f^*$, that is, the

[4] University of Cambridge, Department of Applied Economics, *Exploring 1970*, pp. 7–21. No. 6 in *A Programme for Growth*. Gen. Editor: Richard Stone. (London: Chapman and Hall, 1965).

[5] Stone, Richard, Brown, Alan, and Rowe, D. A., " Demand Analysis and Projections for Britain: 1900–1970 ", in Sandee, J. (ed.), *Europe's Future Consumption* (Amsterdam: North Holland Publishing Co., 1963), pp. 200–225.

[6] Leslie, P. H., " On the Use of Matrices in Certain Population Mathematics ", *Biometrika*, XXXIII, Part III (1945), pp. 183–212.

376   RICHARD STONE

female births in year $\tau - \theta$; and the age-specific male birthrates in the rest
of the first row of J calculate and add together the male births in year $\tau - \theta$.
If we now substitute for $\Lambda^{\tau - \theta}$ from (18) into (16), we obtain

$$\Lambda^{\tau} p = \sum_{\theta=0}^{\tau-1} C^{\theta} J H^{\tau - \theta} f^{*} + C^{\tau} p \tag{19}$$

It will be noticed that in (19) the demographic model, from being an open
model with one exogenous variable, b, has become a closed model, that is a
model which generates all its variables endogenously from given initial
conditions.

   Turning now to the second question, we know that the assumption of
fixed coefficients is only one of those simplifications to which we are forced
to resort in the early stages of building a model. In the real world input
patterns and transition probabilities change and so we must be ready to
allow for such changes. Estimating them may not be easy, and this is not
the place to discuss how to do it; a rough method for dealing with changes
in input patterns is given in *A Computable Model of Economic Growth* [7] and
Input-Output Relationships, 1954–1966, [8] and a suggestion for treating changes
in the transition probabilities as a multiple epidemic process is given in
an earlier article. [9] The point I want to make here is that, once we have
succeeded in estimating these changes, it is not difficult to introduce them
into our original models. The way to do this for the economic model is
indicated in *A Computable Model of Economic Growth* [10] and in my paper
with J. A. C. Brown. [11] For the demographic model, if we let C change with
successive values of Λ^{θ}, then we can re-write (16) as

$$\Lambda^{\tau} p = \Lambda^{\tau} b + \sum_{\theta=1}^{\tau-1} \left(\prod_{\lambda=\tau-1}^{\tau-\theta} \Lambda^{\lambda} C \right) \Lambda^{\tau - \theta} b + \left(\prod_{\theta=\tau-1}^{0} \Lambda^{\theta} C \right) p \tag{20}$$

where Π denotes the operation of forming a product. From the middle term
on the right-hand side of (20) we can see that the multiplier of $\Lambda^{\tau - \theta} b$ is
$[\Lambda^{\tau - 1} C \times \Lambda^{\tau - 2} C \times \ldots \times \Lambda^{\tau - \theta} C]$ in place of C^{θ} as in (16).

   There is one further matter to be settled in this section. Just as in the
economic case Table III added something that was missing from Table II,
so in the demographic case something is missing from Table IV and should
now be added. In dealing with production we saw that intermediate products

[7] University of Cambridge, Department of Applied Economics, *A Computable Model of Econo-mic Growth*, pp. 69–72.
[8] University of Cambridge, Department of Applied Economics, *Input-Output Relationships, 1954–1966*, pp. 22–41. No. 3 in *A Programme for Growth*. General Editor: Richard Stone. (London: Chapman and Hall, 1963).
[9] Stone, Richard, " A Model of the Educational System ", *loc. cit.*
[10] University of Cambridge, Department of Applied Economics, *A Computable Model of Economic Growth*, pp. 73–80.
[11] Stone, Richard, and Brown, J. A. C., " Output and Investment for Exponential Growth in Consumption ", *The Review of Economic Studies*, XXIX, 80 (1962), pp. 241–245.

INPUT-OUTPUT AND DEMOGRAPHIC ACCOUNTING   377

might be made and used within the year; similarly, in the case of population we might want to account for changes of activity within the year. For example, a boy who flows in from the preceding year as a schoolboy may go to a university in the course of the year and thus flow out into the succeeding year as an undergraduate; or a woman who flows in as a typist may get married in the course of the year and flow out as a housewife. To deal with this we must introduce a new matrix, S^* say, at the intersection of the row and column for this year, and replace S by S^{**}. When this is done, the demographic accounting system will appear as in Table V below.

TABLE V

A Demographic Accounting System with Intra-Year Transitions

		Our Country			Elsewhere	Total
		Last year	This year	Next year		
Our country	Last year		$\Lambda^{-1}S^{**}$			
	This year		S^*	S^{**}	d^*	p^*
	Next year					
Elsewhere			b'			
Total			$p^{*\prime}$			

The function of the new matrix, S^*, can best be explained by an example: when an individual moves from category j to category k in the course of the year, this movement is represented in S^* by a -1 at the intersection of row j and column j, balanced by a 1 at the intersection of row j and column k. Thus the sum of the elements of S^* is zero, since in the aggregate all the transfers cancel out. From this it follows that the matrices $\Lambda^{-1}S^{**}$ and S^{**} do not differ in the sum of their elements from $\Lambda^{-1}S$ and S; they do differ from them in the arrangement of their elements, however, because each survivor now enters next year from the activity in which he leaves this year and not from the activity in which he had entered this year. For the same reason the vectors d and p now become d^* and p^*. The vector of primary inputs, b, is, of course, not affected.

378   RICHARD STONE

Like its economic counterpart, the model of this situation is built from three elements. First, the arithmetical identity

$$p^* \equiv \Lambda^{-1}S^{**\prime}i + S^{*\prime}i + b \tag{21}$$

and, second and third, the demographic assumptions

$$S^{*\prime} = C^*\hat{p}^* \tag{22}$$

and

$$S^{**\prime} = C^{**}\hat{p}^* \tag{23}$$

From these we obtain

$$p^* = C^{**}\Lambda^{-1}p^* + C^*p^* + b \tag{24}$$

whose solution for year τ is

$$\Lambda^\tau p^* = \sum_{\theta=0}^{\tau-1} \{ [(I-C^*)^{-1}C^{**}]^\theta (I-C^*)^{-1}\Lambda^{\tau-\theta}b\} + [(I-C^*)^{-1}C^{**}]^\tau p^* \tag{25}$$

corresponding to the last row of (11).

By an extension of the method used to reach (20) we could also allow for changing values of $\Lambda^\theta C^*$ and $\Lambda^\theta C^{**}$.

The Categories in a Demographic Matrix

A preliminary survey shows that in Britain, at any rate for recent years, there exists a considerable amount of relevant statistical material, and suggests that the construction of demographic accounting matrices may be no more difficult than the construction of their economic counterparts. In order to do this, however, it is necessary to have a clear idea of how we are going to define our categories and then find a means of reconciling the classifications used in the different statistical sources with each other and with our own.

In a demographic matrix the primary classification, as I said above, should be by age and the secondary classification should be by activity. Dividing all information into uniform age-groups is not quite so simple as it sounds. An obvious standard to choose would be age last birthday at the end of the calendar year. Much educational information is already available on this basis. But in other cases flows are recorded by the age at which they take place; for example, first employment is recorded by age on entry, death by age at death, and so on. Endless adjustments have therefore to be made; in principle, they could be avoided by retabulating the basic statistics, since information on exact age is usually recorded too.

As concerns the classification by activities, it should be drawn up on the following lines. With minor exceptions, the newly born enter the home of their parents and remain there until, at age two, a few of them begin to go to nursery school. Accordingly, at this age we must establish a new category, requiring a separate row and column in the matrix, so as to distinguish between two-year olds who go to nursery school and two-year olds who stay at home. Apart from the children of immigrants, all two-year olds come from the one-year olds of the year before, all of whom are classified under " home " since no-one goes to school at age one. When we get to age three the supply, again apart from immigrants, comes from two sources: two-year olds who went to school and two-year olds who stayed at home. With the data available in Britain, it is not possible to tell how many children return to the category " home " after a first year at nursery school nor how many go to school for the first time when they are three; it is therefore necessary to make the assumption that all the children who were at nursery school at age two continue in it at age three, and that only the additional three-year old school-goers come directly from " home ". With increasing age more and more children go to school until, when the age of compulsory school attendance is reached, the category " home " becomes virtually empty. Even at this early age it would be possible to distinguish different administrative types of school (independent, direct grant, etc.); but from an educational point of view there would not be much advantage in doing so. An argument for making such distinctions would obtain only if there were significant differences in the economic inputs (teachers, buildings, equipment) used in the different types of school.

Around the age of 11 or 12 most children pass from primary to some form of secondary education. Here again, a purely administrative classification of schools is of only minor interest. It is more useful to group schools into academic types (grammar, secondary modern, comprehensive, etc.) which offer substantially different curricula.

At the age of 15 compulsory education comes to an end and the majority of children leave school and seek employment. Even when employed, however, they may continue to receive education, mainly technical or professional, on a part-time basis. The minority who remain at school normally take public examinations and if successful pass on to a more specialised kind of education in the sixth form. So, from the age of 15 on, it becomes important to distinguish, among those who have left the educational system, between those who attend part-time courses and those who do not; and among those who remain in the educational system, between those who concentrate on science, those who concentrate on the humanities and those who continue to follow a mixed curriculum.

Those who remain at school after the age of 15 gradually drop out of it either into employment or into some other institution of advanced education, such as a technical college or a university. By the age of 25 to 30 even the longest type of formal education, such as medical training or postgraduate work at university, is over and virtually the whole of the male and a large part of the female population is engaged in gainful occupation. From this point we can follow them throughout their working life until, at retiring age, their home or some institution becomes the centre of such activity as is left to them. At age 100 or so the accounts close.

The accounting structure just described relates to a cross-section of human vintages alive in a particular year. In econometric terms, it provides a basis for cross-section analysis of the kind described above under " demographic input-output ". If we could compile a set of tables like Table V stretching over 100 years, we could pick out the information relating to successive ages in each table and thus obtain the elements for a time-series analysis of a particular human vintage.

But we are far from being able to undertake such an exercise; indeed, with the statistics as they are now, it is hard to know how best to classify the population once all regular education has ceased. Fortunately, for the immediate purpose of building models of the flow of students through the educational system this does not matter: the matrices can be partitioned at any age and the analysis concentrated on the earlier ages, on which we have fairly detailed information.

Conclusion

In this paper I have tried to bring together various forms of input-output accounting and analysis suited to dynamic problems. In the usual, static accounting system, the entries all relate to a single time-period and the set of accounts is completely closed. In the alternative, dynamic system suggested here, the inputs for a given period come, either in whole or in part, from the preceding period and the outputs go, either in whole or in part, to the succeeding period.

Two types of model can be built within the framework of this dynamic accounting structure: the conventional input-output model, in which the input coefficients are fixed; and an allocation model, in which the output coefficients are fixed. The conventional model is appropriate to the analysis of production flows; the allocation model to that of demographic flows.

These two models provide us with the main building blocks for an educational model, since as far as the human inputs are concerned the educational system is simply a partition of the demographic system, and as far as the economic inputs are concerned it is a partition of the productive system. A first attempt at combining the two was described in my earlier article.[12]

---

[12] Stone, Richard, "A Model of the Educational System," *loc. cit.*

[28]

Input-output Approach in an Allocation System

By A. GHOSH

I

An input-output transaction matrix may be conceived in terms of an equilibrium position of two sets of interacting forces. The broadest way in which we can define them is to denote one set of forces as technical factors expressed through production functions and the other set as market factors expressed through allocation functions. Though technical factors influence production, it is widely recognised that there are various alternative technical combinations in any economy and under different market situations different combinations are actually taken up. An input-output matrix then represents an equilibrium solution for two sets of equations somewhat analogous to demand and supply functions.

Under a competitive market and non-scarce resources allocation functions will play a minor role in the set up, and special conditions may be formulated under which production coefficients will determine the equilibrium.

But under a monopolistic market with scarce resources allocation functions will determine which among a large group of alternative processes and combinations will be taken up by any particular sector. That is, production functions are forced to play a minor role.

We can in this sense associate with an input-output matrix two sets of coefficients. One of these sets has been familiarised by Leontief as production coefficients, or, technical coefficients. They express the relationship $\qquad x_{ij}=\alpha_{ij}X_j$
where x_{ij} is the output of the ith sector sold to the jth sector and X_j is the output of the jth sector.

We can similarly also assume the existence under different circumstances of the relation $\qquad x_{ij}=A_{ij}X_i$
where x_{ij} is as before the output of the ith industry going to the jth sector and X_i is the output of the ith sector.

According as supply or demand conditions predominate either of the relations may approximate reality or neither of these simplified situations may actually approximate reality at all.

Leontief has formulated an idealised situation where the set α_{ij} is assumed fixed and the set A_{ij} is allowed to change freely with any change in the final demand. Such conditions may be assumed to hold approximately so long as there is no scarce factor and so long as suppliers are able to offer more of any commodity at the existing price.

Leontief's formulation thus takes up for consideration a situation where there is even in the short period a large unused capacity in most sectors such that any change in the final demands do not set

58

up any disturbance in relative prices and certainly do not bring in any question of limited supply.   Ignoring for the moment other criticisms of this simplified approach it may be said that where even in the short period nearly all industries have at their disposal a large surplus of plant and labour the supply curve is bound to be very elastic and the overall situation would be very much dominated by buyers' requirements.   This position is easily illustrated by an advanced capitalist economy in depression.

It is possible to build up a similar model with allocation functions in an economy where different sectors are under monopoly control and all except one resource is scarce.   We can consider a planned economy under centralised control with scarce material resources and productive capacity with ample supply of available labour.   The central authority has for each sector allocation schedules defining national or social welfare and it has been seeking that allocation which maximises welfare subject to possible production combinations.   That is, any feasible combination of inputs which gives a higher welfare value may be preferred to one which may be more efficient as a production combination, but is lower on the welfare scale.   An illustration may be given of a controversy in the Indian second five-year plan which is centred around the objective of reviving cottage industries which are productively less efficient but which gives employment rather than keeping people on a dole.   The objective of the planning authority is not a search for the optimum technical combination of production but for that feasible combination which makes the best use of resource made available for it on the basis of a welfare function.

It is obvious that in cases of this type the production combinations are forced on the industries not by technical considerations but by scarcity and consequent rationing.   In any alternative situation where scarcity has eased or quotas have been changed the industries will seek combinations which are completely different.   Input ratios here, therefore, are conditioned by the assigned quota and any change of the assigned quota will alter such ratios.   If such a situation is postulated, it is evident that the stability of production coefficients cannot by any means be assured for a change in the final demand of the community.

In this paper we shall investigate the use of input-output methods in economies of this type.   This means that our discussion is confined to a consideration of economies with a high rate of investments, with inadequacy of the supply of productive plants and materials and with a rationing system in allocation.

The purpose of the present paper is not to search for optimum allocation combination but to accept that the rationing authorities have in fact arrived at some optimum allocation factors on the basis of a national welfare function and an input-output table gives such a set of allocation coefficients defined by the second set of functions.   For simplicity we assume further that any allocation has corresponding to it at least one feasible combination of products.

In the present paper it is our contention that the general background provided by these economies makes the supply factors of greater predominance and one may consider the second set of coefficients more stable in these economies than the first set defined by Leontief. The basic difference between such economies from that illustrated earlier is that there is an almost unlimited demand for goods stimulated by development plans which is undiminished by higher prices. The only way such a situation can be handled is by rationing, " that is, if price increases prove ineffectual in reducing the expenditure function sufficiently, suppliers [here Govt.[1]] may decide that nevertheless they will produce only the output they desire and allocate it among consumers on some arbitrary rationing basis (first come first served, fixed percentage of purchases in previous years, etc.). In this case it is the spenders who are forced into involuntary actions, they must buy less than they desire ".[2]

In economies of rationing since every sector registers a high demand for the scarce factors the general tendency of the rationing authorities is not to change the relative shares of each sector in the short run since such relative shares are determined by a delicate balancing of different sectors' claims and counter-claims. This tendency considered from the problem of projection makes the allocation coefficient more stable in the short run than production coefficients.

Though such situations are a commonplace feature in controlled economies only under certain conditions, we may imagine a voluntary allocation system being taken up even by free enterprise in scarcity. This might happen when the producer of the scarce article feels that he should keep his market in his grip rather than sell only to the highest bidder. But of course such a situation over the whole economy in a free enterprise is not quite feasible, and sooner or later authority has to step in and dictate the respective quotas on the basis of national needs rather than leave it as a free for all, as happens during wars. Under such basic change in the background it may be of interest to use the second set of coefficients and develop an allocation model as an extension of the original Leontief system.

With this adaptation the Leontief model and its inverse may be used to provide answers to questions which are very similar, though not identical, to those of the conventional input-output model.

II

Our basic model is very similar to the conventional input-output model, that is, we consider the economy as consisting of sectors defined on general economic considerations. We then replace the Leontief production function by a different postulate.

A sector's receipts from every other sector are given linear functions of its own disbursements.

[1] My insertion.
[2] Don Patinkin: "Involuntary Unemployment and the Keynesian Supply Function". *E.J.*, LIX, 1949, p. 375.

Let E_i be the total external outlay of sector i and e_{ij} the outlay of sector i in sector j.   Then we have the identities

$$\sum_j e_{ij} = E_i \ (i \neq j)$$

Consider functions of the form

$$e_{ij} = A_{ij} E_j$$

This implies that the ith sector's outlay in the jth sector is a function of the total outlay of the jth sector.   That is, not production coefficients α_{ij} but supply coefficients A_{ij} are constant.   Any increase of sector j will be allocated in a fixed ratio to all the receipts from other sectors. Then we get a system of homogeneous linear equations

$$\sum_j A_{ij} E_j = E_i \ (i, j = 1, 2 \ldots n)$$

This set of equations leads to the closed system considered by Leontief. As for purposes of projection we are concerned only with the open case we modify slightly the above system by considering E_n as autonomous such that we get now a system in n-1 unknowns

$$\sum_j A_{ij} E_j = E_i - e_{in} \ (i, j = 1, 2, \ldots n-1)$$

where e_{in} is the vector of autonomous outlay elements included in every equation.   The open case thus reduces to

$$(I - A)\ E = e$$

where A is the matrix of coefficient, I a unit matrix and e a column vector of assigned autonomous cost elements in each sector.

The solution vector is given by

$$E = (I - A)^{-1} e$$

In this readapted system the column vector e is best interpreted as the net national income generated in the sectors. E is the vector of total outlay by the different sectors.

For any given vector of national income to be generated we shall get a unique vector of outlays likely to the sectors.   We have thus arrived through this approach not at an estimate of output (value) but at an estimate of likely costs.

The equation system in the open Leontief model is

$$X_i - \sum_j \alpha_{ij} X_j = x_{in} \begin{cases} i, j = 1, 2 \ldots n-1 \\ i \neq j \end{cases}$$

Then we have the solutions

$$X_i = \sum_j \alpha_{ij}^{\bullet} x_{jn}$$

where $\alpha_{ij}^{\bullet}$ are the elements of the inverse of the co-efficient matrix. The income or equivalent employment is obtained by applying the labour input coefficients to the expression for total output in the solution set.   Thus employment

$$x_{ni} = \alpha_{ni} X_i = \alpha_{ni} \sum_j \alpha_{ij}^{\bullet} x_{jn}$$

In exactly similar way, the net output in the present case is obtained
as
$$e_{ni} = A_{ni} E_i = A_{ni} \sum_j A^*_{ij} e_{jn}$$
where e_{jn} are the assigned income to be generated and A^*_{ij} are the
inverse of the coefficient matrix.

We do not thus consider the production possibilities in the system
and the employment or income generation following from a particular
bill of final demand but the income generating or employment possibilities of the system and the resultant net output from the system.

The simplest way of interpreting the use of these cost estimates is
to assume that normally every sector will have to balance its outlay
and its receipts. We then equate the costs to the value of the output
that the sector must produce in order to generate a national income
assigned to it. This approach may be used in a similar way as input-
output approach is used for the location of bottle necks, and for testing
consistency of different bill of goods with different employment
programme.

Let the open allocation model in the base period be
$$E_i - \sum_j A_{ij} E_j - e_{in} = 0 \qquad \left\{ \begin{array}{l} i, j = 1, 2, \ldots n-1 \\ i \neq j \end{array} \right.$$
Then we may write the solution set as
$$E_i = \sum_j A^*_{ij} e_{jn}$$

Let the planning authorities decide that the income in the planned
period in the ith sector will be related to the income in the ith sector
in the base period by the ratio
$$\frac{e^*_{in}}{e_{in}} = \lambda_i$$
where e^*_{in} refers to the planned period and e_{in} to the base period.
Then the costs in the planned period
$$E^*_i = \sum_j A^*_{ij} e^o_{jn}$$
$$= \sum_j \lambda_j A^*_{ij} e_{jn}$$

Let the outputs of sector i be denoted by Q_i and Q^*_i in the two periods
such that $Q^*_i = K_i Q_i$ and let P_i and P^*_i be the respective prices under
equilibrium.

Then $\quad E_i = P_i Q_i, \ E^*_i = P^*_i Q^*_i = P^*_i K_i Q_i$
$$\frac{P_i}{P^*_i} = \frac{K_i E_i}{E^*_i} = \frac{\sum_j K_i A^*_{ij} e_{jn}}{\sum_j \lambda_j A^*_{ij} e_{jn}}$$

The planning authority has the values of λ_j as data in the form of
income ratios between the two periods in different sectors. We may
assume that it has certain tentative estimates of the quantity ratios K_i of
the two periods. Then the new price ratio P_i/P^*_i is determinate. That
is, assuming that the allocation and the suggested income generating

plans will lead to specific changes in output the equilibrium price of the planned period is obtained as a solution. Alternatively, assuming certain price ratios between the current and previous period we can estimate what the equilibrium quantities in different sectors should be. We can thus use this model for the purpose of measuring inflationary effect on prices which may have to be faced due to a particular income generating policy.

Assuming that ratio of prices (quantities) in the planning period should remain as in the base period we get the quantities (prices) that must be obtained in order that the required employment programme is maintained and no sector runs at a loss. Obviously, any sector that reveals here a quantity bottle-neck will be forced to raise prices in order to run without a loss. Quantity bottle-necks thus in this system do not lead to a collapse of the whole system (which would take place with rigid production coefficients) but rather to price changes. Employment, final demand and prices are thus all brought into the picture provided the main background assumptions are assumed in the short run.

The change in the price indices will indicate the extent to which certain sectors are being asked to generate more income without relevant increase in the product. Thus supposing any particular sector is asked to have a higher profit or a higher employment but fails to increase its output in a corresponding way its receipts will exceed costs. Since it has been advised to cover costs it will be forced to raise prices. The relative prices will thus show the extent to which the income generation programme is working in harmony with real output.

III

Goodwin[1] and others have shown that the Keynesian system may be treated as an aggregation of an input-output model. The aggregation in this case cancels all inter-firm transactions leaving only national income. Assuming that aggregated national consumption is related to national income in a non-homogeneous linear form we get the familiar Keynesian equation

$$(I - a)\ Y = I$$

relating income to investment.

Aggregating on similar lines the present model is also reduced to the traditional Keynesian form. It only interprets the " psychological propensity to consume " of a freely spending community as the " allocation decision " of a non-economic authority. Suppose in a community under overall rationing " a " is the marginal propensity to consume as desired by the community and " α " is the marginal rate of consumption spending as determined by the authority. Then for a specific increment of investment $\triangle I$ the desired increment of income of the community will be $\dfrac{1}{1-a} \triangle I$, while the actual rise of income of the

[1] R. M. Goodwin: "The Multiplier as Matrix". *E.J.*, LIX, 1949, pp. 537–555.

community as permitted by the authority will be $\frac{1}{1-\alpha} \triangle I$. If " a " is greater than " α " this will mean a larger desired income compared to the permitted income. $a \triangle y - \alpha.\triangle y$ may be considered as the involuntary saving of the community. The allocation coefficient thus is a realistic concept relevant to income generation under an overall rationing system.

In an economy where demand is outstripping supply and some form of rationing and price control is operating the purchasers are forced to an involuntary saving as far as spending money on a group of commodities is concerned. We define involuntary saving as the saving due to a situation where more demand is forthcoming in the market at a price higher than the present ruling price. Where such involuntary saving exists the basic assumption of a freely moving consumption curve is absent and therefore one can have no idea of the shape of such curve from a study of the earnings, savings and consumption of the community. The consumption to output relation of the community in this case is represented by $\frac{\triangle o_e}{\triangle o_e + \triangle o_i}$ (where o_e and o_i are outputs of consumer goods and investment goods) which equals $\frac{\triangle c}{\triangle y}$ where $\triangle c$ is the actual increment of consumption and $\triangle y$ is the increment of income of the community but is not equal to $\frac{\triangle c'}{\triangle y}$ where $\triangle c'$ is the desired increment of consumption corresponding to that increased income. So long as $\triangle c = \triangle c'$ the stability of $\frac{\triangle c}{\triangle y}$ may be assumed as a community behaviour but otherwise these considerations will not make $\frac{\triangle c}{\triangle y}$ stable. The division of income into spending and saving is thus determined not by the income earner but by the producer or the factors controlling the producer's decision.[1] Unlike the consumption function there is no simple way of determining the shape of the function relating desired production of consumer goods to total output. In most economies of scarcity with large-scale controls the fundamental allocation between consumption and production is determined by a body of socio-economic forces. In the short period we can only accept the constants relating the two as institutional as a given datum and work with it—but to deny its existence in such situations and ignore the constraints to economic behaviour can only lead us to wrong forecasts. The reaction mechanism itself thus ceases to be based on consumer's behaviour and becomes institutional.

Department of Applied Economics,
University of Cambridge.

[1] G. C. Mandal: "An Aspect of Inflation in India, 1939–47". *Bulletin of the International Statistical Institute.* Vol. XXXII: Part III.

Name Index

The International Library of Critical Writings in Economics

90. Women in the Labor Market (Volumes I and II)
   Marianne A. Ferber

91. Market Process Theories (Volumes I and II)
   Peter Boettke and David Prychitko

92. Input–Output Analysis (Volumes I, II and III)
   Heinz Kurz, Erik Dietzenbacher and Christian Lager

93. Mathematical Economics (Volumes I, II and III)
   Graciela Chichilnisky

Future titles will include:

The Economics of Unemployment
P.N. Junankar

The Economics of Energy
Paul Stevens

The Economics of Science and Innovation
Paula E. Stephan and David B. Audretsch

International Finance
Robert Z. Aliber

Welfare Economics
William J. Baumol and Janusz A. Ordover

The Economics of Inequality and Poverty
A.B. Atkinson

The Economics of Crime
Isaac Ehrlich

The Economics of Integration
Willem Molle

The Rhetoric of Economics
Deirdre McCloskey

The Economics of Defence
Keith Hartley and Nicholas Hooper

Consumer Theory
Kelvin Lancaster

The Economics of Business Policy
John Kay

Microeconomic Theories of Imperfect Competition
Jacques Thisse and Jean Gabszewicz

The Economics of Increasing Returns
Geoffrey Heal

The Balance of Payments
Michael J. Artis

Cost-Benefit Analysis
Arnold Harberger and Glenn P. Jenkins

Privatization in Developing and Transitional Economies
Colin Kirkpatrick and Paul Cook

The Economics of Intellectual Property
Ruth Towse

The Economics of Tourism
Clem Tisdell

The Economics of Organization and Bureaucracy
Peter Jackson

The Economics of Commodity Markets
David Greenaway and Wyn Morgan

Realism and Economics: Studies in Ontology
Tony Lawson

New Developments in Game Theory
Eric S. Maskin

The International Economic Institutions of the Twentieth Century
David Greenaway

The Economics of Structural Change
Harald Hagemann, Michael Landesmann and Roberto Scazzieri

Economic Justice
Harold Hochman and Georgio Brosio

The Economics of Famine
Jean Dréze

The Foundations of Regulatory Economics
Robert B. Ekelund

The Economics of the Welfare State
Nicholas Barr

Path Dependence
Paul David

Alternative Theories of the Firm
Richard Langlois, Paul Robertson and Tony F. Yu

Economic Anthropology
Stephen Gudeman

The Economics of Executive Compensation
Kevin F. Hallock and Kevin J. Murphy

The Economics of Marketing
Martin Carter, Mark Casson and Vivek Suneja

Foreign Exchange Intervention: Theory and Evidence
Sylvester C.W. Eijffinger

The Economics of the Mass Media
Glenn Withers

The Foundations of Long Wave Theory
Francisco Lauçã and Jan Reijnders

The Economics of Budget Deficits
Charles Rowley

Economic Forecasting
Terence C. Mills

The Economic Theory of Auctions
Paul Klemperer

Corporate Governance
Kevin Keasey, Steve Thompson and Mike Wright